Reading in Action

Reading in Action

Skills and Strategies
for Engaged College Reading

Eugene Wintner

Northern Essex Community College

PEARSON

Boston Columbus Indianapolis New York San Francisco Upper Saddle River
Amsterdam Cape Town Dubai London Madrid Milan Munich Paris Montreal Toronto
Delhi Mexico City São Paulo Sydney Hong Kong Seoul Singapore Taipei Tokyo

Editor in Chief: Eric Stano
Senior Acquisitions Editor: Nancy Blaine
Editorial Assistant: Jamie Fortner
Marketing Manager: Kurt Massey
Senior Supplements Editor: Donna Campion
Executive Digital Producer: Stefanie Liebman
Senior Digital Editor: Robert St. Laurent
Digital Project Manager: Janell Lantana
Project Coordination and Text Design:
   Electronic Publishing Services Inc., NYC

Art Rendering and Page Makeup: TexTech
Cover Design Manager: John Callahan
Cover Design: Base Art Co.
Cover Image: iStockphoto
Senior Manufacturing Buyer: Dennis Para
Printer/Binder: Courier/Kendallville
Cover Printer: Courier/Kendallville

Credits and acknowledgments borrowed from other sources and reproduced, with permission, in this textbook appear on page 567.

Library of Congress Cataloging-in-Publication Data
Wintner, Eugene.
   Reading in action : skills and strategies for engaged college reading / Eugene Wintner.
      p. cm.
   Includes index.
   ISBN 978-0-205-70752-2
     1. College readers.   I. Title.
PE1417.W58 2012
808'.0427—dc23
                                               2011033013

10 9 8 7 6 5 4 3 2 1—CRK—14 13 12 11

www.pearsonhighered.com

ISBN 10: 0-205-70752-1
ISBN 13: 978-0-205-70752-2

Annotated Instructor's Edition
ISBN 10: 0-205-70754-8
ISBN 13: 978-0-205-70754-6

Brief Contents

Detailed Contents

Preface

Reading in Action, designed for mid-level developmental readers, is built on the premise that the use of active reading strategies fosters engaged reading, which translates to more effective reading and a stronger reader identity. Using varied exercise formats and progressive exercise sequences, including collaborative and online exercises, the text fosters growth in metacognition through a chapter on monitoring comprehension and through a variety of reinforcing exercises and activities included in all chapters. *Reading in Action* also gives significant attention to vocabulary growth through direct instruction, textual vocabulary aids, and in-context practice.

What You Will Find in This Book

***Reading in Action* fosters student engagement.** The success of students in developmental reading courses is largely related to their engagement with the course materials. *Reading in Action* fosters student engagement through its content, organization, and exercise formats. The essential message and meta-message to students throughout the text is that if you become an active and engaged reader, you'll be a better reader and a more successful student. Thus, skills work in the text is presented as deliberate, mental interaction between reader and text. The result is that students take greater ownership of the skills they are practicing and become more likely to apply them in real reading situations.

Modern research tells us that readers construct meaning as they read. Engagement with reading instruction, then, is integrally associated with the student's awareness of his or her own reading processes. The developmental reader needs to forge a positive reader identity. In *Reading in Action*, the process begins in the introductory chapter, "You, the Reader," which asks students to look at their reading histories and their attitudes towards reading, as well as their goals and their reading and learning styles. The process is expedited through the text's emphasis on active reading strategies, and it is reinforced by questions that ask students to reflect on their experiences with the chapter content (i.e., what they've learned from the chapter, how they'll use what they've learned, what engaged them within the chapter). Response questions and reflective questions also accompany the 25 longer readings found at the end of the chapters and in the back of the text. Thus the text's regular attention to metacognition contributes to the student's growing identity as a reader.

***Reading in Action* makes use of varied exercise formats and progressive exercise sequences.** Skills work in the text is couched within the framework of active reading. Generally, skill-building exercise sequences are progressive rather than repetitive. They are carefully structured to move students through an incremental process that culminates with the application of the skills to longer readings. Exercise formats are varied to avoid too much drill work (too much of the same thing can disengage students). Students experience themselves as progressing within and through each chapter, thus staying interested. Most chapters contain exercises that are intended for collaborative classroom work, which also contributes to student engagement. A simple online skills activity is included in each chapter, extending practice through a basic application of chapter skills to the online reading environment. In addition, critical reading skills are introduced gradually, beginning with analysis of supporting details in Chapter 5 and culminating with a full chapter on critical reading in Chapter 10.

Reading in Action **acquaints students with academic disciplines and content.** The 25 readings in *Reading in Action*, and the paragraphs and passages used for skills and strategies practice, have been selected to encourage student engagement with academic reading material. The content is drawn from a wide range of topics and disciplines. The readings provide opportunities for application of skills and strategies and are at varying levels of challenge. Some of the readings and shorter selections are thematically related, offering opportunities for pursuit of topics of interest and for making content connections within the text. Each of the longer reading selections is accompanied by a "Respond to the Reading" activity, which provides questions for reflection on and response to the reading material. Each reading is also followed by a "Webquest," a specific question related to the topic of the reading that students are instructed to answer using an online search. The Webquests can be done by students individually or with partners and are another means of fostering student engagement. The Webquests are not intended to provide complex research experience, but rather to provide simple practice with finding information online and to acquaint the students with some of the concerns that arise when researching online. Suggestions for additional (and in some cases more complex) Webquests are provided in the Instructor's Manual.

Reading in Action **provides substantial vocabulary instruction and practice.** Improving vocabulary skills and increasing word knowledge are critical to the success of developmental readers. *Reading in Action* includes a substantial amount of vocabulary work, which may obviate the need for a supplementary vocabulary book. Vocabulary work is integrated with reading skills work, and the vocabulary words come from the readings and practice material.

Two full vocabulary chapters provide students with instruction and practice in effective use of context and dictionary, and in understanding word structure—the fundamentals for vocabulary building. An appendix introduces students to common roots. Every reading selection is accompanied by a vocabulary exercise. These exercises ask the students to use context clues, the dictionary, and word structure clues to determine the meanings of words from the readings—just as we hope they will do when encountering unfamiliar words when reading on their own. As appropriate, chapter exercises include either vocabulary aids (definitions and pronunciations for words within the passages) or vocabulary in context questions. The Instructor's Manual provides a list of vocabulary words from the exercise material in each chapter.

How This Book Is Organized

Though we know that the skills and strategies we teach are often used simultaneously, or in varying orders, as developmental reading instructors we are constrained to teach these skills and strategies one at a time. To some extent then, the sequence of instruction in any developmental reading course is a matter of preference. The rationale for sequencing in *Reading in Action* is as follows.

Skill and strategy work begins with Chapter 1, which introduces pre-reading strategies. Chapters 2 and 3 are both vocabulary chapters, so that students have basic vocabulary skills in place and can practice and reinforce these skills as the text continues. Main ideas and supporting details are covered in Chapters 4 and 5. When the students are grounded in the basic vocabulary and paragraph skills, they are better prepared to work with the monitoring comprehension practices introduced in Chapter 6. The next two chapters deal with recognizing organization: sentence relationships and transition words in Chapter 7, and logical patterns in Chapter 8. Inference work is contained in Chapter 9, and Chapter 10 is devoted to critical reading skills.

As much as possible, the chapters in *Reading in Action* have been designed to allow instructors flexibility with instructional sequencing. Though logic dictates that certain chapters should follow one another, for the most part the chapters can be taught in alternate sequences with equal benefit. For example, although word structure is covered in Chapter 3, there is no reason why it can't be taught later—or earlier—as the instructor prefers.

On a related note, there is more material in the text than can be taught effectively in a single semester. The intent again is to provide instructors flexibility—by supplying an ample amount of material and exercises from which to choose.

Other Available Resources

Instructor's Manual/Test Bank (ISBN: 020570753X). The Instructor's Manual for *Reading in Action*, in addition to customary contents like answer keys and chapter guides, includes

- A chapter-by-chapter vocabulary list
- Recommendations for related readings for theme-based explorations
- Additional online exercises, including more advanced Webquests
- Additional suggestions for collaborative activities

The test bank includes two sets of review quizzes and a mastery test for each chapter. An answer key is provided. The review quizzes are designed to assess students' knowledge and comprehension of important topics in each chapter. The mastery tests require students to apply skills learned in each chapter.

MyTest Test Bank (ISBN 0205173195). Pearson MyTest is a powerful assessment generation program that helps instructors easily create and print quizzes, study guides, and exams. Select questions from the test bank to accompany

Reading in Action or from other developmental reading test banks; supplement them with your own questions. Save the finished test as a Word document or PDF or export it to WebCT or Blackboard. Available at www.pearsonmytest.com.

PowerPoint Presentation (ISBN 0205210732). PowerPoint presentations to accompany each chapter consist of classroom-ready lecture outline slides, lecture tips and classroom activities, and review questions. Available for download from the Instructor Resource Center.

Answer Key (ISBN 020511721X). The Answer Key contains the solutions to the exercises in the student edition of the text. Available for download from the Instructor Resource Center.

Annotated Instructor's Edition (ISBN 0205707548). An annotated instructor's edition is available for this text. It provides answers to the activities and exercises in the text printed on the write-on lines that follow each exercise.

Acknowledgements

The author would like to thank the following reviewers for their help in shaping the manuscript.

Marilyn Black, Middlesex Community College; Marta Brown, Community College of Denver; Kimberly Carter, Miami Dade College; Shannon Carter, Phoenix College; Ruth Copper, Saginaw Valley State University; Marlys Cordoba, College of the Siskiyous, Melissa Dalton, Lanier Technical College; Nancy Finklea, Hinds Community College; Victoria Gonzalez, Dona Ana Community College; Jan Graham, Mayland Community College; Elizabeth P. Hall, Danville Community College; Nessie Hill, Essex Community College; Kimberly Jones, College of Southern Illinois; Denice Josten, St. Louis Community; Patty Kunkel, Santa Fe CC; Monique Mannering, Brookhaven College; Shirley Melcher, Austin Community College; Mary Nielsen, Dalton State University; Alda Noronha-Ninmo, Miami Dade College; Pam Price, Greenville Tech College; Christine Proctor, St. Louis Community College at Meramec; Regina Ray, Dalton State College; Juliet Scherer, SLCC; Susan Silva, EPCC; Ursula Sohns, LSC-North Harris; Thomas Staael, North Hennepin Community College; Rita Stout, Community College of Denver; Janelle Strik, Yuba College; Majorie Sussman, Miami Dade College; Carol Szabo, Elgin Community College; and Nicole Williams, Community College of Baltimore County Catonsville.

Gene Wintner

Reading in Action

Introduction: You, the Reader

Reading in Action is about you, the reader, for two reasons. The first reason is that *you* are the most important factor in your reading improvement. No matter how good an instructor you have, or how good your textbook is, your improvement will be accomplished through your own effort.

The second reason is that, whether or not you realize it, every time you read you bring your whole self to the experience. You bring to each reading activity all your previous knowledge and experience. You engage your mind and your emotions. You also bring your attitudes and biases. For example, if you enjoy history, when you open a history book you will expect to find the material interesting, and as a result, you probably will.

The Importance of Reading Skills in the Information Age

As a college freshman, you are beginning an important, exciting, and rewarding new stage in your life. Your years in college will be stimulating and challenging ones that will expand your knowledge and provide you with the education you need to enter a worthwhile career.

You may have been advised that in order to be a successful college student, you should improve your reading skills, and that you will need good reading skills to succeed in today's work world. Perhaps your college is requiring you to take a reading improvement course to upgrade your skills, and that is why you are reading this book right now.

Why are reading skills important today? Seventy-five years ago, there were no televisions, no computers, and no videos. Radio was a recent invention, and talking motion pictures were just being released. The primary source of news for most Americans was their local newspaper. To gain information, they read books and magazines. They read fiction books and stories in magazines for entertainment.

Today, as we enter the second decade of the twenty-first century, we live in a world made over by technology—the information age. We can listen to the news on the radio, watch the news on television, or obtain it from the Internet. We have access to a vast amount of information from these sources, and we have more choices for entertainment than any other society in history. Yet, with the popularity of the electronic media, people are reading more today than ever before—whether from books,

1

magazines, or the Internet. The growth of modern technology and the Internet encourages people to read more, since the use of these technologies requires people to read and to think independently. Apparently, in the information age, good reading skills are as valuable as ever before. In fact, as the following cartoon suggests, in some situations reading can even be a lifesaver!

Take a moment now to write answers to the following questions:

- What are your feelings about reading?

  Answers will vary.
  _____

- Do you believe that good reading skills are valuable? Why or why not?

  Answers will vary.
  _____

- How will good reading skills help you achieve the goals that are important to you?

  Answers will vary.
  _____

Goal Setting

You will be more highly motivated to improve your reading skills if you believe that reading can help you achieve the goals that are important and exciting to you. Your goals motivate you and also help you assess your progress.

Read the following excerpt on the importance of goals from the book *Live Your Dreams* by Les Brown, then complete Exercises I.1 and I.2.

1   Goals give you a purpose for taking life on. People who live without goals have no purpose and it is obvious even in their body language. They are on permanent idle, they slouch, they list from side to side. Their conversations dawdle. They telephone you: "Hey, I'm just calling. I wasn't doing anything, so I thought I'd call you." *Well, don't call ME. I'VE got things to do.*

2   Many people just muddle through life. They don't read informational material, they don't even pay attention when they WATCH television. If you ask them what they are watching, they mumble-mouth, *"Nothin', I'm just lookin'."*

3   What are your goals for your career? For your relationships? For your spiritual life? Develop a schedule for the next month, the next six months, the next year, five years, and ten years. Write it all out.

4   *Your goals are the road maps that guide you and show you what is possible for your life.* Life takes on meaning when you become motivated, set goals, and charge after them in an unstoppable manner. Goals help you channel your energy into action. They place you in charge of your life.

Solid Goals

5   You must see your goals clearly and specifically before you can set out for them. Hold them in your mind until they become second nature. Before you go to bed each night, visualize yourself accomplishing your goal. Do the same while you brush your teeth or take a shower in the morning.

6   Goals are not dreamy, pie-in-the-sky ideals. They have everyday practical applications and they should be practical. Your goals should be:

- *Well defined.* You won't know if you've reached them if you haven't established exactly what they are.

- *Realistic.* Not that you can't be president some day, but shooting for state representative might be a wiser first step.

- *Exciting and meaningful to you.* Otherwise, where will your motivation come from?

- *Locked into your mind.*

- *Acted upon.* There is no sense in having a goal if you aren't going to go after it.

7   How do you find your goals? We all have dreams of what we would like to be doing, what we would like to have, who we would like to be with. Think about your dreams. What goal would you go after if you knew you would not fail? If you had unlimited funds? If you had infinite wisdom and ability?

8   One of the most essential things you need to do for yourself is to choose a goal that is important to you. If you need to set goals for your career, find a job or profession that is important to you beyond the bills that it pays.

—Brown, *Live Your Dreams*

EXERCISE I.1 GOAL SETTING

1. List three of your important long-range goals (these may be educational, personal, or career goals):

a. Answers to all will vary. _____

b. _____

c. _____

2. List three of your important goals for the coming week:

a. _Answers to all will vary._____

b. _____

c. _____

3. List three of your important goals for tomorrow:

a. _Answers to all will vary._____

b. _____

c. _____

EXERCISE I.2 READING IMPROVEMENT GOALS

Directions: Using a 1–4 scale, rate the importance of each of the following reading improvement goals for you. Then circle the *three* goals that are the *most important* for you to accomplish this semester.

1 = very important   3 = slightly important

2 = fairly important   4 = of no importance

Answers to all will vary.

{ _____ Improved comprehension

_____ Better concentration

_____ Increased reading speed

_____ Increased vocabulary

_____ Greater reading enjoyment

_____ Improved memory

_____ Increased time for pleasure reading

_____ Other (explain): _____ }

Becoming an Active and Engaged Reader

The key to your success as a college reader is to use active reading strategies to engage fully with your reading material. Successful reading in college does not mean gaining a perfect, instant understanding every time you move your eyes over a line of printed words. Rather, it means maintaining active engagement with whatever you are reading through the application of active reading strategies.

An active reading strategy is anything that you do intentionally to enjoy reading more, improve your comprehension and memory of what you've read, or in any way enhance your reading experience. *Reading in Action* will introduce you to a variety of active reading strategies that will help you become a more engaged reader. Some of these strategies are reading *behaviors,* like previewing a chapter in a textbook before reading it. Some of them are *mental* approaches, like raising questions about your reading material. You will begin working with these strategies in Chapter 1. As you practice with them, you will become more skillful in their use. In addition to these strategies, the following suggestions will also help you become a more engaged and active reader.

1. *Read with purpose.* You will engage more fully with your reading if you view reading as a communication between the author and yourself. Every time you read, you have an opportunity to share the experiences and ideas of another person and to learn something new. Although there are no real formulas for successful reading, having the sincere intention to understand the author's ideas and point of view is always a good starting point.

Active readers are clear about their purpose when they read. When you sit down to read, ask yourself, "What do I hope to learn or gain from the reading? How will reading this material contribute to the achievement of my personal, educational, or career goals?" When reading assigned material, also ask, "What does my instructor want me to learn and remember from the reading?"

2. *Read with full involvement.* Concentration is nothing more or less than bringing your full attention to whatever it is that you are doing at any given time. No one can prevent his or her mind from wandering occasionally, but your mind will wander less frequently if you have chosen to commit your attention to the reading material. The use of the active reading strategies you will learn as you progress through this text will help you read with greater engagement and concentration.

Of course, concentration also depends on interest. When reading on your own, choose materials that motivate and excite you. When reading assigned material, become as interested and as curious about the subject as you can. Remember that interest is in the mind of the beholder—that is, you, the reader. (In Chapters 1 and 6 you will learn some special strategies for increasing interest in assigned readings.)

3. *Read regularly.* Like any other skill, reading improves with practice and experience. As a college student, you may find it helpful to establish regular periods in your daily and weekly schedule for assigned reading and study and to set aside a little time each day for independent reading. Don't wait till you "feel like it" to start reading or studying; let reading become a habit. Find one or two places at home or on campus where you can read without distraction.

> The key to your success as a college reader is to use active reading strategies to engage fully with your reading material.

4. *Respond to what you read.* While reading and after you finish reading something, respond to the material. Note whatever thoughts and feelings arise in response to the material. Do you find yourself agreeing or disagreeing with the author's point of view? Does the information presented relate to any of your previous learning or experiences? Does it seem useful? Also note what questions come to mind while reading and after you finish reading.

5. *Expand your vocabulary.* Many college freshmen report that one of the biggest challenges they face when reading their textbooks is the vocabulary load. *Reading in Action* will teach you to use active reading strategies to expand your vocabulary and meet that challenge. If you are curious about words and motivated to increase your vocabulary, you will become a more successful and more confident reader.

6. *Have confidence in your ability to improve.* There are no perfect readers in the world. Everyone has to work at reading comprehension. Being a confident learner does not mean that you believe you will never make a mistake; it means that you know you can learn from your mistakes and continue to improve through your efforts. Your reading course, your instructor, and your use of this textbook will all help you improve your skills. Believing in yourself will contribute significantly to your progress.

Discovering Your Learning Style and Reading Style

There is no one "right" way of learning. Each of us has a *learning style,* a preferred way of learning ideas and remembering information. Our learning styles reflect our preferences and tendencies for taking in new information, memorizing information, and processing ideas.

Let's take, for example, the relatively simple task of learning a new telephone number. Some people will learn the number by repeating it to themselves over and over. Some will write it down once and then look at it a few times; some will write it several times, or dial it a few times, in order to remember it. None of these methods is better than another; they simply reflect different learning styles.

Learning style is a complex subject—that is, there are several different aspects of learning style and several different ways to analyze learning style. One basic aspect of learning style is related to three modes of learning: visual learning (learning by seeing), auditory learning (learning by hearing), and tactile/kinesthetic learning (learning by touching or moving). Most people use all three modes of learning to some extent. Many people, however, have a preference, slight or strong, for one mode over the others.

- *Visual learners* prefer to *see* the information they are learning. They like pictures and diagrams and tend to visualize—form mental pictures of—what they are learning. A visual learner would want to look at a phone number that he is trying to remember, and might "see" the number in his mind.

- *Auditory learners* prefer to *hear* the information they are learning. They like discussion and are good listeners. They reinforce what they are learning by both speaking and hearing the information. An auditory learner would want to hear and say a phone number that she is trying to remember.

- *Tactile/kinesthetic learners* prefer to *do* something with the information they are learning. The word *tactile* refers to touch; the word *kinesthetic* refers to movement. Tactile/kinesthetic learners are hands-on learners who learn best through physical activity. A tactile/kinesthetic learner would want to write down or dial a phone number that he is trying to remember.

You can discover your learning style by paying attention to your own learning experiences. Think about your most successful learning experiences and how you went about them. The next time you are involved in a learning activity, notice the way or ways that seem most natural for you to approach it. Identify the modes that provide the strongest reinforcement for your learning and memory—in short, which modes make learning easiest for you.

You can also use the Internet to explore your learning style. Use the search term "learning styles" to find Web sites with information about learning styles or the search term "learning styles inventory" to find Web sites that provide exercises that will help you analyze your style.

The term *reading style* refers to your typical approach to reading and to your preferred reading habits. Since reading is a form of learning, your learning style and reading style are closely related. Visual learners, for example, tend to form mental pictures while they are reading. They like to read material that is accompanied by pictures, graphs, charts, and so forth. Auditory learners like to read as if they were pronouncing or hearing the words they are reading in their mind. They tend to read more slowly than visual learners. Tactile/kinesthetic learners are often fidgety readers who don't like to sit still for long periods of time.

Like learning style, reading style is a complex subject with many aspects to it. Reading style includes tendencies and preferences that relate to:

- the speed at which you read and the pacing of your reading.
- the frequency and length of your reading sessions.
- when and where you read.
- your preference for silence or background music while reading.
- the types and formats of reading material you choose.
- the mental processes you typically employ while reading (visualizing, analyzing).
- your reading purposes.
- what you tend to focus on while reading and what you remember from your reading.

You will learn more about your reading style by paying attention to your reading habits and experiences. Notice when, why, and how you typically approach your reading activities. Notice what helps you focus and what goes through your mind while reading (are you forming mental pictures, raising questions, associating the reading material with other experiences, etc.). Right now, you can take a step toward discovering your reading style by completing exercises I.3 and I.4.

EXERCISE I.3 READING HABITS QUESTIONNAIRE

Directions: Answer each question honestly. Completing this questionnaire will make you more aware of your reading habits and interests and will provide information that will help your instructor work with you more effectively.

_____ **1.** How often do you read something that you enjoy?
　　　a. Very often
　　　b. Often
　　　c. Occasionally
　　　d. Rarely or never   Answers will vary.

_____ **2.** Approximately how many hours a week do you read?

    a. None

    b. 1–2

    c. 3–6

    d. 7–10

    e. More than 10   Answers will vary.

_____ **3.** How frequently do you read the newspaper?

    a. Daily

    b. Weekly

    c. Occasionally

    d. Rarely or never   Answers will vary.

4. What newspaper(s) do you read?

Answers will vary.

_____ **5.** How often do you read magazines?

    a. Weekly

    b. Monthly

    c. Occasionally

    d. Rarely or never   Answers will vary.

6. List any magazines you read regularly.

Answers will vary.

_____ **7.** How often do you read and enjoy books?

    a. Frequently

    b. Occasionally

    c. Rarely or never   Answers will vary.

_____ **8.** How many books do you think you've read in your lifetime?

    a. None

    b. 10 or less

    c. 11–25

    d. 26–50

    e. 51–100

    f. More than 100   Answers will vary.

9. Name the last book you read and indicate when you read it.

Answers will vary.

10. Name a book you especially enjoyed and would recommend to others. Include the author's name if you remember it.

Answers will vary.

_____ **11.** How often do you read on the Internet?

    a. Daily

    b. Weekly

    c. Occasionally

    d. Rarely or never   Answers will vary.

12. Which Web sites do you visit most frequently?

<u>Answers will vary.</u>

13. Which types of fiction reading do you enjoy? Check as many as apply:

Answers to all will vary.
- _____ Mystery
- _____ Science fiction
- _____ Romance
- _____ Thrillers
- _____ Classics
- _____ Historical novels
- _____ Other (specify): _____

14. Which of the following nonfiction subjects are of interest to you? Check as many as apply:

Answers to all will vary.
- _____ Sports
- _____ History
- _____ Psychology
- _____ Science
- _____ Technology
- _____ Health/fitness
- _____ Biography
- _____ Other (specify): _____

15. If you do not read much, what is the primary reason you don't read more?
   a. I don't enjoy reading.
   b. I like to read but I'd rather do other things with my time.
   c. I have little free time.
   d. Other (specify): <u>Answers will vary.</u>

16. If you were assigned a research project on a subject of your choice, what subject would you select?

<u>Answers will vary.</u>

EXERCISE 1.4 READING STYLE

Directions: Write simple and honest answers to each of the following questions. When you have finished, read over your answers to form a picture of your reading style. Discuss your answers with your instructor.

1. Where do you usually read? What's the best place for you to read?

<u>Answers will vary.</u>

2. What are the best times of day for you to read? (for example, late morning, early evening)

<u>Answers will vary.</u>

3. Do you read best when it is completely quiet around you, or do you prefer some sound in your environment?

Answers will vary.

4. When is reading most enjoyable for you?

Answers will vary.

5. Do you prefer to read quickly or slowly?

Answers will vary.

6. Do you prefer to read in short spurts or to read steadily for continuous periods of time?

Answers will vary.

7. Do you prefer to read information from print (paper) materials or from electronic screens?

Answers will vary.

8. How often do you form mental pictures of what you're reading?

Answers will vary.

9. How often do you analyze what you're reading?

Answers will vary.

10. Do you enjoy reading aloud?

Answers will vary.

11. How easily do you remember what you've read?

Answers will vary.

12. How often do you skim read?

Answers will vary.

13. Do you look for main ideas or focus on details?

Answers will vary.

14. What are the main reasons why you read?

Answers will vary.

15. Complete this statement: Reading for me is like . . .

Answers will vary.

16. Write *three* different endings to this statement: When I read, I like to . . .

Answers will vary.

Writing Your Reading Autobiography

A reading autobiography is a summary of your life's reading experiences. Writing your reading autobiography in Exercise I.5 provides you with an opportunity to think about how you've come to see yourself as a reader, and how the reading experiences you've had up to now have contributed to your identity as a reader. It is a chance to reflect on the things you've read that have been important to you, and the people who have played a role in your reading history. It is also an opportunity to think about how you've changed over time as a reader, to think about where you are now, and to reassess your current goals as a reader and learner.

EXERCISE **I.5** READING AUTOBIOGRAPHY

Directions: Use lined paper or a word processor to write your reading autobiography. Tell your story as a reader. Your reading autobiography should address at least some of the following questions, but need not answer all of them. Focus on what seems most interesting and important to you.

What are your earliest memories of reading?

When you were a child, did your parents (or any other household members) read to you, or encourage you to read? Did they enjoy reading?

What do you remember about learning to read?

Did you have favorite stories or books growing up?

What school experiences or other life experiences shaped your interest in reading and your feelings about reading? Which books or other readings have had the most influence on you? Which person or persons has most influenced your attitudes towards reading?

What are some of the most positive experiences you've had with reading?

What were your high school reading assignments like?

How have your reading interests and habits changed over time?

How do you feel about reading now? What are your current reading interests and habits?

How would you describe yourself as a reader now? What are your chief strengths as a reader today?

What are your goals for improvement?

Answers will vary.

You, the Reader: Introduction Wrap-up

Directions. At the end of each chapter of *Reading in Action,* you will be asked to write a half-page response to the chapter material. Writing your responses will allow you to evaluate your experiences with the chapter material and to assess your progress with the skills and strategies you are acquiring. Write honest, thorough answers to each question to which you respond.

To conclude your work with this Introduction, write a response to any two of the following questions. You should write a total of at least half a page.

- What were the most important things you learned from this chapter? How will you use what you have learned from this chapter?

- Discuss your goals in coming to college.

- Discuss an important learning experience you had in high school or a book that was especially meaningful to you.

- What parts of the chapter did you find most engaging? What questions do you have about the chapter?

PEARSON
myreadinglab

For support in meeting this chapter's objectives, go to MyReadingLab and select *Reading Skills Diagnostic Pre-Test*.

Using Pre-Reading Strategies

LEARNING OBJECTIVES

In Chapter 1 you will learn to:

- Improve your concentration while reading
- Preview chapters and articles to enhance your concentration, comprehension, and retention
- Connect your prior knowledge and experience with your reading material to increase engagement and enhance your concentration, comprehension, and retention
- Form goal questions from headings and sentences to enhance concentration, comprehension, and retention

CHAPTER CONTENTS

Preparing to Read: Reinforcing Concentration
Active Reading Strategy: Previewing
Active Reading Strategy: Relating to the Subject
Active Reading Strategy: Forming Goal Questions
Skills Online: Previewing Web Sites
Reading 1A: Psychology of Self-Awareness (Psychology)
Reading 1B: Understanding Consumer Behavior (Business)
Chapter 1 Review
Chapter Tests
    Test 1.1: Previewing
    Test 1.2: Relating to the Subject
    Test 1.3: Previewing and Relating
    Test 1.4: Goal Questions from Headings
You, the Reader: Chapter 1 Wrap-up

You learned from the introductory chapter that successful college readers are *active* readers. When they approach reading assignments, they use strategies that help them concentrate better, understand more, and remember more of what they read.

An *active reading strategy* is anything that you do intentionally as a reader to remain engaged while reading and to benefit more from your reading time. A simple example of an active reading strategy that many college readers employ is underlining or highlighting the text. Many students—especially visual and tactile/kinesthetic learners—find that underlining or highlighting helps them stay focused on their reading and encourages them to sift out the main points in the text. An additional benefit is that the underlined material can be reviewed at a later time.

Successful college readers use active reading strategies in three stages: (1) *before* they start reading an assignment; (2) *while* they are reading an assignment; and (3) *after* they finish reading an assignment. Of course, most of the strategies are used while reading, but the strategies used before and after reading also contribute significantly to effective college reading. Table 1.1 lists some of the most important active reading strategies for each of the three stages. You will learn to use these strategies as you progress through the chapters of *Reading in Action*.

In this chapter, we will focus on pre-reading strategies—strategies that you use *before* you actually read through an assignment. Pre-reading strategies prepare you to read an assignment successfully. They are easy to use and highly effective. Most students report that using these strategies increases their concentration, comprehension, and retention, and helps them to be faster and more efficient readers.

Table 1.1   Active Reading Strategies

Strategies to Use before Reading	Strategies to Use while Reading	Strategies to Use after Reading
Previewing	Raising goal questions	Reviewing, summarizing, and self-testing
Relating to the subject	Using context clues	Responding to the material
Raising goal questions	Using the dictionary	Evaluating the author's ideas
	Identifying main ideas and details	
	Monitoring comprehension	
	Visualizing	
	Analyzing	
	Reading aloud	
	Identifying sentence relationships	
	Identifying logical patterns	

Preparing to Read: Reinforcing Concentration

The idea of preparing to read may seem strange to you, but if you want to read with concentration and understanding, a few simple steps can make a big difference to your success. Just as an athlete prepares for a game, or a job hunter prepares for an interview, college readers should prepare themselves to ensure that their reading time will be well spent.

Effective reading requires good concentration, yet many students report difficulty with concentration on their reading assignments. Have you ever noticed what helps you to concentrate when you are reading? Our concentration is affected by both external factors and internal factors. External factors, such as a noisy environment, are sometimes the easiest obstacles to identify. Internal factors, such as a wandering mind, may be harder to pin down.

Identifying the factors that influence your concentration, and controlling them as much as possible, are the first steps in preparing to read. Controlling concentration factors means increasing the ones that help you to concentrate and eliminating or reducing the ones that hinder your concentration. For example, many readers notice that their concentration is better at certain times of day and weaker at other times of day. So, if you notice that your concentration is best in the early evening and weakest in the late evening, you can plan to do as much of your assigned reading as possible in the early evening and avoid reading and studying late at night.

Complete Exercise 1.1 to identify your most important concentration factors and to develop a plan to control them.

EXERCISE 1.1 CONCENTRATION FACTORS

First complete the following sentence; then follow the directions below.

I concentrate best when ___Answers will vary._____

_____

Directions: In the spaces provided, list the three to five factors that have the most effect on your reading concentration. Then explain what you can do to control or influence each factor. An example is provided.

EXAMPLE

Factor: tiredness
How to control/influence: plan to complete reading assignments early in the day; read more difficult material first; maintain a regular schedule and get enough sleep

1. Factor: _____

How to control/influence: ___Answers will vary._____

2. Factor: _____

How to control/influence: ___Answers will vary._____

3. Factor: _____

How to control/influence: Answers will vary. _____

4. Factor: _____

How to control/influence: Answers will vary. _____

5. Factor: _____

How to control/influence: Answers will vary. _____

Active Reading Strategy: Previewing

Engaged reading begins with a preview of your reading material. What exactly does this mean? Simply put, *previewing means looking over a chapter or an article before reading it.* The primary purpose of previewing is to engage with whatever you're reading by gaining an overview of the material and a preliminary orientation to it. Previewing enables you to discover the subject of the chapter or article, the main topics that will be covered, and the basic organization of the chapter or article. Previewing allows you to judge the interest level of the passage, as well as its difficulty or familiarity, and to budget your time more realistically. By previewing, you will know what to look for when you actually read the chapter or article. In short, previewing is like looking at a map before starting on a journey.

Here's what you might look at when previewing a textbook chapter or an article you've been assigned to read:

1. **The Title.** Read and think about the title. What clues does the title provide to the subject and central idea of the passage?

2. **Introduction.** Read any introductory material and the first one or two paragraphs. If chapter objectives are provided, be sure to study them.

3. **Headings and subheadings.** Read each heading and subheading, to determine the topic of each major section in the chapter or article, OR

   First sentences. When you are reading a short article with no headings, read the first sentence of each paragraph. When the topic of a section is not clear from the heading, read the first sentence or two under the heading.

4. **Visuals.** Notice any visual aids, such as pictures, charts and graphs, *italicized print,* and anything else that stands out as you glance over the pages.

5. **Summary/conclusion.** Read the summary or conclusion at the end of the chapter or article. If no summary or conclusion is provided, read the last paragraph.

6. **End-of-chapter material.** In textbook chapters, look over the end-of-chapter material. Sometimes your text will provide a chapter review, a list of important terms, or a set of study questions at the end of the chapter. Previewing this material will help you know what to look for when you read the chapter.

Exactly what you look at when previewing will vary according to the material with which you're working. See Figure 1.1 for an example of a passage in which the previewed elements have been highlighted.

Students sometimes object to previewing because they think it will add time to their reading assignment. In reality, previewing should not take more than a few minutes once you are used to doing it. Those few minutes will contribute substantially to your understanding and memory of what you read. In the long run, previewing may even save you time by enabling you to read with greater efficiency. Previewed material tends to be read faster.

Make previewing a habit. Preview every assignment you are given. You will quickly become a good previewer, and you will enjoy your reading more.

Previewing is like looking at a map before starting on a journey.

FIGURE 1.1   SAMPLE PREVIEW

This figure contains the beginning of a textbook chapter on success in college. The portions of the passage that you would look at while previewing the material are highlighted.

WHERE ARE YOU NOW—*AND WHERE CAN COLLEGE TAKE YOU?*

You are standing at the gateway to a new phase of life. Before you think about moving forward, though, take a look at the road that brought you here. You completed high school or its equivalent. You may have built life skills from experience as a partner or parent. You may have been employed in one or more jobs or completed a tour of duty in the armed forces. You have enrolled in college, found a way to pay for it, signed up for courses, and shown up for class. And, in deciding to pursue a college degree, you made the choice to believe in your ability to accomplish important goals. You have earned this opportunity to be a college student!

What College Can Do For You

Part of what will make your sacrifices worthwhile is for you to understand—and aim to achieve—what you want out of your experience. Students have many different reasons for starting, or returning to, college. The following are just some of many possibilities:

- "I want to earn a better living."
- "I want to get a degree so that I can move ahead in a career."
- "I want to spend time learning new subjects."
- "I just lost my job, so I want to learn new skills."
- "I want to make my parent or spouse happy, and they want me to go to college."
- "I don't really know why I'm here."

Almost all of these reasons for attending college have a specific goal lying within—a degree, earning power, new skills, learning. These goals may change as students gain knowledge and experience through the semesters. Being straight with yourself about why you are here will help you define what you want and begin thinking about how to achieve it over the course of your college years. As for those of you who don't know quite why you are here, even if you don't have a goal now, the experience of college will help you find one.

How can you define your goals so that they give purpose to your educational experience? Looking at the big picture of what college can do for you will give you somewhere to start.

How Education Promotes Life Success

If your work in college only helped you succeed in the classroom, the benefit of your learning wouldn't last beyond graduation day. However, learning is a tool for life, and a college education is designed to serve you far beyond the classroom. Here are a few important "life success goals" that college can help you achieve:

Life Success Goal: Increased Employability and Earning Potential

Getting a degree greatly increases your chances of finding and keeping a high-level, well-paying job. College graduates earn, on average, around $20,000 more per year than those with a high school diploma (see Key 1.1). Furthermore, the unemployment rate for college graduates is less than half that of high school graduates (see Key 1.2).

Life Success Goal: Preparation for Career Success

Your course work will give you the knowledge and hands-on skills you need to achieve your career goals. It will also expose you to a variety of careers related to your major, many of which you may not have even heard of. Completing college will open career doors that are closed to those without a degree.

Life Success Goal: Smart Personal Health Choices

The more educated you are, the more likely you are to take care of your physical and mental health. A college education prepares you with health-related information that you will use over your lifetime, helping you to practice wellness through positive actions and to avoid practices with the potential to harm.

Life Success Goal: Active Community Involvement and an Appreciation of Different Cultures

Going to college prepares you to understand complex political, economic, and social forces that affect you and others. This understanding is the basis for good citizenship and encourages community involvement. Your education also exposes you to the ways in which people and cultures are different and how these differences affect world affairs.

> "A journey of a thousand miles begins with a single step."
> —Lao Tzu

Thinking about these big-picture goals should help you begin to brainstorm, in more detail, what you want out of college. What courses

do you want to take? What kind of schedule do you want? What degree or certificate are you shooting for? Think about academic excellence and whether honors and awards are important goals. If you have a particular career in mind, then consider the degrees and experience it may require. Finally, consider personal growth, and think about the importance of developing friendships with people who will motivate and inspire you.

Now you have an idea of your starting point—where you are now—and you are beginning to develop a picture of your ending point—what you want to have gained by the end of your college experience. The biggest question remains: What gets you from here to there? Not everyone arrives successfully. However, with dedication, hard work, and the power that comes from something called *successful intelligence,* you can make it.

—Carter et al., *Keys to Success,* 5th ed.

Reminder

When previewing a reading assignment, look at the following items:

1. Title
2. Introduction
3. Headings and subheadings, or first sentences of paragraphs when subheadings are absent

4. Visuals
5. Summary or conclusion
6. End-of-chapter material

EXERCISE 1.2 PREVIEWING PRACTICE

Directions: Preview the following passage by reading the *title, first paragraph, headings,* and *last paragraph*. When you have finished your preview, answer the questions that follow the passage.

MAKING TIME FOR FITNESS: FITTING FITNESS INTO A TOO-BUSY SCHEDULE

You know that becoming physically fit can enhance the quality—and quantity—of the years ahead. But you can't seem to find enough time to make fitness work for you. Making time for fitness means setting priorities, sneaking extra activity into daily routines, and scheduling fitness as you would other important events.

Making Fitness a Priority

Ask an expectant parent about the preferred sex of their baby-to-be. The answer? "It doesn't matter, as long as it's healthy." Health is the most precious quality we can wish on a newcomer to the world, and deciding to stay fit and healthy is our way of protecting that gift. You can become more fit by exercising just 20–30 minutes 3 times

a week. Isn't it worth your time to make fitness a priority in your life?

Activating Your Daily Routine

Five minutes of movement here and there does add up to a more active lifestyle. To activate your daily routines, try some of these tips: take the stairs when possible (or walk a few flights and then take the elevator), park your car at the far end of the parking lot, hand-deliver messages at work rather than picking up the phone, and so on. With a little creativity, you'll find dozens of ways to increase the amount of movement in your daily routines.

Scheduling Time for Fitness

Schedule your fitness time as you would an important meeting. Many business people have traded the "business lunch" for an exercise session at the gym. It makes sense—almost half of the North American population exercises regularly. Why not mix business with pleasure? Walk on your lunch hour or, instead of a coffee break, try a stretching break. Rather than joining friends for drinks, get together for a game of softball or a vigorous walk. But whatever you do, stick to your scheduled activity.

There's No Time Like the Present

There's no reason not to do something good for yourself by making fitness one of your daily priorities. By setting aside 20–30 minutes 3 times a week for vigorous activity, and by sneaking extra activity into your daily routines, you can become fitter, happier, and more productive. Why not start right now? What have you got to lose?

—"Making Time for Fitness," Parlay International

1. What is the subject of the passage?

Fitness and exercise

2. What does the author believe is the reason why people don't exercise enough?

People don't make time for it.

3. What suggestions does the author give for making time for fitness?

Make it a priority.

Fit movement into your daily routine.

Schedule exercise time.

Start now.

4. What benefit of physical fitness does the author mention in the first paragraph?

Enhances quality and quantity of life

EXERCISE **1.3** PREVIEWING PRACTICE

Directions: Preview the following passage. When you have finished your preview, answer the questions that follow the passage.

THE FLU

Influenza, or the flu, is second only to the common cold as the most common infectious disease. At some point, virtually everyone suffers a bout with the flu. Most people recover in a week or two, but each year about 20,000 Americans die of complications of the flu. The most vulnerable are the elderly, the very young, and people with a chronic disorder, especially heart or lung disease.

More about Flu

Causes

Flu is caused by 3 principal types of influenza viruses.* The most common strain is *influenza A,* and is responsible for the most serious flu epidemics. About every 3 years, there are widespread epidemics of influenza A, and every 30 to 40 years, there are more serious worldwide

*Note: This article was written before the appearance of the H1N1 flu.

epidemics, called pandemics. The last epidemic was in 1968, and many experts feel that the world is long overdue for another major global outbreak.

Influenza B also causes epidemics about every 5 years, but most cases are relatively mild. The *influenza C* virus is always present, but it only occasionally causes a few local outbreaks of mild flu.

Mode of Transmission

Flu passes from one person to another *through droplets in the air*. When a person with flu coughs or sneezes, millions of viral particles are sprayed into the air. When the flu virus is inhaled, it quickly starts to multiply. The virus spreads so easily that in only a few days a local epidemic may develop. And travelers carry flu far and wide.

Manifestations

After about 48 hours of incubation, the victim suddenly begins to feel very sick. The first symptoms include a fever of *102 to 103°F,* shaking, chills, headache, and a backache and leg pains. Fatigue and weakness are common. The *respiratory symptoms*—a runny or stuffy nose, sore throat, and dry, hacking cough—are mild at first, but worsen in the next few days.

Natural Course

The fever usually lasts for 2 or 3 days, but the other symptoms may last for a week or 10 days. The fatigue and general malaise often last even longer.

Most healthy people recover fully in a few weeks, and are then immune to the particular strain of the flu virus that affected them. *Complications* such as pneumonia or secondary bacterial respiratory infections are most common in the elderly or people weakened by other diseases.

Treatments

Most treatments are aimed at *easing symptoms*. Aspirin or acetaminophen can lower fever. (Note, however, that aspirin should not be given to anyone under age 18 who has a viral illness because it increases the risk of Reye's syndrome, a serious childhood disease that attacks the liver and brain.)

Rest and ample liquids are important. Alcohol should be avoided because it lowers the immune system's ability to fight off the virus.

Antibiotics are of no value against the flu virus, but they may be prescribed for people with chronic lung disease to prevent bronchitis or other bacterial infections.

—*The Complete Guide to Family Health,*
International Masters

1. What is the passage about?
The flu

2. What topics are discussed in the first section ("More about Flu")?
Causes, modes of transmission, manifestations, natural course

3. What is the subject of the last section?
Treatments for flu

4. How many strains of flu are identified in the passage? What are they?
Three: influenza A; influenza B; influenza C

5. What is the most common infectious disease?
The common cold

6. What parts of the passage did you look at for your preview?
Answers will vary but may include title, headings, italics, first and last paragraph.

EXERCISE **1.4** PREVIEWING

Directions: Preview the following passage. When you have finished your preview, answer the questions that follow the passage.

TOUCH

Touching is referred to as either tactile communication or **haptics.** Haptics is one of the most basic forms of communication. "Reach out and touch someone" is a slogan once used by a national phone company. Although the company's advertisement suggests touching in an abstract sense, the idea behind the advertisement is that touch is a personal and powerful means of communication. As one of our most primitive and yet sensitive ways of relating to others, touch is a critical aspect of communication. It plays a significant role in giving encouragement, expressing tenderness, and showing emotional support, and it can be more powerful than words. For example, when you've just received some bad news, a pat on the shoulder from a friend can be far more reassuring than many understanding words.

The kind and amount of touching that is appropriate varies according to the individuals, their relationship, and the situation. Some researchers have set up categories to describe these variations in touch. The categories are functional–professional, social–polite, friendship–warmth, love–intimacy, and sexual arousal.

1. Functional–professional touch is an unsympathetic, impersonal, cold, or businesslike touch. For example, a doctor's touch during a physical examination or an athletic trainer's touch of an injured athlete serves a purely medical, functional purpose. A tailor who takes customers' measurements is another example of functional–professional touching. The person being touched is usually treated as an object or nonperson in order to prevent implying any other messages.

2. Social–polite touch acknowledges another person according to the norms or rules of a society. In our society, the handshake is the most predominant form of polite recognition of another. In many European countries, a kiss is used in place of the handshake to acknowledge another.

3. Friendship–warmth touch expresses an appreciation of the special attributes of others. Friendship–warmth touch is also the most misinterpreted type of touching behavior because it can be mixed or confused with touching related to sex. For example, you see two men meet in an airport, hug, and walk off with their arms around each other. You would probably infer that these two men are close relatives or friends who have not seen each other for a while. Their touching conforms to social expectations about how friends behave in a public context. Their behavior expresses and reinforces the warm feelings they have for each other.

4. Love–intimacy touch usually occurs in romantic relationships between lovers and spouses. It includes caressing, hugging, embracing, kissing, and many other forms of intimate touch. It is highly communicative. Usually this form of touch requires consent between both parties, although one person can initiate love–intimacy touch and the other person being touched may not always reciprocate.

Intimate touch conveys strong caring, devoted, enamored, and loving interpersonal messages. It also complements and validates verbal messages such as "I love you" or "You are someone special in my life." Intimate touch does not necessarily imply sexual involvement. Sometimes confusion between intimate and sexual touch leads to dissatisfaction in some couples' special relationships.

5. Sexual–arousal touch is the most intimate level of personal contact with another. Sexual touch behavior, if mutually desired, is extremely pleasurable for most people, but it can also produce fear and anxiety. This category of touch expresses physical attraction between two consenting individuals.

The meaning of a particular touch depends on the type of touch, the situation in which the touch occurs, who is doing the touching, and the cultural background of those involved. Some cultures are more prone to touching behavior than others. Research has found that people in the United States are less touch-oriented when compared to persons in other cultures. For example, a study examining touching behavior during a one-hour period in a coffeeshop found that people in San Juan, Puerto Rico, touched 180 times in an hour; those in Paris, France, touched 110 times; and those in Gainesville, Florida, touched only 2 times.

Gender differences in touching behavior are also interesting to note. Men tend to touch more than women do, women tend to be touched more often than men, and women seem to value touch more than men do. Gender differences in touching behavior may be partially attributed to men's sexual aggressiveness in our culture and their expression of power and dominance. According to Nancy Henley, men have access to women's bodies, but women do not have the same access to men's bodies. This, according to the research, may be a man's way of exerting power because touch represents an invasion of another's personal space.

—Seiler and Beall, *Communication: Making Connections,* 4th ed.

1. What is the subject of the passage?

Touch

2. How many types of touch are identified? List them?

Five: functional–professional; social–polite; friendship–warmth; love–intimacy;

sexual–arousal.

3. What does *haptics* mean?

Tactile communication (touch)

4. What is the role of touch in communication?

Touch plays an important role: gives encouragement; expresses tenderness; shows

emotional support.

5. What gender differences have been noted regarding the use of touch?

Men touch more; women are touched more; women value touch more.

6. What parts of the passage did you look at for your preview?

Answers will vary, but may include title; headings; first and last paragraph.

EXERCISE 1.5 PREVIEWING

Directions: Preview the following passage. When you have finished your preview, answer the questions that follow the passage.

GOVERNMENT AND POLITICS

Government

The institutions that make authoritative decisions for any given society are collectively known as **government**. In our own national government, these institutions are Congress, the president, the courts, and federal administrative agencies ("the bureaucracy"). Thousands of state and local governments also make policies that

government The institutions and processes through which public policies are made for a society.

influence our lives. There are roughly 500,000 elected officials in the United States, which means that policies that affect you are being made almost constantly.

Because government shapes how we live it is important to understand the process by which decisions are made as well as what is actually decided. Two fundamental questions about governing will serve as themes throughout this book:

How Should We Govern?

Americans take great pride in calling their government democratic. This chapter examines the workings of democratic government; the chapters that follow will evaluate the way American government actually works compared to the standards of an "ideal" democracy. We will continually ask, "Who holds power and who influences the policies adopted by government?"

What Should Government Do?

This text explores the relationship between *how* American government works and *what* it does. In other words, "Does our government do what we want it to do?" Debates over this question concerning the scope of government are among the most important in American political life today. Some people would like to see the government take on more responsibilities; others believe it already takes on too much and that America needs to promote individual responsibility instead.

While citizens often disagree about what their government should do for them, all governments have certain functions in common. National governments throughout the world perform the following functions:

Maintain a national defense. A government protects its national sovereignty, usually by maintaining armed forces. In the nuclear age, some governments possess awesome power to make war through highly sophisticated weapons. The United States currently spends over $500 billion a year on national defense. Since September 11, the defense

budget has increased substantially, in part to cope with the threat of terrorism on U.S. soil.

Provide public services. Governments in this country spend billions of dollars on schools, libraries, hospitals, and dozens of other public institutions. Some of these services, like highways and public parks, can be shared by everyone and cannot be denied to anyone. These kinds of services are called **public goods.** Other services, such as a college education or medical care, can be restricted to individuals who meet certain criteria but may be provided by the private sector as well. Governments typically provide these services to make them accessible to people who may not be able to afford privately available services.

Preserve order. Every government has some means of maintaining order. When people protest in large numbers, governments may resort to extreme measures to restore order. For example, the National Guard was called in to stop the looting and arson after rioting broke out in Los Angeles after the 1992 Rodney King verdict.

Socialize the young. Most modern governments pay for education and use it to instill national values among the young. School curricula typically offer a course on the theory and practice of the country's government. Rituals like the daily Pledge of Allegiance seek to foster patriotism and love of country.

Collect taxes. Approximately one out of every three dollars earned by an American citizen is used to pay national, state, and local taxes— money that pays for the public goods and services the government provides.

All these governmental tasks add up to weighty decisions that our political leaders must make. For example, how much should we spend on national defense as opposed to education? How high should taxes for Medicare and Social Security be? We answer such questions through politics.

---

public goods Goods such as clean air and clean water that everyone must share.

Politics

Politics determines whom we select as our governmental leaders and what policies these leaders pursue. Political scientists often cite Harold D. Lasswell's famous definition of politics: "Who gets what, when, and how." It is one of the briefest and most useful definitions of politics ever penned. Admittedly, this broad definition covers a lot of ground (office politics, sorority politics, and so on) in which political scientists are generally not interested. They are interested primarily in politics related to governmental decision making.

The media usually focus on the *who* of politics. At a minimum, this includes voters, candidates, groups, and parties. *What* refers to the substance of politics and government—benefits, such as medical care for the elderly, and burdens, such as new taxes. In this sense, government and

politics involve winners and losers. *How* people participate in politics is important, too. They get what they want through voting, supporting, compromising, lobbying, and so forth.

The Policymaking System

Americans frequently expect government to do something about their problems. For example, the president and members of Congress are expected to keep the economy humming along; voters will penalize them at the polls if they do not. The **policymaking system** reveals the way our government responds to the priorities of its people. Figure 1.2 shows a skeletal model of this system.

—Edwards et al., *Government in America: People, Politics, and Policy,* Brief 10th ed.

---

politics The process that determines who we select as our governmental leaders and what policies these leaders pursue. Politics produces authoritative decisions about public issues.

---

policymaking system The process by which policy comes into being and evolves over time. People's interests, problems, and concerns create political issues for government policymakers. These issues shape policy, which in turn impacts people, generating more interests, problems, and concerns.

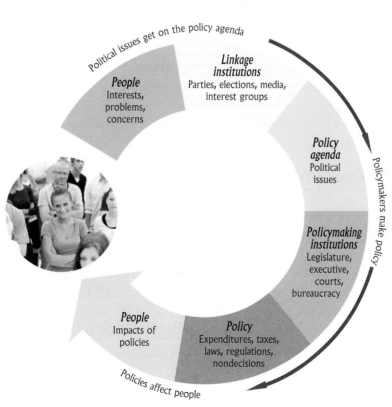

Figure 1.2 The Policymaking System

1. What is the passage about?

Government and politics

2. What two fundamental questions about government are raised in the first section?

How should you govern? What should government do?

3. List the five functions that governments perform.

Maintain a national defense; provide public services; preserve order; socialize the

young; collect taxes

4. What is the author's definition of government? What is the author's definition of politics?

Government: the institutions and processes through which public policies are made for

a society.

Politics: the process that determines who we select as our government leaders and what

policies these leaders pursue.

5. According to Figure 1.2, what is the first step in the policymaking system? What is the last step?

First step: People's interests; problems; concerns (influence policies)

Last step: People are impacted by policies.

6. What parts of the passage did you look at for your preview?

Answers will vary but may include title, headings, graph, first and last paragraphs,

definitions.

Active Reading Strategy: Relating to the Subject

Previewing a chapter or article will give you a general idea of what the chapter or article is about. The next important step is *relating to the subject*. Relating to the subject of your reading material is critical to your engagement with the material. There are several ways you can use this strategy to engage with your material. Your basic goal at this point is to connect with the material in any ways you can. Start by recalling any prior knowledge you have (something you already know) about the subject, or any associations with the subject that come to mind, or any experiences you've had that might relate to the subject. Begin by asking yourself the following questions:

What do I already know about the subject?

What have I previously read or learned about the subject?

What associations do I have with the subject?

What else have I learned that may relate to this subject or help me understand this subject?

What personal experiences have I had that relate to this subject?

Too often, students start reading an assignment with the feeling that they know nothing about it. If you think for a moment, you'll probably realize that you have at least some prior knowledge, association, or experience that relates to the subject matter. Take a few seconds and see what comes to mind. For example, after previewing the passage, "Making Time for Fitness," you could have recalled anything you've previously read or learned about exercise and fitness, or associated the subject with people going to gyms to work out, or you could have thought about your own exercise habits and goals.

Another simple way to relate to the subject is to raise questions about it. As quickly as you can, raise any three or four questions that come to mind about the subject matter. Let the questions flow—do not pause to judge whether or not they are "good" questions. At this stage, all questions are good because they generate curiosity and activate your thinking. Raising questions in this manner will stimulate your curiosity and get you focused on the subject.

For example, here are some questions that might come to mind for the passage "Making Time for Fitness":

How often do most people exercise?

How much exercise is needed to stay fit?

What are the best ways to exercise?

Why do some people avoid exercise?

Relating to the subject is an especially useful engagement strategy for passages that don't look interesting at first glance. Connecting to the subject by relating it to your own experience or simply raising questions will make anything you read more interesting.

EXERCISE 1.6 RELATING TO THE SUBJECT

Directions: Relate to the passage "The Flu" (Exercise 1.3) by answering the following questions. If necessary, preview the passage again before answering the questions.

1. What have you previously read or learned about influenza? What associations do you have with this subject?

   Answers will vary.

2. Have you ever had the flu? What were your symptoms? What treatment did you receive?

   Answers will vary.

3. What would you learn from reading this passage?

The causes of flu; its symptoms; how it spreads; its natural course; how it is treated

4. Write three questions about influenza.

Answers will vary.

EXERCISE 1.7 RELATING TO THE SUBJECT

Directions: Relate to the passage "Government and Politics" (Exercise 1.5) by answering the following questions. If necessary, preview the passage again before answering the questions.

1. What have you previously read or learned about government and politics? What associations do you have with this subject?

Answers will vary.

2. Briefly discuss your views of government and politics. Did you vote in the last election? Why or why not?

Answers will vary.

3. What would you learn from reading this passage?

What government and politics are; the function of government; how policy is made

4. Write three questions about government and politics.

Answers will vary.

EXERCISE 1.8 RAISING QUESTIONS TO RELATE TO THE SUBJECT

Directions: Working with one or more of your classmates, (1) select an object in the room and, as quickly as you can, write ten questions about the object. Then, (2) select one of the following topics and, as quickly as you can, write ten questions about the topic:

- Dreams
- The Common Cold

Answers will vary.

EXERCISE 1.9 PREVIEWING AND RELATING

Directions: Preview the following passage. When you have finished your preview, answer the questions that follow the passage.

UNDERSTANDING THE INTERVIEWING PROCESS

An *employment interview* is a formal meeting during which both you and the prospective employer ask questions and exchange information. These meetings have a dual purpose: (1) The organization's main objective is to find the best person available for the job by determining whether you and the organization are a good match, and (2) your main objective is to find the job best suited to your goals and capabilities.

Adjust your job search to the company's size and hiring practices. Large organizations that hire hundreds of new employees every year typically take a more systematic approach to the recruiting and interviewing process than small local businesses do. In general, the easiest way to connect with a big company is through your campus placement office; the most efficient way to approach a smaller business is often contacting the company directly.

Regardless of which path you choose, interviewing takes time, so start seeking jobs well in advance of the date you want to start work. During downturns in the economy, early planning is even more crucial. Many employers become more selective and many corporations reduce their campus visits and campus hiring programs, so more of the job-search burden falls on you. Whatever shape the economy is in, try to secure as many interviews as you can, both to improve the chances of receiving a job offer and to give yourself more options when you do get offers.

The Typical Sequence of Interviews

Most employers interview an applicant two or three times before deciding to make a job offer. Applicants often face a sequence of interviews, each with a different purpose.

First is the preliminary *screening stage,* which helps employers screen out unqualified applicants. Screening can take place on campus, at company offices, or via telephone or computer. Many companies use standardized evaluation sheets to "grade" the applicants so that all the candidates will be measured against the same criteria. Time is limited, so keep your answers short while providing a few key points that differentiate you from other candidates.

The next stage of interviews helps the organization narrow the field even further. Typically, if you're invited to visit a company, you will talk with a variety of people, including a member of the human resources department, one or two potential colleagues, and your potential supervisor. Your best approach during this *selection stage* of interviews is to show interest in the job, relate your skills and experience to the organization's needs, listen attentively, ask insightful questions, and display enthusiasm.

If the interviewers agree that you're a good candidate, you may receive a job offer, either on the spot or a few days later by phone, mail, or e-mail. In other cases, you may be invited back for a final evaluation by a higher-ranking executive who has the authority to make the hiring decision and to decide on your compensation. An underlying objective of the *final stage* is often to sell you on the advantages of joining the organization.

Common Types of Interviews

Organizations use various types of interviews to discover as much as possible about you and other applicants. A *structured interview* is generally used in the screening stage. Working from a checklist, the interviewer asks you a series of prepared questions in a set order. Although useful for gathering facts, the structured interview is generally regarded as a poor measure of an applicant's personal qualities. Nevertheless, some companies use structured interviews to create uniformity in their hiring process.

By contrast, the *open-ended interview* is less formal and unstructured, more like a conversation between peers. The interviewer poses broad, open-ended questions and encourages you to talk freely. This type of interview is good for bringing out your personality and for testing professional judgment, but remember you're in a business situation so keep your answers focused.

Some organizations perform *group interviews,* meeting with several candidates simultaneously to see how they interact. This type of interview is useful for judging interpersonal skills.

The most unnerving type of interview is the *stress interview,* during which you might be asked pointed questions designed to unsettle you, or you might be subjected to long periods of silence, criticism, interruptions, and/or even hostile reactions by the interviewer. The theory behind this approach is that you'll reveal how well you handle stressful situations, although some experts find the technique of dubious value. If you find yourself in a stress interview, pause for a few seconds to collect your thoughts before continuing, knowing what the interviewer is up to.

As employers try to cut travel costs, the *video interview* is becoming more popular. Many large companies use videoconferencing systems to screen middle-management candidates or to interview new recruits at universities. Experts recommend that candidates prepare a bit differently for a video interview than for an in-person meeting.

- Ask for a preliminary phone conversation to establish rapport with the interviewer.

- Arrive early enough to get used to the equipment and setting.

- During the interview, speak clearly but not more slowly than normal.

- Sit straight and look up.

- Keep your mannerisms lively without looking forced or fake.

Many companies have learned that no strong correlation exists between how well people answer interview questions in a traditional interview and how well they perform real tasks on the job. In response, these firms have begun using the *situational interview,* or *behavioral interview.* During such interviews, you may be asked to explain how you would solve a particular business problem, or you might be asked to lead a brainstorming session, engage in role playing, or even make a presentation. Although situational interviews may strike some candidates as unusual, proponents claim they are much more accurate at predicting success on the job.

What Employers Look for in an Interview

Interviews give employers the chance to go beyond the basic data of your résumé to get to know you and to answer two essential questions. The first is whether you will be a good fit with the organization. For instance, TechTarget, an interactive media company, gives employees an unusual amount of freedom, including the freedom to set their own hours and take as many days off as they want or need—provided they meet their work objectives. To succeed in this environment, employees must be able to handle the responsibility that comes with such independence. As a result, TechTarget's hiring process is focused on filtering out candidates who need a more structured environment.

Some interviewers believe that personal background indicates how well the candidate will fit in, so they might ask about your interests, hobbies, awareness of world events, and so forth. You can expand your potential along these lines by reading widely, making an effort to meet new people, and participating in discussion groups, seminars, and workshops. Interviewers are likely to consider your personal style as well. You can impress them by being open, enthusiastic, and interested. Some interviewers also look for courtesy, sincerity, willingness to learn, and a style that is positive and self-confident.

The second question is whether you can handle the responsibilities of the position. The interviewer should already have some idea of whether you have the right qualifications, based on a review of your résumé. During the interview, you'll probably be asked to describe your education and previous jobs in more depth so that the interviewer can determine how well your skills match the requirements. You may also be asked how you would apply those skills to hypothetical situations on the job.

—Bovee and Thill, *Business Communication Essentials*, 3rd ed.

1. What is the passage about?

   Interviewing for a job

2. What are the purposes of an employment interview?

   Employer's purpose: find the best candidate for the job.

   Candidate's purpose: find a suitable job.

3. What are the three interview stages identified in the passage?

   Screening; selection; final

4. How many types of interviews are identified in the passage? List them.

   Six: structured; open-ended; group; stress; video; situational

5. What will the last section of the passage discuss?

   What employers look for in an interview

6. What have you previously read or learned about job interviews? What associations do you have with this subject?

   Answers will vary.

7. Write three questions about interviews.

   Answers will vary.

8. In the space below, discuss a job interview you've had. If you've never had a job interview, write about how you might prepare for an important job interview.

   Answers will vary.

EXERCISE 1.10 APPLYING PRE-READING STRATEGIES

Directions: Preview a chapter from a textbook you are using in another course or an article you have been assigned to read and answer the following questions.

Title of chapter or article: Answers will vary.

1. What is the subject of the chapter (or article)? What main topics will be discussed?

   Answers will vary.

   _____

2. What have you previously read or learned about this subject? What personal experiences can you relate to the subject? What associations do you have with this subject?

   Answers will vary.

   _____

3. What would you learn from reading this chapter or article?

   Answers will vary.

   _____

4. Write three questions about the subject of the chapter or article.

   Answers will vary.

   _____

   _____

Active Reading Strategy: Forming Goal Questions

Forming goal questions is another great strategy for engaged reading. Active reading is a purposeful activity: it is an active search for meaning. When you read an assignment, you should know why are reading it—that is, what you are trying to learn and remember. You will then be able to judge how well you succeeded with your learning goals.

Previewing enables you to anticipate what you will be reading and to define a general goal for your reading of the chapter or article. For example, after previewing the passage on job interviews, you might express your general goal as "to learn more about employment interviews."

We can focus our reading goals by expressing them as questions. A goal question helps you know what to look for as you read through assigned material. For example, for the passage, "Understanding the Interviewing Process," we might start with the goal question, "What is the interviewing process?" Goal questions are broad or general questions that lead us forward as we read. Goal questions increase our engagement, because when we've formed a goal question, our minds become motivated to find the answer.

Goal questions can be formed while previewing or while reading through a chapter or article. Goal questions are usually formed by changing titles, headings, and subheadings into questions. To make a goal question, simply invert or reword a title, heading, or subheading into a question, using a common question word, like "what" or "how."

For example, for the heading:	*The goal question might be:*
The Typical Sequence of Interviews	What is the typical sequence of interviews?
Common Types of Interviews	What are the common types of interviews?
What Employers Look for in an Interview	What do employers look for in an interview?
Making Time for Fitness	How do you make time for fitness?
Activating Your Daily Routine	How do you activate your daily routine?

Sometimes when you look at a heading or subheading, the best question to raise may not be apparent. When this happens, raise the question that you think is most likely to be addressed, and then as you read, notice if the question is indeed being answered. If it is not, ask yourself what question is being answered by the material in the passage.

Notice that using goal questions is a different strategy from raising questions to relate to the subject. When relating, any and all questions are helpful to stimulate curiosity and interest. With goal questions, you raise only those questions that you expect to be answered in the passage. In short, you use goal questions to predict what to look for while reading and to determine whether or not your goals have been achieved.

EXERCISE 1.11 GOAL QUESTIONS FROM HEADINGS

Directions: Imagine you are reading passages with the following headings. For each heading, write one or two goal questions that would help you know what to look for if you were to read the passage. The first one is done as an example.

1. Changing Unrealistic Views about Marriage

   How can unrealistic views about marriage be changed?

   What are some unrealistic views of marriage?

2. Causes of Prejudice

   What causes prejudice?

   What are some causes of prejudice?

3. Measuring Intelligence

   How is intelligence measured?

   What are the ways by which intelligence is measured?

4. Individual Differences among Newborns

   How do newborns differ from one another?

   What are some individual differences among newborns?

5. How Friendships Develop

How do friendships develop?
_____

What are the stages in the development of a friendship?
_____

6. Stress and Its Consequences

What is stress?
_____

What are the consequences of stress?
_____

7. Pharmacologic Effects of Alcohol

What are the pharmacologic effects of alcohol?
_____

What effects are most common?
_____

8. Superstitions about Money

What are some superstitions about money?
_____

How did superstitions about money arise?
_____

9. Bird Courtship

How do birds court?
_____

What are the stages of the courtship process for birds?
_____

10. The Origins of Jazz

How did jazz originate?
_____

Where and when did jazz originate?
_____

11. The First United States Currency

What was the first U.S. currency?
_____

When was it created?
_____

12. Causes of the Vietnam War

What were the causes of the Vietnam War?
_____

Which causes were most important?
_____

13. The Development of Paper Money

How did paper money develop?
_____

Who first used paper money?
_____

14. Cell Structure

What is the structure of a cell?
_____

What parts make up a cell?
_____

15. Lincoln's Childhood

What was Lincoln's childhood like?

What were the important events of Lincoln's childhood?

EXERCISE 1.12 WORKING WITH GOAL QUESTIONS

Directions: Use the following headings to form a goal question for each of the accompanying passages. After reading each passage, write a brief answer to your question. An example is provided.

EXAMPLE Professional Crime

Goal question: _What is professional crime?_

Although the adage "crime doesn't pay" is familiar, many people do make a career of illegal activities. A professional criminal is a person who pursues crime as a day-by-day occupation, developing skilled techniques and enjoying a certain degree of status among other criminals. Some professional criminals specialize in safe-cracking, hijacking of cargo, pickpocketing, and shoplifting. Such persons can reduce the likelihood of arrest, conviction, and imprisonment through their skill. As a result, they may have long careers in their chosen "professions."

Edwin Sutherland offered pioneering insights regarding professional criminals by publishing an annotated account written by a professional thief. Unlike the person who engages in crime only once or twice, professional thieves make a business of stealing. These criminals devote their entire working time to planning and executing crimes and sometimes travel across the nation to pursue their "professional duties."

—Schaeffer, *Sociology,* 2nd ed.

Answer: _Professional crime is the use of crime as a career or business. Professional criminals often develop special skills to use in their particular lines of crime and engage in crime regularly._

A. The Food Value of Milk

Goal question: What is the food value of milk?

Cow's milk is about 87 percent water and 13 percent solids. The solids contain the nutrients in milk. The body needs five kinds of nutrients for energy, growth, and the replacement of worn-out tissue. These nutrients are (1) carbohydrates, (2) fats, (3) minerals, (4) proteins, and (5) vitamins.

Milk has been called "the most nearly perfect food" because it is an outstanding source of these nutrients. But milk is not "the perfect food" because it lacks enough iron and does not provide all vitamins.

—"Milk," *World Book Encyclopedia*

Answer: Milk contains the five basic nutrients the body needs. It is not a perfect food, however, because it lacks sufficient iron and some vitamins.

B. Printing Paper Money

Goal question: How is paper money printed?

The production of a new bill begins when artists sketch their designs for it. The secretary of the treasury must approve the final design. Engravers cut the design into a steel plate. A machine called a *transfer press* squeezes the engraving against a soft steel roller, making a raised design on the roller's surface. After the roller is heat-treated to harden it, another transfer press reproduces the design from the roller 32 times on a printing plate. Each plate prints a sheet of 32 bills. Separate plates print the front and back of the bills.

Many people believe that the paper used for money is made by a secret process. However, the government publishes a detailed description of the paper so that private companies can compete for the contracts to manufacture it. Federal law forbids unauthorized persons to manufacture any paper similar to that used for money.

The Bureau of Engraving and Printing uses high-speed presses to print sheets of paper currency. The design is printed first. Then the seals, serial numbers, and signatures are added in a separate operation. The sheets are cut into stacks of bills. Imperfect bills are replaced with new ones called *star notes*. Each star note has the same serial number as the bill it replaces, but a star after the number shows that it is a replacement bill. The bills are shipped to Reserve Banks, which distribute them to commercial banks.

Most $1 bills wear out after 18 months in circulation. Larger denominations last for years because they are handled less often. Banks collect worn-out bills and ship them to Federal Reserve banks for replacement. The Reserve Banks destroy worn-out money in shredding machines.

—"Money," *World Book Encyclopedia*

Answer: An artist sketches a design, which is approved by the Secretary of the Treasury. The design is cut into a steel plate, transferred to a steel roller, and then onto a printing plate 32 times. The plate prints a sheet of 32 bills, with separate plates for front and back. High-speed presses are used. The sheets are cut to create individual bills. Imperfect bills are replaced.

C. Circadian Rhythms

Goal question: What are circadian rhythms?

Every plant seems to follow a cycle that includes sleep. Some flowers close their petals at night and open them again in the morning, as if they were aware of the transition between night and day. Scientists call these cycles *circadian rhythms,* which are daily fluctuations comprising a 24-hour period. These cycles are presumed to be present in every living cell.

—Gonzalez-Wippler, *Dreams*

Answer: _Circadian rhythms are the daily cycles believed to occur in all living cells._

_____

_____

_____

_____

D. Other-Imposed Discipline versus Self-Discipline

Goal question: _How is other-imposed discipline different from self-discipline?_

Now let's distinguish between two radically different kinds of control-type discipline. One is externally administered or "other-imposed"; the other is internally administered or self-imposed. Discipline by others versus discipline of oneself; control by others as opposed to self-control.

Everyone is familiar with the term *self-discipline,* but what does it actually mean?

Psychologists use the term *locus of control,* which I think is helpful here. Their investigations show that some people tend to have the locus of control *inside* themselves. With self-discipline, the locus of control is inside the person, but with discipline enforced by others, the locus of control is outside the person—actually inside the controller.

—Gordon, *Teaching Children Self-Discipline*

Answer: _Self-discipline comes from within; the locus of control is inside the person._
Other-imposed discipline comes from outside and from other people.

_____

_____

_____

E. Principles of Criminal Law

Goal question: _What are the principles of criminal law?_

Our system of justice operates on two key principles of criminal law. The first is the presumption of innocence. This means that those accused of crimes are considered innocent until proved guilty. The second principle is the burden of proof, which in criminal cases means that guilt must be proved beyond a reasonable doubt.

Theoretically, determining guilt is a process involving arguing the issues of fact or law in the particular case; in actual practice, however, this seldom happens. In many cases, the existence of guilt is supported by sufficient evidence; in others, where the issues of fact are such that the accused may or may not be found guilty beyond a reasonable doubt, concessions are worked out that may result in a reduced charge if the accused agrees to plead guilty.

—Pursley, *Introduction to Criminal Justice,*
3rd ed.

Answer: <u>There are two key principles: presumption of innocence and burden of proof.</u>

<u>A person is presumed innocent until proven guilty, and guilt must be proved beyond</u>

<u>a reasonable doubt.</u>

SKILLS ONLINE: PREVIEWING WEB SITES

 As a college student, you will be asked to do research in some of your classes, and you will almost certainly use the Internet for much of your research. Previewing Web sites will help you make careful choices about which Web sites to use and wise decisions about which information to trust.

Web sites are organized very differently from printed material, and therefore, previewing a Web site is different from previewing printed material. Here are some guidelines for previewing a Web site:

1. Look for evidence of the Web site's *purpose* and *intended audience*. Is the site selling something, promoting a point of view, or simply giving information? For whom is it intended? You may find a statement of purpose on the home page or on a linked page (such as "About Us").

2. Note the Web site's *domain* (type of Web site): commercial, nonprofit, governmental, educational, and so forth. The domain is an important clue to the Web site's purpose. The domain is indicated by the suffix at the end of the Web site:

   .com = commercial

   .org = organization (often used by nonprofit organizations)

   .gov = governmental

   .edu = educational

   Note that the *.com* suffix is sometimes used by nonprofit organizations as well as by commercial, or profit-making, groups, and that *.org* is not used exclusively by nonprofit organizations.

3. Look for *authorship*. Does the Web site provide the name of an individual or group who published the Web site? If an author's name is provided, are the author's credentials provided?

4. Look for a *date* that indicates how current the Web site is. When was it last updated?

5. Note whether or not the site indicates the *sources* of its information (where it got the information).

6. Look over the *links* that the site contains. Do they seem useful, logical, and adequate? Notice the small print links often found at the bottom of a Web page. These may include a link for a *site map,* which will show the content and organization of the Web site.

7. Note whether the site has any *special features* that might be useful to you or that would distinguish it from other Web sites.

SKILLS ONLINE EXERCISE. PREVIEWING WEB SITES

Directions:

1. Imagine that you are assigned to write a report on a famous person whom you admire. Choose a person you'd like to report on.

2. Connect to the Internet and find two different Web sites that provide information about that person.

3. Preview both Web sites and answer the following questions:

   A. What is the title and URL of each Web site?

      Web site 1: Answers will vary.

      Web site 2: Answers will vary.

   B. Who is the author or publisher of each Web site?

      Web site 1: Answers will vary.

      Web site 2: Answers will vary.

   C. When was each Web site last updated?

      Web site 1: Answers will vary.

      Web site 2: Answers will vary.

   D. Which Web site provides more information about the person?

      Answers will vary.

   E. Which Web site seems easier to navigate and use? Why?

      Answers will vary.

   F. Which Web site seems to contain more reliable information? How can you tell?

      Answers will vary.

   G. Which Web site has more useful links? Explain.

      Answers will vary.

READING 1A

PSYCHOLOGY OF SELF-AWARENESS (PSYCHOLOGY)

by Denis Waitley

Reading 1A is taken from the book *Psychology of Success: Developing Your Self-Esteem*, by Denis Waitley. Dr. Waitley is a widely respected expert on human performance and potential. He is the author of several books, including *The Psychology of Winning*. In this excerpt, Dr. Waitley discusses some of the components of self-awareness and their importance to personal growth.

Pre-Reading Exercise

Directions: Complete this exercise before reading the passage. Preview the passage and answer the following questions.

1. What is the subject of the selection?

   Self-awareness

2. What is self-awareness?

   The ability to look honestly at oneself and accept what one sees

3. What three types of self-awareness are discussed?

   Environmental; physical; mental

4. What comes to mind when you think of the term "self-awareness or self-esteem?" What have you read or learned before on the subject of self-awareness (or self-esteem)?

   Answers will vary.

5. Put yourself in the place of one of your friends or teachers. How would he or she describe you?

   Answers will vary.

6. Write three questions about self-awareness or any of the subtopics in the selection.

   Answers will vary.

Directions: Form a goal question as you come to each subheading within the passage. As you finish each section of the passage, pause to see if you've found an answer to your goal question.

What Is Self-Awareness?

1 One of the most important elements of success is Self-Awareness. *Self-awareness* is the ability to step back from the canvas of life and take a good look at yourself as you relate to your environmental, physical, and mental worlds. It is the ability to accept yourself as a unique, changing, imperfect, and growing individual. It's the ability to recognize your potential as well as your limitations.

2 Self-awareness is self-honesty: seeing yourself, your strengths, and your weaknesses clearly. It is knowing what you have to offer and recognizing that time and effort will be necessary for top achievement. Winners can look in the mirror and see what lies behind their own eyes. You are

a Winner when what you think, how you feel, and what you do all fit together.

Environmental Self-Awareness

3   Winners display an Environmental Self-Awareness. They are aware of how little they really know about anything in their world. They know that what they do know is shaded by their own heredity and environment. Winners are able to accept what is happening around them, and this contributes to their self-awareness. This awareness includes being concerned about the needs of others.

4   Are you open-minded? Do you look at life through your parents' eyes? Are your prejudices inherited from your parents, or are they your own? Environmental self-awareness means realizing that each human being on earth is a person with the equal right to fulfill his or her own potential in life. It is realizing that skin color, religion, birthplace, financial status, or intelligence do not determine a person's worth or value. Environmental self-awareness is accepting the fact that every human being is a unique individual. No two people are exactly alike—not even identical twins.

5   Have you ever heard someone say, "We're not on the same wavelength"? This translates to: "You don't think as I do," or "I don't understand why you think the way you do." It's easy to see why there is so much misunderstanding and fighting in the world, within families and among nations. Everyone sees life through a different camera lens and "hears a different drummer."

Empathy

6   *Empathy* is the awareness of, and sensitivity to, the feelings, thoughts, and experiences of others. It is seeing life through other persons' eyes—experiencing their pain, their curiosity, their hopes, their fears. It is watching marathon runners at the 20-mile mark and feeling your own legs ache.

7   You can feel empathy with anyone—whether that person is of a different generation, a citizen of another country, or simply someone with a different point of view. Instead of being quick to criticize or judge other persons, try to see the situation through their eyes. How do they feel? What are they afraid of? What concerns them most?

8   Perform this "Empathy Checkup" on yourself by changing places with someone else:

- *If I were my husband/wife, how would I like to have a partner like me?* Would I think I was supportive? Independent? Interesting? Understanding? An equal partner?

- *If I were my child, how would I like to have a parent like me?* Would I think I was patient? Encouraging? Positive? Supportive? Nonjudgmental?

- *If I were my instructor, how would I like to have a student like me?* Would I think I showed a lot of effort? A lot of interest? Curiosity? Discipline? Concern for others in class?

- *If I were my boss, how would I like to have an employee like me?* Would I think I was a good worker? Productive? Reliable? Responsible? Nice to work with?

- *How would it feel to be an immigrant just arrived in America?* Would I feel isolated? Frightened? Unsure of whom to trust? Challenged? Optimistic? Hopeful?

- *How does the world appear through the eyes of a child?* Big? Confusing? Exciting? Scary? Hard to understand? Fun?

Adapting

9   Does it bother you to discover that there are so many people around that are different from you? Do you think you might seem strange or different to other people? We need to understand what being human is all about. To be human is to be a changing, growing, imperfect, but amazing living creation. Winners know that they will come across many different people, places, and experiences in their lifetimes. A lot of those people, places, and experiences will seem very strange and unfamiliar. How can you learn to enjoy all the different and unusual things that you come across in life?

10   The answer is to *adapt*. Adapting means being flexible and open to the actions of others. Because Winners are self-aware and have empathy for others, they do not allow others to ruin their day or rain on their parade. Adapting to our environment means being flexible and changing with the times as we need to.

Physical Self-Awareness

11   Our next step is to develop our Physical Self-Awareness. This means understanding that our bodies are machines whose performance depends on good health. We must each treat our body as our one and only transportation vehicle for life. We must care for it with the fuel of good nutrition, activity, and health care. If we are fat and sluggish or thin and nervous because we smoke, drink, eat poorly, or don't exercise, we cannot trade in our bodies for new models. If we abuse them we won't be able to use them as long or as well. You can *do* well only if you *feel* well.

Stress

12   *Stress* is any physical, emotional, or chemical effect that causes tension. It can even be a factor in causing disease. Earl Nightingale, a well-known motivational speaker, told the story of a trip taken with his son to the Great Barrier Reef, which stretches 1,800 miles from New Guinea to Australia. He noticed that the coral growing on the inside of the reef, where the sea was peaceful and quiet in the lagoon, looked pale and lifeless. But the coral on the outside of the reef, constantly beaten by the powerful waves, looked healthy and brightly colored. Earl asked the guide why this was so. "It's very simple," came the reply. "The coral on the lagoon side dies rapidly with no challenge for growth and survival, while the coral facing the open sea thrives and multiplies because it is challenged and tested every day."

13   And so it is with all living things on earth. If we never challenge ourselves, we never have the opportunity to succeed. We can choose to just sit back and wither on the vine. Or we can use the failures and setbacks in our lives to strengthen us and help us guard against anxiety, depression, and other negative responses to stress.

14   Not much has changed since the days of our early ancestors when, at the first sign of danger, the body got ready for "fight or flight." A person would either fight to defend himself against danger or run the other way. Nowadays, we experience at least one or two unpleasant surprises almost every day, and we have to make the decision to fight or walk the other way.

Anger

15   How many complete strangers got you upset and ready to risk your life on the road today? Winners don't overreact to what is happening as the cave dwellers did. They are not quick to anger, with their blood pressures jumping, heart rates quickening, and adrenalin pumping. Every annoying situation is not a struggle for survival, and there are not always tigers ready to pounce.

16   Winners don't let this daily stress destroy their mental and physical health. They don't drink more, smoke more, or pop more pills to escape or cope with the stress. They don't take their anger out on other people. They control their negative feelings and express them in a constructive way. When Winners feel angry or upset they jog around the block, take a long walk, or listen to some soothing music—anything that will relieve their negative feelings in a healthy way. Self-awareness is an important part of the victory over stress. Winners learn how to relax and cope with the ups and downs of everyday life.

17   Expressing joy, love, compassion, and excitement is healthy. But openly expressing hostility, anger, depression, loneliness, or anxiety may not be healthy for us. The only healthy expression of the "fight or flight" response is in the face of a life or death situation. But in most of our daily situations, stress and anger can be dealt with by deep breathing, relaxation, and exercise such as running, aerobics, or basketball.

18   Dr. Hans Selye, one of the first people to study stress, divides people into two categories: racehorses and turtles. A racehorse loves to run and will die from exhaustion if it is corralled or confined in a small space. A turtle will die from exhaustion if forced to run on a treadmill, moving

too fast for its slow nature. We each have to find our own healthy stress level, somewhere between that of the racehorse and the turtle.

Mental Self-Awareness

19   An important part of positive self-awareness is Mental Self-Awareness. This is knowing the potential within our own minds that is just waiting to be challenged. We must ask ourselves, "What is my mental outlook toward life? Do I sell myself short or am I overconfident in my abilities?"

20   Truth and honesty are necessary for any real and lasting success. We must ask ourselves:

"Is this true? Is this honest?" If we can answer yes, or if we can seek out the truth with the help of someone else, we can move ahead and take action.

21   Attitude is the key to healthy self-awareness. In order to feel well and accomplish things in your life, you'll need to develop positive attitudes and positive responses to the pressures in life. The more honest and self-aware you become, the more ways you'll find to Win. Find a new way to Win today!

—Waitley, *Psychology of Success: Developing Your Self-Esteem*

You, the Reader

Interest Rating. Please rate the interest level of the reading on the following scale (circle one):

5—Very interesting   2—A little boring

4—Fairly interesting   1—Very boring

3—Mildly interesting

Difficulty Rating. Please rate the difficulty level of the reading on the following scale (circle one):

5—Very difficult   2—Fairly easy

4—Fairly difficult   1—Very easy

3—Moderate

Comments: Please explain your ratings and make any other comments you wish about the reading.

Answers will vary.

COMPREHENSION QUESTIONS

Directions: For questions 1–5, choose the answer that best completes the statement. For questions 6–10, write your response in the space provided. Base all answers on what you read in the selection. Refer back to the selection as necessary to answer the questions.

_____b_____ **1.** The author believes that it is important to:
a. Criticize yourself.
b. Appreciate people who are different from you.
c. Avoid stress.
d. Learn whether you are a racehorse or a turtle.

_____a_____   **2.** Which of the following is *not* a characteristic of a Winner?
  a. Readiness to defend yourself at all times
  b. The ability to empathize with others
  c. Integrating your thoughts, feelings, and behaviors
  d. Self-awareness

_____d_____   **3.** The author suggests that:
  a. Heredity is more important than environment.
  b. Environment is more important than heredity.
  c. Environmental self-awareness is learned from our parents.
  d. Both heredity and environment contribute to self-awareness.

_____a_____   **4.** Regarding stress, the author believes that:
  a. The level of stress that is desirable varies from person to person.
  b. Turtles adapt better to stress than racehorses.
  c. The less stress in life the better.
  d. Fighting and running away are the best ways to cope with most stressful situations.

_____d_____   **5.** The author uses questions to:
  a. Make the point that many questions in life have no real answers.
  b. Show that he doesn't have all the answers.
  c. Encourage the reader to ask questions.
  d. Encourage the reader's self-awareness.

6. What is Environmental Self-Awareness? Why is it important?

Environmental self-awareness is awareness of the world around us and how little we really

know about it. It involves concern and respect for others. It is important because it enables

us to appreciate differences.

7. What is Physical Self-Awareness? Why is it important?

Physical self-awareness is a respectful awareness of our bodies and their needs.

It is important because our bodies cannot be replaced, and abusing them detracts from

our capacity for growth and joy.

8. The example of the coral reef (in the section headed "Stress") is used to make what point about stress?

Stress or challenge is needed for growth. Coping with stress strengthens us.

9. Are you a racehorse or a turtle? Explain.

Answers will vary.

10. Answer the questions on the "Empathy Checkup" (in the section headed "Empathy") for any *two* of the individuals listed.

Answers will vary.

VOCABULARY EXERCISE

Directions: Write the meaning of the **boldfaced** word in each sentence. You may consult a dictionary as necessary.

1. Self-awareness is the ability to step back from the canvas of life and take a good look at yourself as you relate to your **environmental,** physical, and mental worlds.

Relating to one's surroundings

2. It is the ability to accept yourself as a **unique,** changing, imperfect, and growing individual.

One of a kind

3. It's the ability to recognize your potential as well as your **limitations**.

Restrictions to one's capacities

4. They know that what they do know is shaded by their own **heredity** and environment.

Biological transmission of characteristics

5. **Empathy** is the awareness of, and sensitivity to, the feelings, thoughts, and experiences of others.

Awareness of and sensitivity to feelings, thoughts, and experiences of others

6. If we are fat and **sluggish** or thin and nervous because we smoke, drink, eat poorly, or don't exercise, we cannot trade in our bodies for new models.

Slow; lacking energy

7. The coral on the lagoon side dies rapidly with no challenge for growth and survival, while the coral facing the open sea **thrives** and multiplies because it is challenged and tested every day.

Prospers; grows vigorously

8. We can choose to just sit back and **wither** on the vine.

   Dry up; weaken
   _____

9. They [Winners] control their negative feelings and express them in a **constructive** way.

   Helpful; productive; contributing to improvement
   _____

10. A racehorse loves to run and will die from exhaustion if it is corralled or **confined** in a small space.

    Restricted to a small space; kept in
    _____

RESPOND TO THE READING

Directions: Write a half-page response to either of the following questions.

1. Describe a situation in which you felt stressed or angry and explain how you handled it.

2. How might you apply the author's suggestions to your daily life?

WEBQUEST

Directions: Use the Internet to find the answer to the following question. Write your answer on a sheet of paper. Print out the Web page you used for the answer or copy the URL on your sheet.

List ten techniques or strategies for managing stress.

READING **1B**

UNDERSTANDING CONSUMER BEHAVIOR (BUSINESS)

by Ronald J. Ebert and Ricky W. Griffin

Reading 1B is taken from a business textbook. The selection discusses the importance for marketers (business people) of understanding consumer behavior, but at the same time provides valuable insights from which the ordinary consumer can benefit. As you read the passage, consider your own spending habits in comparison with the authors' ideas about what influences consumer spending.

Pre-reading Exercise:

Directions: Complete this exercise before reading the passage. Preview the passage and answer the following questions.

1. What is the passage about?

   Consumer behavior and the buying process

2. What four types of influences are discussed in the section "Influences on Consumer Behavior"?

   Psychological; personal; social; cultural

3. What are the five stages of the consumer buying process?

   Problem/need recognition; information seeking; evaluation of alternatives; purchase decision;

   post-purchase evaluation

4. In addition to these stages, what other information can be found in Figure 1B.1?

   Personal and environmental factors and marketing factors that influence the process

5. What most influences you when you are making an important purchase?

   Answers will vary.

6. Write three questions about consumer behavior.

   Answers will vary.

Directions: Form a goal question as you come to each subheading within the passage. As you finish each section of the passage, pause to see if you've found an answer to your goal question.

1   Although marketing managers can tell us what features people want in a new refrigerator, they cannot tell us why they buy particular refrigerators. What desire are consumers fulfilling? Is there a psychological or sociological explanation for why they purchase one product and not another? These questions and many others are addressed in the study of **consumer behavior**—the study of the decision process by which people buy and consume products.

consumer behavior Study of the decision process by which people buy and consume products.

Influences on Consumer Behavior

To understand consumer behavior, marketers draw heavily on such fields as psychology and sociology.* By identifying which influences are most active in certain circumstances, marketers try to explain consumer choices and predict future buying behavior.   2

*Note: Psychology is the study of human behavior and the mind. Sociology is the study of group behavior and society.

1. Psychological influences include an individual's motivations, perceptions, ability to learn, and attitudes.

2. Personal influences include lifestyle, personality, and economic status.

3. Social influences include family, opinion leaders (people whose opinions are sought by others), and such reference groups as friends, co-workers, and professional associates.

4. Cultural influences include culture (the way of living that distinguishes one large group from another), subculture (smaller groups with shared values), and social class (the cultural ranking of groups according to such criteria as background, occupation, and income).

3   Although these factors can have a strong impact on a consumer's choices, their effect on actual purchases is sometimes weak or negligible. Some consumers, for example, exhibit high **brand loyalty**—they regularly purchase products

brand loyalty Pattern of regular consumer purchasing based on satisfaction with a product's performance.

because they are satisfied with their performance. Such people are less subject to influence and stick with preferred brands. On the other hand, the clothes you wear and the food you eat often reflect social and psychological influences on your consumer behavior.

The Consumer Buying Process

Students of consumer behavior have constructed various models to help show how consumers decide to buy products. Figure 1B.1 presents one such model. At the core of this and similar models is an awareness of the many influences that lead to consumption. Ultimately, marketers use this information to develop marketing plans.   4

Problem/Need Recognition

This process begins when the consumer recognizes a problem or need. Need recognition also occurs when you have a chance to change your buying habits. When you obtain your first job after graduation, your new income may let you buy things that were once too expensive for you. You may find that you need professional clothing, apartment furnishings, and a car. American Express and Citi cater to such shifts in needs when they market credit cards to college seniors.   5

Information Seeking

Having recognized a need, consumers often seek information. The search is not always extensive, but before making major purchases, most people seek information from personal sources, public sources, and experience.   6

Evaluation of Alternatives

By analyzing product attributes (price, prestige, quality), consumers compare products before deciding which one best meets their needs.   7

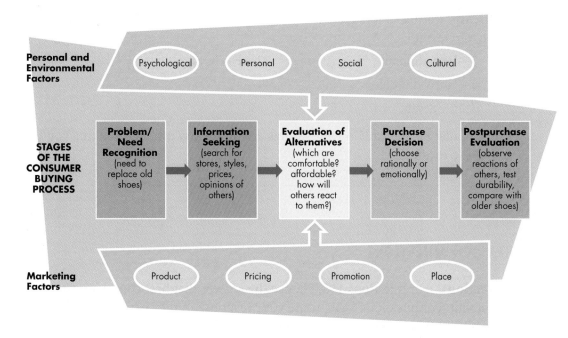

Figure 1B.1 The Consumer Buying Process

Purchase Decision

8   Ultimately, consumers make purchase decisions. "Buy" decisions are based on rational motives, emotional motives, or both. **Rational motives** involve the logical evaluation of product attributes: cost, quality, and usefulness. **Emotional motives** involve nonobjective factors and include sociability, imitation of others, and aesthetics.

> **rational motives** Reasons for purchasing a product that are based on a logical evaluation of product attributes.
> **emotional motives** Reasons for purchasing a product that are based on nonobjective factors.

Postpurchase Evaluation

9   Marketing does not stop with the sale of a product. What happens after the sale is important. Marketers want consumers to be happy after buying products so that they are more likely to buy them again. Because consumers do not want to go through a complex decision process for every purchase, they often repurchase products they have used and liked. Not all consumers are satisfied with their purchases. These buyers are not likely to purchase the same product(s) again and are much more apt to broadcast their experiences than are satisfied customers.

—Ebert and Griffin, *Business Essentials,* 7th ed.

You, the Reader

Interest Rating. Please rate the interest level of the reading on the following scale (circle one):

    5—Very interesting   2—A little boring

    4—Fairly interesting   1—Very boring

    3—Mildly interesting

Difficulty Rating. Please rate the difficulty level of the reading on the following scale (circle one):

5—Very difficult   2—Fairly easy

4—Fairly difficult   1—Very easy

3—Moderate

Comments: Please explain your ratings and make any other comments you wish about the reading.

Answers will vary.

COMPREHENSION QUESTIONS

Directions: For questions 1–5, choose the answer that best completes the statement. For questions 6–10, write your response in the space provided. Base all answers on what you read in the selection. Refer back to the selection as necessary to answer the questions.

c   **1.** Which of the following is *not* identified as a psychological influence?
   a. Motivation
   b. Attitude
   c. Economic status
   d. Ability to learn

b   **2.** The authors state that the four types of influences on consumer behavior:
   a. Always have a strong impact on a consumer's choices.
   b. Sometimes have a weak impact on actual purchases.
   c. Usually don't have much impact on a consumer's choices.
   d. Are never more powerful than brand loyalty.

a   **3.** We can tell from Figure 1B.1 that pricing is:
   a. A marketing factor.
   b. A psychological factor.
   c. A cultural factor.
   d. The most important part of the buying process.

d   **4.** Which of the following would be an example of an *emotional* motive?
   a. Choosing a product whose cost matches your budget
   b. Choosing a higher quality product
   c. Buying something because it will be useful
   d. Buying a product because all your friends have one

d   **5.** We can conclude from the passage that:
   a. Consumers' buying decisions are usually simple.
   b. Brand loyalty is usually the strongest influence.
   c. Rational motives are more powerful than emotional motives.
   d. Buying decisions are often influenced by a variety of factors.

6. Why are marketers interested in psychology and sociology?

Psychology and sociology can help marketers understand consumer influences and choices

and make better predictions about future buying behavior.

7. What do consumers do during the second stage of the buying process (information seeking)?

They gather information and opinions about what they are buying.

8. According to the authors, what are consumers likely to do if they are dissatisfied with a purchase?

They are not likely to buy that product again and are likely to tell others about their

dissatisfaction.

9. Give an example of a *social* influence that has affected you as a consumer.

Answers will vary.

10. In your opinion, what are the best ways to gain information about a product before you purchase it?

Answers will vary.

VOCABULARY EXERCISE

Directions: Write the meaning of the boldfaced word in each sentence. You may consult a dictionary as necessary.

1. Personal influences include lifestyle, personality, and economic **status.**

Standing; rank; position

2. . . . (the cultural ranking of groups according to such **criteria** as background, occupation, and income).

Standards for judging and evaluating

3. . . . their effect on purchases is sometimes weak or **negligible.**

Slight; of small importance

4. Such people are less **subject** to influence and stick with preferred brands.

Liable; affected by; sensitive to

5. **Ultimately,** marketers use this information to develop marketing plans.

Finally; in the end

6. The search is not always **extensive** . . .

Large; wide-ranging

7. By analyzing product **attributes** (price, prestige, quality), consumers compare products before deciding which one best meets their needs.

Qualities; characteristics

8. By analyzing product attributes (price, **prestige,** quality), consumers compare products before deciding which one best meets their needs.

Power to impress or influence

9. Emotional motives involve nonobjective factors and include sociability, imitation of others, and **aesthetics.**

Beauty and its effects; artistry

10. These buyers . . . are much more **apt** to broadcast their experiences than are satisfied customers.

Likely; inclined

RESPOND TO THE READING

Directions: Write a half-page response to either of the following questions.

1. Analyze one of your recent purchases. What did you buy? Why did you buy it? What information did you have about the product before you bought it? Did you compare it with similar products?

2. Thinking about your family and friends as examples, do you think most consumers are influenced more by rational motives or emotional motives? What are the strongest influences on most consumers?

WEBQUEST

Directions: Use the Internet to find the answer to the following question. Write your answer on a sheet of paper. Print out the Web page you used for the answer or copy the URL on your sheet.

How does the U.S. Bureau of Consumer Protection help consumers?

CHAPTER 1 REVIEW

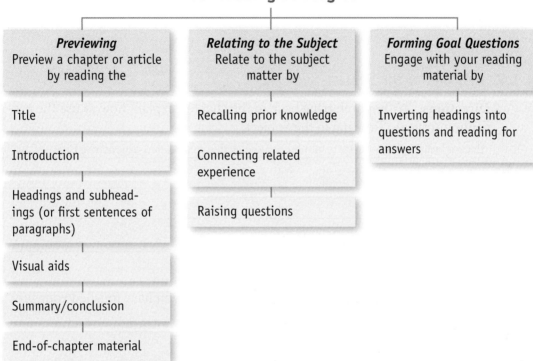

Reinforcing Concentration

Identify and work with external factors that affect your concentration

Identify and work with internal factors that affect your concentration

Pre-Reading Strategies

Previewing
Preview a chapter or article by reading the

- Title
- Introduction
- Headings and subheadings (or first sentences of paragraphs)
- Visual aids
- Summary/conclusion
- End-of-chapter material

Relating to the Subject
Relate to the subject matter by

- Recalling prior knowledge
- Connecting related experience
- Raising questions

Forming Goal Questions
Engage with your reading material by

- Inverting headings into questions and reading for answers

Skills Online: Previewing Web Sites:

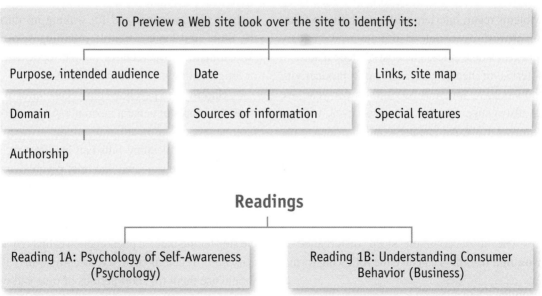

To Preview a Web site look over the site to identify its:

- Purpose, intended audience
- Domain
- Authorship
- Date
- Sources of information
- Links, site map
- Special features

Readings

Reading 1A: Psychology of Self-Awareness (Psychology)

Reading 1B: Understanding Consumer Behavior (Business)

CHAPTER TESTS

TEST 1.1. PREVIEWING

Directions: Without referring back to the chapter, list the six steps you would follow to preview a chapter in a textbook.

Read and think about the title; read introductions; read headings and subheadings or first

sentence of each paragraph; note visuals; read summary or conclusions; review end-of-chapter

material

TEST 1.2. RELATING TO THE SUBJECT

Directions: Without referring back to the chapter, explain how to use the pre-reading strategy "Relating to the Subject."

Engage with the material by recalling prior knowledge and related experience. Raise questions

to stimulate your curiosity about the subject.

TEST 1.3. PREVIEWING AND RELATING

Directions: Preview the following passage. When you have finished your preview, answer the questions that follow the passage.

DISORDERS OF SLEEP

Nearly all of us have trouble falling asleep or staying asleep from time to time. When sleep problems recur, interfere with our ability to function at work or school, or affect our health, they can exact a dear price. The cost of sleep disorders in terms of health and lost work productivity amounts to as much as $35 billion per year. We can also gauge the cost in human lives, with an estimated 1,500 Americans who fall asleep at the wheel killed each year. These grim statistics are understandable given that 30 to 50 percent of people report some sort of sleep problem.

Insomnia

The most common sleep disturbance is **insomnia.** Insomnia can take the following forms:

| insomnia Difficulty falling or staying asleep. |

(a) having trouble falling asleep (regularly taking more than 30 minutes to doze off), (b) waking too early in the morning, and (c) waking up during the night and having trouble returning to sleep. An estimated 15 percent of people report severe or longstanding problems with insomnia.

Short-term psychotherapy can effectively treat most cases of general insomnia. Another common approach to treating insomnia is sleeping pills. Although sleeping pills can be effective, researchers have discovered that brief psychotherapy is more effective than Ambien, a popular sleeping pill. Moreover, longstanding use of many sleeping pills can make it more difficult to sleep once people stop taking them, a phenomenon called *rebound insomnia.* When people try sleeping pills, they should use them for short periods of time and with caution, as there's a risk of dependency.

Narcolepsy

Narcolepsy can appear as almost the opposite of insomnia. In narcolepsy, the most prominent symptom is the rapid and often unexpected onset of sleep. People with narcolepsy can experience episodes of sudden sleep lasting anywhere from a few seconds to several minutes and, less frequently, as long as an hour. The overwhelming urge to sleep can strike at any moment. Surprise, elation, or other strong emotions—even those associated with laughing at a joke or engaging in sexual intercourse—can lead people with narcolepsy to experience *cataplexy,* a complete loss of muscle tone. During cataplexy, people can fall because their muscles become limp as a rag doll. Cataplexy occurs in healthy people during REM sleep. But, in narcolepsy, people experiencing cataplexy remain alert the whole time, even though they can't move. Ordinarily, sleepers don't enter REM sleep for more than an hour after they fall asleep. But when people who experience an episode of narcolepsy doze off, they plummet into REM sleep immediately, suggesting that it results from a sleep–wake cycle that's badly off-kilter. Fortunately, people with narcolepsy can be helped by taking short naps, taking antidepressant and stimulant medication, and avoiding alcohol and caffeine.

Sleep Apnea

Being tired during the day and falling asleep during class or on the job is rarely due to narcolepsy. Many more people with these problems suffer from **sleep apnea,** which afflicts between 2 and 20 percent of the general population, depending on how broadly or narrowly it's defined. Apnea is caused by a blockage of the airway during sleep, as shown in Figure 1.3. This problem causes people with apnea to snore loudly, gasp, and sometimes stop breathing for more than 20 seconds. Struggling to breathe rouses the person many times—often several hundred times—during the night and interferes with sleep, causing

> **narcolepsy** Disorder characterized by the rapid and often unexpected onset of sleep.
> **sleep apnea** Disorder caused by a blockage of the airway during sleep, resulting in daytime fatigue.

fatigue the next day. Yet most people with sleep apnea have no awareness of these multiple awakenings. A lack of oxygen and the buildup of carbon dioxide can lead to many problems, including night sweats, weight gain, fatigue, and an irregular heartbeat. Because apnea is associated with being overweight, doctors typically recommend weight loss as a first option. Many people benefit from wearing a face mask attached to a machine that blows air into their nasal passages, forcing the airway to remain open. Nevertheless, adjusting to this machine can be challenging.

Night Terrors

Night terrors are often more disturbing to onlookers than to sleepers. Parents who witness a child's night terrors can hardly believe that the child has no recollection of what occurred. Screaming, perspiring, confused, and wide-eyed, the child may even thrash about before falling back into a deep sleep. Such episodes usually last for only a few minutes. Despite their dramatic nature, **night terrors** are typically harmless events that take place during deep non-REM sleep (stages 3 and 4). They occur almost exclusively in children, who spend more time than adults in deep stages of sleep. Night

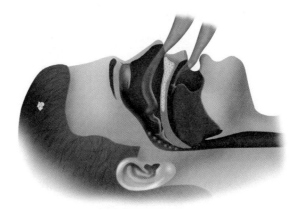

Figure 1.3 Flow of Air and Quality of Sleep
When the flow of air is blocked, as in sleep apnea, the quality of sleep can be seriously disrupted.

> **night terrors** Sudden waking episodes characterized by screaming, perspiring, and confusion followed by a return to a deep sleep.

terrors are often confused with nightmares, which typically occur only during REM sleep. Parents often learn not to overreact and even to ignore the episodes if the child isn't in physical danger. Night terrors occasionally occur in adults, especially when they're under intense stress.

walking like a zombie. In actuality, a sleepwalking person often acts like any fully awake person, although a sleepwalker may be somewhat clumsier. **Sleepwalking** (walking while fully asleep) often involves relatively little activity, but sleepwalkers have been known to drive cars, turn on computers, or fire guns.

For most people, sleepwalking is harmless, and sleepwalkers rarely remember their actions on awakening. But for children and adults who engage in potentially dangerous activities (such as climbing out an open window) while sleepwalking, doors and windows can be wired with alarms to alert others to direct them back to bed. If someone is sleepwalking, it's perfectly safe to wake him or her up, despite what we may have seen in movies.

Sleepwalking

The popular image of a "somnambulist," or sleepwalker, is a person with eyes closed, arms outstretched, and both hands at shoulder height,

> **sleepwalking** Walking while fully asleep.

—Lilienfeld et al., *Psychology: A Framework for Everyday Thinking*

---

1. What is the passage about?

Sleep disorders

2. How many types of sleep disorders are discussed in the passage? List them.

Five: insomnia; narcolepsy; sleep apnea; night terrors; sleepwalking

3. What is narcolepsy?

A disorder characterized by the rapid, often unexpected onset of sleep

4. What causes sleep apnea?

Blockage of the airway during sleep

5. How many Americans die annually because they've fallen asleep while driving?

1,500

6. What have you previously read or learned about sleep disorders?

Answers will vary.

7. How well do you sleep? Have you ever had problems falling or staying asleep?

Answers will vary.

8. Write three questions about sleep disorders.

Answers will vary.

TEST 1.4. GOAL QUESTIONS FROM HEADINGS

Directions: Write a goal question for the following title and headings.

The Constitutional Powers of the President

What are the constitutional powers granted to the President?

Types of Small Business Opportunities

What are some types of small business opportunities?

Planning Your Fitness Program

How do you plan a fitness program?

You, the Reader: Chapter 1 Wrap-up

Directions: Use one or two of the following questions to write a half-page response to Chapter 1.

- What were the most important things you learned from this chapter? How will you use what you have learned from this chapter?
- How have you changed your reading habits in response to the chapter?
- To what extent are you an active reader? Which strategies most help you to engage with your reading?
- What parts of the chapter did you find most engaging? What questions do you have about the chapter?

PEARSON
myreadinglab

For support in meeting this chapter's objectives, go to MyReadingLab and select *Active Reading Strategies.*

CHAPTER 2

Context and Dictionary

LEARNING OBJECTIVES

In Chapter 2 you will learn to:

- Use context clues to determine the meaning of unfamiliar words
- Match dictionary definitions with context to determine the meaning of unfamiliar words
- Use the dictionary's phonetic spelling to determine word pronunciation

CHAPTER CONTENTS

Pre-Reading Exercise for Chapter 2

Directions: Preview the chapter and answer the following questions:

1. What is the chapter about?

   Using context clues and the dictionary

2. What is context?

   The sentence or paragraph surrounding a word

3. What is a definition clue?

   An actual definition of a word found in the context

4. What have you previously learned about using context clues?

   Answers will vary.

5. What do you usually do when you encounter an unfamiliar word while reading? How often do you make use of the dictionary?

   Answers will vary.

6. Write two questions about the content of this chapter.

   Answers will vary.

As a college student, you will be exposed to a wide range of new vocabulary words. Some of these will be subject terms—words that belong to a specific subject—and some will be general vocabulary words that might appear in anything you read. Your response to this vocabulary challenge will be critical to your success as a college reader.

When encountering unfamiliar words, active readers rely heavily on two strategies: using context clues and consulting the dictionary. In Chapter 2 you will learn more about these strategies and practice using them.

Context

The word *context* has two basic meanings. One of the meanings is "circumstances, situation, or surroundings." In other words, the word *context* can refer to whatever circumstance or situation a person, or thing, is in. Everything exists within a context—a set of circumstances, a situation, or surroundings. For example, you are probably reading this chapter now for a class. That class is the *context* in which you are studying this chapter and building your vocabulary.

Look at the cartoon on the next page. What makes the cartoon entertaining?

The humor in the cartoon comes, of course, from the placement of the cat behind the steering wheel of the car (along with the bumper sticker), since we know that cats don't—can't—drive cars. The cat is out of its normal context. Or to look at it another way, in the context of a picture of a car, we expect to see a person driving, and not a cat.

The second meaning of *context* refers specifically to words. When we talk about a word's context, we mean all the words that are around it. That is, a word's context usually consists of the sentence or paragraph within which the word is found. Grasping the meaning of a word involves understanding how the word is used in *context*—in a particular sentence or situation.

You have learned most of the thousands of the words you already know from context. You started learning words at a very early age, long before you learned to read. How do you imagine you learned the word *hot*? Perhaps you burned a finger on the kitchen stove and your mother said to you, "Don't touch that, it's hot!" From that real life context, you learned the meaning of the word *hot*—and of course, you learned not to touch the stove! Growing up, you learned many other words from real-life contexts. After you started reading, you learned to recognize these words in print, and added many other words to your vocabulary from the reading context. Whether from listening or reading, you've learned most of the words you know from context—that is, from the way the words were used.

To some extent, we can say that the meaning of any word depends on its context. For example, a *hot* stove is very different from a *hot* date! Even simple symbols depend on context for meaning. Look at the following symbol. What is it?

O

Now look at the same symbol in these three contexts:

NOT   305   ⚙

You can see that whether the symbol o is a letter, a numeral, or the face of a flower depends on the context in which it is used. In short, whether we are working with symbols or words, we see that their meaning depends on the context in which they're used.

> **Context:** The sentence or paragraph surrounding a word

context	*context*	*context*	*context*	*context*	*context*	*context*	*context*
context	*context*	*context*	**word**	*context*	*context*	*context*	*context*
context	*context*	*context*	*context*	*context*	*context*	*context*	*context*

Figure 2.1 A Word in Context
The context of a word consists of all the words surrounding that word.

Multiple Meanings

Many words have more than one definition. Consider the word *romance*. When you hear or see the word *romance*, you probably think of a love affair, as in "Sally and Harry's romance." But what does *romance* mean in the following sentence?

Our college offers courses in all of the romance languages.

In this sentence, the word *romance* does not refer to a love affair. Romance languages are languages like Spanish, French, and Italian, which were derived from Latin, the language of the *Romans*.

Many of the small, common words in English have multiple meanings. For example, Webster's *New World Dictionary* lists twenty definitions for the word *bat*. Here are five of the definitions, with sentence examples.

1. a club used to strike the ball in baseball and cricket

   The clean-up hitter swung his bat at the first pitch.

2. any stout club, stick, or cudgel

   The mob was armed with rifles, knives, and bats.

3. A blow or hit

   He fell unconscious after receiving a bat on the head.

4. a furry, nocturnal flying mammal

   The bat flew out of the dark cave.

5. to flap

   We watched the bird bat its wings and fly away.

As you can see from these examples, the meaning of *bat* will depend upon the context in which the word is used.

Now complete Exercises 2.1 and 2.2 for practice using context clues for words with multiple meanings.

EXERCISE 2.1 MULTIPLE MEANINGS

Directions: Each of the sentences below contains a common word, but its meaning may be unfamiliar in the given context. Determine the meaning of each bold-faced word from the context and write the meaning in the space provided.

1. After the storm, there was a **run** on batteries. Many of the local stores were completely sold out.

   Big demand

2. When their car broke down, the Mantilla family had to **tap** into their savings to buy another one.

   Draw from

3. The burglars knew they could not sell the stolen jewels to a store, so they tried instead to sell them to a **fence**.

   Person who buys and sells stolen goods

4. No one could tell that the thick black hair on Mr. Jones's head was actually a **rug**.

   Toupee, wig

5. The accident left Harry with a **game** leg that took two months to heal.

   Injured

EXERCISE 2.2 MULTIPLE MEANINGS

Directions: Without consulting a dictionary, write three different meanings for each of the following words. Then write a sentence illustrating each meaning. Write your answers on a separate sheet of paper. An example is provided.

EXAMPLE   Hit

1. to strike

   The fight started when one boy hit the other in the shoulder.

2. a popular movie, song, etc.

   Our radio station always plays the latest hits.

3. to apply oneself to

   Successful college students learn to hit the books on a regular basis.

1. mark ___Answers to all will vary.___

___

2. tip ___Answers to all will vary.___

___

3. fair ___Answers to all will vary.___

___

4. pound ___Answers to all will vary.___

___

5. spring ___Answers to all will vary.___

___

Active Reading Strategy: Using Context Clues

As you read at the beginning of this chapter, as a college reader you are likely to encounter a variety of unfamiliar words when you read your assignments. It will be important for you to understand these words in order to gain a satisfactory understanding of your assignments. How will you handle them? What do you usually do when you encounter an unfamiliar word?

Readers often find clues to the meaning of an unfamiliar word by examining the context in which the word is used. Therefore, *the first strategy when encountering an unfamiliar word is to look for context clues.* A context clue can be anything in the sentence or paragraph that helps you understand the meaning of the unfamiliar word. In other words, when encountering an unfamiliar word, we study the sentence or paragraph containing the word looking for clues to the word's meaning. Consider the following example:

> The children *scurried* out of the classroom as soon as the bell rang at the end of the last period.

From the context of this sentence, what do you think *scurried* means? What clues in the sentence help you to guess the meaning of *scurried*?

Since we know that most children are eager to leave class at the end of the school day, we can guess that *scurried*, in this sentence, probably means "hurried" or "moved fast." The words "as soon as" also suggest that the children are in a hurry to leave.

Let's look at another example:

> Sleep *deprivation* can result in slower reaction time and weakened memory.

From the context of the sentence, what do you think *deprivation* means? What are the clues in the sentence to help guess the meaning of *deprivation*? Logically, we can guess that slower reactions and poorer memory might result from not getting enough sleep. We therefore guess that deprivation means "loss" in this context, or "lack of."

Context clues can be strong or weak. Sometimes, the context makes the meaning of an unfamiliar word obvious. At other times, the context provides no real clue to the word's meaning. Often we are able to get some sense of a word's meaning from context but not necessarily its exact definition. Read the following sentences looking for clues to the meaning of the word *conflagration*:

- The cause of the conflagration was unknown.
- The conflagration probably started in an old, abandoned building.
- The conflagration, which destroyed several buildings, was probably started by children playing with matches.

Which sentence provides the strongest clues? What are those clues? What do you think *conflagration* means?

EXERCISE **2.3** IDENTIFYING CONTEXT CLUES

Directions: In this exercise, you will work with five pairs of sentences. Compare each pair to identify the sentence that provides the stronger context clues, and circle its letter. (You may find it helpful to underline the context clues in that sentence.) Write the meaning of the boldfaced word in the line under the sentences. Try this without consulting a dictionary.

EXAMPLE

Ex. A. My friend Diego has an unusual **surname.**

Ex. B. A woman is likely to change her **surname** when she gets married.

Last name

1A. Joan Twinkletoes was an **obscure** actress from the 1950s.

1B. Joan Twinkletoes was an **obscure** actress until she starred in her first major film.

Unknown

2A. Watching a little television can be a pleasant **diversion**, but watching too much television can turn into a bad habit.

2B. Everyone should set aside a small amount of time each day for **diversion.**

Distraction; entertainment

3A. The program will **terminate** next week.

3B. Miguel was broken-hearted when his girlfriend told him that she wanted to **terminate** their relationship.

End

4A. The **pachyderms** are the most popular animals at the zoo.

4B. **Pachyderms** can use their trunks to pick up objects.

Elephants

(**5A.**) A **tenacious** basketball player will never give up until the final buzzer.

5B. Richard is the most **tenacious** person I know.

Stubborn; persistent

Definition Clues and Synonyms

> **definition clue** an actual definition of a word or term found in the context

Sometimes a writer provides the actual definition of a word or term within the context. We call this a **definition clue**. For example, consider the following sentence:

> Whenever possible, psychologists settle differences by collecting **data** (facts and information).

Notice that the definition of *data* is contained in the parentheses following the word. We can tell from the sentence that *data* means "facts and information." The sentence has provided us with a definition clue for the meaning of the word *data*.

> **synonym** a word with the same meaning or a similar meaning as another word

Synonyms can also be very useful context clues. A **synonym** is a word that has the same meaning, or a similar meaning, as another word. Consider the following example:

> Only the most **affluent**, or wealthy, members of the community could afford to buy the town's most expensive homes.

We can tell from the preceding sentence that *wealthy* is a synonym for *affluent*. In other words, *affluent* means "wealthy".

Punctuation marks (commas, dashes, and parentheses) are often used to indicate a definition clue or synonym. You will need to be an alert reader to recognize these clues.

Here are two more examples:

> **Insulin**, *a hormone produced by the pancreas*, regulates the rate at which sugar in the blood is used by the body. (Definition clue)

> Parents who believe in honesty teach their children not to **prevaricate**—that is, not to lie. (Synonym)

In the first example, the definition for *insulin* follows the word and is separated by commas. In the second example, *lie* and *prevaricate* are synonyms (*prevaricate* means "lie").

Sometimes, a definition clue is not indicated by punctuation marks, but rather by the wording of the sentence:

Capitalism is an economic system that favors private control of business and minimum government regulation of private industry.

In this example, the word *is* following the word *capitalism* suggests that the definition for capitalism is about to be given.

EXERCISE 2.4 DEFINITION CLUES AND SYNONYMS

Directions: Underline the definition clue or synonym for the boldfaced word in each sentence.

EXAMPLE

Whenever possible, psychologists settle differences by collecting **data** (facts and information).

1. **Plagiarism** is the use of someone else's words or ideas without an acknowledgement of that person's authorship.

2. The **mass media**, forms of communication directed to large audiences, have a powerful effect on society.

3. In a troubled society, widespread crime is **engulfing**—surrounding and swallowing up—whole neighborhoods.

4. City planners are trying to determine the best **site** (location) for the new stadium.

5. In most elections, the advantages of **incumbency** (that is, already being in office) help a candidate get reelected.

6. All English majors must take a course in **linguistics**, the study of language.

7. Drug use by professional athletes has come under close **scrutiny**—examination—in recent years.

8. Anthropologists study human **culture**—the ideas, customs, skills, and arts of a people or group.

9. Leonardo Da Vinci was called a **Renaissance man**, meaning a man of the broadest possible learning and a wide range of interests and achievement.

—Janaro and Altshuler, *The Art of Being Human,* 8th ed.

10. Many scientists are concerned about the **greenhouse effect**, the warming of the earth and its atmosphere caused by trapped solar radiation.

Contrast Clues

contrast clue a word or phrase within the context that means the opposite of the unfamiliar word

Contrast clues are another important type of context clue. Contrast means "difference." A contrast clue is a word or phrase within the context that means the opposite of the unfamiliar word. Let's look at an example.

I love volleyball, but I **abhor** tennis.

From this sentence, what do you think *abhor* means? The contrast clue is the word *love*. Abhor, therefore means "hate," the opposite of love.

Contrast clues are often indicated by words such as *but, however, although,* and *than.* In the previous sentence, the word *but* indicates contrast. See Table 2.1 for a more complete list of words and phrases that indicate contrast.

Here is another example of a sentence containing a contrast clue:

Although we were **initially** opposed to the plans, we finally agreed to them after careful study.

In this sentence, the word *although* indicates contrast. The contrast clue for the meaning of the word *initially* is the word *finally. Initially* means the opposite of *finally.* Initially means "at the beginning."

Let's look at a more difficult example of a contrast clue.

Herman Melville's books were more popular with later generations than they were with his **contemporaries**.

In this sentence, the word *than* indicates contrast. Can you tell which word or phrase in the sentence is the opposite of *contemporaries*? The contrast clue is the phrase *later generations*. In the context of this sentence, *contemporaries* means the opposite of *later generations*. Melville's contemporaries, therefore, were the people who lived in his own time.

Table 2.1 Words and Phrases That Signal Contrast

although	than
but	though
conversely	whereas
despite	yet
however	in contrast
nevertheless	in spite of
nonetheless	on the contrary
still	on the other hand

EXERCISE 2.5 CONTRAST CLUES

Directions:

1. Underline the contrast clue within each sentence.

2. Then, in the space provided, write the meaning of the boldfaced word. Do not consult a dictionary.

   EXAMPLE   I love volleyball, but I **abhor** tennis.

   Hate

1. If we are to get along better with others, we must learn to focus on our **commonalities** more than on our <u>differences</u>.

   Similarities
   _____

2. As an army doctor, I expected those wounded in the war to be <u>soldiers</u>, but my first eight patients were **civilians**.

   Ordinary citizens
   _____

3. Some teenagers face unwanted parenthood because they are **naive** about sex and the responsibilities of parenting. However, those who are more <u>sophisticated</u> and <u>worldly</u> wise make more <u>mature</u> choices.

   Unsophisticated; immature
   _____

4. After his injury, the Dodgers' third baseman was welcomed back by his **opponents** as well as his <u>teammates</u>.

   Members of the opposing teams
   _____

5. Though John is <u>eager</u> to buy a new car, he is somewhat **reluctant** to part with his old one.

   Hesitant; holding back; unwilling
   _____

6. More crimes are committed in **urban** areas than in the <u>country</u>.

   City
   _____

7. An increase in taxes can have both **beneficial** and <u>harmful</u> effects on the nation's economy.

   Helpful; good
   _____

8. In dreams, **hostile** acts outnumber <u>friendly acts</u> by more than two to one.

   —Daneri, *"Neuroscience of Sleep"*

   Unfriendly; aggressive
   _____

9. The committee members reached <u>agreement</u> on their goals, but there was considerable **dissent** about the methods that would best achieve those goals.

   Disagreement
   _____

10. Most of her lectures are <u>carefully planned</u>, but sometimes our history professor prefers to lecture **spontaneously**.

    Without plan
    _____

EXERCISE 2.6 DEFINITION CLUES, SYNONYMS, AND CONTRAST CLUES

Directions:

1. Use the context clues to determine the meaning of the boldfaced word in each sentence. Write the meaning in the space marked "meaning."

2. In the space marked "type of clue," indicate which type of clue was used in the sentence (definition clue, synonym, or contrast clue).

EXAMPLE

I love volleyball, but I **abhor** tennis.

meaning: _Hate_

type of clue: _Contrast_

1. **Patronage** is a hiring and promotion system based on political reasons rather than on merit and competence.

   —Edwards et al., *Government in America,* Brief 10th ed.

   meaning: _A hiring and promotion system based on political reasons rather than on merit and competence_

   type of clue: _Definition_

2. Though Hubert's math teacher believed his story that he left his homework at his friend's house, his English teacher remained **skeptical**.

   meaning: _Doubtful; not believing_

   type of clue: _Contrast_

3. A **self-fulfilling prophecy** is a prediction that comes true because you act on it as if it were true.

   —Devito, *The Interpersonal Communication Book,* 12th ed.

   meaning: _A prediction that comes true because you act on it as if it were true_

   type of clue: _Definition_

4. Researchers have discovered more than one hundred viruses, called **rhinoviruses**, that cause the common cold.

   meaning: _Viruses that cause the common cold_

   type of clue: _Definition_

5. Route 12 is normally a very safe road; however, it can become **treacherous** under icy conditions.

   meaning: _Dangerous_

   type of clue: _Contrast_

6. Dreams can express a **moral dilemma**—a conflict between good and bad; between immediate impulses and conscience.

   meaning: _Conflict between good and bad or between immediate impulses and conscience_

   type of clue: _Definition_

7. Inexperienced climbers may find that the **descent** from the mountain top is more difficult than the climb up.

   meaning: _The climb down_

   type of clue: _Contrast_

8. Sylvia's first husband was a **philanderer**, but her second husband proved to be a faithful and true companion.

   meaning: <u>An unfaithful love partner (or one who has affairs with others)</u>

   type of clue: <u>Contrast</u>

9. The convict was **incarcerated** at a maximum security prison where he was imprisoned for most of his life.

   meaning: <u>Imprisoned</u>

   type of clue: <u>Synonym</u>

10. The Fernandez family had hoped to add to their bank account over the winter but were instead forced to **deplete** their savings.

    meaning: <u>Reduce; use up</u>

    type of clue: <u>Contrast</u>

Indirect Context Clues

indirect context clue any clue in the context—other than definition, synonym or contrast—that allows the reader to make a logical guess at the meaning of an unknown word

When definition clues, synonyms, and contrast clues are not available, we rely on **indirect context clues** to guess the meaning of an unfamiliar word. We look for anything else in the sentence that can help us make a logical guess at the meaning of the unknown word. Consider the following sentence from Chapter 1:

> You know that becoming physically fit can **enhance** the quality—and quantity—of the years ahead.

—"Making Time for Fitness," Parlay International

Notice that the previous sentence does not contain a definition clue, synonym, or contrast clue for the word *enhance*. However, we can guess the meaning of *enhance* from the indirect clues in the sentence. We logically interpret that "becoming physically fit" will lead to improved health and longer life. We know that exercise is good for our health. We can therefore guess that *enhance* means "improve."

Let's look at another example of an indirect context clue:

> Everyone at the party was in a **festive** mood, eating and drinking and enjoying the holiday music.

Once again, notice that the sentence contains no definition clue, synonym, or contrast clue. We can still guess the meaning of *festive* from the sentence, however. The sentence tells us that everyone at the party was "eating and drinking and enjoying the holiday music." We know that people are usually in a good mood at parties. We therefore guess that festive means "merry."

EXERCISE **2.7** INDIRECT CONTEXT CLUES

Directions: Use the context clues in each sentence to determine the meaning of the boldfaced word. (You may find it helpful to underline the clues in the sentence.) Write the meaning in the space provided. Do not consult a dictionary.

1. Personal computers have **revolutionized** communication and business practices in the past twenty-five years.

   Changed radically

2. Unusual climate conditions **trigger** frequent thunderstorms in some areas while causing a lack of rainfall in others.

   Cause; set off; initiate

3. A hundred or a thousand years from now, our **descendants** undoubtedly will draw conclusions about our era from the names we use for ourselves and our children.

   Relatives who follow

4. Our early ancestors must have been **baffled** by dreams in which they seemed to move about in distant places and to talk to people long dead.

   —Kagan and Havemann, *Psychology: An Introduction,* 4th ed.

   Puzzled; confused

5. Good vocabulary skills are **paramount** to a college student's success.

   Of great importance

6. During an infant's first year, total sleep time **declines** from an average of sixteen hours to thirteen hours per night.

   —Dement, *The Sleep Watchers*

   Goes down; decreases

7. You will have no trouble finding a book about Shakespeare here. Our library is **replete** with them.

   Filled; plentiful

8. Babe Ruth reached the **pinnacle** of his career in 1927, the year in which he hit sixty home runs.

   Peak; top

9. The suspect demanded that his lawyer be present while the police **interrogated** him.

   Questioned; examined

10. Smoking cigarettes is **detrimental** to your health.

    Harmful

Context Clues in Short Passages

You have learned that context is an important first strategy when encountering new words. You will not always be able to determine a word's meaning from the context, but you should make a habit of looking for context clues whenever you encounter an unfamiliar word.

In your textbooks, definition clues will usually be provided for key terms. Here's an example from a textbook on interpersonal communication (communication between people).

Encoding refers to the act of producing messages—for example, speaking or writing. **Decoding** is the reverse and refers to the act of understanding messages—for example, listening or reading. By sending your ideas via sound waves (in the case of speech) or light waves (in the case of writing), you're putting these ideas into a code, hence encoding. By translating sound or light waves into ideas, you're taking them out of a code, hence decoding. Thus, speakers and writers are called **encoders**, and listeners and readers are called **decoders**. The term **encoding-decoding** is used to emphasize that the two activities are performed in combination by each participant. For interpersonal communication to occur, messages must be encoded and decoded. For example, when a parent talks to a child whose eyes are closed and whose ears are covered by stereo headphones, interpersonal communication does not occur because the messages sent are not being received.

—DeVito, *The Interpersonal Communication Books,* 12th ed.

The preceding paragraph focuses on the definition of two terms, *encoding* and *decoding*. The author provides definition clues in the first two sentences. Encoding is defined as "the act of producing messages." The author clarifies this definition with two examples of encoding: speaking and writing. Decoding is defined as "the act of understanding messages," with listening and reading mentioned as examples of decoding. The remainder of the paragraph continues to discuss and explain these two key terms.

Many of the context clues in your reading will be indirect—that is, no definition, synonym, or contrast will be provided. You can look for other clues in the passage that will help you make a logical guess at the meaning of an unfamiliar word. Let's look at an example—a paragraph about an interesting (and positive) use of rats. Use the context clues to determine the meanings of the boldfaced words.

EXAMPLE

Some people **cringe** when they see a rat, but Bart Weetjens smiles. A Belgian product designer, Weetjens **devised** a way for these often **reviled** rodents to help solve a global problem: how to locate land **mines**, some 60 million of which are scattered in 69 countries. Dogs are often **deployed** to sniff them out, "But I knew rats were easier to train," says Weetjens, who bred them as a boy. Rats are also light, so they don't **detonate** the mines they find; they stay healthy in tropical areas, where many explosives are buried; and they're cheap to breed and raise. Weetjens chose the African giant pouched rat, with its very sensitive nose, for training. More than 30 trained sniffer rats have started sweeping minefields in Mozambique, where they've cleared almost a quarter square mile.

— Mairson, "Ratted Out," *National Geographic*

Now, circle the most likely meanings for the boldfaced words as they are used in the passage.

1. **cringe**

   a. smile

   b. attack

   (c. move back)

2. **devised**

   a. studied

   (b. created)

   c. solved

3. **reviled**

   a. spoken about positively

   (b. spoken about negatively)

   c. treated with respect

4. **mines**

   (a. underground explosives)

   b. places where minerals are found

   c. belonging to me

5. **deployed**

   a. prevented

   b. preferred

   (c. used)

6. **detonate**

   a. touch

   b. discover

   (c. cause to explode)

Analysis

1. We can make a pretty good guess at the meaning of *cringe* from the first sentence. Though there are many things people might do when they see a rat, we know that many people are afraid of rats. We can therefore guess that *cringe* probably means something like "move back." (Note that the contrast clue in the first sentence—"Bart Weetjens *smiles*"—also tells us that cringing must be a *negative* reaction.)

2. Since Weetjens is a designer, and the passage is talking about a new use for rats, we can guess that *devised* means "invented" or "created."

3. Since we know that most people don't like rats, we can guess that *reviled* means "spoken about negatively."

4. Our understanding of the word *mines*, as used in the context of the passage, is necessary to our understanding of the passage. If you are unfamiliar with this use of the word *mines*, the best context clue may be in the third sentence—

"where many explosives are buried." A *mine* is a buried explosive—in other words, an underground bomb.

5. We can guess the meaning of *deployed* from the context as well. Since the passage talks about using rats to find mines, we can be confident that it is also talking about using dogs for this purpose. *Deployed*, then, means "used."

6. Finally, we can also guess what *detonate* means from the context clues. We can tell from the passage that the rats are trained to locate the land mines without causing them to explode, and we can logically guess that a lighter animal, like a rat, would be less likely to cause a mine to explode. Therefore, we can guess that *detonate* means "cause to explode."

In the following exercise, you will practice with short passages. Use the context clues to choose the best meaning for each boldfaced word. Take advantage of definition clues, synonyms, and contrast clues when you encounter them. Remember that sometimes the context clues may be in a sentence that comes before or after the one that contains the word.

EXERCISE **2.8** CONTEXT CLUES IN SHORT PASSAGES

Directions: Use the context clues to determine the meaning of the boldfaced words in each of the following passages. Circle the correct meaning for each word from the multiple choice provided. Do not consult a dictionary.

A. The Manatee

The **manatee**, or sea cow, is a large, **aquatic** mammal that can be found in the shallow coastal waters, rivers, and springs of Florida. Over the past centuries, the number of these unique animals has been **drastically** reduced until today the species is considered endangered throughout its **range**. High **mortality** rates, primarily associated with human activity, continue to reduce the number of these gentle creatures.

In response to an increased awareness of the **plight** of the manatee, governmental agencies, universities, private **conservation** groups, and concerned corporations have joined together to promote research and identify the actions needed to encourage the recovery of manatee populations.

—Van Meter, *The West Indian Manatee in Florida*

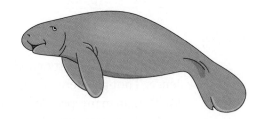

1. manatee	a. cow	(b. sea cow)
	c. mammal	d. coastal water
2. aquatic	a. large	b. of Florida
	(c. living in water)	d. very old
3. drastically	a. slightly	b. recently
	c. carefully	(d. severely)

4. range   a. territory *(circled)*   b. waterway
                   c. life   d. difficulty

5. mortality   a. transportation   b. starvation
                   c. death *(circled)*   d. life span

6. plight   a. location   b. promise
                   c. life   d. difficult situation *(circled)*

7. conservation   a. business   b. environmental *(circled)*
                      c. government   d. university

B. Dealing with Bullies

Like teachers, blackboards, and homework, bullies were once considered to be an **inevitable** fact of school life. This attitude—that schoolchildren could not avoid bullies—was captured in a Simpsons episode **casting** Bart as a victim of Nelson's daily beatings. An alarmed Marge advises her husband Homer to tell the principal, only to have an **appalled** Homer exclaim: "What? And break the code of the schoolyard? I'd rather Bart die."

To help children deal more effectively with bullies, Denver area psychologists **devised** a **bullyproofing** system now in its fourth year at Highline Elementary School. The only way to **neutralize** bullies, they realized, is to **diminish** their opportunities. The best way to do that is to teach **potential** victims **behavioral strategies**—actions they can take—and to provide them with a supportive school community. The result is that bullies find themselves in a world where their challenges go **unheeded**, and their stunts are **ineffective**.

—Rhodes, "A Schoolyard Bully No More," *USA Weekend*

1. inevitable   a. pleasant   b. educational
                    c. unavoidable *(circled)*   d. unnoticed

2. casting   a. portraying *(circled)*   b. protecting
                    c. covering   d. throwing

3. appalled   a. horrified *(circled)*   b. amused
                    c. frightened   d. angry

4. devised   a. learned   b. created *(circled)*
                    c. criticized   d. financed

5. bullyproofing   a. educational   b. encouraging bullies
                       c. proving guilt   d. defending against bullies *(circled)*

6. neutralize   a. weaken *(circled)*   b. support
                    c. find   d. discover

7. diminish   a. increase   b. learn
                    c. reduce *(circled)*   d. encourage

8. potential   a. previous   b. possible *(circled)*
                    c. powerful   d. cowardly

9. behavioral strategies

    a. ideas   b. fighting techniques

    c. rules   (d. actions they can take)

10. unheeded

    a. undefeated   b. exposed

    (c. ignored)   d. recorded

11. ineffective

    (a. unsuccessful)   b. successful

    c. impossible   d. ridiculed

C. Deceiving

We may purposely mislead others by using nonverbal cues to create false impressions or to **convey** incorrect information. Among the most common of such deceiving nonverbal behaviors is the **poker face** that some use when playing cards. **Masking** is a form of **deceiving**. We may try to appear calm when we are really nervous or upset, and we often act surprised, alert, or happy when in fact we are feeling quite the opposite. In addition, we **consciously** try to manage our nonverbal behavior when we give a speech or attend a job interview in order to disguise our true purpose and emotions.

Detecting which nonverbal cues **reveal** when others are being truthful and when they are trying to mislead us is a part of our social behavior. Research indicates that determining whether someone is telling the truth or not relies heavily on nonverbal cues. In general, we are fairly good at successfully recognizing **deception** when we encounter it. We rely on certain cues; for example, **fleeting** facial expressions lasting only a few tenths of a second, changes in voice (pitch of voice often rises when a person is lying), pauses or hesitations, eye shifting or blinking, or hand movement can all help us detect deception. Still, there is no research to support that these types of cues automatically indicate deception. They simply raise the question as to whether a person is telling the truth, but they do not prove anything **absolutely**.

—Seiler and Beall, *Communication: Making Connections,* 4th ed.

1. convey

    a. prove   (b. communicate)

    c. check   d. study

2. poker face

    a. face showing emotion   (b. face not showing emotion)

    c. smiley face   d. face that has been poked

3. masking

    (a. hiding feelings)   b. showing feelings

    c. causing pain   d. wearing a costume

4. deceiving

    a. limiting   b. showing

    c. honesty   (d. deliberately misleading)

5. consciously

    (a. deliberately)   b. by mistake

    c. unknowingly   d. honestly

6. detecting

    a. solving   b. searching

    (c. recognizing)   d. expecting

7. reveal

    a. conceal   b. change

    (c. indicate)   d. influence

8. deception

    a. recognition   b. effort

    c. trouble   (d. dishonesty)

9. fleeting 　　a. running 　　　(b. lasting a short while)

　　　　　　　c. coming down 　　d. dishonest

10. absolutely 　　(a. definitely) 　　b. partially

　　　　　　　c. previously 　　　d. doubtfully

EXERCISE 2.9　CONTEXT CLUES APPLICATION

Directions: Using any source except this textbook (a newspaper, magazine, or another book), identify five unfamiliar words whose meanings you can determine from context clues. On a separate sheet of paper, copy the sentences containing the unfamiliar words, underline the words, and write the words' meanings.

EXERCISE 2.10　WRITING CONTEXT CLUES

Directions: Choose any five of the words listed below (taken from Exercise 2.8). For each word, write an original sentence that provides context clues to the word's meaning. Make sure your context clues are strong enough so that another person could read your sentences and correctly guess the meanings of the words.

convey 　deceive 　detect 　devise 　diminish 　ineffective 　potential 　reveal

Active Reading Strategy: Matching Dictionary Definitions with Context

As you know, you will not always be able to determine a word's meaning from the context alone. When context clues aren't sufficient, we consult the dictionary, looking for a definition that helps us understand the unfamiliar word as it is used in the context of our reading material.

Since many words have more than one meaning or usage, effective use of the dictionary often involves reading or scanning through the definitions to choose the one that best fits the context. For example, consider the following sentence:

> When you disagree, be *diplomatic*: "I can understand how you feel, but I'm sorry I can't feel the same way."

> —Graber, "Take the Sting Out of Criticism," *Reader's Digest*

In the context of this sentence, what do you think *diplomatic* means? Now look at the dictionary entry for *diplomatic*.

dip•lo•mat•ic (dĭp'lə-măt'ĭk) *adj.* **1.** *Abbr.* dipl. Of, relating to, or involving diplomacy or diplomats. **2.** Using or marked by tact and sensitivity in dealing with others. See synonyms at **suave. 3. a.** Of or relating to diplomatics. **b.** Being an exact copy of the original: *a diplomatic edition.* [French *diplomatique,* from New Latin *diplōmaticus,* from Latin *diplōma, diplōmat´-,* letter of introduction. See DIPLOMA.]—**dip'lo•mat'i•cal•ly** *adv.*

Which definition for *diplomatic* best fits the context? You will probably agree that the second definition—"Using or marked by tact and sensitivity in dealing with others"—is the best choice. The second definition not only helps us to understand what the word *diplomatic* means in this context, but it also helps us to better understand the entire sentence. The author is advising us to be tactful and sensitive when we express disagreement.

When consulting a dictionary, then, remember the context! Read through the definitions looking for the one that best matches the context and that best helps you understand the word as it is being used.

Exercises 2.11 through 2.13 will provide practice for matching dictionary definitions with context using common words with multiple meanings.

EXERCISE **2.11** MULTIPLE MEANINGS: DICTIONARY

Directions: Five definitions are shown for each of the following words. Read the definitions and the sentences that follow them. On the line provided, write the number of the definition that best fits the context for each sentence.

A. pitch:

1. a throw; fling; toss
2. a point or degree [emotion was at a high *pitch*]
3. the degree of slope or inclination
4. [Slang] a line of talk, such as a salesman uses to persuade customers
5. *Acoustics* that element of a tone or sound determined by the frequency of vibration of the sound waves reaching the ear

1. Effective speakers learn to control the **pitch** of their voice. _____5_____

2. If you increase the **pitch** of the roof, it will be less likely to leak in a bad storm. _____3_____

B. round:

1. a series or succession of actions, events, etc., that is completed at, or as if at, the point where it began
2. [often pl.] a regular, customary course or circuit, as by a watchman of a station, a doctor of hospital patients, a drinker in a number of bars, etc.
3. a single serving, as of drinks, to each of a group
4. ammunition for a single shot; cartridge, shell, etc.
5. a single outburst, as of applause, cheering, etc.

1. Dr. Santiago did not complete her **rounds** until well after midnight. _____2_____

2. The next **round** is on me! _____3_____

C. pinch:

1. to squeeze between a finger and the thumb or between two surfaces, edges, etc.
2. to nip off the end of (a plant shoot), as for controlling bud development
3. [Slang] to steal

    4. [Slang] to arrest

    5. to cause distress or discomfort to

1. Hunger and thirst **pinched** the desert wanderers throughout the long day. ___5___

2. Hugo Sneakyhand was **pinched** by the police for **pinching** jewelry from the department store. ___4___ ___3___

D. bill:

    1. a statement, usually itemized, of charges for goods or services; invoice

    2. a statement or list, as a menu, theater program, ship's roster, etc.

    3. the entertainment offered in a theater

    4. a draft of a law proposed to a lawmaking body

    5. a bank note or piece of paper money

1. Last month, the Senate failed to pass a **bill** that would have made it illegal to use a cell phone while operating a motor vehicle. ___4___

2. Don't miss the **bill** at the jazz club this weekend. ___3___

E. beat:

    1. to hit or strike repeatedly; pound

    2. to dash repeatedly against [waves beat the shore]

    3. to mix by stirring or striking repeatedly with a utensil; whip (an egg, cream, etc.)

    4. to defeat in a race, contest, or struggle; overcome

    5. to mark (time or rhythm) by tapping, etc.

1. An old, bad joke suggests that chefs are cruel because they **beat** eggs and whip cream. ___3___

2. Vacationers on the coast of Maine enjoy watching the ocean **beat** upon the rocky shoreline. ___2___

F. cross:

    1. to move, pass, or extend from one side to the other side of (a street, river, etc.)

    2. to put or draw (a line, lines, etc.) across

    3. to cancel by marking with a cross or with a line or lines (often followed by *off* or *out*)

    4. *Biology* to cause (members of different species, breeds, varieties) to interbreed

    5. to oppose openly; thwart; frustrate

1. If you **cross** a white rose and a red rose you will get a pink rose. ___4___

2. "Don't **cross** me," the gangster warned, "or you'll be in big trouble." ___5___

EXERCISE 2.12 MULTIPLE MEANINGS: DICTIONARY

Directions: For each of the six words in Exercise 2.11 choose one of the definitions you did *not* use for an answer and, on a separate sheet of paper, write a sentence to illustrate that meaning. Then, switch papers with a classmate and guess which definitions each of you illustrated with your sentences.

EXERCISE 2.13 MATCHING DICTIONARY DEFINITIONS WITH CONTEXT

Directions: Read each sentence and the definitions that follow it carefully; then place a check in front of the definition for the boldfaced word that best matches the context of the sentence.

1. In the army, a corporal is **subordinate** to a sergeant.

    ___√___ subject to or under the authority of a superior

    _____ *Grammar* acting as a modifier

2. Parents should teach their children to **discriminate** between proper and improper behavior.

    _____ to make a distinction in favor of or against a person or thing on the basis of the group, class, or category to which the person or thing belongs rather than according to actual merit

    ___√___ to recognize the difference between; distinguish

3. Your argument will be stronger if you can **cite** several examples to support it.

    ___√___ to mention in support, proof, or confirmation; refer to as an example

    _____ to summon officially or authoritatively to appear in court

4. In the 1950s, the United States Supreme Court ordered public schools in the South to **integrate**.

    _____to bring together or incorporate (parts) into a whole

    ___√___ to give or cause to give equal opportunity and consideration to (a racial, religious, or ethnic group or a member of such a group)

5. Maria's **primary** reason for attending college was to learn as much as she could.

    ___√___ first or highest in rank or importance; chief; principal

    _____ of, pertaining to, or characteristic of primary school; the primary grades

Parts of Speech

Using the dictionary's part of speech labels will often make it easier to find the definition that best fits the context. The part of speech labels tell you the word's grammatical category—whether the word is used as a noun, verb, adjective, and so on. Many English words can be used as more than one part of speech. For example, the word *walk* can be used as a verb or a noun.

Verb usage: My brothers *walk* to school almost every day.

Noun usage: I like to take a *walk* in the early evening.

Dictionaries organize definitions according to parts of speech. If a word is used as more than one part of speech, the dictionary will list all the definitions for the first part of speech (usually starting with the most common one for the given word) before showing the definitions for the next part of speech. Take a look at the entry for the word *cardinal*:

pronunciation   parts of speech

car•di•nal (kär'dn-əl, kärd'nəl) *adj.* **1.** Of foremost importance; pivotal. **2.** Of a dark to deep or vivid red color. —*n.* **1.** *Rom. Cath. Ch.* A member of the Sacred College or College of Cardinals who is appointed by and ranks just below the pope. **2.** A dark to deep or vivid red. **3.** A North American bird, *Richmondena cardinalis*, having a crested head, a short, thick bill, and bright-red plumage in the male. **4.** A short, hooded cloak, originally of scarlet cloth, worn by women in the 18th century. **5.** A cardinal number. [ME < Lat. *cardinalis*, principal, pertaining to a hinge < *cardo*, hinge.] **—car'di•nal•ship'** n.

etymology   derived form

Look at the first line of the entry. After the entry word **car•di•nal** and its pronunciation guide (in parentheses), we see an italicized *adj.* This is a part of speech label, telling us that the dictionary entry for *cardinal* will first list adjective definitions. The adjective definitions are numbered *1* and *2*. After the second adjective definition, the italicized *n.* tells us that noun definitions will come next. How many noun definitions are listed?

Understanding that dictionary definitions are organized by part of speech helps you choose the definition that best fits the context. If you can tell that a word is being used as a noun, for example, you will look at the noun definitions to find the best meaning.

Determine the parts of speech for *cardinal* in the following sentences:

One of the **cardinal** rules of swimming safety is never swim alone.

Her **cardinal** slipped off her shoulders as she fell to the ground.

In the first sentence, *cardinal* is used as an adjective (describing the word *rules*). Adjective definition number 1—"Of foremost importance; pivotal"—fits the context of the sentence very nicely (pivotal means "very important"). The sentence is telling us that "never swim alone" is a very important rule of swimming safety.

In the second sentence, *cardinal* is used as a noun (we can tell from the context that it is an object, something a woman is wearing on her shoulders). Noun definition 4—"A short hooded cloak . . . worn by women in the 18th century"—fits best in the sentence.

If you are unsure about parts of speech, review the Quick Parts of Speech Refresher on the following page.

EXERCISE 2.14 USING PARTS OF SPEECH LABELS

Directions: Review the definitions for each word with the associated parts of speech. Then determine the part of speech for the boldfaced word as used in each sentence. On the line provided, indicate which part of speech is correct for the sentence.

A Quick Parts of Speech Refresher

Nouns

Nouns are words that name people, places, and things. A noun can name a person (*farmer, psychologist*), a place (*home, city*), a living thing (*wolf, tree*), an object (*pencil, textbook*), or an abstract concept (*justice, success*).

Nouns may be preceded by words like *a, an,* and *the (a farmer, an apple, the cat),* which are called articles.

Nouns can be singular (one) or plural (more than one). Plurals are usually formed by adding *–s* or *–es* to the singular (*farmers, wishes*).

Verbs

Most verbs express action (*study, throw, sing*). Other verbs are called state-of-being verbs, which include verbs like *is, are,* and *was*.

Verbs have tenses—for example, past tense, present tense, and future tense. Verbs can add endings to reflect their different tenses (*talked, is talking*).

Verbs sometimes follow the word *to* (*to study, to throw*).

Adjectives

Adjectives describe or modify a noun (a *handsome* farmer, the *largest* city, a *sharp* pencil).

Adverbs

Adverbs modify adjectives (a *very* handsome farmer) or verbs (to study *often*). Many adverbs end in *–ly* (an *especially* sharp pencil).

A. match

noun: any person or thing equal or similar to another in some way
verb: to fit (things) together, make similar or correspond

1. Try to **match** your shirt and your pants before putting them on. _Verb_

2. We love our old car; no matter how much we look, we can't find its **match**.
   Noun

B. merit

noun: worth; value; excellence
verb: to deserve; be worthy of

1. Your suggestion has a lot of **merit**; we'll give it careful thought. _Noun_

2. Your hard work **merits** a pay raise; too bad we can't afford to give you one.
   Verb

C. function

noun: the normal or characteristic action of anything
verb: to act in a required or expected manner; work

1. Sometimes the kitchen table **functions** as a desk for study. _Verb_

2. The usual **function** of the kitchen table is to provide a place to eat meals.
   Noun .

D. ground

noun: the surface of the earth
adjective: of, on, or near the ground

1. There is no **ground** transportation between the two airports. _Adjective_

2. You must travel on the **ground** for three hours to get from one airport to the next. _Noun_

E. static

noun: interference or noises produced by electrical discharges in the atmosphere
adjective: not moving or progressing; at rest; inactive; stationary

1. Until we connected an antenna to our television, **static** prevented us from enjoying our favorite shows. _Noun_

2. The weather hasn't changed in over a week because of the **static** weather front in our region. _Adjective_

EXERCISE 2.15 CONTEXT AND PARTS OF SPEECH

Directions: Use your dictionary to select the definition for each boldfaced word that best fits the context of the sentence. Use parts of speech labels to choose the best definitions. In the spaces provided, write the meanings of the boldfaced words and their parts of speech.

Name of dictionary: _Answers will vary._

1. Most of the **exploits** of Sherlock Holmes are narrated by his friend, Dr. John Watson.
   Meaning: _Acts remarkable for their brilliance or daring; bold deeds_
   Part of speech: _Noun_

2. During the nineteenth century, Chinese laborers were **exploited** to build railroads across the American continent.
   Meaning: _Make profit from the labor of others without providing a just return_
   Part of speech: _Verb_

3. Rude behavior will not be **countenanced** at the Halloween party.
   Meaning: _Tolerated_
   Part of speech: _Verb_

4. A sorrowful expression could be detected on his **countenance**.
   Meaning: _Face_
   Part of speech: _Noun_

5. Politicians often rely on polls to **gauge** public opinion.
   Meaning: _Estimate; judge; appraise_
   Part of speech: _Verb_

6. Most railroad tracks use standard **gauge**.

    Meaning: _Distance between rails of a railroad track_

    Part of speech: _Noun_

7. If you are going to court, make sure you have a skilled **advocate** to represent your case.

    Meaning: _Lawyer_

    Part of speech: _Noun_

8. All of our state representatives **advocate** equal rights for women in all areas of life.

    Meaning: _Support, speak, or write in favor of_

    Part of speech: _Verb_

9. Was I ever surprised when the bone of a **mammoth** was discovered in my backyard!

    Meaning: _Extinct hairy elephant_

    Part of speech: _Noun_

10. College students may regard writing their first research paper as a **mammoth** undertaking.

    Meaning: _Enormous_

    Part of speech: _Adjective_

Usage Labels and Subject Labels

The dictionary uses two other kinds of labels for definitions that can help you select the definition that best fits the context of whatever you're reading. They are called usage labels and subject labels.

Usage Labels   Usage labels tell us something about the way a word, or a particular definition for a word, is used. For example, the usage label *Obsolete (Obs.)* indicates that a word or definition is no longer used in modern English. The usage labels *Slang* and *Colloquial (Col.)* mark words or definitions that are used in informal conversation but not in formal written English.

Understanding the usage labels makes it easier to find the definitions you are looking for. If you are reading something written in modern English, you can ignore a definition that is marked *Obs.* On the other hand, you might need that definition if you are reading something that was written a long time ago. You can ignore slang and colloquial definitions when you are reading formal writing—which is what you will find in most of your textbooks—but might need those definitions when reading dialogue in a novel.

Look at the following examples of usage labels. What would it mean if you were vacationing in the West and someone called you a *dude*? Which definition for *main* is now obsolete?

dude (do͞od, dyo͞od) *n.* **1.** *Informal* An Easterner or city person who vacations on a ranch in the West. **2.** *Informal* A man who is very fancy or sharp in dress and demeanor. **3.** *Slang* **a.** A man; a fellow. **b. dudes** Persons of either sex. ❖ *tr.v.* **dud•ed, dud•ing, dudes** *Slang* To dress elaborately or flamboyantly. [?]

main (mān) *adj.* **1.** Most important; principal. **2.** Exerted to the utmost; sheer: *by main strength.* **3.** *Nautical* Connected to or associated with the mainmast: *a main skysail.* **4.** *Grammar* Of, relating to, or being the principal clause or verb of a complex sentence. **5.** *Obsolete* Of a continuous area or stretch. ❖ *n.* **1.** The chief or largest part: *Your ideas are, in the main, impractical.* **2.** The principal pipe or conduit in a system for conveying gas or other utility. **3.** Physical strength: *fought with might and main.* **4.** A mainland. **5.** The open ocean. **6.** *Nautical* **a.** A mainsail. **b.** A mainmast. [ME < OE *mœgen*, strength.]

Subject Labels   Subject labels are especially important for college students. Subject labels indicate that a definition applies to a particular subject. Examples are *Psych.* (Psychology), *Mus.* (Music), *Bio.* (Biology), and *Bus.* (Business). If you come across an unfamiliar word in a business textbook, then, you might first check the definition labeled *Bus.* On the other hand, you could ignore the definition labeled *Bus.* when you are reading in other subjects.

Look at the following dictionary entry for *rationalize*. What does *rationalize* mean when it is used as a math term?

ra•tion•al•ize (răsh'ə-nə-līz') *v.* **-ized, -iz•ing, -iz•es** —*tr.* **1.** To make rational. **2.** To interpret rationally. **3.** To devise self-satisfying but incorrect reasons for (one's behavior). **4.** *Mathematics* To remove radicals, such as from a denominator, without changing the value of (an expression) or roots of (an equation). **5.** *Chiefly British* To bring modern, efficient methods to (an industry, for example). —*intr.* **1.** To think rationally or rationalistically. **2.** To devise self-satisfying but incorrect reasons for one's behavior. —**ra'tion•al•iz'er** *n.*

EXERCISE 2.16 CONTEXT AND DICTIONARY: SENTENCES

Directions: Use your dictionary to select the definition for each boldfaced word that best fits the context of the sentence. Use parts of speech labels and subject and usage labels when possible. Write the meaning of the boldfaced word in the space provided.

1. A work of art sometimes communicates a message that the artist believes is **imperative** for the public to understand.

Necessary; urgent

2. The first chapter of the textbook **elaborated** on strategies that active readers use before reading an assignment.

State in detail; add more detail

3. Government and politics may **impact** your life in several important ways.

Affect

4. Each survey contains a **battery** of questions that researchers want to investigate.

A group of similar things; set or series; array

5. Many scientists **attribute** recent changes in climate and weather to global warming.

Think of as resulting from; assign

6. The music professor lectured for fifteen minutes on the importance of the **bridge** in classical symphonies.

Connecting passage between two sections of a musical composition

7. Mr. Smith was healthy through most of his life, but became an **invalid** in his seventies after becoming ill with pneumonia.

A weak, sickly individual

8. Hal's English teacher **intimated** that he would not pass the course if he didn't submit his assigned papers.

Hint; imply

9. Businesses do not make much profit on products sold with a small **margin**.

The difference between cost and selling price

10. Although courts were designed to obtain **neutral** and nonpolitical judgments on the application of the law in practice, this has not always been the case.

Not supporting one side or the other in a controversy

EXERCISE 2.17 CONTEXT AND DICTIONARY: PASSAGES

Directions: Read each passage using context clues, and when necessary, the dictionary, to determine the meaning of each boldfaced word. Then, from the multiple choices provided after each passage, circle the meaning that best fits the context.

A. Why We Sleep

Generally speaking, sleep appears to provide a time-out period, so that the body can eliminate waste products from muscles, repair cells, conserve or **replenish** energy stores, strengthen the immune system, and recover abilities lost during the day. When we do not get enough sleep, our bodies operate abnormally. For example, levels of hormones necessary for normal muscle development and proper immune-system **functioning decline.**

Although most people can still get along reasonably well after a day or two of sleeplessness, sleep **deprivation** that lasts for four days or longer becomes uncomfortable and soon becomes unbearable. In animals, forced sleeplessness leads to infections and eventually death, and the same seems to be true for people. In one tragic case, a 51-year-old man **abruptly** began to lose sleep. After sinking deeper and deeper into an exhausted **stupor,** he developed a lung infection and died. An **autopsy** showed that he had lost almost all the large **neurons** in two areas of the **thalamus** that have been linked to sleep and hormonal **circadian** rhythms.

—Wade and Tavris, *Invitation to Psychology,* 4th ed.

1. replenish   a. keep   b. eliminate
              c. refill   d. decrease

2. functioning a. operating   b. playing
               c. repairing   d. beginning

3. decline   a. improve   b. stop
             c. speed up   d. worsen

4. deprivation a. difficulty   b. loss
               c. irregularity   d. interruption

5. abruptly   a. suddenly   b. slowly
             c. intentionally   d. as expected

6. stupor   a. inability to sleep   b. extreme tiredness
            c. loss of communication d. dulled mental state

7. autopsy   a. examination of body after death   b. cause of death
            c. surprising discovery   d. doctor who studies illness

8. neurons   a. muscles   b. nerve cells
            c. internal organs   d. fatty tissue

9. thalamus a. neck and throat region   b. top of the head
            c. a part of the brain   d. upper body

10. circadian a. human   b. animal
              c. occasional   d. daily

B. What Is Crime?

Crime is a natural **phenomenon**, because people have different levels of attachment, motivation, and virtue. If people are to live in society successfully, however, rules are required to make sure they can live together peacefully with a high degree of order. Of course, there will always be some people who do not obey the rules. Therefore, the rules must carry penalties to serve both as a warning and as an enforcement **mechanism**. Rules that **prohibit** certain forms of conduct and maintain social order identify a set of behaviors termed crimes, which form the basis of criminal law. Violations of criminal law are considered crimes against society because they break rules designed for the common good. That is to say, the rules **elevate** the good of the community over the desires of any given individual. Without such a system, **anarchy** would **prevail** as individuals competed to fulfill their own wants and needs without regard for those of others.

The **distinction** between serious and nonserious crimes is related to the possible sentences that can be imposed. Serious crimes that are punishable by **incarceration** for more than one year are called **felonies** in most states. Less serious crimes that are punishable by imprisonment for one year or less are called **misdemeanors**.

—Albanese, *Criminal Justice,* 4th ed.

1. phenomenon   a. mistake   (b. occurrence)
     c. result   d. direction

2. mechanism   a. rule   b. system of government
     (c. tool)   d. officer

3. prohibit   a. eliminate   b. define or describe
     c. support   (d. forbid)

4. elevate   (a. raise)   b. deny
     c. describe   d. benefit

5. anarchy   (a. disorder)   b. order
     c. government   d. law

6. prevail   a. disappear   b. stop
     c. exist   (d. dominate)

7. distinction   a. honor   (b. difference)
     c. definition   d. similarity

8. incarceration   a. punishment   b. death
     (c. imprisonment)   d. the court system

9. felonies   a. crimes   (b. more serious crimes)
     c. less serious crimes   d. harsh punishments

10. misdemeanors   a. crimes   b. more serious crimes
     (c. less serious crimes)   d. mild punishments

EXERCISE 2.18 CONTEXT AND DICTIONARY APPLICATION

Directions: Using any source except this textbook (a newspaper, magazine, or another book), identify three unfamiliar words that you would like to add to your vocabulary. Use context and a dictionary to determine the meaning of each word. On a separate sheet of paper, copy the sentences containing the unfamiliar words, underline the words, and write the dictionary definition that best fits the context.

Using the Dictionary Pronunciation Key

You can use the dictionary to learn the pronunciation of unfamiliar words. The dictionary uses phonetic spelling to show the pronunciation of each entry word. The phonetic spelling is the spelling of the word by sound—the word is spelled exactly as it is pronounced. The phonetic spelling for each entry word is found in parentheses immediately after the word. Accented syllables are marked. Look at the following examples:

phi•los•o•phy (fĭ-lŏs'ə-fē)

gauge (gāj)

Unlike the spelling in written English, each letter in phonetic spelling can have only one sound. For example, the letter *g* has two different sounds in the word *gauge*. In phonetic spelling, however, the letter *g* always stands for the "hard" *g* sound—the sound of the first *g* in *gauge*. When *g* sounds like *j* in a word, as the second *g* in *gauge* does, in phonetic spelling the letter *j* will be used to represent that sound. Notice also that the *ph*'s in philosophy are represented by *f*'s—because that is what they sound like.

Phonetic symbols may vary slightly from dictionary to dictionary. Each dictionary will provide a key to the phonetic symbols it uses. The key lists all the symbols in alphabetical order, with each symbol followed by a common example word containing the sound that the symbol represents. You will find the key at the bottom of the page or in the front of the dictionary in a print dictionary. If you are using an online dictionary, you'll find a link to the key for its phonetic symbols. See key on p. 90.

EXERCISE 2.19 RECOGNIZING PHONETIC SPELLINGS

Directions: Study the phonetic spelling to recognize each word below and then write the word, correctly spelled, in the adjoining space. You may use a dictionary

> **Pronunciation Key from the *American Heritage Dictionary***
>
> ă pat / ā pay / âr care / ä father / b bib / ch church / d deed /
> ĕ pet / ē be / f fife / g gag / h hat / hw which / ĭ pit / ī pie /
> îr pier / j judge / k kick / l lid, needle / m mum / n no, sudden /
> ng thing / ŏ pot / ō toe / ô paw, for / oi noise / ou out /
> ŏŏ took / ōō boot / p pop / r roar / s sauce / sh ship, dish /
> t tight / th thin, path / *th* this, bathe / ŭ cut / ûr urge / v valve /
> w *with* / y yes / z zebra, size / zh vision / ə *a*bout, it*e*m,
> ed*i*ble, gall*o*p, circ*u*s

or spell check to check your spelling. Refer to the preceding key as necessary.
The first one is done as an example.

1.	mŭn'ē	*money*	9.	kôrs	course
2.	ə bŭv'	above	10.	ŭn'yən	onion
3.	fâr	fair/fare	11.	pā'shəns	patients/patience
4.	fär	far	12.	nŏl'ĭj	knowledge
5.	krōōd	crude	13.	mĭs'tə rē	mystery
6.	bôt	bought	14.	mĕzh' ər	measure
7.	shŏŏg'ər	sugar	15.	sī kŏl' ə jē	psychology
8.	kŏl'ĭj	college			

EXERCISE 2.20 JOKES IN PHONETIC WRITING

Directions: The following jokes are written phonetically. Rewrite each joke,
correctly spelled, in the space provided. Check the preceding key when you are
unsure of a phonetic symbol.

1. "Ī kŏod hăv mărēd ĕnēbŏdē ī plēzd."

   "I could have married anybody I pleased."

   "Thĕn hwī är yōō sĭngəl?"

   "Then why are you single?"

   "Ī nĕvər plēzd ĕnēbŏdē."

   "I never pleased anybody."

2. Kēp smīlĭng. Ĭt māks ĕvrēwŭn wŭnder hwŭt yər ŭp tōo.

Keep smiling. It makes everyone wonder what you're up to.

3. ə kŭstəmər wôkd ĭntōo a pĕt shŏp ănd spīd a părət. Hē ămbəld ōvər tōo thə bûrd ănd sĕd, "Hā, stōopid, kăn yōo tôk?"

A customer walked into a pet shop and spied a parrot. He ambled over to the bird

and said, "Hey, stupid, can you talk?"

Thə bûrd ănsərd, "Yes, dŭmē, kăn yōo flī?"

The bird answered, "Yes, dummy, can you fly?"

4. Tōo dôgz wûr chāsĭng tōo răbĭts hwĕn wŭn răbĭt tûrnd tōo thē ŭthər ănd sĕd, "Lĕts stŏp hîr fôr ə fū mĭnĭts ănd outnŭmbər thĕm."

Two dogs were chasing two rabbits when one rabbit turned to the other and said,

"Let's stop here for a few minutes and outnumber them."

5. "Dŏktər, ī hăv thĭs tĕrəbəl prŏbləm. Ī kănt rĭmĕmbər ə thĭng," ĕksklāmd ăn ănkshəs lādē tōo hûr dŏktər.

"Doctor, I have this terrible problem. I can't remember a thing," exclaimed an anxious

lady to her doctor.

"Hou lông hăv yōo hăd thĭs prŏbləm?" the dŏktər ăskd.

"How long have you had this problem?" the doctor asked.

"Hwŭt prŏbləm?" shē rĭplīd.

"What problem?" she replied.

SKILLS ONLINE: USING AN ONLINE DICTIONARY

 Online dictionaries provide basically the same information about words as print dictionaries. However, the information is organized somewhat differently. Because space is not a concern, online dictionaries list definitions one under another, starting a new line for each definition. Online dictionaries may show entries from more than one print dictionary source and contain links to related vocabulary information (such as a listing of synonyms and antonyms from a thesaurus). In addition, some of the phonetic symbols used for pronunciation may be different, and online dictionaries provide a link that enables you to hear the word pronounced.

SKILLS ONLINE EXERCISE. USING AN ONLINE DICTIONARY

Directions: Use an online dictionary to determine the meaning, part of speech, and pronunciation of each of the boldfaced words in the following sentences. If you've never used an online dictionary before, try *dictionary.com* or *yourdictionary.com*, which include links for hearing the words pronounced. Choose the meanings and parts of speech that best fit the context and write your answers in the spaces provided. Copy the phonetic spelling for the words whose pronunciations are unfamiliar to you, and be prepared to pronounce them in class.

1. The motion picture, like other arts, is a **vehicle** of creative expression.

—Janaro and Altshuler, *The Art of Being Human*, 8th ed.

meaning: A medium of communication, expression, or display

part of speech: Noun

pronunciation: Vē'-ĭ-kəl

2. Film is the most **collaborative** of the arts.

—Janaro and Altshuler, *The Art of Being Human*, 8th ed.

meaning: Working together

part of speech: Adjective

pronunciation: Kuh-lab'-er-uh-tĭv *or* kə-lăb'-ə-rə-tĭv

3. Film, like other **genres**, has certain conventions or conditions that the audience must accept.

—Janaro and Altshuler, *The Art of Being Human*, 8th ed.

meaning: A category of artistic endeavor

part of speech: Noun

pronunciation: Zhän'rə

4. The **critical** film viewer is acutely aware of what the camera is up to.

—Janaro and Altshuler, *The Art of Being Human*, 8th ed.

meaning: Involving skilled judgment; characterized by careful, exact evaluation and

judgment

part of speech: Adjective

pronunciation: Krĭt' ĭ-kəl

5. Some **contemporary** filmmakers still prefer to film in black and white.

—Janaro and Altshuler, *The Art of Being Human*, 8th ed.

meaning: Modern; of the present time

part of speech: Adjective

pronunciation: Kən-tĕm' pə-rĕr-ē

Comments: Now, having practiced using with both print and online dictionaries, which do you prefer? Why?

Answers will vary.

READING **2A**

SUCCESS IS A CHOICE (SELF-HELP)

by Rick Pitino

Rick Pitino coached the University of Kentucky's men's basketball team to a national championship in 1996 and is now coaching at the University of Louisville. In this selection, you will learn about his philosophy of success.

Pre-Reading Exercise

Directions: Complete this exercise before reading the passage. Preview the passage and answer the following questions:

1. What is the passage about?

Choosing to succeed
_____

2. What is the author's philosophy of success?

Success comes to those who work hard to earn it.
_____

3. What have you previously read or learned about success?

Answers will vary.
_____

4. What is your definition of success?

Answers will vary.
_____

5. Name a person you know who you believe is successful. Why do you consider that person a success?

Answers will vary.
_____

6. Write three questions about success.

Answers will vary.
_____

_____

_____

_____

Directions: Use context clues and the dictionary to determine the meaning of unfamiliar words in the passage.

1   Winston Churchill's rallying cry for the British people during WW II was simple and succinct: hoping and praying for victory was fine, but deserving it was what really mattered.

2   What does it mean to "deserve victory"?

3   According to Churchill, victory comes only to those who work long and hard, who are willing to pay the price in blood, sweat, and tears. Hard work is also the basic building block of every kind of achievement: Without it, everything else is pointless. You can start with a dream or an idea or a goal, but before any of your hopes can be realized, you truly must deserve your success. This may sound old-fashioned in this age of instant gratification, but from the Sistine Chapel to the first transcontinental railroad to today's space shuttle, there's no mystery as to how these things of wonder were created. They were created by people who worked incredibly hard over a long period of time.

4   If you look closely at all great organizations, all great teams, all great people, the one common denominator that runs through them is a second-to-none work ethic. The intense effort to achieve is always there. This is the one given if you want to be successful. When it comes to work ethic there can be no compromises. Any other promise of achievement is fool's gold.

5   We can see the evidence of fool's gold around us every day. It's the people looking for the quick fix. The easy way to lose weight. The no-pain way to have a better body. The instant way to get rich. The easy, no-assembly-required way to feel better about yourself, as if all you have to do is follow some simple directions and your problems will disappear like frost in the noonday sun.

6   But shortcuts fail.

7   The bottom line: Nothing meaningful or lasting comes without working hard at it, whether it's in your own life or with people you're trying to influence.

8   Take our basketball program at the University of Kentucky: We see ourselves as the hardest-working team in America. That is our standard, the yardstick by which we measure ourselves. We try to live up to it every day.

9   Are we the hardest-working team in America?

10   Who knows?

11   And who cares.

12   The important thing is we believe it. That's our edge. In close games, when the pressure intensifies and the margin between who wins and who loses can be as thin as an eggshell, we believe that all our hard work, all the long hours, and all the perspiration will enable us to come out on top. Why? Because we deserve it. We deserve our victory; we feel we've sweated more blood than our opponents and will earn it the old-fashioned way.

13   In my years of coaching I have worked with many players and seen a variety of attitude problems. Some players were selfish. Some doubted what we were trying to do. Some weren't as committed to the team concept as they should have been. I can live with all that. What I can't live with is a player who won't work hard. If players are willing to give the effort, they have no problem with me.

14   And you know what?

15   What's true on the basketball court is true in business and in life. You want to succeed? Okay, then succeed. Deserve it. How? Outwork everybody in sight. Sweat the small stuff. Sweat the big stuff. Go the extra mile. But whatever it takes, put your heart and soul into everything you do. Leave it all out on the court.

16   But that won't happen unless you choose to make it happen. Success is not a lucky break. It is not a divine right. It is not an accident of birth.

17   Success is a choice.

—Pitino, *Success Is a Choice*

You, the Reader

Interest Rating. Please rate the interest level of the reading on the following scale (circle one):

5—Very interesting   2—A little boring

4—Fairly interesting   1—Very boring

3—Mildly interesting

Difficulty Rating. Please rate the difficulty level of the reading on the following scale (circle one):

5—Very difficult   2—Fairly easy

4—Fairly difficult   1—Very easy

3—Moderate

Comments: Explain your ratings and make any other comments you wish about the reading.

Answers will vary.

COMPREHENSION QUESTIONS

Directions: For questions 1–5, choose the answer that best completes the statement. For questions 6–10, write your response in the space provided. Base all answers on what you read in the selection. Refer back to the selection as necessary to answer the questions.

__b__   **1.** We can tell from the passage that Winston Churchill was:
   a. A basketball coach.
   b. A British leader.
   c. A soldier.
   d. A person who did not understand how to succeed.

__c__   **2.** The author shares Churchill's belief that:
   a. You need luck in order to succeed.
   b. Victory is the result of faith.
   c. Success must be deserved.
   d. Dreams and goals do not contribute to success.

__a__   **3.** The author suggests that the University of Kentucky's basketball team:
   a. Expects to win because of its hard work.
   b. Never loses close games because its players are well prepared.
   c. Is the hardest-working team in America.
   d. Does not perform well except under pressure.

__a__   **4.** The author is most critical of athletes who:
   a. Don't make maximum effort.
   b. Are not committed to the team concept.
   c. Are selfish.
   d. Disobey the coach's advice.

__c__   **5.** When the author refers to people looking for "the quick fix" (paragraph 5), he is suggesting that:
   a. Modern society has made it easier for people to succeed in life.
   b. Modern society has made it more difficult for people to succeed in life.

    c. People expect to find fast, easy ways to succeed.

    d. We are fortunate that quick solutions to problems are more available today.

6. Explain the title and last line of the reading. What does the author mean when he says, "Success is a choice"?

Success results from choosing to work hard at something.

7. Why does the author believe that shortcuts to success fail?

Nothing meaningful or lasting comes without working hard for it.

8. What does the term "fool's gold" mean, as used in paragraphs 4 and 5?

A shortcut or quick fix that looks attractive but doesn't really work

9. If the author were to give a talk at your college, what advice would he probably give to students regarding success in their academic programs?

Work hard to achieve your goals.

10. Do you agree with the author that success is a choice? Why or why not?

Answers will vary.

VOCABULARY EXERCISES

WORDS IN CONTEXT

Directions: Choose the meaning for the boldfaced word or phrase that best fits the context.

   _c_   **1.** Winston Churchill's **rallying cry** for the British people during WW II was simple and succinct: hoping and praying for victory was fine, but deserving it was what really mattered.

    a. Victory

    b. Hidden message

    c. Call to action

    d. A tearful speech

   _c_   **2.** If you look closely at all great organizations, all great teams, all great people, the one **common denominator** that runs through them is a second-to-none work ethic.

    a. Bottom number in a fraction

    b. Something unusual or strange

c. Shared quality or characteristic
d. Popular leader

_b_   **3.** If you look closely at all great organizations, all great teams, all great people, the one common denominator that runs through them is a **second-to-none** work ethic.
a. Second place
b. Equal to or better than the rest
c. Hard to find
d. Happening very quickly

_a_   **4.** In close games, when the pressure **intensifies** and the margin between who wins and who loses is as thin as an eggshell . . .
a. Increases
b. Decreases
c. Stays the same
d. Changes

_d_   **5.** In close games, when the pressure intensifies and the **margin** between who wins and who loses is as thin as an eggshell . . .
a. Amount of effort
b. Limit
c. Increase
d. Difference

CONTEXT AND DICTIONARY

Directions: Use context clues and the dictionary to determine the meaning of the boldfaced word or phrase in each sentence. Write the meaning in the space provided.

1. Winston Churchill's rallying cry for the British people during WW II was simple and **succinct**: hoping and praying for victory was fine, but deserving it was what really mattered.

Short and to the point

2. This may sound old-fashioned in this age of instant **gratification** . . .

Satisfaction

3. When it comes to work **ethic** there can be no compromises.

Standards; principles

4. When it comes to work ethic there can be no **compromises**.

Halfway efforts; concessions; settlements

5. . . . we believe that all our hard work, all the long hours, and all the **perspiration** will enable us to come out on top. . . . We deserve our victory; we feel we've sweated more blood than our opponents.

Sweat; effort

RESPOND TO THE READING

Directions: Write a half-page response to either of the following questions.

1. Describe and discuss a time when you succeeded at something important to you. Why were you successful?

2. In your opinion, why are some people more successful than others at achieving their goals?

WEBQUEST

Directions: Use the Internet to find the answer to the following question. Write your answer on a sheet of paper. Print out the Web page you used for the answer or copy the URL on your sheet.

Find a Web page about a famous person you admire. Read the page and write a paragraph about the obstacles that person faced and what he or she did to overcome them.

READING 2B

ADAPTING TO TODAY'S JOB MARKET (BUSINESS COMMUNICATIONS)

by Courtland Bovee and John Thill

Reading 2B is taken from a business communications textbook. In this excerpt, the authors provide practical advice for finding a satisfying job and starting a promising career. Read the selection to discover what advice the authors offer to today's job seekers.

Pre-Reading Exercise

Directions: Complete this exercise before reading the passage. Preview the passage and answer the following questions:

1. What is the passage about? What goal question might you raise from the title of the passage?
   Finding work suitable to you

   How do you adapt to today's job market?

2. What is listed under the passage's second subheading ("What Do You Want?")?
   Questions about your values, interests, and preferences

3. What is listed under the passage's fourth subheading ("How Can You Make Yourself More Valuable?")?
   Steps toward building a career (or ways to make yourself more valuable)

4. What have you previously learned about developing a career?

   Answers will vary.

5. What is your career goal?

   Answers will vary.

6. Write three questions about career development.

   Answers will vary.

Directions: Use context clues and the dictionary to determine the meaning of unfamiliar words in the passage.

1   Adapting to the workplace is a lifelong process of seeking the best fit between what you want to do and what employers are willing to pay you to do. Start your career quest by figuring out what you want to do, what you have to offer, and how to make yourself more attractive to employers.

What Do You Want to Do?

2   Economic necessities and the vagaries of the marketplace will influence much of what happens in your career, of course; nevertheless, it's wise to start your employment search by examining your own values and interests.

- **What would you like to do every day?** Research occupations that interest you.
- **How would you like to work?** How much variety do you like? Do you prefer to work with products, machines, people, ideas, figures, or some combination?

What specific compensation do you expect? What's your ultimate goal? Are you willing to settle for less money in order to do something you really love?

- **Can you establish some general career goals?** Consider where you'd like to start, where you'd like to go from there, and the ultimate position you'd like to attain.
- **What size company would you prefer?** Do you like the idea of working for a small, entrepreneurial operation or a large corporation?
- **What sort of corporate culture are you most comfortable with?** Casual or formal? Teamwork or individualism? Do you like or loathe competitive environments?
- **What location would you like?** Would you like to work in a city, a suburb, a small town, an industrial area, or an uptown setting?

What Do You Have to Offer?

3   Knowing what you *want* to do is one thing. Knowing what you *can* do is another. You may already have a good idea of what you can offer employers. If not, some brainstorming can help you identify your skills, interests, and characteristics. Start by jotting down ten achievements you're proud of, then think

carefully about what specific skills these achievements demanded of you. As you analyze your achievements, you'll begin to recognize a pattern of skills. Which of them might be valuable to potential employers?

4 Next, look at your educational preparation, work experience, and extracurricular activities. What do your knowledge and experience qualify you to do? What have you learned from volunteer work or class projects that could benefit you on the job? Have you held any offices, won any awards or scholarships, mastered a second language?

5 Take stock of your personal characteristics. Are you aggressive, a born leader? Or would you rather follow? Are you outgoing, articulate, great with people? Or do you prefer working alone? Make a list of what you believe are your four or five most important qualities. Ask a relative or friend to rate your traits as well.

6 If you're having difficulty figuring out your interests, characteristics, or capabilities, consult your college placement office for tests that can help you identify interests, aptitudes, and personality traits.

How Can You Make Yourself More Valuable?

7 While you're figuring out what you want from a job and what you can offer an employer, you can take positive steps now toward building your career:

- **Keep an employment portfolio.** Your portfolio is a great resource for writing your résumé, and it gives employers tangible evidence of your professionalism. Collect anything that shows your ability to perform, whether it's in school, on the job, or in other venues. Many colleges now offer students the chance to create an *e-portfolio*, a multimedia presentation of your skills and experiences. It's an extensive résumé that links to an electronic collection of your student papers, solutions to tough problems, internship and work projects, and anything else that demonstrates your accomplishments and activities. To distribute the portfolio to potential employers, you can burn a CD-ROM or store your portfolio on a website—whether a personal site, your college's site (if student pages are available), or a site such as *www.collegegrad.com.* (However, you *must* check with an employer before including any items that belong to the company or contain sensitive information.)

- **Take interim assignments.** As you search for a permanent job, consider temporary jobs, freelance work, or internships. These short-term assignments help you gain valuable experience, contacts, important references, and items for your portfolio.

- **Continue to polish and update your skills.** Take courses and pursue other educational or life experiences that would be hard to get while working fulltime.

8 Even after an employer hires you, continue to improve your skills in order to distinguish yourself from your peers. Acquire as much technical knowledge as you can, build broad-based life experience, and develop your social skills. Learn to respond to change in positive, constructive ways; doing so will help you adapt if your "perfect" career path eludes your grasp. Learn to see every job or project as an opportunity to learn and expand. And share what you know with others; helping others excel is a skill, too.

—Bovee and Thill, *Business Communication Essentials,* 3rd ed.

You, the Reader

Interest Rating. Please rate the interest level of the reading on the following scale (circle one):

5—Very interesting   2—A little boring

4—Fairly interesting   1—Very boring

3—Mildly interesting

Difficulty Rating. Please rate the difficulty level of the reading on the following scale (circle one):

5—Very difficult   2—Fairly easy

4—Fairly difficult   1—Very easy

3—Moderate

Comments: Explain your ratings and make any other comments you wish about the reading.

Answers will vary.

COMPREHENSION QUESTIONS

Directions: For questions 1–5, choose the answer that best completes the statement. For questions 6–10, write your response in the space provided. Base all answers on what you read in the selection. Refer back to the selection as necessary to answer the questions.

_b_   **1.** The authors state that developing a career in today's job market involves finding a fit between:

    a. Your experience and education.

    b. Your interests and employer needs.

    c. Your ability and your financial needs.

    d. Your financial needs and your employer's financial needs.

_d_   **2.** The authors advise job seekers to:

    a. Accept any job they are offered.

    b. Only accept jobs that pay well and will lead to advancement.

    c. Only accept jobs that are in your career field.

    d. Consider internships and temporary work.

_c_   **3.** The main purpose of an employment portfolio is to:

    a. Practice your communication skills.

    b. Remind you of your accomplishments and boost your confidence.

    c. Collect evidence of your skills and experiences.

    d. Document your educational credentials.

<u> b </u> **4.** After finding a job, you should do all of the following *except*:

    a. Increase your technical knowledge.

    b. Work only on tasks that lead to your perfect career path.

    c. Improve your social skills.

    d. Share what you know and help others to improve.

<u> d </u> **5.** The authors believe that:

    a. Formal education should end once you have found the right job.

    b. You should only take courses related to your career field.

    c. Employers should pay for their employees' courses.

    d. Taking courses can contribute to your value as an employee.

6. According to the authors, how should you begin your career search?

Figure out what you want to do, what you have to offer, and how to make yourself more attractive to employers.

7. What are the advantages of having an e-portfolio?

A portfolio provides tangible evidence of your professionalism. An e-portfolio demonstrates your abilities in a multimedia format that can be extensive and easily distributed to potential employers.

8. Why is it important for job seekers to assess their personal characteristics?

Awareness of your personal characteristics will help you understand what you have to offer and to determine which types of work you are best suited for.

9. What are some strategies for identifying your talents and skills?

Jot down achievements you're proud of and think about what skills they demonstrate.

Identify a pattern of skills that might be valuable to employers.

10. Which of the authors' suggestions do you think is most valuable? Why?

Answers will vary.

VOCABULARY EXERCISES

WORDS IN CONTEXT

Directions: Choose the meaning for the boldfaced word that best fits the context.

<u> d </u> **1.** Start your career **quest** by figuring out what you want to do . . .
    a. Question
    b. Information
    c. Opportunity
    d. Search

<u> b </u> **2.** Consider where you'd like to start . . . and the **ultimate** position you'd like to attain.
    a. First
    b. Final
    c. Expensive
    d. Training

<u> a </u> **3.** Consider where you'd like to start . . . and the ultimate position you'd like to **attain.**
    a. Reach or achieve
    b. Study or learn about
    c. Apply
    d. Imagine

<u> c </u> **4.** Do you like or **loathe** competitive environments?
    a. Love
    b. Enjoy
    c. Hate
    d. Experience

<u> a </u> **5.** . . . doing so will help you adapt if your "perfect" career path **eludes** your grasp.
    a. Escapes
    b. Finds
    c. Comes to
    d. Approaches

CONTEXT AND DICTIONARY

Directions: Use context clues and the dictionary to determine the meaning of the boldfaced word or phrase in each sentence. Write the meaning in the space provided.

1. Economic necessities and the **vagaries** of the job market will influence much of what happens in your career . . .
    Fluctuations; unpredictable changes

    2. What specific **compensation** do you expect?

        Reward; pay

    3. Do you like the idea of working for a small, **entrepreneurial** operation or a large corporation?

        Profit-seeking business

    4. Are you outgoing, **articulate**, great with people?

        Able to express yourself clearly and easily

    5. Your portfolio . . . gives employers **tangible** evidence of your professionalism.

        Concrete; definite; actual

RESPOND TO THE READING

Directions: Write a half-page response to either of the following questions.

    1. Describe your current job, or a job you've had recently. What are its advantages and disadvantages?

    2. What are your career goals? Why is this career ideal for you?

WEBQUEST

Directions: Use the Internet to find the answer to the following question. Write your answer on a sheet of paper. Print out the Web page you used for the answer, or copy the URL on your sheet.

    Research a career that is of interest to you. Find out what training is needed to enter the career, what the job prospects are in that field, and what the average salary is for workers in that field.

Chapter 2 Review

Context

The context is the sentence or paragraph surrounding a word. Many words have more than one meaning. We understand a word as it is used in context. Use context clues to determine the meanings of unfamiliar words.

A *definition clue* is a definition for a word within the context.

A *synonym clue* is another word with the same or a similar meaning.

A *contrast clue* is a word or phrase with an opposite meaning.

An *indirect clue* is anything else that helps us logically guess the meaning.

Dictionary and Context

When context clues aren't sufficient, use the dictionary to determine the meaning of an unfamiliar word.

Find the dictionary definition that best fits the context.

Use *parts of speech* to help choose the best definition.

Use *usage and subject labels* to help choose the best definition.

You can also use the dictionary to determine a word's *pronunciation*. The dictionary uses *phonetic symbols*—letters and markings—to spell a word exactly as it is pronounced.

Skills Online: Using an Online Dictionary

Readings

Reading 2A: Success Is a Choice (Self-Help)

Reading 2B: Adapting to Today's Job Market (Business Communications)

CHAPTER TESTS

TEST 2.1. USING CONTEXT CLUES (SENTENCES)

Directions: Use the context clues to determine the meaning of the boldfaced word in each sentence and write your answer in the space provided. Do not consult a dictionary.

1. Though we had frequent rainfall in the spring, we have had only **sporadic** rainfall this season.

   Occasional

2. Proper care of your automobile will prevent unnecessary **deterioration** of both the inside and the outside of your car.

   Worsening

3. After catching the game-winning pass, the tight end danced **gleefully** in the end zone.

   Happily

4. Anything you do—eating, sleeping, talking, thinking, or sneezing—is a **behavior**.

   Anything you do

5. I love the calm surface of the ocean on a peaceful day, but I also love to watch its **turbulent** waves during stormy weather.

   Rough; agitated; wild

6. If a **scuffle** breaks out, the bartender must decide whether to handle the situation alone or to call the police.

   Fight

7. A **theory** is a general statement about how some parts of the world fit together and how they work.

   A general statement about how some parts of the world fit together and how they work

8. **Hypertension** is the medical term for abnormally high blood pressure.

   Abnormally high blood pressure

9. The American crocodile is so rare that conflicts with people rarely occur. American alligators, on the other hand, are much more **abundant** than crocodiles.

   Plentiful; common

10. The American crocodile is shy of man; American alligators, however, are much less **reclusive**.

    Shy

Test 2.2. Using Context Clues (Passage)

Directions: Use the context clues to determine the meaning of each boldfaced word in the following passage. Circle the correct meaning for each word from the multiple choice provided. Do not consult a dictionary.

AFRICAN BONDAGE

For almost four centuries after Columbus's voyages to the New World, European colonizers **transported** Africans out of their homelands in the largest forced **migration** in history. Estimates vary widely, but the number of Africans brought to the New World was probably not less than 12 million. Millions more **perished** while being marched from the African interior to coastal trading forts or during the passage across the Atlantic. Nearly as many were traded across the Sahara to Red Sea and Indian Ocean slave markets during the centuries from 650 to 1900.

African peoples, fed into the **merciless** slave trade, were **crucially** important in building the first **transoceanic** European colonial empires. Once the slave trade began, **locales** for producing desired **commodities** such as sugar, coffee, rice, and tobacco moved from the Old World to the Americas. This gradually shifted Europe's orientation from the Mediterranean Sea to the Atlantic Ocean. Africa became an essential part of the Atlantic-basin system of trade and communication by providing Europeans with the human labor needed to unlock the profits buried in productive American soils. Without African labor, the overseas colonies of European nations would never have **flourished** as they did.

—Nash et al., *American People,* 5th ed.

1. bondage — a. connection — (b. slavery) — c. cruelty — d. destruction
2. transported — (a. moved) — b. kept — c. influenced — d. harmed
3. migration — a. change — (b. movement from one place to another) — c. destruction — d. arrest of a large group of people
4. perished — a. stayed behind — b. suffered — (c. died) — d. resisted
5. merciless — a. unfortunate — b. expensive — c. unfamiliar — (d. cruel)
6. crucially — a. cruelly — b. surprisingly — c. doubtfully — (d. critically)
7. transoceanic — a. watery — (b. across the ocean) — c. democratic — d. unsuccessful
8. locales — a. people — b. people who live in a certain area — (c. places) — d. reasons
9. commodities — a. foods — b. precious metals — (c. merchandise) — d. necessities
10. flourished — (a. succeeded) — b. troubled — c. failed — d. begun

TEST 2.3. CONTEXT AND DICTIONARY (SENTENCES)

Directions: Read each sentence looking for context clues to determine the meaning of the boldfaced word. When context clues are not sufficient, use your dictionary to select the definition that best fits the context of the sentence. Write the meaning in the space provided.

1. The climate in our nation's capital becomes **equatorial** by late June.

   Like the equator (very warm)

2. We returned to work after a light lunch and a short **respite**.

   A period of rest

3. When Luis came to live with us, we accepted him as an **integral** part of our family.

   Essential; basic

4. Working mothers are hardly a **novelty** or rarity nowadays.

   Something new or unusual

5. The earliest civilizations developed in the **fertile** areas around long rivers.

   Rich; fruitful; producing abundantly

6. By **compressing** time and distance, technology promotes teamwork and improves profits.

   Making more compact; condensing; reducing

7. The completion of a national transportation and communications network was **intricately** linked with economic growth.

   Closely; thoroughly; in great detail

8. She was disappointed when she opened the gift box to find a **hideous** sweater that she knew she'd never wear.

   Very ugly

9. **Mandatory** sentences are designed to require a certain penalty upon conviction in order to guarantee that offenders do not escape punishment.

   Required; compulsory; obligatory

10. Consuming large amounts of sugar during exercise can have a negative effect on **hydration**.

    Amount of water (in the body)

TEST 2.4. CONTEXT AND DICTIONARY (PASSAGE)

Directions: Read the following passage using context clues and, when necessary, the dictionary to determine the meaning of each boldfaced word. Then, from the multiple choices provided after each passage, circle the meaning that best fits the context.

STRESS

Stress! It affects young and old, rich and poor, and people of all racial and **ethnic** groups. Stress is as much a part of daily life as is breathing.

Often, stress is **insidious**, and we don't even notice things that affect us. As we sleep, it **encroaches** on our **psyche** through noise or **incessant** worries. While we work at the computer, stress may interfere in the form of spam on our screens, noise from next door, strain on our eyes, and tension in our backs. The **toll** stress **exacts** from us during a lifetime is unknown, but it is increasingly believed to be much more than an annoyance. Rather, it is a significant health hazard that can rob the body of needed nutrients, damage the **cardiovascular** system, raise blood pressure, and **dampen** the immune system's defenses, all of which leave us **vulnerable** to infections and a host of diseases. In addition, it can drain our emotional reserves; contribute to depression, anxiety, and irritability; and cloud social interactions with hostility and anger. Stress is a major concern in the United States, and it appears to be getting worse.

—Donatelle, *Health: The Basics,* 5th ed.

1. ethnic
   a. human
   b. based on income level
   c. different
   d. cultural

2. insidious
   a. unfamiliar
   b. not easily controlled
   c. very common
   d. not easily noticed

3. encroaches
   a. intrudes
   b. affects
   c. disturbs
   d. surrounds

4. psyche
   a. awareness
   b. mind
   c. life
   d. experience

5. incessant
   a. not stopping
   b. extreme
   c. most serious
   d. personal

6. toll
   a. demand
   b. tax on a purchase or service
   c. cost
   d. number

7. exacts
   a. precise
   b. highly accurate
   c. demands
   d. measures

8. cardiovascular
   a. digestive
   b. of the heart and blood vessels
   c. of breathing
   d. of the muscles and nerves

9. dampen
   a. destroy
   b. make moist or wet
   c. strengthen
   d. weaken

10. vulnerable
   a. prepared
   b. defended against
   c. open
   d. responding

You, the Reader: Chapter 2 Wrap-up

Directions: Use one or two of the following questions to write a half-page response to Chapter 2.

- What were the most important things you learned from this chapter? How will you use what you have learned from this chapter?

- How have you changed your reading and vocabulary habits in response to this chapter?

- Comment on your vocabulary skills. Do you enjoy learning new words? Do you use the context well? Do you like using the dictionary? How can you continue to improve your vocabulary skills?

- What parts of the chapter did you find most engaging? What questions do you have about the chapter?

For support in meeting this chapter's objectives, go to MyReadingLab and select *Vocabulary*.

CHAPTER 3

Understanding Word Structure

LEARNING OBJECTIVES

In Chapter 3 you will learn to:

- Increase your vocabulary by learning the meaning of common prefixes
- Increase your vocabulary skills by learning to recognize base words and suffixes
- Deepen your word knowledge by understanding dictionary etymologies

CHAPTER CONTENTS

Pre-Reading Exercise for Chapter 3

Directions: Preview the chapter and answer the following questions.

1. What is the chapter about?

   Word structure; prefixes; suffixes; etymology

2. How many prefixes are reviewed in this chapter?

   31

3. What is etymology?

   The study of word origins and history

4. What have you previously learned about prefixes and suffixes?

   Answers will vary.

5. What have you previously learned about word origins? Are you curious about word origins? Why or why not?

   Answers will vary.

6. Write two questions about the content of this chapter.

   Answers will vary.

Your vocabulary will increase as you read more and make effective use of context clues and the dictionary. You can also expand your vocabulary by learning about word structure and becoming familiar with common word elements—prefixes, roots, base words, and suffixes. Active readers are curious about words and take advantage of these shortcuts to vocabulary building. In this chapter you will be introduced to thirty-one common prefixes and will learn to distinguish base words from suffixes; you will also learn about etymology (word origins). Information about roots is provided in the Appendix in the back of the text.

Introduction to Word Structure

When we say that words have structure, we mean that words can often be broken up into smaller parts that have meaning. For example, the word *basketball* is a compound word, combining two smaller words—*basket* and *ball*.

Many words contain a meaningful central part called a *root*. A meaningful word part that is attached at the beginning of a word is called a *prefix*; a part attached at the end of a word is called a *suffix*. A word may have no prefix or suffix, or it may have more than one prefix, root or suffix. For example:

pre (prefix) + dict (root) = predict

pre (prefix) + dict (root) + able (suffix) = predictable

un (prefix) + pre (prefix) + dict (root) + able (suffix) = unpredictable

Any whole word (a word that can stand independently) to which word parts can be added is called a *base word*. Prefixes and suffixes are added to base words to form new words. For example:

re (prefix) + decorate (base word) = redecorate

im (prefix) + possible (base word) = impossible

govern (base word) + ment (suffix) = government

color (base word) + ful (suffix) = colorful

Prefix: A word part attached at the beginning of a word
Root: The central part of a word
Suffix: A word part attached at the end of a word
Base word: Any whole word to which word parts can be added

Prefixes

Prefixes are word parts that are attached at the beginning of words. Prefixes often attach to base words to form new words.

im (not)   + possible = impossible (not possible)

tri (three) + angle   = triangle (a geometric figure with three angles)

Prefixes also join with word roots to form new words. A root is the central part of a word, but a root doesn't normally stand alone as a whole word. Many English word roots come from Latin or Greek. (See the Appendix for more information about roots.) For example, *–dict* is a word root, derived from Latin, meaning "say" or "speak." When joined with the prefix *pre–*, meaning "before," the word *predict* is formed—which means, as you know, to <u>say</u> that something will happen <u>before</u> it happens. If the prefix *contra–*, meaning "against" or "opposite," is joined to the root *–dict*, the word *contradict* is formed, meaning "to speak against," or "say the opposite."

The English language uses more than a hundred prefixes; there are thousands of English words that contain prefixes. Learning common prefixes is therefore a great aid to vocabulary building. Study and learn the thirty-one prefixes highlighted in this chapter. Completing the chapter exercises will help you learn the prefixes more quickly and easily.

Keep the following considerations in mind as you review the prefixes:

- Some prefixes have more than one meaning.
- Some prefixes change their spelling and/or pronunciation in different words. For example, the prefix *in–* changes to *ir–* before roots or base words beginning with *r* (*in–* + *responsible* becomes *irresponsible*).
- The meaning of the prefix will not be obvious in some words. For example, the word *prevent* contains the prefix *pre–*, though it may not be obvious how the meaning "before" is part of the meaning of the word *prevent*.

Negative Prefixes

Negative prefixes are prefixes that attach a negative meaning to a base word or root. Most negative prefixes mean *no* or *not*. Sometimes they reverse the meaning of the base word to which they are attached.

Study the negative prefixes in Table 3.1 and then complete Exercises 3.1, 3.2, and 3.3.

Table 3.1 Negative Prefixes

Prefix	Meaning	Example Word
1. un	1. not 2. reverses the action of a verb	unhappy unplug
2. dis	1. not 2. reverses the action of a verb	dissatisfied dismount
3. in, im, il, ir	no, not	inaction impossible illegal irregular
4. a, an	not, without	atypical anarchy
5. mis	wrong	misinterpret

EXERCISE **3.1** NEGATIVE PREFIXES AND BASE WORDS

Directions: Add one of the negative prefixes from Table 3.1 to each of the following words. Then write the meaning of the newly formed word.

EXAMPLES

possible	impossible	not possible
spell	misspell	spell wrong
1. popular	unpopular	not popular
2. probable	improbable	not probable
3. behave	misbehave	behave badly
4. moral	immoral	not moral
5. continue	discontinue	reverse of continue or not continue
6. complete	incomplete	not complete
7. tie	untie	reverse of tie
8. responsible	irresponsible	not responsible
9. please	displease	reverse of please
10. legible	illegible	not legible

EXERCISE 3.2 NEGATIVE PREFIXES

Directions: Complete each sentence by filling in the meaning of the negative prefix in the underlined word.

EXAMPLE

John has <u>mis</u>placed his keys; he's put them in the <u>wrong</u> place.

1. An <u>unintentional</u> error is one that was <u>not</u> done intentionally.

2. When you <u>disregard</u> advice, you do <u>not</u> follow the advice.

3. A politician who <u>misuses</u> the power of his office uses his power in the <u>wrong</u> way.

4. <u>Irreconcilable</u> differences can <u>not</u> be made up.

5. An <u>asymmetrical</u> design is one that is <u>without</u> symmetry.

EXERCISE 3.3 NEGATIVE PREFIXES

Directions: Working with a classmate, on a separate sheet of paper list two additional example words for each negative prefix listed in Table 3.1. Write the words' meanings next to them. You should not use the example words from Table 3.1 or words from Exercises 3.1 and 3.2.

Number Prefixes

English has prefixes for the numbers 1 through 10, and for some higher numbers as well. English also uses prefixes that refer to indefinite quantities. Table 3.2 contains some of the most common of these prefixes. Study the prefixes in Table 3.2 and then complete Exercises 3.4, 3.5, and 3.6.

Table 3.2 Number Prefixes

Prefix	Meaning	Example Word
6. uni	one	unicycle
7. mono	one	monotheism
8. bi	two	bicycle
9. tri	three	tricycle
10. deci, deca	ten	decimeter
11. cent, centi	hundred	centigram

The following prefixes refer to quantities, but not to specific numbers:

Prefix	Meaning	Example Word
12. poly	many, several	polygon
13. multi	many, several	multivitamin
14. semi	half, partly	semicircle

EXERCISE 3.4 NUMBER PREFIXES AND BASE WORDS

Directions: Add one of the number prefixes from Table 3.2 to each of the following words. Then write the meaning of the newly formed word. There may be more than one correct answer for some words.

EXAMPLE

angle	triangle	a figure with three angles
1. monthly	bimonthly	every two months or twice a month
2. graph	polygraph	lie detector (graphs multiple body functions)
3. rail	monorail	one-rail train
4. liter	decaliter	ten liters
5. form	uniform	having one/the same form
6. partisan	bipartisan	of two parties
7. lingual	trilingual	speaks three languages
8. gram	centigram	one hundredth of a gram
9. media	multimedia	using many media
10. formal	semiformal	somewhat formal

EXERCISE 3.5 NUMBER PREFIXES

Directions: Complete each sentence by filling in the meaning of the prefix in the underlined word.

1. Bigamy is the illegal practice of having ____two____ husbands or wives.

2. A monomial is a mathematical expression consisting of ____one____ term(s).

3. A semester is ____half____ of an academic year.

4. A centennial is a period of ____one hundred____ years.

5. The decathlon is an athletic contest consisting of ____ten____ events.

6. A unilateral withdrawal of troops occurs when only ____one____ side withdraws.

7. An athletic contest consisting of ____two____ events is called a biathlon.

8. A trio is a group of ____three____ people.

9. Polytheism is the belief in ____many____ gods.

10. A semidetached house is ____partly____ separated from another house.

EXERCISE 3.6 NUMBER PREFIXES

Directions: Working with a classmate, on a separate sheet of paper list two additional example words for each number prefix listed in Table 3.1. Write the words' meanings next to them. You should not use the example words from Table 3.2 or words from Exercises 3.4 and 3.5.

Other Common Prefixes

There are many other common prefixes that will help you expand your vocabulary. Table 3.3 will introduce you to some of the most frequently encountered prefixes. Study the prefixes in Table 3.3 and then complete Exercises 3.7, 3.8, and 3.9.

EXERCISE 3.7 COMMON PREFIXES AND BASE WORDS

Directions: Add one of the prefixes from Table 3.3 to each of the following words. Then write the meaning of the newly formed word. There may be more than one correct answer for some words.

Table 3.3 Common Prefixes

Prefix	Meaning	Example Word
15. in, im, il, ir	in, into	inhale, import, illustrate, irritate
16. ex, e	out	exhale, eject
17. pre	before	predict
18. post	after	postpone
19. inter	between	intercept
20. intra	within	intrastate
21. bene	good, well	benefit
22. male, mal	bad	malevolent, malodorous
23. anti	against	antiwar
24. con, com, col, cor, co	with, together	connect, company, colleague, correspond, co-owner
25. de	down, away from	descend
26. dis	away, apart	dismiss
27. re	again, back	repeat, reverse
28. sub	under	submarine
29. super	above, over	supervise
30. syn, sym	with, together, same	synchronize, sympathy
31. trans	across, changing	transmit, transition

EXAMPLE

marine	submarine	under water
1. game	pregame	before the game
2. migrate	immigrate	move into
3. session	intersession	between sessions
4. operate	cooperate	work together

5. form	transform	change forms
6. freeze	antifreeze	substance that prevents (works against) freezing
7. conscious	subconscious	level of mind below consciousness
8. natural	supernatural	beyond (above) natural law
9. cover	recover	cover again or get better/get back
10. nutrition	malnutrition	bad nutrition

EXERCISE 3.8 COMMON PREFIXES

Directions: Complete each sentence by filling in the meaning of the prefix in the underlined word.

1. A <u>pre</u>monition is a feeling about something ___before___ it happens.

2. <u>Post</u>war elections occur ___after___ a war.

3. <u>Intra</u>cellular activities occur ___inside___ a cell.

4. An <u>e</u>migrant is a person moving ___out___ of a country.

5. <u>Mal</u>icious remarks are remarks that say ___bad___ things about someone.

6. A <u>bene</u>volent person is kindly, or disposed to do ___good___ .

7. A <u>sub</u>terranean home is ___under___ the ground.

8. To <u>dis</u>pel a child's fear is to help the child push her fear ___away___ .

9. To <u>de</u>celerate is to slow ___down___ .

10. In a <u>sym</u>phony, all the instruments play ___together___ (the conductor hopes).

EXERCISE 3.9 COMMON PREFIXES

Directions: Working with a classmate, on a separate sheet of paper, list two additional example words for each prefix listed in Table 3.3. Write the words' meanings next to them. You should not use the example words from Table 3.3 or words from Exercises 3.7 and 3.8.

Learning the Prefixes

Find a strategy consistent with your learning style that will help you lock the meanings of the prefixes into your memory. Many students find that using index cards is a simple and helpful method for learning prefixes. Make a card for each prefix. Write the prefix on the front of the card; write the meaning of the prefix and an example word on the back of the card (see Figure 3.1). Study the prefixes in groups (for example: negative prefixes; number prefixes; divide the common prefixes into two or three groups) and test yourself until you're confident that you've learned them.

FRONT   **BACK**

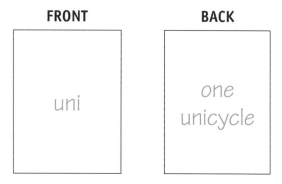

Figure 3.1   Index Cards for Learning Prefixes

Index cards provide visual, tactile, and kinesthetic reinforcement. If you pronounce the prefixes and their meanings as you review them, you'll add auditory reinforcement as well. (If you prefer, go to the Web site *www.quizlet.com,* which allows you to create flash cards that you can either print out or use online for review. Quizlet also provides games and other learning activities that can make learning vocabulary easier and more fun.)

Table 3.4 lists all the prefixes we've studied in this chapter with their meanings and example words. You can use the table to review the prefixes, test yourself, and to prepare your index cards.

Table 3.4   Prefix Review

Prefix	Meaning	Example Word
1. un	1. not 2. reverses the action of a verb	unhappy unplug
2. dis	1. not 2. reverses the action of a verb	dissatisfied dismount
3. in, im, il, ir	no, not	inaction impossible illegal irregular
4. a, an	not, without	atypical anarchy
5. mis	wrong	misinterpret
6. uni	one	unicycle
7. mono	one	monotheism
8. bi	two	bicycle
9. tri	three	tricycle
10. deci, deca	ten	decimeter
11. cent, centi	hundred	centimeter
12. poly	many, several	polygon
13. multi	many, several	multivitamin
14. semi	half, partly	semicircle
15. in, im, il, ir	in, into	inhale, import, illustrate, irritate

(continued)

Table 3.4   *(continued)*

Prefix	Meaning	Example Word
16. ex, e	out	exhale, eject
17. pre	before	predict
18. post	after	postpone
19. inter	between	intercept
20. intra	within	intrastate
21. bene	good, well	benefit
22. male, mal	bad	malevolent, malodorous
23. anti	against	antiwar
24. con, com, col, cor, co	with, together	connect, company, colleague, correspond, co-owner
25. de	down, away from	descend
26. dis	away, apart	dismiss
27. re	again, back	repeat, reverse
28. sub	under	submarine
29. super	above, over	supervise
30. syn, sym	with, together, same	synchronize, sympathy
31. trans	across, changing	transmit, transition

Suffixes

Suffixes are word parts added at the ends of words. Suffixes may be added to base words to form new words, or to roots to form a word.

contempt (base word) + ible (suffix) = contemptible

cred (root)   + ible (suffix) = credible

Some suffixes have specific meanings. For example, the suffix –*itis*, used in medical terms, means "inflammation," which is the body's reaction to certain unfavorable conditions. *Appendicitis* is inflammation of the appendix; *dermatitis* is skin inflammation; *sinusitis* is sinus inflammation. Some suffixes, however, are not so easily defined, but mostly serve a grammatical purpose. The suffix –*ed*, for example, is added to verbs to form the past tense. The suffix –*ment*, usually defined as "act or state of," changes a verb to a noun, as in the word *government*.

Recognizing suffixes makes it easier to pronounce words and understand their meaning and usage. Sometimes a reader will come across what appears to be an unfamiliar word that, if studied, proves to be a familiar word with a suffix added. For example, you may never have seen the word *suggestible* before, but a second look will reveal that it contains the common word *suggest* and the suffix –*ible*, which means "able." *Suggestible* means able to be influenced by suggestion.

A knowledge of suffixes will also help you use the dictionary more effectively. If you are looking up a word containing a suffix in the dictionary, you often find the base word or a related form of the word included in the definition.

uis1For example, the first definition for the word *depletion* in *Webster's New World Dictionary* is "a depleting or being depleted." If you don't know the meaning of *deplete*, this definition won't help you at all until you look up and understand the definition of *deplete*.

In some cases, especially in traditional paper dictionaries, you may not find any definition provided for a word containing a suffix. Instead, the word will be listed under its base word. For example, the word *deployment* might be listed at the end of the entry for *deploy*, with no separate definitions for *deployment* shown—so you will use the definitions for *deploy* to understand what *deployment* means.

Spelling Changes with Suffixes

Sometimes when a suffix is added to a base word, there is a change to the spelling at the end of the base word. In some cases, the last letter of the base word is dropped when a suffix is added. This often occurs when the base word ends with *e*.

like + able = likable

fortune + ate = fortunate

In some cases, the spelling of the last letter changes. This often occurs when the last letter of the base word is *y*; the *y* usually changes to an *i*:

happy + ness = happiness

vary + ation = variation

These spelling changes sometimes make it more difficult to recognize the base word.

The exercises that follow will provide practice with recognizing base words and suffixes. Before you complete the exercises, review Table 3.5, "Common Suffixes." Refer to the table as necessary to complete the exercises.

Table 3.5   Common Suffixes

Noun Suffixes

Suffix	Meaning	Example Words
ance, ence	act or quality of	endurance, persistence
ant, ent	person who	defendant, resident
cy	act or state of	democracy
ee, er, or	person who	referee, writer, prosecutor
ion, ation, sion	act or state of	separation, formation, comprehension
ist	person who	columnist
ity	condition or quality of	diversity
ment	act or state of	enchantment
ness	state of	fairness
ship	quality or state of	leadership

(continued)

Table 3.5 *(continued)*

Adjective Suffixes

Suffix	Meaning	Example Words
able, ible	able or able to be	likable, reversible
al	relating to	natural
ant, ent	performing or being	defiant, insistent
ate	having or tending to	affectionate
ful	having, full of	colorful
ic	like, having the nature of	angelic
ive	doing or tending to	attractive
less	lacking, not having	worthless
ly	like	fatherly
ous	having, full of	glamorous
y	having, tending to	rainy, sleepy

Verb Suffixes

Suffix	Meaning	Example Words
ate	make, cause to	liquidate
en	make, cause to	fasten
ify, fy	make, form into	beautify
ize	cause to, become like	modernize

Adverb Suffix

Suffix	Meaning	Example Words
ly	in a specified manner (indicates how something is done)	slowly

EXERCISE 3.10 BASE WORDS AND SUFFIXES

Directions: Divide each of the following words into a base word and a suffix. If the spelling in the base word has been changed, write the correct spelling of the base word.

EXAMPLE

government	govern	ment
happily	happy	ly
1. completeness	complete	ness
2. transferable	transfer	able
3. employee	employ	ee
4. complexity	complex	ity
5. democratic	democrat	ic

6. judgment	judge	ment
7. normalcy	normal	cy
8. contributor	contribute	or
9. conversation	converse	ation
10. universal	universe	al
11. courageous	courage	ous
12. comparable	compare	able
13. accountant	account	ant
14. glorify	glory	fy
15. forgetful	forget	ful
16. magnetize	magnet	ize
17. penniless	penny	less
18. daily	day	ly
19. confident	confide	ent
20. ridiculous	ridicule	ous

EXERCISE 3.11 RECOGNIZING BASE WORDS

Directions: Complete each sentence by filling in the base word from the boldfaced word that follows the sentence. If the spelling in the base word has been changed, write the correct spelling of the base word.

EXAMPLE

Come here and be as ___quick___ as you can. (**quickly**)

1. The ___infant___ was crying because she was hungry. (**infancy**)

2. If you can't ___resist___ all those sweet desserts, you are not likely to lose weight. (**resistance**)

3. All major religions teach people to have ___compassion___ for others. (**compassionate**)

4. General education requirements at many colleges include a course in ___psychology___. (**psychologist**)

5. This semester you are becoming a more ___active___ reader. (**activate**)

6. Relationships are more successful when partners ___communicate___ honestly with each other. (**communicative**)

7. A serious artist must ___dedicate___ himself to his art. (**dedication**)

8. "Don't worry about breaking up with your boyfriend," her friends advised, "there are ___plenty___ of fish in the sea." (**plentiful**)

9. *The Lord of the Rings* is a popular __fantasy__ that was written by J. R. R. Tolkien and made into a successful film series. (**fantasize**)

10. We will start with __simple__ problems and work up to more difficult ones. (**simplify**)

EXERCISE 3.12 ADDING SUFFIXES TO BASE WORDS

Directions: Add a suffix from Table 3.5 to each of the following words to form a new word. Be sure to write the correct spelling of the new word. There may be more than one correct answer for some words.

EXAMPLE

glory	*glorious*
1. establish	establishment
2. occupy	occupant; occupation
3. clumsy	clumsiness; clumsily
4. thought	thoughtful
5. depend	dependable; dependent
6. scandal	scandalous
7. measure	measurement; measurable
8. hero	heroic
9. hesitate	hesitation
10. fashion	fashionable

EXERCISE 3.13 ADDING SUFFIXES TO BASE WORDS

Directions: Complete each sentence with a word formed by adding a suffix from Table 3.5 to the boldfaced base word at the end of the sentence. Be sure to write the correct spelling of the new word.

EXAMPLE

We woke to a __glorious__ morning with a clear blue sky and a hint of warmth already in the air. (**glory**)

1. __Tighten__ the ropes to the stakes carefully when pitching your tent. (**tight**)

2. The children aroused her __motherly__ instincts. (**mother**)

3. Take time to __familiarize__ yourself with the list of common suffixes. (**familiar**)

4. The prisoners of war had been held in __captivity__ for almost three full years. (**captive**)

5. Pets offer people affection and ___companionship___ . (**companion**)

6. Slang should be avoided in ___formal___ writing (**form**).

7. The ___congregation___ grew in membership from year to year. (**congregate**)

8. Take your time; don't make a ___weighty___ decision too quickly. (**weight**)

9. You may move into the apartment once the current ___occupant___ has moved out. (**occupy**)

10. You will get better gas mileage if you increase your speed more ___gradually___ . (**gradual**)

EXERCISE `3.14` BASE WORDS AND SUFFIXES

Directions: Working with a classmate, on a separate sheet of paper list ten words that contain a base word and a suffix. You may find them in any print material you have with you, or you can think of your own example words. Your words must contain a suffix found in Table 3.5, but you may *not* use the example words from the table or any of the words in Exercises 3.10 through 3.13.

For each word you list, write the base word, the suffix, and the meaning of the word.

EXAMPLE

| motivate | motive + ate | to provide a motive or reason for doing something |

Etymology

Have you ever wondered where words come from? The study of word origins and word histories is called **etymology**.

The etymology of some words is obvious. Words like *sandal* and *window* contain the base words from which they are derived. But the origins of most words will not be obvious. For example, why do we call a sandwich a *sandwich*? After all, there is no sand in it!

A standard college dictionary will explain the etymology of most entry words. This information is enclosed within brackets before or after the definitions for the word. For example:

> **etymology**
> the study of word origins and word histories

sand•wich (sănd'wĭch, săn'-) *n.* **1a.** Two or more slices of bread with a filling such as cheese placed between them. **b.** A partly split long or round roll with a filling. **c.** One slice of bread covered with a filling. **2.** Something resembling a sandwich. ❖ *tr.v.* **-wiched, -wich•ing, -wich•es 1.** To make into or as if into a sandwich. **2.** To insert (one thing) tightly between two others esp. of differing character or quality. [After John Montagu, 4th Earl of *Sandwich* (1718–92).]

The etymology for the word *sandwich* explains that the word comes from the name of an Englishman who was the Earl of Sandwich. (The story is that he loved to gamble and started eating sandwiches so he could eat without leaving the gambling table.) Many other English words come from people's names or the names of places.

Of course, most words do not have such colorful origins. Because historically English has been a borrowing language, many English words are derived from words in other languages, especially Latin and Greek. Look at the etymology for the word *cardinal*.

> **car•di•nal** (kär'dn-əl, kärd' nəl) *adj.* **1.** Of foremost importance; pivotal. **2.** Of a dark to deep or vivid red color. —*n.* **1.** *Rom. Cath. Ch.* A member of the Sacred College or College of Cardinals who is appointed by and ranks just below the pope. **2.** A dark to deep or vivid red. **3.** A North American bird, *Richmondena cardinalis*, having a crested head, a short, thick bill, and bright-red plumage in the male. **4.** A short, hooded cloak, originally of scarlet cloth, worn by women in the 18th century. **5.** A cardinal number. [ME < Lat. *cardinalis*, principal, pertaining to a hinge < *cardo*, hinge.] —**car'di•nal•ship'** *n.*

The etymology for *cardinal* shows that the word is derived from a Middle English (ME) word which in turn was derived from the Latin word *cardinalis*, meaning "principal," or "pertaining to a hinge" (the etymology goes on to show that *cardinalis* contains the root word *cardo*, meaning "hinge").

The etymological information in the dictionary will sometimes tell you about a word's prefix or suffix. For example:

> **an•tip•a•thy** (ăn-tĭp'ə-thē) *n., pl.* -**thies 1.** A strong feeling of aversion or repugnance. **2.** An object of aversion. [Lat. *antipathia* < Gk. *antipatheia* < *antipathĕs*, of opposite feelings : *anti-*, anti- + *pathos*, feeling; see PATHOS.]

The etymology for the word *antipathy* shows that it comes from a Latin word, which came from a Greek word, and that it contains the prefix *anti–* (which, as you know, means "against") and the root *pathos* meaning feeling.

Although you do not have to learn a word's etymology to understand its meaning, learning the etymology has several benefits. Learning a word's etymology can strengthen your understanding of the word and reinforce your memory of its meaning. Over time, paying attention to etymology will expand and deepen your general vocabulary knowledge. Besides, as you've seen in some of our examples, word etymologies are sometimes quite interesting.

Complete Exercises 3.15 and 3.16 for practice with etymology.

EXERCISE 3.15 ETYMOLOGY

Directions: Use your dictionary to determine the etymology of the underlined word in each of the following sentences. Then mark the sentence True (T) or False (F).

EXAMPLE

False   The word <u>cardinal</u> is derived from a Greek word meaning "strange."

_T_   **1.** The word <u>silhouette</u> is derived from the name of an eighteenth-century French minister.

_F_   **2.** The word <u>alumnus</u> is derived from a Spanish word meaning "school graduate."

_T_   **3.** The word <u>bikini</u> comes from the name of an island where the atom bomb was tested.

_T_   **4.** The word <u>abduct</u> is derived from Latin, and contains the prefix _ab-_, meaning "away."

_F_   **5.** The word <u>motive</u> derives from a Latin word which meant "purpose."

EXERCISE 3.16 ETYMOLOGY

Directions: Look up each of the following words in your dictionary and read the etymology for the word. Then explain the etymology in the space provided.

EXAMPLE

cardinal   _comes from cardinalis, a Latin word meaning principal or pertaining to a hinge_

1. alligator

from _el lagarto,_ Spanish, meaning the lizard

2. hippopotamus

from the Greek _hippopotamos,_ meaning river horse

3. boycott

after Captain C. C. Boycott, a land agent ostracized by his neighbors

4. hamburger

from Hamburg, a city in Germany

5. import

from Latin _importare,_ to bring in (_in_ + _portare,_ to carry)

SKILLS ONLINE: LEARNING MORE PREFIXES AND SUFFIXES

 Directions:

1. Go online to learn three new prefixes. Find a Web site that lists prefixes and locate three prefixes that were not presented in this chapter. On a separate sheet of paper, list the three prefixes with their meanings and an example word for each.

2. Go online to discover three new suffixes. Find a Web site that lists suffixes and locate three suffixes that were not presented on Table 3.5 (pp. 121–122). On a separate sheet of paper, list the three suffixes, their meanings, and an example word for each.

3. Print out the Web pages you used for your answers or copy the URLs on your sheet.

READING **3A**

THE MYTH AND REALITY OF
MULTITASKING (GENERAL INTEREST)
by Edward M. Hallowell

Reading 3A is taken from the book *Crazy Busy*. In this passage, the author discusses multi-tasking. Read the selection to learn what the author thinks about multitasking.

Pre-Reading Exercise

Directions: Complete this exercise before reading the passage. Preview the passage and answer the following questions.

1. What is the passage about?
   Multitasking

2. What is multitasking?
   Doing two or more things at the same time

3. How does the author feel about multitasking?
   He believes you can't really do it—that you lose something when you try.

4. What have you previously learned about multitasking?
   Answers will vary.

5. How often do you multitask?
   Answers will vary.

6. Use the title to write a goal question for the passage.
   Answers will vary.

Directions: As you read the passage, use word structure (prefixes, base words, and suffixes), as well as context and the dictionary, to determine the meaning of unfamiliar words.

1   "Multitasking" refers to a mythical activity in which people believe they can perform two or more tasks simultaneously as effectively as one. To appreciate how faulty this notion is, consider how you behave in your car when you get lost. As you focus and try to get your bearings, one of the first things you do is turn down the radio. Why? Because you want to pay single-minded attention to the task of finding your way. The second "task" of listening to the radio detracts from the attention you can pay to the task of finding your way.

2   Or imagine playing tennis. You hit the ball and immediately get ready to make your next shot. You focus single-mindedly on the ball; the better the player you are, the more focused you become. You put all your energy, experience, instinct, and thought into each shot as well as the shot you plan to hit next and what you imagine your opponent will do. The game becomes mental as well as physical, like human chess.

3   Now imagine playing tennis with two balls. You have to keep track of both, running each down, watching your opponent do the same, as you frantically try to keep two balls in play at once. There is no way your game with two balls could be as good as your game with one.

4   Multitasking is like playing tennis with two balls, or three, or four. Some people say they pay better attention when they multitask. For a person to do better performing two tasks at once, it must mean that she was not fully engaged with the first task and needed two tasks to get her adrenaline flowing, thus boosting her performance. While this can happen, it would make more sense to try to fully engage with the first task.

5   That modern life forces a person to perform several tasks seemingly at once may well be true. But it is a myth that you can perform two tasks simultaneously as well as you can perform one. It is fine to believe that multitasking is a skill necessary in the modern world, but to believe it is an equivalent substitute for single-minded focus on one task is incorrect.

6   It may be convenient or necessary to multitask, to talk on the telephone as you write an e-mail and watch the stock prices stream across your computer screen; or to put clothes in the dryer as you play with your toddler and talk to your real estate agent on the phone. However, you will not be doing any of those tasks as effectively as you would if you were doing them one at a time.

7   The adrenaline rush you get from the excitement of multitasking may help you in the short run, but it cannot be sustained. Furthermore, even when the adrenaline is at its peak, your performance doing three tasks at once will not be as good as if you were doing just one.

8   Multitasking can get you into trouble when the tasks are important. I have a lawyer friend who told me how he negotiated an extraordinary deal for himself with several adversaries. He got concessions he never had thought possible. When they reconvened the following year to discuss business, the adversaries asked my friend how on earth he had persuaded them to consent to a deal that was so lopsided against them. He told them he had given the negotiation his full attention, while they had all been pecking away on their BlackBerrys. They had consented to what he proposed without fully focusing on what they were consenting to. It was all legal but done under the influence of BlackBerrys.

9   Each time you introduce a new object of attention into what you are doing, you dilute your attention on any one object. If, say, you are talking on the telephone and writing an e-mail, neither task receives the benefit of your full attention. As you blip back and forth between the two, you are liable to miss an item in one task while you are blipped over to the other task, just as my friend's adversaries did at their meeting while they worked on their BlackBerrys.

10   The time you spend on one task may be brief—say, one second or one-tenth of one second—before you switch to another, but at no time are you truly multitasking. You are only doing a series of tasks in rapid sequence, one after the other, over and over again. You may be able to watch four television shows at once, but this is only because you are good at inferring what you missed on one when you come back to it later. You may be able to carry on four conversations

simultaneously, but again, you will necessarily miss bits of each. You may pull it off, but no conversation will get your full attention.

11 If none of what you are doing requires your full attention, it is fine to multitask. Just be aware that you may make mistakes, miss key bits of information, be impolite, and fail to produce your best work.

12 Sometimes people do what is (erroneously) called multitasking because each of the activities is so boring, they want to do them in rapid succession to bring some excitement to the process, as if playing tennis with one ball were just too dull. Perhaps if your opponent is inferior, it might make sense for you to have to hit two balls and she just one. This is fine, as long as none of what you are doing is important.

13 But sometimes people try to play tennis with two balls in big matches against strong opponents. They want to be able to switch from one task to another the minute the first task becomes difficult. Instead of bearing with the difficult task, running down the tough shot, or sitting back and thinking about the problem, they simply hop off to a new task and hit the second ball. By the end of the day, they have done a lot of mediocre work and lost the match.

14 Multitasking ineffectively—what I call "frazzing"—is a common mistake that busy people make, frantically hoping that it will work. If the task matters, it is better that you do it by itself. That way you can give it your full attention.

15 There is an exception. You can ride a bicycle and ponder quantum mechanics at the same time. If you're good, you could ride a bicycle and mix pancake batter at the same time. This is because the riding of the bicycle is done on automatic pilot. You have practiced riding bikes long enough for the skill to be embedded in your brain's automatic pilot, the cerebellum.

16 If you have practiced a piece on the piano long enough, you could play it and read a book at the same time. You lose something, though: It is unlikely the piece would be played as beautifully as if you were giving it your full attention. The shadings and expressions that make a piece of music beautiful require conscious attention, not just automatic pilot. There is an energy, only partly understood, that conscious human attention alone can convey. That's why human interactions convey emotion far more vividly than electronic.

17 While there is a place for what is commonly called multitasking, the notion that it is as effective as single tasking is wrong. When what you are doing is important, multitasking is a practice to be avoided. Just think of it as playing tennis with two balls.

—Hallowell, *Crazy Busy*

You, the Reader

Interest Rating. Please rate the interest level of the reading on the following scale (circle one):

5—Very interesting   2—A little boring

4—Fairly interesting   1—Very boring

3—Mildly interesting

Difficulty Rating. Please rate the difficulty level of the reading on the following scale (circle one):

5—Very difficult   2—Fairly easy

4—Fairly difficult   1—Very easy

3—Moderate

Comments: Please explain your ratings and make any other comments you wish about the reading.

Answers will vary.

COMPREHENSION QUESTIONS

Directions: For questions 1–5, choose the answer that best completes the statement. For questions 6–10, write your response in the space provided. Base all answers on what you read in the selection. Refer back to the selection as necessary to answer the questions.

_d_   **1.** The author compares multitasking with playing tennis with two balls to show that:
   a. It is impossible to multitask.
   b. Multitasking makes activities more challenging.
   c. Multitasking makes activities more fun.
   d. Multitasking divides your attention and weakens your performance.

_d_   **2.** Multitasking successfully is possible when:
   a. Both tasks are familiar and enjoyable.
   b. The tasks are both important to you.
   c. You are well rested and highly motivated.
   d. You can do one of the tasks automatically.

_b_   **3.** The author's lawyer friend was able to negotiate an extraordinary deal because:
   a. He was an expert multitasker.
   b. His adversaries were multitasking and he was not.
   c. He was a better multitasker than this adversaries.
   d. His adversaries didn't understand how to use their BlackBerrys.

_a_   **4.** When you are multitasking, you are actually:
   a. Moving your attention rapidly from one task to another.
   b. Constantly keeping your full attention on two or more tasks.
   c. Raising and lowering your adrenaline level in a steady rhythm.
   d. Adjusting your attention level according to your priorities.

_c_   **5.** Which of the following best summarizes the author's view of multitasking?
   a. Everyone should learn to multitask well because multitasking is necessary in today's world
   b. Multitasking is a skill that requires a lot of practice
   c. Modern life may require multitasking, but multitasking weakens performance
   d. Multitasking is impossible and should always be avoided

6. Why does the author describe multitasking as "mythical"?

He believes no one can really do two different things at the same time.

Instead, you repeatedly move your attention from one to the other.

7. Why is multitasking sometimes necessary in modern life?

Answers will vary.

8. When is it most important to avoid multitasking?

When you are doing something important

9. What are the chief disadvantages of multitasking?

Multitasking divides your attention and weakens your performance. You will

miss things as your attention moves around. Quality of work will decline.

10. Do you agree with the author's criticisms of multitasking? Why or why not?

Answers will vary.

VOCABULARY EXERCISES

Pronunciation Guide (see p. 90 for list of phonetic symbols)

mediocre	(mē′dē-ō′kər)
mythical	(mĭth′ĭ-kəl)
simultaneously	(sī′məl-tā′nē-əs-lē)

WORDS IN CONTEXT

Directions: Choose the meaning for the boldfaced word that best fits the context.

__b__   **1.** "Multitasking" refers to a **mythical** activity in which people believe they can perform two or more tasks simultaneously as effectively as one.
   a. Real; proved true
   b. Falsely believed; not true
   c. Popular
   d. Very old

__a__   **2.** "Multitasking" refers to a mythical activity in which people believe they can perform two or more tasks **simultaneously** as effectively as one.
   a. At the same time
   b. One following after another
   c. Very fast
   d. Effectively

__d__   **3.** The adrenaline rush you get from the excitement of multitasking may help you in the short run, but it cannot be **sustained**.
   a. Stopped
   b. Supported
   c. Made faster; speeded up
   d. Kept up

___c___ **4.** Each time you introduce a new object of attention into what you are doing, you **dilute** your attention on any one object.
   a. Strengthen
   b. Increase
   c. Weaken
   d. Control

___b___ **5.** But sometimes people try to play tennis with two balls in big matches against strong opponents . . . By the end of the day, they have done a lot of **mediocre** work and lost the match.
   a. Excellent
   b. Not very good
   c. Contributing to victory
   d. Interesting

Using Word Structure Clues

Part I

Directions: The boldfaced word in each of the following sentences contains a prefix you learned in this chapter. For each boldfaced word, identify the prefix and the meaning of the prefix. Then write the meaning of the word. Use context and a dictionary as well as the prefix to determine the word's meaning.

1. "**Multitasking**" refers to a mythical activity in which people believe they can perform two or more tasks simultaneously as effectively as one.

   prefix = __multi__   prefix meaning = __many, several__
   multitasking means __doing several things at once__

2. The second "task" of listening to the radio **detracts** from the attention you can pay to the task of finding your way.

   prefix = __de__   prefix meaning = __down, away__
   detracts means __takes away from__

3. You put all your energy, experience, **instinct**, and thought into each shot as well as the shot you plan to hit next . . .

   prefix = __in__   prefix meaning = __in, into__
   instinct means __inborn or natural tendency__

4. He got **concessions** he never had thought possible.

   prefix = __con__   prefix meaning = __with, together__
   concessions means __things granted or yielded; going with what someone else wants__

5. When they **reconvened** the following year to discuss business . . .

   prefix = __re__   prefix meaning = __again__
   reconvened means __met again__

6. That's why human **interactions** convey emotion far more vividly than electronic.

prefix = _inter_   prefix meaning = _between_

interactions means _actions between (people)_

Part II

Directions: Divide each word into a base word and suffix.

	Base word	**Suffix**
1. activity	active	ity
2. frantically	frantic	ally
3. performance	perform	ance
4. excitement	excite	ment
5. negotiation	negotiate	ion
6. vividly	vivid	ly

RESPOND TO THE READING

Directions: Write a half-page response to either of the following questions.

1. Describe a recent situation when you were multitasking. Why were you multitasking? How well did you perform the tasks? Would you have been better off not multitasking?

2. Are Americans too busy? Discuss.

WEBQUEST

Directions: Use the Internet to find the answers to the following questions. Write your answers on a sheet of paper. Print out the Web page(s) you used for the answers or copy the URL(s) on your sheet.

What is attention deficit hyperactivity disorder (ADHD)? What are its symptoms? How common is it?

READING 3B

FRIENDSHIP
(INTERPERSONAL COMMUNICATION)
by Joseph A. DeVito

Reading 3B is taken from an interpersonal communication textbook. Interpersonal communication is the study of interactions and relationships between individuals. This excerpt discusses the nature of friendship and the different types of friendship.

Pre-Reading Exercise

Directions: Complete this exercise before reading the passage. Preview the passage and answer the following questions.

1. What is the passage about?
   Friendship and types of friendships

2. What will be discussed in the first main section?
   What friendship is and the characteristics of friendships

3. How many types of friendship are identified? What are they?
   Three: friendship of reciprocity; friendship of receptivity; friendship of association

4. What is the subject of the last paragraph?
   Face-to-face vs. online friendships

5. What have you previously read or learned about friendship?
   Answer will vary.

6. Write a goal question for each of the following headings:

   Definition and Characteristics
   What is the definition of friendship, and what are its characteristics?

   Friendship Types
   What types of friendship are there?

Directions: As you read the passage, use word structure (prefixes, base words, and suffixes) as well as context and the dictionary, to determine the meaning of unfamiliar words.

1   Friendship has engaged the attention and imagination of poets, novelists, and artists of all kinds. On television, friendships have become almost as important as romantic pairings. And friendship also interests a range of interpersonal communication researchers. Throughout your life you'll meet many people, but out of this wide array you'll develop few relationships you would call friendships. Yet despite the low number of friendships you may form, their importance is great.

Definition and Characteristics

2   Friendship is an *interpersonal relationship* between two interdependent persons that is *mutu-* *ally productive* and *characterized by mutual positive regard*. First, friendship is an interpersonal relationship; communication interactions must have taken place between the people. Further, the relationship involves a "personalistic focus"; friends react to each other as complete persons, as unique, genuine, and irreplaceable individuals.

3   Second, friendships must be mutually productive—they cannot be destructive to either person. Once destructiveness enters into a relationship, it can no longer be characterized as friendship. Lover relationships, marriage relationships, parent–child relationships, and just about any other possible relationship can be either destructive or productive, but friendship

must enhance the potential of each person and can only be productive.

4   Third, friendships are characterized by mutual positive regard. Liking people is essential if we are to call them friends. Three major characteristics of friendship—trust, emotional support, and sharing of interests—facilitate mutual positive regard.

5   When friends are especially close, the actions of one will impact more significantly on the other than they would if the friends were merely casual acquaintances. The closer friends are, the more interdependent they become. At the same time, however, the closer friends are, the more independent they are of, for example, the attitudes and behaviors of others. Also, the less they are influenced by the societal rules that govern more casual relationships. Close friends are likely to make up their own rules for interacting with each other; they decide what they will talk about and when, what they can say to each other without offending and what they can't; when and for what reasons they can call each other, and so on.

6   In North America friendships clearly are a matter of choice; you choose—within limits—who your friends will be. And most researchers define friendship as a voluntary relationship, a relationship of choice. The density of U.S. cities and the ease of communication and relocation does make many friendships voluntary. But throughout human history in many parts of the world—for example, in small villages miles away

from urban centers, where people are born, live, and die without venturing much beyond their community—relationships traditionally have not been voluntary. In these settings you simply form relationships with those in your village. You don't have the luxury of selecting certain people to interact with and others to ignore. You must interact with and form friendships and romantic relationships with members of the community simply because these are the only people you come into contact with on a regular basis. This situation is changing rapidly, however, as Internet use becomes near universal. With access to people from all over the world via the Internet, more and more relationships will become voluntary.

Friendship Types

7   Not all friendships are the same. But how do they differ? One way of answering this question is by distinguishing among three major types: friendships of reciprocity, receptivity, and association.

8   The *friendship of reciprocity* is the ideal type, characterized by loyalty, self-sacrifice, mutual affection, and generosity. A friendship of reciprocity is based on equality: Each individual shares equally in giving and receiving the benefits and rewards of the relationship.

9   In the *friendship of receptivity*, in contrast, there is an imbalance in giving and receiving; one person is the primary giver and one the primary receiver. This is a positive imbalance, however,

because each person gains something from the relationship. The different needs of both the person who receives and the person who gives affection are satisfied. This is the friendship that may develop between a teacher and a student or between a doctor and a patient. In fact, a difference in status is essential for the friendship of receptivity to develop.

10   The *friendship of association* is a transitory one. It might be described as a friendly relationship rather than a true friendship. Associative friendships are the kind we often have with classmates, neighbors, or coworkers. There is no great loyalty, no great trust, no great giving or receiving. The association is cordial but not intense.

11   Another way to look at friendship types is to compare face-to-face and online friendships. Not surprisingly, there is not yet enough research to draw clear distinctions between face-to-face and online friendships. Nevertheless, some differences are coming to light. For example, one study found that people viewed opposite-sex face-to-face friendships as more intimate than online friendships. Female–female online and face-to-face friendships, however, were rated equally— and male–male online friendships were rated as more intimate than face-to-face friendships. Another study found that face-to-face friendships involved more interdependence, greater breadth and depth, greater understanding, and greater commitment. Over time, however, as both types of friendships improved, the differences between face-to-face and online friendships decreased.

—DeVito, *The Interpersonal Communication Book,* 12th ed.

You, the Reader

Interest Rating. Please rate the interest level of the reading on the following scale (circle one):

5—Very interesting   2—A little boring

4—Fairly interesting   1—Very boring

3—Mildly interesting

Difficulty Rating. Please rate the difficulty level of the reading on the following scale (circle one):

5—Very difficult   2—Fairly easy

4—Fairly difficult   1—Very easy

3—Moderate

Comments: Please explain your ratings and make any other comments you wish about the reading.

Answers will vary.

COMPREHENSION QUESTIONS

Directions: For questions 1–5, choose the answer that best completes the statement. For questions 6–10, write your response in the space provided. Base all answers on what you read in the selection. Refer back to the selection as necessary to answer the questions.

_____b_____ **1.** One way that friendship differs from marriage or a love relationship is that:
    a. Marriage and love relationships can never be destructive.
    b. Friendships cannot be destructive.
    c. Friendships are more important than marriage or a love relationship.
    d. Friendships are a matter of choice.

_____c_____ **2.** The author states that the closer friends are:
    a. The more likely they are to have arguments.
    b. The less dependent they become on one another.
    c. The less dependent they become on the attitudes of others.
    d. The less their actions impact upon one another.

_____a_____ **3.** The author implies that you cannot be friends with:
    a. Someone you don't like.
    b. Someone from a different cultural background.
    c. Someone with whom you've never had a face-to-face interaction.
    d. Your teacher or doctor, unless you are a teacher or doctor yourself.

_____c_____ **4.** Emilio and Sal are classmates. They enjoy working with each other in class, e-mail each other about assignments, and sometimes have lunch together. When the semester is over, they have no more contact. Which type of friendship do they have?
    a. A friendship of reciprocity
    b. A friendship of receptivity
    c. A friendship of association
    d. An involuntary friendship

_____d_____ **5.** A study comparing online and face-to-face friendships found that:
    a. There are no differences between online and face-to-face friendships.
    b. Online friendships last longer than face-to face friendships.
    c. Women prefer online friendships over face-to-face friendships.
    d. Face-to-face friendships involve greater commitment.

6. How does the author define friendship?

Friendship is an interpersonal relationship that is mutually productive and

characterized by mutual positive regard.

7. What are the three major characteristics of friendship?

Trust, emotional support, and sharing of interests

8. According to the author, why is it easy to form voluntary friendships in the United States? Why is it necessary to have involuntary friendships in small villages in other parts of the world?

In the U.S. there are a lot of people in the cities, and it's easy to communicate

and relocate. In small villages you only have the opportunity to form relationships

with the people in your village.

9. Which is the ideal type of friendship? Why?

The friendship of reciprocity is the ideal type because it involves an equal giving

and receiving.

10. In your opinion, why are friendships important?

Answers will vary.

VOCABULARY EXERCISES

Pronunciation Guide (see p. 90 for list of phonetic symbols)

array	(ə-rā')
facilitate	(fə-sĭl'-ə-tāt')
mutually	(myōō'chōō-ə-lē)
reciprocity	(rĕs'ə-prŏs'ĭ-tē)
transitory	(trăn'-sə-tôr'-ē)

WORDS IN CONTEXT

Directions: Choose the meaning for the boldfaced word that best fits the context.

   c   **1.** Throughout your life you'll meet many people, but out of this wide **array** you'll develop few relationships you would call friendships.
     a. Travel
     b. Geographic area
     c. Large group
     d. Knowledge

   d   **2.** Second, friendships must be **mutually** productive—they cannot be destructive to either person.
     a. Unusually
     b. Contributing to success
     c. Affecting one person more than other
     d. Experienced by each toward the other

   b   **3.** Three major characteristics of friendship—trust, emotional support, and sharing of interests—**facilitate** mutual positive regard.
     a. Get in the way of
     b. Encourage; make easier
     c. Cause to become friends
     d. Discourage; make difficult

   a   **4.** . . . in small villages miles away from urban centers, where people are born, live, and die without **venturing** much beyond their community . . .
     a. Going into unfamiliar territory
     b. Staying in one place
     c. Having a lot of information
     d. Learning

_b_ **5.** In the friendship of receptivity, in contrast, there is an imbalance in giving and receiving: one person is the **primary** giver and one the **primary** receiver.
   a. Only
   b. Main
   c. Occasional
   d. Generous

Using Word Structure Clues

Part I

Directions: The boldfaced word in each of the following sentences contains a prefix you learned in this chapter. For each boldfaced word, identify the prefix and the meaning of the prefix. Then write the meaning of the word. Use context and the dictionary as well as the prefix to determine the word's meaning.

1. And friendship also interests a range of **interpersonal** communication researchers.
   prefix = _inter_   prefix meaning = _between_
   interpersonal means _between people_

2. . . . friends react to each other as complete persons, as unique, genuine, and **irreplaceable** individuals.
   prefix = _ir_   prefix meaning = _not_
   irreplaceable means _not replaceable_

3. When friends are especially close, the actions of one will **impact** more significantly on the other than they would if the friends were merely casual acquaintances.
   prefix = _im_   prefix meaning = _in; into_
   impact means _influence, affect_

4. This situation is changing rapidly, however, as Internet use becomes near **universal**.
   prefix = _uni_   prefix meaning = _one_
   universal means _used by everyone_

5. The friendship of **reciprocity** is the ideal type, characterized by loyalty, self-sacrifice, mutual affection, and generosity.
   prefix = _re_   prefix meaning = _back_
   reciprocity means _mutal actions; giving back to each other_

6. In the friendship of receptivity, in contrast, there is an **imbalance** in giving and receiving . . .
   prefix = _im_   prefix meaning = _not_
   imbalance means _lack of balance_

7. The friendship of association is a **transitory** one.

prefix = _trans_   prefix meaning = _across; change_

transitory means _changing rapidly; not long-lasting_

8. Not surprisingly, there is not yet enough research to draw clear **distinctions** between face-to-face and online friendships.

prefix = _dis_   prefix meaning = _away, apart_

distinctions means _differences; telling apart_

Part II

Directions: Divide each word into a base word and a suffix.

	Base Word	**Suffix**
1. friendship	friend	ship
2. imagination	imagine	ation
3. productive	product	ive
4. characterize	character	ize
5. acquaintance	acquaint	ance
6. societal	society	al
7. density	dense	ity
8. receptivity	receptive	ity

RESPOND TO THE READING

Directions: Write a half-page response to either of the following questions.

1. Discuss and analyze one of your friendships. Which type of friendship is it? Why is the friendship important to you?

2. Can online friendships be as rewarding as face-to-face friendships? Discuss.

WEBQUEST

Directions: Use the Internet to find the answer to the following question. Write your answer on a sheet of paper. Print out the Web page you used for the answer or copy the URL on your sheet.

Find a quotation about friendship that agrees with your view of friendship. Copy the quotation on your sheet and include the name of the quotation's author if it is provided. Explain why you like the quotation and what it has to say about friendship.

CHAPTER 3 REVIEW

Words often have meaningful parts: prefixes, roots, base words, and suffixes.

Prefixes

A *prefix* is attached at the beginning of a word.

Negative prefixes attach a negative meaning, such as *no* or *not*, to a base word or root.

Number prefixes represent specific numbers or indefinite quantities.

Other common prefixes have a wide range of meanings.

Base Words and Suffixes

A *base word* is a whole word to which word parts can be added.
A *suffix* is attached at the end of a word.
Suffixes often change the parts of speech of the base words to which they attach.

Etymology

Etymology is the study of word origins.

A word's etymology is usually explained in the dictionary as part of the word entry. The etymology is enclosed in brackets.

Many English words come from words in other languages, especially Latin and Greek.

Learning a word's etymology can be interesting and can strengthen your understanding of the word.

Skills Online: Learning More Prefixes and Suffixes

Readings

Reading 3A: The Myth and Reality of Multitasking (General Interest)

Reading 3B: Friendship (Interpersonal Communication)

CHAPTER TESTS

TEST 3.1. PREFIXES

Directions: *Without looking back in this chapter or consulting a dictionary,* (1) identify the prefix in each of the following words, and (2) write the meaning of the prefix.

EXAMPLE

unconcerned	un	not
1. illiterate	il	not
2. misjudge	mis	wrong
3. atheist	a	not; without
4. disuse	dis	not
5. uncover	un	reverses the action
6. unicorn	uni	one
7. decagon	deca	ten
8. semisweet	semi	half; partly
9. multipurpose	multi	many; several
10. bifocals	bi	two

TEST 3.2. PREFIXES

Directions: *Without looking back in this chapter or consulting a dictionary,* (1) identify the prefix in each of the following words, and (2) write the meaning of the prefix.

EXAMPLE

unconcerned	un	not
1. imprison	im	in; into
2. precondition	pre	before
3. correlation	cor	with; together
4. benefactor	bene	good
5. dismiss	dis	away; apart
6. translate	trans	across; change
7. subculture	sub	under

8. emit	e	out	
9. international	inter	between	
10. superintendent	super	above; over	

TEST 3.3. SUFFIXES

Directions: Divide each of the following words into a base word and a suffix. If the spelling in the base word has been changed, write the correct spelling of the base word.

EXAMPLES

government	govern	ment
happily	happy	ly
1. hesitation	hesitate	ion
2. beautify	beauty	fy
3. energize	energy	ize
4. merciful	mercy	ful
5. senseless	sense	less

TEST 3.4. ETYMOLOGY

Directions: Use your dictionary to find the etymology for each of the following words. Explain the etymology in the space provided.

1. frankfurter
from Frankfurt, a city in Germany

2. ambition
from the Latin *ambitio,* a going around to solicit votes

3. hacienda
from the Spanish *facienda,* meaning employment or estate (which was derived from Latin)

4. incentive
from the Latin *incinere,* to sing

5. telescope
from the Italian *telescopio*; coined by Galileo; from the Greek *teleskopos,* seeing from a distance.

You, the Reader: Chapter 3 Wrap-up

Directions: Use one or two of the following questions to write a half-page response to Chapter 3.

- What were the most important things you learned from this chapter? How will you use what you have learned from this chapter?

- How have you changed your reading and vocabulary habits in response to this chapter?

- How might an understanding of word structure and etymology help you to be a more engaged college reader and student?

- What parts of the chapter did you find most engaging? What questions do you have about the chapter?

PEARSON
myreadinglab

For support in meeting this chapter's objectives, go to MyReadingLab and select *Vocabulary*.

CHAPTER

4

Paragraph Logic: Topic and Stated Main Idea

LEARNING OBJECTIVES

In Chapter 4 you will learn to:

- Distinguish between general and specific ideas
- Identify the topic of a paragraph
- Recognize stated main ideas in paragraphs

CHAPTER CONTENTS

Pre-Reading Exercise for Chapter 4

Directions: Preview the chapter and answer the following questions.

1. What is the chapter about?

   Identifying topics and stated main ideas in paragraph.

2. What is a topic?

   A topic is the subject or focus of a whole paragraph.

3. What is a main idea?

   A main idea is a general point developed in the paragraph about the topic.

4. What have you previously learned about recognizing main ideas in paragraphs?

   Answers will vary.

5. When you read textbook material, do you usually focus on general ideas or on specific information? Explain.

   Answers will vary.

6. Write two questions about the content of this chapter.

   Answers will vary.

You know that effective reading involves the use of active reading strategies. Perhaps the most practical active reading strategies for college readers are those we use to recognize main ideas. As a college student, you will be asked to read a wide variety of materials. Given the amount of reading required and the difficulty level of some of the material, you won't necessarily understand and remember everything you read. However, you will want to make every effort to understand and remember the most important ideas and information in your material—the main ideas.

Recognizing main ideas is not always an easy task. One of the most common complaints of college readers is that they are unable to distinguish the more important ideas from the less important. When they are reading their textbooks, everything seems important; they are unsure about what to underline or highlight, what to include in their textbook notes, and what to focus on when they study for a test.

In Chapters 4 and 5 you will learn to use active strategies to recognize the main ideas in your reading. Practice with the chapter exercises will enable you to apply these strategies with increasing skillfulness.

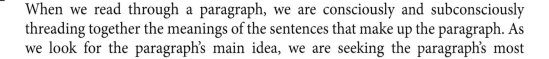

General vs. Specific

When we read through a paragraph, we are consciously and subconsciously threading together the meanings of the sentences that make up the paragraph. As we look for the paragraph's main idea, we are seeking the paragraph's most important point. The main idea is usually a *general* idea—that is, an idea that summarizes or ties together the specific information in the paragraph. When we read through a paragraph, in other words, one of the things we look for is the relationship between general and specific ideas.

What is the difference between a general and specific idea? Consider the following statements:

Ana loves baseball.

Ana loves sports.

Which is the more general statement? The second statement, "Ana loves sports," is more general, because "sports" is a broader, more inclusive—or more *general*—concept than "baseball." Baseball is one type of sport; there are many others. This makes "baseball" a more specific term than "sports"; therefore the sentence "Ana loves baseball" is more specific than the sentence "Ana loves sports."

Let's look at another example. Compare the following phrases:

- television sitcoms
- television programs

Which is the more general phrase? You probably agree that the second phrase—"television programs"—is more general. Why? Sitcoms are a specific type of television program. All television sitcoms are television programs, but not all television programs are sitcoms. There are many other types of television programs as well. "Television programs" is therefore a broader phrase—it includes more—than "television sitcoms."

Whether comparing words, phrases, or sentences, the more general term or statement is the one that includes more. *More general means broader, wider. More specific means narrower.*

General vs. Specific

More general = broader, including more
More specific = narrower, including less

Exercises 4.1 and 4.2 will provide practice with recognizing general vs. specific terms. Exercises 4.3 and 4.4 will provide practice with writing general and specific terms.

EXERCISE 4.1 GENERAL VS. SPECIFIC

Directions: Circle the more *general* word or phrase in each line.

1. (insects)   ants

2. (restaurants)   fast-food restaurants

3. spinach   (green vegetable)

4. women   (females)

5. (ocean)   Atlantic Ocean

6. rap music   (music)

7. plural nouns   (nouns)

8. (Shakespeare's plays)   Shakespeare's tragedies

9. sociology   (behavioral science)

10. gasoline   (fuel)

EXERCISE 4.2 GENERAL AND SPECIFIC

Directions: In the spaces provided below each line, list the terms in order, with the most general at the top and the most specific at the bottom. An example is provided.

EXAMPLE

animal, horse, mammal
animal **(most general)**

_____

mammal

_____

horse **(most specific)**

_____

1. minor-league baseball, sport, baseball

sport
_____

baseball
_____

minor league
_____

2. orange, citrus fruit, fruit

fruit
_____

citrus fruit
_____

orange
_____

3. president, modern American president, American president

president
_____

American president
_____

modern American president
_____

4. book, textbook, history textbook

book
_____

textbook
_____

history textbook
_____

5. wristwatch, expensive wristwatch, watch

watch
_____

   wristwatch
_____

      expensive wristwatch
_____

6. breakfast, meal, food

food
_____

   meal
_____

      breakfast
_____

7. jazz musician, musician, performing artist

performing artist
_____

   musician
_____

      jazz musician
_____

8. addition, mathematics, arithmetic

mathematics
_____

   arithmetic
_____

      addition
_____

9. parrot, bird, talking bird

bird
_____

   talking bird
_____

      parrot
_____

10. active reading strategies, previewing, pre-reading strategies

active reading strategies
_____

   pre-reading strategies
_____

      previewing
_____

EXERCISE 4.3 BE MORE GENERAL

Directions: Write a more general word or phrase for each of the following terms. An example is provided.

EXAMPLE

ice cream sundae

dessert
_____

1. Cheerios

   cereal (sample answer; accept reasonable alternatives)

2. Labrador retriever

   dog (sample answer; accept reasonable alternatives)

3. North America

   continent (sample answer; accept reasonable alternatives)

4. armed robbery

   crime (sample answer; accept reasonable alternatives)

5. reading *Sports Illustrated* magazine

   leisure reading (sample answer; accept reasonable alternatives)

EXERCISE 4.4 BE MORE SPECIFIC

Directions: Write a more specific word or phrase for each of the following terms. An example is provided.

EXAMPLE

appliance

refrigerator

1. jewelry

   necklace (sample answer; accept reasonable alternatives)

2. emotion

   love (sample answer; accept reasonable alternatives)

3. residence

   apartment (sample answer; accept reasonable alternatives)

4. American history

   history of the American Civil War (sample answer; accept reasonable alternatives)

5. the human digestive system

   the stomach

Active Reading Strategy: Identify the Paragraph's Topic

Almost everything you read is organized in paragraphs. But what makes a group of sentences a paragraph? You have probably learned that a paragraph is a group of sentences that are all about the same topic. The topic is the subject, or focus, of the entire paragraph. Identifying the topic answers the question, "who or what is the whole paragraph about?"

Identifying the topic of a paragraph is a practical and important strategy. Identifying the topic helps your mind connect the various ideas and information contained in the paragraph and is a first step towards recognizing the main idea. Identifying the topic also helps you to take effective notes from the text material. Naming the paragraph's topic is like providing your mind with a title for the paragraph.

To identify the topic of a paragraph, discover the common subject or focus of all the sentences within the paragraph. Ask yourself "who or what is the whole paragraph about," and answer the question in a short phrase (two to six words).

Let's look at an example.

A regular program of aerobic exercise improves the efficiency of your cardiovascular and respiratory systems. As a benefit of regular exercise, the heart is able to pump more blood with each stroke, thus lowering resting heart rate. Additionally, the body's capacity to distribute oxygen to working muscles is improved while the muscles responsible for respiration are strengthened.

—Donatelle and Davis, *Health: The Basics,* 2nd ed.

The preceding paragraph contains three sentences. What is the common subject of the three sentences? In other words, who or what is the whole paragraph about? Each sentence talks about regular exercise and its benefits. Therefore, the topic of the paragraph is "the benefits of regular aerobic exercise."

The topic must be general enough to include the whole paragraph. For example, "distributing oxygen to working muscles" would be too specific (too narrow) for the topic of the previous paragraph, because the *whole* paragraph is not about how exercise distributes oxygen to working muscles. Only the last sentence mentions this benefit.

On the other hand, the topic should not be too general (too broad) compared to the content of the paragraph. For example, "improving your health" would be too general for the topic of the previous paragraph. Though exercise will improve your health, the paragraph focuses on one particular way to improve your health—regular, aerobic exercise.

Naming the topic with just one word usually results in too broad a topic statement. For example, you might be tempted to say that the topic of the preceding paragraph is "exercise." Though the paragraph is indeed about exercise, the single word *exercise* is too broad a heading for the paragraph's topic. There are many aspects of exercise that are not discussed in the paragraph. Since the paragraph focuses on "the benefits of regular aerobic exercise," this would be a more accurate way of stating its topic. When you identify the topic of a paragraph, then, you may start with one word, but you will usually need to create a phrase to focus the topic more specifically.

Let's look at one more example.

Before the Civil War, America's colleges were small institutions with religious roots, training students for the higher professions of medicine, teaching, ministry, and law. Only a fraction of Americans attended college, and the education they received was based on beliefs whose truth was taken for granted. The Puritan divines who founded Harvard College in 1636 understood their task to be the education of Christian gentlemen, schooled in the classics and devoted to God. They knew the answer to the question of what living is for, and saw that their students learned it.

—Kronman, *"Why Are We Here?"*

Which of the following phrases do you think best expresses the topic for the preceding paragraph? Which best tells us who or what the whole paragraph is about?

- history of American colleges
- American colleges before the Civil War
- Puritan education at Harvard College

The whole paragraph is not about the Puritans' approach to education at Harvard, so "Puritan education at Harvard College" is too narrow to be the topic of the paragraph. The paragraph does not talk about the entire history of American colleges—only before the Civil War—so "history of American colleges" is too broad to be the topic of the paragraph. "American colleges before the Civil War" is the phrase that best expresses the topic of the paragraph, because this is what the whole paragraph is about. The first sentence introduces the topic, providing information about the size and purpose of America's colleges before the Civil War. The second sentence adds to the information in the first sentence, telling us that not many people attended college then, and that the education was based on beliefs whose truth was assumed. The last two sentences use the Puritans and Harvard College as an example.

In sum, the topic should fit the paragraph the way a well-made garment fits the body. Just as a shirt can be too big or too small for its wearer, a topic can be too big (too broad) or too small (too narrow) for its paragraph.

> **Identifying the Topic of a Paragraph**
>
> The topic is the subject or focus of the whole paragraph.
>
> The topic answers the question "who or what is the whole paragraph about?"
>
> The topic should be expressed in a short phrase of two to six words.

Exercises 4.5, 4.6, and 4.7 will provide practice with identifying the topic.

EXERCISE 4.5 IDENTIFYING THE TOPIC

Directions: Write the topic for each of the following sets of words or phrases. Express your topic in a short phrase of two to six words.

EXAMPLE

dog   cow
tiger   whale

Topic: _Types of mammals_ _____

SET 1

pen	crayon
pencil	marker

Topic: _Writing utensils_

SET 2

automobile	sailboat
bicycle	jet plan

Topic: _Vehicles of transportation_

SET 3

radio	newspaper
magazine	television

Topic: _Mass media_

SET 4

Marilyn Monroe	Hank Aaron
Richard Nixon	Eleanor Roosevelt

Topic: _Famous Americans_

SET 5

drawing a picture	playing a computer game
taking a stroll	reading a mystery

Topic: _Leisure activities_

EXERCISE 4.6 IDENTIFYING THE PARAGRAPH TOPIC

Directions: Place a check in front of the phrase that best states the topic for each paragraph. Use context clues, word structure clues, and the dictionary, as well as the marginal definitions provided, to determine the meaning of unfamiliar words.

1. The earliest Americans, whom **archaeologists** call *Paleo-Indians,* traveled in small bands, tracking and killing mammoths, bison, and other large game. Paleo-Indians were resourceful hunters who crafted sharp stone points for their spears. Their efficiency may have led to overhunting, for by 9000 B.C. mammoths, mastodons, and other game had become extinct. The world's climate also grew warmer, turning grasslands into deserts and reducing the animals' food supply, hastening their disappearance. This meant that humans had to find other food sources.

> **archaeologist** scientist who studies the ancient past

—Goldfield et al, *The American Journey: A History of the United States,* Portfolio ed.

___ tracking of large game by early Americans

___ history of the early Americas

_√_ Paleo-Indians' search for food

2. The modern justice process begins with investigation. When a crime has been committed, it is often discovered and reported to the police. On occasion, a police officer on routine patrol discovers the crime while it is still in progress. Evidence is gathered at the scene when possible, and a follow-up investigation attempts to reconstruct the likely sequence of activities. A few offenders are arrested at the scene of the crime; some are apprehended only after an extensive investigation. In such cases, an arrest warrant issued by a magistrate or another judge provides the legal basis for an apprehension by police.

—Schmalleger, *Criminal Justice: A Brief Introduction,* 7th ed.

____ issuing an arrest warrant

_√_ investigating a crime

____ the criminal justice system

populous
containing many people

regime
government in power

impoverished poor

3. The People's Republic of China is the world's most **populous** nation, home to one-fifth of the 6.5 billion people living on Earth at the start of 2006. When Mao Zedong founded the country's current **regime** 57 years earlier, roughly 540 million people lived in a mostly rural, war-torn, **impoverished** nation. Mao believed population growth was desirable, and under his leadership China grew and changed. By 1970, improvements in food production, food distribution, and public health allowed China's population to swell to approximately 790 million people. At that time, the average Chinese woman gave birth to 5.8 children in her lifetime.

—Withgott and Brennan, *Essential Environment: The Science Behind the Stories,* 2nd ed.

_√_ population growth in China

____ Mao's desire for population growth

____ the nation of China

correspondent
person employed to write and send news reports

4. Radio news came into its own in World War II, when the networks sent **correspondents** abroad. Americans, eager for news from Europe, developed the habits of listening to the likes of Edward R. Murrow and other giants of mid-20th century journalism, including Walter Cronkite. As a medium of instantaneous reporting, radio offered news on breakthrough events even before newspapers could issue special extra editions. The term *breaking news* emerged for something for which radio was uniquely suited.

—Vivian, *The Media of Mass Communication,* 7th ed.

____ Americans and the news

____ sending correspondents abroad

_√_ emergence of radio news

5. The process of acquiring language begins in the first months, with crying and cooing. Even at this early stage, babies are highly responsive to the pitch, intensity, and sound of language, and they react to the emotions and rhythms in voices. When most adults

speak to babies, their pitch is higher and more varied than usual, and their intonation is exaggerated. Adult use of baby talk, which researchers call *parentese*, has been documented all over the world, from Sweden to Australia to Japan. Parentese helps babies learn the melody and rhythm of their native language.

—Wade and Tavris, *Invitation to Psychology,* 4th ed.

___√___ beginnings of language acquisition

_____ parentese

_____ language acquisition

EXERCISE 4.7 WRITING THE TOPIC

Directions: Write the topic for each of the following paragraphs in the space provided. Express the topic in a short phrase of two to six words that tells who or what the whole paragraph is about. Use context clues, word structure clues, and the dictionary, as well as the marginal definitions provided, to determine the meaning of unfamiliar words.

rigorous
strict

stringent
demanding

1. Today's new teachers must meet **rigorous** national and state standards for entering the profession that did not exist a decade ago. Requirements for entering teacher education programs in colleges and universities are now more **stringent** than admission requirements for most other professions. Grade point averages of 3.0 and higher are becoming more common requirements for admission; tests and other assessments must be passed before admission, at the completion of a program, and for state licensure. Clearly, not everyone can teach. Teaching is becoming a profession that attracts the best and brightest college students into its ranks.

—Johnson et al., *Foundations of American Education,* 14th ed.

Topic: _(qualifications of) today's teachers_

impiety
lack of respect for God and religion

corrupt
make dishonest or immoral

2. Socrates was an Athenian philosopher. He wrote no books, but taught his pupils by word of mouth, discussing points of philosophy with them and questioning accepted opinions. Socrates and his pupils pointed out weak points in the government, and in people's beliefs. This made them very unpopular with Athenian politicians. Eventually his enemies charged him with **impiety** and **corrupting** the young. He was sentenced to death by drinking poison. We know about Socrates' ideas because they were written down by some of his pupils, including Plato.

—Peach and Millard, *The Greeks*

Topic: _Socrates, an Athenian philosopher_

3. The growing influence of street gangs has had a harmful impact on the health of our country. Drug abuse, gang shootings, beatings, thefts, carjackings, and the possibility of being caught in the middle between gangs at war have led to whole neighborhoods being held hostage by gang members. Once thought to be a **phenomenon** that occurred only in inner-city areas, gang violence now also occurs in both rural and

**phenome-
non** event, occurrence

suburban communities, particularly in the southeast, southwest, and western regions of the country.

—Donatelle and Davis, *Health: The Basics,* 2nd ed.

Topic: <u>Harmful influence of street gangs</u>

4. Most people do not have any idea of the importance of small businesses in our economy. The news media devote so much time to employment and problems in big businesses such as automobiles, steel, and textiles that you might think that the economy is dominated totally by large businesses. Yet large companies (more than 1,000 employees) created only 6 percent of the new jobs since 1975. Since 1979, large companies actually lost about 600,000 jobs. Ninety percent of the nation's new jobs in the private sector are in small businesses. More than half of the new jobs are with companies with fewer than 20 employees. Even in the **sluggish** economic climate of the early 1990s, employment in small business increased by 1.77 percent, compared to only a 0.62 percent employment increase in large companies. That means there is a very good chance that you will either work in a small business someday or start one.

> **sluggish**
> slow,
> inactive

—Nickels et al., *Understanding Business,* 3rd ed.

Topic: <u>Importance of small businesses</u>

5. The Civil War had many causes, but slavery was clearly the key issue. During the war (1861–1865), abolitionists kept up their antislavery pressure. They were rewarded when President Abraham Lincoln issued the Emancipation Proclamation, which provided that all slaves in states in active rebellion against the United States would automatically be freed on January 1, 1863. Designed as a measure to gain favor for the war in the North, the Emancipation Proclamation did not free all slaves—it freed only those who lived in the Confederacy. Complete abolition of slavery did not occur until congressional passage and **ultimate ratification** of the Thirteenth Amendment in 1865.

> **ultimate**
> final
> **ratification**
> approval

—O'Connor and Sabato, *The Essentials of American Government,* 3rd ed.

Topic: <u>Slavery and the Civil War</u>

Active Reading Strategy: Identify Stated Main Ideas

After you have identified the topic of a paragraph, you will next want to identify the paragraph's main idea. As we have previously suggested, reading for main ideas is perhaps the most important active reading strategy for college readers. As you read from paragraph to paragraph in your texts and other assignments, identifying the main ideas will not only help you determine what is most important to understand and remember, but it will also enable you to see how ideas are related from one paragraph to the next.

What Is a Main Idea?

Most textbook writing is *expository* writing—that is, writing whose main purpose is to explain ideas and give information (some other types of writing are *narrative*, which tells a story; *descriptive*, which describes a person, place, or object; and *persuasive*, which attempts to influence the reader's opinions and/or behaviors). As you now know, an expository paragraph has a topic—its particular subject or focus. An expository paragraph also contains supporting details—specific information that the author wants to communicate about the topic. In addition, an expository paragraph has a **main idea—the most important point the paragraph makes about its topic. The main idea is usually a general point** that is developed throughout the paragraph. It is the single idea that all the paragraph's details support. To look at it another way, **the main idea summarizes, or generalizes from, all the details contained in the paragraph** (see Figure 4.1).

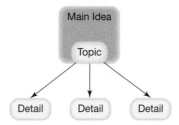

Figure 4.1   Topic, Main Idea, and Details

To identify the main idea of a paragraph, first identify the topic. Next, ask yourself, "what is the general point, or the most important point, that the whole paragraph makes about the topic?" What point summarizes, or generalizes from, all the details within the paragraph?

For an example, let's take another look at our paragraph about the benefits of regular exercise.

A regular program of aerobic exercise improves the efficiency of your cardiovascular and respiratory systems. As a benefit of regular exercise, the heart is able to pump more blood with each stroke, thus lowering resting heart rate. Additionally, the body's capacity to distribute oxygen to working muscles is improved while the muscles responsible for respiration are strengthened.

—Donatelle and Davis, *Health: The Basics,* 2nd ed.

We have already stated that the topic of this paragraph is "the benefits of regular aerobic exercise." To find the main idea, we ask ourselves, what is the general or most important point the paragraph makes about the benefits of regular aerobic exercise? You probably will agree that the main idea, stated in the first sentence of the paragraph, is that regular exercise contributes to the efficiency of our cardiovascular and respiratory systems. The supporting details in this paragraph are stated in the second and third sentences. They explain the specific ways that regular exercise benefits the cardiovascular and respiratory systems—pumping more blood, lowering resting heart rate, distributing more oxygen to muscles, and strengthening respiratory muscles (see Figure 4.2).

Let's look at another example:

Regardless of the field you're in or the career you choose, your chances of being hired by an organization are better if you possess strong communication skills. Out of 120 job descriptions appearing in one issue of the *National Business Employment Weekly* (published by the *Wall Street Journal*), almost every listing included this requirement: "The persons we seek must have strong oral

Topic:	benefit of regular aerobic exercise	
Main Idea:	A regular program of aerobic exercise improves the efficiency of your cardio-vascular and respiratory systems.	
Supporting Details:	As a benefit of regular exercise, the heart is able to pump more with each stroke, thus lowering resting heart rate.	Additionally, the body's capacity to distribute oxygen to working muscles is improved while the muscles responsible for respiration are strengthened.

Figure 4.2   Topic, Main Idea and Details of Paragraph on the Benefits of Regular Aerobic Exercise

and written communication skills." From chief financial officer to product manager, from senior economist to personnel analyst, from senior sales representative to petroleum buyer—these positions will be filled by people who can communicate well.

—Bovee and Thill, *Business Communication Today,* 5th ed.

The *topic* of the paragraph is "the importance of strong communication skills." The *main idea*, or general point, of the paragraph, stated in the first sentence, is that you need strong communication skills to be hired for almost any job. The paragraph's *details* support the main idea by telling us that almost all of the job listings in the *National Business Employment Weekly* include the statement that applicants must have strong communication skills (sentence two), and by listing several examples of jobs that require strong communication skills (sentence three) (see Figure 4.3).

Topic:	importance of strong communication skills	
Main Idea:	Regardless of the field you're in or the career you choose, your chances of being hired by an organization are better if you possess strong communication skills.	
Supporting Details:	Out of 120 job descriptions appearing in one issue of the *National Business Employment Weekly* (published by the *Wall Street Journal*), almost every listing included this requirement: "The persons we seek must have strong oral and written communication skills."	From chief financial officer to product manager, from senior economist to personnel analyst, from senior sales representative to petroleum buyer—these positions will be filled by people who can communicate well.

Figure 4.3   Topic, Main Idea and Details of Paragraph on the Importance of Strong Communication Skills

Topic = The subject of the entire paragraph
Answers the question, "who or what is the whole paragraph about?"

Main Idea = The most important point the paragraph develops about the topic
Answers the question, "What main point does the writer wish to communicate about the topic?"

Details = The specific information about the topic of the paragraph that supports and develops the main idea

General vs. Specific Sentences

The main idea is often stated in one or two sentences within a paragraph. Some paragraphs contain no stated main idea. Instead, the main idea is *implied*, or suggested, by the details of the paragraph, and the reader must *infer* the main idea. In this chapter, we will focus on paragraphs with stated main ideas. We will work with implied main ideas in Chapter 5.

The sentence that states the main idea is often the most general sentence in the paragraph. In our paragraph about strong communication skills, for example, the first sentence (main idea) is more general than the two following sentences (supporting details):

General: Regardless of the field you're in or the career you choose, your chances of being hired by an organization are better if you possess strong communication skills.

Specific: Out of 120 job descriptions appearing in one issue of the *National Business Employment Weekly* (published by the *Wall Street Journal*), almost every listing included this requirement: "The persons we seek must have strong oral and written communication skills."

Specific: From chief financial officer to product manager, from senior economist to personnel analyst, from senior sales representative to petroleum buyer—these positions will be filled by people who can communicate well.

In short, distinguishing between general and specific sentences is an important strategy for recognizing stated main ideas in paragraphs. Remember, the general idea is the broader, more inclusive idea. Specific ideas are narrower ideas, such as examples and individual facts.

Complete Exercises 4.8 and 4.9 to practice recognizing general sentences.

EXERCISE ▣4.8 GENERAL VS. SPECIFIC SENTENCES

Directions: For each pair of sentences, place a check on the line in front of the more general sentence.

▐EXAMPLE▌

___ Ana loves baseball.

_√_ Ana loves sports.

1.

___ For example, taking a friend's high-powered prescription painkiller for your headache is a misuse of that drug.

_√_ Drug misuse involves the use of a drug for a purpose for which it was not intended.

—Donatelle, *Health; The Basics*, 6th ed.

2.

___ To maximize its production, beekeepers in Egypt floated their hives down the Nile to areas of abundant bloom, with some success.

√ The cultivation of honey is an age-old pursuit.

—Levy, "The Vanishing," *OnEarth*

3.

√ Although teamwork has many advantages, it also has a number of potential disadvantages.

___ Unsuccessful teamwork can waste time and money.

—Bovee and Thill, *Business Communication Essentials,* 3rd ed.

4.

___ Most of us can easily remember the tune of our national anthem, how to use an automated teller machine, the most embarrassing experience we ever had, and hundreds of thousands of other bits of information.

√ Human beings are capable of astonishing feats of memory.

—Wade and Tavris, *Invitation to Psychology,* 4th ed.

5.

√ With only a few exceptions, any food that has not been heavily processed contains most nutrients, although in widely varying amounts.

___ Green peppers are especially high in vitamin C, and dairy products are especially high in calcium—but both nutrients also are found in a great many other foods, just in smaller amounts.

—Nestle, "How to get the Nutrients You Need," *Parade Magazine*

6.

√ In word and deed, Americans have long demonstrated that we, the people, value our wild places.

___ In 1872, Congress held hearings to create Yellowstone as the first national park.

—Linden, "The Call of the Wild," *Parade Magazine*

7.

√ Millions of young people in the second half of the 1960s expressed their alienation from American society by sampling drugs or chasing the rainbow of a youth culture.

___ Some just smoked marijuana, grew long hair, and listened to psychedelic rock.

—Goldfield et al., *The American Journey,* Portfolio ed.

8.

___ The unemployed construction worker does not seek work as a certified public accountant.

√ The unemployed seek jobs consistent with their skills, qualifications, and work experience.

—Gregory, *Essentials of Economics,* 4th ed.

9.

___ The cooperation that comes naturally in small communities high in the Andes Mountains of Peru is very different from the competitive lifestyle that is natural to so many people living in, say, Chicago or New York.

√ No way of life is "natural" to humanity, even though most people around the world view their own behavior that way.

—Macionis, *Society: The Basics,* 9th ed.

10.

√ During the uneasy and turbulent times of pre-Revolutionary America, various resistance groups began to organize, often in secret.

___ In 1765, in opposition to the Stamp Act imposed by Parliament, several of these early interest groups became collectively known as the Sons of Liberty.

—Shea et al., *Living Democracy,* Brief National Professional ed.

EXERCISE 4.9 TOPIC AND MAIN IDEA

Directions: This exercise consists of five groups of sentences. Each group was once a paragraph, but the sentences have been rearranged so that they are no longer in their original order. For each group of sentences:

- Write the topic. Tell who or what the paragraph is about in a short phrase (two to six words).
- Write the letter of the general sentence that states the main idea for the group.

EXAMPLE

a. Most important of all, friendships can help us to grow and develop as individuals.

b. The most basic of these is survival—friendships provide mutual protection.

c. Friendships serve many human needs.

d. In addition to that need, friendships also help us to avoid loneliness, gain approval for ourselves, and increase our certainty about our own behavior.

—Derlega and Janda, *Personal Adjustment: The Psychology of Everyday Life,* 3rd ed.

Topic: _Benefits of friendship_

Main Idea: _c_

1. a. It is an issue that captured the attention of the president and has been debated in the highest court of our land and in Congress.

b. It is the most frequent cause of disputes between spouses.

c. Strict discipline, including the right (and duty) of parents to punish their children, is a critical plank in the platform of the Moral Majority and so-called family life advocates.

d. Discipline has recently surfaced as a very important issue in our nation—in fact, throughout the world.

e. And it has shown up in opinion polls as the number one concern of parents.

f. It is the subject of spirited debates in PTA chapters, at school faculty meetings and within boards of education.

—Gordon, *P.E.T.*

Topic: <u>Importance of discipline</u>

Main Idea: <u>d</u>

2. a. Notice that two co-workers sit closer to each other than do the employee and the "boss."

b. You will discover that the closer an individual chooses to sit to another, the more comfortable that person feels about the relationship.

c. In business, the more confident a person is, the closer he or she will decide, even subconsciously, to sit to a partner or associate.

—Halloran, *Applied Human Relations: An Organizational Approach,* 2nd ed.

Topic: <u>Sitting distance</u>

Main Idea: <u>b</u>

3. a. In 1997, family therapist Michael Gurian's book *The Wonder of Boys* urged us to examine how we manage and respond to boy culture.

b. William Pollock, Ph.D.'s, 1998 book *Real Boys* used groundbreaking research from Harvard Medical School to examine why so many boys were sad, confused, even violent, and called for an understanding of what boys experience.

c. Researchers have been zeroing in on boys for the last decade, examining what makes them tick and how we all can better understand them and meet their needs.

d. Two years later, Michael Thompson, Ph.D., co-authored *Raising Cain*, urging us to broaden our definition of masculinity and to save boys from the tyranny of toughness.

—Orcutt, "What's Up with Boys?" *Boston Parents Paper*

Topic: <u>Research about boys</u>

Main Idea: <u>c</u>

4. a. In my relationships with people, I have found that it does not help, in the long run, to act as though I were something that I am not.

b. It does not help to act calm and pleasant when actually I am angry and critical.

c. It does not help to act as though I know the answers when I do not.

d. It does not help for me to act as though I were full of assurance if actually I am frightened and unsure.

—Rogers, *On Becoming a Person*

Topic: ___Honesty in relationships (or not acting dishonestly in relationships)___

Main Idea: __a_____

5. a. In some cases, if the loss of sleep continues, the person begins to develop marked paranoid symptoms.

b. He also feels lightheaded and often hears a buzzing sound in his ears.

c. After three nights without sleep, the average person complains of itchy eyes and begins to see double.

d. He is unable to count past 15, and cannot concentrate on any subject for longer than a few minutes.

e. Actual sleep deprivation, where a person loses more than one night's sleep, does tend to affect the organism, impairing several faculties of the body.

—Gonzalez-Wippler, *Dreams and What They Mean to You*

Topic: ___Sleep deprivation_____

Main Idea: __e_____

Stated Main Ideas

A stated main idea is a main idea that is stated by the writer in one or two sentences within a paragraph. Stated main ideas are great aids to the alert reader. They provide clear and recognizable statements of the writer's main points and help readers anticipate as they read. **To identify the stated main idea in a paragraph, look for the sentence that expresses the most important or most emphasized point that the paragraph develops about the topic**. Ask yourself which sentence best summarizes, or generalizes from, the details within the paragraph. This will usually (but not always) be the most general sentence within the paragraph. When you have correctly identified the main idea, you can see how all the other sentences in the paragraph support or develop the point expressed in the main idea statement.

Let's look at another example. Read the following paragraph and answer the questions that follow it.

EXAMPLE

Jackie Robinson was indeed a great athlete. Raised by his mother in Pasadena, California, he went to UCLA, where he was a brilliant football and basketball player and a long-jumper who would surely have been in the Olympics had the 1940 games not been canceled by war. In major-league baseball, his eleven-year career with the Brooklyn Dodgers earned him the rare honor of election to the Hall of Fame in his first year of eligibility. He batted over .300 for six consecutive years, accumulating a lifetime average of .311. Twice he led the National League in stolen bases. In 1949, when he was named Most Valuable Player, he led the league not only in stolen bases but in batting, scoring 122 runs and driving in 124. Still more indicative of his achievement was his team's unprecedented success in the years of his fiery play; the Dodgers won six National League pennants and their only world championship.

—Kagan, "The Indispensable Man," *Commentary*

1. What is the topic of the paragraph?

Jackie Robinson (and his athletic talents)

___c___ **2.** Most of the details in the paragraph:
   a. Explain why Robinson became a great athlete
   b. List examples of Robinson's contributions to baseball
   c. Give evidence of Robinson's greatness as an athlete
   d. Provide reasons why Robinson became the first African American to play major league baseball

___d___ **3.** The main idea or general point of the paragraph is:
   a. Jackie Robinson was an unusual man.
   b. The Dodgers would not have won the World Series without Jackie Robinson.
   c. Jackie Robinson was a brilliant football and basketball player.
   d. Jackie Robinson was a great athlete.

4. Underline the sentence within the paragraph that states the main idea.

Answers

1. The topic of the paragraph is "Jackie Robinson," or "Jackie Robinson's talents."

2. Statement c is the best answer. Most of the details provide evidence of Robinson's greatness: his batting average, MVP award, stolen bases records, early induction into the Hall of Fame, and the Dodgers' success are all mentioned by the author to provide evidence of Robinson's athletic greatness.

3. Statement d is the best answer, expressing the general point of the paragraph—the point supported and developed by the paragraph's details. Statement a is too general, because the paragraph focuses only on Jackie Robinson's athletic talents and achievements. Statement b is a conclusion that might be drawn from the paragraph but not a generalization of the paragraph's details. Statement c is a specific detail within the paragraph.

4. You should have underlined the first sentence. The rest of the sentences are details supporting the general statement made in the first sentence.

Figure 4.4 provides an outline and block diagram for the Jackie Robinson paragraph.

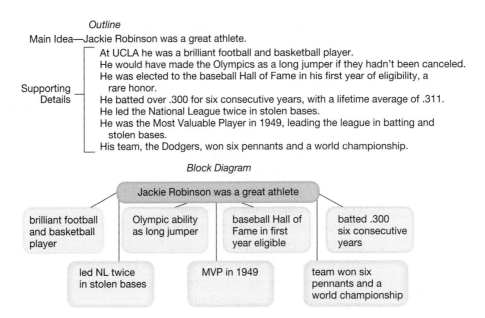

Outline

Main Idea—Jackie Robinson was a great athlete.

Supporting Details
- At UCLA he was a brilliant football and basketball player.
- He would have made the Olympics as a long jumper if they hadn't been canceled.
- He was elected to the baseball Hall of Fame in his first year of eligibility, a rare honor.
- He batted over .300 for six consecutive years, with a lifetime average of .311.
- He led the National League twice in stolen bases.
- He was the Most Valuable Player in 1949, leading the league in batting and stolen bases.
- His team, the Dodgers, won six pennants and a world championship.

Block Diagram

Jackie Robinson was a great athlete

- brilliant football and basketball player
- Olympic ability as long jumper
- baseball Hall of Fame in first year eligible
- batted .300 six consecutive years
- led NL twice in stolen bases
- MVP in 1949
- team won six pennants and a world championship

Figure 4.4   Paragraph Outline and Block Diagram, Sample Paragraph

Locating Stated Main Ideas

The main idea may be stated anywhere within a paragraph—at the beginning, middle, or end. Active readers are sensitive to the flow of ideas through a paragraph and look for clues to the location of the main idea. Highlighting or underlining stated main ideas is a simple and effective strategy.

The main idea is often stated in the first sentence of a paragraph. The rest of the paragraph provides details to support and develop the main point. When the main idea is in the first sentence, it is often a simple, general statement, followed by examples or explanation.

Main Idea
Detail
Detail
Detail

EXAMPLE 1   **Stated Main Idea in First Sentence**

If life stages affect our dreams, so do our attitudes. Studies by University of Pennsylvania professor emeritus Aaron Beck show that angry people act out their anger in their dreams. Other research shows that depressed people sometimes dream they're victims of rejection, humiliation, or abandonment. People with "thin boundaries"—unusual openness, vulnerability, difficulty standing up for themselves—are likely to suffer from nightmares.

—Von Kreisler, "Why We Dream What We Dream," *Reader's Digest*

In the preceding paragraph, the main idea is a simple, general statement at the beginning of the paragraph, telling us that attitude affects dreams. It is followed by details which provide examples of how various attitudes affect people's dreams.

Sometimes the main idea is stated at the end of a paragraph. The details are provided first, leading up to a conclusion or generalization in the last sentence.

EXAMPLE 2   Stated Main Idea in Last Sentence

Today's new teachers must meet rigorous national and state standards for entering the profession that did not exist a decade ago. Requirements for entering teacher education programs in colleges and universities are now more stringent than admission requirements for most other professions. Grade point averages of 3.0 and higher are becoming more common requirements for admission; tests and other assessments must be passed before admission, at the completion of a program, and for state licensure. Clearly, not everyone can teach. Teaching is becoming a profession that attracts the best and brightest college students into its ranks.

—Johnson et al., *Foundations of American Education*, 14th ed.

The preceding paragraph begins with specific information—details—about the requirements for becoming a teacher today. The main idea is stated as a general conclusion at the end of the paragraph—that the teaching profession is now attracting some of the best college students.

The main idea may also be stated in the middle of a paragraph. For most readers, this placement makes the main idea more difficult to detect. The alert reader, however, may notice a shift in a middle sentence to a general point, often signaled by a transition word or phrase. (See Table 4.1 for a list of transition words and phrases that signal a change of thought.) When the main idea is found in a middle sentence, the first sentence of the paragraph may serve as an introduction to the topic or a transition sentence (a bridge from the previous paragraph), or may be a specific detail. The sentences following the main idea statement will provide details that directly support the main idea.

EXAMPLE 3   Stated Main Idea in a Middle Sentence

You don't need to be a health expert to know that there are **physiological** differences between men and women. Although much of male and female anatomy is identical, it's clear that many major medical differences exist. Many diseases—osteoporosis, thyroid disease, lupus, and Alzheimer's disease, for example—are far more common in women than in men. Diseases may show up differently in men than in women—research suggests that hypertension treatment for men may not be beneficial to white women, for example. Finally, although women live longer than men, they don't necessarily have a better quality of life.

—Donatelle and Davis, *Health: The Basics*, 2nd ed.

physiological pertaining to the body and its processes

Table 4.1   Transition Words That Signal a Change of Thought

although	conversely	however	nevertheless	nonetheless
rather	though	yet	on the contrary	on the other hand

The first sentence of the preceding paragraph is an introductory statement, reminding the reader that we all know that men and women are physiologically different. The word *although* at the beginning of the second sentence indicates that the writer is going to shift from the introductory statement to a different point—in this case, the paragraph's main idea, that men and women have medical differences. Note that the remaining sentences provide details to support the second sentence by listing examples of some of the medical differences.

In some paragraphs, the main idea is stated in both the first *and* last sentences. The paragraph begins with a general statement—the main idea. Details are presented in the middle sentences. Then the author returns to the main idea in the last sentence, usually rewording or refining the main idea in some way.

This type of paragraph is similar to a paragraph in which the main idea is expressed in the first sentence. The alert reader will notice, however, that in this type of paragraph, instead of ending the paragraph with an additional detail, the author concludes the paragraph by returning to the main idea.

EXAMPLE 4   **Stated Main Idea in First and Last Sentences**

In today's world, it is difficult to imagine U.S. schools and classrooms without technology. An expectation exists that nearly all schools and classrooms will have access to computers in some form. Other technologies such as videotapes, DVDs, television, calculators, digital cameras, and overhead projectors are found in most schools and available to most classrooms. We are teaching and learning in a technology-rich environment.

—Johnson et al., *Foundations of American Education*, 14th ed.

The author begins the preceding paragraph with the main idea—a general statement that tells us that nowadays it is hard to imagine U.S. schools and classrooms without technology. The next two sentences provide details, identifying the types of technology we have and expect to have in our classrooms. The last sentence returns to the main idea with a general, concluding statement. Note that even though the first sentence and last sentences are worded differently, they both express essentially the same point.

Exercises 4.10 through 4.12 will provide practice with paragraph logic. Exercises 4.13 through 4.16 will provide additional practice with recognizing topics and stated main ideas.

EXERCISE 4.10 PARAGRAPH LOGIC

Directions: Read each paragraph and answer the questions that follow.

A. <u>Books were valued during the Colonial period.</u> In Massachusetts in 1638, the pilgrims set up Cambridge Press, the first book producer in what is now the United States. Just as today, personal libraries were a symbol of the intelligentsia. John Harvard of Cambridge, Massachusetts, was widely known for his personal collection of 300 books, a large library for the time. When Harvard died in 1638, he bequeathed his books to Newtowne College, which was so grateful that it renamed itself for him. Today it's Harvard University.

—Vivian, *The Media of Mass Communication,* 4th ed.

1. Who or what is the whole paragraph about? Write the topic in a short phrase of two to six words.

   Books in colonial time

2. Underline the sentence that states the paragraph's main idea (general point). If the main idea is stated in the first and last sentences, underline both of those sentences.

3. List one supporting detail contained in the paragraph.

   The pilgrims set up Cambridge Press in 1638, the first book producer in the U.S.

   (sample answer; accept any detail)

4. *Vocabulary in context:*

   _b_ The *intelligentsia* (ĭn-tĕl'ə-jĕnt'sē-ə) are people who are:
   a. Rich
   b. Intelligent
   c. Government agents

   _c_ When John Harvard *bequeathed* his books to Newtowne College, he:
   a. Sold them to the college
   b. Reviewed them for the college
   c. Left them to the college in his will

B. When casual users were asked about their current reasons for marijuana use, two answers—"to feel good" and "to have a good time"—prevailed overwhelmingly. In contrast, while regular marijuana users all continued to cite these two reasons, large numbers additionally responded, "to get away from my problems" (37%) or "to help me get through the day" (29%). <u>Using marijuana as a means of escaping or coping with problems thus strongly distinguishes the regular daily user of marijuana from the casual user.</u>

—McClellan et al., *Escape from Anxiety and Stress*

1. Who or what is the whole paragraph about? Write the topic in a short phrase of two to six words.

Marijuana users

2. Underline the sentence that states the paragraph's main idea (general point). If the main idea is stated in the first and last sentences, underline both of those sentences.

3. List one supporting detail contained in the paragraph.

Casual users use marijuana to feel good and have a good time. (sample answer; any

detail)

4. *Vocabulary in context:*

____a____ When two answers *prevailed overwhelmingly*, they:
    a. Were the answers that most casual users gave
    b. Were the only answers that casual users gave
    c. Were the answers that a few casual users gave

C. <u>The story of how names came down to our time is a record that can be told in terms of people.</u> In ancient days almost all peoples gave each of their children only one personal name, individually selected and tailored to fit a particular child. As population groups increased in number, it became necessary to expand the name pools. Instead of remaining unique to one person, names began to be reused for succeeding generations. "Son of" suffixes and prefixes came into use. Distinguishing nicknames became names in themselves.

—Turner, *The Very Best Book of Baby Names*

1. Who or what is the whole paragraph about? Write the topic in a short phrase of two to six words.

History of names

2. Underline the sentence that states the paragraph's main idea (general point). If the main idea is stated in the first and last sentences, underline both of those sentences.

3. List one supporting detail contained in the paragraph.

In ancient days, people gave children just one name. (sample answer; accept any

detail)

4. *Vocabulary in context:*

____b____ If a name remained *unique* to a person, that name:
    a. Was the name the person used most of the time
    b. Was used only for that person
    c. Was used for that person and for a few others

D. Some social scientists believe that society still operates more smoothly when the sexes specialize in different roles—the male as breadwinner and link between the family and the outside world; the female as the source of affection and support within the family. Many observers, however, have concluded that there is no longer any need in our modern society for men to be masculine and women to be feminine. They point out that physical strength is no longer important. There are very few jobs in the industrial system that cannot be performed as well by a woman as by a man. In a world of nuclear weapons, aggressiveness of the kind that can lead to warfare is disastrous. The population explosion has turned large families into a liability instead of an asset—and women, in the age of birth control, have fewer children and more years to live after the last of them has gone to school or left home. Because they are not necessarily immobilized by children and are free to enter the work force, they're no longer dependent on men to support them.

—Kagan and Havemann, *Psychology*

1. Who or what is the whole paragraph about? Write the topic in a short phrase of two to six words.

Gender roles

2. Underline the sentence that states the paragraph's main idea (general point). If the main idea is stated in the first and last sentences, underline both of those sentences.

3. List one supporting detail contained in the paragraph.

There are few jobs that women can't do as well as men. (sample answer; accept any

detail)

4. *Vocabulary in context:*

___a___ If large families have become a *liability* rather than an *asset*, large families are:
  a. More of a disadvantage than an advantage
  b. More of an advantage than a disadvantage
  c. Becoming more common

___c___ If women are no longer *immobilized* by children, they:
  a. No longer wish to have children
  b. Are not able to take care of their children
  c. Are no longer prevented from other activity by having children

E. Newborn babies sleep an average of 17–18 hours a day. Adolescents sleep approximately 10–11 hours in a 24-hour period, while young adults spend an average of eight hours a night sleeping. Elderly people, on the other hand, seldom sleep more than six hours during the night. This seems to indicate that we require less sleep as we grow older, but still, on the whole, we spend approximately one-third of our lives sleeping.

—Gonzalez-Wippler, *Dreams*

1. Who or what is the whole paragraph about? Write the topic in a short phrase of two to six words.

   Sleep needs

2. Underline the sentence that states the paragraph's main idea (general point). If the main idea is stated in the first and last sentences, underline both of those sentences.

3. List one supporting detail contained in the paragraph.

   Newborns sleep 17–18 hours a day. (sample answer; accept any detail)

EXERCISE 4.11 PARAGRAPH LOGIC

Directions: Read each paragraph and answer the questions that follow.

A. <u>In some ways cell phones and other technology devices facilitate friendships for the technologically astute child, but in other ways they hinder social-skill development.</u> Kids have access to each other and the larger world to a much greater extent than they ever did before, but less effort is required for them to communicate. Cell phones, the Internet, e-mail, and instant messaging reduce human contact and yet, paradoxically, make people constantly available and endlessly distractible.

   —Osit, *Generation Text*

1. Who or what is the whole paragraph about? Write the topic in a short phrase of two to six words.

   Technology and social skills

2. Underline the sentence that states the paragraph's main idea (general point). If the main idea is stated in the first and last sentences, underline both of those sentences.

3. List one supporting detail contained in the paragraph.

   Kids have more access to each other through technology devices. (sample answer;

   accept any detail)

4. *Vocabulary in context:*

   ___a___ If cell phones and other technology devices *facilitate* friendships, they:
      a. Make friendships easier.
      b. Make friendships more difficult.
      c. Make friendships undesirable.

   ___b___ A technologically *astute* child:
      a. Doesn't understand how to use technology.
      b. Understands how to use technology.
      c. Has no experience with technology.

___c___ Reducing human contact and making people constantly available are *paradoxical* because:
   a. They are not important.
   b. One causes the other.
   c. You wouldn't expect them both to be true because they're contradictory.

B. Profit, then, defines business. But what is it? <u>Simply, profit is the difference between a business's total revenues or sales receipts and the total of its production costs, operating expenses, and taxes.</u> Go back to our bread example. The bakery has to pay for its raw materials (flour, butter or shortening, yeast, salt), equipment (mixers, ovens, wrapping machines), employees, and the energy it uses. When the bakery sells the bread to the supermarket, it charges more than the cost of making the bread. That extra part of the selling price is profit.

—Straubb and Kossen, *Introduction to Business*

1. Who or what is the whole paragraph about? Write the topic in a short phrase of two to six words.

Profit in business

2. Underline the sentence that states the paragraph's main idea (general point). If the main idea is stated in the first and last sentences, underline both of those sentences.

3. List one supporting detail contained in the paragraph.

The bakery has to pay for raw materials, equipment, employees, and energy. (sample

answer; accept any detail)

C. <u>Though most Americans have jobs, many white-collar and blue-collar workers report considerable dissatisfaction.</u> Many persons identity themselves not in terms of their employment, but by how they spend their time outside of the office or factory. Many seem resigned to their jobs, spending the time at work waiting for the next holiday, 3-day weekend, or vacation period. As an indication of this dissatisfaction, the number of absentee workers in automobile factories is particularly high. On an ordinary day in such factories, about 5 percent of the work force may be absent. On a typical Monday or Friday, the absentee rate may jump to about 15 percent.

—Derlega and Janda, *Personal Adjustment*

1. Who or what is the whole paragraph about? Write the topic in a short phrase of two to six words.

Americans' job dissatisfaction

2. Underline the sentence that states the paragraph's main idea (general point). If the main idea is stated in the first and last sentences, underline both of those sentences.

3. List one supporting detail contained in the paragraph.

Many identify with the activities outside of work rather than their work. (sample

answer; accept any detail)

D. Sometimes, the influence of others can be a powerful social support for our positive behavior changes. At other times, we are influenced to drink too much, party too hard, eat too much, or engage in some other negative action because we don't want to be left out or because we fear criticism. Learning to understand the subtle and not-so-subtle ways in which our families, friends, and other people have influenced and continue to influence our behaviors is an important step toward changing our behaviors.

—Donatelle and Davis, *Health: The Basics,* 2nd ed.

1. Who or what is the whole paragraph about? Write the topic in a short phrase of two to six words.

The influence of others

2. Underline the sentence that states the paragraph's main idea (general point). If the main idea is stated in the first and last sentences, underline both of those sentences.

3. List one supporting detail contained in the paragraph.

The influence of others sometimes supports our positive behavior changes. (sample

answer; accept any detail)

4. *Vocabulary in context:*

___a___ The *subtle* and not-so-*subtle* ways that people influence us are:
   a. The ways that are hard to notice and the ways that are obvious.
   b. The friendly and unfriendly ways.
   c. The ways people ask for favors and the ways they do favors for others.

E. Hypnotized people cannot be forced to do things against their will. Like drunkenness, hypnosis can be used to justify letting go of inhibitions ("I know this looks silly, but after all, I'm hypnotized"). Hypnotized individuals may even comply with a suggestion to do something that seems embarrassing or dangerous. But the individual is choosing to turn responsibility over to the hypnotist and to cooperate with the hypnotist's suggestions. There is no evidence that hypnotized people will do anything that actually goes against their morals or that constitutes a real threat to themselves or others.

—Wade and Tavris, *Invitation to Psychology,* 4th ed.

1. Who or what is the whole paragraph about? Write the topic in a short phrase of two to six words.

Behavior under hypnotism

2. Underline the sentence that states the paragraph's main idea (general point). If the main idea is stated in the first and last sentences, underline both of those sentences.

3. List one supporting detail contained in the paragraph.

   Hypnosis can be used to justify letting go of inhibitions. (sample answer; accept any

   detail)

4. *Vocabulary in context:*

   c   When a person lets go of an *inhibition*, she:
       a. Carefully controls her behavior.
       b. Asks someone for help with something.
       c. Does something she wouldn't normally do.

   c   To *comply* with a suggestion is to:
       a. Ignore the suggestion.
       b. Understand the suggestion.
       c. Follow the suggestion.

EXERCISE 4.12 PARAGRAPH LOGIC

Directions: Read each paragraph and answer the questions that follow.

A. The New World reflected the diverse experiences of the peoples who built it. Improving economic conditions in the fifteenth and early sixteenth centuries propelled Europeans overseas to seek new opportunities for trade and settlement. Spain, Portugal, France, and England competed within Europe, and their conflict carried over into the Americas. Native Americans drew upon their familiarity with the land and its resources, their patterns of political and religious authority, and their systems of trade and warfare to deal with the European newcomers. Africans were brought to the Americas by the Europeans to work as slaves. They too would draw on their cultural heritage to cope with a new land and a harsh life.

—Goldfield et al., *The American Journey*

1. Who or what is the whole paragraph about? Write the topic in a short phrase of two to six words.

   The New World and its diversity

2. Underline the sentence that states the paragraph's main idea (general point). If the main idea is stated in the first and last sentences, underline both of those sentences.

3. List one supporting detail contained in the paragraph.

   Europeans sought new opportunities for trade and settlement. (sample answer;

   accept any detail)

4. *Vocabulary in context:*

_____b_____ When improving economic conditions *propelled* Europeans overseas:
    a. The economic conditions prevented Europeans from traveling.
    b. The economic conditions motivated Europeans to travel.
    c. The economic conditions made traveling more expensive.

B. Beside a spitting fire a mother croons softly to a fitful child. Asking protection from a raging storm, a clan raises its chanted invocation to the gods. Preparing for the hunt, a band of men rouse their courage with a rhythmic song. Perhaps even before humans first spoke, they were singing. From the beginning, then, music has been part of every human culture. Yet, as much as it surrounds us, music is also the most elusive art. Its history is often lost in the dying chord—unrecorded, unpreserved, but unforgettable. Maybe that's why we're always humming that tune that rattles in our head—to keep in touch with the music.

—Bishop, *A Beginner's Guide to the Humanities,* 2nd ed.

1. Who or what is the whole paragraph about? Write the topic in a short phrase of two to six words.

Universality of music

2. Underline the sentence that states the paragraph's main idea (general point). If the main idea is stated in the first and last sentences, underline both of those sentences.

3. List one supporting detail contained in the paragraph.

A clan chants to the gods for protection from a storm. (sample answer; accept any

detail)

4. *Vocabulary in context:*

_____b_____ When a mother *croons* to a *fitful* child, she:
    a. Talks to a child who is falling asleep.
    b. Sings to a restless child.
    c. Yells at a child who is misbehaving.

_____a_____ When a clan raises a chanted *invocation* to the gods, they:
    a. Call upon the gods.
    b. Create a statue to please the gods.
    c. Sacrifice animals to please the gods.

_____c_____ If music is the most *elusive* art, it is the art that is:
    a. Most popular.
    b. Most studied; most researched.
    c. Hardest to grasp or define.

C. A study of drinking at college parties found that students who did not drink believed the risk of being caught was very high if they committed a crime. Those who drank most heavily condemned crime less strongly and believed the risk of being caught was low. <u>A major implication of this research is that it may be possible to reduce crime by preventing heavy drinking.</u>

—Albanese, *Criminal Justice,* 3rd ed.

1. Who or what is the whole paragraph about? Write the topic in a short phrase of two to six words.

Crime and drinking

2. Underline the sentence that states the paragraph's main idea (general point). If the main idea is stated in the first and last sentences, underline both of those sentences.

3. List one supporting detail contained in the paragraph.

Students who didn't drink believed there was a high risk of being caught if they

committed a crime. (sample answer; accept any detail)

4. *Vocabulary in context:*

__c__ To *condemn* crime is to:
  a. Commit crime.
  b. Be afraid of becoming a victim of crime.
  c. Disapprove of crime.

D. <u>Almost everything people do with their cars causes some form of pollution.</u> Driving creates auto exhaust, which spews out chemicals and poisons the air. Oil spills and the dumping of auto-related refuse pollute the water supply. Auto "graveyards" and tire dumps deface the landscape, and highway runoff is a major source of soil pollution. Making and using cars may be one of humankind's most polluting activities.

—Rock, *The Automobile and the Environment*

1. Who or what is the whole paragraph about? Write the topic in a short phrase of two to six words.

Cars and pollution

2. Underline the sentence that states the paragraph's main idea (general point). If the main idea is stated in the first and last sentences, underline both of those sentences.

3. List one supporting detail contained in the paragraph.

Driving creates auto exhaust, which pollutes the air. (sample answer; accept any

detail)

4. *Vocabulary in context:*

__a__ To *spew out* chemicals is to:
  a. Release them or send them out.
  b. Control them.
  c. Change them into a harmless substance.

___a___ Auto-related *refuse* is:
  a. Waste material; trash.
  b. Building material.
  c. A problem when a car doesn't start.

___b___ To *deface* the landscape is to:
  a. Beautify it.
  b. Make it uglier.
  c. Remove it.

E. Diabetes is a serious, widespread, and costly chronic disease, affecting not just the more than 18 million Americans who must live with it, but their families and communities. Between 1990 and 2000, diagnosed diabetes increased 49 percent among U.S. adults, which gives it the dubious distinction of being the fastest growing chronic disease in American history. A recent CDC study indicated that diabetes seems to be increasing even more dramatically among younger adults—up by almost 70 percent among those in their thirties. More than 2,200 people are diagnosed with diabetes each day in America, and more than 200,000 die each year of related complications, thus making diabetes the sixth leading cause of death in America today.

—Donatelle, *Health: The Basics,* 6th ed.

1. Who or what is the whole paragraph about? Write the topic in a short phrase of two to six words.

Diabetes, a serious disease

2. Underline the sentence that states the paragraph's main idea (general point). If the main idea is stated in the first and last sentences, underline both of those sentences.

3. List one supporting detail contained in the paragraph.

Diabetes increased 49% among U.S. adults between 1990 and 2000. (sample

answer; accept any detail)

4. *Vocabulary in context:*

___c___ A *chronic* disease:
  a. Causes death.
  b. Only affects people in their senior years.
  c. Lasts a long time.

___b___ A *dubious distinction* is:
  a. An honor to be proud of.
  b. Recognition for something negative or undesirable.
  c. A difference that goes unnoticed.

EXERCISE `4.13` PARAGRAPH WRITING

Directions: On a separate sheet, write two different paragraphs about the same topic. In your first paragraph, place the sentence that states the main idea at the beginning. In your second paragraph, place the sentence that states the main idea at the end. You may choose your own topic or write about one of the following suggested topics. Each paragraph you write should contain four to six sentences.

Suggested topics:

- Your current job
- Problems with the economy
- The police
- A memorable teacher

EXERCISE `4.14` SHARING PARAGRAPHS

Directions: Using the paragraphs you wrote for Exercise 4.13:

1. Exchange paragraphs with a classmate. Don't tell your partner which sentences you intended to be the stated main ideas.

2. Read each other's paragraphs and identify the sentences in them that state the main ideas.

3. Return the paragraphs to each other and see if you agree about the placements of the stated main ideas. If you disagree, share your points of view with each other.

SKILLS ONLINE: FINDING STATED MAIN IDEAS

Go online to find three paragraphs that contain stated main ideas. Print out the paragraphs and cut and tape them onto a sheet of paper. Write the topic for each paragraph and highlight or underline the sentence that states the main idea. Remember to include the URL for each paragraph.

Choose your paragraphs from any interesting articles you find on the Web. You may search topics of your own interest or choose topics related to the paragraphs you read in this chapter. If you prefer, try using "Stated Main Ideas" as a search term to find a Web site that provides paragraphs from which you can choose.

READING `4A`

THE EYEWITNESS ON TRIAL

by Carole Wade and Carol Tavris

Reading 4A is taken from a psychology textbook chapter on memory. Psychologists are interested in understanding how human memory works. Research suggests that our memory is not always as trustworthy as we believe it to be. Our reading will discuss the unreliability of eyewitness memory.

Pre-Reading Exercise

Directions: Complete this exercise before reading the passage. Preview the passage and answer the following questions.

1. What is the passage about?

   Eyewitnesses' reliability

2. What point do the authors wish to make about eyewitness testimony?

   The authors suggest that eyewitness testimony is often mistaken.

3. What information is provided in Figure 4A.1?

   Two students' drawings of the same face, with one affected by misleading information

4. What have you previously read or learned about eyewitness testimony?

   Answers will vary.

5. Name a TV show or movie you've seen in which eyewitness testimony played an important part. Was the witness's testimony reliable? Explain.

   Answers will vary.

6. Write three questions about eyewitness testimony.

   Answers will vary.

Directions: While reading, pause after each paragraph to identify its topic. If the paragraph has a stated main idea, highlight it or underline it. Use context, the dictionary, and word structure clues to determine the meanings of unfamiliar words.

1   Without the accounts of eyewitnesses, many guilty people would go free. But eyewitness testimony is not always reliable, even when the witness is certain about the accuracy of his or her report. Lineups—a staple of TV shows like *Law and Order*—don't necessarily help, because witnesses may simply identify the person in the line who looks most like the perpetrator of the crime. As a result, some convictions based on eyewitness testimony turn out to be tragic mistakes.

2   Eyewitnesses are especially likely to make mistaken identifications when the suspect's ethnicity differs from their own. When people say of another group, "They all look alike to me," often, unfortunately, they are telling the truth. Because of unfamiliarity with or prejudice toward other ethnic groups, the eyewitness may focus solely on the ethnicity of the person they see committing a crime ("He's black"; "He's white"; "He's an Arab") and ignore the distinctive features that would later make identification more accurate.

3   In a program of research spanning more than three decades, Elizabeth Loftus and her colleagues have shown that the memories of eyewitnesses are also influenced by the way in which questions are put to the witness and by suggestive comments made during an interrogation or interview. In one classic study, the researchers showed how even subtle changes in the wording of questions can lead a witness to give different answers. People first viewed short films depicting car collisions. Afterward, the researchers asked some of them, "About how fast were the cars going when they hit

each other?" Other viewers were asked the same question, but with the verb changed to *smashed, collided, bumped,* or *contacted.* Estimates of how fast the cars were going varied, depending on which word was used. *Smashed* produced the highest average speed estimates (40.8 mph), followed by *collided* (39.3 mph), *bumped* (38.1 mph), *hit* (34.0 mph), and *contacted* (31.8 mph).

4   In a similar study, the researchers asked some participants, "Did you see a broken headlight?" but asked others, "Did you see the broken headlight?" The question with *the* presupposes a broken headlight and merely asks whether the witness saw it, whereas the question with *a* makes no such presupposition. People who received questions with *the* were far more likely to report having seen something that had not really appeared in the film than were those who received questions with *a.* If a tiny word like *the* can lead people to "remember" what they never saw, you can imagine how the leading questions of police detectives and lawyers might influence a witness's recall.

5   Misleading information from other sources, too, can profoundly alter what witnesses report. Consider what happened when students were shown the face of a young man who had straight hair, then heard a description of the face supposedly written by another witness—a description

that wrongly said the man had light, curly hair (see Figure 4A.1). When the students reconstructed the face using a kit of facial features, a third of their reconstructions contained the misleading detail, whereas only 5 percent contained it when curly hair was not mentioned.

6   Leading questions, suggestive comments, and misleading information affect people's memories not only for events they have witnessed but also for their own experiences. Researchers have successfully used these techniques to induce people to "recall" complicated events from early in life that never actually happened, such as getting lost in a shopping mall, being hospitalized for a high fever, being harassed by a bully, or spilling punch all over the mother of the bride at a wedding. In one such study, when people were shown a phony Disneyland ad featuring Bugs Bunny, about 16 percent later recalled having met a Bugs character at Disneyland. In later studies, using several versions of the ad, the percentages were even higher. Some people even claimed to remember shaking hands with the character, hugging him, or seeing him in a parade. But these "memories" were impossible, because Bugs Bunny is a Warner Bros. creation and would definitely be rabbit non grata at Disneyland!

—Wade and Tavris, *Invitation to Psychology,* 4th ed.

Figure 4A.1   The Influence of Misleading Information
In a study described in the text, students saw the face of a young man with straight hair and then had to reconstruct it from memory. On the left is one student's reconstruction in the absence of misleading information about the man's hair. On the right is another person's reconstruction of the same face after exposure to misleading information that mentioned curly hair.

You, the Reader

Interest Rating. Please rate the interest level of the reading on the following scale (circle one):

5—Very interesting	2—A little boring
4—Fairly interesting	1—Very boring
3—Mildly interesting	

Difficulty Rating. Please rate the difficulty level of the reading on the following scale (circle one):

5—Very difficult	2—Fairly easy
4—Fairly difficult	1—Very easy
3—Moderate	

Comments: Please explain your ratings and make any other comments you wish about the reading.

Answers will vary.

COMPREHENSION QUESTIONS

PART I. TOPIC AND STATED MAIN IDEA EXERCISE

Directions: Refer to the indicated paragraphs to choose the best answer for each question.

___b___ **1.** In the first paragraph, which sentence states the main idea?
  a. The first sentence
  b. The second sentence
  c. The last sentence

___a___ **2.** In the second paragraph, which sentence states the main idea?
  a. The first sentence
  b. The second sentence
  c. The last sentence

___b___ **3.** What is the topic of paragraph 3?
  a. The importance of words
  b. How question wording affects eyewitnesses' memories
  c. Inconsistent estimates of car speeds

___a___ **4.** What is the topic of paragraph 5?
  a. How misleading information affects witnesses
  b. How curly hair can mislead a witness
  c. Unreliable memory of witnesses

_____a_____ **5.** In paragraph 6, which sentence states the main idea?
    a. The first sentence
    b. The third sentence
    c. The last sentence

PART II. PASSAGE COMPREHENSION

Directions: For questions 1–5, choose the answer that best completes the statement. For questions 6–10, write your response in the space provided. Base all answers on what you read in the selection. Refer back to the selection as necessary to answer the questions.

_____b_____ **1.** The main point of the passage is that:
    a. Eyewitness testimony should be disregarded because it is never correct.
    b. Eyewitness testimony is not always reliable.
    c. Never trust your memory.
    d. Research shows that eyewitnesses are influenced by the way questions are worded.

_____c_____ **2.** The authors state that lineups are unreliable because:
    a. The people in the line usually all look alike.
    b. Prejudice leads most witnesses to identify people they don't like as perpetrators.
    c. Witnesses identify the person in the line who looks most like the perpetrator.
    d. Witnesses don't usually remember what the perpetrator looked like.

_____a_____ **3.** Loftus's research showed that:
    a. The wording of a question can influence a witness's memory.
    b. The wording of a question does not influence a witness's memory.
    c. Eyewitnesses frequently lie when they don't remember something.
    d. Television programs do not accurately portray eyewitness testimony.

_____c_____ **4.** Figure 4A.1 is used to show that:
    a. Witnesses have difficulty recognizing a person who has changed his hairstyle.
    b. People have difficulty remembering faces.
    c. Misleading information can alter memory.
    d. Eyeglasses make it harder to remember a person's appearance.

_____d_____ **5.** Bugs Bunny is mentioned in the last paragraph as an example of:
    a. How advertisements are used to mislead the public.
    b. How researchers help people reconstruct accurate memories.
    c. How the wording of a question influences memory.
    d. How people may think they remember something that never actually happened.

6. What are some possible consequences of inaccurate eyewitness testimony?

Innocent people may be convicted.

7. How does ethnicity affect eyewitness identifications?

Eyewitnesses make more mistakes when the suspect's ethnicity is different from their

own.

8. In the study discussed in paragraph 3, why do you think the changing of the verb influenced the witnesses' estimates of the cars' speeds? Why might *smashed* have produced the highest speed estimates?

Different verbs imply different speed. Smashed suggests the highest speed because

it implies damage.

9. List two examples of events that people were made to "recall" that never really happened.

Any two: getting lost in a mall; being hospitalized for a high fever; being harassed by

a bully; spilling punch all over the mother of the bride at a wedding

10. Have the authors convinced you that eyewitness testimony is unreliable? Why or why not?

Answers will vary.

Vocabulary Exercises

Pronunciation Guide (see p. 90 for list of phonetic symbols)

ethnicity	(ĕth-nĭs'ĭ-tē)
harassed	(hə-răst', hăr'əst)
interrogation	(ĭn-tĕr'ə-gā' shən)
non grata	(nŏn grä'tə)
subtle	(sŭt'l)

Words in Context

Directions: Choose the meaning for the boldfaced word that best fits the context.

___b___ **1.** . . . because witnesses may simply identify the person in the line who looks most like the **perpetrator** of the crime.
   a. Victim
   b. Committer; person guilty of
   c. Officer of the law
   d. Witness; one who sees

_____c_____ **2.** . . . the eyewitness may . . . ignore the **distinctive** features that would later make identification more accurate.
  a. Attractive
  b. Hard to notice
  c. Different
  d. Similar

_____b_____ **3.** . . . the researchers showed how even **subtle** changes in the wording of questions can lead a witness to give different answers.
  a. Obvious
  b. Slight, small
  c. Easy to understand
  d. Illogical; making no sense

_____d_____ **4.** People first viewed short films **depicting** car collisions.
  a. Lacking; without
  b. Researching
  c. Contributing to
  d. Showing

_____a_____ **5.** . . . being hospitalized for a high fever, being **harassed** by a bully . . .
  a. Bothered
  b. Criticized
  c. Sickened; made ill
  d. Approached

USING WORD STRUCTURE CLUES

Directions: Identify the prefix and the meaning of the prefix in the boldfaced word in each of the following sentences. Use context and the dictionary as well as the word structure clues to determine the word's meaning.

1. . . . eyewitnesses are also influenced by . . . suggestive comments made during an **interrogation** or interview.
   prefix = _inter_____   prefix meaning = _between_____
   interrogation means _questioning or examination_____

2. The question with *the* **presupposes** a broken headlight . . .
   prefix = _pre_____   prefix meaning = _before_____
   presupposes means _assumes, supposes a preexisting condition_____

3. **Misleading** information from other sources, too, can profoundly alter what witnesses report.
   prefix = _mis_____   prefix meaning = _wrong_____
   misleading means _lead into wrong thinking_____

4. When the students **reconstructed** the face using a kit of facial features . . .
   prefix = _re_____   prefix meaning = _again_____
   reconstructed means _constructed again; recreated; rebuilt_____

5. Researchers have successfully used these techniques to **induce** people to "recall" complicated events from early in life that never actually happened . . .

prefix = ___in___   prefix meaning = ___in, into___

induce means ___influence, lead into doing___

CONTEXT AND DICTIONARY

Directions: Use context and the dictionary to determine the meaning of the boldfaced word in each sentence. Use word structure clues when applicable.

1. Lineups—a **staple** of TV shows like *Law and Order*—don't necessarily help . . .

   basic or principal feature

2. Eyewitnesses are especially likely to make mistaken identifications when the suspect's **ethnicity** differs from their own.

   cultural group or background

3. In a program of research **spanning** more than three decades . . .

   extending; covering

4. Misleading information from other sources, too, can **profoundly** alter what witnesses report.

   significantly

5. . . . Bugs Bunny is a Warner Bros. creation and would definitely be rabbit **non grata** at Disneyland!

   unwelcome

RESPOND TO THE READING

Directions: Write a half-page response to either of the following questions.

1. How can we tell if our memories are trustworthy? Do you generally trust your own memory? Do you generally trust other people's memories? Why or why not? Discuss.

2. If you were a defense lawyer in a criminal case, how would you use the information in the passage to plan your client's defense?

WEBQUEST

Directions: Use the Internet to find the answers to the following questions. Write your answers on a sheet of paper. Print out the Web page you used for the answers or copy the URL on your sheet.

Who is Jill Price? What is unusual about her memory?

READING 4B

SIGNIFICANCE OF MOVIES (COMMUNICATION/MEDIA)
by John Vivian

Reading 4B is taken from a mass media textbook. The term *mass media* refers to the means of communication that reach very large numbers of people—such as television and the Internet. This excerpt is from a chapter about motion pictures and focuses on their significance.

Pre-Reading Exercise

Directions: Complete this exercise before reading the passage. Preview the passage and answer the following questions.

1. What is the passage about?
   Movies and their influence

2. What are the topics of the four main sections in the passage?
   Movie power; cocoon experience; movies and mores; global role

3. What information is contained in the table near the end of the passage?
   The table compares the domestic and foreign box office for seven American films.

4. What have you previously read or learned about movies?
   Answers will vary.

5. How often do you watch movies? Name one or two of your favorite films.
   Answers will vary.

6. Using the title and headings, write three goal questions for the passage.
   Answers will vary.

Directions: While reading, pause after each paragraph to identify its topic. If the paragraph has a stated main idea, underline it. Use context, the dictionary, and word structure clues to determine the meanings of unfamiliar words.

Movie Power

1   As Dan Brown's thriller *The Da Vinci Code* picked up steam en route to becoming a mega-selling book, the debate intensified on his account of Catholic church history. It was a big deal—but nothing compared to the fury that occurred when Sony moved Ron Howard's movie adaptation toward release. The full crescendo came when the movie premiered. The unprecedented dialogue demonstrates the impact of movies as a storytelling and myth-making medium, which, for mass audiences, can far exceed the impact of other media for at least short windows of time.

2   Movies with religious themes can strike loud chords, as did Mel Gibson's *Passion of the Christ* and Martin Scorsese's *Last Temptation of Christ*. But movies have an impact on other hot-button issues. Consider *Brokeback Mountain*, which catapulted homosexual affections into a

new territory of public dialogue. The short story in the *New Yorker* magazine on which *Brokeback* was based had made merely a ripple in the mass consciousness. Al Gore's documentary *An Inconvenient Truth* gave new urgency in 2006 to finding solutions for global warming. Michael Moore and other docu-ganda producers have stirred significant issues far beyond what magazine and newspaper articles had been doing for years. *Guess Who's Coming to Dinner*, with a theme that was interracially edgy for the 1960s, moved the public toward broader acceptance.

Cocoon Experience

3   Why the powerful and immediate effect of movies? There may be a clue in one of Thomas Edison's first shorts, which included ocean waves rolling toward a camera on a beach. Audiences covered their heads, such was their **suspension of disbelief**. Instinctively they expected to be soaked. Natural human skepticism gets lost in the darkened cocoon of a movie-house auditorium, compounding the impact of what's on-screen (see Figure 4B.1).

Although moviegoers are insulated in a   4
dark auditorium, the experience is communal. You're not the only one sobbing or terrified or joyous. Among your fellow viewers is a reinforcement of emotions that other media can't match. A newspaper article, for example, may be read by thousands, but the experience is individual and apart. The emotional impact is less.

> **suspension of disbelief** Occurs when you surrender doubts about the reality of a story and become caught up in the story.

Figure 4B.1 Suspension of Disbelief
People are carrying their experiences and realities with them when they sit down for a movie. As a storyteller, a movie director needs quickly to suck the audience into the plot—to suspend disbelief, as novelists call it. Master directors, like James Cameron, best known for *Titanic,* strive to create this new reality in opening scenes to engross viewers in the story as it unfolds.

Television, watched at home, often alone, is similarly disadvantaged, although television has most of the accoutrements of movies—visuals, motion and sound.

5   At their most potent, movies need to be seen in a theater. A movie may be good on a DVD at home, as computer downloads or as pay-per-view on television—but nothing compares to the theater phenomenon.

Movies and **Mores**

6   As an especially powerful medium, movies have been targets of censors and the moral police from almost the beginning. In retrospect, some concern has been darkly comical—like attempts in 1896 to ban *Dolorita in the Passion Dance*. Provocative or not, nobody has ever made the case that *Dolorita* corrupted anybody. Movies can be successful at moving emotions at the moment, but as for changing fundamentals in lifestyle or triggering aberrant behavior, the jury remains out.

7   More clear is that movies can sensitize people to issues with sympathetic or deleterious portrayals. Such was the case in 2005 with *Brokeback Mountain*. A generation earlier, *Guess Who's Coming to Dinner* had done the same. Conversely, terrorists have received no slack in the ever-growing volume of action movies. Knowing the value of on-screen portrayals, special-interest groups have worked to eliminate negative stereotypes. It's wrong, say Italian-American organizers, for organized-crime characters always to carry Italian surnames. Feminists have gone after lopsided portrayals of women in homemaker and subordinate roles. Minority groups have leveled similar charges. The result, although hard to prove, has been a new **Hollywood** sensitivity to these issues that proba-

bly is playing out slowly in general attitudes in society.

Global Role

8   After Europe and its promising young film industry were devastated by World War I, Hollywood filled a void by exporting movies. Thus began Hollywood's move toward global pre-eminence in filmmaking. It happened again in World War II. The U.S. government declared movies an essential wartime industry for producing military training and propaganda films. After the war, Europe again in ruins, Hollywood was intact and expanded its exports.

9   Today, movies are among the few products that contribute positively to the balance of trade for the United States. More movies are exported than imported. Indeed, the potential for foreign box office presence is essential for Hollywood in working out the financial details for film projects. Movie proposals with good prospects for a foreign box office revenue are more likely to get a green light. Consider this mid-2006 snapshot of leading Hollywood films:

Box Office Receipts (in billions)

	U.S.	Foreign
X-Men: Last Stand	$231.2	$205.5
The Da Vinci Code	213.2	515.1
Cars	205.9	64.6
Ice Age: The Meltdown	194.3	446.9
Superman Returns	141.6	35.8
Pirates of the Caribbean: Dead Man's Chest	135.6	48.6
Mission: Impossible III	133.0	219.4

10   About 60 percent of U.S. film exports go to Europe, 30 percent to Asia. It is action films that do best abroad. There usually is minimal dialogue to impede the transcultural experience. Media

---

mores (pronounced mô'-rās) Society's rules about right and wrong behavior.

Hollywood A Los Angeles enclave that was the early center of U.S. filmmaking, now more a metaphor for the industry.

scholar George Gerbner once explained it this way: "Violence travels well."

11   Although Hollywood historically has been globally dominant in filmmaking, significant film industries have emerged elsewhere. In India, the film capital Mumbai, formerly Bombay and nicknamed Bollywood, outproduces Hollywood with 900 to 1,200 films a year, compared to 700 or so from U.S. studios. China and Hong Kong each put out more than 100 films a year. In Africa the Nigerian film industry has come to be called Nollywood.

—Vivian, *The Media of Mass Communication*, 9th ed.

You, the Reader

Interest Rating. Please rate the interest level of the reading on the following scale (circle one):

5—Very interesting   2—A little boring

4—Fairly interesting   1—Very boring

3—Mildly interesting

Difficulty Rating. Please rate the difficulty level of the reading on the following scale (circle one):

5—Very difficult   2—Fairly easy

4—Fairly difficult   1—Very easy

3—Moderate

Comments: Please explain your ratings and make any other comments you wish about the reading.

Answers will vary.

COMPREHENSION QUESTIONS

PART I. TOPIC AND STATED MAIN IDEA EXERCISE

Directions: Refer to the indicated paragraphs to choose the best answer for each question.

___c___ **1.** In the first paragraph, which sentence states the main idea?
   a. The first sentence
   b. The second sentence
   c. The last sentence

___b___ **2.** In the second paragraph, which sentence states the main idea?
   a. The first sentence
   b. The second sentence
   c. The last sentence

_____b_____ **3.** What is the topic of paragraph 4?
   a. Watching movies
   b. The communal aspect of movie-watching
   c. Movies vs. television

_____a_____ **4.** What is the topic of paragraph 6?
   a. Movie censorship
   b. *Dolorita in the Passion Dance*
   c. Movies and lifestyle

_____a_____ **5.** In paragraph 7, which sentence states the main idea?
   a. The first and last sentences
   b. The second sentence
   c. The fifth sentence

PART II: COMPREHENSION QUESTIONS

Directions: For questions 1–5, choose the answer that best completes the statement. For questions 6–10, write your response in the space provided. Base all answers on what you read in the selection. Refer back to the selection as necessary to answer the questions.

_____c_____ **1.** The main point of the passage is that:
   a. Movies are now being produced all over the world.
   b. Movies can have an impact on hot-button issues.
   c. Movies are an important medium with a great deal of influence.
   d. Movies have an advantage over other media because they provide a communal experience.

_____c_____ **2.** The author suggests that one reason for movies' powerful effect is that:
   a. Most people can afford to watch them.
   b. Today's films use advanced technology.
   c. Movies encourage a suspension of disbelief.
   d. Movies can be watched in a variety of formats.

_____a_____ **3.** We can tell that *Dolorita in the Passion Dance* was:
   a. An early movie that some people considered improper.
   b. The first porno film.
   c. A true story.
   d. The most popular film of the 1890s.

_____d_____ **4.** The author states that special-interest groups:
   a. Are unaware of the power of movies.
   b. Create films to further their interests.
   c. Have been ignored by modern filmmakers.
   d. Have attempted to eliminate negative stereotypes in films.

_____b_____ **5.** We can tell from the box office information provided in the table that:
   a. Most American films earn more abroad than in the U.S.
   b. The foreign box office earnings of American films are significant.

c. American films are usually not successful in other countries.

d. The popularity of American films is increasing in other countries.

6. What does a movie audience do when they suspend disbelief? How does suspension of disbelief contribute to a movie's powerful effect?

The audience relates to the movie as if it were real; they give up doubts about

reality. This draws them into the film; they get caught up in the story.

7. What is a *cocoon*? What does the author mean when he refers to movie watching as a "cocoon experience"?

A cocoon is a protective covering that separates you from the world outside.

The author suggests that in a movie theater we forget about the world outside and

enter the world of the movie.

8. The author states that movies have an impact on important social issues. What evidence does he provide to support this claim?

The author identifies films that have had an impact on social issues: *Brokeback*

Mountain, Guess Who's Coming to Dinner, An Inconvenient Truth. He also reports that

minority groups and special-interest groups are sensitive to film portrayals of their

members.

9. What is Bollywood?

Bollywood is India's film capital (Mumbai).

10. Do you agree with the author's statement that "movies need to be seen in a theater" to have the most powerful effect? Explain your answer.

Answers will vary.

VOCABULARY EXERCISES

Pronunciation Guide (see p. 90 for list of phonetic symbols)	
communal	(kə-myōō'nəl)
deleterious	(dĕl'ĭ-tîr'ē-əs)
preeminence	(prē-ĕm'ə-nəns)
unprecedented	(ŭn-prĕs'ĭ-dĕn'tĭd)

WORDS IN CONTEXT

Directions: Choose the meaning for the boldfaced word that best fits the context.

_____c_____ **1.** Although moviegoers are insulated in a dark auditorium, the experience is **communal**. You're not the only one sobbing or terrified or joyous.
   a. Happy
   b. Sad
   c. Shared
   d. Isolated

_____a_____ **2.** As an especially powerful **medium**, movies have been targets of censors and the moral police from almost the beginning.
   a. Means of communication
   b. Something that is neither good nor bad
   c. Source of revenue
   d. Invention

_____b_____ **3.** More clear is that movies can sensitize people to issues with sympathetic or **deleterious** portrayals.
   a. Sympathetic
   b. Negative; harmful
   c. Hard to understand
   d. Crude; gross

_____c_____ **4.** After Europe and its promising young film industry were devastated by World War I, Hollywood filled a **void** by exporting movies.
   a. Continent
   b. Something not allowed or accepted
   c. Emptiness; gap
   d. Audience or market

_____d_____ **5.** Although Hollywood historically has been globally **dominant** in film-making, significant film industries have emerged elsewhere.
   a. Unimportant; insignificant
   b. Unsuccessful
   c. Weak
   d. Influential; prominent

USING WORD STRUCTURE CLUES

Directions: Identify the prefix and the meaning of the prefix in the boldfaced word in each of the following sentences. Use context and the dictionary as well as the word structure clues to determine the word's meaning.

1. The **unprecedented** dialogue demonstrates the impact of movies as a storytelling and myth-making medium.

prefix = ___un___   prefix meaning = ___not___

unprecedented means ___having no precedent; never done before___

2. Feminists have gone after lopsided portrayals of women in homemaker and **subordinate** roles.

prefix = _sub_   prefix meaning = _under_

subordinate means _under another's authority; lower in rank, status_

3. Thus began Hollywood's move toward global **preeminence** in filmmaking.

prefix = _pre_   prefix meaning = _before_

preeminence means _superiority; dominance_

4. There usually is minimal dialogue to **impede** the transcultural experience.

prefix = _im_   prefix meaning = _in, into_

impede means _obstruct; get in the way of; interfere with_

5. There usually is minimal dialogue to impede the **transcultural** experience.

prefix = _trans_   prefix meaning = _across, change_

transcultural means _across cultures_

CONTEXT AND DICTIONARY

Directions: Use context and the dictionary to determine the meaning of the boldfaced word in each sentence. Use word structure clues when applicable.

Pronunciation Guide (see p. 90 for list of phonetic symbols)	
aberrant	(ăb'ər-ənt, ə-bĕr' ənt)
accoutrements	(ə-kōō'tər-mənts)
crescendo	(krə-shĕn'dō)
phenomenon	(fĭ-nŏm'ə-nŏn')
provocative	(prə-vŏk'ə-tĭv)
skepticism	(skĕp'tĭ-sĭz'əm)

1. The full **crescendo** came when the movie premiered.

force; intensity; climax; peak of intensity

2. Natural human **skepticism** gets lost in the darkened cocoon of a movie house auditorium . . .

doubt; disbelief

3. Television . . . is similarly disadvantaged, although television has most of the **accoutrements** of movies . . .

trappings; accessories; "stuff"

4. A movie may be good on a DVD at home . . . but nothing compares to the theater **phenomenon**.

experience; occurrence

5. In **retrospect**, some concern has been darkly comical . . .

looking back
_____

6. **Provocative** or not, nobody has ever made the case that Dolorita corrupted anybody.

stirring up feelings, thoughts, desires or actions
_____

7. Provocative or not, nobody has ever made the case that *Dolorita* **corrupted** anybody.

made impure or morally unsound; perverted
_____

8. Movies can be successful at moving emotion at the moment, but as for changing fundamentals in lifestyle or triggering **aberrant** behavior . . .

abnormal
_____

9. . . . special-interest groups have worked to eliminate negative **stereotypes**.

a fixed image of a group allowing for no individual variation
_____

10. The U.S. government declared movies an essential wartime industry for producing military training and **propaganda** films.

spreading of ideas and information to promote one's cause
_____

RESPOND TO THE READING

Directions: Write a half-page response to either of the following questions.

1. Discuss a movie that had an important influence on you. Describe the film and explain how and why it influenced you.

2. Do you agree with the author's statement that movies can have a powerful influence on people and on society? Why or why not?

WEBQUEST

Directions: Use the Internet to find the answers to the following questions. Write your answers on a sheet of paper. Print out the Web page(s) you used for the answers or copy the URL(s) on your sheet.

What is a "talkie?" What was the first "talkie?" When was it made?

CHAPTER 4 REVIEW

General vs. Specific Ideas

Active readers distinguish between general and specific ideas. An idea is more *general* if it is broader and includes more; an idea is more *specific* if it is narrower and includes less.

Paragraph Topic

Every paragraph has a *topic*—a specific subject or focus. Identifying the topic of a paragraph is an important active reading strategy. To identify the topic, ask yourself who or what the whole paragraph is about and answer in a short phrase (two to six words).

Stated Main Ideas

Each expository paragraph also has a *main idea*, which may be stated in one or two sentences within the paragraph. To recognize the main idea, look for a general sentence that states the most important point the paragraph develops about its topic. It is useful to highlight or underline this sentence.

Skills Online: Finding Stated Main Ideas

Readings

| Reading 4A: The Eyewitness on Trial (Psychology) | Reading 4B: Significance of Movies (Communication/Media) |

CHAPTER TESTS

TEST 4.1. PARAGRAPH LOGIC

Directions: Read each paragraph and answer the questions that follow. Use context, the dictionary, and word structure clues to determine the meanings of unfamiliar words.

A. Most Americans have never heard of the East German Trabant or its compatriot, the Wartburg, or of cars like the Zaz Zaporojetz (U.S.S.R.), Skoda (Czechoslovakia), Dacia (Romania), Jaefang (China), Maruti Udyog (India) or Sevel (Argentina). Nor are they likely to see them in an auto-dealer showroom any time soon. But cars like these are being bought in growing numbers as consumers in Eastern Europe, Asia and Latin America rush to buy cars. Rising consumer demand is creating an explosion in the world's car population.

—Schaeffer, "Car Sick: Automobiles Ad Nauseam," *Greenpeace Magazine*

1. Who or what is the whole paragraph about? Write the topic in a short phrase of two to six words.

Growing world demand for cars

2. Underline the sentence that states the paragraph's main idea (general point). If the main idea is stated in the first and last sentences, underline both of those sentences.

3. List one supporting detail contained in the paragraph.

Most Americans haven't heard of the Trabant, the Wartburg . . . (sample answers;

accept any detail)

B. The worst habitat destruction is still to come. We are just starting in earnest to destroy tropical rain forests. These forests cover only 6 percent of Earth's surface but harbor at least half of its species. Brazil's Atlantic forest and Malaysia's lowland forest are nearly gone, and most forests in Borneo and the Philippines will be logged within the next two decades. By the middle of the century the only large tracts of tropical rain forest likely to be standing intact will be in parts of Zaire and the Amazon Basin.

—Diamond, "Playing Dice with Megadeath," *Discover*

1. Who or what is the whole paragraph about? Write the topic in a short phrase of two to six words.

Destruction of the rain forests

2. Underline the sentence that states the paragraph's main idea (general point). If the main idea is stated in the first and last sentences, underline both of those sentences.

3. List one supporting detail contained in the paragraph.

Tropical rain forests cover 6% of the Earth's surface but support at least half its species.

(sample answer; accept any detail)

C. Aserinsky and Kleitman were astounded to discover that adults show a period of rapid eye movement, just as the infants had shown. They were able to awaken their adult subjects during a REM period and ask them what they were experiencing. Almost invariably, the sleepy subject would say he had been in the middle of a dream. This discovery had immediate impact. At last dreams could be scientifically observed and measured. What further unlocking of the secret of dreams might not be possible? Dream and sleep labs sprang up throughout the world. Today, more than two dozen dream labs exist in the United States alone. The study of dreams has become a significant and respectable scientific exploration, one that can directly benefit you.

—Garfield, *Creative Dreaming*

1. Who or what is the whole paragraph about? Write the topic in a short phrase of two to six words.

The study of dreams

2. Underline the sentence that states the paragraph's main idea (general point). If the main idea is stated in the first and last sentences, underline both of those sentences.

3. List one supporting detail contained in the paragraph.

Aserinsky and Kleitman discovered that adults, like infants, showed rapid eye

movement. (sample answers; accept any detail)

D. Infants will not grow normally without the touch of others. This need is usually met in the everyday intimate transactions of diapering, feeding, burping, powdering, fondling, and caressing that nurturing parents give their babies. Something about being touched stimulates an infant's chemistry for mental and physical growth. Infants who are neglected, ignored, or for any reason do not experience enough touch, suffer mental and physical deterioration even to the point of death.

—James and Jongeward, *Born to Win*

1. Who or what is the whole paragraph about? Write the topic in a short phrase of two to six words.

Infants' need for touch

2. Underline the sentence that states the paragraph's main idea (general point). If the main idea is stated in the first and last sentences, underline both of those sentences.

3. List one supporting detail contained in the paragraph.

The need is met in everyday activities like diapering, feeding, burping, etc. (sample

answer; accept any detail)

E. How many times have you had a conversation with someone and not heard a word that was said? Have you ever wanted to shake anyone and force him or her into "paying attention" to you while you were speaking? Most people have these experiences from time to time. <u>Listening is a form of *paying attention*, which is an active process involving much more than hearing and seeing.</u> When we pay attention to each other, we are *focusing* our awareness on what is being said and are excluding other external and internal stimuli. This is not always easy, since our senses are constantly scanning the environment for incoming stimuli, much like switched-on radar screens, and our minds are often preoccupied with our own thoughts.

—Halloran, *Applied Human Relations*

1. Who or what is the whole paragraph about? Write the topic in a short phrase of two to six words.

Paying attention

2. Underline the sentence that states the paragraph's main idea (general point). If the main idea is stated in the first and last sentences, underline both of those sentences.

3. List one supporting detail contained in the paragraph.

Most people have the experience of not being paid attention to. (sample answer;

accept any detail)

TEST 4.2. PARAGRAPH LOGIC

Directions: Read each paragraph and answer the questions that follow. Use context, the dictionary, and word structure clues to determine the meanings of unfamiliar words.

A. <u>*Developmental psychology* is the study of how humans grow, develop, and change throughout the life span.</u> Some developmental psychologists specialize in the study of a particular age group on the continuum from infancy, childhood, and adolescence, through early, middle, and late adulthood, to the end of the life span. Others concentrate on a specific area of interest, such as physical, cognitive, or language development or emotional or moral development.

—Wood et al., *The World of Psychology*, 5th ed.

1. Who or what is the whole paragraph about? Write the topic in a short phrase of two to six words.

Developmental psychology

2. Underline the sentence that states the paragraph's main idea (general point). If the main idea is stated in the first and last sentences, underline both of those sentences.

3. List one supporting detail contained in the paragraph.

Some developmental psychologists specialize in particular age groups. (sample

answer; accept any detail)

B. How will the economy's output be divided among the members of society? Will everyone get an equal share? Will a few get most of the output? Will differences in wealth be allowed to persist over generations? <u>The law of scarcity teaches a hard lesson: All wants cannot be satisfied, and therefore, there will be both winners and losers in the struggle for goods.</u>

—Gregory, Essentials of Economics, 4th ed.

1. Who or what is the whole paragraph about? Write the topic in a short phrase of two to six words.

The law of scarcity

2. Underline the sentence that states the paragraph's main idea (general point). If the main idea is stated in the first and last sentences, underline both of those sentences.

3. List one supporting detail contained in the paragraph.

Will everyone get an equal share in the economy? (sample answer; accept any detail)

C. <u>Music aficionados quibble about who invented the term *rock 'n' roll*. There is no doubt, though, that Memphis disc jockey Sam Phillips was a key figure.</u> From his job at WREC, Phillips found an extra $75 a month to rent a 20-foot-by-35-foot storefront, the paint peeling from the ceiling, to go into business recording, as he put it, "anything, anywhere, anytime." His first jobs, in 1949, were weddings and bar mitzvahs, but in 1951 Phillips put out his first record, "Gotta Let You Go" by blues singer Joe Hill Louis, who played his own guitar, harmonica and drums for accompaniment. In 1951 Phillips recorded B. B. King and then Jackie Breston's "Rocket 88," which many musicologists call the first rock 'n' roll record. Phillips sold his early recordings, all by black musicians, mostly in the blues tradition, to other labels.

—Vivian, The Media of Mass Communication, 7th ed.

1. Who or what is the whole paragraph about? Write the topic in a short phrase of two to six words.

Sam Phillips (rock 'n' roll pioneer)

2. Underline the sentence that states the paragraph's main idea (general point). If the main idea is stated in the first and last sentences, underline both of those sentences.

3. List one supporting detail contained in the paragraph.

Phillips rented a storefront to go into business recording "anything, anytime, anywhere."

(sample answer; accept any detail)

D. No film genre is more historically associated with Hollywood than the Western tale of good and evil. In one film after another, bad guys menaced the decent folks in a town that was often the same studio back-lot set, complete with horses, a stagecoach, the jail, the general store, the saloon, and a dusty main street, scene of a thousand shootouts. Actors embodied their time-honored personae of cowboys, sheriffs, outlaws, and marshals, to the delight of loyal fans. Some of the characters had recognizable historical names, such as Wyatt Earp, Doc Holliday, Jesse and Frank James, and Billy the Kid. Others were purely fictional. All became part of an American morality myth, so much so that children continue to play the parts and tourists continue to visit the ghost towns where scenes from the basic Western are reenacted in an authentic setting.

—Janaro and Altshuler, *The Art of Being Human*, 8th ed.

1. Who or what is the whole paragraph about? Write the topic in a short phrase of two to six words.

   Hollywood's Westerns

2. Underline the sentence that states the paragraph's main idea (general point). If the main idea is stated in the first and last sentences, underline both of those sentences.

3. List one supporting detail contained in the paragraph.

   In many films, bad guys threatened the decent folks on the same studio set. (sample

   answer; accept any detail)

E. Although infants are largely in their own little worlds, almost immediately after birth, they soon begin to take a keen interest in others. Infants prefer looking at faces over just about all other visual information. In fact, as early as 4 days after birth, infants show a marked preference for Mommy's face compared with that of other women. Infants are profoundly interested in other people, and this is a good thing.

—Lilienfeld et al., *Psychology: A Framework for Everyday Thinking*

1. Who or what is the whole paragraph about? Write the topic in a short phrase of two to six words.

   Infants' interest in others

2. Underline the sentence that states the paragraph's main idea (general point). If the main idea is stated in the first and last sentences, underline both of those sentences.

3. List one supporting detail contained in the paragraph.

   Infants prefer looking at faces over other visual information. (sample answer; accept

   any detail)

You, the Reader: Chapter 4 Wrap-up

 Directions: Use one or two of the following questions to write a half-page response to Chapter 4.

- What were the most important things you learned from this chapter? How will you use what you have learned from this chapter?
- How have you changed your reading habits in response to this chapter?
- What strategies most help you recognize main ideas when you read? What sometimes makes it difficult to recognize the main ideas?
- What parts of the chapter did you find most engaging? What questions do you have about the chapter?

myreadinglab

For support in meeting this chapter's objectives, go to MyReadingLab and select *Main Idea*.

CHAPTER

5

Paragraph Logic: Main Ideas and Supporting Details

LEARNING OBJECTIVES

In Chapter 5 you will learn to:

- Identify three common purposes of supporting details
- Outline and diagram a paragraph's main idea and details
- Determine the main idea of a paragraph in which the main idea is implied

CHAPTER CONTENTS

Pre-Reading Exercise for Chapter 5

Directions: Preview the chapter and answer the following questions.

1. What is the chapter about?

   Main ideas and supporting details: purpose of details, diagramming paragraphs, implied

   main ideas

2. Name three purposes of supporting details.

   Examples, evidence, reasons

3. What is an implied main idea?

   An implied main idea is a main idea that is not stated within the paragraph.

4. What have you previously learned about supporting details?

   Answers will vary.

5. What experience do you have working with outlining, diagramming, or mapping ideas in a paragraph or passage? Why might these be helpful strategies?

   Answers will vary.

6. Write two questions about the content of this chapter.

   Answers will vary.

In Chapter 4, you learned to identify the topic of a paragraph and to recognize stated main ideas. In Chapter 5, we will continue working with paragraph strategies and skills, focusing on purposes of supporting details, paragraph outlining and diagramming, and paragraphs with implied main ideas.

Purposes of Supporting Details

The details within a paragraph play a wide variety of roles consistent with the paragraph's purpose. In descriptive paragraphs, the details will contain specific bits of descriptive information. In narrative paragraphs, the details will relate the specific events of the narrative. In expository paragraphs, the details will support and develop the main idea. Active readers connect the details in a paragraph to the main idea by noting these relationships.

In this section, we will focus on three important ways in which details in expository paragraphs support the main idea:

- by giving *examples* of the main point
- by providing *evidence* that supports the main point
- by explaining *reasons* (or causes) for the main point

These are not the only purposes of supporting details in expository paragraphs, but they are among the most common.

Imagine that you were asked to write a paragraph about popular sports in your home town (or city or county). Your main idea is going to be that team sports are very popular in your area. How would you support this main idea? What details would you include in your paragraph?

- You might choose to support the main idea with *examples*. You could list examples of some of the teams or team sports that are especially popular in your area.
- You might support the main idea with *evidence*. The evidence could be the sell-out crowds at your home teams' home games, or how much the next day's conversations around town are invariably about what happened in the teams' games.
- You might support the main idea with *reasons*. You could explain why team sports are popular in your area—perhaps because certain teams have been successful or exciting to watch, or perhaps because of the tradition and history of sports in your area.

Of course, you could support the main idea with a combination of the three types of details. In any case, you will find that the details in expository paragraphs will often be one of these three types: examples, evidence, or reasons.

Examples

Authors commonly use *examples* to illustrate or flesh out a main point. Examples can bring a general idea to life or make an abstract idea more concrete for the reader.

Paragraph with Supporting Details That Provide Examples   Here is a paragraph we looked at in Chapter 4 that uses examples to support the main idea.

Friendships serve many human needs. The most basic of these is survival—friendships provide mutual protection. In addition to that need, friendships also help us to avoid loneliness, gain approval for ourselves, and increase our certainty about our own behavior. Most important of all, friendships can help us grow and develop as individuals.

—Derlega and Janda, *Personal Adjustment: The Psychology of Everyday Life,* 3rd ed.

In the preceding paragraph, the main idea is a simple, general point, stated in the first sentence: friendships serve many human needs. Sentences two, three, and four all provide *examples* of the types of human needs that friendships serve: protection, avoiding loneliness, gaining approval, increasing certainty about our behavior, and individual growth. The examples make the authors' general point about friendship more real and more complete for the reader.

Evidence

Authors support main ideas with *evidence*, either when they are making a claim that may not be readily accepted by the reader without the evidence, or when they simply want to strengthen a claim with impressive support. The evidence helps to convince the reader that the author's point is valid. The evidence often consists of data in the form of statistics (number facts), or references to previous research.

Paragraph with Supporting Details That Provide Evidence

Incarceration costs average around $62 per inmate per day at both the state and federal levels when all types of adult correctional facilities are averaged together. Prison systems across the nation face spiraling costs as the number of inmates grows and as the age of the inmate population increases. The cost of running the nation's correctional programs approached $64 billion in 2003, of which more than half, or $39 billion, went to run state prisons.

—Schmalleger, *Criminal Justice: A Brief Introduction,* 7th ed.

In the preceding paragraph, the author's main point is stated in the second sentence. He claims that U.S. prison costs are increasing significantly—"spiraling." To support this point, the author provides *evidence*—statistical data—to support his claim. In the first sentence, he refers to the high daily per inmate cost in state and federal prisons. In the last sentence, he refers to the annual cost in 2003 of almost $64 billion.

Reasons

Reasons are *explanations* that clarify the main idea. Authors support main ideas with *reasons* when they want to explain why something has occurred or why the main idea is or might be true.

Paragraph with Supporting Details That Provide Reasons

All human cultures develop religious or philosophical systems. Some scientists have even debated whether humans are somehow "hardwired" biologically to tend toward religious beliefs. Regardless of the outcome of that debate, clearly religion and philosophy meet profound human psychological needs. They offer people explanations of where they and their societies came from, why they exist, and what the future holds for them, in this life and beyond.

—Craig et al., *The Heritage of World Civilizations,* 8th ed.

In the preceding paragraph, the main idea is stated in the first sentence, which tells us that all civilizations—all human cultures—have religious and philosophical systems. Notice that the rest of the paragraph—sentences two, three, and four—does not provide examples of cultures with religious or philosophical systems, or factual evidence to support the authors' point. Instead, the details in the paragraph provide *reasons* that might explain why all civilizations have religion or philosophy. The authors offer both biological and psychological *explanations*—humans may be biologically programmed to be religious; religion and philosophy serve important psychological needs; religion and philosophy answer important questions for people.

Find strategies that will help you recognize the purpose of supporting details while you read. Here are a few suggestions.

- When a supporting detail contains number facts or refers to research, it is almost certainly *evidence.*

- Details that answer the question *why* are usually *reasons*. If you could logically put the word *because* in front of the detail, it's probably a reason.

- When an author names people, places, things, etc., that are specific instances of the general idea, the details are *examples*. If you could logically put the phrase *for example* in front of the detail, it's probably an example.

- Pay attention to the wording of the detail statement. Transition words and phrases can be clues to the purpose of a detail. Phrases like *because of* or *due to* indicate reasons. Phrases like *for instance* or *such as* indicate examples. See Table 5.1 for transitions words that signal the purpose of a supporting detail.

- Paragraphs can contain more than one type of supporting detail. Sometimes even a single sentence may contain two types of supporting details.

Table 5.1 Transition Words That Signal the Purpose of a Detail

Signaling *Example*: for example, for instance, such as, specifically, in particular

Signaling *Reason*: because of, due to, for, for this reason, in that, since

Signaling *Evidence*: there are no transition words for evidence, but watch for number facts and references to research

Let's try applying these suggestions to some main idea and detail statements. Each of the following pairs of sentences consists of a main idea and a supporting detail. Identify the purpose of the supporting detail by writing Example, Evidence, or Reason on the line below the detail, and briefly explain your answer. Review the following sample and then complete the three practice pairs.

> **SAMPLE**
>
> *Main Idea*: Friendships serve many human needs.
> *Supporting Detail*: The most basic of these is survival—friendships provide mutual protection.
>
> —Derlega and Janda, *Personal Adjustment: The Psychology of Everyday Life*, 3rd ed.
>
> Example—The detail gives an example of one of the needs that friendships serve.

A. *Main Idea*: The United States has by far the world's highest incarceration (imprisonment) rate.
   Supporting Detail: With 5 percent of the world's population, our country now houses nearly 25 percent of the world's reported prisoners.

   —Webb, "Why We Must Fix Our Prisons," *Parade Magazine*

   _____

B. *Main Idea*: Many people equate brains with computers.
   Supporting Detail: They process a lot of information, and in older models they freeze a lot.

   —Roizen and Oz, *You: The Owner's Manual*

   _____

C. *Main Idea*: Whatever else may be said about rock 'n' roll, in the early 1950s, the appearance in the mainstream market of African American artists recording rhythm and blues for independent labels turned all the rules of the music industry upside down.

Supporting Detail: In 1953, for example, the Orioles, a black group originally from Baltimore, recorded "Crying in the Chapel," a sentimental country song, for Jubilee, an independent record label.

—Garofalo, *Rockin' Out: Popular Music in the U.S.A.*, 4th ed.

Analysis:

A. The detail provides <u>evidence</u> to support the author's claim that the U.S. has the highest incarceration (imprisonment) rate in the world. Note the number facts—the percentages—in the detail statement.

B. The detail provides a <u>reason</u> why people equate brains with computers. In other words, the detail is explaining why people think of brains as being like computers. Note that you could logically insert the word <u>because</u> in front of the detail statement: "Many people equate brains with computers [because] they process a lot of information. . . ." (You probably also noted the author's attempt at humor in the detail, poking a little fun at aging brains.)

C. Did you notice the phrase "for example" in the supporting detail? This was not a trick question. The detail provides an <u>example</u> of an African American group recording for an independent record label and changing the practices of the music industry in the 1950s.

> **Three Common Purposes of Supporting Details**
>
> **Examples:** specific instances of the main idea; examples flesh out the main idea, making it clearer for the reader
> **Evidence:** information that supports and strengthens a claim made in the main idea; usually consists of number facts or research
> **Reasons:** explanations that clarify the main idea; reasons answer the question *why*

Exercises 5.1, 5.2, and 5.3 will provide practice with identifying the purpose of supporting details.

EXERCISE 5.1 SUPPORTING DETAILS

Directions: Each pair of sentences in this exercise consists of a main idea and a supporting detail. Read each pair of sentences and check the answer that best states the purpose of the supporting detail.

1. *Main Idea*: Now, thanks in large part to years of misunderstanding, sharks are threatened.

Supporting Detail: More than 100 million sharks of all species are slaughtered each year for their fins, livers, meat, or just because they're in the way.

—Christrup, "Sharks on the Line," *Greenpeace Magazine*

The supporting detail:

___X___ a. Lists reasons why sharks are killed
_____ b. Provides examples of the ways in which sharks are killed
_____ c. Provides reasons why people don't understand sharks

2. *Main Idea*: Advertising is a major component of modern economies.
Supporting Detail: In the United States the best estimates are that advertisers spend about 2 percent of the gross domestic product to promote their wares.

—Vivian, *The Media of Mass Communication*, 9th ed.

The supporting detail:

_____ a. Gives examples of popular types of advertisements
___X___ b. Provides evidence of the importance of advertising to modern economies
_____ c. Explains why advertising has become so important to modern economies

3. *Main Idea*: Although involuntary smokers breathe less tobacco than active smokers do, they still face risks from exposure to tobacco smoke.
Supporting Detail: Sidestream smoke actually contains more carcinogenic substances than the smoke that a smoker inhales.

—Donatelle and Davis, *Health: The Basics*, 2nd ed.

The supporting detail:

_____ a. Gives examples of illnesses caused by sidestream smoke
___X___ b. Explains why sidestream smoke is harmful
_____ c. Both *a* and *b*

4. *Main Idea*: Emotionally healthy people are usually able to respond in a stable and appropriate manner to upsetting events.
Supporting Detail: When they feel threatened, they are not likely to react in an extreme fashion, behave inconsistently, or adopt an offensive attack mode.

—Donatelle and Davis, *Health: The Basics*, 2nd ed.

The supporting detail:

_____ a. Explains why healthy people respond more stably to upsetting events
_____ b. Provides examples of the ways healthy people respond to upsetting events
___X___ c. Provides examples of the ways healthy people do not respond to upsetting events

5. *Main Idea*: The United States has become one of the largest Spanish-speaking nations in the world.
Supporting Detail: Thirty-one million Americans speak Spanish at home.

—Henslin, *Sociology: A Down-to-Earth Approach*, 9th ed.

The supporting detail:

_____ a. Gives examples of American families who speak Spanish
___X___ b. Gives evidence that supports the idea that many Americans speak Spanish
_____ c. Provides reasons why Spanish is popular in the United States

EXERCISE 5.2 SUPPORTING DETAILS

Directions: Each of the following pairs of sentences consists of a main idea and a supporting detail. Identify the purpose of the supporting detail by writing Example, Evidence, or Reason on the line below the detail, and briefly explain your answer. An example is provided.

EXAMPLE

Main Idea: Friendships serve many human needs.
Supporting Detail: The most basic of these is survival—friendships provide mutual protection.

—Derlega and Janda, *Personal Adjustment: The Psychology of Everyday Life,* 3rd ed.

Example: The detail gives an example of one of the needs that friendships serve.

1. *Main Idea:* Drug misuse and abuse are problems of staggering proportions in our society.
   Supporting Detail: Each year drug and alcohol abuse contributes to the deaths of more than 120,000 Americans.

   Donatelle, *Health: The Basics,* 6th ed.

   Evidence: The detail cites the number of deaths (to which substance abuse has

   contributed) as evidence of the extent of the problem.

2. *Main Idea:* Scientists are finding ways to counteract the food-allergy boom.
   Supporting Detail: In clinical studies across the country, doctors and researchers are experimenting with new methods such as Chinese herbs to neutralize the allergic switches.

   Flynn, "What You Can Do about Food Allergies," *Parade Magazine*

   Example: The detail provides an example (Chinese herbs) of one of the ways

   scientists are fighting food allergies.

3. *Main Idea:* Play is a fundamental need, just like air, water, and the five food groups.
   Supporting Detail: It teaches us trust, cooperation, respect for others, sharing, mastery, and many of life's other lessons.

   Tait, "Let's Play," *Parade Magazine*

   Reason: The detail provides a reason (or reasons) why play is needed.

4. *Main Idea:* Education is valuable because it raises income.
   Supporting Detail: A woman who has completed four years of college will earn on average 78 percent more per year than a woman who has completed only four years of high school.

   —Curry et al., *Sociology for the 21st Century,* 5th ed.

Evidence: The detail provides evidence of the value of education by comparing

income levels and education levels. (Also accept "Example" if logically supported.)

5. *Main Idea:* There is no doubt that studying animal intelligence is challenging and exciting.
Supporting Detail: There is still much to learn, and surprises are always forth-coming.

—Beckoff, *Animals Matter*

Reason: The detail gives a reason or reasons why studying animal intelligence is

exciting and challenging.

6. *Main Idea:* Noise-induced hearing loss is the most common kind of hearing disability in the United States, and in most circumstances, it's preventable.
Supporting Detail: A California study reported that 61 percent of college fresh-men showed a measurable hearing loss in the high-frequency ranges caused by prolonged exposure to loud noise.

—Campbell, *The Mozart Effect*

Evidence: The detail cites a study showing a high percentage of students affected

by noise.

7. *Main Idea:* In Western societies, sculpture was long obsessed with the imitation of ancient Greek and Roman styles.
Supporting Detail: George Washington was portrayed as the Roman soldier-farmer Cincinnatus.

—Bishop, *A Beginner's Guide to the Humanities,* 2nd ed.

Example: The detail gives an example of a sculpture (Washington, an American)

based on a classical model.

8. *Main Idea:* In spite of, or perhaps because of, the fact that it is legal and socially approved, alcohol is America's number-one drug problem.
Supporting Detail: Alcohol is a highly addictive drug with potentially devastat-ing long-term effects.

—Morris and Maisto, *Understanding Psychology,* 8th ed.

Reason: The detail gives a reason or reasons why alcohol is a problem. (It's addictive;

has devastating long-term effects.)

9. *Main Idea:* Successful cities tend to be located in places that give them eco-nomic advantages.
Supporting Detail: Portland got its start in the mid-nineteenth century as pio-neers arriving by the Oregon Trial settled where the Willamette River flowed into the Columbia River.

—Withgott and Brennan, *Essential Environment: The Science Behind the Stories,* 2nd ed.

Example: The detail uses Portland as an example of a city whose location helped

it become successful.

10. *Main Idea:* Methamphetamine has inflicted many cruelties on children.
Supporting Detail: Nationally, 62 percent of the counties surveyed in 2005 reported increases in meth-related domestic violence.

— Rader, "How Could We Not Have Known?" *Parade Magazine*

Evidence: The detail cites survey data showing a high percentage of counties

reporting problems with meth-related violence.

EXERCISE 5.3   TOPIC, MAIN IDEA, AND SUPPORTING DETAILS

Directions: For each of the following paragraphs, write the topic, underline the sentence that states the main idea, and identify the purpose of the supporting details. Use context clues, word structure clues, and the dictionary as well as the vocabulary notes provided to determine the meaning of unfamiliar words.

A. Although cigarette smoking is dangerous for all women, it presents special risks for pregnant women and their fetuses. Each year in the United States, approximately 50,000 miscarriages are **attributed** to smoking during pregnancy. On average, babies born to mothers who smoke weigh less than those born to nonsmokers, and low birth weight is correlated with many **developmental** problems. Pregnant women who stop smoking in the first three or four months of their pregnancies give birth to higher-birth-weight babies than do women who smoke throughout their pregnancies. Infant **mortality** rates are also higher among babies born to smokers. Moreover, research indicates that babies born to women who smoke during pregnancy are more likely to die of sudden infant death syndrome (SIDS) than are babies born to mothers who do not smoke. SIDS, or "crib death," occurs when an infant, usually under one year of age, dies during its sleep for no apparent reason.

— Donatelle and Davis,
Health: The Basics, 2nd ed.

> **attribute** consider to be caused by
> **developmental** relating to stages of growth and development

> **mortality** death

1. What is the topic of the paragraph?   smoking and pregnancy

2. Underline the main idea.

3. Choose the best answer. The supporting details in the paragraph:
   a. Give reasons why pregnant women smoke.
   b. Explain how cigarette smoke affects the fetus.
   c. Provide evidence and examples of the risks of smoking during pregnancy.

B. Like most of us, I have borne our usual prejudices toward rodents. On the surface, it may seem that there is not much about these "lower mammals" to admire, with their ordinary bodies and apparently humble lifestyles lived mainly out of our view. But there's more to rodents than we may realize. Not only are they fabulously diverse and successful—they number around 1,200 species, and there is estimated to be about one Norway rat for every human—they are also clever and complex.

— Balcombe, *Second Nature*

1. What is the topic of the paragraph?   appreciating rodents

2. Underline the sentence that states the main idea.

3. Choose the best answer. The supporting details in the paragraph:
   a. Explain why people don't admire rodents and also what is admirable about them.
   b. Provide evidence of rodents' diversity and success.
   c.) Both *a* and *b*

C. In reality, people's role performance—their actual role behavior—often does not match the behavior expected by society. Some doctors do not give their patients the best possible care. Some parents mistreat their children. In some cases, the problem arises because role behaviors considered appropriate in a subgroup are considered inappropriate in the larger society. Even when [a person] is trying to fulfill a role in the manner expected by society, it is often difficult to achieve a close match between actual performance and expectations. This is partly due to the fact that each of us is asked to perform many roles, some of them contradictory.

—Thomas, *Sociology: The Study of Human Relationships*, 5th ed.

1. What is the topic of the paragraph? role performance

2. Underline the main idea.

3. Choose the best answer. The supporting details in the paragraph:
   a. Give examples of people whose behavior is not consistent with their role expectations.
   b. Explain why behavior and role expectations sometimes don't match.
   c.) Both *a* and *b*

D. In interpersonal communication, you can reach another person with what you have to say. At a rally, you can reach a few dozen. Even at a super-rally, like an evangelist at a football stadium, the maximum audience is the seating of the stadium. With mass communication, however, a message can be **amplified** so millions of people pick it up. This potential for mass communication to reach such vast audiences, and perhaps motivate them to action, is its greatest advantage over other communication forms, and is the reason why the study of mass communication is important.

—Vivian, *The Media of Mass Communication*, 4th ed.

amplified increased; expanded

1. What is the topic of the paragraph? advantages of mass communication

2. Underline the main idea.

3. Choose the best answer. The supporting details in the paragraph:
   a. Provide several examples of the various forms of mass communication.
   b.) Explain the limits of other forms of communication compared with mass communication.
   c. Provide evidence of the influence of mass media on our society.

E. Until recently there was no conception among the Navajo of joint property ownership between husband and wife. A woman controls the hogan, built on land that was set aside for her by her family; she owns the children, which belong to her clan, her sheep, the product of her sheep and other livestock, her jewelry and all blankets she might weave, and the income from the sale of any of her property. A husband owns what he has inherited from his own family and all goods which he has bought out of his own earn- ings, which, nowadays, often includes a pickup truck. Either partner may sell or trade what he owns, though one usually consults with the other about any major transaction.

—Locke, *The Book of the Navajo*

1. What is the topic of the paragraph?   <u>Navajo property ownership</u>

2. Underline the main idea.

3. Choose the best answer. Most of the details in the paragraph:
   a. Explain why the Navajo husband and wife don't share property.
   ⓑ Give examples of the property owned by the Navajo husband and wife.
   c. Explain how couples decide what may be sold.

Active Reading Strategy: Outlining and Diagramming Paragraphs

We can illustrate the relationship between the main idea and supporting details with an informal outline or with a block diagram. There are several benefits to paragraph outlining and diagramming. First, outlining or diagramming a paragraph makes the relationship between the ideas in the paragraph clear. Second, because outlining or diagramming a paragraph requires you to think carefully about a paragraph, it strengthens both your understanding of that particular paragraph and your paragraph reading skills in general. Third, outlining and diagramming a paragraph makes the information in the paragraph more visual, which for many students means that the information becomes easier to understand and remember. Finally, this practice provides a foundation for developing effective notetaking skills, which are essential to your success in college courses.

How to Outline a Paragraph

In an informal paragraph outline, we write the main idea at the left margin, and then list and indent the details below the main idea.

> Main Idea
> > Supporting Detail
> > Supporting Detail
> > Supporting Detail

Clearly, a successful paragraph outline requires that we first accurately identify the main idea. It is a good strategy to start by mentally identifying the paragraph's topic; then locate the stated main idea. Place the main idea at the top of the outline, regardless of its location in the paragraph.

Let's look at an example which you may remember from Chapter 4.

If life stages affect our dreams, so do our attitudes. Studies by University of Pennsylvania professor emeritus Aaron Beck show that angry people act out their anger in their dreams. Other research shows that depressed people sometimes dream they're victims of rejection, humiliation, or abandonment. People with "thin boundaries"—unusual openness, vulnerability, difficulty standing up for themselves—are likely to suffer from nightmares.

—Von Kressler, "Why We Dream What We Dream,"
Reader's Digest

After reading this paragraph we can determine that the topic of the paragraph is "attitudes' effect on dreams." The main idea is stated in the first sentence, a general statement which tells us that our attitudes affect our dreams. To begin outlining the paragraph, we'll write down the main idea, starting at the left margin.

Our attitudes affect our dreams.

The second, third, and fourth sentences in the paragraph contain supporting details—evidence and examples that support the statement that our attitudes affect our dreams. To complete our paragraph outline, we'll work a sentence at a time, listing and indenting the supporting details under the main idea.

Our attitudes affect our dreams.
   Studies show that angry people act out their anger in dreams.
   Research shows that depressed people dream they're victims of rejection,
      humiliation, and abandonment.
   People with thin boundaries are likely to suffer from nightmares.

Let's look at one more example, a slightly more difficult paragraph from a book about William Shakespeare.

William Shakespeare was born into a world that was short of people and struggled to keep those it had. In 1564 England had a population of between three million and five million—much less than three hundred years earlier, when plague began to take a continuous, heavy toll. Now the number of living Britons was actually in retreat. The previous decade had seen a fall in population nationally of about 6 percent. In London as many as a quarter of the citizenry may have perished.

—Bryson, *Shakespeare: The World as Stage*

The preceding paragraph is about England's population during Shakespeare's time. We might express the topic as "England's population in Shakespeare's time," or "England's population in the sixteenth century." Which sentence states the main idea or general point of the paragraph? You probably agree that the main idea is stated in the first sentence, which tells us that when Shakespeare was born, England didn't have a large population and, in fact, was struggling to maintain the population level it had. Let's start our outline by placing the main idea at the left margin.

When Shakespeare was born, England had a small population that it was struggling
   to maintain.

Note that we've reworded the main idea for our outline to make it clearer.

The details in the second, third, fourth, and fifth sentences support the main idea by giving evidence of the low population and providing a reason why the population was low—the plague, which took many lives throughout Europe in the Middle Ages (Shakespeare was born just after the end of the Middle Ages). Let's list the details under the main idea, indenting each one.

> When Shakespeare was born, England had a small population that it was struggling to maintain.
>> The population in England in 1564 was 3–5 million, much lower than 300 years before when plague started to reduce it.
> The population was actually decreasing.
> The population had decreased by about 6 percent in the previous decade.
> London lost perhaps one-fourth of its population.

Exercises 5.4 and 5.5 will provide practice with outlining paragraphs. Remember to mentally identify the topic of each paragraph before locating the main idea and completing your outline.

EXERCISE 5.4 OUTLINING PARAGRAPHS

Directions: Each of the paragraphs in this exercise is followed by a partial outline of the paragraph's main idea and supporting details. After reading each paragraph, complete the accompanying paragraph outline by filling in the missing supporting details, and when necessary, the main idea, in the spaces provided. Then, answer the question (found below the outline) about the purpose of the paragraph's supporting details. Use context clues, word structure clues, and the dictionary as well as the vocabulary notes provided to determine the meaning of unfamiliar words.

1. Books were valued during the Colonial period. In Massachusetts in 1638, the pilgrims set up Cambridge Press, the first book producer in what is now the United States. Just as today, personal libraries were a symbol of the intelligentsia. John Harvard of Cambridge, Massachusetts, was widely known for his personal collection of 300 books, a large library for the time. When Harvard died in 1638, he bequeathed his books to Newtowne College, which was so grateful that it renamed itself for him. Today it's Harvard University.

—Vivian, *The Media of Mass Communication*, 7th ed.

Complete the outline:

Books were valued during the Colonial period.
> The pilgrims started Cambridge Press, the first U.S. book producer, in 1638.
> Having a personal library was considered a sign of intelligence.
>> John Harvard was known for his large personal library (300 books).
>> When he died he left his books to Newtowne College, which renamed itself for him—today it's Harvard University.

Supporting Details Question (check the better answer):

The supporting details in the preceding paragraph:

_____✔ a. Provide evidence of the importance of books in the Colonial period.

_____ b. Explain why people in the Colonial period liked to read books.

2. Proteins perform many different **functions** in organisms. An especially important role is played by *enzymes,* proteins that guide almost all of the chemical reactions that occur inside cells. Because each enzyme assists only one or a few specific reactions, most cells contain hundreds of different enzymes. Other types of proteins are used for energy storage or structure. Proteins may also function in transport or movement (for example, a protein carries oxygen in the blood, and others help muscle cells move).

—Audesirk et al., *Life on Earth,* 5th ed.

function purpose; action

Complete the outline:

Proteins perform a variety of functions.

One important role is played by enzymes, which are proteins that govern most of the chemical reactions happening inside cells.

Each enzyme assists only one or a few reactions, so most cells contain hundreds of different enzymes.

Other types of proteins are used for energy storage or structure.

Proteins can also function in transport or movement.

Supporting Details Question (check the better answer):

The supporting details in the preceding paragraph:

_____ a. Provide evidence from research studies proving the importance of proteins.

_____✔ b. Provide examples of the different functions performed by proteins.

3. A study of drinking at college parties found that students who did not drink believed the risk of being caught was very high if they committed a crime. Those who drank most heavily condemned crime less strongly and believed the risk of being caught was low. A major implication of this research is that it may be possible to reduce crime by preventing heavy drinking.

—Albanese, *Criminal Justice,* 3rd ed.

Complete the outline:

Preventing heavy drinking may help reduce crime.

Students who didn't drink believed there was a high risk of being caught if they committed a crime.

Students who drank more condemned crime less strongly and believed there was a low risk of being caught.

Supporting Details Question (check the better answer):

The supporting details in the preceding paragraph:

_____ a. List the reasons why college students drink.

___✔___ b. Provide evidence of a link between crime and drinking.

4. Everyone has the potential to be motivated. Your challenge as you begin college is to identify and activate your personal motivators—the forces that move you forward. For example, you may be motivated to learn a **marketable** skill so you can support yourself and your family or to study a subject that has always fascinated you. Motivators can change with time and situations. Though good grades may be all that interest you at the beginning of the semester, as time passes you may wish to learn as much as you can about a subject you have grown to love.

—Carter et al., *Keys to Success: Building Successful Intelligence for College, Career, and Life,* 5th ed.

marketable usable for sale or earnings

Complete the outline:

Your challenge as you begin college is to identify and activate your personal motivators. Everyone has the potential to be motivated.

You may be motivated to learn a marketable skill or to study a subject that

fascinates you.

Motivators can change with time and situations.

Good grades may motivate you at first, but you may grow to love a subject

and wish to learn as much as you can about it.

Supporting Details Question (check the better answer):

The supporting details in the preceding paragraph:

___✔___ a. Provide examples of things that might motivate you in college.

_____ b. Provide evidence of the importance of motivation to success in college.

EXERCISE 5.5 OUTLINING PARAGRAPHS

Directions: On a separate sheet of paper, make a paragraph outline for each of the following paragraphs. Then briefly explain the purpose of the paragraph's supporting details. Use context clues, word structure clues, and the dictionary as well as the vocabulary notes provided to determine the meaning of unfamiliar words.

See Instructor's Manual for sample answers.

1. The story of how names came down to our time is a record that can be told in terms of people. In ancient days almost all peoples gave each of their children only one personal name, individually selected and tailored to fit a particular child. As population groups increased in number, it became necessary to expand the name pools. Instead of remaining unique to one person, names began to be reused for succeeding generations. "Son of" suffixes and prefixes came into use. Distinguishing nicknames became names in themselves.

—Turner, *The Very Best Book of Baby Names*

2. Organisms detect and respond to **stimuli** in their environments. For example, plants grow toward a source of light. Some kinds of bacteria can move to get away from a poisonous chemical.

stimuli things that cause responses

Animals can also respond to stimuli inside their bodies. For example, when you feel hungry, you sense the contractions of your empty stomach and the low levels of sugars and fats in your blood. You then respond by finding some food and eating.

—Audesirk et al., *Life on Earth,* 5th ed.

3. In schools many girls and boys perform differently in academic subjects and behave differently in the classroom. Males outperform females in the highest levels of mathematics and physics, but the differences are declining as more high school girls take higher level math and science courses. Girls continue to be ahead of boys in reading and writing

proficiencies. In the classroom "boys tend to be louder, more physically aggressive, and more prone to attention-getting devices…than are girls, resulting in more teacher attention going to boys."

—Johnson et al.,
Foundations of American Education, 14th ed.

proficiency: skill; ability

4. According to the Uniform Crime Report, 17 percent of all persons arrested nationally are under eighteen and 46 percent are under age twenty-five. This age pattern does not vary much by type of crime, with 46 percent of violent crime arrests (including homicide) and 58 percent of property crime

arrests involving people under age twenty-five. This finding suggests that the majority of crimes are committed by young people, although not necessarily juveniles. Juveniles represent less than 20 percent of all arrests, a number that has been dropping steadily.

—Albanese, *Criminal Justice,* 3rd ed.

How to Diagram a Paragraph

Diagramming a paragraph (also referred to as *mapping* a paragraph) is similar to outlining a paragraph, and has similar benefits. The primary difference between diagramming and outlining paragraphs is that diagramming makes the relationship of ideas within the paragraph more strongly visual. Diagramming is therefore often preferred by visual learners.

There are several ways to go about diagramming a paragraph. In this section we will work with a block diagram—meaning that when creating the diagram, we place the ideas into blocks, with the main idea centered at the top of the diagram and the supporting details in a row below it.

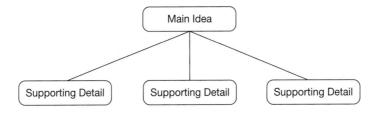

Before you diagram a paragraph, mentally identify the topic of the paragraph. Then determine which sentence states the main idea and start your diagram by placing that sentence in the top block of your diagram, centered. Next, list each detail in a block underneath the main idea, going in a row across the page. Draw a line connecting each detail to the main idea. The connecting line emphasizes the fact that the detail is supporting the main idea.

Let's look at the paragraph about dreams again as an example:

If life stages affect our dreams, so do our attitudes. Studies by University of Pennsylvania professor emeritus Aaron Beck show that angry people act out their anger in their dreams. Other research shows that depressed people sometimes dream they're victims of rejection, humiliation, or abandonment. People with "thin boundaries"—unusual openness, vulnerability, difficulty standing up for themselves—are likely to suffer from nightmares.

—Von Kressler, "Why We Dream What We Dream,"
Reader's Digest

As we have previously noted, the main idea is stated in the first sentence of the paragraph. To start our diagram, we place the main idea in a block centered on the page.

> Our attitudes
> affect our dreams.

Next, we note that the paragraph contains three supporting details. We'll place them in three blocks under the main idea and draw lines to connect the supporting detail blocks to the main idea block.

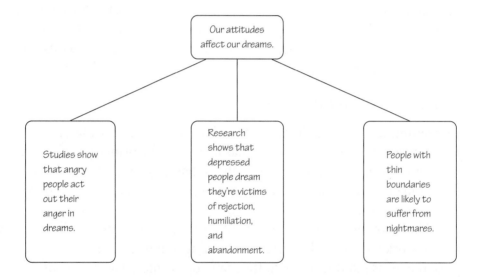

Now our paragraph diagram is complete.

Exercises 5.6 and 5.7 will provide practice with diagramming and help you determine whether outlining or diagramming is more useful to you. Remember to mentally identify the topic of each paragraph before locating the main idea and completing your diagram.

EXERCISE 5.6 DIAGRAMMING PARAGRAPHS

Directions: Each of the paragraphs in this exercise is followed by an incomplete diagram of the paragraph's main idea and supporting details. After reading each paragraph, complete the accompanying paragraph diagram by filling in the missing supporting details, and when necessary, the main idea, in the blocks provided. Then, answer the question (found below the diagram) about the purpose of the paragraph's supporting details. Use context clues, word structure clues, and the dictionary as well as the vocabulary notes provided to determine the meaning of unfamiliar words.

1. Sometimes, the influence of others can be a powerful social support for our positive behavior changes. At other times, we are influenced to drink too much, party too hard, eat too much, or engage in some other negative action because we don't want to be left out or because we fear criticism. Learning to understand the subtle and not-so-subtle ways in which our families, friends, and other people have influenced and continue to influence our behaviors is an important step toward changing our behaviors.

—Donatelle and Davis, *Health: The Basics,* 2nd ed.

Complete the diagram:

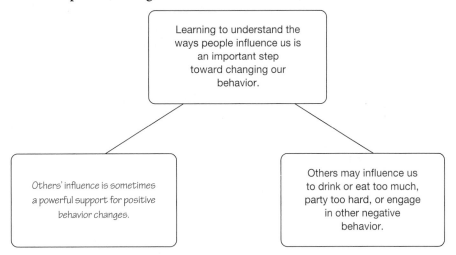

Learning to understand the ways people influence us is an important step toward changing our behavior.

Others' influence is sometimes a powerful support for positive behavior changes.

Others may influence us to drink or eat too much, party too hard, or engage in other negative behavior.

Supporting Details Question (check the better answer):

The supporting details in the preceding paragraph:

_____ a. Provide evidence that the influence of others can cause positive behavior changes.

___✔___ b. Compare the ways others can influence us and list examples of negative influences.

2. Lincoln has lived on at the center of American popular culture. On TV right now, a bank commercial portrays a President Lincoln complaining that no one seems to save his pennies anymore. Even those Americans most ignorant of presidential history will encounter Lincoln cars, Lincoln Logs, companies, schools and cities named for Lincoln. A **formidable** engine of the Lincoln legend is the fact that in many states, especially Illinois ("Land of Lincoln"), Lincoln's birthday has been celebrated as a holiday, and schoolchildren are annually taught to understand and respect the Great Emancipator.

—Beschloss, "Why Lincoln Matters,"
USA Today Weekend Magazine

formidable powerful; forceful

Complete the diagram:

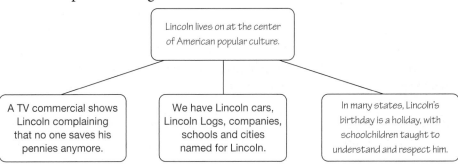

Lincoln lives on at the center of American popular culture.

A TV commercial shows Lincoln complaining that no one saves his pennies anymore.

We have Lincoln cars, Lincoln Logs, companies, schools and cities named for Lincoln.

In many states, Lincoln's birthday is a holiday, with schoolchildren taught to understand and respect him.

Supporting Details Question (check the better answer):

The supporting details in the preceding paragraph:

✔ a. Provide examples of the ways that Lincoln lives on in American culture.

___ b. Explain why Lincoln was an important president.

3. *Developmental psychology* is the study of how humans grow, develop, and change throughout the life span. Some developmental psychologists specialize in the study of a particular age group on the **continuum** from infancy, childhood, and adolescence, through early, middle, and late adulthood, to the end of the life span. Others concentrate on a specific area of interest, such as physical, **cognitive**, or language development or emotional or **moral** development.

—Wood et al., *The World of Psychology,* 5th ed.

continuum continuous series of stages

cognitive relating to mental processes
moral relating to right and wrong

Complete the diagram:

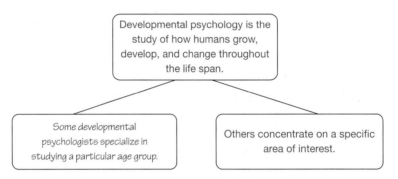

Supporting Details Question (check the better answer):

The supporting details in the preceding paragraph:

___ a. Provide reasons why developmental psychology is an important and interesting subject.

✔ b. Lists examples of the areas in which developmental psychologists specialize.

4. Known for its informality and diversity, American culture proved powerfully attractive to peoples all over the world, partly because racial and ethnic diversity was more pronounced in the United States than in any other major power. African Americans, Latino Americans, and Asian Americans, all figured **prominently** in the popular realms of sports, music, and films. Television was the leading medium for this culture of entertainment, beaming CNN, MTV, ESPN, and "reality" shows around the world. From jazz to rock 'n' roll to rap, American popular music spread across the globe, as did American jeans and sneakers, symbols of informality and comfort. Hollywood's movies **dominated** cinemas and DVD players everywhere, providing 85 percent of films screened in Europe.

—Jones et al., *Created Equal: A History of the United States,* 3rd ed.

prominently significantly

dominate have most power and influence

Complete the diagram:

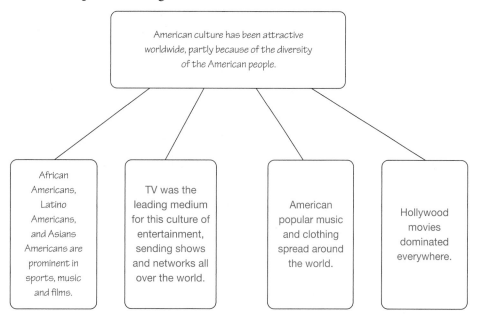

Supporting Details Question (check the better answer):

The supporting details in the preceding paragraph:

_____ a. Compare American culture with the cultures of other nations.

___✔___ b. Provide examples and evidence of the popularity of American culture.

EXERCISE 5.7 DIAGRAMMING PARAGRAPHS

Directions: On a separate sheet of paper, make a block diagram for any *two* of the following paragraphs. Then briefly explain the purpose of the paragraph's supporting details. Use context clues, word structure clues, and the dictionary as well as the vocabulary notes provided to determine the meaning of unfamiliar words.

1. Newborn babies sleep an average of 17–18 hours a day. Adolescents sleep approximately 10–11 hours in a 24-hour period, while young adults spend an average of eight hours a night sleeping. Elderly people, on the other hand, seldom sleep more than six hours during the night. This seems to indicate that we require less sleep as we grow older, but still, on the whole, we spend approximately one-third of our lives sleeping.

—Gonzalez-Wippler, *Dreams*

2. Schooling also provides opportunities for students to develop their social skills by interacting with others. In this process, students should learn to respect others; they also learn a set of rules for working appropriately with peers and adults. Although schools usually do not provide a course that teaches skills in social development, appropriate behavior is constantly reinforced by teachers and other school professionals in the classroom and on the playground.

—Johnson et al., *Foundations of American Education,* 14th ed.

3. For Latinos, country of origin is highly significant. Those from Puerto Rico, for example, feel that they have little in common with people from Mexico, Venezuela, or El Salvador—just as earlier immigrants from Germany, Sweden, and England felt they had little in common with one another. A sign of these divisions is that many refer to themselves in terms of their country of origin, such as puertorriquenos or cubanos, rather than as Latino or Hispanic.

—Henslin, *Sociology: A Down-to-Earth Approach,* 9th ed.

4. When Queen Elizabeth I passed away in 1603, several important elements were already in place to help England compete for colonial outposts. The trade in wool had prompted many large landholders to fence in their fields and turn to raising sheep. This "enclosure" movement pushed thousands of tenants off the land, and these uprooted people flocked to urban centers in search of work, forming a supply of potential colonists. Also, the country had an expanding fleet of English-built ships, sailed by experienced mariners. In addition, England had a group of seasoned and ambitious leaders. A generation of soldiers (many of them younger sons of the property-holding **elite** known as the gentry) had fought in Europe or participated in the brutal colonization of Ireland.

—Jones et al., *Created Equal: A History of the United States,* 3rd ed.

elite upper class

Have you determined whether you prefer outlining or diagramming? Exercise 5.8 will give you a choice as you continue to practice. If you're not sure which is better for you, try doing some of each.

EXERCISE 5.8 OUTLINING AND DIAGRAMMING PARAGRAPHS

Directions: On a separate sheet of paper, make an outline *or* a block diagram for each of the following paragraphs. Then briefly explain the purpose of the paragraph's supporting details. Use context clues, word structure clues, and the dictionary as well as the vocabulary notes provided to determine the meaning of unfamiliar words.

1. Americans have many things in common in addition to their political culture. Most Americans share a common language—English—and have similar **aspirations** for themselves and their families. Most agree that they would rather live in the United States than anywhere else, and that democracy, with all of its warts, is still the best system for most. Most Americans highly value education and want to send their children to the best schools possible, viewing an education as the key to success.

—O'Connor and Sabato, *American Government: Continuity and Change,* 2006 ed.

aspiration desire; ambition

2. Among offenders in prison for any crime, more than 75 percent have used drugs in the past, about 57 percent use drugs regularly, and about 30 percent had used drugs at the time of the offense. More than 52 percent of inmates state that they were under the influence of drugs or alcohol at the time of the offense. The evidence is quite strong, therefore, that use of drugs and alcohol is **correlated** with criminal behavior.

—Albanese, *Criminal Justice,* 3rd. ed.

correlated related; connected

3. Economic agents specialize. Some people sell; others program computers. Some people specialize in law; others in medicine. Iowa farmland is used for corn; Kansas farmland for wheat. Japan specializes in electronics and compact cars; the United States in commercial aircraft and wheat. Individuals, businesses, and countries cannot afford to be jacks-of-all-trades. They increase their material well-being by doing what they do better than others.

—Gregory, *Essentials of Economics,* 4th ed.

4. All organisms must obtain *energy*—the ability to do work, such as carrying out chemical reactions, growing leaves, or contracting a muscle. Plants and some single-celled organisms capture the energy of sunlight and store it in sugar molecules, a process called *photosynthesis*. Organisms that are not capable of photosynthesis obtain energy by extracting it from energy-containing molecules. In most cases, these energy-rich molecules are obtained by consuming the bodies of other organisms. Some kinds of single-celled organisms, however, extract energy from molecules found in the surrounding environment.

—Audesirk et al., *Life on Earth,* 5th ed.

Active Reading Strategy: Recognizing Implied Main Ideas

 You have learned how to analyze paragraphs in which the main idea is stated. In some paragraphs, however, there is no sentence that states the main idea. Instead, each sentence contains a supporting detail. The main idea is implied by the paragraph's details; the reader must therefore *infer,* or interpret, the main idea from the paragraph's details.

Active readers know that they have to approach paragraphs with implied main ideas differently from how they approach paragraphs with stated main ideas. Implied main ideas can be more difficult for the reader because an extra mental step—inferring the main idea from the details—must be taken. To identify an implied main idea, always start by identifying the paragraph's topic, asking yourself who or what the whole paragraph is about, and remembering to express the topic in a short phrase (two to six words). Then ask yourself what general point about the topic is implied by the supporting details. *Always express the main idea in a complete sentence,* so that the point is clear and definite.

Let's look at an example.

Good team collaborators are willing to exchange information, examine issues, and work through conflicts that arise. They trust each other, working toward the greater good of the team and organization rather than focusing on personal agendas. The most effective teams have a clear sense of purpose, communicate openly and honestly, reach decisions by consensus, think creatively, and know how to resolve conflict.

—Bovee and Thill, *Business Communication Essentials,* 3rd ed.

The preceding paragraph consists of three sentences. Notice that no sentence states the main idea for the whole paragraph. Instead, each sentence lists some of the characteristics of good collaborators (people working with others) and good teams. What is the paragraph's topic? You probably agree that the *whole* paragraph is about good teamwork; we can state the topic as "good teamwork," or "characteristics of effective teamwork." What is the main idea of the paragraph? What general point is supported and developed by the paragraph's details?

Let's list the details.

- Good collaborators exchange information, examine issues, and work through conflicts.
- They trust each other and place the good of their group above their personal preferences.
- The best teams are clear about their purpose, communicate well, make decisions by consensus, think creatively, and can resolve conflict.

What general point is implied, or suggested, by the paragraph's details? Since each sentence lists specific characteristics of good team players or good teams, we might express the main idea in a simple generalization, such as "There are several important qualities that characterize good teamwork;" or "Good collaborators and effective teams have several important qualities." We could also state the main idea by making a generalization about the qualities: "Good teamwork involves effective communication and the ability to effectively handle conflicts."

Let's work with another example. Read the following paragraph and answer the questions that follow it.

Americans spend billions of dollars each year on unconventional treatments—herbs, massage, self-help groups, megavitamins, folk remedies, and homeopathy—for a variety of illnesses and conditions. In one survey, the National Science Foundation found that 88% of Americans believe that there are valid ways of preventing and curing illnesses that are not recognized by the medical profession. Moreover, a growing number of people are turning to alternative health care providers for treatment of their mental health problems. And college-educated Americans are more likely to use unconventional treatments than those who have less education.

—Wood et al., *Portable Psychology*

1. What is the topic of the paragraph? Answer in a short phrase of two to six words.

   Answer provided below.

2. What is the main idea developed by the details of the paragraph? Write one complete sentence.

   Answer provided below.

Analysis: The paragraph consists of four sentences. No sentence states the main idea for the whole paragraph. Instead, each sentence provides specific information about Americans' interest in alternative medicine. The topic might therefore be expressed as "Americans' interest in alternative medicine" or "growing use of alternative medical treatments." The details tell us:

- Americans spend billions on various forms of alternative medical treatment.
- A survey found that most Americans believe that there are valid ways to treat illness that the medical profession doesn't recognize.

- People are seeking alternative treatments for mental health problems.
- College-educated people are more likely to use alternative medical approaches than those with less education.

We can state the paragraph's main idea by summarizing or generalizing for the details: "Many Americans are turning to alternative approaches for treating their health problems."

As you practice with Exercises 5.9 and 5.10, apply the guidelines we have just reviewed. First identify the paragraph's topic. Then ask yourself what general point about the topic is developed and implied by the paragraph's details. Remember that the main idea must be expressed in a complete sentence.

> An **implied main idea** is a main idea that is not stated by any sentence within the paragraph.

EXERCISE 5.9 IMPLIED MAIN IDEAS

Directions: Read each paragraph and answer the questions that follow it. Remember that the main idea must be expressed in a complete sentence. Use context clues, word structure clues, and the dictionary as well as the vocabulary notes provided to determine the meaning of unfamiliar words.

1. Each of us has positive and negative emotions that govern moods and behaviors throughout the day. We often take joy, happiness, and contentment for granted since we tend not to notice the *absence* of stress and distress. However, we typically are aware of negative emotions, such as jealousy, hatred, and anger, because they **deplete** our energy reserves and cause us problems in interacting with others.

—Donatelle, *Health: The Basics*, 6th ed.

> **deplete** use up, drain

Which of the following best expresses the *topic* of the paragraph? (check one)

_____ Emotions

___✔___ Awareness of positive and negative emotions

_____ Awareness of negative emotions

___c___ Which of the following best expresses the *implied main idea* of the paragraph?

    a. How emotions affect us

    b. We often don't notice our positive emotions.

    c. We tend to be more aware of our negative emotions than our positive emotions.

    d. Negative emotions deplete energy and cause problems.

2. It is difficult to assess the position of women in Egyptian society, because our pictorial and textual evidence comes almost entirely from male sources. Women's prime roles were connected with the management of the household. They could not hold office, go to **scribal** schools, or become **artisans**. Nevertheless, women could own and control property, sue for divorce, and, at least in theory, enjoy equal legal protection.

—Craig et al., *The Heritage of World Civilizations,* 8th ed.

| scribal of scribes, people who wrote and copied |

| artisan craftsperson |

Which of the following best expresses the *topic* of the paragraph?

_____ Women's roles in society

_____ Egyptian women's property rights

__✔__ Women's roles in Egyptian society

__b__ Which of the following best expresses the *implied main idea* of the paragraph?

a. It is hard to know about the position of women in Egyptian society.
b. Egyptian women managed the household and had some legal rights but did not enjoy equal status with men.
c. Women in ancient Egypt could own property but could not hold office or become artisans.
d. Women in Egyptian society

3. Today, some members of Congress criticize the movie industry and reality television shows including *Survivor* and *The Bachelor* for **pandering** to the least common denominator of society. Other groups criticize popular performers such as Eminem for lyrics that promote violence in general, and against women in particular. Janet Jackson's "wardrobe malfunction" as well as Kid Rock's antics at the 2004 Super Bowl, however, launched renewed calls for increased restrictions, the **imposition** of significant fines on broadcasters, and greater regulation of the airwaves.

—O'Connor and Sabato, *American Government: Continuity and Change,* 2006 ed.

| pander cater to; indulge |

| imposition placing |

Which of the following best expresses the *topic* of the paragraph?

__✔__ Criticisms of broadcast media and performers

_____ Improper song lyrics

_____ Congress's criticism of movies and television

__d__ Which of the following best expresses the *implied main idea* of the paragraph?

a. Since 2004, Congress has been calling for increased regulation of the media.
b. Congress has been critical of movies and television shows.
c. Today's media and popular performers should provide more wholesome entertainment.
d. Congress and other groups have criticized the broadcast media and popular performers and called for increased regulation of public broadcasting.

4. A growing number of immigrant students are populating schools in large cities. Even small cities and rural areas are now home to immigrant families and their children. In fact, nearly one in five students speaks a language other than English at home. The rates are much higher for some groups. Sixty-five percent of Asian American children and 68 percent of Latino children are English language learners.

—Johnson et al., *Foundations of American Education,* 14th ed.

Which of the following best expresses the *topic* of the paragraph?

_____ Education in the twenty-first century

_____ Immigrant students in cities

___✔__ English language learners in our schools

__a__ Which of the following best expresses the *implied main idea* of the paragraph?

    a. Many of the students in our schools are English language learners.
    b. Immigrants account for most of our cities' students.
    c. Sixty-eight percent of Latino children are English language learners.
    d. Why the number of immigrant students is growing

5. Cholesterol is a steroid with a bad reputation. Why are so many products now advertising themselves as "cholesterol free" or "low in cholesterol"? After all, cholesterol is a **crucial** component of cell membranes. It is also the raw material for the production of bile (which helps us digest fats), vitamin D, and both male and female sex hormones.

—Audesirk et al., *Life on Earth,* 5th ed.

crucial necessary, essential

Which of the following best expresses the *topic* of the paragraph?

_____ The dangers of cholesterol

_____ Avoiding cholesterol

__✔__ Cholesterol, a needed steroid

__d__ Which of the following best expresses the *implied main idea* of the paragraph?

    a. Cholesterol has a bad reputation.
    b. Cell membranes need cholesterol.
    c. Benefits of cholesterol
    d. Despite its bad reputation, cholesterol is actually needed by our bodies.

EXERCISE 5.10 IMPLIED MAIN IDEAS

Directions: Read each paragraph and answer the questions that follow it. Remember that the main idea must be expressed in a complete sentence. Use context clues, word structure clues, and the dictionary as well as the vocabulary notes provided to determine the meaning of unfamiliar words.

1. Altogether, every year Americans throw out 160 million tons of commercial and residential trash. That's 25 pounds per person per week—more than enough to bury 2,700 football fields in a layer ten stories high. That's twice as much trash as Japan or Europe generates. Add in all the industrial nonhazardous waste and the oil, natural gas, and mining wastes, and it comes out to a total of 11 billion tons of nonhazardous solid waste a year—in the U.S. alone. Industry generates the greatest portion of what environmentalists call the waste stream, an estimated 7.6 billion tons.

—Langone, *Our Endangered Earth*

Which of the following best expresses the *topic* of the paragraph?

_____ Trash

✔____ America's production of trash and waste

_____ Industrial waste produced in America

_a____ Which of the following best expresses the *implied main idea* of the paragraph?

   a. The United States generates a huge amount of trash and waste.
   b. The United States generates more trash than Japan.
   c. American industry's huge waste stream
   d. Waste production is harming the American environment.

2. Research done by Lyman Steil, an authority on communications, indicates that people on the average listen effectively to only about 25 percent of what they hear. He states further that the ability to listen well is not an **inherent** trait. It is a learned behavior. When we come into this world, we don't have a built-in knowledge of how to listen well. That skill must be developed. Unfortunately, it is not developed well systematically in our school systems. We teach reading, writing, speaking, and numerous other abilities, but not listening. In the business world Steil has found that, as one advances in management, listening ability becomes increasingly critical.

—Halloran, *Applied Human Relations*

inherent inborn

Which of the following best expresses the *topic* of the paragraph?

_____ Lyman Steil

_____ Listening's importance in the business world

✔____ Listening skills

_d____ Which of the following best expresses the *implied main idea* of the paragraph?

   a. Lymen Steil's research on listening
   b. The average person listens effectively to 25 percent of what he or she hears.
   c. Our schools don't teach students how to listen.
   d. Listening is an important skill that needs to be learned and developed.

3. To the outsiders who came to the United States—European settlers and their descendants—the native people came to be known as American Indians. By the time that the Bureau of Indian Affairs (BIA) was organized as part of the War Department in 1824, Indian-white relations had already included three centuries of mutual misunderstanding. As we saw earlier, many bloody wars took place during the nineteenth century, and a significant part of the nation's Indian population was wiped out. By the end of the nineteenth century, schools for Indians operated by the BIA or church missions, often segregated, prohibited the practice of Indian cultures. Yet such schools did little to make the children effective competitors in white society.

—Schaeffer, *Sociology*

Which of the following best expresses the *topic* of the paragraph?

_____ Wars between whites and Native Americans

__✔__ Misunderstanding and mistreatment of Native Americans

_____ Native American schooling

__c__ Which of the following best expresses the *implied main idea* of the paragraph?

a. BIA and church schools prohibited the practice of Indian cultures.
b. The history of Indian-white relations
c. Throughout U.S. history, Native Americans have been misunderstood and mistreated.
d. American minority groups are often mistreated.

4. You can fly from the East to the West Coast on the same day and read the same Associated Press stories word for word. Newspaper publishers learned long ago that sharing stories via AP could reduce costs. Although the audience is worse off for the lack of diverse coverage, nobody seems to mind much. This also has happened in network television. Whereas ABC, CBS and NBC once took pride in never using video their crews had not shot, the networks today have scaled back coverage to save costs and all **subscribe** to the same video coverage from outside sources: APTV, Reuters and Worldwide Television News.

—Vivian, *The Media of Mass Communications,* 4th ed.

subscribe pay to receive a service, publication, etc.

Which of the following best expresses the *topic* of the paragraph?

__✔__ Uniformity of news coverage

_____ Uniformity of American culture

_____ Reading the news

__b__ Which of the following best expresses the *implied main idea* of the paragraph?

a. You can read the same newspaper stories anywhere in the United States.
b. American news coverage has become increasingly uniform.
c. Television networks have saved costs by subscribing to the same news service.
d. The need for more diversity in the news

5. At first glance, heroin's psychological effects might appear mostly pleasurable. Users often experience a sense of the **euphoria** that **opiate** users may experience. But the pleasurable effects of heroin are limited to the 3 or 4 hours that the usual dose lasts. If people addicted to heroin don't take another dose within 4 to 6 hours, they experience *heroin withdrawal syndrome,* with symptoms like abdominal cramps, vomiting, craving for the drug, yawning, runny nose, sweating, and chills. With continued heroin use, the drug's euphoric effect gradually diminishes. The addict may continue using heroin as much to avoid withdrawal symptoms as to experience the intense high of the first few injections.

—Lilienfeld et al., *Psychology: A Framework for Everyday Thinking*

euphoria	feeling of well-being; high
opiate	opium-based drug

Which of the following best expresses the *topic* of the paragraph?

✔ Effects of heroin

_____ Drug addiction

_____ The pleasurable effects of heroin

c Which of the following best expresses the *implied main idea* of the paragraph?

a. Heroin withdrawal syndrome
b. Heroin users experience a very pleasurable euphoria.
c. The pleasurable effects of heroin are soon replaced by withdrawal symptoms and then the need to use the drug to avoid them.
d. Heroin withdrawal syndrome involves a variety of very unpleasant symptoms.

Main Ideas and Supporting Details in Short Passages

We have been practicing paragraph skills and strategies in this and the previous chapter with individual paragraphs. In most of your college courses, however, you will not be asked to analyze single paragraphs. Rather, you will be actively looking for main ideas (whether stated or implied) and supporting details as you read assigned articles or book chapters, paragraph by paragraph.

We will therefore practice now with short passages that will provide you with an opportunity to apply the paragraph skills and strategies you've developed to short selections from college textbooks. Use the strategies you've learned to identify the main ideas and purposes of the supporting details in the passages in Exercise 5.11. You will continue to practice these skills as you work with the end-of-chapter readings.

EXERCISE 5.11 MAIN IDEAS AND SUPPORTING DETAILS IN SHORT PASSAGES

Directions: Read the following passages, looking for the main ideas and supporting details in each paragraph. Then complete the accompanying exercises.

A. The mass media can be wonderful enter-tainers, bringing together huge audiences not otherwise possible. More people cried at the movie *Titanic* than read all of the dozens of books about the tragedy. More people hear the Counting Crows on records or the radio than ever attend one of their concerts. Count the seats in Jimmy Buffett's bar in Key West, even calculate standing room only crowds, and contrast that with the audience for his signature song, "Margaritaville," in even one television appearance.

Almost all mass media have an entertain-ment component, although no medium is wholly entertainment. The thrust of the U.S. movie in-dustry is almost all entertainment, but there can be a strong informational and persuasive ele-ment. Even the most serious newspaper has an occasional humor column. Most mass media are a mix of information and entertainment—and also persuasion.

—Vivian, *The Media of Mass Communication*, 7th ed.

1. What is the topic of the whole passage?

The mass media (functions of)

2. Underline the sentence that states the main idea in paragraph 1.

3. Underline the sentence that states the main idea in paragraph 2.

_c_ **4.** The details in the first paragraph support the claim that:
   a. Movies are the most popular form of entertainment.
   b. Mass media entertainment is more enjoyable than other forms of entertainment.
   c. Mass media entertainment reaches a large audience.

_a_ **5.** The details in the second paragraph:
   a. Provide examples of the mixed functions of mass media.
   b. Provide evidence of the superiority of mass media entertainment.
   c. Explain why the mass media must serve a variety of purposes.

_c_ **6.** Which of the following statements best expresses the main idea of the whole passage?
   a. Mass media entertainment attracts huge audiences.
   b. No mass medium is wholly entertainment.
   c. The mass media provide entertainment but also have other functions.
   d. Entertainers should use the mass media if they want to become popular.

B. You may have wondered what it means if someone is "color blind." Does that person see the world in black and white? No—the term *color blindness* refers to an inability to distinguish certain colors from one another. About 7% of males experience some kind of difficulty in distin-guishing colors, most commonly red from green.

By contrast, fewer than 1% of females suffer from color blindness (This sex difference is explained by the fact that genes for color vision are carried on the X chromosome.).

Research has shown that color blindness can have degrees; it isn't simply a matter of either-you-have-it-or-you-don't. And why are

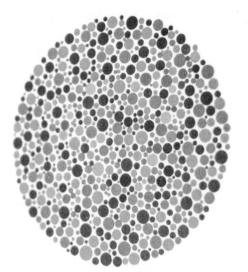

some of us better able to make fine distinctions between colors, as we must do when sorting black and navy blue socks, for instance? These differences appear to be related to the number of color vision genes individuals have. Researchers have found that, in people with normal color vision, the X chromosome may contain as few as two or as many as nine genes for color perception. Those who have more of such genes appear to be better able to make very fine distinctions between colors. (See Figure 5.1 for a sample color blindness test.)

—Wood et al., *The World of Psychology*,
5th ed.

Figure 5.1 The Ishihara Test for Red-Green Color Blindness.

If you can't see the two-digit number, you probably have red-green color blindness. This condition is common, especially among males.

1. What is the topic of the whole passage?

Color blindness

2. Underline the sentence that states the main idea in paragraph 1.

_____c_____ **3.** Which of the following statements best expresses the main idea of paragraph 2?

a. Color blindness is related to our genes.
b. The X chromosome in people with normal vision contains more genes for color vision than the X chromosome in people who are color blind.
c. There are differences in color perception among people with normal color perception as well as people who are color blind.
d. Color blindness is an either-or condition: either you have it or you don't.

_____b_____ **4.** The details in paragraph 1:

a. Explain what causes color blindness.
b. Compare the frequency of color blindness in males and females.
c. Provide examples of what the world looks like to a person who is color blind.

_____a_____ **5.** In paragraph 2, the details:

a. Explain why some people can distinguish color differences better than others.

    b. Provide evidence to support the claim that it's hard to tell who really is color blind.

    c. Provide examples of several tasks in which color recognition is important.

_b_   **6.** The main idea of the whole passage is that:

    a. Most people are color blind to some extent.

    b. Color blindness is the inability to distinguish certain colors, and can vary in degree.

    c. People who are color blind do not see the world in black and white.

    d. Everyone is color blind to some extent, but some people are more color blind than others.

Vocabulary in Context

_b_   **7.** Color *perception* is:

    a. Color blindness

    b. Color recognition

    c. The ability to use colors artistically

C. We live at a turning point. Beginning in 2008 or 2009, for the first time in human history, more people are living in urban areas than in rural areas. This shift from the countryside into towns and cities, or *urbanization*, is arguably the single greatest change our society has undergone since its transition from a nomadic hunter-gatherer lifestyle to a sedentary agricultural one. As we design our new urban-centered world, and as human population and resource consumption increase, the ways we apportion land for different uses and the ways we manage natural resources take on increasing importance.

Urban areas are sinks for resources and cannot function without a steady supply of goods and raw materials from source areas beyond their borders. Cities and suburbs depend on the food and fiber that agricultural lands supply. They rely on mineral resources from land where minerals are extracted. They need timber and other forest products from land where forests are managed. And as we manage these types of lands and the extraction of resources from them, we also require that some land be left undeveloped, so that natural ecosystems continue to function, providing vital ecosystem services, homes for wildlife, and areas of wilderness.

—Withgott and Brennan, *Essential Environment: The Science Behind the Stories,* 2nd ed.

1. What is the topic of the whole passage?

   Urbanization and natural resources

_c_   **2.** Which of the following statements best expresses the main idea of paragraph 1?

    a. We live at an important time.

    b. Urbanization is the movement of people from the countryside into cities and towns.

    c. The increase in urbanization requires us to think more carefully about how we use land and natural resources.

    d. More people live in cities than ever before.

_____b_____ **3.** The details in the first paragraph:

  a. Provide examples of better ways to use land.

  b. Explain why land use and resource management are taking on increasing importance.

  c. Explain why more people are living in cities.

_____b_____ **4.** Which of the following statements best expresses the main idea of paragraph 2?

  a. Urban areas are sinks for resources.

  b. While urban areas need to draw on resources from beyond their borders, we must also protect and conserve some land in order to sustain natural ecosystems.

  c. Cities need minerals from the areas where minerals are obtained, and timber and wood products from forested land.

  d. Cities are threats to the future of wildlife.

_____a_____ **5.** In paragraph 2, the details:

  a. Provide examples of the kinds of resources cities need to import.

  b. Explain what will happen if we don't manage resources carefully.

  c. Provide evidence of the claim that cities cannot function without a steady supply of goods and raw materials from outside areas.

_____c_____ **6.** Which of the following statements best expresses the main idea of the whole passage?

  a. Urbanization is the most important change in society's history.

  b. Cities and suburbs depend upon natural resources from surrounding regions.

  c. With urbanization, careful management of natural resources and preservation of natural ecosystems have become especially important.

  d. Natural ecosystems will vanish soon if we don't protect them.

Vocabulary in Context:

_____a_____ **7.** When society undergoes a *transition*:

  a. Society changes

  b. Society stays the same

  c. Society is destroyed and disappears

_____a_____ **8.** A change from a *nomadic* hunter-gatherer lifestyle to a *sedentary* agricultural one is a change from:

  a. Moving to find food to staying in one place to farm.

  b. Staying in one place to farm to moving to hunt.

  c. Hunting in the same place to moving about to herd animals.

_____c_____ **9.** The ways we *apportion* land for different use are the ways we:

  a. Sell the land to different buyers.

  b. Destroy the land and make it unfit for further use.

  c. Distribute or assign the land for different purposes.

<u> b </u> **10.** When minerals are *extracted* from land they are:

        a. Added to the land.

        b. Taken from the land.

        c. Studied within the land.

SKILLS ONLINE: WORKING WITH PARAGRAPHS

Directions: Find one paragraph with a stated main idea and one paragraph with an implied main idea from any online reading(s). Print out both paragraphs, remembering to include the URLs from your sources.

1. The paragraph with the stated main idea must contain at least four sentences. On the back of the sheet or on a separate sheet, make a diagram of the paragraph's main idea and supporting details. Below your diagram, briefly explain the purpose of the supporting details.

2. The paragraph with the implied main idea must contain at least three sentences. Under the paragraph, write the topic and the main idea. Remember to express the topic in a short phrase (two to six words) and to express the main idea in a complete sentence.

READING 5A

2008: AN ELECTION ABOUT CHANGE (GOVERNMENT)

by George C. Edwards et al.

Reading 5A is taken from a chapter in an American Government textbook on campaigns and voting behavior. The passage discusses the historic election in 2008 of Barack Obama, forty-fourth president of the United States.

Pre-Reading Exercise

Directions: Complete this exercise before reading the passage. Preview the passage and answer the following questions.

1. What is the passage about?

   The presidential election of 2008

2. Who was Obama's opponent in the election?

   John McCain

3. Name two other politicians who are mentioned in the passage.

   (Any two) Williams Jennings Bryan, Hillary Clinton, Sarah Palin, George W. Bush

4. Did you follow the 2008 campaign and election? What do you remember about the campaign and election?
   Answers will vary.

5. What have you previously read or learned about the election and President Obama?
   Answers will vary.

6. Write three questions about the election of 2008 or about President Obama.
   Answers will vary.

Directions: While reading, pause after each paragraph to identify its main idea. If the paragraph has a stated main idea, underline it. If the main idea is implied, infer it from the paragraph and state it in a complete sentence. Use context, the dictionary, and word structure clues to determine the meanings of unfamiliar words.

See Instructor's Manual for implied main ideas.

1   Late in the 2008 presidential campaign, Barack Obama told a crowd of supporters in Detroit that, "You couldn't have written a novel with all the crazy stuff that has happened in this election." Indeed, Obama's rise from an obscure Illinois state senator in 2004 to the nation's first successful African-American candidate for president in 2008 was truly incredible.

2   Like the great 19th century orator, William Jennings Bryan, Barack Obama was catapulted to national prominence as the result of a debut speech that electrified the Democratic Convention. Most notable in Obama's nationally televised address in 2004 was when he said:

> There is not a liberal America and a conservative America—there is the United States of America. There is not a Black America and a White America and Latino America and Asian America—there is the United States of America. The pundits like to slice-and-dice our country into Red States and Blue States; Red States for Republicans, Blue States for Democrats. But I've got news for them, too. We worship an "awesome God" in the Blue States, and we don't like federal agents poking around in our libraries in the Red States. We coach Little League in the Blue States and yes, we've got some gay friends in the Red States. There are patriots who opposed the war in Iraq and there are patriots who supported the war in Iraq. We are one people, all of us pledging allegiance to the stars and stripes, all of us defending the United States of America.

With this message of unity and multi-culturalism, Obama was viewed as a rising star and potential presidential candidate from his first day as a U.S. Senator in 2005. Within two years he had two books on the best-seller list—an autobiography entitled *Dreams from My Father* and a collection of policy proposals entitled *The Audacity of Hope*.

3   By the time Obama declared his presidential candidacy in February 2007, he had built a national constituency and established himself as the primary alternative to the front-runner, Senator Hillary Clinton. On a cold day in Springfield, Illinois, he proclaimed that, "I recognize there is a certain presumptuousness—a certain audacity—to this announcement. I know I haven't

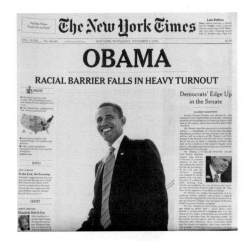

Newsstands from New York to Seattle quickly sold out of newspapers declaring Barack Obama the nation's first African-American president, as some jubilant customers picked up multiple copies as keepsakes. The *New York Times* and the *Chicago Tribune* in Obama's hometown were among papers that restarted their printing presses to produce additional copies across the country.

spent a lot of time learning the ways of Washington. But I've been there long enough to know that the ways of Washington must change." Indeed, his call for change resonated slightly more effectively than Clinton's emphasis on experience in the Democratic primaries. With strong support from young people, the highly educated, and African-Americans, Obama eked out one of the closest nomination victories ever, as he and Senator Clinton contested all 50 states from January to June.

4   In contrast, the Republican presidential nomination was wrapped up faster and more decisively by Senator John McCain. Nevertheless, he too seemed to be an improbable nominee, having long been viewed with suspicion by the party's conservative base. But in 2008, when even many Republicans wanted change, his reputation as a maverick (someone who thinks independently and doesn't always toe the party line) had special appeal. And when he surprised everyone with his historic choice of the first Republican woman to be nominated for vice president—Alaska's little-known Governor Sarah Palin—he energized the party's base and took a short-lived lead in the polls.

2008

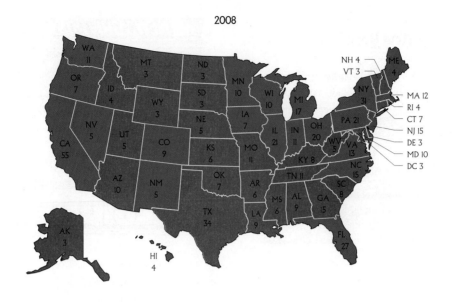

2004

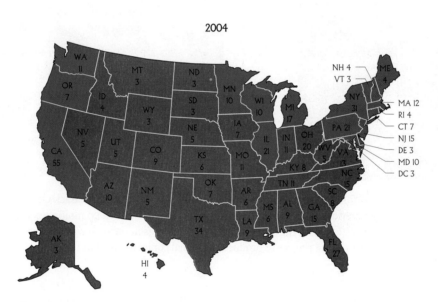

Figure 5A.1 The Electoral College Results for 2004 and 2008

These two maps show the number of votes each state had in the electoral college in 2004 and 2008 and which states were carried by the Democrats (blue) and Republicans (red).

5   As the Fall campaign began, the race seemed to be shaping up as a close battle between Obama's perceived advantages on economic issues and personal intelligence versus McCain's perceived advantages on foreign policy issues and political experience. But then the nation's agenda changed dramatically as a credit crisis rocked the financial markets in late September. McCain took an aggressive approach, even suspending his campaign in order to try to stitch together a congressional coalition to address the crisis. Obama, on the other hand, approached the situation coolly, noting that the campaign should go on as presidents have to work on multiple things all the time. When McCain's fellow Republicans in the House of Representatives voted against the financial bailout bill that both candidates had endorsed, his leadership image clearly suffered. Furthermore, the intense focus on the economy for the rest of the campaign provided Obama with opportunities

to emphasize his popular plans for a middle-class tax cut, extension of health care coverage, and programs to support education.

6   Obama also gained ground on McCain as voters compared the choices for vice president. Although Sarah Palin proved to be an effective stump speaker, her one-on-one interviews with the anchors of ABC and CBS News revealed apparent gaps in her knowledge of policies in the view of many observers. By election day, exit polls found that just 38 percent of voters thought she was qualified to assume the presidency compared to 66 percent for Democratic vice presidential nominee Joe Biden.

7   Most importantly, Obama was able to inextricably link McCain to President George W. Bush, whose 70 percent disapproval rating was the worst ever recorded. In their final televised debate, McCain looked right at Obama and said, "I'm not George Bush. If you wanted to run against President Bush, you should have run four years ago." In turn, the Obama campaign responded with a powerful ad that tied the two together by

showing a clip in which McCain acknowledged he had voted with President Bush 90 percent of the time.

8   The people's verdict in 2008 was that it was time for a change in Washington. Obama carried 53 percent of the popular vote compared to 46 percent for McCain and 1 percent for third party candidates. As shown in Figure 5A.1, this translated into a 365–173 margin in the electoral college, with the Democrats winning 9 states they had lost in 2004—Florida, Ohio, Indiana, Iowa, New Mexico, Colorado, Nevada, North Carolina, and Virginia.

9   The results of the 2008 election show how important it is to understand how the electoral college works. In presidential elections, once voters make their decisions it is not just a simple matter of counting the ballots to see who has won the most support nationwide. Instead, the complicated process of determining electoral college votes begins.

—Edwards et al., *Government in America: People, Politics, and Policy,* 10th ed.

You, the Reader

Interest Rating. Please rate the interest level of the reading on the following scale (circle one):

    5—Very interesting   2—A little boring

    4—Fairly interesting   1—Very boring

    3—Mildly interesting

Difficulty Rating. Please rate the difficulty level of the reading on the following scale (circle one):

    5—Very difficult   2—Fairly easy

    4—Fairly difficult   1—Very easy

    3—Moderate

Comments: Please explain your ratings and make any other comments you wish about the reading.

Answers will vary.

COMPREHENSION QUESTIONS

PART I. MAIN IDEAS AND SUPPORTING DETAILS

   c   **1.** The main idea of the first paragraph is:
  a. Obama was surprised to win the election.
  b. In 2004, Obama had been an obscure senator from Illinois.
  c. Obama's success in the election is a remarkable story.
  d. No one thought an African American could become president.

   b   **2.** The main idea of paragraph 3 is:
  a. Hillary Clinton was the front-runner in the Democratic primary.
  b. Obama's message and support base enabled him to overcome Clinton's lead and win the Democratic nomination by a small margin.
  c. Obama had the support of young people and the highly educated.
  d. Clinton's emphasis on experience did not appeal to the Democratic voters.

   a   **3.** The supporting details in paragraph 4 provide:
  a. Reasons for McCain's campaign successes.
  b. Evidence of McCain's popularity and leadership qualities.
  c. Examples of McCain's campaign ads and slogans.

   a   **4.** The details in paragraph 5 provide:
  a. Reasons why Obama won the election.
  b. Evidence of Obama's popularity with young and educated voters.
  c. Examples of Obama's campaign ads and slogans.

   a   **5.** Which sentence states the main idea of paragraph 6?
  a. The first sentence
  b. The second sentence
  c. The last sentence

PART II. PASSAGE COMPREHENSION

Directions: For questions 1–5, choose the answer that best completes the statement. For questions 6–10, write your response in the space provided. Base all answers on what you read in the selection. Refer back to the selection as necessary to answer the questions.

   b   **1.** The authors compare Obama with William Jennings Bryan because:
  a. Both were the most famous African American politicians of their time.
  b. Both were skilled speakers who achieved fame through their speeches.
  c. Both were elected president because they could inspire people with their speeches.
  d. Both promoted a message of unity and multiculturalism that inspired the nation.

_____a_____ **2.** The authors suggest that Obama's success in the primary and the national election was largely due to:
  a. His message of change.
  b. His opponents' failure to take advantage of his mistakes.
  c. His being an African American.
  d. The media favoring him over his opponents.

_____b_____ **3.** The authors suggest that one important reason why McCain lost the election was:
  a. His age.
  b. Obama's success in linking him with George W. Bush.
  c. His reputation as a maverick.
  d. His foreign policy experience.

_____a_____ **4.** Which of the following states were carried by the Republican candidate in 2004 and the Democratic candidate in 2008?
  a. Ohio and Colorado
  b. Nevada and Utah
  c. New Mexico and Missouri
  d. Indiana and Illinois

_____d_____ **5.** Which of the following is *not* identified in the passage as a factor in Obama's political success?
  a. His authorship of two books
  b. His running mate
  c. The nation's financial crisis
  d. His foreign policy experience

6. Reread the quote in paragraph 2 from Obama's 2004 speech. What is the main point of his speech?

There is only one America, and we are one people. (sample answer)

7. What were John McCain's chief strengths as a presidential candidate?

Foreign policy expertise; political experience

8. Why did voters ultimately prefer Joe Biden over Sarah Palin for vice president?

Palin's interviews revealed gaps in her knowledge of policies; voters viewed

Biden as more qualified.

9. Name three states that voted for the Democratic presidential candidate in both 2004 and 2008.

See Figure 5A.1. (any blue state in 2004)

10. In your opinion, why did Obama win the election?

Answers will vary.

VOCABULARY EXERCISES

Pronunciation Guide (see p. 90 for list of phonetic symbols)

audacity	(ô-dăs'ĭ-tē)
catapulted	(kăt'ə-pŭlt'ĭd)
coalition	(kō'ə-lĭsh'ən)
debut	(də-byōō')
inextricably	(ĭn-ĕk strĭk'ə-blē)
resonated	(rĕz'ə-nāt'ĭd)

WORDS IN CONTEXT

Directions: Choose the meaning for the boldfaced word or phrase that best fits the context.

_c_   **1.** Obama's rise from an **obscure** Illinois state senator in 2004 to the nation's first successful African-American candidate for president . . .
   a. Famous
   b. Unsuccessful
   c. Unknown
   d. Experienced

_a_   **2.** . . . Obama was **catapulted** to national prominence as the result of a debut speech . . .
   a. Moved quickly
   b. Moved slowly
   c. Advised
   d. Prevented from achieving

_b_   **3.** . . . Obama was catapulted to national **prominence** as the result of a debut speech . . .
   a. Government
   b. Fame; importance
   c. Movement
   d. Argument

_d_   **4.** Indeed, his call for change **resonated** slightly more effectively than Clinton's emphasis on experience in the Democratic primaries.
   a. Recovered
   b. Caused disagreement
   c. Inspired curiosity
   d. Related well; struck a chord

_b_   **5.** . . . Obama **eked out** one of the closest nomination victories ever . . .
   a. Won by a large amount
   b. Won by a small amount
   c. Lost by a small amount
   d. Overcame

CONTEXT AND DICTIONARY

Directions: Use context and the dictionary to determine the meaning of the boldfaced word in each sentence. Use word structure clues when applicable.

1. . . . Obama was catapulted to national prominence as the result of a **debut** speech . . .

   First (before a national audience, in this context) public appearance

2. . . . "I recognize that there is a certain presumptuousness—a certain **audacity**— to this announcement."

   Boldness; daring

3. But in 2008, when even many Republicans wanted change, his reputation as a **maverick** (someone who thinks independently and doesn't always toe the party line) had special appeal.

   Someone who thinks independently and doesn't always toe the party line

4. . . . suspending his campaign . . . to stitch together a congressional **coalition** to address the crisis.

   Group including diverse factions

5. . . . Obama was able to **inextricably** link McCain to President George W. Bush . . .

   Not able to release or disconnect from

RESPOND TO THE READING

Directions: Write a half-page response to either of the following questions.

1. Has President Obama fulfilled his campaign promise to bring change to our country and government? Discuss and explain.

2. What are the qualities of a great president? Name one or two of your favorite presidents and explain why you admire them.

WEBQUEST

Directions: Use the Internet to find the answers to the following questions. Write your answers on a sheet of paper. Print out the Web page you used for the answers or copy the URL on your sheet.

Who was William Jennings Bryan? When did he live? For what is he most famous?

NEW WAYS TO STOP CRIME
(CRIMINAL JUSTICE)

by David Baldacci

David Baldacci is a popular fiction writer who has written several best-selling thrillers. In this article he writes about Cathy Lanier, the chief of police in Washington, D.C. The article discusses Lanier's personal and career path and her work as police chief. Read the article to learn more about this unusual woman and her approach to policing.

Pre-Reading Exercise

Directions: Complete this exercise before reading the passage. Preview the passage and answer the following questions.

1. What is the passage about?

   Cathy Lanier and her approach to stopping crime

2. What is unusual about Lanier's career?

   She is D.C.'s first female police chief. (sample answer)

3. From previewing the article, what can you tell about Lanier's approach to fighting crime?

   She believes police forces must be proactive; she wants to be accessible to the

   community. (sample answer)

4. What have you previously read or learned about women police officers?

   Answers will vary.

5. Do you think women can be as effective as men at police work? Why or why not?

   Answers will vary.

6. Write three questions about the Cathy Lanier or about stopping crime.

   Answers will vary.

Directions: While reading, pause after each paragraph to identify its main idea. If the paragraph has a stated main idea, underline it. If the main idea is implied, infer it from the paragraph and state it in a complete sentence. Use context, the dictionary, and word structure clues to determine the meanings of unfamiliar words.

See Instructor's Manual for implied main ideas.

1   As chief of police in Washington, D.C., Cathy L. Lanier never has the luxury of easing into the day. Her mornings begin with a jolt at 5 a.m., when the BlackBerry messages start arriving from Joe Persichini, assistant director of the FBI's D.C. field office. These urgent missives cover terrorism, joint-task-force missions, and current national-security intelligence. Lanier's schedule

is punishing, to say the least. And thanks to her discipline and commitment, the 42-year-old has attracted national attention as one of the most successful big-city police chiefs in America.

2   For much of the last decade, D.C. had one of the highest murder rates among America's large cities. However, as of mid-July, its homicide rate is 14% lower than at this time last year, putting the city on track to have one of its lowest murder rates in years. During Lanier's two and a half years on the job as top cop, other categories of major crime have fallen as well, and the force's closure rate on homicides in 2008 was the highest on department record.

3   Lanier is D.C.'s first female police chief—a white woman in a police department that is mostly male in a city that is mostly black. She says simply, "To be able to lead other officers takes credibility and trust." Those are qualities that she has built up in 19 years on the force.

4   Her early life did not portend such achievement. She grew up with two brothers in a Maryland suburb. She got pregnant at 14, dropping out of school after ninth grade to have a son and marry the father. By 18, she was divorced. Instead of continuing on a downward spiral, Lanier got a GED and enrolled in college. She joined the police force, partly because of its tuition-reimbursement program, and became an officer at 23. While working full time, she earned undergraduate and master's degrees from Johns Hopkins University. She holds another master's from the Naval Postgraduate School and is also a graduate of the FBI Academy.

5   Lanier's first on-the-job experience of violence came when, on patrol with a partner, she confronted five large men with pockets full of drugs. She was punched in the face and had to hold her own in a fight until backup arrived. "I got my butt kicked," she says without a trace of bruised ego. In another episode, a domestic-violence call had her charging to the aid of a woman who had been severely injured by her deranged companion. Lanier was within seconds of shooting the man before officers came to assist her. In 19 years on the force, she has fired her gun only once—at two attacking pit bulls.

6   Then, as a young officer, Lanier made a potentially bridge-burning move. After being

Under Lanier, cops are part of the community not the opposition.

sexually harassed by a superior who went unpunished, she (and another female colleague) sued the very police department that she now heads.

7   "In the early 1990s, there was a different culture in the department than there is today," Lanier explains. "Back then, the culture dictated that it was okay to make explicit sexual comments and have inappropriate contact with female officers. I brought a lawsuit with the goal of changing that culture and hopefully helping others going through the same thing." Although the superior denied wrongdoing, Lanier and her fellow officer received $75,000 each in a settlement of the case. Today, the D.C. police force is approximately 25% female.

8   Broad-shouldered and 6 feet tall, Lanier cuts an imposing figure. She is known for speaking bluntly. At a recent press conference held after a bloody Fourth of July weekend in which six people were shot to death in D.C., she warned the killers: "We're out looking, and if we don't have you yet, we will have you very soon."

9   Lanier's crime-fighting philosophy is based on the principle that today's police forces must be proactive rather than reactive. "We can no longer

wait for crime to come to us but need to look at the history and the trends and project from there."

10   Lanier uses real-time statistics to figure out how and where to allocate officers. "In D.C.," she explains, "3% of the addresses account for 50% of the violent crime. We use sophisticated formulas gleaned from arrest records to identify potential offenders." She and her officers track these MVPs (most violent persons) and make sure they know the cops are watching.

11   People have disagreed with some of Lanier's tactics. She has used curfews and surveillance cameras in high-crime areas and initiated new search-and-seizure methods to get guns off the street. After a burst of fatal shootings in the Trinidad section in May 2008, Lanier instituted five days of checkpoints so that any driver wishing to enter the area was stopped by officers.

12   Arthur Spitzer, legal director for the ACLU's Washington office, denounced it as "Baghdad, D.C." Mary Cheh, a City Council member and law professor at George Washington University, called it "outrageous."

13   Lanier counters, "While scholars of constitutional law pick our activities and methods apart,

> "We can't wait for crime to come to us," Lanier says.

I have personally heard from citizens who are grateful for our presence and actually ask us to use checkpoints and curfews in their neighborhoods. I once heard an analogy comparing the checkpoints to airport security: Although it was a little inconvenient, it saved lives."

14   Another initiative that has drawn some controversy is called All Hands on Deck. Over a weekend, every available police officer—from rookie to detective—is on duty and on patrol, saturating the city. Lanier intends this periodic program to serve as part anti-crime sweep, part get-to-know-your-local-police event. "It's important that officers interact with citizens," Lanier says. "That way they're seen as part of the community and not the opposition." While it's hard to assess if community relations have improved, in two weekends this spring, the police made 887 arrests and seized thousands of dollars in drugs.

15   Being accessible to D.C. residents is one of Lanier's top priorities. She gives her business card to everyone she meets and her private cellphone number to anyone who asks. Last July, she was lying in bed on a brutally hot night when she received a call from a mother of seven who lived in one of the city's poorest areas. They were roasting to death, the woman told Lanier, because the building had no air conditioning. Lanier bought the woman an AC unit and delivered it herself. Yet, she says, "I still felt guilty that eight people were huddled in one room to escape 100-degree heat."

16   Of course, she must always be available for the district's most important resident, President Barack Obama. Her police department assists the U.S. Secret Service in providing his protection. For the inauguration in January, Lanier meticulously mapped out the miles-long parade route and the entire National Mall in square-foot increments to make sure that there was adequate security coverage. Whenever the President goes for a ride, she must supply major manpower. "When he wants to go from the White House to the National Cathedral, which is less than three miles, it takes 150 officers on duty, plus a standing force at the destination," she says. "I have to pull those bodies from somewhere. It makes crime planning a real challenge."

17   Despite her elevated title, Lanier is still very much a beat cop at heart. She regularly attends morning roll calls, rotating among D.C.'s seven police districts so that officers can see and talk to her. She monitors radio calls from her car—Cruiser One—so she can hear how her people are responding. A cop recently wounded on duty found Chief Lanier sitting next to him in the ambulance on the ride to the hospital. She has also created a website that officers can use to contact her directly. She says, "It's so they can reach me with no buffer."

18   Officer Raymond Hawkins patrols D.C.'s Fifth District. Of Lanier, he says, "She's pushed a scout car just like I do. She knows what it's like to walk the pavement. She hears crime stats all day long, but what she really wants to know is, How's it going on your beat? She's very approachable. But if you go to her with a problem, you'd better have a solution, too. She'll give you resources if

you have an answer she thinks will work, but having no solution is unacceptable to her."

19   Chief Lanier credits her success to the love and support of her mother, herself a single parent. "My mother could have given up on me when I didn't make the decisions that everyone else thought I should, but she didn't, and that's when I learned that compassion, understanding, and patience would be the most important characteristics that I employed in my chosen profession. My greatest strength as a police officer is my ability to relate to anyone, no matter their background."

20   Lanier feels that her unconventional history helps her identify with the city residents whom she's trying to keep safe. "Being a single mom at age 15 and also a high school dropout, it teaches you things about life that no other experience can. I could have easily gone down the wrong path. I know that a single positive mentor in someone's life can make all the difference."

21   She adds, "The best thing we can do sometimes as police officers is get out of our cruisers and throw the ball with kids, let them wear our hats, or just give them a hug. It's often as simple as that."

—Baldacci, "New Ways to Stop Crime,"
Parade Magazine

You, the Reader

Interest Rating. Please rate the interest level of the reading on the following scale (circle one):

5—Very interesting   2—A little boring

4—Fairly interesting   1—Very boring

3—Mildly interesting

Difficulty Rating. Please rate the difficulty level of the reading on the following scale (circle one):

5—Very difficult   2—Fairly easy

4—Fairly difficult   1—Very easy

3—Moderate

Comments: Please explain your ratings and make any other comments you wish about the reading.

Answers will vary.

COMPREHENSION QUESTIONS

PART I. MAIN IDEAS AND SUPPORTING DETAILS

____b____ **1.** The main idea of the first paragraph is:
  a. Cathy Lanier is the chief of police in Washington, D.C.
  b. Cathy Lanier is the busy and successful chief of police in Washington, D.C.
  c. Cathy Lanier has an unusual job.
  d. Cathy Lanier begins her day at 5 a.m. when she starts getting messages from the FBI.

___c___   **2.** The supporting details in paragraph 2 provide:
  a. Reasons why Washington, D.C. has high crime rates.
  b. Examples of the strategies Lanier has used to reduce crime.
  c. Evidence of Lanier's success in reducing crime in Washington, D.C.

___c___   **3.** The main idea of paragraph 4 is:
  a. Cathy Lanier dropped out of school after becoming pregnant at 14.
  b. Cathy Lanier obtained a GED and then went to college.
  c. Cathy Lanier overcame early life problems to become a successful policewoman with an extensive education.
  d. Cathy Lanier has earned two master's degrees and is a graduate of the FBI Academy.

___b___   **4.** The supporting details in paragraph 11 provide:
  a. Evidence of the effectiveness of Lanier's tactics.
  b. Examples of Lanier's controversial tactics.
  c. Explanations of why people disagree with some of Lanier's tactics.

___a___   **5.** Which sentence states the main idea of paragraph 15?
  a. The first sentence
  b. The second sentence
  c. The last sentence

PART II. PASSAGE COMPREHENSION

Directions: For questions 1–5, choose the answer that best completes the statement. For questions 6–10, write your response in the space provided. Base all answers on what you read in the selection. Refer back to the selection as necessary to answer the questions.

___b___   **1.** In the 1990s, Lanier helped changed the culture of her police department by:
  a. Becoming the first woman chief of police.
  b. Bringing a lawsuit to fight sexual harassment.
  c. Almost shooting a man in a domestic violence case.
  d. Fighting with a male officer.

___a___   **2.** Lanier's approach to police work includes all of the following *except*:
  a. A refusal to discuss her tactics with the community and its leaders.
  b. A police force that is proactive rather than reactive.
  c. Working with the community.
  d. The use of statistics to determine how and where to allocate officers.

___d___   **3.** What was Lanier's response to Spitzer's and Cheh's criticism of her tactics?
  a. She did not respond to their criticisms
  b. She agreed with their criticisms and changed her tactics
  c. She accused her critics of being soft on crime
  d. She said that citizens supported the curfews and checkpoints

___c___   **4.** For Obama's inauguration, Lanier:
  a. Rode in the President's car to protect him.
  b. Provided the President with bodyguards from her staff.

    c. Mapped out the parade route to make sure that security was adequate.

    d. Advised the President and his staff regarding their choice of routes and vehicles.

_b_   **5.** We can tell from the passage that Lanier:

    a. Blames her mother for her early life problems.

    b. Can still identify with her beat cops.

    c. Does not really want to be chief of police.

    d. Has difficulty identifying with the city residents.

6. List some of the problems that Lanier faced in her early life.

She got pregnant at 14 and dropped out of school to have the baby and

marry the father. She was divorced by 18.

7. Describe Lanier's first on-the-job experience of violence.

She was on patrol with a partner and confronted five large men with pockets

full of drugs. She was punched in the face and had to fight until backup

arrived.

8. What is Lanier's All Hands on Deck initiative?

On some weekends, all available officers are on duty and on patrol. She

intends this as an anti-crime initiative and an attempt to improve community

relations.

9. How has Lanier's personal history helped her to understand and identify with Washington's residents?

Being a young single mom and a high school dropout has helped her

understand what it's like to face serious problems and need some guidance.

10. Do you agree with Lanier's use of curfews and checkpoints to control crime? Why or why not?

Answers will vary.

Vocabulary Exercises

Pronunciation Guide (see p. 90 for list of phonetic symbols)

allocate	(ăl'ə-kāt')
initiated	(ĭ-nĭsh'ē-āt'ĭd)
meticulously	(mĭ-tĭk'yə-ləs-lē)
periodic	(pĭr'ē-ŏd'ĭk)
proactive	(prō-ăk'tĭv)
saturating	(săch'ə-rāt'ĭng)

WORDS IN CONTEXT

Directions: Choose the meaning for the boldfaced word or phrase that best fits the context.

___a___ **1.** Broad-shouldered and 6 feet tall, Lanier cuts an **imposing** figure.
   a. Impressive
   b. Hard to notice
   c. Curvy
   d. Typical

___b___ **2.** Lanier's crime-fighting philosophy is based on the principle that today's police forces must be **proactive** rather than reactive.
   a. Looking back; reacting to what is happening
   b. Looking ahead; anticipating what might happen
   c. Using methods from the past
   d. Available

___d___ **3.** Lanier uses real-time statistics to figure out how and where to **allocate** officers.
   a. Train
   b. Criticize
   c. Study
   d. Place

___a___ **4.** She has . . . **initiated** new search-and-seize methods to get guns off the street.
   a. Introduced; put into practice
   b. Ended, stopped
   c. Copied or borrowed from another organization
   d. Reviewed

___c___ **5.** For the inauguration in January, Lanier **meticulously** mapped out the miles-long parade route and the entire National Mall . . . to make sure that there was adequate security coverage.
   a. Quickly
   b. Cooperatively; with help from others
   c. Carefully
   d. Easily

CONTEXT AND DICTIONARY

Directions: Use context and the dictionary to determine the meaning of the boldfaced word in each sentence. Use word structure clues when applicable.

1. These urgent **missives** cover terrorism, joint-task-force missions, and current national security intelligence.

Messages; communications

2. Back then, the culture dictated that it was okay to make **explicit** sexual comments and have inappropriate contact with female officers.

   Fully and clearly expressed; direct; definite

3. Arthur Spitzer, legal director for the ACLU's Washington office, **denounced** it as "Baghdad, D.C." Mary Cheh, a City Council member and law professor at George Washington University, called it "outrageous."

   Criticized; condemned

4. "I once heard an **analogy** comparing the checkpoints to airport security."

   Comparison

5. Another initiative that has drawn some **controversy** is called All Hands on Deck.

   Disagreement; debate; argument

6. Over a weekend, every available police officer . . . is on duty and on patrol, **saturating** the city.

   Filling

7. Lanier intends this **periodic** program to serve as part anti-crime sweep, part get-to-know-your-local-police event.

   Occasional; occurring from time to time

RESPOND TO THE READING

Directions: Write a half-page response to either of the following questions.

1. What makes Cathy Lanier a good police chief and policewoman? What do you most admire about her?

2. What do you think are the most effective ways for the police to control and prevent crime in the communities they serve?

WEBQUEST

Directions: Use the Internet to find the answers to the following questions. Write your answers on a sheet of paper. Print out the Web pages you used for the answers or copy the URLs on your sheet.

1. Approximately how many people are murdered in the United States each year?

2. Which state has the highest murder rate?

CHAPTER 5 REVIEW

Purposes of Supporting Details

Active readers identify the purpose of supporting details in paragraphs. Three common purposes of supporting details are to provide *examples*, *evidence*, or *reasons*.

Examples are specific instances (people, places, things, etc.) that illustrate the main idea.	*Evidence* is information, often number facts or research, that supports a claim stated in the main idea.	*Reasons* are explanations of the main idea, telling why something happened or why the main idea is true.

Outlining and Diagramming Paragraphs

Outlining or *diagramming a paragraph* is a useful strategy that helps clarify the relationship between the main idea and the paragraph's supporting details.

Create an *informal paragraph outline* by placing the main idea at the top of the outline and indenting the supporting details under it.	Create a *paragraph diagram* or *map* by placing the main idea in a rectangular block at the top of the diagram and placing the supporting details in blocks under it. Draw lines to connect the details to the main idea.

Implied Main Ideas

In some paragraphs, the main idea is *implied* rather than stated. Determine the main idea of this type of paragraph by first identifying the topic and then identifying the general point about the topic implied by the paragraph's details. Always express the main idea in a complete sentence.

Skills Online: Working with Paragraphs

Readings

Reading 5A: 2008: An Election about Change (Government)	Reading 5B: Who Are the Police? (Criminal Justice)

CHAPTER TESTS

TEST 5.1. SUPPORTING DETAILS

Directions: Each pair of sentences below consists of a main idea and a supporting detail. Identify the purpose of the supporting detail by writing Example, Evidence, or Reason on the line below the detail and briefly explain your answer.

1. *Main Idea:* Felonies are serious crimes.

   Supporting Detail: They include murder, rape, aggravated assault, robbery, burglary, and arson.

   —Schmalleger, *Criminal Justice: A Brief Introduction,* 7th ed.

   Example: The detail lists examples of serious crimes.

   _____

2. *Main Idea:* The use of tobacco products is costly to all of us in terms of lost productivity and lost lives.

   Supporting Detail: Estimates show that tobacco use causes over $167 billion in annual health-related economic losses.

   —Donatelle, *Health: The Basics,* 8th ed.

   Evidence: The detail gives evidence—a dollar amount—of health-related costs

   associated with tobacco use.

3. *Main Idea:* We may purposely mislead others by using nonverbal cues to create false impressions or to convey incorrect information.

   Supporting Detail: Among the most common of such deceiving nonverbal behaviors is the poker face that some use when playing cards.

   —Seiler and Beall, *Communication: Making Connections,* 4th ed.

   Example: The detail gives an example (the poker face) of a deliberately

   misleading nonverbal use.

4. *Main Idea:* The American people have a tremendous appetite for magazines.

   Supporting Detail: According to magazine industry studies, almost 90 percent of U.S. adults read an average ten issues a month.

   —Vivian, *The Media of Mass Communication,* 9th ed.

   Evidence: The detail provides statistical evidence of U.S. magazine readership.

   _____

5. *Main Idea:* The American colonists rejected a system with a strong ruler, as in the British monarchy, as soon as they declared their independence.

   Supporting Detail: Many of the colonists had fled Great Britain to avoid religious persecution and other harsh manifestations of power wielded by King George II.

   —O'Connor and Sabato, *American Government: Continuity and Change,* 2006 ed.

   Reason: The detail gives a reason why colonists rejected a system with a

   strong ruler.

TEST 5.2. OUTLINING AND DIAGRAMMING PARAGRAPHS

Directions: On a separate sheet of paper, make an outline or diagram of the main idea and supporting details in the following paragraph. Then briefly explain the purpose of the paragraph's supporting details.

Short-term memory (STM) holds the information that we are thinking about or are aware of at any given moment. When you listen to a conversation or a song on the radio, when you watch a television show or a football game, when you become aware of a leg cramp or a headache—in all these cases, you are using STM both to hold onto and to think about new information coming in from the sensory registers. Short-term memory has two primary tasks: to store new information briefly and to work on that (and other) information. Short-term memory is sometimes called *working memory*, to emphasize the active or working component of this memory system.

—Morris and Maisto, *Understanding Psychology*, 8th ed.

TEST 5.3. IMPLIED MAIN IDEAS

Directions: Read each paragraph and answer the questions that follow it. Remember that the main idea must be expressed in a complete sentence.

1. How significant is the Internet as a mass medium? Estimates are that the number of users in the United States is well past 200 million—75 percent of the population. In only a few years the Internet has become a major medium for advertising. In 2005 advertisers spent $12.9 billion for space on Internet Web sites, up 34 percent from the year before and wholly one-fifth of what was spent on television. More than half of new-car buyers based their choice on information they had found on the Internet.

—Vivian, *The Media of Mass Communication*, 9th ed.

Which of the following best expresses the *topic* of the paragraph?

_____ The importance of the mass media

___✔___ The significance of the Internet

_____ Advertising space on Web sites

___b___ Which of the following best expresses the *implied main idea* of the paragraph?
  a. Growth of the Internet
  b. The Internet has become a very significant mass medium.
  c. Advertisers are now spending more money on the Internet than on television.
  d. More than 200 million Americans use the Internet.

2. In the 1950s, most students came from families with both a mother and a father. In the subsequent fifty years, more and more students have been raised by single mothers and now by a growing number of single fathers. Some students do not live with either parent but stay instead with relatives or in a foster home. As society becomes more tolerant of a variety of family structures and as adults become more open about their sexual orientation, teachers will also be introduced to lesbian and gay parents who may be living with a partner or separated from a partner.

—Johnson et al., *Foundations of American Education*, 14th ed.

Which of the following best expresses the *topic* of the paragraph?

_____ The family

_____ Students with single parents

___✔___ The increasing diversity of students' families

___d___ Which of the following best expresses the *implied main idea* of the paragraph?

    a. Today's teachers face a variety of challenges.

    b. Today's teachers are likely to encounter students whose parents are gay or lesbian.

    c. Diversity among the families of today's schoolchildren

    d. Today's teachers work with students from a wide variety of families.

3. Some evidence suggests that exercise may boost feel-good endorphins, relieve muscle tension, help you sleep, and reduce the stress hormone cortisol. According to the Mayo Clinic, it also increases body temperature, which can have a calming effect. If nothing else, it gives you a break from thinking about the things that are making you depressed or stressed. It may even be helpful just to get out and interact with other people. So, the next time you're having a bad day, go for a walk with friends or work out to your favorite music.

—O'Shea, "Get a Better Mood Fast," *Parade Magazine*

Which of the following best expresses the *topic* of the paragraph?

___✔___ Benefits of exercise

_____ How to be healthy

_____ How exercise affects hormones

___c___ Which of the following best expresses the *implied main idea* of the paragraph?

    a. The benefits of exercising

    b. Exercise causes your body to produce the right amount of hormones.

    c. Exercise helps you feel better.

    d. Exercise is helpful because it gets you to interact with other people.

4. Satellite technology is only one of the ways children access the world. According to the Cellular Telecommunications and Internet Association, cell phone use has skyrocketed from 4.3 million users in the United States in 1990 to 254 million by February 2008. Children and adolescents represent a rapidly growing sector of that market. Internet subscriptions have increased 300% from 18 million subscribers in the mid-1990s to 66.2 million in 2007, with Internet access for almost nine out of every ten children living in a household with a computer and with 30 percent to 40 percent yearly increases in Internet subscribers.

—Osit, *Generation Text*

Which of the following best expresses the *topic* of the paragraph?

_____ Technology

___✔___ Children's increasing use of modern technology

_____ Increasing use of the Internet

___a___ Which of the following best expresses the *implied main idea* of the paragraph?

    a. Today's children are using modern technologies to access the world around them.

    b. Children and today's technology

    c. Cell phone use has skyrocketed in the last twenty years.

    d. Satellite technology allows today's children to make increasing use of the Internet.

5. Edgar Allan Poe's early detective fiction tales starring the fictitious C. Auguste Dupin laid the groundwork for future detectives in literature. Sir Arthur Conan Doyle said, "Each of Poe's detective stories is a root from which a whole literature has developed. . . . Where was the detective story until Poe breathed the breath of life into it?" The Mystery Writers of America have named their awards for excellence in the genre the "Edgars." Poe's work also influenced science fiction, notably Jules Verne, who wrote a sequel to Poe's novel *The Narrative of Arthur Gordon Pym of Nantucket* called *An Antarctic Mystery*, also known as *The Sphinx of the Ice Fields*. Science fiction author H. G. Wells noted, "*Pym* tells what a very intelligent mind could imagine about the south polar region a century ago."

—"Edgar Allan Poe," *Wikipedia*

Which of the following best expresses the *topic* of the paragraph?

_____ Poe's detective fiction

_____ The life of Edgar Allan Poe

___✔___ Poe's literary influence

___c___ Which of the following best expresses the *implied main idea* of the paragraph?

    a. Poe's detective fiction was the start of the modern detective story.

    b. Poe's work influenced the development of science fiction.

    c. Poe's detective stories and science fiction influenced the development of these genres (types of literature).

    d. Poe's importance in the world of literature

TEST 5.4. MAIN IDEAS IN SHORT PASSAGES

Directions: Read the following passage, looking for the main idea and supporting details in each paragraph. Then complete the accompanying exercise.

Even though violence has long been a concern in American society, not until 1985 did the U.S. Public Health Service formally identify violence as a leading public health problem that contributed significantly to death and disability rates. The Centers for Disease Control and Prevention (CDC) created the Division of Violence Prevention and considers violence a chronic disease that is pervasive at all levels of American society. Vulnerable populations, such as children, women, black males, and the elderly, were listed as being at high risk.

Recent numbers indicate that we have made dramatic improvements in certain areas. Since 1973, Federal Bureau of Investigation (FBI) statistics show that overall crime and certain types of violent crime actually have decreased each year. In addition, a recent Department of justice report suggests that colleges and universities are relatively safe. However, many question the accuracy of such reports, since petty theft, date rape, fighting, and other common campus incidents are not always reported to police. Although a person's chances of being murdered or violently assaulted may have declined, the odds of being a victim of burglary, theft, and minor assault in general are on the increase.

Violence affects everyone directly or indirectly. Although the direct victims of violence

and those close to them obviously suffer the most, others suffer in various ways because of the climate of fear that violence generates. Women are afraid to walk alone at night. The elderly are often afraid to go out even in the daytime. Since terrorist episodes such as the 2001 World Trade Center attack, some people are afraid to fly, to work in tall buildings, or to live in heavily populated areas. The cost of homeland security is staggering. International travelers often fear coming to the United States just as Americans fear traveling to other regions of the world where U.S. citizens have been attacked. The news media broadcast stories of children dodging bullets in city neighborhoods or drivers being carjacked. Even people who live in supposedly safe areas can become victims of violence within their own homes or at the hands of family members.

—Donatelle, *Health: The Basics,* 6th ed.

1. What is the topic of the whole passage?

Violence in the U.S.

_a_ **2.** Which of the following statements best expresses the main idea of paragraph 1?
   a. Violence has become a leading public health concern in the United States.
   b. Violence is a chronic disease.
   c. Children, women, black males and the elderly are especially vulnerable to violence.
   d. The government must take steps to reduce violence in the United States.

_c_ **3.** Which of the following statements best expresses the main idea of the second paragraph?
   a. The odds of being a victim of burglary, theft, and minor assault are on the increase.
   b. FBI data shows an annual decrease in certain types of violent crime.
   c. There is evidence that violence is decreasing, but not for all types of crimes.
   d. Violence is increasing for most but not all crimes.

_c_ **4.** In paragraph 2, the details in the second and third sentences:
   a. Explain why violence is decreasing.
   b. Give examples of violent crimes that are increasing.
   c. Provide evidence of the decrease in violent crime.

5. Underline the sentence that states the main in paragraph 3.

_____b_____ **6.** Most of the details in paragraph 3:
   a. Explain why people commit violent acts.
   b. Give examples of how Americans are affected by violence.
   c. Provide evidence of an increase in crime.

_____a_____ **7.** Which of the following statements best expresses the main idea of the whole passage?
   a. Violence is now considered a serious public health concern which may affect everyone.
   b. Americans are more fearful since the terrorist attacks of 9/11.
   c. Violent crime is decreasing in the United States, but the risk of being a crime victim is still high for certain types of crimes.
   d. The government must do more to protect its law-abiding citizens from criminals.

You, the Reader: Chapter 5 Wrap-up

Directions: Use one or two of the following questions to write a half-page response to Chapter 5.

- What were the most important things you learned from this chapter? How will you use what you have learned from this chapter?
- How have you changed your reading habits in response to this chapter?
- Which strategies most help you to engage with paragraph reading? What most helps you to recognize the purpose of supporting details?
- What parts of the chapter did you find most engaging? What questions do you have about the chapter?

PEARSON
myreadinglab

For support in meeting this chapter's objectives, go to MyReadingLab and select *Supporting Details*.

Monitoring and Clarifying Comprehension

LEARNING OBJECTIVES

In Chapter 6 you will learn to:

- Monitor your comprehension while reading
- Use active reading strategies to clarify your comprehension
- Paraphrase an author's ideas

CHAPTER CONTENTS

Making Sense
Active Reading Strategy: Monitoring Comprehension
Anticipating the Text
Using Active Reading Strategies to Clarify and Strengthen Comprehension
Active Reading Strategy: Paraphrasing
When the Going Gets Tough
Skills Online: Monitoring Your Comprehension Online
Reading 6A: *Waking Up to Our Dreams* (Psychology)
Reading 6B: *Nutrition: Eating for Optimum Health* (Health)
Chapter 6 Review
Chapter Tests
    Test 6.1. Monitoring Comprehension
    Test 6.2. Paragraph Sense
    Test 6.3. Clarifying Comprehension
    Test 6.4. Paraphrasing
    Test 6.5. Clarifying Comprehension
You, the Reader: Chapter 6 Wrap-up

Pre-Reading Exercise for Chapter 6

Directions: Preview the chapter and answer the following questions.

1. What is the chapter about?

   Strategies for monitoring and clarifying comprehension

2. What does a reader do when he monitors his comprehension?

   He evaluates how well he understands what he's read.

3. List two strategies for clarifying comprehension.

   Answers will vary; see Table 6.1.

4. What have you previously learned about monitoring or clarifying comprehension?

   Answers will vary.

5. What strategies do you usually employ when you read something that doesn't make sense to you?

   Answers will vary.

6. Write two questions about the content of this chapter.

   Answers will vary.

Active readers do not necessarily understand everything they read. They do know, however, that reading is a communication process, and that the use of active reading strategies will enhance their understanding and memory of what they read. They are also able to recognize when their comprehension is not satisfactory and can identify the reasons for comprehension challenges. They can then use appropriate strategies to clarify and strengthen their understanding.

Making Sense

Monitor means "watch" or "check on"—especially for quality control. Monitoring comprehension involves evaluating how well we understand what we're reading. When we monitor our comprehension, we have an awareness of whether or not what we're reading makes sense to us. It's as if there's a small part of our mind that's watching while we're reading to see if we're "getting it." We can call that part of our mind the monitor. Actually, we have a monitor for a variety of tasks, not just for reading. If you're watching a movie, for example, and something doesn't make sense to you, a part of your mind notices that you just saw something that you didn't understand.

If our monitor is working when we're reading and we understand the material, we say that the material "makes sense." Actually, it's not the material itself that makes sense; it's our minds that are making sense—building the meaning—of what we're reading. Conversely, then, the monitor's job is to recognize when we don't make sense out of what we are reading—in other words, when we're not understanding the material.

Exercises 6.1, 6.2, and 6.3 will put your monitor to work. They will give you practice with material that doesn't make sense because a word or phrase that doesn't belong has been inserted into the sentence or passage. You will practice monitoring your comprehension by looking for the misplaced word or phrase. If you are monitoring successfully, you will be able to identify the words and phrases that don't make sense—don't belong—in the context of the exercise material.

EXERCISE 6.1 SENTENCE SENSE

Directions: Each of the following sentences contains a word that doesn't belong. Cross out the mistakenly placed word so that the sentence makes sense. An example is provided.

EXAMPLE

Tombstones originated as a way of keeping the dead in the underground ~~airport~~.

1. Anthropologists have found evidence that funeral traditions existed ~~winter~~ during the Neanderthal age.

2. Different cultures have ~~never~~ different ways of mourning their dead.

3. Family life in Sparta was severely limited because both boys and girls ~~today~~ spent long hours in physical training.

4. From the ages of seven ~~decades~~ to thirty, boys received instruction in the art of waging war.

5. The Spartans were obedient ~~athletes~~ to the laws of their land.

6. During World War II, German invaders devastated ~~repeated~~ some of Russia's richest agricultural regions.

7. The Russians suffered heavy ~~television~~ losses in World War II.

8. During World War II the war department finally approved the training ~~horror~~ of African American pilots.

9. In 1941 Benjamin O. Davis Jr. became the first ~~incredible~~ African American to lead a squadron of pilots.

10. Heredity plays an important role in the obesity of children ~~singing~~.

EXERCISE 6.2 PARAGRAPH SENSE

Directions: Each paragraph contains a word or phrase that doesn't belong. Cross out the mistakenly placed word or phrase so that the paragraph makes sense. When crossing out a phrase, make sure you eliminate every word that doesn't belong—and only the words that don't belong—so that the remaining paragraph reads correctly. An example is provided.

EXAMPLE

When registering for online services under a screen name, it can be tempting to think your identity is a secret to other users. Many people will say or do things on the Internet that they would never do in real life because they believe that they are acting anonymously. However, most blogs, e-mail and instant messenger services, and social networking sites are tied to your real identity ~~and your neighbor's home~~ in some way. While your identity may be superficially concealed by a screen name, it often takes little more than a quick Google search to uncover your name, address, and other personal and possibly sensitive information.

—Ebert and Griffin, *Business Essentials,* 7th ed.

1. Good study skills will not only allow you to learn material thoroughly and permanently. If you must look to someone else for an interpretation or an explanation, you cannot be an intellectually free person. To become an independent student, you must have the desire and the courage to open a textbook, ~~jump up and down~~, and to read it, study it, and think about it.

—Pauk, *How to Study in College*

2. Your M.D. may be a top specialist, but if he or she isn't a good communicator, your health can suffer. You should feel free to ask questions ~~and call your friends~~ without being hurried. Your doctor should not repeatedly use terms that you don't understand, which can compromise treatments. Every prescription should be fully explained, including potential side effects. And your phone messages should be returned promptly. If your doctor doesn't meet these criteria, discuss your concerns and be prepared to switch.

—Listfield, "Health Style Cheat Sheet," *Parade Magazine*

3. Individuals should have a wide range of work experiences ~~and blueberry muffins~~ in order to make a decision about a career. Vocational preparation should combine project interests with actual practice in different fields. College level courses, on the other hand, may also provide useful training for a satisfying life. Persons are taught to think logically in solving problems and are exposed to experiences that help them identify and develop their attitudes toward various careers.

—Derlega and Janda, *Personal Adjustment*

4. In baseball's earliest decades, players didn't think in terms of hitting for power, and neither did managers ~~or housewives~~. During the first 75 years of baseball history, the strategies traditionalists still prize today evolved and then came to dominate the game: bunting, moving runners over with ground balls, and the hit-and-run. Even had players tried to hit home runs, conditions were stacked against them. They couldn't swing for the fences, because there often weren't any fences at baseball's first fields.

—Keating, "The Game That Ruth Built," *The Boston Globe*

5. History, someone said, surveys the past in order to find what it is that makes us human. The Greeks also invented another way of exploring our humanity: the tragic drama. Greek tragedies were short, tense plays that explored the meaning behind the suffering caused by some unintended harmful act. Even for the poorest Greek, these tragedies became a passion. At a festival held in Athens once a year, audiences of many thousands sat on stone in open-air theaters for as much as ten hours a day, on four consecutive days. Each day they watched four or five ~~3-D cartoon~~ dramas.

—Davis, *The Human Story*

EXERCISE 6.3 PARAGRAPH SENSE

Directions: Each paragraph contains a word or phrase that doesn't belong. Cross out the mistakenly placed word or phrase so that the paragraph makes sense. When crossing out a phrase, make sure you eliminate every word that doesn't belong—and only the words that don't belong—so that the remaining paragraph reads correctly.

1. People like newspapers. Some talk affectionately of curling up in bed on a leisurely Sunday morning with their paper. The news and features give people something in common to talk about. Newspapers are important in ~~dead~~ people's lives, and as a medium they adapt to changing lifestyles. The number of Sunday newspapers, for example, grew from 600 in the 1970s to almost 900 today, reflecting an increase in people's weekend leisure time for reading and shopping. Ads in Sunday papers are their guide for shopping excursions.

—Vivian, *The Media of Mass Communication,* 7th ed.

2. By age two, children realize that they are a girl or a boy; by five or six, they have learned their gender and stereotypical behavior. In most cultures, boys are generally socialized toward achievement and self-reliance, girls ~~with bicycles~~ toward nurturance and responsibility. In the United States, differences in the expectations and behaviors of the two genders may be rooted in their groups' ethnicity, religion, and socioeconomic status.

—Johnson et al., *Foundations of American Education,* 14th ed.

3. Today we face dietary choices and nutritional challenges that our grandparents never dreamed of, such as exotic foreign foods; dietary supplements; ~~rap and hip-hop;~~ artificial sweeteners; no-fat, low-fat, and artificial-fat alternatives; and cholesterol-free, high-protein, low-carbohydrate, and low-calorie products. Thousand of alternatives bombard us daily. Caught in the crossfire of advertised claims by the food industry and advice provided by health and nutrition experts, most of us find it difficult to make wise dietary decisions. The good news is that, according to the American Dietetic Association, more Americans are seeking out information on food and nutrition and taking action to improve their habits than ever before.

—Donatelle, *Health: The Basics,* 6th ed.

4. The subject of blues music is almost always what we might expect: the empty aftermath of a once burning passion. The songs ~~and textbooks~~ are written from either a male or a female point of view. Men sing of the faithlessness of women, and women return the compliment about men. Probably the most famous of all the blues songs is "St. Louis Blues" by W. C. Handy (1873–1958), who also composed "Beale Street Blues." If jazz is strongly associated with New Orleans, the headquarters of the blues was Memphis, and it was on Beale Street that many of the great blues clubs were located, attracting visitors from all over the world.

—Janaro and Altshuler, *The Art of Being Human,* 8th ed.

5. The subject line in an e-mail might seem like a minor detail, but it's actually one of the most important parts of every e-mail message because it helps recipients decide which messages to read and when to read them. Missing or poorly written subject lines often result in messages being deleted without even being opened. To capture ~~or lose~~ your audience's attention, make sure your subject line is both informative and compelling. Do more than just describe or classify message content. Use the opportunity to build interest with key words, quotations, directions, or questions.

—Bovee and Thill, *Business Communication Essentials,* 3rd ed.

Active Reading Strategy: Monitoring Comprehension

Of course, the material we normally read will not contain words or phrases that don't belong. (At least, I certainly hope not!) Usually, when something we're reading doesn't make sense to us, it means that our minds haven't been able to make sense of—construct the meaning from—the material.

It is our monitor's job to evaluate how well we've understood what we've read. We call the process by which we evaluate our understanding of reading material *monitoring comprehension*. Monitoring comprehension includes judging how well you have understood the material and identifying the reasons for any comprehension challenges.

To judge your understanding, interrupt your reading from time to time. Instead of reading steadily along, make a habit of pausing at the end of each section in your textbook, or after any challenging paragraph, to see if you've understood what you've just read. How can you be sure that you've understood the material? One simple strategy is to mentally summarize the main ideas and important details from the material. In other words, explain to yourself what you've just read—at least the most important ideas and information. If you cannot adequately summarize for yourself the main ideas and important details, assume that your comprehension was not satisfactory. Then you will want to identify the reasons for any comprehension challenges so that you can respond to them. The reasons will often be obvious. The most common interferences with comprehension are

1. poor concentration

2. unfamiliar vocabulary

3. confusing sentences (typically long sentences that don't "make sense" as you read them)

4. unfamiliar subject/lack of background knowledge

5. abstract material (*abstract* means not concrete, referring to something that can't be seen or heard or touched; this means you are reading about ideas and theories rather than people or things)

Monitoring Comprehension

The process by which we evaluate our understanding of reading material
Monitoring comprehension includes:

- judging how well you have understood the material, and
- identifying the reasons for any comprehension challenges

Complete Exercise 6.4 for practice with monitoring comprehension—judging your understanding and identifying comprehension challenges.

EXERCISE 6.4 MONITORING COMPREHENSION AND IDENTIFYING COMPREHENSION CHALLENGES

Directions: After reading each pair of passages, identify which passage was more difficult to understand. Then, explain which of the five factors previously listed made that passage more challenging. You may also identify any additional factors that contributed to difficulty.

SET 1

A. If you are one of the millions of people who try to get a "healthy tan" each year, think again. As the primary cause of more than 1.3 million cases of skin cancer in the United States this year, many of which will disfigure or permanently change the person's appearance, the sun may just be the skin's public enemy number one. Skin cancer is the most common cancer in the United States today and accounts for nearly 2 percent of all cancer deaths.

—Donatelle, *Health: The Basics*, 6th ed.

B. Melanocytes are protective cells that produce melanin. Our skin contains different amounts of the pigment melanin, which gives the skin various colors. When UV radiation strikes the skin, melanin reacts to absorb the radiation and protect the skin. Melanin causes a tan in two stages. First, melanin near the skin's surface is oxidized to a dark brown, giving a tan in about an hour. This tan gives limited protection, but it fades within a day. In the second stage, new melanin is produced and carried upward with the keratinocytes, spreading the tan through the skin. This tan takes a few days to develop.

—Baxter, "Sun Alert," *Chem Matters*

In which passage was it more difficult to understand the main idea and important details?

Answers will vary.

Why? Which factors made the passage more challenging?

Answers will vary.

SET 2

A. Besides explicit advocacy and its immediate, obvious effects, recorded music can have subtle impact on the course of human events. Elvis Presley, "the white boy who sang colored," hardly realized in the mid-1950's that his music was helping pave the way for American racial integration. It was the black roots of much of Presley's music, as well as his suggestive gyrations, that made him such a controversial performer. Whatever the fuss, white teenagers liked the music, and it blazed a trail for many black singers who became popular beyond the black community. A major black influence entered mainstream American culture. There also was a hillbilly element in early rock, bringing the concerns and issues of poor rural whites—another oppressed, neglected minority—into the mainstream consciousness. Nashville ceased to be an American cultural ghetto.

—Vivian, *The Media of Mass Communication*, 4th ed.

B. Rock-and-roll music really began to make an impact in 1955, however, when Bill Haley's "Rock Around the Clock" was rereleased as part of the sound track for the popular Hollywood film *The Blackboard Jungle*. The song had already been a modest hit for the singer when it was originally released the year before. With the exposure provided by the film, however, the record rose steadily up the charts to become the first rock-and-roll record to reach number one on the *Billboard* pop singles chart. "Rock Around the Clock" also climbed to number 14 on the rhythm-and-blues charts—the best indication of what young black record buyers wanted to hear. With his gum-smacking, finger-snapping dance music, Haley had finally found a sound that both black and white listeners could enjoy. It proved to be a formula for instant success. By 1956, the former Pennsylvania disc jockey had sold more than three million records.

—Shirley, *History of Rock and Roll*

In which passage was it more difficult to understand the main idea and important details?

Answers will vary.

Why? Which factors made the passage more challenging?

Answers will vary.

SET 3

A. Did you know that our food system is a major contributor to global warming? The U.S. food system uses between seventeen and nineteen percent of the total energy supply in the country, contributing a significant amount of greenhouse gas emissions to the atmosphere every day.

How is this possible?

On large-scale, modernized industrial farms, greenhouse gases are created in a multitude of ways. Pesticide and fertilizer applications, irrigation, lighting, transportation, and machinery are powered by greenhouse gas-emitting fossil fuels. The production of synthetic fertilizers and pesticides alone requires the equivalent use of more than 123 million barrels of oil, making them one of the largest contributors to greenhouse gas emissions in agriculture.

Once our food is grown, it is transported throughout the country to grocery stores and markets. The average American meal has traveled about 1,500 miles before it arrives on your plate. All told, the U.S. food system uses the equivalent of more than 450 billion gallons of oil every year.

—Weber, *FOOD, Inc.*

B. Most urban shoppers know that food is produced on farms. But most of them do not know what farms, or what kind of farms, or where the farms are, what knowledge or skills are needed in farming, or how farming today bears little resemblance to farming as practiced a hundred years ago. Farming in 1908 was what we today call organic farming, and most farms raised both crops and animals. We produce much more food today than we did a century ago, and humankind is better off because of it. The proportion of the earth's people who live with hunger has been consistently reduced, in large part because of American food production. We can be proud of what our farmers have accomplished.

But there have been many unsustainable negative side effects of the large-scale industrial agriculture that has developed since our grandfather's day. Soil erosion has carried away a significant portion of our topsoil, and the remaining soil has been depleted of its nutrients. The fertilizers used to replace the nutrients are made from ever more expensive petroleum and replace only some of the lost nutrients. In addition, these artificial fertilizers commonly contain poisonous heavy metals. Pesticides are sprayed on crops on nearly all farms today, and residues are often still present in small amounts on the produce when they reach the supermarket, though they are invisible to us as we pick up and inspect them.

—Blatt, *America's Food: What You Don't Know about What You Eat*

In which passage was it more difficult to understand the main ideas and important details?

Answers will vary.

Why? Which factors made the passage more challenging?

Answers will vary.

Anticipating the Text

When we are monitoring our comprehension successfully and understanding what we are reading, our minds can often anticipate, or predict, what will come next with a high degree of accuracy. For example, when we understand a heading or subheading in a textbook, we can form a goal question to anticipate or predict what will be discussed under that heading. When we recognize a stated main idea, we may predict that a supporting detail will follow.

Sometimes anticipation means having a sense of what will be said in the next sentence or next paragraph; often it is a subconscious sense of what the next word might be. In the next two exercises, you will practice anticipating the text by filling in blank spaces in the passages. If you are monitoring effectively and understanding the passage, you will be able to accurately insert the missing words.

EXERCISE 6.5 ANTICIPATING THE TEXT

Directions: Fill in each blank space with the word that you think is most consistent with the meaning of the passage. There may be more than one possible answer for a blank, but you should write only one answer for each blank.

Note: Accept synonyms or logical alternative answers.

TEENAGERS NEED HELP TO FORM BETTER SLEEP HABITS

Teenagers need as much (1) ___sleep___ as the rest of us: Adolescents who get a good night's sleep do better in school and on standardized (2) ___tests___ than those who don't get enough, they have less anxiety, and they're less (3) ___likely___ to get into car accidents.

But many factors conspire against a good night's sleep, including early-morning school start times, heavy (4) ___homework___ loads, after-school jobs—and even doctors' lack of training. In response to more and more research about the risks of sleep (5) ___loss___, doctors, policy makers, and (6) ___parents___ have proposed solutions that include simply educating doctors better and (7) ___developing___ new kinds of drugs to maximize people's productivity.

Left to their own devices, (8) ___teenagers___ sleep about nine hours a night, studies show. Generally, they go to bed later and wake up (9) ___later___ than younger children and adults, perhaps due to hormonal-induced changes in circadian rhythm.

But in reality, most American teenagers get far less sleep, regardless of their biological clocks. Hormones don't explain why Swiss children go to (10) ___bed___ almost an hour earlier than (11) _____American_____ kids. Some researchers point to the excessive homework here.

Plus, 30 percent of teenagers are (12) _____working_____ for more than 20 hours weekly, and they have (13) _____more_____ symptoms of daytime sleepiness than those who don't work jobs. Finally, only one in 20 high school students have a (14) _____bed time_____ set by parents—and most just fall asleep after watching television, socializing, or (15) _____doing_____ homework, rather than following a set routine.

—Sanghavi, "Teenagers Need Help to Form Better Sleep Habits," *The Boston Globe*

EXERCISE 6.6 ANTICIPATING THE TEXT

Directions: Fill in each blank space with the word that you think is most consistent with the meaning of the passage. There may be more than one possible answer for a blank, but you should write only one answer for each blank.

Note: Accept synonyms or logical alternative answers.

COMMUNICATION AND CAREER DEVELOPMENT

Most of us aspire to (1) _____succeed_____ in our chosen careers. We enter college to better ourselves and to prepare for satisfying jobs. Communication plays an important role in career success. Leaders in education, business, and industry have identified several critical life skills that are necessary to function successfully in the workforce, and (2) _____communication_____ is one of the most valued areas of expertise. For example, several recent studies reinforce what previous research had already (3)_____shown_____: Employers want workers at all levels who know how to (4) _____communicate_____.

In other (5)_____words_____, effective workplace communicators can explain ideas clearly and give (6) _____clearer_____ directions. Effective communicators are good listeners who work well with (7) _____others_____ and represent their companies well in small- and large-group settings. Too often, employers (8) _____find_____ that these skills are lacking in their employees. Introductory courses in communication, such as the one for which you are reading this (9) _____book_____, focus on these skills.

Personnel directors have described their needs in prospective (10) _____employees_____ as follows: Send me people who know how to speak, listen, and think, and I'll do the rest. I can train people in their specific job (11) _____requirements_____, as long as they listen well, know how to think, and can (12) _____express_____ themselves well. In fact, most careers involve contact with others and require the (13) _____employee_____ to communicate effectively with them. Business and industry often look for the most competent communicators when they (14) _____hire_____ new employees. So, although some companies provide on-the-job (15) _____training_____ in communication skills, it is by far most advantageous to develop excellent speaking, listening, and analytical abilities before applying for the exciting job that could launch or enhance your career.

—Seiler and Beall, *Communication: Making Connections,* 7th ed.

Using Active Reading Strategies to Clarify and Strengthen Comprehension

Of course, when your comprehension isn't satisfactory, you will want to do something to improve it. For example, if after reading a paragraph you are not feeling clear about its main idea, you'll want to employ the strategies or steps that will help you to understand the paragraph better and capture its main point.

Clarifying comprehension is the process of strengthening your comprehension through the use of one or more active reading strategies. Although there is no simple formula for clarifying your comprehension, there is a wide variety of active reading strategies that you can use to effectively increase your comprehension. You have already learned some of these strategies in Chapters 1 through 5 of this textbook. Which strategies will help you the most depends largely upon the reasons for the comprehension difficulties, as well as your learning style. Strategies that you generally use to concentrate better and understand more are likely to be useful when clarifying material that doesn't make sense upon first reading.

Let's take a closer look at some of these strategies.

Improving Concentration. You will likely find your concentration improved through the use of any active reading strategy. However, when concentration lags, what will help you to concentrate better depends on the reasons for your lack of concentration. Concentration problems come from external (outside of yourself) and internal (inside of yourself) sources. If the source is external (for example, noise), you will want to change the environment (control the noise) or choose a different environment (read in another room). If the source is internal (for example, you're worried or upset about something), you need to recognize what's distracting you and do something about it. A simple, practical strategy is to *identify the internal distraction* and promise yourself that you'll deal with it at a later time. For example, if you were having trouble concentrating because you were worrying about one of your friends, you might tell yourself, "I am worried about Ramona. I will call her tonight."

Your mind will usually be able to put a problem aside when it knows that the problem will be dealt with at a later time. If there are several things on your mind, list them on a piece of paper with brief comments about how you are going to deal with them.

College readers sometimes believe that lack of concentration is a response to material that isn't interesting. Keep in mind that interest comes from the reader, not the material, and that the effective use of active reading strategies usually sends boredom packing. If you are feeling bored with an assignment, first make an effort to become more interested (you might try a strategy such as *raising questions* about the material, or *marking the material* while you read). Look for a way to connect with and relate to the material. Second, remind yourself of the *purpose* of the reading assignment (what you want to learn and what your instructor wants you to learn from the assignment); this should also help you stay focused on the reading task.

One final point about concentration: Aids to concentration vary from person to person. For example, some people need absolute quiet to concentrate while reading, whereas others concentrate better with music playing softly in the background. Revisit your work on Exercise 1.1 on pages 15–16. Have you successfully identified the conditions which will best support your concentration?

Working with Unfamiliar Vocabulary. Of course, if unfamiliar vocabulary is interfering with your comprehension, you will want to use the strategies you learned in the first two chapters of this book: *context clues, dictionary consultation*, and *word structure clues.*

Untangling Confusing Sentences. When you are reading a confusing sentence, it is often helpful to *break the sentence down*. What is the subject of the sentence, and what point is the writer making about the subject of the sentence? Try to *simplify* or *paraphrase* the sentence (explain it to yourself in your own words). *Visualizing* (picturing in your mind) and *reading aloud* can also be helpful strategies with difficult sentences.

Reading about an Unfamiliar Subject. *Rereading* is often necessary when reading unfamiliar content. Also, ask yourself what *prior knowledge* or experience you have that might relate to the subject and can help you understand the material better. You may occasionally need to obtain a piece of *background information* from another source (your instructor, online, etc.). Use your paragraph skills to *identify topics and main ideas.*

Understanding Abstract Material. When reading abstract material (material that deals with ideas and theories rather than people or things), find ways to make the material more meaningful and concrete. Think of *real-life situations* and concrete examples that might relate to the concepts you're reading; examples from your own life experience are especially helpful. Any prior knowledge you have that relates to the subject may be helpful as well. *Rereading* will often be necessary when reading material that is abstract. Your paragraph skills—especially identifying main ideas—can likewise be helpful when you are working with abstract material.

See Table 6.1 for a list of strategies for clarifying comprehension.

> **Clarifying comprehension** is the process of strengthening your comprehension through the use of one or more active reading strategies.

Table 6.1   Strategies for Clarifying Comprehension

Cause of Difficulty	Clarifying Strategies
Poor concentration	Use active reading strategies
	Raise questions
	Reread
	Clarify your purpose
	Identify causes of concentration problem and respond to them
	Mark the material
Unfamiliar vocabulary	Use context clues
	Use a dictionary
	Identify word structure (prefix/suffix)
Confusing sentences	Break the sentence down
	Paraphrase: simplify the sentence in your own words
	Visualize
	Reread
	Read aloud
Unfamiliar subject/lack of background knowledge	Relate with something from your experience
	Recall related prior knowledge
	Identify and obtain missing information
	Reread
	Identify paragraph topics and main ideas
Abstract material	Relate with something from your experience
	Think of real-life examples and applications
	Recall related prior knowledge
	Reread
	Identify paragraph topics and main ideas

EXERCISE 6.7 MONITORING AND CLARIFYING COMPREHENSION

Directions: Read each of the following passages and underline any unfamiliar words and confusing sentences you encounter. Notice what's going on in your mind while you're reading; feel free to jot down your questions and thoughts. Use the strategies in Table 6.1 to clarify your comprehension as needed. Then answer the questions that follow the passage.

A. GENERATION TEXT:
THE WORLD AT THEIR FEET—AND FINGERTIPS

The cell phone is a prime example of how easily kids adapt to the frequent changes in technology, how they use technology to suit their needs and desires, and in turn, how technology is shaping their attitudes, behaviors, and values.

In some ways cell phones and other technology devices facilitate friendships for the technologically astute child, but in other ways they hinder social-skill development. Kids have access to each other and the larger world to a much greater extent than they ever did before, but less effort is required for them to communicate. Cell phones, the Internet, e-mail, and instant messaging reduce human contact and yet, paradoxically, make people constantly available and endlessly distractible.

As another teenage patient tells me, when a high school student wants to talk to a friend sitting on the other side of the school cafeteria, he may be more inclined to call or text the friend on his cell phone than to walk across the room. If he were to walk across the cafeteria to speak to his friend, he may encounter a teacher or another kid he doesn't want to talk to. When he approaches the friend, he may have to wait to speak with him so as not to interrupt a conversation. He then must establish eye contact, read nonverbal cues in the conversation, and react to body language.

—Osit, *Generation Text: Raising Well-Adjusted Kids in an Age of Instant Everything*

1. Using a 1 to 5 scale (5 = excellent; 4 = good; 3 = fair; 2 = poor; 1 = very poor), rate your comprehension of the passage.

   Answers will vary.

2. What prior knowledge or experience helped you understand the passage?

   Answers will vary.

3. What other background information would be helpful for reading this passage?

   Answers will vary.

4. What did you visualize or imagine while reading the passage?

   Answers will vary.

5. Which strategies did you use while reading the passage? (Check any that you used.)

   Answers will vary.

   _____ Rereading

   _____ Marking the material

   _____ Using context clues

   _____ Consulting the dictionary

   _____ Word structure clues

   _____ Analyzing or paraphrasing confusing sentences

   _____ Visualizing

   _____ Reading aloud

   _____ Relating to prior knowledge

   _____ Relating to the material

   _____ Thinking of real-life examples

   _____ Other (explain): _____

6. Which strategy or strategies were most helpful? Explain.

   Answers will vary.

7. What is the main point of the passage? Answer in a complete sentence of your own wording.

   Modern technology both helps and hinders the social development of children and

   teenagers. (sample answer)

B. REINFORCEMENT/BEHAVIOR MODIFICATION

Some companies try to control workers' behavior through systematic rewards and punishments for specific behaviors. Such companies first try to define the specific behaviors that they want their employees to exhibit (working hard, being courteous to customers, and stressing quality) and the specific behaviors they want to eliminate (wasting time, being rude to customers, and ignoring quality). Then they try to shape employee behavior by linking positive reinforcement with desired behaviors and punishment with undesired behaviors.

Positive reinforcement is used when a company or manager provides a reward when employees exhibit desired behaviors. When rewards are tied directly to performance, they serve as positive reinforcement. For example, paying large cash bonuses to salespeople who exceed quotas prompts them to work even harder during the next selling period. John Deere has adopted a reward system based on positive reinforcement. The firm gives pay increases when its workers complete college courses and demonstrate mastery of new job skills.

Punishment is designed to change behavior by presenting people with unpleasant consequences if they exhibit undesired behaviors. Employees who are repeatedly late for work, for example, may be suspended or have their pay docked. Similarly, when the National Football League or Major League Baseball fines or suspends players found guilty of substance abuse, the organization is seeking to change players' behaviors.

—Ebert and Griffin, *Business Essentials,* 7th ed.

1. Using a 1 to 5 scale (5 = excellent; 4 = good; 3 = fair; 2 = poor; 1 = very poor), rate your comprehension of the passage.

   Answers will vary.

2. What prior knowledge or experience helped you understand the passage?

   Answers will vary.

3. What other background information would be helpful for reading this passage?

   Answers will vary.

4. What did you visualize or imagine while reading the passage?

   Answers will vary.

5. Which strategies did you use while reading the passage? (Check any that you used.)

   Answers will vary.

   _____ Rereading

   _____ Marking the material

   _____ Using context clues

   _____ Consulting the dictionary

   _____ Word structure clues

   _____ Analyzing or paraphrasing confusing sentences

   _____ Visualizing

   _____ Reading aloud

   _____ Relating to the material

_____ Relating to prior knowledge

_____ Thinking of real-life examples

_____ Other (explain): _____

6. Which strategy or strategies were most helpful? Explain.

Answers will vary.
_____

7. What is the main point of the passage? Answer in a complete sentence of your own wording.

Companies use rewards and punishments to control their employee's behavior.
_____

(sample answer)
_____

C. INVISIBILITY CLOAKS

If you're a fan of Harry Potter, then you're quite familiar with the concept of an invisibility cloak. In his first year at Hogwarts Academy, Harry receives an invisibility cloak that used to belong to his father. As its name suggests, the invisibility cloak renders Harry invisible when he slips beneath the shining, silvery cloth.

This seems perfectly believable when you're reading about a fictional world filled with witches, wizards and centuries-old magic; but in the real world, such a garment would be impossible, right? Not so fast. With optical-camouflage technology developed by scientists at the University of Tokyo, the invisibility cloak is already a reality.

Optical camouflage delivers a similar experience to Harry Potter's invisibility cloak, but using it requires a slightly more complicated arrangement. First, the person who wants to be invisible (let's call her Person A) dons a garment that resembles a hooded raincoat. The garment is made of a special material that we'll examine more closely in a moment. Next, an observer (Person B) stands before Person A at a specific location. At that location, instead of seeing Person A wearing a hooded raincoat, Person B sees right through the cloak, making Person A appear to be invisible.

—"How Invisibility Cloaks Work," *www.howstuffworks.com*

Optical camouflage technology won't make you invisible to multi-eyed Beholder monsters—or even to stray cats and squirrels.

1. Using a 1 to 5 scale (5 = excellent; 4 = good; 3 = fair; 2 = poor; 1 = very poor), rate your comprehension of the passage.

Answers will vary.

2. What prior knowledge or experience helped you understand the passage?

Answers will vary.

3. What other background information would be helpful for reading this passage?

Answers will vary.

4. What did you visualize or imagine while reading the passage?

Answers will vary.

5. Which strategies did you use while reading the passage? (Check any that you used.)

Answers will vary.

_____ Rereading

_____ Marking the material

_____ Using context clues

_____ Consulting the dictionary

_____ Word structure clues

_____ Analyzing or paraphrasing confusing sentences

_____ Visualizing

_____ Reading aloud

_____ Relating to the material

_____ Relating to prior knowledge

_____ Thinking of real-life examples

_____ Other (explain): _____

6. Which strategy or strategies were most helpful? Explain.

Answers will vary.

7. What is the main point of the passage? Answer in a complete sentence of your own wording.

Scientists are using optical camouflage to develop a real invisibility cloak. (sample answer)

Active Reading Strategy: Paraphrasing

In the previous section, we identified paraphrasing (expressing an author's ideas in different words) as a tool for clarifying comprehension. Active readers will use this strategy when unsure about something in their reading. They rephrase the author's ideas for themselves in wording that makes sense to them (for example, rephrasing a stated main idea to ensure that its meaning is clear). If reading comprehension is the process of making someone else's (the author's) ideas our own, then we must paraphrase to be sure that we've grasped the author's thoughts. Paraphrasing, therefore, helps us to monitor as well as to clarify our comprehension.

When you paraphrase, your goal is to rephrase the author's ideas *without changing the meaning*. Imagine that you are trying to explain to another person what you have read, using your own wording in place of the author's as much as possible.

To get the most from this strategy, follow these guidelines.

1. Before you paraphrase, clarify the meaning of any unfamiliar words in the statement.

2. If you are paraphrasing a long or complicated sentence, first identify the subject of the sentence and then look for the basic point the sentence expresses about that subject.

3. Your paraphrase may be shorter and simpler than the original statement, but always paraphrase in complete sentences.

4. You may change the order of the author's statement.

5. When you have finished writing a paraphrase, compare your paraphrase with the author's statement to be sure you've accurately captured the author's meaning.

Let's look at an example. Imagine you are reading a chapter in a communications textbook about cultural differences and you come across the following sentence.

Author's statement: Cultures, of course, differ in a wide variety of ways; and for purposes of communication, the difference that probably comes to mind first is that of languages.

—DeVito, *The Interpersonal Communication Book,* 12th ed.

You decide to paraphrase the sentence to make sure its meaning is clear and to help you remember the point. As you reread and think about the sentence, you recognize that the sentence consists of two parts. The first part of the sentence tells you that cultures are different in a variety of ways. The second part of the sentence tells you that language is probably the most obvious of the differences (for communication purposes). You might then paraphrase as follows.

Paraphrase: There are many ways in which cultures vary, and when thinking about communication, language is perhaps the most obvious of these differences.

Notice that the preceding paraphrase carries the same meaning as the author's original statement, but it is worded differently.

If you wanted to simplify the sentence further, you could shorten and simplify your paraphrase.

Simplified paraphrase: Language differences are perhaps the most obvious of the many differences between cultures.

Note that in the simplified paraphrase, the basic meaning of the sentence has been retained. Also note that the order of the original sentence has been changed—which is okay to do when paraphrasing.

Let's look at another example. This one's from a nutrition chapter in a health textbook.

> *Author's statement:* Although the importance of proteins in the body should not be underestimated, it is carbohydrates that supply us with the energy needed to sustain normal daily activity.
>
> —Donatelle, *Health: The Basics,* 6th ed.

In analyzing this sentence, we realize that the main point of the sentence is expressed in the second half of the sentence, which tells us that carbohydrates are our primary nutritional source for daily energy. We also notice that before stating that point, the sentence reminds us of the importance of proteins. We can paraphrase as follows.

> *Paraphrase:* Proteins are important, but it is carbohydrates that give us the energy we need for our regular, day-to-day activities.

Exercises 6.8, 6.9, and 6.10 will provide practice with paraphrasing.

EXERCISE 6.8 PARAPHRASING

Directions: Each statement in this exercise is followed by two possible paraphrases. Check the paraphrase that more accurately expresses the point of the original statement. An example is provided.

EXAMPLE

> *Author's statement:* Dreams presumably have always fascinated humanity, for they seem to free us from all limitations of space or time.
> —Kagan and Havemann, *Psychology: An Introduction,* 4th ed.

Choose the better paraphrase:

_√_ People have always been curious about dreams because they free us from the restrictions of waking life.

_____ Humanity has always been fascinated by dreams, we assume, because they cannot go beyond the limits of time and space.

1. *Author's statement:* The studies have shown quite clearly that sleep is by no means a state of suspended animation in which body and brain are shut down for a time.
—Kagan and Havemann, *Psychology: An Introduction,* 4th ed.

Choose the better paraphrase:

_____ We learn from studies that sleep is similar to suspended animation, a condition in which the body and brain stop functioning.

_√_ The mind and body do not stop being active when we sleep.

2. *Author's statement:* Personal worth and self-identity are heavily influenced by the opportunity to work and by the type of work one chooses to do.

    —Derlega and Janda, *Personal Adjustment: The Psychology of Everyday Life,* 3rd ed.

    Choose the better paraphrase:

    __√__   A person's work has an important impact on his or her identity and self-esteem.

    _____   It is difficult to feel good about yourself if you're unhappy with your job.

3. *Author's statement:* Dropouts tend to be deficient in basic reading, language arts, and mathematics skills, and often they are children of high school dropouts.

    —Johnson et al., *Introduction to the Foundations of American Education,* 10th ed.

    Choose the better paraphrase:

    __√__   Dropouts often lack basic educational skills, and their parents were likely to have been dropouts.

    _____   Parents of dropouts have poor reading and math skills, causing their children to become dropouts as well.

4. *Author's statement:* In the United States, Canada, and other developed nations, many cities by the mid-twentieth century had accumulated more people than these cities had jobs to offer.

    —Withgott and Brennan, *Essential Environment: The Science Behind the Stories,* 2nd ed.

    Choose the better paraphrase:

    _____   Cities in the United States, Canada, and elsewhere welcomed immigration in the mid-twentieth century but failed to meet the needs of the people coming in.

    __√__   By the middle of the twentieth century, population growth had exceeded employment opportunities in cities in the U.S., Canada, and other developed countries.

5. *Author's statement:* From the very early days of the republic, political leaders recognized the importance of public opinion and used all the means at their disposal to manipulate it for political purposes.

    —O'Connor and Sabato, *American Government: Continuity and Change,* 2006 ed.

    Choose the better paraphrase:

    __√__   Politicians have always understood the importance of public opinion and have tried to influence it however they could.

    _____   Throughout the republic's history, political leaders who recognized that public opinion had to be manipulated were more successful in achieving their political goals and ambitions.

EXERCISE `6.9` PARAPHRASING

Directions: In the space provided, write a one-sentence paraphrase for each of the following statements. Your paraphrase should be a complete sentence that accurately restates the author's point without copying the author's words.

1. Understanding our interactions with the world around us is vital because we depend utterly on our environment for air, water, food, shelter, and everything else essential for living.

   —Withgott and Brennan, *Essential Environment: The Science Behind the Stories,* 2nd ed.

   We need to understand our interactions with our environment because it provides us

   with all the things we need to live. (sample answer)

2. In spite of society's messages about the need for diet and exercise, numerous studies on eating patterns suggest that Americans are doing worse with each successive decade.

   —Donatelle, *Health: The Basics,* 6th ed.

   Even though we know the importance of diet and exercise, studies show that

   Americans' eating habits are getting worse. (sample answer)

3. Although people hold many different perspectives on education, most agree that teaching is a profession that is critical to the well-being of youth and of society.

   —Johnson et al., *Foundations of American Education,* 14th ed.

   People have different views of education, but most people believe that teachers are

   very important. (sample answer)

4. The basic idea behind self-esteem is that when you feel good about yourself— about who you are and what you're capable of doing—you will perform better.

   —DeVito, *The Interpersonal Communication Book,* 12th ed.

   The idea behind self-esteem is that you will be more successful if you feel good

   about yourself and your abilities. (sample answer)

5. Men are more likely than women to make comments throughout the stream of conversation rather than wait until the other person finishes speaking.

   —Beck, *Love Is Never Enough*

   Men interrupt more than women. (sample answer)

EXERCISE 6.10 PARAPHRASING

Directions: In the space provided, write a one-sentence paraphrase for each of the following statements. Your paraphrase should be a complete sentence that accurately restates the author's point without copying the author's words.

1. Victory comes only to those who work hard, who are willing to pay the price in blood, sweat, and tears.

   —Pitino, *Success Is a Choice*

   Success requires hard work. (sample answer)

2. Empathy is the awareness of, and sensitivity to, the feelings, thoughts, and experiences of others.

—Waitley, *Psychology of Success,* 2nd ed.

Empathy is understanding how someone else feels and thinks. (sample answer)

3. The national data on dropouts point to the desperate need for the school and society to find ways to keep children in school and to teach them at least basic life skills—not only for their own good but also for the good of society.

—Johnson et al, *Introduction to the Foundations of American Education,* 10th ed.

Information on dropouts tells us that we must prevent children from leaving school

and help them learn fundamental life skills, for society's sake as well as

the children's. (sample answer)

4. The power of music to set the mood in a movie depends on the fact that most people react in the same way to the same music.

—Gard, "Music 'n' Moods," *Current Health 2*

Because we tend to react similarly to the same music, music can be used to

establish mood in a movie. (sample answer)

5. Gestures not only facilitate communication but, since they differ around the world, can also lead to misunderstanding, embarrassment, or worse. To get along in another culture, then, it is important to learn the gestures of that culture.

—Henslin, *Essentials of Sociology,* 3rd ed.

We can avoid misunderstandings by realizing that the meaning of gestures varies

from culture to culture. (sample answer)

When the Going Gets Tough

The instruction and exercises in this chapter have encouraged you to do something that you, and most readers, don't usually do—that is, to pay close attention to your reading *processes.* When you are reading casually, or reading easy material, it may not be necessary to monitor your comprehension carefully or to be thorough in your use of clarifying strategies. However, when you are reading challenging material, or reading an assignment for a college class in which you are expected to learn and remember new information and ideas, monitoring your comprehension and using effective clarifying strategies are critical to your success.

In short, when the going gets tough, active readers monitor and clarify their comprehension! Exercise 6.11 contains two passages that are typical of the kinds of material you will read in college courses. Imagine that you are reading each passage for a course in which you are expected to learn and remember the main ideas and important details from the passage. Monitor your comprehension carefully and use the clarifying strategies that will best help you to understand each passage.

EXERCISE 6.11 CLARIFYING COMPREHENSION

Directions: Read each passage using the clarifying strategies that are most help-ful to you. Feel free to jot down questions and thoughts while reading. When you have finished reading, answer the questions that follow the passage.

A. DEVIANCE AND CRIME

While most people will admit to breaking the law sometime during their lives, almost all of us oppose serious violations. And while our everyday life may be orderly, there are times when life is less orderly—when murder, scandal, and other normative violations take place. In fact, these violations occur often enough that deviance and crime have become fields of specialization practiced by sociologists and criminologists.

What is deviance? Technically, *deviance* is any violation of a widely held norm. In practice, however, most deviance is ignored, mildly pun-ished, regarded as amusing, or even supported. It is one thing to mug a person and quite another to wear cutoff blue jeans to a formal banquet. All deviance involves violating norms, but some norms attract the attention of the authorities. An act that has been declared illegal by some author-ity is called a *crime*. The authority might be the formal government of an industrial society or the council of a small town or village. Regardless of

the type, however, authorities tend to criminalize acts that severely upset societal order and that cannot be easily controlled.

Not all crimes are deviant acts, and not all deviant acts are crimes. Murder and incest are both deviant and criminal, whereas piercing your eyebrows to insert a ring, though not criminal, is mildly deviant in most American communities. However, since body piercing is becoming more popular in the United States, within the near future perhaps only the most extreme forms of it will be considered deviant. Scalping—illegally selling tickets to an event—is a crime in some localities, but the practice is so common that in most places, it is not considered to be deviant. Similarly, driving a few miles per hour over the speed limit posted on an interstate highway is technically a crime, but the police usually give drivers some leeway before pulling them over.

—Curry et al., *Sociology for the Twenty-First Century*, 5th ed.

1. *Vocabulary:* List two unfamiliar words from the passage.
   Answers will vary.

   Which strategy or strategies did you use to understand these words?
   Answers will vary.

2. *Sentences:* Underline one difficult sentence from the passage.
   Which clarifying strategy or strategies did you use to understand the sentence?
   Answers will vary.

3. What prior knowledge do you have of this subject?
   Answers will vary.

4. What was the biggest challenge in understanding the passage?

Answers will vary.

5. Which strategy or strategy most helped you to clarify your understanding of the passage?

Answers will vary.

6. What is *deviance*?

Deviance is violation of a norm—behaving differently from what is normal and

expected.

7. What is *crime*?

A crime is an act that has been made illegal by an authority.

8. How does society respond to deviance?

Most deviance is ignored, punished lightly, or sometimes supported or enjoyed.

Laws are made against more serious forms of deviance.

9. What is the main idea of the last paragraph in the passage?

Crime and deviance are not the same; not all crimes are deviant acts,

and not all deviant acts are crimes.

10. Paraphrase the following sentence:
However, since body piercing is becoming more popular in the United States, within the near future perhaps only the most extreme forms of it will be considered deviant.

With body piercing becoming more common in the U.S., soon most body

piercing will probably not be viewed as deviant. (sample answer)

B. LOVE

Despite the sentiment in poems and songs that love is timeless, it must be considered in the context of history. Love has meant different things at different times and places, including its relative unimportance for people in desperate circumstances. Cultural anthropologists, for example, once discovered that people in a certain remote area of Africa had no word that translates as "love," though parents probably showed affection for their young by teaching them how to survive in a hostile environment. As you may have guessed, their vocabulary was filled with words that relate to survival strategies, all with favorable connotations. They seemed, however, to have little need for words that refer to tight family bonds and none for words indicating romance between adults.

Imagine the difficulty of having a meaningful discussion about love between people from totally different backgrounds—one waiting for romance and passion, with a wide choice of partners, the other obediently preparing to marry a stranger in a match arranged by the parents of the couple.

In the classical world of Greece and Rome the word *love* can be found in poetry, philosophy, and mythology, but a citizen of that world, alighting from a time machine in our era, might not understand axioms such as "Love is blind" or "Love is the answer." The time traveler, hearing the latter, might wittily retort, "To what question?"

The Greeks made a famous distinction between *eros*, or love as physical lust, and *agape*, in which a spiritual and intellectual relationship is more important than a strictly physical one. Though the Romans are famous for their wine-filed orgies, they recognized the distinction as well, and that distinction is still with us.

—Janaro and Altshuler, *The Art of Being Human,* 8th ed.

1. *Vocabulary*: List two unfamiliar words from the passage.

   Answers will vary.

   Which strategy or strategies did you use to understand these words?

   Answers will vary.

2. *Sentences*: Underline one difficult sentence from the passage. Which clarifying strategy or strategies did you use to understand the sentence?

   Answers will vary.

3. What prior knowledge do you have of this subject?

   Answers will vary.

4. What was the biggest challenge in understanding the passage?

   Answers will vary.

5. Which strategy or strategy most helped you to clarify your understanding of the passage?

   Answers will vary.

6. Why might a citizen of ancient Greece or Rome not understand our view of love today?

   Love meant something different to them than it means to us. (sample answer)

7. According to the passage, under what circumstances is love relatively unimportant?

   Love is relatively unimportant when people are in desperate circumstances

   and have to focus on survival.

8. What is the difference between *eros* and *agape*?

Eros is sexual love or lust; agape is a mental and spiritual bond.

9. What is the main point that the authors make about love?

Love must be understood in historical context—its meaning has differed

in different times and places.

10. Paraphrase the following sentence:

Despite the sentiment in poems and songs that love is timeless, it must be considered in the context of history.

Songs and poems may suggest that love is timeless, but love must be understood in

historical context. (sample answer)

SKILLS ONLINE: MONITORING YOUR COMPREHENSION ONLINE

   Directions:

1. Choose one of the following topics.

- Freud's dream theories
- organic food
- global warming

2. Read two different Web pages about your topic from two different Web sites, monitoring and clarifying your comprehension as necessary. Then answer the following questions.

a. Which page was easier to understand? Why?
b. Which clarifying strategies did you use while reading the Web pages? Which ones were most helpful?
c. How are the challenges of online reading different from the challenges of textbook reading? Which strategies are most useful for online reading?
d. Briefly summarize what you learned (about the topic you selected) from the two Web pages you read.

3. Remember to include the URLs of the Web sites on your paper or print out the pages you read.

READING 6A

WAKING UP TO OUR DREAMS (PSYCHOLOGY)

by Robert Moss

Robert Moss is the author of *The Secret History of Dreaming* and several other books about dream potential. Read the selection to learn how Moss believes dreams can benefit us in our daily lives.

Pre-Reading Exercise

Directions: Complete this exercise before reading the passage. Preview the passage and answer the following questions.

1. What is the passage about?

   Dreams and how they can help us

2. How does the author feel about dreams?

   The author feels that dreams are important and valuable. (sample answer)

3. Name two possible benefits of dreams that are mentioned in the passage.

   Any two: warn of dangers/challenges; warn of internal danger; aid in learning and memory;

   contribute to creativity; solve problems; deal with emotional issues

4. Does the picture accompanying the passage successfully capture the feeling of a dream? Why or why not?

   Answers will vary.

5. What have you previously read or learned about dreams?

   Answers will vary.

6. Does the passage seem easy to understand, or is it difficult? Explain your answer.

   Answers will vary.

Directions: Monitor and clarify your comprehension while reading the passage. Underline unfamiliar words and confusing sentences.

1   Here's an open secret: Dreaming isn't really about sleeping; it's about waking up. Dreams wake us up to the challenges and opportunities that lie ahead. They can tell us what we need to know and alert us to actions we need to take.

2   Throughout history—from ancient shamans to the Bible to Freud—men and women have been fascinated by dreams and have pondered their meaning. Current research indicates that dreaming has a real, practical function but also

Source: "Waking Up to Our Dreams" from *Parade*, October 28, 2007. © 2007 Robert Moss. Initially published in *Parade Magazine*. All rights reserved. Used by permission of *Parade* and the author.

Dreams can make us smarter, more creative and better able to cope with problems.

that it can spark our imaginations in unexpected ways. Best of all, one doesn't have to be especially "adept" at dreaming: The power of dreams is accessible to everyone.

3   New studies confirm that all of us have dreams—even those who never recall them—every night for 90 minutes to three hours, in four or five cycles. MRI images and PET scans show that specific areas of the brain are triggered at regular intervals, giving us dream imagery.

4   Until recently, many scientists dismissed the idea that there was rich meaning in dreams, believing instead that dreams were initiated by random firings of the brainstem during REM (rapid eye movement) sleep. But evidence has been accumulating that dreams also can originate during other phases of sleep, when the higher visual and emotional centers of the brain are activated. This suggests that our dreams are not strange results of meaningless biological processes. Rather, they are produced by the part of the brain tied to motivation, goals and desires.

5   Dreams may even be related to survival itself. Antti Revonsuo, a psychology professor in Finland, theorizes that dreaming is central to human evolution. "A dream's biological function is to simulate threatening events and to rehearse threat perception and threat avoidance," he explains. That is, our dreams can warn us of challenges ahead and give us a chance to rehearse efficient responses—including getting out of the way.

6   I once dreamed of a car accident on a hill east of Troy, N.Y. Several weeks later, driving on the same hill, I found my view of a curve in the road obscured by a delivery truck ahead. I remembered my dream and slowed almost to a stop—avoiding a head-on collision with an 18-wheeler.

7   Dreams also can alert us to dangers that are internal. They may tell us what is going on inside our bodies and what we need to do to stay healthy. Mary Agnes Twomey, a registered nurse in Baltimore, dreamed she'd traveled inside her body and found it was like a boiler room

A dream may be sending a message about your health.

in danger of blowing up. Upon waking, she made a doctor's appointment and learned she had an ulcer that needed treatment. Other people have reported dreams that alerted them to illnesses ranging from breast cancer to heart disease.

8   Whether or not you believe that dreams serve as warnings, studies suggest that they play a critical role in learning and memory.

9   "Dreams allow us to play and experiment with new conditions or find novel solutions," says Richard C. Wilkerson, operations director of the International Association for the Study of Dreams. "They allow us to explore unusual areas of life and practice new behaviors."

10   One fertile source of creativity is the ability to make new and unexpected connections—something we do all the time when we dream. In dreams, "connections are made more easily than in waking, more broadly and loosely," says Dr. Ernest Hartmann, a professor of psychiatry at Tufts University who has written widely on sleep and dreaming. But he adds, "The connections are not random. They are guided by the emotional concerns of the dreamer." In dreams you may gain new insights about personal relationships or develop exciting new ideas.

11   Many artists have experienced this phenomenon: Paul McCartney awoke with the music for the Beatles' hit "Yesterday" in his mind. Architect Frank Gehry has said that his building designs were influenced by his dreams.

12   "The waking mind is thinking inside the box; the dreaming mind is thinking outside the box," explains David Kahn, a professor at Harvard Medical School.

13   This may be why solutions to nagging problems often come to us in dreams. Robyn Johnson, a consultant for nonprofit organizations in Washington state, needed to produce a fund-raiser for a city park. She dreamed that Annie Oakley rode into the park on her horse, urging her to produce a children's storybook to be given to every guest. She followed Oakley's advice, to great success.

14   Not least, dreams can help us deal with emotional hurdles. Marlene Cantor at the May Institute in Massachusetts has discovered recurring themes in the dreams of middle-aged women. One woman dreamed night after night of going to a house that was falling into disrepair. It began to

crumble around her, and one night she saw the roof falling in. In another dream, she saw a beautiful young girl run out of the house and into the path of a speeding car. She wept as the girl died in her arms. In sharing these dreams, the woman reflected that the first symbolic dreamscape might express her fears about her aging body. And perhaps in weeping over the young girl's death, she was mourning the death of her younger self.

15   "Most of these women had never really talked to anyone—not family, not even thera-pists—about what they were feeling," Cantor recalls. "Telling their dreams brought them a tremendous sense of relief, of coming out of silence and solitude."

Whether we share our dreams or reflect on them privately, we'd all do well to wake up to their power. Amid the stress and clutter of everyday life, our dreams can help us discover what's most important.   16

—Moss, "Waking Up to Our Dreams," *Parade Magazine*

You, the Reader

Interest Rating. Please rate the interest level of the reading on the following scale (circle one):

5—Very interesting   2—A little boring

4—Fairly interesting   1—Very boring

3—Mildly interesting

Difficulty Rating. Please rate the difficulty level of the reading on the following scale (circle one):

5—Very difficult   2—Fairly easy

4—Fairly difficult   1—Very easy

3—Moderate

Comments: Please explain your ratings and make any other comments you wish about the reading.

Answers will vary.

MONITORING AND CLARIFYING COMPREHENSION EXERCISE

1. Using a 1 to 5 scale (5 = excellent; 4 = good; 3 = fair; 2 = poor; 1 = very poor), rate your comprehension of the passage.

   Answers will vary.

2. What prior knowledge or experience do you have that helped you understand the passage?

   Answers will vary.

3. What other background information would be helpful for reading this passage?

   Answers will vary.

4. What did you visualize or imagine while reading the passage?

   Answers will vary.

5. Which strategies did you use while reading the passage? (Check any that you used):

   Answers will vary.

   _____ Rereading

   _____ Marking the material

   _____ Using context clues

   _____ Consulting the dictionary

   _____ Analyzing word structure

   _____ Analyzing or paraphrasing confusing sentences

   _____ Visualizing

   _____ Reading aloud

   _____ Relating to the material

   _____ Relating to prior knowledge

   _____ Thinking of real-life examples

   _____ Other (explain): _____

6. Which strategy or strategies were most helpful? Explain.

   Answers will vary.

7. Choose the better paraphrase for the following sentence:

   Author's statement: Until recently, many scientists dismissed the idea that there was rich meaning in dreams, believing instead that dreams were initiated by random firings of the brainstem during REM (rapid eye movement) sleep.

   Choose the better paraphrase:

   _____ a. Scientists have recently learned that dreams are caused by brain activity during certain phases of sleep.

   __√___ b. Until recently, scientists had thought that dreams were not meaningful and were caused by brainstem firings during REM sleep.

8. What were the most important things you learned from the passage about dreams?

   Answers will vary.

COMPREHENSION QUESTIONS

Directions: For questions 1–5, choose the answer that best completes the statement. For questions 6–10, write your response in the space provided. Base all answers on what you read in the selection. Refer back to the selection as necessary to answer the questions.

___d___ 1. When the author says that dreaming is about waking up, he means that:
   a. Dreams cause us to wake up from our sleep.
   b. If we didn't dream, we would never wake up.
   c. Dreaming is similar to being awake.
   d. Dreams alert us to challenges and opportunities in our waking lives.

_____a_____ **2.** Research indicates that:
  a. Everyone dreams every night.
  b. Most people do not realize that they dream.
  c. Dreams are meaningless creations of the visual and emotional centers of the brain.
  d. Dreams occur only during REM sleep.

_____c_____ **3.** The author refers to one of his own dreams as an example of how dreams:
  a. Can help us with health problems.
  b. Encourage creative thinking.
  c. Can alert us to danger.
  d. Solve emotional problems.

_____d_____ **4.** The main idea of paragraph 7 is:
  a. Mary Agnes Twomey dreamed that she traveled inside her body.
  b. People have had dreams about heart disease.
  c. Dreams are the best way to recognize illness.
  d. Dreams can alert us to internal dangers to our health.

_____b_____ **5.** Antti Revonsuo believes that dreams:
  a. Are meaningless patterns created by the brainstem.
  b. Help us deal with possible threats.
  c. Enable us to predict the future.
  d. Are usually misunderstood and misinterpreted.

6. What does the author mean when he says that "one doesn't have to be especially 'adept' at dreaming"?

Dreaming requires no special skills.

7. According to the author, how has scientific thinking about dreams changed in recent times?

Until recently, most scientists believed that dreams were the result of

brainstem firings during REM sleep and not particularly meaningful. New

research supports the idea that dreams are meaningful.

8. Describe Mary Agnes Twomey's dream. How did the dream help her?

She dreamed she was traveling inside her body and it was like a boiler

room in danger of blowing up. She saw a doctor and found out she had an

ulcer that needed treatment.

9. How do dreams contribute to creative thinking?

Dreams allow the mind to experiment and make new connections.

10. Do you agree with the author's statement about dreams that "we'd all do well to wake up to their power"? Why or why not?

Answers will vary.

VOCABULARY EXERCISES

> **Pronunciation Guide** (see p. 90 for list of phonetic symbols)
>
> obscured   (ŏb-skyoŏrd')
> phenomenon   (fĭ-nŏm'ə-nŏn)
> shaman   (shä'mən)
> simulate   (sĭm'yə-lāt')

WORDS IN CONTEXT

Directions: Choose the meaning for the boldfaced word or phrase that best fits the context.

_a_ **1.** A dream's biological **function** is to simulate threatening events and to rehearse threat perception and threat avoidance.
  a. Purpose
  b. History
  c. Material
  d. Problem

_c_ **2.** A dream's biological function is to **simulate** threatening events and to rehearse threat perception and threat avoidance.
  a. Cause
  b. Prevent
  c. Imitate; create a likeness of
  d. Draw the attention away from

_a_ **3.** I found my view of a curve in the road **obscured** by a delivery truck ahead.
  a. Hidden
  b. Reflected
  c. Made easier
  d. Made clear

_b_ **4.** Dreams allow us to play and experiment with new conditions or find **novel** solutions.
  a. Old; no longer useful
  b. New; inventive
  c. Coming or copied from a book
  d. Extremely odd

_b_ **5.** Telling their dreams brought them a tremendous sense of relief, of coming out of silence and **solitude**.
  a. Conversation
  b. Aloneness; isolation
  c. Unfamiliarity
  d. Excitement

CONTEXT AND DICTIONARY

Directions: Use context and the dictionary to determine the meaning of the boldfaced word in each sentence. Use word structure clues when applicable.

1. Throughout history—from ancient **shamans** to the Bible to Freud . . .

   Healers and/or spiritual guides in certain cultures
   _____

2. One **fertile** source of creativity is the ability to make new and unexpected connections . . .

   Rich; fruitful; productive
   _____

3. Many artists have experienced this **phenomenon**.

   Occurrence; special occurrence; circumstance or experience
   _____

4. Marlene Cantor . . . has discovered **recurring** themes in the dreams of middle-aged women.

   Repeating; re-occurring
   _____

5. In sharing these dreams, the woman reflected that the first **symbolic** dreamscape might express her fears about her aging body.

   Standing for or representing (another thing or level of meaning)
   _____

RESPOND TO THE READING

Directions: Write a half-page response to either of the following questions.

1. Describe and discuss one of your own dreams. What happened in the dream? What was the setting? What does the dream mean to you?

2. Can dreams predict future events? Can they warn us of dangers in waking life? Discuss your opinion regarding the power of dreams.

WEBQUEST

Directions: Use the Internet to find the answer to the following question. Write your answer on a sheet of paper. Print out the Web page you used for the answer or copy the URL on your sheet.

What causes nightmares?

READING 6B

NUTRITION: EATING FOR OPTIMUM HEALTH (HEALTH)

by Rebecca Donatelle

Reading 6B is taken from a health textbook. In this selection, the author talks about the importance of nutrition, offering information and advice on how to maintain a healthy diet. Read the selection to learn what the author has to say about food, nutrition, and health.

Pre-Reading Exercise

Directions: Complete this exercise before reading the passage. Preview the passage and answer the following questions.

1. What is the passage about?

   Nutrition and healthy eating

2. What will the author discuss under the first subheading ("Assessing Eating Behaviors: Are You What You Eat?")

   Influences on eating behaviors

3. What will the author discuss under the second subheading ("Eating for Health")?

   A healthy diet

4. What have you previously read or learned about diet and nutrition?

   Answers will vary.

5. How much do you pay attention to the nutritional value of the food you eat?

   Answers will vary.

6. Write three questions about diet and nutrition.

   Answers will vary.

Directions: Monitor and clarify your comprehension while reading the passage. Underline unfamiliar words and confusing sentences.

1   When was the last time you ate something without thinking about how much fat or carbohydrates or how many calories it contained? Can you remember when you last went out to dinner with friends and didn't "think twice" before ordering the fried foods or high-calorie desserts? Do you eat "differently" around your health-conscious friends from when you eat alone? If so, you are not alone. Clearly, Americans are trying to heed expert advice and the multiple pressures to eat low-fat, high-fiber foods and to consume fewer calories overall. However, knowing what to eat, how much to eat, and how to choose from a media-driven array of foods and nutrition advice can be mind-boggling.

2   The good news is that in survey after survey, 60 to 80 percent of food shoppers say they read food labels before selecting products; consume more vegetables, fruits, and lower-fat foods; and are cutting down on portion sizes and total calories. Diet book sales are at an all time high as millions of people make the leap toward healthy eating. The not-so-good news is that overweight and obesity rates continue to rise, making the United States one of the "fattest" nations in the world. In fact, although we report that increasing numbers of us read labels and are trying to eat more healthfully, in the same surveys nearly 78% of all adults indicate that they were not eating the recommended servings of fruits and vegetables and that they are still eating too many refined carbohydrates and high-fat foods.

3   Although the U.S. Food and Drug Administration (FDA), the U.S. Department of Agriculture (USDA), and several professional groups do a remarkable job in helping to protect our foods and

It takes information and planning to make healthy food choices, whether you are eating in the dining hall, or cooking your meals at home.

supplements, recommending foods we should eat, and supporting research to provide sound dietary advice, they can't possibly regulate every dietary claim or food product on the market or monitor individual behaviors. That means that the responsibility for making wise dietary decisions is largely yours.

4   Just how important is sound nutrition? A landmark review of over 4,500 research studies concluded that widespread consumption of 5 to 6 servings of fruits and vegetables daily would lower cancer rates by over 20 percent in the global population. Although no newer estimates of the global contribution of nutrition to cancer have been published, many documented studies and organizations indicate that undernutrition and overnutrition play major roles in global population health. Indeed, undernutrition, overnutrition, and diet-related chronic diseases account for more than half of the world's diseases and hundreds of millions of dollars in public expenditure.

5   Research has also emphasized the impact of diet and nutrition on cardiovascular disease, diabetes, and a host of other chronic and disabling conditions. The evidence is compelling and clear. Your health depends largely on what you eat and how much you eat throughout your life.

Assessing Eating Behaviors: Are You What You Eat?

6   True **hunger** occurs when there is a lack or shortage of basic foods needed to provide the energy and nutrients that support health. When we are hungry, chemical messages in the brain, especially in the hypothalamus, initiate a physiological response that prompts us to seek food. Few Americans have experienced the type of hunger that continues for days and threatens survival. Most of us eat because of our **appetite**, a learned psychological desire to eat that may or may not have anything to do with feeling hungry. Appetite can be triggered by smells, tastes, and other triggers such as certain times of day, special occasions, or proximity to a favorite food.

7   Hunger and appetite are not the only forces involved in our physiological drive to eat. Other

hunger The physiological impulse to seek food, prompted by the lack or shortage of basic foods needed to provide the energy and nutrients that support health.
appetite The desire to eat; normally accompanies hunger but is more psychological than physiological.

factors that influence when, how, and what we eat include the following:

- *Cultural and social meanings attached to food.* Cultural traditions and food choices give us many of our *food preferences.* We learn to like the tastes of certain foods, especially the foods we grew up eating. A yearning for sweet, salty, or high-fat foods can evolve from our earliest days.

- *Convenience and advertising.* That juicy burger on TV looked really good. You've got to have it.

- *Habit or custom.* Often we select foods because they are familiar and fit religious, political, or spiritual views.

- *Emotional comfort.* Eating it makes you feel better—a form of reward and security. We derive pleasure or sensory delight from eating the foods and reward ourselves with foods.

- *Nutritional value.* You think the food is good or bad for you, or it may help you maintain your weight.

- *Social interaction.* Eating out or having company over for a meal is an enjoyable social event.

- *Regional/seasonal trends.* Some foods may be favored in your area by season or overall climate.

8   With all of the factors that influence our dietary choices and the wide array of foods available, the challenge of eating for health increases daily. Fortunately, we have a wealth of solid information that serves as a foundation for our decisions. **Nutrition** is the science that investigates the relationship between physiological function and the essential elements of the foods we eat. With our country's overabundance of food and vast array of choices, media that "prime" us to want the tasty morsels shown in advertisements, and easy access to almost every type of **nutrient** (proteins, carbohy-

drates, fats, vitamins, minerals, and water), Americans should have few nutritional problems. However, these "diets of affluence" contribute to many major diseases, including obesity-related problems with heart disease; cancer; diabetes; high blood pressure; cirrhosis of the liver; varicose veins; gout; gallbladder disease; respiratory problems; abdominal hernias; flat feet; injuries to the knees, hips, and other weight-bearing joints; complications in pregnancy and surgery; and even higher accident rates, to name but a few.

Eating for Health

Generally, a healthful diet provides the proper   9
combination of energy and nutrients. It is sufficient to keep us functioning well in our daily activities. A healthful diet should be.

- *Adequate.* It provides enough of the energy, nutrients, and fiber to maintain health and essential body functions. A **calorie** is the unit of measurement used to quantify the amount of energy we obtain from a particular food. Everyone's energy needs differ (Table 6B.1). For example, a small woman who has a sedentary lifestyle may need only 1,700 calories of energy to support her body's functions, whereas a professional biker may need several thousand calories of energy to be up for his competition.

- *Moderate.* The quantity of food you consume can cause you to gain weight. Moderate caloric consumption, portion control, and awareness of the total amount of nutrients in the foods you eat are key aspects of dietary health.

- *Balanced.* Your diet should contain the proper combination of foods from different groups.

- *Varied.* Eat a lot of different foods each day. Variety helps you avoid boredom and can make it easier to keep your diet interesting and in control.

- *Nutrient dense.* Nutrient density refers to the proportion of vitamins, minerals,

nutrition The science that investigates the relationship between physiological function and the essential elements of foods eaten.
nutrients The constituents of food that sustain humans physiologically: proteins, carbohydrates, fats, vitamins, minerals, and water.

calorie A unit of measure that indicates the amount of energy obtained from a particular food.

Table 6B.1   Estimated Daily Calorie Needs

	Calorie Range		
	Sedentary[a]	→	Active[b]
Children			
2–3 years	1,000	→	1,400
Females			
4–8 years	1,200	→	1,800
9–13	1,600	→	2,200
14–18	1,800	→	2,400
19–30	2,000	→	2,400
31–50	1,800	→	2,200
51+	1,600	→	2,200
Males			
4–8 years	1,400	→	2,000
9–13	1,800	→	2,600
14–18	2,200	→	3,200
19–30	2,400	→	3,000
31–50	2,200	→	3,000
51+	2,000	→	2,800

[a] A lifestyle that includes only the light physical activity associated with typical day-to-day life.
[b] A lifestyle that includes physical activity equivalent to walking more than 3 miles per day at 3 to 4 miles per hour, in addition to the light physical activity associated with typical day-to-day life.

Source: Department of Agriculture Center for Nutrition Policy & Promotion, April 2005, www .MyPyramid.gov.

and other nutrients compared to the number of calories. In short, the foods you eat should have the biggest nutritional bang for the calories consumed. Making each bite count and not wasting calories on foods that give you little nutritional value are also keys to healthful eating.

In a 30-year study of changes in consumption, women's overall caloric intake increased by 22 percent and men's by 7 percent. Are we eating more food, or is it what we are eating? Trends indicate that it isn't actual amounts of food, but the number of calories in the foods we choose to eat (Figure 6B.1). When these trends are combined with our increasingly sedentary lifestyle, it is not surprising that we have seen a dramatic rise in obesity.   10

Americans typically get approximately 38 percent of their calories from fat, 15 percent from proteins, 22 percent from complex carbohydrates, and 24 percent from simple sugars. Nearly one-third of the calories we consume come from junk foods with no real nutritional value. Sweets and desserts, soft drinks, sugary fruit juice beverages, and alcoholic beverages make up 25 percent of those calories, and another 5 percent come from salty snacks and fruit-flavored drinks. In sharp contrast, healthy foods such as vegetables and fruit make up only 10 percent of our total calories.   11

—Donatelle, *Health: The Basics,* 8th ed.

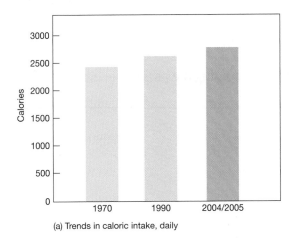

(a) Trends in caloric intake, daily

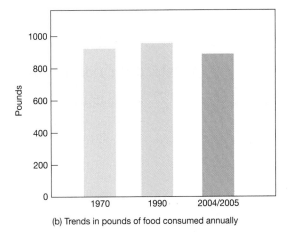

(b) Trends in pounds of food consumed annually

Figure 6B.1   Trends in Caloric Intake and Food Consumption

Source: United States Department of Agriculture, "Food consumption Patterns: How We've Changed, 1970–2005," December 2005, www.usda.gov.

You, the Reader

Interest Rating. Please rate the interest level of the reading on the following scale (circle one):

5—Very interesting   2—A little boring

4—Fairly interesting   1—Very boring

3—Mildly interesting

Difficulty Rating. Please rate the difficulty level of the reading on the following scale (circle one):

5—Very difficult   2—Fairly easy

4—Fairly difficult   1—Very easy

3—Moderate

Comments: Please explain your ratings and make any other comments you wish about the reading.

Answers will vary.

MONITORING AND CLARIFYING COMPREHENSION EXERCISE

1. Using a 1 to 5 scale (5 = excellent; 4 = good; 3 = fair; 2 = poor; 1 = very poor), rate your comprehension of the passage.

   Answers will vary.

2. What prior knowledge or experience do you have that helped you understand the passage?

   Answers will vary.

3. What other background information would be helpful for reading this passage?

   Answers will vary.

4. What did you visualize or imagine while reading the passage?

   Answers will vary.

5. Which strategies did you use while reading the passage? (Check any that you used):

Answers will vary.

_____ Rereading

_____ Marking the material

_____ Using context clues

_____ Consulting the dictionary

_____ Analyzing word structure

_____ Analyzing or paraphrasing confusing sentences

_____ Visualizing

_____ Reading aloud

_____ Relating to the material

_____ Relating to prior knowledge

_____ Thinking of real-life examples

_____ Other (explain): _____

6. Which strategy or strategies were most helpful? Explain.

Answers will vary.

7. Choose the better paraphrase for the following sentence:

Author's Statement: With all of the factors that influence our dietary choices and the wide array of foods available, the challenge of eating for health increases daily.

Choose the better paraphrase:

_____ a. A healthy diet is more important than ever because modern life is full of many stresses.

__√__ b. Eating for health has become more difficult because there are so many things that affect our food choices and so many food choices available to us.

8. What were the most important things you learned from the passage about diet and nutrition?

Answers will vary.

COMPREHENSION QUESTIONS

Directions: For questions 1–5, choose the answer that best completes the statement. For questions 6–10, write your response in the space provided. Base all answers on what you read in the selection. Refer back to the selection as necessary to answer the questions.

___c___   **1.** An important concern regarding American health and diet is:
  a. The lack of information available about good nutrition.
  b. The popularity of diet books.
  c. The increase in the number of overweight individuals.
  d. The lack of access to healthy foods.

___a___   **2.** Decisions about what we eat are influenced:
  a. By a wide variety of factors.
  b. Mostly by our cultural heritage.
  c. Mostly by our knowledge of nutrition.
  d. Almost entirely by our appetite.

___d___   **3.** Which of the following is *not* a characteristic of a healthy diet?
  a. It provides the amount of calories needed by the individual.
  b. It consists of foods high in nutrients.
  c. It consists of a variety of foods.
  d. It consists of eating the same foods every day.

___b___   **4.** The author states that cancer rates would be lowered if:
  a. People reduced their caloric intake.
  b. More fruits and vegetables were consumed.
  c. The U.S. Food and Drug Administration protected our foods better.
  d. Carbohydrate consumption was reduced.

___c___   **5.** Figure 6B.1 shows that:
  a. Americans have been reducing their caloric intake and the amount of food they eat.
  b. Both caloric intake and the amount of food consumed have risen steadily since 1970.
  c. Caloric intake has increased while the amount of food consumed has decreased.
  d. Caloric intake has decreased while the amount of food consumed has increased.

6. What is the difference between hunger and appetite?

Hunger is the physiological response to lack of food; appetite is a learned

psychological desire to eat.

7. List three factors that influence the amount of calories an individual needs.

Gender, age, lifestyle

8. According to Table 6B.1, how many calories does an active 16-year-old female need daily?

2,400

9. What are some challenges to maintaining a healthy diet?

There are many foods and food choices available; we may be influenced

by commercials or other people; we are surrounded by high-calorie foods

with little nutritional value.

10. Which of the factors listed on p. 296 have the most influence on your food choices? Explain.

Answers will vary.

VOCABULARY EXERCISES

Pronunciation Guide (see p. 90 for list of phonetic symbols)	
affluence	(ăf'l$\overline{oo}$-əns)
array	(ə-rā')
expenditure	(ĕk-spĕn'də-chər)
hypothalamus	(hī'pō-thăl'ə-məs)
obesity	(ō-bē'sĭ-tē)
physiological	(fĭz'ē-ə-lŏj'ĭ-kəl)
proximity	(prŏk-sĭm'ĭ-tē)
sedentary	(sĕd'n-tĕr'ē)

WORDS IN CONTEXT

Directions: Choose the meaning for the boldfaced word that best fits the context.

c   **1.** The not-so-good news is that overweight and **obesity** rates continue to rise, making the United States one of the "fattest" nations in the world.
  a. Health
  b. Disease
  c. Extreme fatness
  d. Underweight

d   **2.** Indeed, undernutrition, overnutrition, and diet-related chronic diseases account for . . . hundreds of millions of dollars in public **expenditure**.
  a. Savings
  b. Health threats
  c. Policies
  d. Spending

a   **3.** Appetite can be triggered by smells, tastes, and other triggers such as certain times of day, special occasions, or **proximity** to a favorite food.
  a. Nearness
  b. Frequent eating of
  c. Preference
  d. Memory

<u> a </u> **4.** With all of the factors that influence our dietary choices and the wide **array** of foods available, the challenge of eating for health increases daily.
    a. Range
    b. Knowledge
    c. Desire
    d. Influence

<u> c </u> **5.** . . . media that "**prime**" us to want their tasty morsels shown in advertisements . . .
    a. Teach
    b. Discourage
    c. Stimulate
    d. Choose

CONTEXT AND DICTIONARY

Directions: Use context and the dictionary to determine the meaning of the boldfaced word in each sentence. Use word structure clues when applicable.

1. Indeed, undernutrition, overnutrition, and diet-related **chronic** diseases account for . . . hundreds of millions of dollars in public expenditure.

   Lasting a long time

2. When we are hungry, chemical messages in the brain, especially in the **hypothalamus,** initiate a physiological response that prompts us to seek food.

   A part of the brain that regulates many basic body functions

3. When we are hungry, chemical messages in the brain, especially in the hypothalamus, initiate a **physiological** response that prompts us to seek food.

   Physical; bodily

4. We derive pleasure or **sensory** delight from eating the foods and reward ourselves with food.

   Relating to the senses

5. However, these "diets of **affluence**" contribute to many major diseases ...

   Wealth

6. For example, a small woman with a **sedentary** lifestyle may need only 1,700 calories of energy to support her body's functions . . .

   Involving much sitting; inactive

RESPOND TO THE READING

Directions: Write a half-page response to either of the following questions.

1. Discuss your own diet and eating habits. What do you eat in a typical week? How could your diet be improved?

2. Why are so many people unsuccessful in their attempts to lose weight? What do you think are the best ways to reach and maintain a healthy body weight?

WEBQUEST

Directions: Use the Internet to find the answers to the following questions. Write your answers on a sheet of paper. Print out the Web page you used for the answers or copy the URL on your sheet.

What is a food pyramid? How might a food pyramid be used to develop and maintain a healthy diet?

CHAPTER 6 REVIEW

Making Sense

When we monitor comprehension, we notice whether or not what we're reading makes sense to us. We develop an awareness of how well we're understanding what we're reading. We can strengthen our monitoring process by interrupting our reading from time to time to assess our understanding of the material. When comprehension is not satisfactory, we identify the reasons for it. Comprehension challenges usually result from either *poor concentration; unfamiliar vocabulary; confusing sentences; an unfamiliar subject; a lack of background knowledge;* or *abstract material.* When we are monitoring our comprehension successfully and our understanding of the material is good, we can often anticipate or predict what will come next in the text.

Clarifying Comprehension

We use active reading strategies to clarify and strengthen our comprehension. We choose strategies that are consistent with our learning style and that respond to the specific challenges we're tackling. These strategies include *strategies for improving concentration; vocabulary strategies; identifying topics and main ideas of paragraphs; rereading; marking the material; analyzing sentences; paraphrasing; visualizing; reading aloud; relating or connecting with the material; recalling prior knowledge; obtaining background information;* and *thinking of real-life examples.* It is especially important to use these strategies when reading more advanced material or when we need to remember new ideas and information from the reading material.

Paraphrasing

When we paraphrase, we express an author's ideas in different words. Paraphrasing is a useful strategy for clarifying comprehension. Paraphrasing helps us make the author's ideas our own.

Skills Online: Monitoring Your Comprehension Online

Readings

Reading 6A: Waking Up to Our Dreams (Psychology)

Reading 6B: Nutrition: Eating for Optimum Health (Health)

CHAPTER TESTS

TEST 6.1. MONITORING COMPREHENSION

Directions: Answer the following questions without looking back in the chapter.

1. Name and explain the two steps involved in monitoring comprehension.

   The first step is interrupting your reading to judge how well you've understood the

   material. The second step is identifying the reasons for any comprehension

   difficulties.

2. Briefly explain why it is important for college readers to monitor their comprehension.

   College readers must be independent readers. They must be able to make accurate,

   independent judgments of their comprehension.

TEST 6.2. PARAGRAPH SENSE

Directions: Each paragraph contains a word or phrase that doesn't belong. Cross out the mistakenly placed word or phrase so that the paragraph makes sense. When crossing out a phrase, make sure you eliminate every word that doesn't belong—and only the words that don't belong—so that the remaining paragraph reads correctly. An example is provided.

EXAMPLE

When registering for online services under a screen name, it can be tempting to think your identity is a secret to other users. Many people will say or do things on the Internet that they would never do in real life because they believe that they are acting anonymously. However, most blogs, e-mail and instant messenger services, and social networking sites are tied to your real identity ~~and your neighbor's home~~ in some way. While your identity may be superficially concealed by a screen name, it often takes little more than a quick Google search to uncover your name, address, and other personal and possibly sensitive information.

—Ebert and Griffin, *Business Essentials,* 7th ed.

1. What is the most popular and widely consumed drug in the United States? Caffeine. Almost half of all Americans drink coffee every day, and many others consume caffeine in some other form, mainly for its well-known "wake-up" effect. Drinking coffee is legal, even socially encouraged. Many people believe caffeine is not a drug and not really addictive. Coffee, soft drinks, ~~cotton shirts~~, and other caffeine-containing products seem harmless. If you share these attitudes, think again; research in the past decade has linked caffeine to certain health problems.

—Donatelle, *Health: The Basics,* 8th ed.

2. In France in 1422, Charles VII, a boy of seventeen, inherited the throne and the problems that his father, who was often mad, had never solved. A major problem was the noblemen, the castle dwellers who would take no orders from the king. The other problem was the English, who had raided France since early in the 1300s in what was now the "Hundred Years' War." The English ruled great chunks of northern and southwestern France, including the capital, Paris. Charles lacked the money for an army ~~or air force~~ strong enough to drive them out.

—Davis, *The Human Story*

3. Consumer income affects demand because, as income rises, people tend to spend more on most goods and services. Prior to graduation, a young couple's combined income was $6000 per year ~~whenever it rained~~, and now it is $60,000 per year. The dramatic rise in income will cause a substantial increase in their purchases of goods and services; they may buy a new car, better cuts of meat, and new wardrobes. Purchases of some goods and services would actually fall with the rise in income. Instead of riding a city bus, they now drive to work in a new car. Instead of eating macaroni and cheese at home, they eat out.

—Gregory, *Essentials of Economics,* 4th ed.

TEST 6.3. CLARIFYING COMPREHENSION

Directions: Without looking back in this chapter, name two strategies that you could use when encountering each of the following comprehension obstacles. (Any two of the answers provided in each case)

Poor concentration   Use active reading strategies; raise questions; reread; mark the material; clarify purpose; identify causes and respond

Unfamiliar vocabulary   Use context clues; use dictionary; identify word structure

Confusing sentences   Break sentences down; paraphrase; visualize; reread; read aloud

Unfamiliar subject   Relate; recall prior knowledge; identify and obtain missing information; reread; identify topic and main idea

Abstract material   Relate; think of real life examples; recall prior knowledge; reread; identify topic and main idea

TEST 6.4. PARAPHRASING

Directions: Paraphrase any *two* of the following sentences. Your paraphrase should be one complete sentence of your own wording that accurately reflects the meaning of the original sentence.

1. All societies have particular ways of encouraging and enforcing what they view as appropriate behavior while discouraging and punishing what they consider to be improper conduct.

Every society has its own ways to encourage desired behaviors and discourage undesired behaviors. (sample answer)

2. A person's work is an important factor in determining personal identity and satisfaction in life.

—Derlega and Janda, *Personal Adjustment: The Psychology of Everyday Life,* 3rd ed.

Work contributes significantly to how a person sees herself and to her fullfillment in life. (sample answer)

3. Given the contrast between the conversational styles of men and women, the conditions are ripe for conflicts to arise.

—Beck, *Love Is Never Enough*

Gender differences in conversational style often contribute to conflict between

men and women. (sample answer)

TEST 6.5. CLARIFYING COMPREHENSION

Directions: Read the following passage using the clarifying strategies that are most helpful to you. Then answer the questions that follow the passage.

EARLY DAYS OF ROCK & ROLL

When rock and roll was forming, in the 1940s and 1950s, people weren't constantly bombarded with music and entertainment. There weren't televisions droning in every den and living room; radio stations didn't broadcast around the clock. The media provided only a portion of most people's musical nourishment, and these media weren't nationally standardized or programmed from one central source. Local radio stations might carry national network programming during certain hours, but most of their shows were locally generated, and responsive to the tastes of the area. Radio-station program directors were not the powers they later became; disc jockeys played whatever they liked, or whatever their audience wanted to hear. There were local hits, records that sold almost exclusively within a given area, and local artists whose styles—familiar to their fans—might differ considerably from national norms. When a performer or group established a solid regional following, there was often a small record company in the area that would take a chance on them, hoping for national hits but making records that largely reflected local trends. These were the labels that first gave rock and roll a hearing, and later the labels with the first rock and roll hits: Sun in Memphis,

Chess in Chicago, King/Federal in Cincinnati, Los Angeles's Imperial and Specialty with their strong New Orleans connections, and so on.

The men who ran these labels, and the singers and musicians who performed on the records, have become visionaries in retrospect. But they were hardly revolutionaries. Even a man as creative and outspoken as Sun's founder, Sam C. Phillips, who gave Elvis, Howling Wolf, Jerry Lee Lewis, B. B. King, Johnny Cash, Carl Perkins, and Ike Turner their first shots at recording, was solidly rooted in the swing-band era of popular music. Phillips's first job in Memphis was engineering network radio broadcasts by nationally known dance bands from the swank roof garden of Memphis's Peabody Hotel. He was an avid follower of the big bands, and once told me that his favorite record of all time was "T. D.'s Boogie Woogie" by the Tommy Dorsey Orchestra. In New Orleans, Dave Bartholomew, who produced all Fats Domino's hits and led the band that played on Little Richard's breakthrough recordings, was a jazz trumpeter by training and inclination, another key creator of rock and roll's first generation whose tastes and values were shaped by the swing era.

—Palmer, *Rock & Roll: An Unruly History*

1. *Vocabulary*: List two unfamiliar words from the passage.

Answers will vary.

Which strategy or strategies did you use to understand these words?

Answers will vary.

2. *Sentences*: Underline one difficult sentence from the passage.

   Which clarifying strategy or strategies did you use to understand the sentence?

   Answers will vary.

   _____

3. What prior knowledge do you have of this subject?

   Answers will vary.

4. What was the biggest challenge in understanding the passage?

   Answers will vary.

5. Which strategy or strategies most helped you to clarify your understanding of the passage?

   Answers will vary.

6. How was the music world of the 1940s different from the music world of today?

   In the 1940s they didn't have media playing music all the time. A lot of the music

   people heard was local. (sample answer)

7. How did local radio stations contribute to the development of rock and roll?

   In the '40s and '50s the DJs played pretty much what they wanted and what their

   audiences liked. Artists had local hits and local followings. Successful artists made

   records on local labels that contributed to the launching of rock and roll. (sample answer)

8. How did Sam Phillips contribute to the development of rock and roll?

   Sam Phillips founded Sun in Memphis and gave many rock and roll greats their

   first shots at recording, including Elvis, Jerry Lee Lewis, Johnny Cash, and B. B. King.

   (sample answer)

9. What is the main idea of the first paragraph in the passage?

   When rock and roll was forming in the '40s and '50s, the music world was very

   different from today. (sample answer)

10. Choose the better paraphrase for the following sentence.

    Author's statement: "There weren't televisions droning in every den and living room; radio stations didn't broadcast around the clock."

    Choose the better paraphrase:

    __√__ a. People didn't have television sets on all around their homes and radio stations weren't available at all times.

    _____ b. Televisions weren't popular and radio stations didn't broadcast late at night.

You, the Reader: Chapter 6 Wrap-up

Directions: Use one or two of the following questions to write a half-page response to Chapter 6.

- What were the most important things you learned from this chapter? How will you use what you have learned from this chapter?
- How have you changed your reading habits in response to this chapter?
- Which strategies most help you to engage with your reading? Which strategies most help you to strengthen and clarify your comprehension?
- What parts of the chapter did you find most engaging? What questions do you have about the chapter?

For support in meeting this chapter's objectives, go to MyReadingLab and select *Memorization and Concentration.*

Connecting Ideas: Sentence Relationships and Transition Words

---

Pre-Reading Exercise for Chapter 7

Directions: Preview the chapter and answer the following questions.

1. What is the chapter about?
   Relationships between sentences and transition words
   _____

2. Name the four types of sentence relationships discussed in this chapter.
   Sequence; Addition; Contrast; Reason
   _____

3. What is a transition word?
   A transition word is a word that indicates the relationship between sentences or ideas.
   _____

4. What have you previously learned about how sentences and ideas in a paragraph or passage relate?
   Answers will vary.
   _____

5. What have you previously learned about signal words?
   Answers will vary.
   _____
   _____

6. Write two questions about the content of this chapter.
   Answers will vary.
   _____
   _____

In Chapter 6 you learned some strategies for monitoring and clarifying your comprehension. One important part of monitoring comprehension is noticing whether the relationships between the ideas and sentences in a paragraph or passage (or even, in complex sentences, the ideas within a sentence) are clear. It's possible to understand all the sentences in a given paragraph or passage but fail to see how some of them connect; then the material won't make complete sense.

Chapter 7 will provide some useful strategies for identifying and clarifying relationships between ideas and sentences.

Active Reading Strategy: Identifying Sentence Relationships

 What's wrong with the following paragraph?

Nobody is born knowing how to add and subtract. It is important to recognize the main ideas when reading in your textbook. How can you tell what tomorrow's weather will be like? After all, a better education leads to a brighter future.

You noticed, of course, that although each of the sentences in the preceding paragraph is clear, the paragraph makes no sense because the sentences have nothing to do with one another. In other words, there is no logical *relationship* between any of the sentences.

Normally (and thankfully) when we are reading, the sentences are related. Recognizing *how* the ideas and sentences are related strengthens both comprehension and retention of your reading material.

There are of course many ways in which sentences or ideas can be related. In Chapter 5, for example, you learned three ways that a paragraph's details can relate to the paragraph's main idea (example, evidence, and reason). Effective reading also includes understanding how the details in a paragraph relate to one another, and how ideas relate from paragraph to paragraph. In this chapter we will focus on four of the most common sentence relationships found in college texts:

- *Sequence*: relates in time order
- *Addition*: adds similar information
- *Contrast*: presents a different or opposing idea
- *Reason*: provides reason, cause, explanation

Active readers use these sentence relationships as tools to monitor, clarify, and strengthen their comprehension and retention.

Sequence

Sequence in reading material means that one event or step follows another in time. As a logical relationship between sentences, sequence means that the events or steps in one sentence come before—or after—the events or steps in another sentence. Consider the following example.

John went to the store. He bought a loaf of bread and a gallon of milk.

In this example, John *first* went into the store, and *then* he bought bread and milk. The events in the second sentence occurred *after* the events in the first sentence. These two sentences are therefore related by sequence.

Here's another example of sequence:

From the mouth, food passes into the esophagus, a 9- to 10-inch tube that connects the mouth and stomach. A series of contractions and relaxations by the muscles lining the esophagus gently move food to the next digestive organ, the stomach.

—Donatelle, *Health: The Basics*, 6th ed.

The preceding passage describes a sequence of steps in the digestion of food. The step in the second sentence (muscle activity moving food down the esophagus to the stomach) occurs after the step in the first sentence (food moving from the mouth to the esophagus).

Sequence is used in narrative writing (writing that tells a story). You will find sequence in historical material, and also in science and technical material when steps in a process are presented.

EXERCISE 7.1 SEQUENCE

Directions: Write two sentences that are related by sequence.

Answers will vary.

Addition

When an author adds *similar* information to what he or she has previously stated, we have the logical relationship called *addition*. In other words, the information in a given sentence is adding on to the information in the preceding sentence by continuing with similar information. Consider the following example.

> Reading—whether it's a book, newspaper, or the Internet—is a powerful means of obtaining information. Reading for many people can also be a source of great pleasure.

In this example, the first sentence describes one important benefit of reading—gaining information. The second sentence identifies another, or *additional*, benefit of reading—pleasure. In other words, the second sentence adds to the first sentence with similar information.

Here is another, more complex example of addition.

> Sculpture possesses what a painting can only pretend to have: real, solid, three-dimensional existence. Sculptures are not in some other world that we must imagine; they are bodies in the same world as we are bodies.
>
> —Bishop, *A Beginner's Guide to* the *Humanities,* 2nd ed.

In this example, the first sentence makes a point about sculpture—that sculpture is physical and three-dimensional. What does the second sentence add? The second sentence further explains the same point by reminding us that sculptures are not imaginary but occupy space in the real world (which we know is three-dimensional) just as people's bodies do. In short, the second sentence adds to the point in the first sentence by explaining it further in different words.

Addition is used whenever an author simply wants to add more information that is similar or to enlarge on a previous sentence; you'll find addition relationships throughout texts of virtually all subjects.

EXERCISE 7.2 ADDITION

Directions: Write two sentences that are related by addition.

Answers will vary.

_____

_____

Contrast

Contrast means difference or dissimilarity. When we contrast things, we identify the ways in which they are different from each other. You will remember that in Chapter 2 we looked at contrast clues for vocabulary. We determined the meaning of unfamiliar words from other words in the context with opposite meanings.

Sentence meanings may also stand in contrast. Often an author will present an idea and then introduce an opposing, or different, idea in a following sentence. When this occurs, we have the logical relationship we call contrast. Consider the following example.

> Linda is a talented athlete who has succeeded with almost every sport she's played. Golf, however, is one sport that Linda doesn't play well, despite her repeated attempts to master the game.

In this example, the second sentence provides information that contrasts with the information in the first. Instead of adding to the first sentence (for instance, by saying more about the sports that Linda plays well), the second sentence contrasts with the first sentence by talking about a sport she doesn't play well.

Here is another example of contrast.

> Often, we think of stress as an externally imposed factor. But for most of us, stress results from an internal state of emotional tension that occurs in response to the various demands of living.
>
> —Donatelle, *Health: The Basics,* 6th ed.

In this example, the second sentence contrasts with the first sentence by providing a different view of stress. The first sentence tells us that we think of stress as coming from outside of ourselves; the second sentence tells us that in reality stress usually comes from inside ourselves. In other words, in the second sentence the author changes our understanding of stress by presenting a contrasting view of it.

In short, contrast is used when an author wants to introduce or present differing ideas. Contrast may be found in textbooks of all subjects.

EXERCISE 7-3 CONTRAST

Directions: Write two sentences that are related by contrast.

Answers will vary.

Reason

Reason, our fourth type of sentence relationship, occurs when the information in one sentence provides a reason, cause, or explanation for an event or statement in another sentence. For example, in Chapter 5 we noted that a detail in a paragraph sometimes supports the main idea by providing a reason, or explanation, for it.

There are also other ways that authors use the logical relationship *reason.* In historical material, for example, an event in one sentence may be a cause of something that happens (a result) in another sentence. Sometimes, in expository material, an idea in one sentence may be a logical conclusion from an idea stated in another sentence.

Let's look at a simple example of sentences related by *reason.*

> Everyone had a great time at Mike's party last weekend. Mike therefore decided to plan another party soon.

In this example, Mike's decision to plan a second party was the result of the success of his first party. In other words, the *reason* for the second party was the success of the first party. Here's another simple example.

> The wide receiver injured his hand on the last play of the game. Consequently, he will be sidelined for practice this week and for the next game.

In this example, the information in the second sentence—that the receiver will miss practice and a game—is the result of the event (the reason) in the first sentence—that he injured his hand.

Now let's look at a more complicated example from an education textbook.

> Culturally relevant teaching validates the cultures of students and communities. As a result, students begin to feel that teachers care about them, which is a first step in building a foundation for trust between teachers and students who are from different groups.
>
> —Johnson et al., *Foundations of American Education,* 14th ed.

In this example, the first sentence states that teaching that is culturally relevant validates (values and supports) students' cultures and communities. The second sentence describes a *result* of culturally relevant teaching—students feel that their teachers care about them, which helps build trust. The first sentence is the *reason* for the *result* described in the second sentence.

You will find reason in textbooks of all subjects whenever an author wants to answer the question "why." Reason is especially important in historical and scientific material. It is important in any subject when a theory is being explained.

EXERCISE 7.4 REASON

Directions: Write two sentences that are related by reason.

Answers will vary.

_____

_____

Sentence Relationships

Sequence: the events or steps in one sentence come before or after the events or steps in the preceding sentence

Addition: a sentence adds information that is similar to the information in the previous sentence

Contrast: a sentence presents a differing or opposing idea from the previous sentence

Reason: the information in one sentence provides a reason, cause, or explanation for an event or statement in the preceding or following sentence

EXERCISE **7.5** RECOGNIZING SENTENCE RELATIONSHIPS

Directions: Review the sentences you wrote for Exercises 7.1 through 7.4, rewriting them if necessary. Then, working with one of your classmates, select one of your sentence pairs at random and read it to your partner; your partner must guess which relationship your sentences illustrate. Alternate reading your sentence pairs until you and your partner have read and guessed the relationship for each pair. If you disagree on a pair, share your different points of view.

EXERCISE **7.6** SENTENCE RELATIONSHIPS

Directions: Read each pair of sentences and decide how they are related. In the space provided, write Sequence, Addition, Contrast, or Reason to indicate which relationship is used to connect the sentences, and briefly explain your answer. An example is provided.

EXAMPLE

Everyone had a great time at Mike's party last weekend. Mike therefore decided to plan another party soon.

Reason: everyone having a great time at the first party is the reason why

Mike is planning another party.

1. If you are like many Americans, you already take multivitamins or other supplements at least occasionally. You probably take them because you don't always eat carefully, and you want to make sure you get the vitamins and minerals you need.

   —Nestle, "How to Get the Nutrients You Need," *Parade Magazine*

   Reason: The second sentence states the reasons why people take vitamins and

   supplements.

2. The traditional American Dream is based on the belief that hardworking citizens can better their lives, pay their monthly bills without worry, give their children a start to an even better life, and still save enough to live comfortably after they retire. But many average Americans are struggling—squeezed by rising costs, declining wages, credit-card debt, and diminished benefits, with little left over to save for retirement.

   —Wallechinsky, "Is the American Dream Still Possible?" *Parade Magazine*

   Contrast: The sentences contrast the American Dream with the realities of

   struggling Americans.

3. There are ads on TV, ads on the Internet, ads in video games. There are ads for breakfast cereals, ads for fast-food burgers, ads for candy treats.

   —Smith, "Ad Infinitum," *The Boston Globe*

   Addition: The second sentence adds more ads.

4. If you're having problems with technology, you probably figure it's your own fault. But here's the good (and bad) news: It's not.

—Maeda, "How to Keep It Simple," *Parade Magazine*

Contrast: The sentences contrast blaming yourself (for problems with technology)

with the "news" that it's not your fault.

5. We all love a bargain. So, when we go to the store with $100 to spend, we naturally look for the most for our money.

—Lindstrom, "Buyer Beware," *Parade Magazine*

Reason: Loving a bargain is the reason we look for the most for our money.

6. In 2005 a video-playing Internet device introduced by Apple fully liberated viewers from planting themselves before large and stationary television sets. By 2008 handheld iPods could store as many as 150 hours of video and display the images on a 2 1/2-inch color screen.

—Vivian, *The Media of Mass Communication,* 9th ed.

Sequence: The events in the second sentence follow the events in the first sentence.

7. At the beginning of the 20th century, the federal government continued to extend protection of wildlands through national parks and wildlife refuges. Later, state governments expanded parks and open spaces as voters authorized bond issues to finance land acquisitions.

—Linden, "The Call of the Wild," *Parade Magazine*

Sequence: The events in the second sentence came after the events in the first

sentence.

8. Children who are responsible for their own care after school experience more accidents and injuries. They are also at risk of behavior problems, lower social competence, and poorer academic performance.

—Johnson et al., *Foundations of American Education,* 14th ed.

Addition: The second sentence adds more risk factors for children who are

responsible for their own after school care.

9. In the movie *Footloose,* the village elders of a Midwestern town try to keep their youngsters from dancing. They suspect that dancing will encourage drinking, drugs, and unbridled lovemaking.

—Janaro and Altshuler, *The Art of Being Human,* 8th ed.

Reason: The second sentence gives the reason the elders didn't want youngsters

dancing (It would encourage drinking, drugs and sex).

10. On September 6, 1901, an anarchist named Leon Czolgosz shot President McKinley during a public reception at the Pan-American Exposition at Buffalo, New York. Eight days later McKinley died and Theodore Roosevelt became president of the United States.

—Garraty and Carnes, *The American Nation: A History of the United States,* 10th ed.

Sequence: The events in the second sentence come after the events in the first

sentence.

EXERCISE 7-7 SENTENCE RELATIONSHIPS

Directions: Each sentence below is followed by two other sentences. Choose the sentence which connects to the first sentence by the indicated relationship. An example is provided.

EXAMPLE

Bribery involves the voluntary giving or receiving of anything of value with the intent to influence the action of a public official.

—Albanese, *Criminal Justice,* 3rd ed.

Check the sentence that relates to the previous sentence by addition:

_____ On the other hand, intentionally preventing a public servant from lawfully performing an official function is obstruction of justice.

___√___ The more important the official act to be performed is, the more serious the penalty.

—Albanese, *Criminal Justice,* 3rd ed.

1. Most people speak at about 120 to 150 words per minute.

—Bovee and Thill, *Business Communication Essentials,* 3rd ed.

Check the sentence that relates to the previous sentence by contrast:

_____ The exact rate at which we speak varies according to person and circumstance.

___√___ However, humans can process audio information at up to 500 words per minute or more.

—Bovee and Thill, *Business Communication Essentials,* 3rd ed.

2. College students often face a challenge when trying to eat healthy foods.

—Donatelle, *Health: The Basics,* 6th ed.

Check the sentence that relates to the previous sentence by reason:

___√___ Some students live in dorms and do not have their own cooking or refrigeration facilities.

_____ Buy fruits and vegetables in season whenever possible for their lower cost, higher nutrient quality, and greater variety.

—Donatelle, *Health: The Basics,* 6th ed.

3. At age 2, children may call all large animals by one name (say, "horsie") and all small animals by another (say, "bug").

—Wade and Tavris, *Invitation to Psychology,* 4th ed.

Check the sentence that relates to the previous sentence by sequence:

_√_ At 4, they may protest that a sibling has more fruit juice when it is only the shapes of the glasses that differ, not the amount of juice.

_____ Children do not think the way adults do.

—Wade and Tavris, *Invitation to Psychology,* 4th ed.

4. Music can be found in every nook of human society.

—Bishop, *A Beginner's Guide to the Humanities,* 2nd ed.

Check the sentence that relates to the previous sentence by addition:

_____ However, the types of instruments used and the types of songs that are sung vary significantly from culture to culture.

_√_ In fact, we can measure the diversity of our society by the differences in its music.

—Bishop, *A Beginner's Guide to the Humanities,* 2nd ed.

5. Advertising contributes to prosperity.
Check the sentence that relates to the previous sentence by reason:

_____ However, advertising has no role and serves no purpose when survival is the question.

_√_ By dangling desirable commodities and services before mass audiences, advertising can inspire people to greater individual productivity so that they can have more income to buy the things that are advertised.

—Vivian, *The Media of Mass Communication,* 9th ed.

Active Reading Strategy: Recognizing Transition Words

Transition words are words that indicate the relationships between sentences or ideas. Authors use *transition words* to make these relationships clear. Active readers, then, are alert to these words and use them to anticipate and clarify the relationships between the ideas and sentences they are reading.

In Chapters 4 and 5, we looked at a few examples of transition words that helped to identify the location of stated main ideas (Chapter 4) and the purposes of supporting details (Chapter 5). In this chapter, we will focus on the transition words that signal our four common types of sentence relationships.

Transition Words That Indicate Sequence

Sequence is indicated by transition words that suggest relationship in time. These include words like *before, after, then, when,* and *next.* Read the following paragraphs from a history text, noting the italicized transition words for sequence.

Before the national convention there were two serious Republican contenders. The energetic Nelson A. Rockefeller, who had been elected governor of New York in 1958, represented the liberal wing. But in December 1959, finding that the party leaders would not support him, he withdrew from the race.

When the Republicans met in Chicago in July 1960, the road was cleared for Vice-President Richard M. Nixon of California. He was nominated for President. *Then* Henry Cabot Lodge, Jr., a former senator from Massachusetts and now ambassador to the UN, was chosen for second place because of his experience in foreign affairs.

—Boorstin and Kelley, *A History of the United States*

In the preceding paragraph, transition words (*before, when, then*) are used along with dates to clarify the order of events leading up to the nomination of Richard Nixon for president in 1960. It is not unusual for dates and other specific time references (words like *yesterday, the year before*, etc.) to work with transition words to indicate sequence. See Table 7.1 for a list of transition words for sequence.

Table 7.1 Transition Words That Indicate Sequence

after	meanwhile	previously	while
before	next	then	first, second, third, etc.
later	now	when	one, two, three, etc.

Transition Words That Indicate Addition

The transition words that indicate addition are words that signal that the author will add more information similar to what is in the previous sentence. They include words like *also, furthermore, moreover*, and—of course—*additionally*. The transition word *also* was used in one of the previous examples for addition:

Reading—whether it's a book, newspaper, or the Internet—is a powerful means of obtaining information. Reading for many people can *also* be a source of great pleasure.

In this example, the word *also* indicates to the reader that in the second sentence the author is adding another benefit of reading to the one he listed in the first sentence.

The following paragraph provides another example of the use of a transition word for addition:

Several factors have led to dramatic growth in two-income families. The high cost of housing and the maintenance of a comfortable lifestyle have made it difficult if not impossible for many households to live on just one income. *Furthermore*, many women today simply want a career outside of the home.

—Nickels et al., *Understanding Business*

In this paragraph, the word *furthermore* is a transition word indicating that the author wants to add another factor that explains the dramatic growth in two-income families. See Table 7.2 for a list of transition words for addition.

Table 7.2   Transition Words That Indicate Addition

also	besides	moreover	as well
additionally	finally	similarly	in addition
again	furthermore	too	
another	likewise		

Transition Words That Indicate Contrast

The transition words that indicate contrast between sentences are similar to the ones we listed in Chapter 2 to indicate contrast clues for vocabulary and those we listed in Chapter 4 to indicate change of thought: words like *but, however,* and *though*. They signal the introduction of an opposing idea or a different line of thought about the topic.

Here is an example that we looked at earlier in this chapter.

Often, we think of stress as an externally imposed factor. *But* for most of us, stress results from an internal state of emotional tension that occurs in response to the various demands of living.

—Donatelle, *Health: The Basics,* 6th ed.

In this paragraph, the transition word *but* signals the introduction of a contrasting idea: that stress comes from our internal state rather than from an external factor. Here is another example from a health textbook.

With increasing maturity, most people learn to control outbursts of anger in a socially acceptable and rational manner. *However,* some people go through life acting out their aggressive tendencies in much the same ways they did as children or as their families did.

—Donatelle, *Health: The Basics,* 6th ed.

In these sentences the transition word *however* signals the contrast the author draws between people who have learned to control anger and people who go through life acting out of their anger.

Transition words like *though, although,* and *while* are often used at the beginning of a sentence to signal that there will be contrast within the sentence. Here is an example from a health book chapter on skin.

Though anything from cat claws to razor blades can disturb the structure of your skin, the greatest enemy, when exposed to it in large amounts, is the sun.

—Roizen and Oz, *You: The Owner's Manual*

In this sentence, the author contrasts the idea in the first part of the sentence— that there are many things that can harm your skin—with the idea in the second part of the sentence—that the greatest danger to your skin is actually the sun. The transition word *though* prepares the reader for contrast within the sentence. See Table 7.3 for a list of transition words for contrast.

Table 7.3   Transition Words That Indicate Contrast

although	however	still	in contrast
but	instead	though	in spite of
conversely	nevertheless	yet	on the contrary
despite	rather	while (meaning *although*)	on the other hand

Transition Words That Indicate Reason

Transition words that indicate reason show that one idea can be concluded from another, or that one event is the result of another event. They signal that the information or event in one sentence is the cause, explanation or reason for the information or event in another sentence.

They are similar to the transition words listed in Chapter 5 for supporting details that provide reasons, and include *therefore*, *thus*, and *consequently*, as well as phrases like *as a result*.

The following is an example from the previous section on reason.

The wide receiver injured his hand on the last play of the game. *Consequently*, he will be sidelined for practice this week and for the next game.

The word *consequently* signals that the receiver's injury is the reason for his being sidelined for the next week.

Now read the following paragraph from a sociology text.

Many single parents complain that their lives are lonely. If the parent works outside of the home during the day—and then must prepare dinner and care for the child in the evening—there will be little time and energy left for socializing with adults or pursuing hobbies. *As a result*, single parents have banded together to form organizations such as Parents Without Partners, which provide emotional support, social functions, and contacts for sharing of child care.

—Schaefer, *Sociology*

In the preceding paragraph, the reasons for the formation of organizations like Parents Without Partners is given in the first two sentences (single parents being lonely and busy). The phrase *as a result* signals the transition to the result or effect of the reason—the forming of the organizations. See Table 7.4 for a list of transition words for reason.

Table 7.4   Transition Words That Indicate Reason

accordingly	hence	therefore	as a result
because	then	as a consequence	for this reason
consequently	thus		

Transition words are words that indicate the relationship between sentences or ideas.

EXERCISE 7.8 RECOGNIZING TRANSITION WORDS

Directions: Circle the transition word in each of the following statements. Then in the space provided, identify the relationship that is indicated by the transition word (write Sequence, Addition, Contrast, or Reason) and briefly explain your answer. An example is provided.

EXAMPLE

(Though) anything from cat claws to razor blades can disturb the structure of your skin, the greatest enemy, when exposed to it in large amounts, is the sun.

—Roizen and Oz, *You: The Owner's Manual*

Contrast: the sentence contrasts the various dangers to skin with its main

enemy, the sun.

1. Proteins are the key elements of enzymes that control chemical activities in the body. (Moreover,) proteins aid in the transport of iron, oxygen, and nutrients to all body cells.

—Donatelle, *Health: The Basics,* 6th ed.

Addition: The second sentence adds more uses of proteins in the body.

2. (Although) you may think you're sitting still, Earth's spin is actually moving you along at hundreds of miles per hour.

—Suplee, *Everyday Science*

Contrast: The sentence contrasts the perception of not moving with the reality that

the Earth is spinning.

3. Imhotep was the architect of the first pyramid. He was (also) a high priest and a doctor and may have had something to do with introducing the calendar.

—Chisholm and Millard, *Early Civilization*

Addition: The second sentence adds more information about Imhotep.

4. Our judicial system is designed to guarantee legal justice for individuals and groups. Social justice, (on the other hand,) focuses on how we help others in the community who are not as advantaged as we are.

—Johnson et al., *Foundations of American Education,* 14th ed.

Contrast: The sentence contrasts legal justice with social justice.

5. There are now more gangs that involve more students in our schools than ever before. (In addition) to the problems that these people bring to the school, they have become violent in their neighborhood communities.

—Johnson et al., *Introduction to the Foundations of American Education,* 10th ed.

Addition: Second sentence adds more problems from gangs.

6. While inertia constantly urges a planet to fly off in a straight line, gravity just as constantly tugs it toward the sun. The result: a stable, smoothly curved orbit.

—Suplee, *Everyday Science*

Reason: The balancing of the forces of inertia and gravity is the reason for our

planet's stable curved orbit.

7. The earliest people were nomads who travelled from place to place, hunting animals and collecting wild plants to eat. Then slowly a more settled way of life developed, based on farming.

—Chisholm and Millard, *Early Civilization*

Sequence: The events in the second sentence occur after the events in the first

sentence.

8. One of the cornerstones of teaching is knowledge about teaching and learning and the development of skills and dispositions to help students learn. Therefore, teacher candidates study theories and research on how students learn at different ages.

—Johnson et al., *Foundations of American Education*, 14th ed.

Reason: The importance of teachers' knowledge and skills is the reason why teacher

candidates study theories and research on learning.

9. According to one Egyptian legend, the world started with an ocean in darkness. Then a mound of dry land rose up and the sun god Re appeared. He created light and all things.

—Chisholm and Millard, *Early Civilization*

Sequence: The events in the second and third sentence come after the events in

the first sentence.

10. Your rewards and reinforcers may initially come from others, but as you see positive changes in yourself, you will begin to reward and reinforce yourself

—Donatelle, *Health: The Basics*, 6th ed.

Contrast: The sentences contrast rewards and reinforcers coming from others to

those coming from yourself.

EXERCISE 7.9 USING TRANSITION WORDS

Directions: Complete each statement by inserting the appropriate transition word(s) from the following list.

but	despite	for example	furthermore	however
in addition	next	therefore	thus	while

1. Research shows that attendance is a critical factor in student success. ___Therefore or thus___, all college orientation programs should inform new students of the importance of attending their classes.

2. A regular exercise program contributes significantly to the health of the cardio-vascular system. In addition or furthermore, exercise is a great aid to stress reduction.

3. ___While___ it's usually bad behavior that gets an athlete a spot on the six o'clock news, many high-profile players work hard to be positive role models to children.

   —Globus, "Athletes As Role Models," *Current Health 2*

4. Studies show that laughter stimulates the immune system by increasing the number and activity of natural killer cells and other antibodies. In addition or furthermore, laughing exercises your lungs and increases the amount of oxygen in your blood.

   —Grand, "Human Helps," *Current Health 2*

5. Bodily reactions are the most obvious aspect of our emotional experience, because we can observe them easily. They include, ___for example___, the blush of embarrassment and the sweating palms that accompany nervousness.

   —DeVito, *The Interpersonal Communication Book*, 12th ed.

6. There are several current theories about the origin of human language, ___but___ none have yet been proven.

7. The first step in preparing your résumé is to make a list of all your work experiences. ___Next___, list your educational experiences and credentials, including all degrees, diplomas, and certificates you have attained.

8. ___Despite___ increasing confidence in the economy, consumer spending was up only slightly in the last three months.

9. Members of groups who have experienced discrimination can easily describe the power relations among groups. ___However___, members of groups who do not normally experience discrimination have a more difficult time acknowledging that differences in power and advantage exist.

   —Johnson et al., *Introduction to the Foundations of American Education*, 10th ed.

10. Most of us learned that the United States is a just and democratic society. Therefore or thus, it is difficult for us to confront the contradictions that support racism.

    —Johnson et al., *Introduction to the Foundations of American Education*, 10th ed.

EXERCISE 7.10 TRANSITION WORDS AND SENTENCE RELATIONSHIPS IN PARAGRAPHS

Directions: Read each paragraph and answer the questions that follow. Use context clues, word structure clues, and the dictionary as well as the vocabulary notes provided to determine the meaning of unfamiliar words.

A. In an attempt to preserve their bodies forever, the Egyptian kings had **massive** tombs built for themselves and their families. Pyramid-shaped tombs were introduced during the Old Kingdom. However, pyramids were frequently robbed, so the New Kingdom kings chose to be buried in tombs cut deep into the sides of cliffs.

massive very large

—Chisholm and Millard, *Early Civilization*

1. Circle the transition word(s) used in the paragraph.

2. Which relationship does the transition word indicate (Sequence, Addition, Contrast, or Reason)? Briefly explain your answer.

Contrast: The sentences contrast the preservation in the tombs with the

pyramids being robbed.

c 3. The main idea of the paragraph is:
   a. Pyramids were often robbed.
   b. The Egyptians wanted to be buried in large tombs to show the world their importance.
   c. Egyptian kings built tombs to preserve their bodies but later had to bury them in cliffs to avoid robbery.

B. When you find yourself being criticized, determine if the criticism is **valid**. Tell yourself to consider the source. If the source is an expert, or is powerful—your boss, for instance—you'll be wise to listen. Next ask yourself if you've heard this criticism before. When we're criticized repeatedly for the same things, we probably should pay attention.

valid well-founded

—Graber, "Take the Sting Out of Criticism," *Reader's Digest*

1. Circle the transition word(s) used in the paragraph.

2. Which relationship does the transition word indicate (Sequence, Addition, Contrast, or Reason)? Briefly explain your answer.

Sequence: The fourth sentence tells you what to do when being criticized

after you've taken the previous step of considering the source.

a 3. The main idea of the paragraph is:
   a. There are several things you should consider when you're being criticized.
   b. Pay attention to criticism you've heard before.
   c. Pay attention to criticism from your boss.

C. Use of students' prior knowledge and experiences with the subject matter is also critical in providing meaningful learning experiences in the classroom. Students make sense of new information in different ways. Therefore, the teacher must be able to teach the same concept by explaining it in different ways, relating it to something meaningful in the student's life and demonstrating it with multiple representations. For most beginning teachers, **repertoires** are rather limited; with experience, good teachers are able to draw on many different strategies to take advantage of a student's unique learning style and cultural patterns.

—Johnson et al., *Introduction to the Foundations of American Education,* 10th ed.

repertoire group or range of methods

1. Circle the transition word(s) used in the paragraph.

2. Which relationship does the transition word indicate (Sequence, Addition, Contrast, or Reason)? Briefly explain your answer.

   Reason: The reason teachers should teach a concept in different ways is

   that students have different ways of learning.

b 3. The main idea of the paragraph is:
   a. Students learn in different ways.
   b. Effective teachers use different teaching strategies to address students' different learning styles and backgrounds.
   c. Good teachers take advantage of students' prior knowledge.

D. Like family, hometown environments also mold behaviors. If you **deviated** from the actions expected in your hometown, you probably suffered strange looks, **ostracism** by some high school **cliques,** and other negative social reactions. The more you value the opinions of other people, the more likely you are to change a behavior that offends them. If you couldn't care less what they think, you probably brush off their negative reactions or suggested changes. How often have you told yourself, "I don't care what so-and-so thinks, I'll do what I darn well please?"

(Although) most of us have thought or said these words, we in fact all too often care too much about what even the insignificant people in our lives think. We say certain things, act in a **prescribed** manner, and respond in a specific way because our culture, our upbringing, and our need to be liked by others pressure us to do what we believe they think is the right thing. In general, the lower your level of self-esteem and **self-efficacy**, the higher the chances that others will influence your actions.

—Donatelle and Davis, *Health: The Basics,* 2nd ed.

---

deviate behave differently
ostracism exclusion
clique small, exclusive group

---

prescribed expected; established
self-efficacy belief in one's ability to succeed

---

1. Circle the transition word(s) used in the paragraph.

2. Which relationship does the transition word indicate (Sequence, Addition, Contrast, or Reason)? Briefly explain your answer.

   Contrast: The sentences in the middle of the paragraph contrast our

   telling ourselves that we don't care what others think with the fact that we do

   care what they think.

c 3. The main idea of the paragraph is:
   a. Hometown environments mold behavior.
   b. If you don't care what others think, you are likely to ignore their reactions and suggestions.
   c. We are often influenced by what others think, especially if our self-esteem is low.

E. The Japanese are among the most highly educated people in the world. All young people finish junior high school, 94 percent attend high school, and nearly a third enroll in college. Students in Japan spend more time in school than U.S. students. The school day is longer, the school week is five and a half days, and the school year is broken only by a short summer vacation of a little over a month in late July and August, a New Year's holiday, and a break before the start of the school year at the beginning of April. (In addition,) students are assigned daily homework, beginning in the first grade, and a large percentage of them spend their summer va-

cation studying. **Discrepancies** in the quality of education across rural, urban, and suburban schools are limited as measured by the achievement of students in higher education.

—Johnson et al., *Introduction to the Foundations of American Education,* 10th ed.

discrepancy difference

1. Circle the transition word(s) used in the paragraph.

2. Which relationship does the transition word indicate (Sequence, Addition, Contrast, or Reason)? Briefly explain your answer.

   Addition: The sentence adds more information about students and

   education in Japan.

_____a_____ 3. The main idea of the paragraph is:
   a. The Japanese are among the most highly educated people in the world.
   b. Japanese students spend more time in school than U.S. students.
   c. In Japan, students in rural, urban and suburban schools do equally well.

EXERCISE 7.11 USING TRANSITION WORDS

Directions: On a separate sheet of paper, write a paragraph on the topic of your choice in which you use any three of the following transition words: *although, as a result, as well, despite, furthermore, however, in addition, nevertheless, therefore, though, thus.*

EXERCISE 7.12 TRANSITION WORDS AND SENTENCE RELATIONSHIPS IN SHORT PASSAGES

Directions: Read each passage, underlining transition words and noticing sentence relationships while you read. Then answer the questions that follow the passage.

A. WITHOUT A MAP

1   Each fall, billions of birds undertake a migratory odyssey that can span the globe or carry them only a few states away. They fly thousands of miles toward warmer climates or more abundant food—then reverse their trips each spring.

2   Despite the regularity of these journeys, scientists know surprisingly little about bird migration. How do birds know where to go? What exact routes do they take to reach their destinations?

3   Now, scientists have new tools that many believe will revolutionize bird migration research. Tracking technologies like satellite transmitters and GPS units—formerly too bulky to be placed on any but the largest birds—now fit on duck-sized birds without hindering their flight.

4   Scientists can now map complete migration routes for individual birds from the comfort of their offices, in contrast to the demands of previous research methods—such as bird banding—which

provided only the start and finish-point of a bird's travels.

5   "There will be a tremendous number of new things to learn from these tracks covering the individual full journey over the years," said ornithologist Thomas Alerstam of Lund University in Sweden.

6   The new techniques come at a time of increasingly urgent questions about bird migration.

Birds' extinction rates now average one species a year, according to a July report in the Proceedings of the National Academy, raising the stakes for protecting migratory habitats and understanding how birds cope with climate change.

7   Moreover, as bird flu wings its way across Eurasia on the backs of wild swans and bird-carried West Nile virus spreads in the United States, migration routes have a direct impact on human health.

8   And the miniaturized technology is already shedding light on how birds use signals to navigate.

9   Birds use both geographic cues like the sun and magnetic cues from the earth's magnetic field to orient themselves as they migrate, Alerstam said. But scientists don't yet know which sense the birds rely on the most, or how birds cope if their different methods provide conflicting information.

—Moreira, "Without a Map," *The Boston Globe*

1. What transition word is used in paragraph 1? Then

   What relationship does it indicate? Sequence

2. What transition word is used in paragraph 2? Despite

   What relationship does it indicate? Contrast

3. What transition word is used in paragraph 3? Now

   What relationship does it indicate? Sequence

4. Which relationship connects the sentences in paragraph 6? Explain your answer.

   Reason: The second sentence states the reason (high extinction rates) for the urgent

   concern about bird migration.

5. In paragraph 7, the word *moreover* indicates what relationship? Addition

6. Why are scientists better able to track bird migrations now?

   New tracking technologies/techniques enable scientists to track the birds' migration

   better.

7. According to paragraphs 6 and 7, why is it important to research bird migration?

   Birds' extinction rates are high, and birds are spreading diseases.

8. Explain the contrast in the last paragraph. What two ideas are being contrasted?

The sentences contrast our knowledge of birds' use of geographic and magnetic cues

with scientists' lack of knowledge of which sense is used most or how birds cope

with conflicting information.

_____b_____ **9.** The main idea of the passage is:
   a. Birds have instincts that enable them to migrate great distances yearly.
   b. Modern technology is enabling scientists to better understand and track birds' migration patterns.
   c. Scientists know surprisingly little about bird migration.

10. *Vocabulary in Context:*

   _____a_____ A *migratory odyssey* is:
      a. A long journey from one place to another.
      b. A method of flying.
      c. A trip around the world.

   _____b_____ *Miniaturized* technology is:
      a. Very large.
      b. Very small.
      c. Untried; experimental.

B. A NEW MOVE FOR AFRICAN AMERICAN RIGHTS

(1) In 1955, soon after *Brown II*, the civil rights movement took another step forward—this time in Montgomery, Alabama. (2) Rosa Parks, the local NAACP's Youth Council adviser, decided to challenge the constitutionality of the segregated bus system. (3) First, Parks and other NAACP officials began to raise money for litigation and made speeches around town to garner public support. (4) Then, on December 1, 1955, Rosa Parks made history when she refused to leave her seat on a bus to move to the back to make room for a white male passenger. (5) She was arrested for violating an Alabama law banning integration of public facilities, including buses. (6) After she was freed on bond, Parks and the NAACP decided to enlist city clergy to help her cause. (7) At the same time, they distributed 35,000 handbills calling for African Americans to boycott the Montgomery bus system on the day of Parks's trial. (8) Black ministers used Sunday services to urge their members to support the boycott. (9) On Monday morning, African Americans walked, carpooled, or used black-owned taxicabs. (10) That night, local ministers decided that the boycott should be continued. (11) A new, twenty-six-year-old minister, Martin Luther King Jr., was selected to lead the newly formed Montgomery Improvement Association.

(1) As the boycott dragged on, Montgomery officials and local business owners began to harass the city's African American citizens. (2) The residents held out, despite suffering personal hardship for their actions, ranging from harassment to bankruptcy to job loss. (3) In 1956, a federal court ruled that the segregated bus system violated the equal protection clause of the Fourteenth Amendment. (4) After a year of walking, black Montgomery residents ended their protest when city buses were ordered to integrate. (5) The first effort at nonviolent protest had been successful. (6) Organized boycotts and other forms of nonviolent protest, including sit-ins at segregated restaurants and bus stations, were to follow.

—O'Connor and Sabato, *American Government: Continuity and Change*, 2006 ed.

1. Which transition words in the first paragraph indicate sequence?

Soon after, first, then, when, after

2. What were the first things Rosa Parks did to challenge segregated busing?

She raised money for litigation and made speeches.

3. What was the next thing Rosa Parks did to challenge segregated busing?

She refused to yield her seat to a white passenger.

4. What happened to Rosa Parks as a result of her refusal to yield her bus seat?

She was arrested.

5. What relationship connects sentences 6, 7, and 8 in the first paragraph? Explain your answer.

Addition: Sentences 7 and 8 add the other things that were done to support the boycott.

6. What relationship connects sentences 9 and 10 in the first paragraph? Explain your answer.

Sequence: The sentences progress from morning to night (on the Monday of the boycott).

7. Which transition word in the second paragraph indicates contrast?

Despite

8. According to the second paragraph, why was it difficult for the African American residents of Montgomery to maintain their boycott?

They were harassed and faced bankruptcy and job loss.

___c___ 9. Which of the following sentences best summarizes the events described in the second paragraph?
   a. Montgomery officials and business owners harassed the city's African American citizens in order to destroy their boycott.
   b. The success of the boycott led to other forms of nonviolent protest.
   c. The Montgomery boycott was successful despite the harassment from the white community and led to other forms of nonviolent protest.

10. *Vocabulary in Context:*

_____a_____ When *boycotting* the bus system, Montgomery's African Americans:
a. Refused to ride the buses.
b. Tried to damage the buses.
c. Refused to yield their seats on the buses.

_____c_____ In *harassing* the African American citizens of Montgomery, the city officials:
a. Ignored them.
b. Followed them and recorded their activities.
c. Made efforts to bother and trouble them.

C. GENDER, CULTURE, AND LOVE

1   Which sex is more romantic? Which sex truly understands true love? Which sex falls in love but won't commit? Pop-psych books are full of answers, along with advice for dealing with all those love-challenged heartbreakers who love you and leave you (fools that they are). But all stereotypes oversimplify. Neither sex loves more than the other in terms of love at first sight, passionate love, or companionate love over the long haul. Men and women are equally likely to suffer the heart-crushing torments of unrequited love. They are equally likely to be securely or insecurely attached. Both sexes suffer mightily when a love relationship ends, assuming they did not want it to.

2   However, women and men do differ, on average, in how they *express* love. Males in many cultures learn early that revelations of emotion can be construed as evidence of vulnerability and weakness, which are considered unmasculine. Thus, men in such cultures often develop ways of revealing love that differ from the ways women do. In contemporary Western society, many women express feelings of love in words, whereas many men express these feelings in actions—doing things for the partner, supporting the family financially, or just sharing the same activity, such as watching TV or a football game together. Similarly, many women tend to define intimacy as shared revelations of feelings, but many men define intimacy as just hanging out together.

3   These gender differences in ways of expressing the universal motives of love and intimacy do not just pop up out of nowhere; they reflect social, economic, and cultural forces. For example, for many years, Western men were more romantic than women in their choice of partner, and women in turn were far more pragmatic than men. One reason was that a woman did not just marry a man; she married a standard of living. Therefore, she could not afford to marry someone unsuitable or waste her time in a relationship that was not going anywhere, even if she loved the guy. She married, in short, for extrinsic reasons rather than intrinsic ones. In contrast, a man could afford to be sentimental in his choice of partner. In the 1960s, two-thirds of a sample of college men said they would not marry someone they did not love, but only one-fourth of the women ruled out the possibility.

—Wade and Tavris, *Invitation to Psychology*

1. What transition word is used in paragraph 1? __But_____

What relationship does it indicate? __Contrast_____

2. What relationship connects the last three sentences of paragraph 1? Explain your answer.

Addition: These sentences add more ways in which the genders are equal (do not differ).

3. What is the relationship between the last sentence of paragraph 1 and the first sentence of paragraph 2?

Which transition word indicates that relationship?

Contrast; However

4. What transition word in paragraph 2 indicates reason? Thus

Explain your answer—what reason and result are explained in the paragraph?

Men in many cultures think it is unmasculine to reveal emotions. Because

of this they develop alternative ways to express love.

5. Which transition word in paragraph 3 indicates reason? Reason or therefore

Explain your answer—what reason and result are explained in the paragraph?

Women being economically dependent on their husbands is the reason why

women were pragmatic in choosing a marriage partner.

6. Which transition word in paragraph 3 indicates contrast? In contrast, but

Who or what is contrasted?

A woman's circumstance is contrasted with a man's; he can afford to marry for love.

7. According to the authors, what are some of the similarities between men's and women's experiences with love?

They are similar in how much and how strongly they love; they are equally likely to

suffer from unreturned love; they have similar feelings of security and insecurities;

they suffer equally when a relationship ends.

8. According to the authors, what are some of the differences between men's and women's attitudes toward love?

Men are less likely to show or verbalize their emotion. They are more likely to show

feelings through action or by sharing experiences. Women are more likely to express

their feelings directly and verbally, and view intimacy as a sharing of feelings. Historically,

women have been more practical than men in their choices of partners.

_b_ **9.** The main idea of the second paragraph is:
a. Men and women have different views of intimacy.
b. Men and women express love differently.
c. Men are afraid to express love.

_b_ **10.** *Vocabulary in Context:*

The *torments* of *unrequited* love are:
a. The exciting feelings that accompany first love.
b. The pains associated with unreturned love.
c. The doubts experienced in the early stages of a relationship.

___a___   To *construe revelations* of emotion as evidence of *vulnerability* is to:
   a. Interpret expressions of emotions as evidence of weakness.
   b. Encourage expressions of emotion as evidence of honesty.
   c. Interpret expressions of emotions as evidence of strength.

___b___   If women were more *pragmatic* in their choice of marriage partners, they were more:
   a. Romantic.
   b. Practical.
   c. Uncertain.

___c___   If a woman married for *extrinsic* reasons rather than *intrinsic* ones, she:
   a. married for more important reasons.
   b. married for love rather than for practical purposes.
   c. married for practical considerations rather than her feelings.

SKILLS ONLINE: RECOGNIZING TRANSITION WORDS AND SENTENCE RELATIONSHIPS

Directions:

1. Working with a classmate, choose any two of the sentence relationships we have been working with in this chapter (Sequence, Addition, Contrast, Reason).

2. For each of the relationships you've chosen, find one online article in which that relationship is used. The article must contain at least one transition word indicating that relationship.

3. Print the articles and underline the transition words. For each article, add a brief explanation of how the author uses the relationship in the article.

READING **7A**

CAN ANIMALS TALK? (NATURE)

by James Trefil

Reading 7A is from Trefil's book *Are We Unique?*, which examines the differences between human and animal life. In this excerpt, the author focuses on communication between animals and humans.

Pre-Reading Exercise

Directions: Complete this exercise before reading the passage. Preview the passage and answer the following questions.

1. What is the passage about?
   Communication with animals

2. How many sections does the passage contain? ___3___

Name the subject of each section:

Clever Hans; Humans Talking to Animals; What Can Animals Do?

3. Which types of animals are discussed in the passage?

A horse; dogs; a parrot; crows

4. What have you previously read or learned about animal communication?

Answers will vary.

5. Do you have any pets? How well do you think they understand you? How well do you understand them?

Answers will vary.

6. Does the passage seem easy to understand, or difficult? Explain your answer.

Answers will vary.

Directions: Circle transition words and note sentence relationships while reading the passage. Monitor and clarify your comprehension as you read. Use context, the dictionary, and word structure clues to determine the meanings of unfamiliar words.

It seems this guy walked into a country store and saw a dog playing checkers with the storekeeper.
"What a smart dog," he exclaimed.
"Oh, he ain't so smart," the storekeeper replied. "I can beat him three games out of four."
Traditional Story

Clever Hans

1   At the turn of the nineteenth century, a rather strange chain of events transpired in Germany. A retired schoolteacher named Wilhelm von Osten set out to teach Hans, his horse, to do arithmetic. So successful was he that he soon found himself on tour, performing for delighted audiences. The routine would go like this: Von Osten would ask Hans something like "How much is two plus three?" Hans would (then) start to paw the ground with his hoof—one, two, three, four, five times. (Then) he would stop. What's more, Hans was able to deal with complex questions. "How many umbrellas are there in the room, Hans?" or "What is the date next Thursday?" Invariably, Hans would tap out the answer. What more proof of animal intellect

could you want? Here was a horse that was not only smart enough to do arithmetic, but could communicate his answers in a meaningful way to a rapt human audience! Observers at the time compared him to a smart fourth grader, and gave him the name "Clever Hans" *(der kluge Hans).*

2   Alas, it was not to be. The horse became so famous that in 1904 the German Board of Education set up a commission to study him. They quickly found that there was no obvious chicanery involved—von Osten was clearly an honest man (for the record, he never charged admission for Hans' performances). (Nevertheless,) some simple tests began to show that all was not as it seemed. Hans was asked to read a number written on a card. If he could see the questioner, his answers were correct over 90 percent of the time. If the questioner stood off to the side while the horse wore blinders, (however,) his accuracy rate dropped to 6 percent. Close observations of the questioners finally provided the key to the Clever Hans phenomenon. It turned out that when people asked Hans a question, they would bend

over slightly to watch his foot. When he got to the right answer, every observer would unconsciously give a little upward jerk of his head. No one was aware of doing this, but clearly Hans had learned to recognize this movement.

3   Von Osten was as surprised as anyone by this result—there had been, after all, no attempt to hoodwink anybody. Nevertheless, the incident cast a pall over the field of animal–human communication for generations. Even today, researchers in the field have to be very careful that they're not simply reproducing what has come to be called the "Clever Hans effect."

4   Having said this, however, it seems to me that one very important point is often missed in discussions of Clever Hans: He had to be one very smart horse to learn to read unconscious signals from his trainers. That he couldn't do arithmetic as well shouldn't obscure that simple fact.

Humans Talking to Animals

5   I have been around dogs all my life, so I know from personal experience that communication between species is possible. Anyone who has been to a canine obedience class (or, better yet, sheepdog trials) knows that dogs can understand, interpret, and act upon commands from humans. In a similar vein, anyone who has been to one of the numerous Sea Worlds that dot the landscape knows that porpoises and seals can do the same. Communications from humans to other species is an everyday occurrence, hardly worth commenting upon.

6   In the same way, animals can communicate with humans to some degree. To take dogs as an example again, most humans can distinguish readily between an approach by a friendly dog (head up, tail wagging, loud bark) and an unfriendly one (head low, bristles up, low growl). We all recognize what ethologists call a "play bow" (rear up, tail wagging, front legs on ground from elbows forward) and know how to respond to it. We can even, with some experience, learn some simple canine etiquette. When a friendly dog approaches, for example, we practice interspecies courtesy by holding our hand out for the dog to smell before we pet it—a simple accommodation to the fact that the dog's view of the world is much more olfactory than ours.

7   I should point out, however, that it is all too easy for people to fool themselves into thinking that because we can communicate or establish some sort of relationship with an animal, the animal must somehow think and see the world as we do. *Nothing could be further from the truth!* Except for a few species such as dogs, with whom we have enjoyed a long association, the minds of other

animals are fundamentally foreign to us. You can see evidence for this in the many stories of people who raise wild animals from birth, only to have the animals turn on them one day without, so far as the human can tell, any provocation whatsoever.

What Can Animals Do?

8   At the level of naming things, recognizing words, and being able to answer simple questions, there's no doubt that animals can function in the verbal sphere. Perhaps the most striking example of this rule is an African gray parrot named Alex. Alex has been trained in language since 1977, and by now his vocabulary includes more than ninety words. He can name objects ("What's this?" "green key") and count to six with a little better than 80 percent accuracy.

9   This work shows that even an animal with a brain as small as a parrot's can learn some aspects of language.

10   As an aside, I should say that Alex's ability to count shouldn't surprise you. Hunters have known for generations that crows can count. The knowledge comes from observing that crows who see a hunter enter a blind won't come near it until the hunter leaves, and they'll do the same if two hunters enter the blind and one leaves. Only if three hunters enter the blind and two leave will the crows believe it's empty.

—Trefil, *Are We Unique?*

You, the Reader

Interest Rating. Please rate the interest level of the reading on the following scale (circle one):

5—Very interesting	2—A little boring
4—Fairly interesting	1—Very boring
3—Mildly interesting	

Difficulty Rating. Please rate the difficulty level of the reading on the following scale (circle one):

5—Very difficult	2—Fairly easy
4—Fairly difficult	1—Very easy
3—Moderate	

Comments: Please explain your ratings and make any other comments you wish about the reading.

Answers will vary.

SENTENCE RELATIONSHIPS AND TRANSITION WORDS EXERCISE

1. Which transition word indicates sequence in paragraph 1? <u>then</u>

    What did Hans do when von Osten asked him an arithmetic question?

    <u>Hans pawed the ground with his hoof.</u>

2. List two transition words used to indicate contrast in paragraph 2:

    <u>Nevertheless</u>   <u>However</u>

What ideas or information are contrasted?

Hans's apparent ability vs. the reality; Hans's success when seeing the questioner vs. when he wore blinders.

3. What transition word is used in paragraph 3? _Nevertheless_

What sentence relationship does it indicate? _Contrast_

4. What transition words indicate addition in paragraph 6?

In the same way; an example; again

What information is added?

Examples of animal to human communications—specifically dogs

5. Which transition word in paragraph 7 indicates contrast? _However_

Which ideas are contrasted?

The idea in paragraph 6 that humans can understand some dog behaviors is contrasted with people fooling themselves into thinking that animals think and see the world as we do.

COMPREHENSION QUESTIONS

Directions: For questions 1–5, choose the answer that best completes the statement. For questions 6–10, write your response in the space provided. Base all answers on what you read in the selection. Refer back to the selection as necessary to answer the questions.

_a_   **1.** Clever Hans was a horse who seemed to be able to
   a. Add and count.
   b. Subtract and multiply.
   c. Understand most human language.
   d. Read people's minds.

_a_   **2.** We can infer from the article that von Osten:
   a. Really believed that Hans could do arithmetic.
   b. Deliberately tried to fool people in order to get their money.
   c. Was a well-trained scientist.
   d. Suspected that Hans couldn't really add.

_b_   **3.** We can conclude from the passage that:
   a. Parrots are smarter than dogs.
   b. Humans can communicate with dogs more easily than with most other species.
   c. Porpoises and seals are the friendliest animals.
   d. Most animals can be trained.

<u>d</u>   **4.** Regarding dogs, the author believes that:

    a. Most people cannot tell a friendly dog from an unfriendly dog.

    b. Most dogs cannot be trained.

    c. It is more difficult for people to communicate with dogs than with other animals.

    d. Dogs can understand human commands.

<u>b</u>   **5.** The parrot Alex has demonstrated the ability to do *all* of the following *except:*

    a. Count to six.

    b. Distinguish between quantities of two and three.

    c. Name objects.

    d. Learn vocabulary.

6. List several of the tricks that Hans performed.

He answered addition questions and counted. He told what the date would be on a given day.

7. How did the commission discover that Hans could not really do arithmetic?

They put blinders on him before asking him questions and his accuracy rate dropped from 90% to 6%. They discovered that he was responding to human body language.

8. What evidence does the author provide to show that people and animals can sometimes communicate?

He gives examples of dogs, porpoises, and seals responding to human commands. He points out that most people can distinguish between a friendly dog and an unfriendly dog.

9. In a complete sentence of your own wording, state the main idea for paragraph 7.

Most animals think and see the world very differently from how humans think and see the world. (sample answer)

10. In your opinion, how well can humans and animals understand each other?

Answers will vary.

VOCABULARY EXERCISES

Pronunciation Guide (see p. 90 for list of phonetic symbols)

chicanery	(chĭ-kā′nə-rē)
etiquette	(ĕt′ĭ-kĭt′)
obscure	(ŏb-skyo͞or′)
olfactory	(ŏl-făk′tə-rē)
pall	(pôl)
provocation	(prŏv′ə-kā′shən)

WORDS IN CONTEXT

Directions. Choose the meaning for the boldfaced word that best fits the context.

__b__   **1.** At the turn of the nineteenth century, a rather strange chain of events **transpired** in Germany.
   a. Were predicted
   b. Occurred
   c. Caused shock
   d. Ended

__c__   **2.** They quickly found that there was no obvious **chicanery** involved—von Osten was clearly an honest man (for the record, he never charged admission for Hans's performances).
   a. Mistake
   b. Honesty
   c. Deliberate trickery
   d. Magic

__a__   **3.** Von Osten was as surprised as anyone by this result—there had been, after all, no attempt to **hoodwink** anybody.
   a. Fool
   b. Train or educate
   c. Be honest; tell the truth to
   d. Cause injury to; damage

__c__   **4.** We practice interspecies courtesy by holding our hand out for the dog to smell before we pet it—a simple accommodation to the fact that the dog's view of the world is much more **olfactory** than ours.
   a. Having to do with sight
   b. Having to do with hearing
   c. Having to do with smell
   d. Unusual

__d__   **5.** At the level of naming things, recognizing words, and being able to answer simple questions, there's no doubt that animals can function in the **verbal sphere**.
   a. The earth's environment
   b. The world of human logic and complex reasoning
   c. The world of family relationships
   d. The world of words

CONTEXT AND DICTIONARY

Directions: Use context and the dictionary to determine the meaning of the boldfaced word in each sentence. Use word structure clues when applicable.

1. Here was a horse that . . . could communicate his answers in a meaningful way to a **rapt** human audience.

   Engrossed; enchanted; completely absorbed

2. Nevertheless, the incident cast a **pall** over the field of animal–human communication for generations.

   Shadow; darkness; gloom

3. That he couldn't do arithmetic as well shouldn't **obscure** that simple fact.

   Hide; conceal

4. We can even, with some experience, learn some simple canine **etiquette**.

   Rules of proper behavior

5. You can see evidence for this in the many stories of people who raise wild animals from birth, only to have the animals turn on them one day without, so far as the human can tell, any **provocation** whatsoever.

   Cause; instigation

RESPOND TO THE READING

Directions: Write a half–page response to either of the following questions.

1. Can animals learn language? Discuss.

2. Are humans responsible for the welfare of animals? Is it okay for people to experiment with animals for the sake of scientific research? Discuss.

WEBQUEST

Directions: Use the Internet to find the answer to the following question. Write your answer on a sheet of paper. Print out the Web page you used for the answer or copy the URL on your sheet.

How successfully did Koko the gorilla learn human language?

READING 7B

DARWIN AND THE THEORY OF EVOLUTION (BIOLOGY)

by William P. Cunningham and Mary Ann Cunningham

Reading 7B, taken from an environmental science textbook, provides a brief account of the work of Charles Darwin, the nineteenth–century scientist who proposed the theory of evolution. Read the selection to learn how Darwin developed his theory and how his theory is viewed by modern scientists.

Pre-Reading Exercise

Directions: Complete this exercise before reading the passage. Preview the passage and answer the following questions.

1. What is the passage about?

   Darwin; evolution; and the voyage of the *Beagle*

2. Who was Charles Darwin?

   Darwin was a scientist interested in the origin of species. He developed the theory of

   evolution.

3. When was Darwin's theory first published?

   About 150 years ago

4. What have you previously learned about Darwin and evolution?

   Answers will vary.

5. Write two questions about Darwin and evolution.

   Answers will vary.

6. Does the passage seem easy to understand, or difficult? Explain your answer.

   Answers will vary.

Directions: Circle transition words and note sentence relationships while reading the passage. Monitor and clarify your comprehension as you read. Use context, the dictionary, and word structure clues to determine the meanings of unfamiliar words.

1   Why do living things vary so much, and how is it that they fit so neatly into their environment and their biological communities? These questions, at the core of environmental science today, inspired Charles Darwin to explore the origin of species a century and a half ago. Darwin's work demonstrates the importance of careful observation, cautious explanation, and a

willingness to consider new ideas, even controversial ones.

2   Darwin was only 22 years old when he set out on his epic five-year voyage aboard the ship *Beagle*, which left England in 1831 to map sailing routes around South America. Initially an indifferent student, Darwin had found inspiring professors in his last years in college. One of these helped him get a position as an unpaid naturalist on board the *Beagle*. Darwin turned out to be an inquisitive thinker, an avid collector of specimens, and a careful reader of explorers, natural historians, and geologists.

3   After four years of exploring and collecting, Darwin reached the Galápagos Islands. Six hundred miles from the coast of Ecuador, these islands are isolated from the mainland and from each other by strong, cold currents and high winds. By then, Darwin had read and seen enough to recognize that numerous species on each island occurred nowhere else in the world. Yet, their features suggested common ancestors on the South American mainland. The finches were especially interesting: each island had its own species, marked by distinct bill shapes, which graded from large and parrot-like to small and warbler-like. Each bird's beak type was suited to an available food source on its island. It seemed obvious that, somehow, these birds had been modified to survive in their distinct environments.

4   To convince others that species could adapt to their environments, and to make a useful contribution to scientific understanding, Darwin had to come up with an *explanation* of *how* they did so. Shortly after his return to England, he read an essay by the Reverend Thomas Malthus, proposing that humans invariably reproduce beyond the carrying capacity of their resources, after which famine, disease, and competition eliminate the surplus population. Here Darwin found a plausible explanation for evolution: species produce many offspring, but only the fittest survive to reproduce again; poorer competitors do not reproduce and pass on their traits.

5   It's important to note that Darwin wasn't the first to think about biological evolution. Many people in his time understood that organisms could share common ancestors but drift apart over time. Darwin spent a great deal of time, for example, interviewing animal and plant breeders about how traits changed from generation to generation. What was missing—and what Darwin supplied with his brilliant insights about natural selection—was how this process works in nature. Darwin didn't know, however, how characteristics were passed from generation to generation. Only after many years of further research were Ernst Mayer and others able to put together a modern synthesis that explains the genetic basis of evolution.

6   An overwhelming majority of biologists now consider the theory of evolution through natural selection to be the cornerstone of their science. A huge body of evidence from both laboratory and field studies supports this theory. Neither Darwin nor his ideas are above scrutiny, however. Darwin believed, for example, that evolution probably proceeds very slowly and gradually. In 1972, the Harvard paleontologist Stephen Jay Gould challenged this idea of gradualism, suggesting instead that species and biological communities go through long periods of relatively little change, but then have brief episodes of very rapid evolutionary development. Gould called this punctuated equilibrium. Darwin's work remains one of our foremost examples of bold, creative thinking and meticulous observation. A good theory is able to explain new evidence as it accumulates; it is also a springboard for further exploration and debate. How species multiply and how they interact are aspects of evolution that scientists continue to explore and debate almost 150 years after Darwin's theory was first published.

7   For further reading, see Charles Darwin, *The Voyage of the* Beagle (1837) and *On the Origin of Species by Means of Natural Selection* (1859).

—Cunningham and Cunningham, *Principles of Environmental Science*, 3rd ed.

You, the Reader

Interest Rating. Please rate the interest level of the reading on the following scale (circle one):

> 5—Very interesting   2—A little boring
>
> 4—Fairly interesting   1—Very boring
>
> 3—Mildly interesting

Difficulty Rating. Please rate the difficulty level of the reading on the following scale (circle one):

> 5—Very difficult   2—Fairly easy
>
> 4—Fairly difficult   1—Very easy
>
> 3—Moderate

Comments: Please explain your ratings and make any other comments you wish about the reading.

Answers will vary.

SENTENCE RELATIONSHIPS AND TRANSITION WORDS EXERCISE

1. What transition word indicates sequence in paragraph 3? After

How long did it take Darwin to reach the Galapagos Islands? Four years

2. What transition word indicates contrast in paragraph 3? Yet

What ideas or information are being contrasted?

Darwin's observation that the species on each island occurred nowhere else is

contrasted with their features suggesting common ancestry on the South

American mainland.

3. What transition word indicates sequence in paragraph 4? After

When did Darwin read Malthus's essay? after returning to England

4. What transition word is used in paragraph 5? However (also but); after

What relationship does it indicate? Contrast; sequence

5. What transition word indicates contrast in paragraph 6? However (also but, instead)

What ideas or information are being contrasted?

Support for Darwin's theory is contrasted with the idea that it is not above scrutiny;

Darwin's theory is contrasted with Gould's; long periods with little change are

contrasted with brief periods of rapid change.

COMPREHENSION QUESTIONS

Directions: For question 1–5, choose the answer that best completes the statement. For questions 6–10, write your response in the space provided. Base all answers on what you read in the selection. Refer back to the selection as necessary to answer the questions.

_b_   **1.** The theory of evolution is:
   a. Rejected as outdated by most modern scientists.
   b. Accepted by most modern biologists, though it is still being modified.
   c. Accepted by all modern scientists as fact which cannot be changed or expanded.
   d. Accepted by some modern biologists, but rejected by many.

_c_   **2.** The passage states that one of Darwin's college professors:
   a. Encouraged him to study evolution.
   b. Discouraged him from studying evolution.
   c. Helped him get a job on the _Beagle_.
   d. Taught Darwin the scientific method.

_a_   **3.** The authors suggest that all of the following qualities helped Darwin succeed as a scientist _except_:
   a. Stubbornness.
   b. Curiosity.
   c. Openness to new ideas.
   d. Being a careful reader.

_b_   **4.** Thomas Malthus provided Darwin with:
   a. A job in England after his voyage.
   b. An explanation for evolution.
   c. Guidelines for experimentation and research.
   d. A theory and information about genes.

_d_   **5.** When Darwin proposed his theory, he did not understand:
   a. Why there was a need for species to change.
   b. Malthus's ideas about competition and overpopulation.
   c. That organisms could share common ancestors.
   d. The role of genes in evolution.

6. What did Darwin want to discover?

   Darwin wanted to discover why living things vary, why they fit their

   environment, and how they evolved.

7. What did Darwin learn from the finches in the Galápagos?

   By observing the finches Darwin learned that they had adapted to their

   distinct environments.

8. How did Stephen Jay Gould modify Darwin's theory?

   Gould suggests that evolution was not always gradual; it could happen

   rapidly at times.

9. Why do the authors consider Darwin's theory of evolution to be a good theory?

Darwin's theory is supported by a large body of evidence. It can explain

new evidence and lead to new ideas.

10. Do you consider Darwin's theory to be a good theory? Why or why not?

Answers will vary.

VOCABULARY EXERCISES

Pronunciation Guide (see p. 90 for list of phonetic symbols)

avid	(ăv'ĭd)
controversial	(kŏn'trə-vûr'shəl)
equilibrium	(ē'kwə-lĭb'rē-əm)
invariably	(ĭn-vâr'ē-ə-blē)
meticulous	(mĭ-tĭk'yə-ləs)
scrutiny	(skrōōt'n-ē)
synthesis	(sĭn'thĭ-sĭs)

WORDS IN CONTEXT

Directions: Choose the meaning for the boldfaced word that best fits the context.

___d___ **1.** Darwin's work demonstrates . . . a willingness to consider new ideas, even **controversial** ones.
 a. Hard to understand
 b. Easy to understand
 c. Previously studied
 d. Arguable; debatable

___a___ **2.** Darwin was only 22 years old when he set out on his **epic** five year voyage aboard the ship *Beagle.*
 a. Long and adventurous
 b. Boring or monotonous
 c. Unpleasant
 d. Carefully planned

___b___ **3.** Darwin turned out to be . . . an **avid** collector of specimens . . .
 a. Sloppy
 b. Enthusiastic
 c. Not very interested
 d. Not very skilled

___d___ **4.** Neither Darwin nor his ideas are above **scrutiny**, however.
 a. Frequent error
 b. Scientific law
 c. Rejection; throwing away
 d. Examination

___c___ **5** Darwin's work remains one of our foremost examples of bold, creative thinking and **meticulous** observation.
    a. Creative
    b. Careless
    c. Careful
    d. Technical

CONTEXT AND DICTIONARY

Directions: Use context and the dictionary to determine the meaning of the boldfaced word in each sentence. Use word structure clues when applicable.

1. Initially an **indifferent** student, Darwin had found inspiring professors in his last years in college.

   Mediocre; not very good; or, not caring; not very interested

2. Darwin turned out to be an **inquisitive** thinker . . .

   Curious, questioning

3. Shortly after his return to England, he read an essay . . . proposing that humans **invariably** reproduce beyond the carrying capacity of their resources . . .

   Virtually always; without change

4. Only after many years of further research were Ernst Mayer and others able to put together a modern **synthesis** that explains the genetic basis of evolution.

   Combination

5. Gould called this punctuated **equilibrium**.

   Balance

RESPOND TO THE READING

Directions: Write a half–page response to either of the following questions.

1. What qualities of Darwin made him a successful scientist? What qualities are needed today to be a successful scientist?

2. What are you most curious about? If you had an opportunity to study and research a topic of your choice, what topic would you pick and how would you go about researching it?

WEBQUEST

Directions: Use the Internet to find the answers to the following questions. Write your answers on a sheet of paper. Print out the Web pages you used for the answers or copy the URLs on your sheet.

What species in your state are threatened with extinction? Why are they becoming extinct? Is anything being doing to protect them?

CHAPTER 7 REVIEW

Sentence Relationships

Active readers note the relationships or connections between the ideas and sentences they are reading.

Recognizing sentence relationships helps to monitor, clarify, and strengthen comprehension and retention.

Four common sentence relationships are:

Sequence—the sentences are related by time order

Addition—one sentence adds similar information to the information in a previous sentence

Contrast—the sentences present different or opposing ideas

Reason—one sentence provides a reason, cause, or explanation for a result described in another sentence.

Transition Words

Transition words are words that indicate the relationships between sentences or ideas.

There are transition words for each of the four common sentence relationships.

Transition words for *sequence* include *then, when, before, after*.

Transition words for *addition* include *also, in addition, as well, furthermore*

Transition words for *contrast* include *but, however, despite, though*

Transition words for *reason* include *therefore, thus, because, as a result*

Skills Online: Recognizing Transition Words and Sentence Relationships

Readings

Reading 7A: Can Animals Talk? (Nature)

Reading 7B: Darwin and the Theory of Evolution (Biology)

CHAPTER TESTS

TEST 7.1. SENTENCE RELATIONSHIPS

Directions: Read each pair of sentences and decide how they are related. In the space provided, write Sequence, Addition, Contrast, or Reason to indicate which sentence relationship is used to connect the sentences and briefly explain your answer.

1. At 23, Mary Wells began writing ad copy for a department store in her native Youngstown, Ohio. The next year she was in New York doing Macy's fashion ads.

   —Vivian, *The Media of Mass Communication*, 2006 update

   Sequence: The event in the second sentence follows the event in the first sentence.

2. Poets speak in a language charged with rhythm and rhyme. They break their utterances into lines that stop and start, sounding out a cadence and taking a shape.

   —Bishop, *Beginner's Guide to the Humanities*, 2nd ed.

   Addition: The second sentence adds information about what poets do (with language).

3. The roots of theater must lie somewhere in the human gene. Other animals pretend—the nesting bird that feigns an injury to protect its young—but only humans don a mask and pretend to be someone else.

   —Bishop, *Beginner's Guide to the Humanities*, 2nd ed.

   Contrast: The second sentence contrasts human pretending (acting) with animals

   pretending (for protection). or Reason: Humans act because theater is in our genes.

4. At some point, humans learned to speak to one another. They may have done this because they were developing a richer culture that depended on communication.

   —Davis, *The Human Story*

   Reason: The second sentence offers a reason why humans learned to speak to

   one another.

5. Unless working parents have been lucky enough to arrange a flexible schedule that allows them to be home when their children are not in school, they are not available to care for their children during the period immediately after school. The result is children of all ages being left alone or in the care of others.

   —Johnson et al., *Foundations of American Education*, 14th ed.

   Reason: Parents being unavailable is the reason why children are left alone or in

   the care of others.

TEST 7.2. TRANSITION WORDS

Directions: Without looking back in the text, identify the sentence relationship indicated by each of the following transition words by writing Sequence, Addition, Contrast, or Reason on the line next to the word.

1. therefore   <u>Reason</u>

2. but   <u>Contrast</u>

3. however   <u>Contrast</u>

4. then   <u>Sequence</u>

5. thus   <u>Reason</u>

6. furthermore   <u>Addition</u>

7. after   <u>Sequence</u>

8. also   <u>Addition</u>

9. though   <u>Contrast</u>

10. consequently   <u>Reason</u>

TEST 7.3 TRANSITION WORDS AND SENTENCE RELATIONSHIPS

Directions: After reading each paragraph, (1) circle the transition word, and (2) in the space provided, identify the sentence relationship that is indicated by the signal word (write Addition, Contrast, Reason, or Sequence). Briefly explain your answer.

1. The length of time required to learn English varies. Most students become conversationally fluent within two or three years. However, young people may require five to seven years to reach the proficiency necessary for success in academic subjects such as social studies and English. Students who are conversationally fluent may be immersed in English-only classrooms without appropriate support to ensure that they can function effectively in academic work. These students may fall further behind their classmates in conceptual understanding of the subjects being taught.

—Johnson et al., *Foundations of American Education*, 14th ed.

<u>Contrast: The sentence contrasts most students becoming conversationally fluent in two to three</u>

<u>years with the need for five to seven years to each academic proficiency.</u>

2. Ethics, an individual's system of moral principles, plays a key role in communication. As speakers, we are responsible for what we tell others. We should always hold the highest ethical standards. We must communicate with honesty, sincerity, and integrity. In addition, a responsible, ethical speaker presents worthwhile and accurate information in a fair manner. Communication scholar David Zarefsky says, "Speech has tremendous power and the person who wields it bears great responsibility . . . both speakers and listeners should seek high standards of ethical conduct."

—Seiler and Beall, *Communication: Making Connections*, 7th ed.

<u>Addition: The sentence adds to what ethical speakers must do.</u>

3. Nearly one in five residents of the United States speaks a language other than English at home. As a result, a growing number of English language learners are found in schools across the country. A number of students use a dialect that is not standard English in their home environments.

—Johnson et al., *Foundations of American Education*, 14th ed.

Reason: That nearly one in five residents speaks a language other than English at home is

the reason why the number of English language learners in schools is increasing.

4. While some black Southerners asserted their rights as workers on Southern farms, others affirmed their freedom by moving to towns and cities. Even (before) the war, the city had offered slaves and free black people a measure of freedom unknown in the rural South. (After) the war, African Americans moved to cities to find families, seek work, escape the tedium and supervision of farm life, or simply test their right to move about. Between 1860 and 1870, the official African-American population in every major Southern city rose significantly.

—Goldfield et al., *The American Journey: A History of the United States*

Sequence: The sentences tell when slaves /African Americans moved to cities. (Also, "while" in

first sentence indicates contrast.)

5. (While) most people will admit to breaking the law sometime during their lives, almost all of us oppose serious violations. And (while) our everyday life may be orderly, there are times when life is less orderly—when murder, scandal, and other normative violations take place. In fact, these violations occur often enough that deviance and crime have become fields of specialization practiced by sociologists and criminologists.

—Curry et al., *Sociology for the Twenty-First Century,* 5th ed.

Contrast: The first sentence contrasts occasional law violations with opposition to serious violations.

The second sentence contrasts our orderly everyday lives with times when life is less orderly.

TEST 7.4. TRANSITION WORDS AND SENTENCE RELATIONSHIPS IN A SHORT PASSAGE

Directions: Read the following passage, noticing transition words and logical relationships while you read. Then answer the questions that follow the passage.

The Importance of Effective Listening

1   From the time we get up in the morning until we end the day, we are constantly listening to something. Yet most of us give little thought to the role that listening plays in our everyday experiences. Parents and children both complain, "They don't listen to me." A similar refrain may be heard from relationship partners, workers and bosses, teachers and students. You might even have heard a friend say to you, "You really ought to listen to yourself." As simple as listening appears to be, many of us are not efficient listeners.

2   According to a survey of executives by Office Team, a leading staffing service in Menlo Park, California, 14 percent of each work week is wasted because of poor communication between staff and managers—amounting to seven weeks per year. Jim Presley, former vice president of professional services at SeeCommerce, a company that developed applications allowing customers to visualize supply chains and form collaborative groups, says that effective listening can improve sales by 30 to 40 percent. Students, too, seem to have trouble as listeners. Informal surveys of our colleagues reveal that the instructors believe the "failure to listen" is one of the major problems in their students. There is little doubt that communicating, and in particular, listening, plays a significant role in society. Because we spend so much time as *consumers* of communication, we need to learn as much as we can about effective listening. In the global community

in which we live and work, listening carefully to the messages conveyed by people of other cultures and backgrounds is a skill required to succeed in many areas of life.

Listening and Hearing: Is There a Difference?

3   Because most of us take listening for granted, we tend to think of it as a simple task. However, listening is actually quite complex. Scholars agree that listening, like communication in general, is a process and that it is closely linked to the thinking process. Wolvin and Coakley suggest that listening is a distinct behavior that is separate from other intellectual activities. They acknowledge, however, that much of the research closely links listening with reasoning, comprehension, and memory. Listening scholars and teachers agree that hearing and listening are not the same. It is impossible to listen to sounds without first hearing them, but it is possible to hear sounds without listening to them. What distinguishes listening from hearing?

4   Communication scholars suggests that the major difference between listening and hearing is the difference between active and passive processes. Hearing is passive. If you have normal hearing, your ears receive sounds. You don't have to work at hearing; it just happens. People can have excellent hearing and be terrible listeners. Listening, on the other hand, is active and requires energy and desire. The ILA defines listening as "the process of receiving, constructing meaning from, and responding to spoken or nonverbal massages."

—Seiler and Beall, *Communication: Making Connections,* 7th ed.

1. What transition word indicates contrast in paragraph 1? _Yet_

How does the idea expressed in the second sentence contrast with the first sentence?

The second sentence points out that we don't appreciate the importance of listening,

contrasted with the first sentence pointing out that we do it all day long.

2. What transition word indicates addition in paragraph 2? _Too_

Explain the addition (what idea is being added?)

Students also have trouble listening.

3. What transition word indicates reason in paragraph 2? _Because_

According to paragraph 2, why is it important to learn about effective listening?

We spend a lot of time as consumers of communication.

4. What transition word indicates contrast in paragraph 3? _However (used twice)_

What ideas are contrasted?

We think listening is simple but it is really complex. Or, two scholars view listening

as a separate behavior but admit that much research links listening to other

mental activities.

5. What transition word indicates reason in paragraph 3? _Because_

What reason and result are explained in the first sentence of the paragraph?

Reason: We take listening for granted. Result: we think listening is a simple task.

6. What transition word or phrase indicates contrast in paragraph 4?

On the other hand

What is being contrasted in this paragraph?

Listening is contrasted with hearing. Hearing is passive while listening is active.

7. Explain the difference between hearing and listening.

Hearing is passive reception of sound through the ears. Listening is active, requiring

energy and desire.

8. According to the passage, who has problems with effective listening?

Everyone

9. According to the passage, why is it important to be an effective listener?

We do a lot of listening; listening will contribute to success in school, at work, and in

other areas of life.

10. According to the passage, how is the scholar's view of listening different from the average person's view of listening?

The average person takes listening for granted, thinks it's simple, and doesn't think

much about it. The scholar sees listening as a complex process distinct from hearing

and linked to other mental processes.

You, the Reader: Chapter 7 Wrap-up

Directions: Use one or two of the following questions to write a half-page response to Chapter 7.

- What were the most important things you learned from this chapter? How will you use what you have learned from this chapter?
- How have you changed your reading habits in response to this chapter?
- Which sentence relationship is easiest for you to recognize? Why? Which one is most difficult for you to recognize? Why?
- What parts of the chapter did you find most engaging? What questions do you have about the chapter?

For support in meeting this chapter's objectives, go to MyReadingLab and select *Patterns of Organization*.

Logical Patterns

LEARNING OBJECTIVES

In Chapter 8 you will learn to:

- Identify five common logical patterns
- Use the patterns to better understand and remember what you read
- Diagram the patterns to reinforce understanding and memory

CHAPTER CONTENTS

Pre-Reading Exercise for Chapter 8

Directions: Preview the chapter and answer the following questions.

1. What is the chapter about?

    Logical patterns; recognizing organization

2. What is chronological order? With which sentence relationship is it associated?

    Chronological order is time order and is related to sequence.

3. What is compare-contrast?

    Compare-Contrast shows similarities and/or difference between people, things, etc.

4. What have you previously learned that is related to the logical patterns discussed in this chapter?

    Answers will vary.

5. What experience do you have diagramming or mapping the ideas in a passage?

    Answers will vary.

6. Write two questions about the content of this chapter.

    Answers will vary.

In Chapter 7, you learned to identify sentence relationships and to recognize transition words. Building upon what you learned in Chapter 7, in Chapter 8 you will learn how to recognize logical patterns that writers use to organize paragraphs and larger sections of material, and you will learn how to use these patterns to improve your understanding and retention of what you read.

Logical patterns are tools that enable writers to order their ideas and information and to make the relationships between ideas clearer to the reader. The patterns are tools for readers as well: Active readers look for these patterns to help them understand the organization of the material they're reading.

As you will see, logical patterns are closely associated with sentence relationships. In fact, some of the patterns build on the sentence relationships, extending the relationship to a whole paragraph or longer section of material. For example, *chronological order*, the first pattern we will study in this chapter, is related to the sentence relationship *sequence*. When sequence is extended through a paragraph or passage, the writer is using *chronological order*.

Writers use a wide variety of logical patterns. In this chapter, we will review five of the most common of them:

- *Chronological (time) order*: the material is organized by time sequence
- *Listing*: the material is organized into a list
- *Compare-contrast*: the material presents similarities and/or differences between two or more people, places, ideas, etc.

- *Cause-effect*: the material explains how one event is the cause of another, or the effect (result) of another

- *Definition*: the material presents a definition that is supported by examples or other explanation

Chronological Order

The word *chronological* comes from the Greek root *chron–*, meaning time. Chronological order means time order. When a writer uses chronological order, the material is presented in a time sequence. Events are described and discussed in the order in which they actually occurred.

Chronological order is the primary pattern for narrative writing (writing which tells a story), whether the narrative is true or fictional. It is common in history books, which follow sequences of events through time. Chronological order is also used for directions or steps in a process when the steps must be followed in a particular order.

Chronological order is of course closely related to the sentence relationship *sequence*. The transition words that indicate sequence are essentially the same as the transition words that indicate chronological order. Dates or other time markers (days of the week, hours in the day) are also clues to chronological order. In short, any wording that indicates that the events in a given sentence are following the events in a preceding sentence is a clue to chronological order. See Table 8.1 for transition words indicating chronological order.

When you recognize that the writer is using chronological order, you know that one of your main tasks as an active reader is to understand and remember the narrated sequence of events. Let's look at an example.

After Don Pancho's death, Nane's family fell apart. His father began to drink, and jobs became more scarce. Nane felt his father's pain as he bowed his head before the patrons and searched for work. He wanted nothing more than to escape, but there was nowhere to go. He decided if he couldn't run from his pain, he'd numb it. At twelve years of age, he started sniffing glue. By thirteen, he'd smoked his first joint. When he was seventeen, he tried LSD. He returned from Vietnam a heroin addict.

—Townsend, "Viva! Barrios Unidos," *Stone Soup for the World*

Note that the paragraph begins with the transition word *after*. The relationship that connects most of the sentences in the paragraph is sequence. The last three sentences begin with references to Nane's age, in time order: "At twelve

Table 8.1   Transition Words for Chronological Order

after	later	previously	first, second, third, etc.
before	next	then	in the past
currently	now	today	one, two, three, etc.
formerly	presently	when	

years of age"; "By thirteen"; and "When he was seventeen." These clues indicate a paragraph using chronological order.

The events in the paragraph might be ordered as follows.

1. Don Pancho died.

2. Nane's father started drinking and couldn't find work.

3. Nane started sniffing glue at age twelve.

4. He smoked his first joint at age thirteen.

5. He tried LSD at the age of seventeen.

6. He became a heroin addict during the Vietnam War.

> *In short,* to check for chronological order, ask yourself: does the passage discuss events or steps that follow one after another?

EXERCISE 8.1 WORKING WITH CHRONOLOGICAL ORDER

Directions: Read each passage and complete the accompanying exercises.

A. Joanne Alter was well aware of the problems in Chicago's public schools; as a county officeholder she sometimes visited them. The first woman elected to county-wide office, she was ending an eighteen-year career in elective politics. In her mid-sixties, it was time for her to retire.

One day she talked with a third-grade teacher at the Byrd Academy. The teacher was concerned that her students were struggling to learn, oppressed by fear, and starving for love and positive role models. On an impulse, Joanne volunteered to help the kids learn to read and— just as important—to let them know that someone besides their teacher believed in them, too.

On Joanne's first day of class, as she was leaving home, she met her neighbor, Marion Stone, in the elevator of her apartment building. Joanne explained the school's need and invited Marion to join her, and the two decided to go together. They had a terrific time in the classroom. The young children, delighted to have their attention, begged them to come back. That was the modest beginning of a program called Working in the Schools (WITS).

—Alter, "Working in the Schools," *Stone Soup for the World*

1. What transition words or other clues in the passage indicate chronological order?"

"One day" and "On Joanne's first day" are phases that suggest chronological order.

Other clues are references to time ("It was time to retire.")

2. Number the following events in the order in which they occurred:

___6___ The Working in the Schools program was started.

___3___ Joanne talked with a third-grade teacher and offered to help in the classroom.

___1___ Joanne Alter visited Chicago's public schools while holding a county office.

___5___ The two women went into the classroom together.

___2___ Joanne was about to retire.

___4___ Joanne met her neighbor Marion and invited her to join her.

B. In 1765 the colonists called for the Stamp Act Congress, the first official meeting of the colonies and the first step toward a unified nation. Nine of the thirteen colonies sent representatives to a meeting in New York City, where a detailed list of Crown violations of their fundamental rights was drawn up.

The Stamp Act Congress and its petitions to the Crown did little to stop the onslaught of taxing measures. In 1767 Parliament imposed duties on all kinds of colonial imports, including tea. Response from the Sons of Liberty was immediate. A boycott was announced, and almost all colonists gave up their favorite drink in a united show of resistance to the tax and British authority. Tensions continued to run high, especially after the British sent 4,000 troops to Boston. On March 5, 1770, English troops opened fire on a mob that included disgruntled dock workers, whose jobs had been taken by British soldiers, and members of the Sons of Liberty who were taunting the soldiers in front of the Boston Customs House. Five colonists were killed in what became known as the "Boston Massacre." Following this confrontation, all duties except those on tea were lifted. The tea tax, however, continued to be a symbolic irritant. In 1772, at the suggestion of Samuel Adams, Boston and other towns around Massachusetts set up Committees of Correspondence to articulate ideas and keep communications open around the colony. By 1774 twelve colonies had formed committees to maintain a flow of information among like-minded colonists.

—O'Connor and Sabato,
The Essentials of American Government, 3rd ed.

1. What transition words or other clues in the passage indicate chronological order?
   first; following; dates follow chronological sequence

2. Number the following events in the order in which they occurred:

   __3__ The colonists boycotted tea.

   __1__ Nine colonies sent representatives to the Stamp Act Congress.

   __2__ Parliament imposed taxes on tea and many other imports.

   __7__ Committees of Correspondence were established in Massachusetts.

   __6__ The British stopped taxes on all goods except tea.

   __5__ British soldiers killed five colonists in the Boston Massacre.

   __8__ Twelve of the colonies formed committees to share information.

   __4__ Four thousand British troops were sent to Boston.

Diagramming Chronological Order

Just as diagramming a paragraph makes the relationship of the main idea and details in the paragraph clearer, diagramming a passage to reflect its logical pattern makes the relationship of the ideas in the passage clearer. A passage diagram can also be a useful way to store information for later study.

A passage diagram serves as a map of what is important to learn and remember from the material. Passage diagrams that are consistent with the logical pattern used in the passage will make it easier for you to learn and remember the material.

Diagramming a passage using chronological order will clarify your understanding of the passage and reinforce your memory of the order of events. Diagramming a passage using chronological order is similar to creating a timeline for the main events in the passage.

LISTING **359**

To diagram a passage using chronological order, simply place each important event in a box or circle and draw arrows between the boxes or circles to illustrate the order of the events. See Figures 8.1 and 8.2 for examples of chronological order diagrams.

Figure 8.1 Chronological Order Diagram

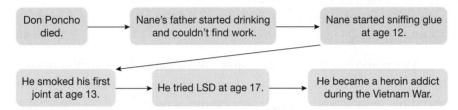

Figure 8.2 Sample Diagram, "Nane" Passage

EXERCISE 8.2 DIAGRAMMING CHRONOLOGICAL ORDER

Directions: On a separate sheet of paper, diagram the important events of either Passage A or Passage B from Exercise 8.1.

See Instructor's Manual.

Listing

You have probably had the experience of making a shopping list before going into a store. Perhaps you've made lists of things that were important to do in a coming day or week. Most people use listing as a practical life tool. Authors use listing, too—as a simple way of organizing some of the material they are writing.

Listing is a commonly used pattern that you will find in virtually any college textbook. In the listing pattern, the author lists related points of information. Lists may be contained in a sentence, a paragraph, or a longer section of material. The listed information may be presented in a logical order (such as more important to less important), or in random order. The active reader should ask, "What material is being listed? What is the purpose of the listing? Are the items listed in a particular order?"

Listing is associated with the sentence relationship *addition*. Each item in the list adds to the items previously listed.

Authors will sometimes use transition words to indicate listing (they will be similar to those that indicate addition). However, some of the transition words for listing are the same as the transition words for chronological order. When these transition words are used, the reader must rely on the context to distinguish between the two patterns. See Table 8.2 for transition words that indicate listing.

Table 8.2   Transition Words for Listing

another	next	first of all, etc.
finally	then	for one thing
last	first, second, third, etc.	one, two, three, etc.

The following is an example of a paragraph that uses listing.

During your career you may be called on to give speeches and presentations for all sorts of reasons. If you're in the human resources department, you may give orientation briefings to new employees or explain company policies, procedures, and benefits at assemblies. If you're a department supervisor, you may conduct training programs. If you're a problem solver or consultant, you may give analytical presentations on the merits of various proposals.

—Bovee and Thill, *Business Communication Today*

The preceding paragraph begins with a general point (the main idea)—that during your career you may be asked to give speeches and presentations. In the next three sentences, the author lists examples of the kinds of speeches and presentations you may be asked to give. Note that sentences two, three, and four begin with similar wording: "If you're in . . . you may . . . ." The parallel structure of these three sentences suggests that the paragraph contains listing. Note also that the second sentence ends with a brief listing of three things you might be asked to explain, with commas separating them ("*policies, procedures,* and *benefits* at assemblies").

The information in the paragraph might be listed as follows:

Speeches and Presentations You Might Give During Your Career

If you're in human resources:
    orientation briefings to new employees
    explanations of company policies, procedures, and benefits at assemblies
If you're a department supervisor:
    training programs
If you're a problem solver or consultant:
    analytical presentations on the merits of proposals

Today's textbook authors often use visual cues to indicate listing. For example, bullets are commonly used to show a listing pattern. Numbers may also be used to show listing, but numbers, like certain transition words, can also indicate chronological order. When numbers are used for a list, the pattern may also be called *enumeration*.

Let's look at an example of the listing pattern in which bullets are used.

DELIVERING THE SPEECH

When it's time to deliver the speech, you may feel a bit of stage fright. Most people do, even professional actors. A good way to overcome your fears is to rehearse until you're thoroughly familiar with your material. Communication professionals have suggested other tips:

- Prepare more material than necessary. Extra knowledge, combined with a genuine interest in the topic, will boost your confidence.
- Think positively about your audience, yourself, and what you have to say. See

LISTING   **361**

yourself as polished and professional, and your audience will too.

■ Be realistic about stage fright. After all, even experienced speakers admit that they feel butterflies before they address an audience. A little nervous excitement can actually provide the extra lift that will make your presentation sparkle.

■ Use the few minutes while you're arranging your materials, before you actually begin speaking, to tell yourself you're on and you're ready.

■ Before you begin speaking, take a few deep breaths.

■ Have your first sentence memorized and on the tip of your tongue.

■ If your throat is dry, drink some water.

—Bovee and Thill,
Business Communication Today

In the introductory paragraph of the preceding passage, the authors tell us to expect to be a little nervous before giving a speech—it's normal. They then offer a way to deal with the fears (rehearse thoroughly). Next, they wish to share several more tips for dealing with the fears, and proceed to list them with bullets. The bullets make the listing visually clear—you can tell you have a list before you even read the suggestions. Do you think the tips are listed in any particular order?

Let's look at a short passage about responding to criticism that uses enumeration (listing with numbers):

Behavior experts say we should avoid destructive responses and we should also help our critics. Here's how:

1. Be quiet and listen. Rein in your emotions and try to hear what your critic is actually saying.

2. Ask for more information, if needed. A simple "Can you be more specific?" is a good way to start.

3. Ask for a solution, or for help in finding one. "What specifically would you like me to do?" often clears the air.

—Graber, "Take the Sting Out of Criticism,"
Reader's Digest

Here the author offers three suggestions for responding to criticism and has chosen to number them. The numbering makes clear to the reader how many suggestions are listed.

In short, to check for listing, ask yourself, does the passage contain related ideas or points of information that are organized into a list?

EXERCISE 8.3 WORKING WITH LISTING

Directions: Read each passage and complete the accompanying exercises.

A. Virtually all that most white Americans know about the largest Indian tribe in the United States is that they are called the Navajo; the women weave beautiful blankets and dress in long full skirts and loose blouses of bright-colored velveteen, and the men make silver jewelry and often wear their hair long and banded with colorful silk scarves; they live in funny-looking little round houses called hogans, and the smiling children herd the family sheep.

—Locke, *Book of the Navajo*

1. What is listed in this paragraph?

The paragraph lists the limited information known by most white Americans about the Navajo.

2. What transition words or other clues in the passage indicate listing?

Listing is indicated by punctuation (semicolons and commas); and with the word "and."

3. Name five facts about the Navajo listed within the passage.

Any 5: their name; women weave beautiful blankets; women dress in long skirts and loose blouses of bright velveteen; men make silver jewelry; men wear hair long and banded with colorful silk scarves; they live in hogans; children herd sheep

4. Is some of the information listed more important to remember than other information in the paragraph? Explain your answer.

Probably not—it's a simple list of facts about the Navajo people.

5. Is the information listed in this paragraph placed in any special order? Explain your answer.

It goes from the women to the men to the children.

B. If diabetes is not kept under control, the disease affects almost every organ system. Those that are especially vulnerable include:

The heart and blood vessels. Diabetes greatly increases the risk of heart disease and stroke, and it contributes to high blood pressure and hardening of the arteries. Diabetics also tend to have high levels of cholesterol and triglycerides, another fat that circulates in the blood.

Eyes. Diabetes, which damages the tiny blood vessels in the eye, is the leading major cause of adult blindness. It also causes cataracts.

Kidneys. In the United States, diabetes is the leading cause of kidney failure.

Legs and feet. Damaged blood vessels and nerves result in reduced blood flow to the lower legs and feet. This can lead to diabetic ulcers—chronic skin sores. In a distressing number of cases, amputations are needed.

Nerves. Diabetes commonly causes tingling, numbness, and nerve pain (neuropathy). Nerve damage and impaired circulation can also lead to sexual impotence.

The good news is that these consequences can be prevented by making sure that blood glucose levels are normal.

—"Diabetes, Type II," from *The Complete Guide to Family Health*

1. What is the main point of the passage?

Diabetes is a serious illness that can affect almost any organ system if uncontrolled.

2. What is listed in the passage?

The organs and systems affected by diabetes and some ways the disease affects them

LISTING **363**

3. What transition words or other clues in the passage indicate listing?

The organ and systems affected are in boldfaced type, each starting a new

paragraph.

4. Name five organs or organ systems that may be affected by diabetes.

Any five: heart, blood vessels, eyes, kidneys, legs, feet, nerves

5. What are some of the ways that diabetes can affect the heart and blood vessels?

Increases risk of heart disease and stroke; contributes to high blood pressure and

hardening of the arteries; diabetics tend to have high cholesterol and triglyceride

levels.

Diagramming the Listing Pattern

There are several ways to diagram a passage that uses the listing pattern. You can make a simple diagram of the items being listed, placing each in a box or circle under their general heading or topic. An alternative, if there are not too many items listed, is to place the topic in a circle and draw lines from the circle to represent the listed items, writing each item on one of the lines. See Figures 8.3, 8.4, and 8.5.

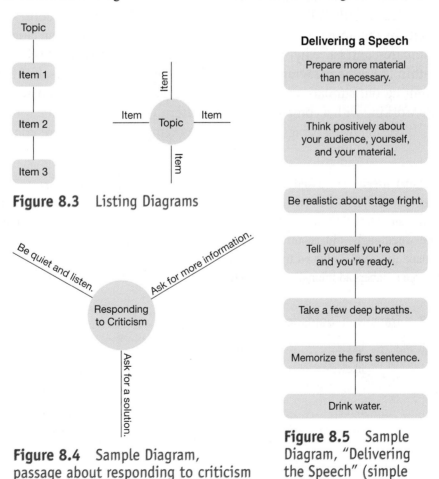

Figure 8.3 Listing Diagrams

Figure 8.4 Sample Diagram, passage about responding to criticism (alternative form)

Figure 8.5 Sample Diagram, "Delivering the Speech" (simple outline form)

EXERCISE **8.4** DIAGRAMMING LISTING

Directions: On a separate sheet of paper, diagram the important information from Passage A *or* Passage B in Exercise 8.3.

See Instructor's Manual.

Compare-Contrast

The human mind has a natural tendency to compare people, places, things, and ideas. With the compare-contrast pattern, authors discuss similarities and/or differences (comparison includes both similarities and differences; contrast refers only to differences) between two or more people, places, groups, theories, or other items. The compare-contrast pattern is often used in social science readings and may be found in other subject areas as well. When noticing compare-contrast, the active reader looks to identify the key points of similarity and/or difference that the author describes.

The compare-contrast pattern is of course closely associated with the sentence relationship *contrast*. The transition words for compare-contrast are pretty much the same as the transition words for contrast, with the addition of transition words and phrases indicating similarity. See Table 8.3 for a list of the transition words indicating compare-contrast.

You will often find transition words when the compare-contrast pattern is used. In the absence of transition words, you may find other clues indicating compare-contrast. Anytime two people, groups, places, or ideas are discussed within the same paragraph or in nearby paragraphs, ask yourself if the author is pointing out similarities or differences between them. If the answer is yes, you are working with a compare-contrast pattern.

The following paragraph provides an example of the compare-contrast pattern:

When casual users were asked about their current reasons for marijuana use, two answers—"to feel good" and "to have a good time"—prevailed overwhelmingly. In contrast, while regular marijuana users all continued to cite these two reasons, large numbers additionally responded: "to get away from my problems" (37%) or "to help me get through the day" (29%). Using marijuana as a means of escaping or coping with problems thus strongly distinguishes the regular daily user of marijuana from the casual user.

—McClellan et al., *Escape from Anxiety and Stress*

Table 8.3 Transition Words for Compare-Contrast

although	like	than	in a similar fashion
but	likewise	though	in contrast
conversely	nevertheless	yet	in spite of
despite	rather	while (meaning *although*)	in the same way
however	similarly		on the contrary
instead	still		on the other hand

The preceding paragraph compares casual marijuana users with regular marijuana users. Note that two of the reasons mentioned are the same for both groups: "to feel good" and "to have a good time." Regular users, however, added two reasons that casual users did not include: "to get away from problems" and "to get through the day." These two reasons create a contrast between the two groups—note the use of the transition words "in contrast" that begin sentence two.

The compare-contrast in the passage can be displayed as follows:

Casual users:	*Regular users:*	
to feel good	to feel good	(same)
to have a good time	to have a good time	(same)
	to get away from problems	(different)
	to get through the day	(different)

Note also that the main idea in this paragraph is stated in the general sentence at the end of the paragraph that explains the difference—the contrast—between the two groups of users.

> *In short*, to check for compare-contrast, ask yourself: does the author point out any similarities and/or differences between two or more people, groups, places, ideas, and so on?

EXERCISE 8.5 WORKING WITH CAMPARISON–CONTRAST

Directions: Read each passage and complete the accompanying exercises.

A. Some of the writing you'll do on the job requires very little planning. For a memo to your staff regarding the company picnic or a letter requesting information from a supplier, you can often collect a few facts and get right down to writing. In other cases, however, you won't be able to start writing until you've done extensive research. The research often covers both the audience you'll be writing to and the subject matter you'll be writing about. Technology can help you with planning tasks, with research tasks, and with outlining your thoughts once you've done your research.

—Bovee and Thill, *Business Communication Today*

1. What is being compared or contrasted in the paragraph?
   <u>Writing on the job that requires very little planning vs. writing on the job that requires</u>
   <u>considerable planning and research</u>

2. Write one complete sentence to express the paragraph's main idea.
   <u>Some writing on the job requires little planning, but some requires considerable</u>
   <u>planning and research.</u>

3. What transition words or other clues in the passage indicate compare-contrast?
   <u>In other cases; however</u>

4. What specific writing task mentioned in the passage requires little planning?

A memo to staff about a company picnic, *or* a letter requesting information from a

supplier

5. What will you need to research when a writing task requires more planning?

You need to research your audience and the subject matter.

B. The most frequently expressed complaint women have about men is that men don't listen. Either a man completely ignores her when she speaks to him, or he listens for a few beats, assesses what is bothering her, and then proudly puts on his Mr. Fix-It cap and offers her a solution to make her feel better. He is confused when she doesn't appreciate this gesture of love. No matter how many times she tells him that he's not listening, he doesn't get it and keeps doing the same thing. She wants empathy, but he thinks she wants solutions.

The most frequently expressed complaint men have about women is that women are always trying to change them. When a woman loves a man, she feels responsible to assist him in growing and tries to help him improve the way he does things. She forms a home-improvement committee, and he becomes her primary focus. No matter how much he resists her help, she persists—waiting for any opportunity to help him or tell him what to do. She thinks she's nurturing him, while he feels he's being controlled. Instead, he wants her acceptance.

—Gray, *Men Are from Mars, Women Are from Venus*

1. Who or what is being compared or contrasted in the passage?

Complaints women have about men vs. complaints men have about women

2A. What is the main idea of the first paragraph?

Women's primary complaint about men is that they don't listen.

2B. What is the main idea of the second paragraph?

Men's primary complaint about women is that they're trying to change them.

3. What transition words or other clues in the passage indicate compare-contrast?

The parallel beginnings of the two paragraphs with the genders reversed; but, while,

instead

4. What does a man think a woman wants when she is expecting him to listen empathetically?

He thinks she wants a solution to a problem.

5. What does a man want when a woman feels she's nurturing him by helping him improve?

He wants acceptance.

Diagramming Compare-Contrast

To diagram a passage using the compare-contrast pattern, place the points of comparison or contrast in boxes or circles in two columns. Use the top box or circle in each column to head the column. Place related points of comparison or contrast side by side. See Figures 8.6 and 8.7.

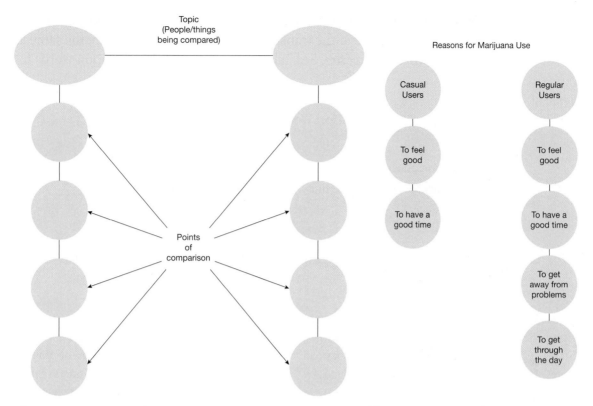

Figure 8.6 Comparison–Contrast Diagram

Figure 8.7 Sample Diagram, paragraph about marijuana use

EXERCISE 8.6 DIAGRAMMING COMPARISON-CONTRAST

Directions: On a separate sheet of paper, diagram the important information from Passage A *or* Passage B in Exercise 8.5.

See Instructor's Manual.

Cause-Effect

In virtually every field of study, there will be times when we ask the question *why*? An historian, for example, might ask why a war started. A psychologist might ask why a person has certain character traits. An environmentalist might ask why a given species has become endangered. When we ask the question *why*, we are seeking a *cause*.

We also sometimes want to know what results will follow a certain action or set of circumstances. For example, the sociologist or psychologist might ask, what happens to someone who grows up in a deprived environment? An historian might ask, what happened as a result of a war?

When an author is discussing the reasons for something, or the results of something, she is using the cause-effect pattern. Cause-effect patterns are common in history, social science, and science textbooks. The active reader will identify the causes and effects discussed in the passage and determine which ones are important to remember.

The cause-effect pattern is most closely associated with the sentence relationship *reason*, and some of the transition words for cause-effect are the same as the transition words for *reason*. See Table 8.4 for a list of the transition words for cause-effect.

Table 8.4   Transition Words for Cause-Effect

because	then	as a consequence
consequently	therefore	as a result
hence	thus	for this reason
since	whereas	

The following is a paragraph from a history textbook that uses cause-effect:

During this period, hardships in Western Europe led to increased immigration to the United States, especially from Ireland and the German states. For the long-suffering people of Ireland, by the early nineteenth century life had become more precarious than ever. Over the generations, small farm plots had been subdivided among heirs to the point that most holdings consisted of fewer than fifteen acres. At the same time, the population of Ireland had grown exponentially—to more than 4 million people in 1800. England treated Ireland like a colony that existed purely for the economic gain of the mother country (or, in the eyes of the Irish, an occupying power). A series of English laws and policies mandated that farmers export most of the island's grain and cattle, leaving the impoverished people to subsist mainly on a diet of potatoes. Then, beginning in 1845, a blight devastated the potato crop. In the next five years, a million people died and another million fled to the United States. The great Irish migration had begun.

—Jones et al., *Created Equal*

The preceding paragraph explains the cause of the great Irish migration to the United States, which occurred in the middle of the nineteenth century. The paragraph begins with a general statement that indicates cause-effect: notice the words "led to" in that sentence. In other words, "hardships in western Europe" is the cause in this sentence, and "increased immigration to the United States" is the effect. The paragraph proceeds to talk specifically about the conditions that led to, or caused, the Irish migration: farms getting smaller while the population increased; English laws and policies forcing the Irish to live mostly on their potato crop; and the failure of the potato crop due to blight, leading to death for many and migration for others.

The information in this paragraph can be viewed in this way:

Hardships in Western Europe	*caused*	increased immigration to the United States
Smaller farms, increased population, English policies, and a potato blight	*caused*	the great Irish migration

Let's look at another example of cause-effect:

Almost everything people do with their cars causes some form of pollution. Driving creates auto exhaust, which spews out chemicals and poisons the air. Oil spills and the dumping of auto-related refuse pollute the water supply. Auto "graveyards" and tire dumps deface the landscape, and highway runoff is a major source of soil pollution. Making and using cars may be one of humankind's most polluting activities.

—Rock, *The Automobile and the Environment*

The preceding paragraph focuses on the *effects* of auto use. The first sentence contains the transition word "cause" and introduces the general point of the paragraph—that cars cause pollution. The next three sentences identify specific types of pollution that result from auto use: air pollution from auto exhaust; water pollution from auto-related refuse; and landscape defacement and soil pollution from auto graveyards, tire dumps, and highway runoff.

The information in the paragraph may be thought of in this way:

Auto use	*causes*	pollution
Auto exhaust	*causes*	air pollution
Oil spills and dumping of auto-related refuse	*cause*	water pollution
Auto graveyards and tire dumps	*cause*	land defacement
highway runoff	*causes*	soil pollution

Since a cause-effect situation may involve events that occur one after another, the cause-effect pattern sometimes overlaps with chronological order. When this occurs, the active reader will ask himself if the author is explaining reasons for the events (cause-effect) or merely telling what happened (chronological order).

Let's look at a passage in which cause-effect overlaps with chronological order.

China had a major opium addiction problem among its citizens. It sought to bar imports of opium, chiefly from Britain, which had damaged Chinese society and drained wealth overseas. Britain, seeking to end trade restrictions imposed by China, used this as an opportunity for war. In the first Opium War (1839–1842), Britain forced China to expand trade and to cede Hong Kong. A second war (1856–58) opened more Chinese ports. With the loss to Britain, addiction in China increased. By the end of the century, there were nearly ninety million opium addicts in the country.

—Terkel, *Should Drugs Be Legalized?*

You probably noted that the events in the preceding paragraph are in time order:

1. China had an opium problem.
2. China barred opium imports from Britain.
3. Britain started a war with China.
4. Britain forced China to expand trade and cede Hong Kong (first Opium War).

5. A second war opened more Chinese ports.

6. Addiction in China increased.

You probably also noticed that the author is suggesting that the events in the paragraph *caused* one another. The Chinese barred opium imports *because* they had an opium problem. Britain started a war with China *because* their trade had been restricted. China expanded trade and ceded Hong Kong *because* they lost the first war and later opened more ports *because* they lost the second war. Finally, addiction to opium increased in China *because* Britain could now export more opium to China. In paragraphs of this type, the alert reader will recognize the cause-effect pattern along with chronological order.

> *In short*, to check for cause-effect, ask yourself: is the author explaining why something happened or the results of something that happened?

EXERCISE 8.7 WORKING WITH CAUSE AND EFFECT

Directions: Reach each passage and complete the accompanying exercises.

A. Starting in the early seventeenth century, colonists came to the New World for a variety of reasons. Often it was to escape religious persecution. Others came seeking a new start on a continent where land was plentiful. The independence and diversity of the settlers in the New World made the question of how best to rule the new colonies a tricky one. More than merely an ocean separated England from the colonies; the colonists were independent people, and it soon became clear that the Crown could not govern the colonies with the same close rein used at home. King James I thus allowed some local participation in decision making through arrangements such as the first elected colonial assembly, the Virginia House of Burgesses, and the elected General Court that governed the Massachusetts Bay Company and that colony after 1629. Almost all the colonists agreed that the king ruled by divine right; but English monarchs allowed the colonists significant liberties in terms of self-government, religious practices, and economic organization. For 140 years, this system worked fairly well.

—O'Connor and Sabato, *The Essentials of American Government*, 3rd ed.

1. What is the main idea of the paragraph?

   Because he could not closely govern the colonies, the English king allowed them

   some degree of self-government.

2. What transition words or other clues in the passage indicate the cause-effect pattern?

   reasons; "made the question"; thus

3. According to the passage, what caused the colonists to come to the New World?

   A variety of reasons—some were escaping religious persecution, others sought a

   new start in a new land.

4. Name one important result (effect) of the independence and diversity of the colonists.

Their independence and diversity made it difficult to rule them.

5. Why did King James allow the colonists to have some self-government?

He realized that it would be difficult to rule them because of their independence

and because they were separated by an ocean.

B. In the game of basketball, trash talking is part of the deal. While you're playing, people be saying they're better than you, that you can't play, or just insult you. It puts people on the spot. Like, I'm playing, and this guy playing defense on me is saying, "You're not going to score nothing. I'm going to score more than you. Let met get the ball." So when someone's trash talking, you have to prove yourself to him, but mostly to yourself. No matter what they say, you can't believe them.

When I'm feeling good about myself, trash talking is not a problem. But if I start a game and miss my first five shots, I feel that's how I'm going to play the whole game. If I make the first five shots, I have more confidence. I'm ready for trash talking. It depends on how I start. If it's a great start, that's how I'm going to finish it. If I have a bad start, that's how I'm going to finish.

I think trash talking can also give you confidence, but my dad doesn't like it when I do it. But I think it works. Like, I would say, "You can't score on me." You try to get them out of their game. You get them so mad they're not into the game, they're into you. So you take them out of the game and put yourself in the game more.

—Alicea, *The Air Down Here*

1. What is the author's main point about trash talking?

Trash talking is a part of the game of basketball and affects people's play.

2. What transition words or other clues in the passage indicate the cause-effect pattern?

"Puts people in the spot"; "depends on"; "give you confidence"

3. According to the passage, what are some of the *effects* of trash talking?

Trash talking puts pressure on the opponent, who may feel he has to prove himself.

4. What are some of the causes of trash talking?

Trash talking may be caused by the desire to out-psych one's opponent or build

one's own confidence.

5. According to the author, how does confidence affect his trash talking and basketball play?

He plays better when he's more confident. He is unaffected by trash talking when he's

confident. He also says that trash talking can increase your confidence.

Diagramming Cause-Effect

How you diagram a passage using the cause-effect pattern will depend upon whether the passage is explaining the causes for something or discussing the effects of something. If there are several effects for one cause, place the cause on top and the effects under it. If there are several causes for one event, place the causes on top and the effect (resulting event) below them. You can use arrows to emphasize the cause-effect relationship. See Figures 8.8, 8.9, and 8.10.

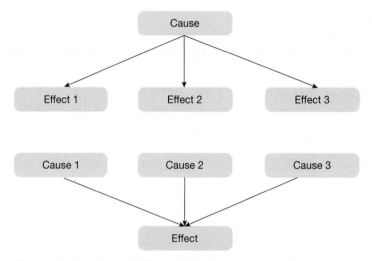

Figure 8.8 Cause-Effect Diagrams

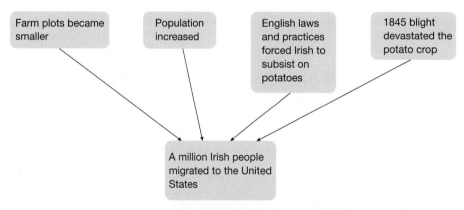

Figure 8.9 Sample Diagram, paragraph about the great Irish migration

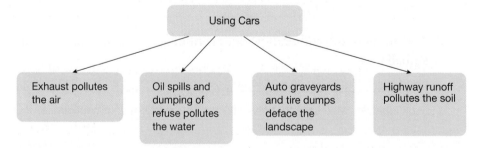

Figure 8.10 Sample Diagram, paragraph about cars causing pollution

EXERCISE 8.8 DIAGRAMMING CAUSE-EFFECT

Directions: On a separate sheet of paper, diagram the important information from Passage A *or* Passage B in Exercise 8.7.

See Instructor's Manual.

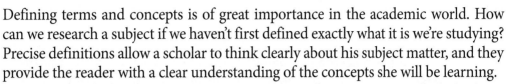

Definition

Defining terms and concepts is of great importance in the academic world. How can we research a subject if we haven't first defined exactly what it is we're studying? Precise definitions allow a scholar to think clearly about his subject matter, and they provide the reader with a clear understanding of the concepts she will be learning.

The definition pattern is common in college freshman textbooks, which introduce students to the terminology used in college disciplines. The active reader is alert to definitions when they are presented in the text. The challenge for the student is first to understand the definition, and then of course to remember the new term and its meaning.

When the definition pattern is used, the definition is often followed by further explanation that may include examples to clarify the meaning. The alert reader will pay careful attention to the explanation and examples, because they may be of great help in understanding the new term.

Although there is no set of transition words for the definition pattern, this pattern is normally easy to recognize. Textbooks will usually place new terms in boldfaced print or italics. Today's textbooks often repeat key definitions in the margins of the text as well. Definitions can also be recognized by the author's wording: when the word "is" follows a new term, a definition is likely to follow.

The definition pattern is not directly associated with any of the sentence relationships reviewed in Chapter 7. However, you may notice the use of the *addition* relationship when the definition pattern is used, as the author adds examples or explanation to clarify the meaning of a term.

The following is an example of a paragraph that uses the definition pattern.

Hypnosis is a trancelike state of concentrated and focused attention, heightened suggestibility, and diminished response to external stimuli. In the hypnotic state, people suspend their usual rational and logical ways of thinking and perceiving and allow themselves to experience distortions in perceptions, memories, and thinking. Under hypnosis people may experience positive hallucinations, in which they see, hear, touch, smell or taste things that are not present in the environment. Or they may have negative hallucinations and fail to perceive those things that are present.

—Wood and Wood, *The World of Psychology,* 2nd ed.

The primary purpose of the preceding paragraph is to provide the reader with a definition of hypnosis. The definition is stated in the first sentence, in which the word "hypnosis" is italicized. The authors then clarify the definition with an explanation of what happens in the hypnotic state and some examples of things that hypnotized people may experience.

Let's look at another example of a paragraph that uses the definition pattern.

Profit, then defines business. But what is it? Simply, profit is the difference between a business's total revenues or sales receipts and the total of its production costs, operating expenses, and taxes. Go back to our bread example. The bakery has to pay for its raw materials (flour, butter or shortening, yeast, salt), equipment (mixers, ovens, wrapping machines), employees, and the energy it uses. When the bakery sells the bread to the supermarket, it charges more than the cost of making the bread. That extra part of the selling price is profit.

—Straub and Kossen, *Introduction to Business*

In the preceding paragraph, the authors use the question in the second sentence to lead the reader to the definition of profit in the third sentence. The rest of the paragraph clarifies the definition through the use of one extended example (the bakery).

In short, to check for the definition pattern, ask yourself: is the passage primarily concerned with defining an important term?

EXERCISE 8.9 WORKING WITH DEFINITION

Directions: Read each paragraph and answer the accompanying questions.

A. Demand is the quantity of a good or service consumers are willing and able to buy at a given price. Usually the quantity demanded changes as price changes, and we can use a demand curve to represent this change. Thus, you might be willing to pay someone $1 to wash your car each week. But you might have the car washed only every two weeks if the price rose to $2, and not at all at a price of $20. At $20, you would either wash the car yourself or leave it dirty!

—Zikmund et al., *Business*

1. Underline the sentence that contains the definition of demand.

2. The authors clarify the definition of demand by:

   (a.) Discussing one common example.

   b. Listing and discussing several examples.

   c. Explaining what causes demand.

3. How does price affect demand?

   Demand decreases as price increases.

4. Explain what *demand* means in a complete sentence of your own wording.

   Demand is how much consumers will buy at a given price level. (sample answer)

B. By the time we reach adulthood, experience has taught us a large number of simple, predictable associations. We know, for example, that a long day at the beach may result in a painful sunburn and that a gas station should be our next stop when the fuel gauge reads empty. We have also learned sophisticated, complicated processes, such as how to drive a car and how to appreciate music ranging from Bach to Hootie and the Blowfish. Some people learn socially deviant behaviors, such as stealing and drug abuse. <u>In general, learning is the process by which people acquire new knowledge.</u> <u>Psychologists define learning as a relatively permanent change in an organism that occurs as a result of experiences in the environment and that is often seen in overt behavior.</u> This definition of learning has three important parts: (1) experience in the environment, (2) change in the organism, and (3) permanence.

—Lefton, *Psychology,* 6th ed.

1. Underline the two sentences that define learning.

2. In the first half of the paragraph, the author provides:

    ⓐ Several examples of learning.

    b. One extended example of an important learning experience.

    c. An explanation of how people learn.

3. In the last sentence, the author:

    a. Distinguishes between three different types of learning.

    b. Compares and contrasts the psychologists' definition of learning with the general definition.

    ⓒ Identifies the important elements of the psychologists' definition of learning.

4. From your own experience, give an example of learning that would be consistent with the psychologists' definition.

    Answers will vary.

Diagramming the Definition Pattern

Diagramming passages using the definition pattern is simple. Place the definition in a box or circle and use boxes or circles underneath it for useful examples or explanations that support the definition. If more than one term is being defined, you might use a diagram similar to the comparison-contrast diagram. See Figures 8.11 and 8.12.

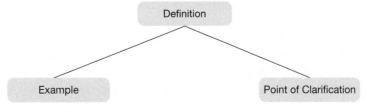

Figure 8.11 Definition Pattern Diagram

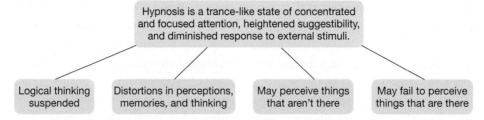

Figure 8.12 Sample Diagram, passage about hypnosis

EXERCISE 8.10 DIAGRAMMING THE DEFINITION PATTERN

Directions: On a separate sheet of paper, diagram the definition and important supporting information from Passage A *or* Passage B in Exercise 8.9.

See Instructor's Manual.

> **Logical patterns** are tools that enable writers to order their ideas and information and to make the relationship between ideas clearer to the reader.
>
> Active readers look for these patterns to help them understand the organization of the material they're reading.

Active Reading Strategy: Recognizing Logical Patterns

As we have already seen, it is not unusual to find more than one logical pattern in a passage, or even in a single paragraph. Typically, however, there is one primary pattern that is most useful for understanding and remembering the important points. Use the "in short" questions reprinted below to help you recognize the primary pattern. Look for the pattern that best helps you connect and understand the most important points in the passage. Within a paragraph, the primary pattern will normally be linked with

> **"In Short" Questions to Recognize Logical Patterns**
>
> - To check for **chronological order**, ask yourself, does the passage discuss events or steps that follow one after another?
> - To check for **listing**, ask yourself, does the passage contain related ideas or points of information that are organized into a list?
> - To check for **compare-contrast**, ask yourself, does the author point out any similarities and/or differences between two or more people, groups, places, ideas, etc.?
> - To check for **cause-effect**, ask yourself, is the author explaining why something happened or the results of something that happened?
> - To check for the **definition** pattern, ask yourself, is the passage primarily concerned with defining an important term?

the main idea. For example, in the compare-contrast paragraph on marijuana users (p. 364), the main idea is expressed in the last sentence, contrasting two types of marijuana users. In the definition paragraph on hypnosis (p. 373), the main idea is expressed in the first sentence, which provided the reader with the definition of hypnosis.

Let's look at a paragraph from a computer science textbook that uses two patterns.

An operating system is the software that controls the computer's use of its hardware resources such as memory and disk storage space. An operating system works like an air traffic controller to coordinate the activities within the computer. Just as an airport cannot function without air traffic controllers, a computer cannot function without an operating system.

—Parsons and Oja, *Computer Concepts*

In the preceding paragraph, we find both definition and compare-contrast. The paragraph begins with the definition of *operating system* and then compares an operating system to an air traffic controller (or more exactly, draws an analogy between an operating system and an air traffic controller). Which is the primary pattern? Is the main concern of the paragraph to tell us what an operating system is or to point out the ways that operating systems and air traffic controllers are similar? You probably agree that the main concern of this paragraph is to tell us what an operating system is, and that the main idea—the definition of an operating system—is stated in the first sentence. We then understand that the comparison or analogy with an air traffic controller is meant to help the reader better understand the definition of operating system. We therefore consider the *primary* pattern in this paragraph to be definition.

EXERCISE 8.11 RECOGNIZING LOGICAL PATTERNS IN SENTENCES

Directions: Identify the primary logical pattern in each of the following sentences. Write Chronological Order, Listing, Compare-Contrast, Cause-Effect, or Definition for your answer in the space provided and briefly explain your answer. An example is provided.

EXAMPLE

Although violence has long been a concern in American society, not until 1985 did the U.S. Public Health Service formally identify violence as a leading public health problem.

Donatelle, *Health: The Basics*, 6th ed.

Compare-Contrast—the sentence contrasts the long concern with violence with the recent recognition by the government of violence as a leading public health problem.

1. From ancient times, parents from most language groups were guided in choosing names by such things as birth time events, physical characteristics, hopes for future prosperity, wealth, fame, or martial prowess, references to higher powers, and ordinary vocabulary words.

—Turner, *The Very Best Book of Baby Names*

Listing: the sentence lists things from which names were chosen.

2. In conversations, women hold eye contact more than men, but men have their own brand of eye contact: staring.

—Macionis, *Sociology,* 11th ed.

Compare-Contrast: the sentence contrasts women's and men's use of eye contact in conversations.

3. Sally sat in the driver's seat, fastened the seat belt, and started the ignition.

Chronological Order: the sentence describes Sally's actions in the order in which they were done.

4. Radioactivity occurs because a few elements are just too big or ungainly to be stable.

—Suplee, *Everyday Science*

Cause-Effect: the sentence explains the cause of radioactivity (unstable elements).

5. Do not go on a camping trip without a flashlight, raincoat, knife, and rope or twine.

Listing: the sentence lists essential items to bring on a camping trip.

6. A newspaper chain is a company that owns several newspapers.

—Vivian, *The Media of Mass Communication,* 2006 ed.

Definition: the sentence defines newspaper chain.

7. A slice of cheese has more protein than a slice of bread.

Compare-Contrast: the sentence compares protein in cheese and bread.

8. Peers, like parents, shape the expression of personality traits, causing us to emphasize some attributes or abilities and downplay others.

—Wade and Tavris, *Invitation to Psychology,* 4th ed.

Cause-Effect: the sentence states that peers affect how personality is shaped and how specific traits are developed or suppressed.

9. Power is the ability to carry out one's will, even over the resistance of others

—Henslin, *Sociology: A Down-to-Earth Approach,* 7th ed.

Definition: the sentence defines power.

10. When baking a cake, be sure to preheat the oven before you mix the ingredients.

Chronological Order: the sentence tells the correct sequence when baking a cake.

EXERCISE 8.12 RECOGNIZING LOGICAL PATTERNS IN PARAGRAPHS

Directions: Read each paragraph and answer the questions that follow.

A. They may not have been born free, but more and more animals are being set free by zoos determined to help endangered species hang on. Because of these efforts, some species driven to extinction in the wild decades ago now roam free once again.

—Biondo, "Born to Be Wild," *USA Weekend Magazine*

1. What is the paragraph's primary logical pattern (Chronological Order, Listing, Compare-Contrast, Cause-Effect, or Definition)? Explain your answer.

Cause-Effect: setting animals free is the cause; species roaming free is the effect.

2. What transition words or other clues in the paragraph indicate this pattern?

Because (of)

___a___ **3.** The main idea of the paragraph is:
   a. Zoos are helping endangered species to survive by setting them free.
   b. Most animals are better off in the wild than in the zoo.
   c. Many zoo animals today are threatened with extinction and will not survive unless they are returned to the wilderness.

B. The National Science Foundation defines **alternative medicine** as any treatment or therapy that has not been scientifically demonstrated to be effective. Even a simple practice such as taking vitamins sometimes falls into this category. For instance, if you take vitamin C to protect yourself against the common cold, you are using alternative medicine because vitamin C has not been scientifically proven to prevent colds.

—Wood et al., *Portable Psychology*

1. What is the paragraph's primary logical pattern (Chronological Order, Listing, Compare-Contrast, Cause-Effect, or Definition)? Explain your answer.

Definition: the paragraph defines alternative medicine and gives an example of it.

2. What transition words or other clues in the paragraph indicate this pattern?

"defines"; boldface term

___c___ **3.** The main idea of the paragraph is:
   a. Taking vitamin C is an example of alternative medicine because vitamin C has not been scientifically proven to prevent colds.
   b. Alternative medicine should be avoided until it has been scientifically proven.
   c. Alternative medicine is any treatment or therapy that hasn't been scientifically proven to be effective.

C. After reading about the death of pioneer glider Otto Lilienthal in 1896, the Wright brothers became interested in flying. They began serious reading on the subject in 1899, and soon obtained all the scientific knowledge of aeronautics then available. That same year they experimented for a day or two with a five-foot biplane kite. The Wrights selected for their experiments a narrow strip of sand called Kill Devil Hill, near the little settlement of Kitty Hawk, N.C. In 1900, they experimented at Kitty Hawk with their first man-carrying gilder. It measured 16 feet from wing tip to wing tip, and cost $15 to build.

—"Wright Brothers," *World Book Encyclopedia*

1. What is the paragraph's primary logical pattern (Chronological Order, Listing, Compare-Contrast, Cause-Effect, or Definition)? Explain your answer.

   Chronological Order: the paragraph narrates the sequence of events leading to the

   Wright brothers' first flight.

2. What transition words or other clues in the paragraph indicate this pattern?

   After; soon; that same year; dates (1896, 1899, 1900)

_b_ 3. Which sentence best summarizes the paragraph?
   a. The Wright brothers experimented at Kitty Hawk with their first man-made glider.
   b. The Wright brothers began experimenting with flight around the turn of the century (1899–1900).
   c. Otto Lilienthal inspired the Wright brothers to learn more about flying.

D. Most people do not have any idea of the importance of small businesses in our economy. The news media devote so much time to employment and problems in big businesses such as automobiles, steel, and textiles that you might think that the economy is dominated totally by large businesses. Yet large companies (more than 1,000 employees) created only 6 percent of the new jobs since 1975. Since 1979, large companies actually lost about 600,000 jobs. Ninety percent of the nation's new jobs in the private sector are in small businesses. More than half of the new jobs are with companies with fewer than 20 employees. Even in the sluggish economic climate of the early 1990's, employment in small businesses increased by 1.77 percent compared to only a 0.62% employment increase in large companies. That means there is a very good chance that you will either work in a small business someday or start one.

—Nickels et al., *Understanding Business*

1. What is the paragraph's primary logical pattern (Chronological Order, Listing, Compare-Contrast, Cause-Effect, or Definition)? Explain your answer.

   Compare-Contrast: the paragraph contrasts small and larger businesses.

2. What transition words or other clues in the paragraph indicate this pattern?

   Yet; alternation between information about small and large businesses

_b_ 3. The main idea of the paragraph is:
   a. Most people today work for a small business.
   b. Small businesses play an important role in our economy.
   c. Large companies have created only 6 percent of the new jobs since 1975.

E. By the age of two we are more capable of doing things for ourselves—not to mention all the other things we *want* to do for ourselves. Much to our delight we walk, we talk, we feed ourselves, and we even try dressing ourselves. We are very curious about the world that we can now explore. We realize that we can express our needs; only they're not as simple as they once were. Our language, with its limited vocabulary, hasn't quite caught up with our thinking and feeling capacity, so we are often frustrated communicators. We also are beginning to recognize that there are "others" out there and that we don't always get the response we want from them.

—Johnson and Goodman, *The Essence of Parenting*

1. What is the paragraph's primary logical pattern (Chronological Order, Listing, Compare-Contrast, Cause-Effect, or Definition)? Explain your answer.

   Listing: the paragraph lists the things we can do at the age of two.

2. What transition words or other clues in the paragraph indicate this pattern?

   "Other things"; also punctuation (commas for series); parallel constructions

   (sentences and clauses starting with "we")

_c_ 3. The main idea of the paragraph is:
   a. Two-year-olds are very curious about the world around them.
   b. At the age of two we become able to express ourselves and communicate with the people around us.
   c. By the age of two we can do more things for ourselves and are more aware of ourselves and the people around us.

EXERCISE 8.13 WRITING LOGICAL PATTERNS

Directions: For each logical pattern, write an original sentence in which you use that pattern.

Chronological Order

   Answers will vary.

Listing

   Answers will vary.

Compare-Contrast

   Answers will vary.

Cause-Effect

   Answers will vary.

Definition

_____

Answers will vary.

_____

_____

EXERCISE 8.14 RECOGNIZING LOGICAL PATTERNS

Directions: Review the sentences you wrote for Exercises 8.13, rewriting them if necessary. Then, working with one of your classmates, select one of your sentences at random and read it to your partner; your partner must guess which pattern your sentence illustrated. Alternate reading your sentences until you and your partner have read and guessed the pattern for each one. If you disagree on any, share your different points of view.

EXERCISE 8.15 LOGICAL PATTERNS IN SHORT PASSAGES

Directions: Note logical patterns while reading each of the following passages; then answer the questions that follow the passage.

A. LEMON AID: CLUES TO SPOT A CLUNKER

1  When shopping for a used car, a few simple measures can help you separate the peaches from the lemons. Here are some safeguards endorsed by Austin Davis, the third-generation owner of a Houston car repair shop:

2 **When meeting with a private seller,** inspect the car first thing in the morning—after it has sat at that location overnight (as opposed to having been driven to a different location, such as a parking lot). This allows you to check under the chassis for leaked fluids.

3 **Arrive at least 15 minutes** before the designated meeting time to ensure the owner isn't "prepping" the car by taking special measures to hide problems.

4 **When you start the car**, have a friend stand off to one side to check the tailpipe for signs of smoke.

- *White smoke* often results from water or antifreeze entering the cylinders (the white smoke is steam). It could suggest the engine will overheat.
- *Blue smoke* is caused by engine oil entering the cylinders and may suggest failed gaskets or O-rings.

- *Black smoke*, typically the least problematic, usually means excess fuel is entering the engine's cylinders. It may signal problems with the carburetor, the fuel pump, the fuel injector, or the computer sensors.

5 **When you take a test-drive**, head for a highway with a solid side wall, jersey wall, or median barrier. This gives you a chance to roll down the window—with the stereo off—and listen for any untoward noises echoing off that hard surface. Ideally, you should hear nothing more than the sound of the car's tires on the road.

6 **Check the car body** for straight and even seams in the doors, hood, and trunk; deviations could betray a previous wreck. Place a magnet over a piece of cloth and gently drag it along each steel body panel; if it won't adhere in certain places, that indicates a putty "body" filler was used for a repair. Check the underside of both the hood and the trunk to make sure the paint color is consistent with the rest of the body.

7 **Examine tires** for even wear and uniform size and manufacturer. Is the spare tire properly inflated? If not the seller may have been a neglectful owner.

8   **Bounce each corner** of the car; it should rock only once or twice before coming to a stop.

9   **Check the interior carpeting** for signs of water damage or excessive wear (and compare that to the mileage). Pay special attention to the carpeting just beneath the dashboard; stains there may indicate a leaky heater or air conditioner.

—Kirchheimer, *Scam Proof Your Life*

1. What is the primary logical pattern used in this passage? Explain your answer.

Listing: the passage lists things to check when shopping for a used car.

2. What transition words or other clues in the passage indicate this pattern?

Boldface type; bullets; wording ("here are some . . .") and colon at end of first

paragraph

3. Are the suggestions listed in the passage presented in any particular order? Explain your answer.

Partially chronological: starts with arrival, then starting the car, then test drive; finishes

with list for inspection of car (body, tires, bounce corners, interior carpeting)

4. In the context of this passage, what are *peaches* and *lemons*?

Peaches are good cars; lemons are bad cars.

5. Where in the passage does the author use compare-contrast?

Under "when you start the car," the author contrasts three different colors of exhaust

smoke and the different problems they may indicate.

_____d_____ **6.** Which of the following statements best expresses the main idea of the passage?
 a. Never trust a used car dealer.
 b. It is important to bring a friend along when shopping for a used car.
 c. Shopping for a used car can be fun.
 d. Following a few suggestions will help you buy a better used car.

7. *Vocabulary in Context*

_____b_____ *Safeguards endorsed* by Austin Davis are:
 a. Improvements that he designed.
 b. Suggestions to protect the buyer that he approves.
 c. Rules that he has written for auto dealers.

_____a_____ A car's *chassis* (chăs'ē) is its:
 a. Frame.
 b. Wheels.
 c. Rear portion.

8. On a separate sheet of paper, diagram the important information from Passage A.
 See Instructor's Manual.

B. TREASON AND ESPIONAGE

1   Felonies, misdemeanors, offenses, and the people who commit them constitute the daily work of the justice system. However, special categories of crime do exist and should be recognized. They include treason and espionage, two crimes that are often regarded as the most serious of felonies. **Treason** has been defined as "a U.S. citizen's actions to help a foreign government overthrow, make war against, or seriously injure the United States." In addition to being a federal offense, treason is also a crime under the laws of most states. Hence treason can be more generally defined as the attempt to overthrow the government of the society of which one is a member. The legislatures of some states, like California, have defined the crime of treason; in other states, the crime is defined in the state constitution. Florida's constitution, for example, which mirrors wording in the U.S Constitution, says, "Treason against the state shall consist only in levying war against it, adhering to its enemies, or giving them aid and comfort, and no person shall be convicted of treason except on the testimony of two witnesses to the same overt act or on confession in open court."

2   **Espionage,** an offense akin to treason, but which can be committed by noncitizens, is the "gathering, transmitting, or losing" of information related to the national defense in such a manner that the information becomes available to enemies of the United States and may be used to their advantage. In 1999, for example, one of the most significant espionage cases ever came to light. It involved the theft of highly classified American nuclear weapons secrets by spies working for the People's Republic of China. Over at least three decades, beginning in the 1960s, Chinese spies apparently stole enough weapons-related information to advance China's nuclear weapons program into the modern era. Were it not for the missile and bomb information gathered by the spies, congressional officials said, China's nuclear weapons technology might still be where America's was in the 1950s.

3   Another example of espionage is the crime committed by former FBI agent Robert Hanssen. In July 2001 he pleaded guilty in U.S District Court in Alexandria, Virginia, to 15 counts of espionage and conspiracy against the United States. Hanssen admitted to having passed U.S. secrets to Moscow from about 1979 until 2001, when undercover investigators caught him leaving a package for his Russian handlers under a wooden footbridge in a Virginia park. The 25-year agency veteran had accepted more than $1.4 million in cash and diamonds from the Russians in return for disclosing secret and highly sensitive information, including U.S. nuclear warfare plans, advanced eavesdropping technology, and the identities of U.S. spies working overseas. Government officials feared that the information Hanssen provided had resulted in the deaths of a number of U.S. agents working in Russia. Prosecutors described the damage done to national security by Hanssen's spying as extremely grave. In return for his full cooperation in assessing the damage he had caused, Hanssen was spared the death penalty. Instead, he was sentenced to life in prison without possibility of parole.

—Schmalleger, *Criminal Justice: A Brief Introduction,* 7th ed.

1. What is the primary logical pattern used in this passage? Explain your answer.

Definition: the passage defines treason and espionage.

2. What transition words or other clues in the passage indicate this pattern?

Boldfacing of the two terms; "has been defined"; "can be more generally defined"; "have defined"; "espionage is."

3. Name one other logical pattern used in the passage and tell where it is used.

Compare-Contrast: in paragraph 1 (states' treatment of treason); chronological order

in paragraphs 2 and 3 (in the examples of espionage)

___d___ **4.** The author clarifies the meaning of *espionage* by:
  a. Providing a listing of espionage cases.
  b. Repeating the definition in different words.
  c. Pointing out the differences between espionage and other major crimes.
  d. Providing examples of significant cases of espionage.

___c___ **5.** *Treason* is best understood as:
  a. A serious felony.
  b. A crime against the state in which one lives.
  c. An attempt to overthrow your own government.
  d. Espionage against the United States.

___b___ **6.** Which of the following statements best expresses the main idea of the passage?
  a. In addition to felonies and misdemeanors, there are special categories of crimes.
  b. Treason and espionage are special categories of serious crimes involving acts against a government.
  c. Treason involves a U.S. citizen acting against his or her own country.
  d. Treason is a serious crime, and espionage is the most serious form of treason.

7. *Vocabulary in Context*

___c___ *Adhering* to our nation's enemies means:
  a. Fighting against them.
  b. Learning about them.
  c. Supporting them.

___b___ Extremely *grave* damage to national security is:
  a. Damage to our national cemeteries.
  b. Serious damage; very harmful damage.
  c. Permanent damage; damage that can never be repaired.

8. On a separate sheet of paper, diagram the important information from Passage B.
See Instructor's Manual.

C. FITNESS ISN'T HEALTH

Health, fitness and performance are three separate and poorly correlated phenomena.

1. Health is generally defined as the freedom from disease.

2. Fitness strictly relates to your ability to meet the demands of your environment.

3. Performance is how well you accomplish a task.

You can be healthy without being fit. You can be in poor health and perform superbly. Sick athletes break records all the time. Every Olympic competition is populated by athletes with colds, fevers, infections and diarrhea. They invariably compete, and perform to their level.

The idea that sports make you healthy is a shibboleth. Sports can actually hurt you. They're not unhealthy *per se,* but they can be.

You don't have to be fit to be healthy. If health is defined as lack of disease, then fitness is not health. Only when your definition of health includes functional wellness—meaning the ability to cope with your environment—do health, fitness, and performance coincide.

I was at a faculty picnic a few years back, swimming with a colleague of mine, John Sellwood. He was dying of lung cancer. One lung had been removed; the other was infected. He was to go into the hospital the next day. Both of us had been college swimmers. We'd been swimming for a while when he said, "I'll race you fifty yards."

"You've already given me my handicap," I said, and I thought it gave me an unfair advantage. We started off even. I didn't deliberately let him beat me, but he did. The next day he entered the hospital, and a month later he was dead. I can think of no better illustration of the lack of correlation between health and performance.

—Morehouse and Gross,
Total Fitness in 30 Minutes a Week

1. What is the primary logical pattern used in this passage? Explain your answer.

Compare-Contrast: the passage focuses on the differences between health, fitness, and performance.

2. What transition words or other clues in the passage indicate this pattern?

"Separate and poorly correlated"; "lack of correlation between"; opposing ideas in sentences and paragraphs ("you can be . . . without . . . ")

3. Name one other logical pattern used in the passage and tell where it is used.

Definition is used at the beginning (defining the three terms); chronological order is used in the story at the end.

4. According to the author, what are the differences between health, fitness, and performance?

Health refers to whether or not you're sick; fitness refers to your physical conditioning at any point in time; performance refers to how well you actually do a particular thing.

5. What examples does the author provide to illustrate the difference between health and performance?

Olympic athletes performing while sick; story about author's colleague with cancer beating him in a swimming race

_a_ **6.** Which of the following statements best expresses the main idea of the passage?
   a. Health, performance, and fitness are not the same.
   b. Health is more important than fitness.
   c. Performance is not the same as fitness.
   d. You can be healthy without being fit.

7. *Vocabulary in context*

___a___   *Poorly correlated phenomena* are:
   a. Circumstances that have little connection with each other.
   b. Events that depend on one another.
   c. Circumstances that are hard to control.

___c___   When the author says that the idea that sports make you healthy is a *shibboleth*, he means that this idea:
   a. Is true.
   b. Is popular.
   c. Is a myth; is false.

8. On a separate sheet of paper, diagram the important information from Passage C.
   See Instructor's Manual.

D. AMERICAN FEMINISM

Many people believe that the feminist movement is a new and recent development in American history. But, in fact, the fight for women's rights dates back at least as far as colonial times. On March 31, 1776, months before the signing of the Declaration of Independence, Abigail Adams wrote to her husband, John Adams, later the nation's second president:

> I desire you would Remember the Ladies, and be more favourable and generous to them than your ancestors. Do not put such unlimited power in the hands of Husbands. Remember all Men would be tyrants if they could. If particular care and attention is not paid to the Ladies, we are determined to foment a Rebellion, and will not hold ourselves bound by any Laws in which we have no voice, or representation.

In a formal sense, the American feminist movement was born in upstate New York, in a town called Seneca Falls, in the summer of 1848. On July 19, the first women's rights convention began, attended by Elizabeth Cady Stanton, Lucretia Mott, and other pioneers in the struggle for women's rights. The first wave of *feminists*, as they are currently known, battled ridicule and scorn as they fought for legal and political equality for women. They were not afraid to risk controversy on behalf of their cause; in 1872 Susan B. Anthony was arrested for attempting to vote in that year's presidential election.

Ultimately, the early feminists won many victories, among them the passage and ratification of the Nineteenth Amendment to the Constitution, which granted women the right to vote in national elections beginning in 1920. But suffrage did not lead to other reforms in women's social and economic position, and the women's movement became a much less powerful force for social change in the early and middle twentieth century.

The second wave of American feminism emerged in the 1960s and came into full force in the 1970s. In part, the movement was inspired by the publication of two pioneering arguments for women's rights: Simone de Beauvoir's book *The Second Sex* and Betty Friedan's book *The Feminine Mystique*. In addition, the general political activism of the 1960s led women—many of whom were working for black civil rights or against the war in Vietnam—to reexamine their own powerlessness as women. The sexism often found within allegedly progressive and radical political circles made many women decide that they needed to establish their own movement for "women's liberation."

—Schaeffer, *Sociology*

1. What is the primary logical pattern used in this passage? Explain your answer.

Chronological Order: the passage reviews some of the major events in the history of the American feminist movement (in time order).

2. What transition words or other clues in the passage indicate this pattern?

"dates back"; "colonial time"; before; "was born"; first; second; dates (1776–1970s)

3. Name one other logical pattern used in the passage and tell where it is used.

Cause-Effect is used in the last paragraph (two books inspired the movement; political activism led to reexamination of roles).

4. According to the author, when and where did the American feminist movement begin?

Seneca Falls, NY in the summer of 1848

5. What inspired the second wave of American feminism?

De Beauvoir's *The Second Sex* and Friedan's *The Feminine Mystique* and the growing awareness of sexism within progressive movements

__c__ **6.** Which of the following statements best expresses the main idea of the passage?
   a. The American feminist movement has faced many problems.
   b. The feminist movement is a recent development in American history.
   c. The American feminist movement has a long and interesting history.
   d. Women should have the same political rights as men.

7. *Vocabulary in Context:*

__b__ When Abigail Adams wrote that "all Men would be *tyrants* if they could," she was accusing men of wanting to be:
   a. Equal with their wives.
   b. The bosses.
   c. Aggressive and violent.

__a__ To *foment* a rebellion is to:
   a. Start one.
   b. Stop one.
   c. Criticize one.

__c__ *Suffrage* is:
   a. Suffering.
   b. A person's social and economic position.
   c. The right to vote.

b A group that is *allegedly* progressive:
    a. Is truly progressive.
    b. Claims to be progressive but perhaps isn't really progressive.
    c. Is against being progressive.

8. On a separate sheet of paper, diagram the important information from Passage D.

    See Instructor's Manual.

E. PHARMACOL OGIC EFFECTS OF ALCOHOL

1 It would be inaccurate to claim that the major mood-altering effects of alcohol are due only to the drinking environment. Clearly, if this were true, alcohol would not be used as widely as it is. In fact, alcohol has a number of pharmacologic properties that cause it to alter sensations, feelings, and abilites, regardless of the social setting.

2 Virtually all drugs have varied and increasingly stronger effects as they are used over a period of time and in greater doses. This is especially true for alcohol.

3 The dual nature of alcohol's effects has been known since alcohol was first used. Initially, alcohol is a stimulant and releaser of energy, but over time, and at larger doses, it acts as a strong depressant. One chemist, noting these contradictory characteristics, has called alcohol a "great deceiver."

4 Many studies have focused on alcohol's mood-changing qualities. The data are very clear. Using low doses of alcohol for short periods appears to liven spirits and produce greater happiness in normal people. Low doses also appear to reduce feelings of anxiety and depression in both normal and depressed people. High doses of alcohol, or moderate doses over longer periods, do not have mood-elevating effects on either of these groups of people. On the contrary, these higher doses can cause increased anxiety and depression in both normal and depressed people. Among alcoholics, the higher doses produce variable effects, none of them clearly positive.

5 Despite these findings, most people who use alcohol tend to remember only the light-use, low-dose, positive effects. They may recall how small amounts of alcohol helped lift their mood and relieve tension when a personal problem had made them depressed, frustrated, or insecure. Even heavy drinkers and alcoholics usually believe that using alcohol will raise their mood, decrease their anxiety, and improve their sleep.

6 These erroneous impressions have also been studied. Apparently, people in general, and heavy drinkers in particular, selectively remember the initial, low-dose, pleasant effects of alcohol and are generally less able to recall the later, high-dose, unpleasant effects. This phenomenon may be due to memory impairment caused by higher doses of alcohol, and is probably one of the reasons why heavy drinkers continue to abuse alcohol despite its adverse effects.

—McClellan et al., *Escape from Anxiety and Stress*

1. What is the primary logical pattern used in this passage? Explain your answer.

    Cause-Effect: the passage focuses on the physiological effects of alcohol.

2. What transition words or other clues in the passage indicate this pattern?

    Effects (several times); due to; cause; reasons why

3. Name one other logical pattern used in the passage and tell where it is used.

    Compare-Contrast is used in paragraph 3 (stimulant vs. depressant) and in paragraphs

    4–6, contrasting low dose effects and high dose effects.

4. According to the author, what are the effects of low doses of alcohol?

Using low doses for short periods livens spirits, increases happiness (in normal

people), and reduces anxiety and depression.

5. According to the author, what are the effects of high doses of alcohol?

High doses do not elevate mood; high doses can increase anxiety and depression.

___b___ **6.** Which of the following statements best expresses the main idea of the passage?
  a. People should consume less alcohol.
  b. Using alcohol in low doses usually produces positive effects, whereas high doses produce harmful effects which may not be recognized or remembered by the user.
  c. High doses of alcohol impairs memory, which explains why it is hard to stop drinking.
  d. Low doses of alcohol have positive effects, including reduction of anxiety and depression.

7. *Vocabulary* in Context:

___a___ Alcohol's *pharmacologic* properties are its:
  a. Drug or chemical properties.
  b. Positive effects.
  c. Negative effects.

___b___ *Erroneous* impressions are:
  a. Correct.
  b. Mistaken.
  c. Long-lasting.

___b___ The *adverse* effects of alcohol are its:
  a. Positive effects.
  b. Harmful effects.
  c. Neutral effects (neither positive nor harmful).

8. On a separate sheet of paper, diagram the important information from Passage E.
  See Instructor's Manual.

EXERCISE 8.16 RECOGNIZING LOGICAL PATTERNS

Directions

1. Using a textbook from another course or independent reading material from any source, find two paragraphs or short passages that illustrate any two different logical patterns you have learned in this chapter.

2. Photocopy the paragraphs and tape them on a sheet of paper. On a separate sheet, name the logical pattern for each of your passages and briefly explain your answers.

3. In class, exchange passages with a classmate; read each other's passages to identify the primary logical patterns. If you disagree about the patterns, share your different points of view.

SKILLS ONLINE: USING GRAPHIC ORGANIZERS

 Directions: The types of diagrams we have been working with in this chapter are sometimes called *graphic organizers*. Go online to find a graphic organizer that you like for the compare-contrast pattern or a graphic organizer that you like for the cause-effect pattern (use search terms such as "compare-contrast graphic organizer" or "cause-effect graphic organizer"). Print a copy and bring it to class for application with passages from the chapter.

See Instructor's Manual.

READING 8A

SOJOURNER TRUTH
(AMERICAN HISTORY)

by John Garraty and Mark C. Carnes

Reading 8A, taken from an American history textbook, provides a short bio-graphical sketch of Sojourner Truth, a woman who was born into slavery, but who became a free woman and fought against slavery and for women's rights. Read the selection to learn about this remarkable woman.

Pre-Reading Exercise

Directions: Complete this exercise before reading the passage. Preview the passage and answer the following questions.

1. What is the passage about?

   Sojourner Truth's experiences as a slave and free woman

2. Who was Sojourner Truth?

   Sojourner Truth was born a slave. She gained her freedom, became a preacher, and

   worked against slavery and subordination of women.

3. Where and when was she born?

   She was born at the end of the eighteenth century is Ulster County, NY.

4. What have you previously learned about slavery? Have you previously learned anything about Sojourner Truth?

   Answers will vary.

5. What will you learn from reading this passage?

   Answers will vary, but should say something about Sojourner Truth's life and experiences.

6. Does the passage look interesting? Why or why not?

   Answer will vary.

Directions: Note logical patterns while reading the passage. Monitor and clarify your comprehension as you read. Use context, the dictionary, and word structure clues to determine the meanings of unfamiliar words.

1   Isabella was the youngest of ten, or perhaps twelve, children; she was born in 1797, or perhaps 1799. Most details of her early life are unknown. No one bothered to record them because she was a slave. We do know that she was born in Ulster County, New York and that her owner was Colonel Ardinburgh, a Dutch farmer. He grew tobacco, corn and flax. Because the rocky hills west of the Hudson River could not sustain large farms, he could make use of only a handful of slaves. He therefore sold most of the slave children, includ-ing Isabella's siblings, when they were young.

5   In 1810 she was sold to John Dumont, a farmer. She remained with him for nearly eighteen years. Though she came to regard him "as a God," she claimed that his wife subjected her to cruel and "unnatural" treatment. What exactly transpired, she refused "from motives of delicacy" to say. Historian Nell I. Painter contends that the mistress likely abused her sexually.

6   In 1815 Dumont arranged for Isabella to marry another of his slaves. (Slave marriages were recognized by law in most northern states, but not in the South.) Isabella had no say in the choice of a husband, who had previously been mated to at least two other slaves. She had five children by him.

7   Isabella labored in the fields, sowing and harvesting crops. She also cooked and cleaned the house. In recognition of her diligence, Dumont promised to set her free on July 4, 1826, exactly one year prior to the date set by the New York State legislature to end slavery. But during that final year Isabella injured her hand and could not work as effectively as before. On the promised date of liberation, Dumont reneged on his promise to release her. Isabella chafed at his decision but said nothing. She dutifully spun 100 pounds of wool—the amount of labor she thought she owed him—and then, as winter was setting in, she heard the voice of God tell her to leave. She picked up her baby and walked to a neighbor's house. When Dumont came to collect her, the neighbor—Isaac Van Wagenen—paid him $25 for Isabella and the baby and set them free. In gratitude, Isabella took the surname Van Wagenen.

8   But Isabella learned that her five-year-old son, Peter, had been sold to a planter in Alabama, where no date had been set for the ending of slavery. She angrily confronted the Dumonts, who scoffed at her concern for "a paltry nigger." "I'll have my child again," Isabella retorted. She consulted with a Quaker lawyer, who assured her that New York law forbade such sales. He filed suit in her behalf and, in 1828, the boy was returned.

9   Now on her own, Isabella went to New York City. During these years New York City, like much of the nation, was awash in religious ferment. Isabella, whose views on religion were a

2   Isabella's mother used to tell her of the time when Ardinburgh had gathered up her five-year-old brother and three-year-old sister to take them for a sleigh ride. They were initially delighted, but when he tried to lock them into a box, the boy broke free, ran into the house and hid under a bed. He was found and both children were dragged away, never to be seen by their parents again. Isabella lived in terror of being similarly torn from her parents.

3   In 1807 Ardinburgh died. His heirs sold his "slaves, horses, and other cattle" at auction. A local farmer bought Isabella for $100. Her parents, too old and decrepit to be of value, were given their freedom. Destitute and virtually homeless, they died shortly afterward.

4   Isabella, who spoke only Dutch, found herself at odds with her new master and his family. Sometimes she did not understand what they wanted her to do. "If they sent me for a frying pan, not knowing what they meant, perhaps I carried them the pot-hooks," she recalled. "Then, oh! How angry mistress would be with me." Once, for an order that she did not understand, the master whipped her with a bundle of rods. The lacerations permanently scarred her back.

complex amalgam of African folkways, spiritualism, temperance, and dietary asceticism, was attracted to various unorthodox religious leaders. The most curious of these was Robert Matthews, a bearded, thundering tyrant who claimed to be the Old Testament prophet Matthias. He proposed to restore the practices of the ancient patriarchs, especially an insistence that men dominate women. Matthews converted Elijah Pierson, a wealthy New York merchant, and persuaded him to finance a religious commune. Matthews acquired a house in the town of Sing Sing, named it Mount Zion, housed nearly a dozen converts, and ruled it with an iron hand. Isabella was among those who joined the commune.

10   In 1834, Pierson died. Local authorities, who had heard stories of sexual and other irregularities at Mount Zion, arrested Matthews on charges of poisoning Pierson. This sensational story boosted sales of the city's penny press, then in its infancy. When one published story accused Isabella of the murder, she sued the author for libel and collected a judgment of $125.

11   Isabella then gravitated to William Miller, a zealot who claimed that the world would end in 1843. When it did not, his movement did.

12   Although she had nearly always been subject to the authority of powerful men, Isabella had by this time become a preacher. Tall and severe in manner, she jabbed at the air with bony fingers and demanded the obedience she had formerly given to others. Now she changed her name to Sojourner Truth—a journeyer conveying God's true spirit—and embarked on a career of antislavery feminism.

—Garraty and Carnes, *The American Nation:
A History of the United States,* 10th ed.

You, the Reader

Interest Rating. Please rate the interest level of the reading on the following scale (circle one):

      5—Very interesting   2—A little boring

      4—Fairly interesting   1—Very boring

      3—Mildly interesting

Difficulty Rating. Please rate the difficulty level of the reading on the following scale (circle one):

      5—Very difficult   2—Fairly easy

      4—Fairly difficult   1—Very easy

      3—Moderate

Comments: Please explain your ratings and make any other comments you wish about the reading.

Answers will vary.

LOGICAL PATTERNS EXERCISE

1. What is the primary logical pattern used in the passage? Explain your answer.

Chronological Order: the passage follows some of the major events in the first parts

of Sojourner Truth's life (in time order).

2. What transition words or other clues are used in the passage to indicate this pattern?

"early life"; "the time when"; "afterward"; "final year"; then; when; now; dates

throughout passage (1797–1843)

3. Name one other logical pattern that is used in the passage. Tell where it is used and explain how it is used.

Cause-Effect is used in paragraph 1 (farming conditions affecting numbers of slaves).

There is slight use of cause-effect (or suggestions of it) in most paragraphs. The

various components contributing to Isabella's religious views are listed in paragraph 9.

4. What transition words or other clues are used in the passage to indicate this pattern?

In paragraph 1, the words "because" and "therefore" indicate cause-effect.

In paragraph 4, "if-then" suggests cause-effect.

5. In the space provided, list or diagram the most important events of the passage.

Isabella was born in Ulster County, New York, in 1797 or 1799, as a slave owned by Colonel Ardinburgh.

Ardinburgh died in 1807 and Isabella was sold to a local farmer. Her parents were set free and soon died.

In 1810 Isabella was sold to John Dumont, another farmer.

In 1815 she was married by arrangement to another slave (she subsequently had five children by him).

Dumont promised to set her free on July 4, 1826, but reneged.

Isabella paid him, in wool, what she thought she owed him and left him (inspired by the voice of God).

Isabella sued for the return of her son (1828).

She went to New York where she became involved with religious cults.

One cult leader died in 1834 and another was arrested for poisoning him. Isabella sued an author who accused her of the murder. She then followed another zealot who predicted the world would end in 1843, whose movement ended when the world didn't.

Isabella became a preacher and embarked on a career of antislavery feminism.

COMPREHENSION QUESTIONS

Directions: For questions 1–5, choose the answer that best completes the statement. For questions 6–10, write your response in the space provided. Base all answers on what you read in the selection. Refer back to the selection as necessary to answer the questions.

b   **1.** How many slave owners did Isabella work for?
- a. Two
- b. Three
- c. Four
- d. Five

d   **2.** The passage suggests that Isabella had problems with her second master and his family because:
- a. She was stubborn.
- b. She was the first slave they owned.
- c. They made no attempt to understand her.
- d. She spoke only Dutch and did not always understand them.

c   **3.** Isabella became a free woman:
- a. On July 4, 1826.
- b. When the New York legislature ended slavery in that state.
- c. After being sold to Isaac Van Wagenen.
- d. When she paid John Dumont with 100 pounds of wool.

a   **4.** While in New York City, Isabella:
- a. Was influenced by a man who claimed to be a prophet.
- b. Became the leader of a commune.
- c. Married a preacher.
- d. Murdered Elijah Pierson after joining his commune.

d   **5.** Which of the following words does *not* describe Sojourner Truth?
- a. Determined
- b. Religious
- c. Courageous
- d. Violent

6. How did Isabella regain possession of her son Peter?

She hired a lawyer who filed a suit to have the boy returned.

7. Who was Elijah Pierson? What happened to him?

Pierson was a New York merchant who became a follower of Robert

Matthews, a religious zealot. Pierson financed a commune for Matthews.

Pierson died in 1834, and Matthews was arrested for poisoning him.

8. Why were Isabella's parents freed when Colonel Ardinburgh died? Why wasn't Isabella freed with them?

   They were too old to work. She was sold because she could still be of use

   as a slave.

9. What can we tell from the passage about Isabella's religious beliefs and practices?

   Isabella was very religious. She "heard the voice of God" and was guided by

   her beliefs, which were formed from a mix of different traditions and practices.

   She naively followed men who claimed to be prophets. She became a preacher.

10. What can we tell from the passage about Isabella's personality and character?

    Answers will vary. She might be described as determined, courageous,

    patient, strong, spiritual, and religious.

VOCABULARY EXERCISES

Pronunciation Guide (see p. 90 for list of phonetic symbols)	
amalgam	(ə-mǎl'gəm)
asceticism	(ə-sět' ə-sĭz' əm)
decrepit	(dĭ-krěp'ĭt)
lacerations	(lǎs'ə-rā'shənz)
patriarchs	(pā'trē-ärks')
reneged	(rĭ-něgd')

WORDS IN CONTEXT

Directions: Choose the meaning for the boldfaced word or phrase that best fits the context.

_____c_____ 1. Her parents, too old and **decrepit** to be of value, were given their freedom.
   a. Expensive
   b. Rebellious
   c. Weakened by age
   d. Confused

_____b_____ 2. **Destitute** and homeless, they died shortly afterward.
   a. Free
   b. Poor
   c. Searching; trying to find something
   d. Living in an institution

_a_   **3.** The **lacerations** permanently scarred her back.
     a. Wounds
     b. Insults
     c. Weapons
     d. Pains

_b_   **4.** In recognition of her **diligence**, Dumont promised to set her free on July 4, 1826.
     a. Desire for freedom
     b. Hard work
     c. Learning; education
     d. Honesty

_a_   **5.** On the promised date of liberation, Dumont **reneged** on his promise to release her.
     a. Went back on
     b. Repeated
     c. Fulfilled; carried out
     d. Planned for the future

CONTEXT AND DICTIONARY

Directions: Use context and the dictionary to determine the meaning of the boldfaced word in each sentence. Use word structure clues when applicable.

1. During these years New York City, like much of the nation, was **awash** in religious ferment.

   Filled or crowded with

2. During these years New York City, like much of the nation, was awash in religious **ferment.**

   Agitation; unrest; excitement; commotion

3. Isabella, whose views on religion were a complex **amalgam** of African folkways, spiritualism, temperance . . .

   Mix; combination

4. Isabella, whose views on religion were a complex amalgam of African folkways, spiritualism, **temperance** . . .

   Avoidance of alcoholic beverages

5. . . . a complex amalgam of African folkways, spiritualism, temperance, and dietary **asceticism** . . .

   Self-denial and self-discipline

6. Isabella . . . was attracted to various **unorthodox** religious leaders.

Unconventional; unusual

7. He proposed to restore the practices of the ancient **patriarchs** . . .

Male leaders of families or groups; forefathers

RESPOND TO THE READING

Directions: Write a half-page response to either of the following questions.

1. What were Sojourner Truth's chief strengths and weaknesses? What do you most admire about her?

2. What parts of Isabella's story are most remarkable to you? Why? What else would you like to know about her and her life?

WEBQUEST

Directions: Use the Internet to find the answers to the following questions. Write your answers on a sheet of paper. Print out the Web page you used for the answers or copy the URLs on your sheet.

What happened in Sojourner Truth's life after 1843? When did she die?

READING 8B

STRESS AND THE MIND
(PSYCHOLOGY)

by Carole Wade and Carol Tavris

Reading 8B is taken from a psychology textbook chapter on stress and health. In this excerpt, the authors discuss two types of mental outlooks, optimism and pessimism, and the ways that these outlooks may contribute to stress and health. Read the excerpt to find out what psychologists have to say about optimism and pessimism.

Pre-Reading Exercise

Directions: Complete this exercise before reading the passage. Preview the passage and answer the following questions.

1. What is the passage about?
   Optimism, pessimism, and the sense of control

2. What will be discussed in the last section of the passage?
   Locus of control

3. What is the main point of the introductory paragraph?
   Some people make themselves unhappy while others stay serene in trying circumstances—

   because they have different outlooks. (sample answer)

4. What have you previously learned about optimism and pessimism?
   Answers will vary.

5. Do you know anyone whom you would describe as an optimist or someone you would describe as a pessimist? Briefly describe that person.
   Answers will vary.

6. Write three questions about optimism and pessimism.
   Answers will vary.

Directions: Note logical patterns while reading the passage. Monitor and clarify your comprehension as you read. Use context, the dictionary, and word structure clues to determine the meanings of unfamiliar words.

Stress and the Mind.

1   Some people manufacture their own misery. Send them to a beach for a week to escape the pressures of civilization, and they take along a suitcase full of worries and irritations. Others stay serene in the midst of chaos and conflict; they seem to carry along their own inner tranquilizer. These two kinds of people are distinguished by how they explain events and by the degree of control they feel they have over what happens of them.

Is the glass half full or half empty?

Optimism and Pessimism

2 When something bad happens to you, what is your first reaction? Do you tell yourself that you will somehow come through it okay, or do you gloomily mutter, "More proof that if something can go wrong for me, it will"?

3 In a fundamental way, optimism—the general expectation that things will go well in spite of occasional setbacks—makes life possible. If people are in a jam but believe things will get better eventually, they will keep striving to make that prediction come true. Even despondent fans of the Chicago Cubs, who have not won the World Series in living memory, maintain a lunatic optimism that "there's always next year." If the Boston Red Sox could do it in 2004, their first World Series win since 1918, surely there is hope!

4 Optimism is also a lot better for your health and well-being than pessimism is. This does not mean that an optimistic outlook will always prolong the life of a person who already has a serious illness: A team of Australian researchers who followed 179 patients with lung cancer over a period of eight years found that optimism made no difference at all in who lived, or in how long they lived. But optimism does seem to produce good health and even prolong life in people without life-threatening illnesses whereas the "catastrophizing" style of pessimists is associated with untimely death.

5 Optimists do not deny their problems or avoid facing bad news; rather, they regard the problems and bad news as difficulties they can overcome. They may have better health than

pessimists, therefore, partly because they take better care of themselves. They are more likely than pessimists to be active problem solvers, get support from friends, and seek information that can help them. They do not give up at the first sign of a setback or escape into wishful thinking. They keep their sense of humor, plan for the future and reinterpret the situation in a positive light. Pessimists, in contrast, often do self-destructive things: They drink too much, smoke, fail to wear seat belts, drive too fast, and refuse to take medication for illness. This may be why pessimists, especially males, are more likely than optimists to die in accidents or as a result of violence.

6   Pessimists, naturally, accuse optimists of being unrealistic, and often that is true! Yet health and well-being often depend on having some "positive illusions" about yourself, your abilities, and your circumstances. Positive illusions have both psychological benefits and physiological ones. Optimism is directly associated with better immune function, such as a rise in the natural killer cells that fight infection. And people who see themselves in "self-enhancing" ways—thinking, for example, that they are smarter and healthier than average—also show immunological benefits. They have lower physiological activation in the face of chronic difficulties, thereby reducing the wear and tear on their body's regulatory systems.

Can pessimists be cured of their gloomy outlook? Optimists, naturally, think so. One way is by teaching pessimists to follow the oldest advice in the world: to count their blessings instead of their burdens. Even among people with serious illnesses, such as a neuromuscular disease, a focus on the positive aspects of life increases well-being and reduces the number of physical symptoms they report.   7

The Sense of Control

Optimism is related to another important   8 cognitive ingredient in health: having an internal locus of control. **Locus of control** refers to your general expectation about whether you can control the things that happen to you. People who have an *internal locus of control* ("internals") tend to believe that they are responsible for what happens to them. Those who have an *external locus of control* ("externals") tend to believe that their lives are controlled by luck, fate, or other people. Having an internal locus of control is associated with good health, academic achievement, political activism, and emotional well-being.

—Wade and Tavris, *Invitation to Psychology,* 4th ed.

> **locus of control** A general expectation about whether the results of your actions are under your own control (internal locus) or beyond your control (external locus).

You, the Reader

Interest Rating. Please rate the interest level of the reading on the following scale (circle one):

    5—Very interesting   2—A little boring

    4—Fairly interesting   1—Very boring

    3—Mildly interesting

Difficulty Rating. Please rate the difficulty level of the reading on the following scale (circle one):

    5—Very difficult   2—Fairly easy

    4—Fairly difficult   1—Very easy

    3—Moderate

Comments: Please explain your ratings and make any other comments you wish about the reading.

Answers will vary.

LOGICAL PATTERNS EXERCISE

1. What is the primary logical pattern used in the passage? Explain your answer.

Compare-Contrast: the passage contrasts optimism and pessimism.

2. What transition words or other clues are used in the passage to indicate this pattern?

But; than, whereas; rather; in contrast; yet

3. Name one other logical pattern that is used in the passage. Tell where it is used and explain how it is used.

Paragraph 5 lists characteristics of optimists and pessimists. Cause-effect is used in

paragraph 3–5 and 7 (and is implied by the correlations in 6 and 8).

4. What transition words or other clues are used in the passage to indicate this pattern?

"If . . . they will" (paragraph 3); "seem to produce" (4); because; "may be why"; result (5)

5. What are some of the chief differences between optimists and pessimists?

Optimists expect things to go well; they regard problems as difficulties they can

overcome; they take better care of themselves; they are more likely to be active

problem-solvers and get social support; they don't give up easily; they keep their

sense of humor; they plan for the future; they usually interpret a situation in a

positive light.

Pessimists do self-destructive things. They expect things to go badly.

COMPREHENSION QUESTIONS

Directions: For questions 1–5, choose the answer that best completes the statement. For questions 6–10, write your response in the space provided. Base all answers on what you read in the selection. Refer back to the selection as necessary to answer the questions.

_____b_____ **1.** In general, optimists and pessimists are distinguished by:
    a. How they deal with vacation time.
    b. How they explain events and how much control they feel they have over what happens to them.
    c. How they view other people.
    d. How realistic they are about their health and how much treatment they seek for health problems.

___d___ **2.** The authors suggest that:
   a. Optimists always live longer than pessimists.
   b. Optimists are more likely to survive life-threatening illnesses.
   c. Optimists are more realistic than pessimists.
   d. Optimists are often unrealistic.

___b___ **3.** Regarding control, pessimists are more likely than optimists to believe that:
   a. They control their own destinies.
   b. What happens to them is the result of luck or fate.
   c. Other people's behaviors are not as important as their own in determining what happens to them.
   d. They are responsible for what happens to them.

___c___ **4.** According to the authors, pessimists are more likely than optimists to do all of the following *except*:
   a. Drink too much.
   b. Refuse medication.
   c. Get support from friends.
   d. Fail to wear seat belts.

___d___ **5.** Having illusions about yourself and your abilities:
   a. Is more common among pessimists than among optimists.
   b. Always leads to health problems or performance problems.
   c. Is a result of having an external locus of control.
   d. Can be positive and contribute to well-being.

6. How do the authors define optimism?

The general expectation that things will go well despite occasional setbacks

7. Explain the difference between an internal locus of control and an external locus of control. Which do the authors believe is better?

People with an internal locus of control believe they are responsible for what

happens to them. People with an external locus of control believe that their

lives are controlled by fate, luck, or other people. The author states than an

internal locus of control is associated with better health, academic

achievement, and emotional well-being.

8. Why do optimists tend to have better health than pessimists?

They take better care of themselves; they are more likely to be active

problem-solvers. Maybe also because they have more social support.

(sample answer)

9. What do the authors advise pessimists to do in order to become more optimistic?

Count their blessings instead of their burdens. Focus on the positive.

10. Are you an optimist or a pessimist? Explain.

Answers will vary.

VOCABULARY EXERCISES

Pronunciation Guide (see p. 90 for list of phonetic symbols)

catastrophizing	(kə-tăs'trə-fīz' ĭng)
chaos	(kā'ŏs')
neuromuscular	(no͞or'ō-mŭs'kyə-lər)
physiological	(fĭz'ē-ə-lŏj'ĭ-kəl)

WORDS IN CONTEXT

Directions: Choose the meaning for the boldfaced word or phrase that best fits the context.

_d_ **1.** Others stay **serene** in the midst of chaos and conflict . . .
　a. Afraid
　b. Excited
　c. Discouraged
　d. Calm

_a_ **2.** Even **despondent** fans of the Chicago Cubs, who have not won the World Series in living memory . . .
　a. Discouraged
　b. Excited
　c. Angry
　d. Recent

_c_ **3.** Positive illusions have both psychological benefits and **physiological** ones.
　a. Mental
　b. Unknown
　c. Physical; of the body
　d. Future; possible

_a_ **4.** Optimism is directly associated with better **immune** function, such as a rise in the natural killer cells that fight infection.
　a. Protecting from disease
　b. Causing illness
　c. Mental; psychological
　d. Relating to rest and sleep

<u>a</u>   **5.** Optimism is related to another important **cognitive** ingredient in health: having an internal locus of control.
a. Mental
b. Of the body and its processes
c. Relating to doctors and medicine
d. Inherited; genetic

CONTEXT AND DICTIONARY

Directions: Use context and the dictionary to determine the meaning of the boldfaced word in each sentence. Use word structure clues when applicable.

1. Others stay serene in the midst of **chaos** and conflict . . .

Disorder; confusion

2. . . . the "**catastrophizing**" style of pessimists is associated with untimely death.

Considering situations as disasters, or worse than they really are

3. They have lower physiological activation in the face of **chronic** difficulties . . .

Lasting a long time

4. Even among people with serious illnesses, such as a **neuromuscular** disease . . .

Affecting both nerves and muscles

5. Optimism is related to another important cognitive ingredient in health: having an internal **locus** of control.

Location; place

RESPOND TO THE READING

Directions: Write a half-page response to either of the following questions.

1. Why are some people optimists and some people pessimists? Discuss.

2. Do you believe that you are responsible for what happens to you, or do you believe that your life is controlled by luck, fate, or other people? Explain and discuss.

WEBQUEST

Directions: Use the Internet to find the answers to the following questions. Write your answers on a sheet of paper. Print out the Web page(s) you used for the answers or copy the URL(s) on your sheet.

Who was Norman Vincent Peale? What famous book did he write?

CHAPTER 8 REVIEW

Logical Patterns

Authors use *logical patterns* to organize ideas and information and to clarify relationships between ideas. Active readers look for these patterns to better understand the organization of the material they're reading. Recognizing logical patterns contributes to better understanding and retention.

Common Logical Patterns

Five common logical patterns are

Chronological order, in which the passage discusses events or steps that follow one another in time

Listing, in which related ideas or points of information are presented in a list

Compare-Contrast, in which similarities and/or differences are described and discussed

Cause-Effect, in which the passage discusses reasons, explanations and results

Definition, in which the passage focuses on defining an important term or terms.

Diagramming Logical Patterns

Active readers create diagrams reflecting a passage's logical order as an aid to comprehension and memory and as a study aid.

Skills Online: Using Graphic Organizers

Readings

| Reading 8A: Sojourner Truth (American History) | Reading 8B: Stress and the Mind (Psychology) |

CHAPTER TESTS

TEST 8.1. LOGICAL PATTERNS IN PARAGRAPHS

Directions: Identify the primary logical pattern in each of the following paragraphs. Write Chronological Order, Listing, Compare-Contrast, Cause-Effect, or Definition for your answer in the space provided and briefly explain your answer.

1. Given the forces in the contemporary workplace, employers are looking for people who are able and willing to adapt to the new dynamics of the business world, can survive and thrive in fluid and uncertain situations, and continue to learn throughout their careers. Companies want team players with strong work records, leaders who are versatile, and employees with diversified skills and varied job experience. In addition, most employers expect college graduates to be sensitive to intercultural differences and to have a sound understanding of international affairs. In fact, in some cases, your chances of being hired are better if you've studied abroad, learned another language, or can otherwise demonstrate an appreciation of other cultures.

   —Bovee and Thill, *Business Communication Essentials,* 3rd ed.

   Pattern: _Listing_____

   Explain your answer:

   The paragraph lists the things employers are looking for in an employee.

2. In general, extinction occurs when environmental conditions change rapidly or severely enough that a species cannot adapt genetically to the change; natural selection simply doesn't have enough time to work. All manner of environmental events can cause extinction, from climate change to the rise and fall of sea level, to the arrival of new harmful species, to severe weather events such as extended droughts. In general, small populations and species narrowly specialized on some particular resource or way of life are most vulnerable to extinction from environmental change.

   —Withgott and Brennan, *Essential Environment:*
   The Science Behind the Stories, 2nd ed.

   Pattern: _Cause-effect_____

   Explain your answer:

   The paragraph explains the causes of extinction.

3. A *monopoly* is one seller of a good that has no close substitutes, with considerable control over price and protection from competition by barriers to entry. In a monopoly, there is a single firm facing no direct competition from other firms that produce the same, or a very similar, product. Water, electric, and gas companies are the best examples. Although there are substitutes, such as natural gas for electricity, there are no *close* substitutes. Pure monopolies come and go. Long-distance telephone service was a virtual monopoly of AT&T until the development of microwave and wireless transmission enabled companies like Sprint and MCI to offer alternative services. The railroads had a monopoly over

long-distance transportation until the advent of trucking and air transportation. Today's "monopolies" appear to be computer companies like Microsoft and Intel that dominate operating systems or microchip processing.

—Gregory, *Essentials of Economics,* 4th ed.

Pattern: _Definition_

Explain your answer:

The paragraph defines monopoly.

4. To understand taste, we must distinguish it from flavor—a complex interaction of taste and smell. Try holding your nose when you eat. You will notice that most of the food's flavor will disappear, and you will experience only the basic taste qualities: *sweet, sour, salty,* and *bitter.* You get the taste, but not the flavor.

—Morris and Maisto, *Understanding Psychology,* 8th ed.

Pattern: _Compare-contrast_

Explain your answer:

The paragraph contrasts taste and flavor.

5. In 1825, the same year the Erie Canal was completed, the world's first general-purpose railroad, the Stockton and Darlington, opened in England. The construction of the first American railroads began in the late 1820s, and they all pushed outward from seaboard cities eager to connect to the Western market. The Baltimore and Ohio crossed the Appalachians and connected Baltimore with Wheeling, Virginia, on the Ohio River. The Boston and Worcester linked New England and the eastern terminus of the Erie Canal at Albany. By 1840, U.S. rails had become the most dynamic booster of interregional trade. Whereas the canal network stopped expanding after 1840, the railroads tripled their mileage in the 1840s. By 1849 trunk lines from Atlantic Coast cities had reached the great Lakes and the Ohio Valley and were about to enter the Mississippi Valley.

—David Goldfield et al., *The American Journey: A History of the United States,* portfolio ed.

Pattern: _Chronological order_

Explain your answer:

The paragraph presents a sequence of events in the growth of railroads in the

nineteenth century.

TEST 8.2. LOGICAL PATTERNS IN SHORT PASSAGES

Directions: Note logical patterns while reading the following passages; then answer the questions that follow them.

A. PREPARING FOR TODAY'S DYNAMIC WORKPLACE

Good communication skills are more vital today than ever before because people need to adapt to a workplace that is constantly changing. Effective communication will help you meet challenges such as advances in technology, the need to manage vast amounts of information, the growth of globalization and workforce diversity, and the increasing use of teams in the workplace.

Communicating amid advancing technology. From instant messaging (IM) and blogs to wireless networks and video-enabled mobile phones, technology has revolutionized the way businesspeople communicate. Used intelligently, these tools can increase the speed, reach, and effectiveness of your communication efforts and enable you to collaborate with others virtually anywhere on Earth, any time of the day. In almost every aspect of business these days, you'll be expected not only to communicate well but to do so using a variety of communication technologies.

Communication in the age of information. In today's workplace you must know how to find, evaluate, process, and share information effectively and efficiently. Plus, you must be able to use what information you receive to make strong, speedy decisions. Unfortunately, people are so inundated with information today that they tend to ignore messages they see as less important. Your challenge is to get your audience's attention so that they will read and respond to your messages.

Communication globally and within a culturally diverse workforce. Chance are good that your business career will require you to communicate across national or cultural borders. For instance, of the top ten export markets for U.S. products, only two (Canada and Great Britain) have English as an official language, and Canada has two official languages, English and French. Within the United States, some companies and brands that you may think of as American (including Ben & Jerry's, Dr. Pepper, Pillsbury, Carnation, and Shell Oil) are in fact owned by organizations based in other countries. Moreover, the workforce in both the United States and other countries is becoming more diverse as countries look worldwide for talent and employees look worldwide for opportunities. To communicate effectively with these varied audiences, you'll have the challenge of understanding other people's backgrounds, personalities, and perceptions.

Communicating in team-based organizations. Many successful companies today no longer limit decisions to a few managers at the top of a formal hierarchy. These organizations use teams and flexible industry partnerships to collaborate and make fast decisions. Before you can function in a team-based organization, you must understand how groups interact. You must be a good listener and correctly interpret the nonverbal cues you receive from others. Such interaction requires a basic understanding of the communication process in organizational settings.

—Bovee and Thill, *Business Communication Essentials,* 3rd ed.

1. What is the primary logical pattern used in this passage? Explain your answer.

   Listing: the passage lists challenges in the workplace for which good communication

   skills will be needed.

2. Name one other logical pattern used in the passage and tell where it is used.

   Cause-Effect is used at various points. In paragraph 2, for example: people being

   inndated with information causes messages to be ignored if they're seen as less

   important. (sample answer)

3. What are some of the challenges mentioned by the authors that you can meet more successfully with effective communication skills?

Dealing with advances in technology; managing vast amounts of information;

communicating globally and with a diverse workforce; working with teams

_____c_____ **4.** Regarding global communication and cultural diversity, the authors suggest that:

a. All jobs in business require international communication.

b. Workplace diversity is a greater challenge than international communication.

c. Both workplace diversity and international communication pose challenges for today's workers.

d. Most American companies are owned by organizations based in other countries where English is not the official language.

_____b_____ **5.** Which of the following statements best expresses the main idea of the passage?

a. You cannot succeed in business if you don't have good teamwork skills.

b. Good communication skills help workers adapt to challenge and change.

c. Workers today must make effective use of communication technologies.

d. Globalization is changing the American workplace at a rapid pace.

6. On a separate sheet of paper, diagram the important information from the preceding passage.

See Instructor's Manual.

B. ENVIRONMENTAL SCIENCE EXPLORES OUR INTERACTIONS WITH THE WORLD

Understanding our relationship with the world around us is vital because we depend utterly on our environment for air, water, food, shelter, and everything else essential for living. However, our actions modify our environment. Many of these actions have enriched our lives, bringing us longer life spans, better health, and greater material wealth, mobility, and leisure time—but they have also often degraded the natural systems that sustain us. Impacts such as air and water pollution, soil erosion, and species extinction compromise human well-being, pose risks to human life, and endanger our ability to build a society that will survive and thrive in the long term. The elements of our environment were

functioning long before the human species appeared, and we would be wise to keep these elements in place.

Environmental science is the study of how the natural world works, how our environment affects us, and how we affect our environment. We need to understand our interactions with our environment because such knowledge is essential for devising solutions to our most pressing challenges. It can be daunting to reflect on the sheer magnitude of environmental dilemmas that confront us today, but with these problems also come countless opportunities for devising creative solutions.

Environmental scientists study the issues most centrally important to our world and its future. Right now, global conditions are changing more quickly than ever. Right now, through science, we are gaining knowledge more rapidly than ever. And right now, the window of opportunity for acting to solve problems is still open. With such bountiful challenges and opportunities, this particular moment in history is indeed an exciting time to be alive—and to be studying environmental science.

—Withgott and Brennan, *Essential Environment: The Science Behind the Stories*, 3rd ed.

1. What is the primary logical pattern used in this passage? Explain your answer.

   Cause-Effect: the passage discusses how we affect the environment and how the environment affects us.

2. Name one other logical pattern used in the passage and tell where it is used.

   Definition: Environmental science is defined in paragraph 2.

3. According to the authors, why is it important to study environmental science?

   The study of environmental science will lead to solutions to current problems.

4. What are some of the ways that human activity has affected our natural environment?

   We have polluted air, water, and soil; we have caused the extinction of other species.

___d___ 5. Which of the following statements best expresses the main idea of the passage?
   a. Environmental science is the study of how the natural world works, and how the environment affects our daily lives.
   b. Today's environmental problems bring opportunities for creative solutions, but if we don't act soon, there will be no environment left to save.
   c. In order to enrich our lives and increase our wealth, we humans have often degraded the natural systems that sustain us.
   d. An understanding of environmental science will help us deal with current environmental problems and sustain the natural systems on which we depend.

6. On a separate sheet of paper, diagram the important information from the preceding passage.
   See Instructor's Manual.

You, the Reader: Chapter 8 Wrap-up

Directions: Use one or two of the following questions to write a half-page response to Chapter 8.

- What were the most important things you learned from this chapter? How will you use what you have learned from this chapter?
- How have you changed your reading habits in response to this chapter?

- How can recognizing logical patterns help you understand and remember more of what you read?

- What parts of the chapter did you find most engaging? What questions do you have about the chapter?

PEARSON
myreadinglab

For support in meeting this chapter's objectives, go to MyReadingLab and select *Patterns of Organization*.

CHAPTER

9 Inference

LEARNING OBJECTIVES

In Chapter 9 you will learn to:

- Make logical inferences from what you read
- Infer an author's purpose
- Infer an author's tone

CHAPTER CONTENTS

Making Inferences
    Literal vs. Inferential Comprehension
    Inference and Humor
    Making Logical Inferences
Active Reading Strategy: Inferring the Author's Purpose
    Infer the Author's Purpose from the Context and the Content
    Authors' Three Main Purposes
Active Reading Strategy: Inferring the Author's Tone
Skills Online: Identifying the Author's Purpose
Reading 9A: *I Am Crow Dog* (American History)
Reading 9B: *Listening* (Interpersonal Communication)
Chapter 9 Review
Chapter Tests
    Test 9.1. Inference
    Test 9.2. Purpose and Tone
    Test 9.3. Inference
You, the Reader: Chapter 9 Wrap-up

414

Pre-Reading Exercise for Chapter 9

Directions: Preview the chapter and answer the following questions.

1. What is the chapter about?

   Making inferences
   _____

2. What is inference?

   Inference is the reasoning process by which we interpret what we read and draw
   _____
   conclusions from stated information.
   _____

3. What is author's tone?

   Tone refers to the tone of voice the author would use if he/she were reading
   _____
   the material aloud.
   _____

4. What have you previously learned about making inferences?

   Answers will vary.
   _____

5. How do you identify the author's purpose when you read?

   Answers will vary.
   _____

   _____

6. Write two questions about the content of this chapter.

   Answers will vary.
   _____

   _____

Reading comprehension involves understanding not only what is directly stated, but also what is implied, or suggested, by what an author has written. Inference, when reading, is the reasoning process by which we interpret what we read and draw conclusions from the author's stated information. We sometimes refer to this process as "reading between the lines."

Making Inferences

Webster's *New World Dictionary* defines the word *infer* as "to conclude or decide from something known or assumed; derive by reasoning, draw a conclusion." Inference is a natural reasoning skill that we use everyday. When you wake up in the morning, look out your window and see a clear, blue sky and think, "it's going to be a nice day," you've made an inference. Inference is the process of reasoning or drawing conclusions from what we know and from what we perceive through our senses.

We frequently make inferences about people based on their appearance and other nonverbal cues. For example, what might you infer about a person who during a job interview is hesitant to make eye contact and uses a lot of "ums" and "ahs" when answering questions?

We also make inferences about people's feelings based on their facial expressions. Look at the faces shown on the next page and make an inference about what each person is feeling.

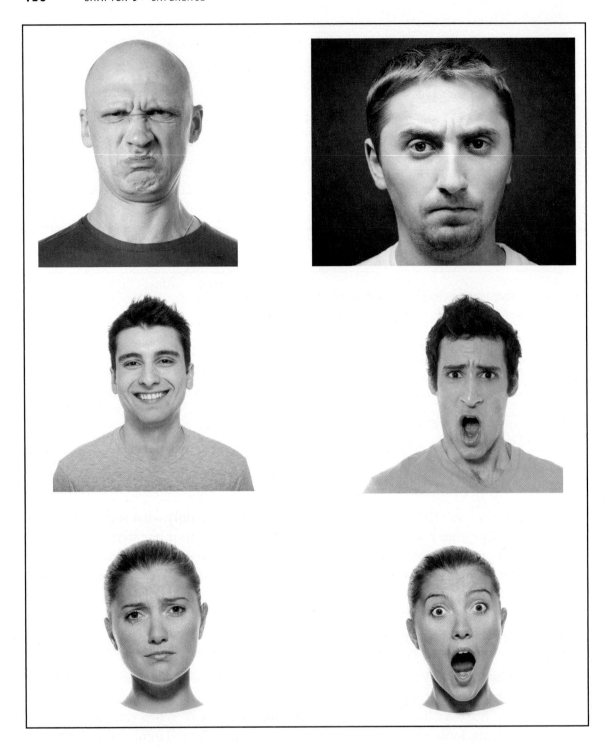

Which person is sad?
Which person is happy?
Which person is angry?
Which person is surprised?
Which person is afraid?
Which person is disgusted?

We use inference in a wide variety of contexts. When you watch a movie, for instance, you make inferences about the characters, the events, and the location of the story, based on what you see on the screen and what you hear (the dialogue, tone of voice, background music, etc.). We also use inference to interpret what we're seeing when we look at pictures. Take a look at the photo above. What inferences do you make about the picture? What might you infer about the people in the picture? Where are they? What are they doing?

Literal vs. Inferential Comprehension

Inference is an important part of the reading process. Reliable inferences—inferences that are based on sound reasoning—are essential for good reading comprehension. For example, in Chapter 5 you learned to infer main ideas when they weren't stated within their paragraphs. In Chapters 7 and 8 you worked on improving your skill with making inferences about sentence relationships and logical patterns. (Because authors don't announce, "I'm relating these sentences by sequence," or "I'm using compare-contrast now," the reader must infer these relationships and patterns.)

We can think of reading comprehension as having two levels. The first level is the *literal* level of comprehension. At the literal level we understand what is actually stated in the material. The second level is the *inferential* level of comprehension—that is, the level at which we make inferences and interpret what is stated. When we infer main ideas, sentence relationships, and logical patterns, we are functioning at the inferential level of comprehension.

Let's consider another example of how we make inferences when reading. Read the following sentences.

Timothy glanced nervously at his watch. "Where was she?" he wondered.

On the literal level, we understand from the first sentence that someone named Timothy is looking at his watch and that he is feeling nervous. A literal question about the sentence might be, "What did Timothy do?" (Answer: he glanced nervously at his watch.) From the second sentence, we may begin to make some inferences about Timothy and why he is nervous. For example, we might infer that Timothy is waiting for someone he was supposed to meet and that she is late. An inference question about these sentences might be: "Why was Timothy nervous?" (Possible answer: the woman he is supposed to meet is late. Note that until we read more, we don't have enough information to be completely confident about this inference.)

Since no writer can spell out everything he may want to communicate, we must make inferences—read between the lines—whenever we read. In other words, we use inference skills in virtually all reading situations. Whether you are reading a textbook, newspaper, novel, poem, or comic, you will use inference to gain a full understanding and appreciation of your material.

> **Inference,** when reading, is the reasoning process by which we interpret what we read and draw conclusions from the author's stated information.

Inference and Humor

Inference often plays an important role in understanding a joke or comic. Look at the comic strip below.

The humor in this cartoon is based on some simple inferences:

- How does the boy in the first frame feel about his sandcastle? What response does he want from his friend?

- Who is under the bucket in the second picture? How can you tell?

- How did the bucket get there? What is the girl's reaction?

Let's look at another example. Read the following joke about two men who love baseball.

Tom and Steve were lifelong friends who both loved baseball. As they grew on in years, they made a pact that whoever died first would contact the other to let him know if there was baseball in heaven.

Several years later Tom dies. After a few weeks pass, Steve is awakened in the middle of the night by Tom's voice.

"Tom, is that you? Are you in heaven?" Steve asked.

"Yes, Steve, it's me, Tom, and I am in heaven. It's pretty cool up here."

"So tell me, Tom, is there baseball up there?"

"Well, Steve, I have some good news and bad news for you. The good news is that there is baseball up here in heaven. We play every week."

"That's great, Tom. Whatever could be the bad news?"

"You're pitching next Sunday."

To appreciate this joke, we have to make an inference from the last line. What bad news do we infer when Tom tells Steve that he'll be pitching in heaven next Sunday?

Making Logical Inferences

Good inference is always based on sound reasoning. Readers often insert their own ideas and opinions into what they're reading, rather than logically interpreting the author's statements. Since we often don't notice our inferences, the challenge for active readers is to become more aware of the inferences they're making and to monitor them so that they become more attuned with the writer's intended meanings.

Let's look at some examples of inference at work in nonfiction material. Read the following paragraph, taken from a book about relationships between men and women.

Even couples with only mild difficulties in communicating can have important misunderstandings. Marjorie, for example, wanted Ken to invite her to a favorite cocktail lounge overlooking a bay to celebrate their anniversary. She archly asked him, "Ken, do you feel like going out for a drink tonight?" Ken, who was feeling tired, missed the hidden message contained in her question. He responded, "No, I'm too tired." Marjorie was extremely disappointed. Only after feeling hurt and sorry for herself did she realize that she had not communicated to Ken her real desire—to celebrate their anniversary. When she later made clear her true wish, he readily agreed to celebrate.

—Beck, *Love Is Never Enough*

Which of the following statements can be logically inferred from the passage? Place a check in front of each statement that is a logical inference based on what you have read.

____√____   **1.** Marjorie and Ken are probably married.

_____   **2.** Marjorie and Ken have been married for a long time.

_____   **3.** Ken does not enjoy going out for drinks with his wife.

_____√_____   **4.** If Marjorie had expressed her wish more clearly, Ken would have probably agreed.

_____√_____   **5.** All couples can have communication problems.

Analysis: Statements 1, 4, and 5 are logical inferences based on the passage.

> Statement 1 can be inferred from the first two sentences, which indicate that the passage is discussing couples and that Marjorie and Ken are celebrating their anniversary.

> Statement 2 cannot be inferred from the passage; there is nothing in the passage to indicate how long they have been married.

> Statement 3 cannot be inferred from the passage; the passage suggests that Ken did not want to go out for a drink with Marjorie because he was tired.

> Statement 4 can be inferred from the fact that Ken readily agreed to celebrate once Marjorie communicated her wishes more clearly.

> Statement 5 can be inferred from the passage's first sentence.

Now let's look at an example from a history book.

Vietnam had been part of a French colony called Indochina since the late 19th century. Then, beginning during World War II, the Vietnamese Communist party under the leadership of Ho Chi Minh fought the French to regain their country's independence. This war ended in 1954. The French and the Vietnamese communists agreed to divide Vietnam temporarily into two parts, North and South Vietnam. The communists believed that a nationwide election would soon establish a new government that would reunite the two parts. Instead, however, a new government was formed in South Vietnam, with the support of the United States, to counter the communist government in North Vietnam, which was backed by China and the Soviet Union (now Russia). The split of Vietnam became permanent. The election was never held, and civil war erupted.

—Takaki, *Strangers at the Gate Again*

Which of the following statements can be logically inferred from the passage? Place a check in front of each statement that is a logical inference based on what you have read.

_____√_____   **1.** Vietnam had once been an independent country.

_____   **2.** The Vietnamese army was stronger than the French army.

_____   **3.** The civil war began in the early 1950s.

_____√_____   **4.** The United States did not want to see North and South Vietnam united under a communist government.

_____√_____   **5.** The civil war might have been avoided if the planned election had been held.

Analysis: Statements 1, 4 and 5 can be inferred from the passage.

Statement 1 can be inferred from the second sentence, which states that the Vietnamese were fighting to *regain* their independence.

Statement 2 cannot be inferred from the passage. There is no information in the passage suggesting whose army was stronger.

Statement 3 cannot be inferred from the passage. Since the war for independence from the French ended in 1954, the civil war must have started after that date.

Statement 4 can be inferred from the fact that the United States supported the government in South Vietnam "to counter the communist government" in North Vietnam.

Statement 5 can be inferred from the passage's last sentence, which implies that the war broke out because no election was held.

Now it's time to practice! The exercises that follow will help you to monitor your inferences and to sharpen your inference skills. In some exercises, you will be asked to choose the better inferences and to explain your answers. In some exercises, you will be asked to identify the sentences in the passage that support the better inferences. The practice will help you to notice the reasons why, when reading, some inferences are better than others, and to better monitor your inferential comprehension.

EXERCISE 9.1 INFERENCE FROM SENTENCES

Directions: Each of the sentences in this exercise is followed by two possible inferences. Check the better inference and briefly explain your answer. An example is provided.

EXAMPLE

After an arrest and search have been carried out, the police have the authority to interrogate the arrested person.

—Albanese, *Criminal Justice,* 3rd ed.

_____ The police always interrogate a person immediately after arrest.

___✓___ The police do not have the authority to interrogate a person before arrest.

Explain: *The sentence suggests that arrest must precede interrogation, but does not suggest how soon after arrest interrogation occurs.*

1. Our ability to listen can be affected by our day-to-day health and state of mind, and can in turn have an effect on those states.

—Campbell, *The Mozart Effect*

___✓___ A person with a bad cold might not listen as well as he normally does.

_____ Healthy people are almost always good listeners.

Explain: The sentence implies that illness can impair listening.

2. Rock and roll's coming in the mid-fifties was not so much a single event or series of events as an opening of America's sonic floodgates.

—Palmer, *Rock & Roll: An Unruly History*

_____ A series of successful concerts in the mid-fifties contributed to the beginnings of rock and roll.

___√___ Rock and roll had a major impact on American music in the 1950s.

Explain: The sentence implies that the advent of rock and roll was a major, rapid

change in American music ("opening of . . . sonic floodgates").

3. From the high mountains to the vast polar ice sheets, the world is losing its ice faster than anyone thought possible.

—Appenzeller, "The Big Thaw," *National Geographic*

_____ There will soon be no ice left on the surface of our planet.

___√___ Scientists are surprised at the current rate of ice melt.

Explain: The sentence implies that everyone is surprised at how fast the ice is melting.

4. India and China are the giants of the earth, big in hills and plains, but even more in people.

—Davis, *The Human Story*

___√___ India and China are the most populous nations on the earth.

_____ People in India and China are taller than people in other countries.

Explain: "Giants . . . in people" implies a large population.

5. Although both given names and surnames affect the sense of identity and destiny, nicknames, pet names, and being called names have even more influence on some people.

—James and Jongeward, *Born to Win*, 3rd ed.

___√___ A nickname can have a powerful positive effect on a person's identity.

_____ Nicknames should not be used because they can harm a person's self-image.

Explain: The sentence implies that nicknames can be influential, which implies

the possibility of a positive effect.

6. Many are not satisfied with their jobs, but the problem can be much worse for the majority of American youth who have little or no college education.

—Derlega and Janda, *Personal Adjustment: The Psychology of Everyday Life*, 3rd ed.

_____ Most Americans don't like their jobs and wish they'd stayed in school longer.

___√___ Workers with college degrees are less likely to be dissatisfied with their jobs than workers who have no college education.

Explain: The sentence implies a relationship between education level and job

satisfaction or dissatisfaction.

7. Franklin D. Roosevelt (FDR) took office in 1933, in the midst of the Great Depression, during which as many as 25 percent of the U.S. workforce was unemployed.

—O'Connor and Sabato, *The Essentials of American Government,* 3rd ed.

_____√_____ Roosevelt was deeply concerned about reducing unemployment in the U.S.

_____ The Great Depression began near the end of 1932.

Explain: <u>A high unemployment rate would have to be of concern for a president.</u>

8. When I was a teenager growing up in New Jersey in the 1980s, my girlfriends and I were obsessed with Duran Duran.

—Majewski, "Teens & Celebrities," *USA Weekend Magazine*

_____√_____ Duran Duran was a popular rock group of the 1980s.

_____ The author of this sentence was a popular teenager.

Explain: <u>Teenagers are more likely to be obsessed with popular music groups.</u>

9. Although oil prices will undergo cyclical ups and downs resulting from short-term factors such as seasonal demand fluctuations, overall, oil will become increasingly expensive.

—Keith, "Crude Awakening," *Bostonia*

_____ Oil prices will rise at a steady rate over the next two years.

_____√_____ Two years from now, oil prices will be higher than they are today.

Explain: <u>"Ups and downs" suggests that the rise will not be steady, but the end of the</u>

<u>sentence supports the prediction of higher prices in the future.</u>

10. Although various immune cells (known collectively as *white blood cells*) and chemicals can be found throughout the body, their main mode of transportation is a thick liquid called *lymph* that, like blood, circulates through its own collection of vessels.

—James, "Immunity All-Stars," *Energy Times*

_____ Lymph is a body fluid thicker than blood that often flows through the same vessels that blood flows through.

_____√_____ White blood cells do not always travel through blood vessels.

Explain: <u>Lymph has its own vessels, and lymph transports white blood cells.</u>

EXERCISE 9.2 INFERENCE FROM SHORT PARAGRAPHS

Directions: Each of the paragraphs in this exercise is followed by two possible inferences. Check the better inference and briefly explain your answer.

1. Summer is the most popular time of year for American brides to don a white gown and say "I do." But in Kenya and India, November ushers in wedding season, and brilliant colors are a symbol of joy.

—"Brides Unveiled," *National Geographic*

_____ The United States is the only country where it is customary for brides to wear white.

___√___ The color of a bridal gown is determined primarily by custom and culture.

Explain: The examples in the paragraph suggest that color is related to custom

and culture.

2. Few tasks present people with as monumental a challenge and few tasks are as far-reaching in their consequences as the challenge of learning to read. In describing his own childhood agonies with the printed word, Nobel Prize winner John Steinbeck once wrote, "Some people there are who, being grown, forget the horrible task of learning to read. It is perhaps the greatest single effort that the human undertakes, and he must do it as a child."

—Trelease, *The Read-Aloud Handbook*

___√___ John Steinbeck found learning to read difficult.

_____ John Steinbeck believed that children are taught to read at too young an age.

Explain: "His own childhood agonies" suggests that Steinbeck had trouble learning

to read.

3. Meteorites are hot rocks. This month, collectors at the Tucson Gem and Mineral Show in Arizona were bidding nearly $5000 per gram for slivers from some rare ones. Whole meteorites that exploded from the moon or Mars can have a price tag in the millions.

—Brown, "Prospectors," *The Boston Globe*

___√___ Some people search for fragments of meteorites.

_____ Because meteorites have traveled through space, their temperature is higher than other rocks.

Explain: "Hot" in this context implies popularity and desirability; monetary value would

motivate search.

4. One of the great broken promises of the twentieth-century view of the future, right up there with personal jet-packs, was the promise of artificial intelligence. AI was supposed to lead to computers that wouldn't just calculate and organize, but reason and analyze; computers that could really think, like HAL in "2001" or KITT on the 1980s TV show "Knight Rider." (Of course, HAL turned out to be a homicidal psychopath and KITT was a smug know-it-all, but still, it seemed like a good idea).

—Spurgeon, "Souls of a New Machine," *The Boston Globe*

_____ The author watched "Knight Rider" frequently.

___√___ Personal jet-packs did not become available in the twentieth century.

Explain: Personal jet-packs are mentioned as a broken promise, which implies they

didn't happen.

5. A frequent activity of family life in the slave quarters was telling stories. The folktale was an especially useful and indirect way in which older slaves could express hostility toward their masters, impart wisdom to the young, teach them how to survive, portray and mock their own weaknesses, and entertain themselves.

—Nash et al., *The American People,* 5th ed.

_____ Folktales were told mostly to pass the time when the slaves weren't working.

____√____ Slaves couldn't openly express hostility toward their masters.

Explain: "Indirect way" implies slaves couldn't openly express hostility toward their masters.

EXERCISE 9.3 INFERENCE FROM SHORT PARAGRAPHS

Directions: Each of the paragraphs in this exercise is followed by two possible inferences. Check the better inference and briefly explain your answer.

1. Men are less likely than women to ask personal questions. Men are prone to think, "If she wants to tell me something, she'll tell me without my asking." A woman might reflect, "If I don't ask, he'll think that I don't care." For men, questions may represent intrusive meddling and an invasion of privacy; for women, however, they are a sign of intimacy and an expression of caring.

—Beck, *Love Is Never Enough*

____√____ Men are more likely to ask questions to gain information than to promote intimacy.

_____ Intimacy is not important to men.

Explain: The passage implies that men ask fewer questions and see questions as practical/informational rather than personal.

2. People have been fascinated with movies almost from the invention of the technology that made it possible, even when the pictures were nothing more than wobbly, fuzzy images on a whitewashed wall. The medium seemed to possess magical powers. With the introduction of sound in the late 1920s, and then color and a host of later technical enhancements, movies have kept people in awe. Going to the movies remains a thrill—an experience unmatched by other media.

—Vivian, *The Media of Mass Communication,* 4th ed.

____√____ Television does not have the same hold on people as movies do.

_____ Before they had sound, movies didn't attract large audiences.

Explain: "Unmatched by other media" implies that television can't do what a movie can do.

3. Authors will sometimes report on research studies or surveys to support their point of view. A study may supply strong and valid evidence to support an argument. Nevertheless, the critical reader will want to know how reliable the study was and whether other studies yielded the same results.

—Wintner, *The Reading Quest*

_____ Authors rely on research to convince their readers of their opinions and will sometimes falsify information in order to persuade the reader.

___√___ Authors do not always rely on research or surveys to support their opinions.

Explain: "Sometimes" doing something means that sometimes you don't do it. (In this case, report on research studies . . .)

4. Nobody wakes up in the morning and says, "Gee, I think I'll get addicted to drugs today." It just sort of happens. The first drug I tried was alcohol when I was 14 or 15. I liked it, but it didn't become the center of my life. Then a friend offered me some marijuana. I definitely did not like marijuana—it made me feel paranoid— but I still used it frequently, mostly to feel like I fit in. Since I was around other people who were using drugs, it seemed normal to start using cocaine, and then heroin. By the time I was 19, I was definitely a heroin addict.

—Scheller, "My Name Is Eric, and I'm an Addict," *Current Health 2*

___√___ The author believes that her drug addiction was largely the result of her social circumstances.

_____ The author enjoyed cocaine even less than marijuana, but used it to fit in with her friends.

Explain: The author says she used marijuana mostly to fit in and used other drugs because people around her were using them.

5. The car, and the roads it travels on, will be revolutionized in the twenty-first century. The key to tomorrow's "smart cars" will be sensors. "We'll see vehicles and roads that see and hear and feel and smell and talk and act," predicts Bill Spreitzer, technical director of General Motors Corporation's ITS program, which is designing the smart car and road of the future.

—Kaku, *Visions: How Science Will Revolutionize the 21st Century*

_____ The best "smart cars" will be produced by General Motors.

___√___ In the future, vehicles will be equipped with sensors that will make driving safer.

Explain: The paragraph states that sensors will be the key to tomorrow's "smart cars".

EXERCISE 9.4 FINDING SUPPORT FOR INFERENCES

Directions: Each passage below is followed by four inferences that can be reasonably drawn from the passage. After reading the passage, study each inference and indicate which sentence or sentences in the passage support the inference. Write the sentence number(s) on the line before the inference. An example is provided. Use context clues, word structure clues, and the dictionary as well as the vocabulary notes provided to determine the meaning of unfamiliar words.

EXAMPLE

(1) Obviously, if we are spending immense amounts of time and money in successfully teaching children to read but they in turn are choosing *not* to read, we can only conclude that something is wrong. (2) In concentrating exclusively on teaching the child *how* to read, we have forgotten to teach him to *want* to read. (3) There is the key: desire. (4) It is the prime mover, the magic ingredient. (5) There is no success story written today—whether in the arts, business, education, athletics—in which desire does not play the leading role. (6) Somehow we lost sight of the teaching precept: What you make a child love and desire is more important than what you make him learn.

—Trelease, *The Read-Aloud Handbook*

Inferences:

___1___ **1.** A great deal of money has been invested in teaching children to read.

___1, 2___ **2.** It is possible to learn to read without being motivated to want to read.

___2, 6___ **3.** The author believes that we must do more to get children to want to read.

___5___ **4.** Desire is essential for success in any field.

A. (1) Elephants have strong feelings. (2) They experience joy, grief, and depression, and they mourn the loss of their friends. (3) Elephants live in **matriarchal** societies in which strong social bonds among individuals endure for decades. (4) They also have great memory. (5) Shirley and Jenny, two female elephants who were unintentionally reunited after living apart for twenty-two years, showed that they truly had missed one another when they were separated. (6) At different times, each was brought to the Elephant Sanctuary in Hohenwald, Tennessee, founded and run by Carol Buckley, so that they could live out their lives in peace, absent the abuse they had suffered in the entertainment industry. (7) Upon their initial meeting, when Shirley was introduced to Jenny, there was an ur-gency in Jenny's behavior. (8) She wanted to get into the same stall with Shirley. (9) Loud roars **emanated** from deep in each elephant's heart as if they were old friends. (10) Rather than being cautious and uncertain about one another, they touched one another through the bars separating them and remained in close contact. (11) Their keepers were intrigued by how outgoing each was. (12) A search of records showed that Shirley and Jenny had lived together twenty-two years before in the same circus when Jenny was a calf and Shirley was in her twenties. (13) They still remembered one another, as individuals, when they were **inadvertently** reunited.

—Bekoff, *Minding Animals: Awareness, Emotions, and Heart*

matriarchal having a female leader

emanated came from **inadvertently** not intentionally

Inferences:

___5___ **1.** When Shirley and Jenny were brought to the sanctuary, its founder did not realize that they had been in the same circus.

___6___ **2.** The elephants had been mistreated when they were circus animals.

___11___ **3.** The elephant keepers expected Shirley and Jenny to be more cautious with each other.

___8, 9, 10___ **4.** Shirley and Jenny were happy to see each other.

B. (1) Scientists working in the Canadian Arctic have discovered fossils of a fish that had fins like limbs, capturing in stone the crucial period in evolution when creatures climbed from water onto land.

(2) The new species, named Tiktaalik roseae, lived about 375 million years ago, and was a sharp-toothed predator that resembled a crocodile and grew to at least 9 feet in length. (3) Like its fish ancestors, Tiktaalik had scales, but also a number of **innovations**, including fins with an elbow joint that could lift the animal from the ground.

(4) "It is like a fish that can do a push up," said Neil H. Shubin, a **paleontologist** at the University of Chicago and one of the principal scientists. (5) The team, which also included a Harvard University scientist, describes the find in the journal *Nature* today.

(6) Scientist hailed the long-sought discovery of the transition from sea to land. (7) In the story of life on earth, these fish fossils mark what is considered one of the major transitions, along with such milestones as the first multicellular organism or the first warm-blooded animal. (8) The find, scientists said, provides the clearest picture yet of this moment, as well as clues to how such major shifts in evolution happen. (9) The fossils are especially interesting, they said, because they show the beginning of the basic human body plan: Over the course of **eons**, Tiktaalik's front fins became the human arm and hand.

—Cook, "Fossil Discovery Fills a Piece of Evolutionary Puzzle," *The Boston Globe*

innovation new feature
paleontologist scientist who studies prehistoric life forms

eon very long period of time

Inferences:

___6___ **1.** Scientists believe that sea animals preceded land animals.

__7, 9__ **2.** Scientists believe that the human body evolved from earlier life forms.

__1–4__ **3.** Tiktaalik could swim.

_1–4, 6_ **4.** Tiktaalik could move on land.

C. (1) Two "superpowers" emerged from World War II. (2) America had escaped the devastation and was rich, productive, and the sole possessor of "the bomb." (3) Russia had been flattened in the war, but it **garrisoned** 3 million soldiers, the biggest army in the world. (4) Americans believed themselves the guardians of freedom and free enterprise (or capitalism). (5) The Russians saw themselves as leaders of a worldwide socialist (or communist) revolution. (6) To some extent both countries' sweeping global goals were covers for their national objectives and the pleasure that they took in holding power.

(7) Stalin, still the **autocrat** of Russia after twenty years, focused—no, **obsessed**—about the danger of encirclement by "capitalist" nations. (8) He resolved to guard his borders, especially from Germany, which had battered Russia both in World War I and World War II. (9) So Russia turned the smaller Eastern European nations that it held at the end of the war—Poland, Czechoslovakia, Hungary, Bulgaria, and Romania—into satellites. (10) Each was ruled by communists, who took orders from Russia. (11) Russia's domination of Eastern Europe shocked the western, democratic nations. (12) Winston Churchill coined a phrase; he said an "iron curtain" had descended in the midst of Europe.

garrison station and maintain (soldiers)

autocrat ruler; dictator
obsess think about constantly

(13) The superpowers, each fearful of the other, did the things they had to for their safety and their sense of mission. (14) They **propagandized**, argued, bluffed, and blustered. (15) Truman stated that America would "contain" communism everywhere in order "to assist free peoples who are resisting attempted **subjugation**." (16) The Russians talked as tough as Truman. (17) Nikita Khrushchev once told the West that "history is on our side. (18) We will bury you." (19) He was speaking of an economic triumph but was widely understood to mean much more.

—Davis, *The Human Story*

propagandize spread ideas or rumors to influence public opinion	**subjugation** control; domination

Inferences:

<u>2, 3</u> **1.** Russia suffered more severe damages in World War II than the United States.

<u>12</u> **2.** The "iron curtain" was the dividing line between communist and noncommunist nations in Europe, and not an actual curtain.

<u>7, 8</u> **3.** Stalin was the leader of Russia during World War II.

<u>19</u> **4.** Khrushchev's threat ("we will bury you") was political as well as economic.

D. (1) A mother we know was describing her two children: "My daughter has always been difficult, intense, and **testy**," she said, "but my son is the opposite, **placid** and good-natured. (2) They came out of the womb that way." (3) Was this mother right? (4) Is it possible to be born touchy or good-natured? (5) Or was she treating her two babies differently?

(6) For centuries, efforts to understand why people differ from one another have swung from biological answers ("it's in their nature; they are born that way") to learning and environmental ones ("it's all a matter of nurture—how they are raised and the experiences they have"). (7) The nature-nurture debate has been one of the longest-running either-or arguments in philosophy and psychology. (8) Edward L. Thorndike, one of the leading psychologists of the early 1900s, staked out the nature position by claiming that "in the actual race of life . . . the chief determining factor is heredity."

(9) But in stirring words that became famous, his **contemporary**, behaviorist John B. Watson, insisted that experience could write virtually any message on the blank slate of human nature:

> Give me a dozen healthy infants, well-formed, and my own specified world to bring them up in and I'll guarantee to take any one at random and train him to become any type of specialist I might select—doctor, lawyer, artist, merchant-chief and yes, even beggar-man and thief, regardless of his talents, **penchants**, tendencies, abilities, vocations, and race of his ancestors.

(10) Today, almost all psychologists who study personality regard biology and experience as interacting influences, each shaping the other over time. (11) "The nature-nurture debate is over," said one researcher.

—Wade and Tavris, *Invitation to Psychology*, 4th ed.

testy irritable **placid** calm	**contemporary** person living at the same time **penchant** inclination; liking

Inferences:

___2___ **1.** The mother believed that her children were born with their personality differences.

___8___ **2.** Thorndike believed that nature was more powerful than nurture.

___6___ **3.** "Nurture" refers to learning and experience.

__10, 11__ **4.** The author believes that human personality is shaped by both nature and nurture.

EXERCISE 9.5 INFERENCE

Directions: Each passage in this exercise is followed by five statements. *Three* of the five statements are logical inferences. (1) Circle the numbers of the *three* statements that can be logically inferred from the passage, and (2) indicate which sentence or sentences in the passage support the inferences by writing the sentence number(s) on the line before the inference. An example is provided. Use context clues, word structure clues, and the dictionary as well as the vocabulary notes provided to determine the meaning of unfamiliar words.

EXAMPLE

(1) Vietnam had been part of a French colony called Indochina since the late 19th century. (2) Then, beginning during World War II, the Vietnamese Communist party under the leadership of Ho Chi Minh fought the French to regain their country's independence. (3) This war ended in 1954. (4) The French and the Vietnamese communists agreed to divide Vietnam temporarily into two parts, North and South Vietnam. (5) The communists believed that a nationwide election would soon establish a new government that would reunite the two parts. (6) Instead, however, a new government was formed in South Vietnam, with the support of the United States, to counter the communist government in North Vietnam, which was backed by China and the Soviet Union (now Russia). (7) The split of Vietnam became permanent. (8) The election was never held, and civil war erupted.

—Takaki, *Strangers at the Gate Again*

___2___ **(1.)** Vietnam had once been an independent country.

_____ **2.** The war for independence ended in 1954, when the Vietnamese were defeated by the French.

_____ **3.** The civil war began in the early 1950s.

___6___ **(4.)** The United States did not wish to see North and South Vietnam united under a communist government.

___8___ **(5.)** The civil war might have been avoided if the planned election had been held.

A. A POLICE FORCE THAT WORKS

(1) Lt. Dewey Hosmer of the San Jose Police Department scans the computer screen in his squad car, looking for trouble. (2) Most nights, he finds it.

(3) "Here's an assault," he says, tracing a finger down the glowing screen, a **luminous rogues**' gallery of crimes in progress. (4) "Here's another assault . . . a hit-and-run . . . a burglary . . . a drunk driver . . . another assault . . ."

(5) The screen blinks and a new item appears at the top of the screen: Code 1072. (6) "A stabbing," Hosmer says. (7) "Let's check it out."

(8) When Hosmer arrives at the scene, a cheap hotel near downtown, two officers already are there. (9) A heavily tattooed 27-year-old man, blood dribbling from a wound in his shoulder, is being questioned in the parking lot. (10) Nearby, his 36-year-old girlfriend sobs quietly. (11) After questioning, the police believe the woman stabbed the man with a kitchen knife after he assaulted her. (12) "This is the third time she's stabbed me," the man tells the officers.

(13) "What can I say?" the man shrugs. (14) "I love her. (15) Love does strange things."

(16) For every **corrupt** cop who has made headlines recently, thousands of police officers like Hosmer quietly go about serving their communities, cleaning up messy disputes and sorting out the strange things people do for love.

(17) "Law enforcement is going to have to answer for the Mark Fuhrmans for a long time," Hosmer says, referring to the **infamous** Los Angeles police detective who figured in the O. J. Simpson trial. (18) "We all grind our teeth about that, but we can't fix it overnight. (19) All we can do is show up day in and day out, and do the right thing."

—McNichol, "Do the Right Thing," *USA Today Weekend Magazine*

luminous lighted up **rogue** villain; dishonest person

corrupt dishonest **infamous** notorious; having a bad reputation

_____ **1.** Most San Jose Police Department squad cars do not have computer screens.

<u>11, 12</u> (**2.**) The 27-year-old man was stabbed by his girlfriend.

_____ **3.** The 36-year-old woman stabbed her boyfriend because she was jealous of his relations with other women.

<u>17</u> (**4.**) Mark Fuhrman was a police detective whose involvement in the O. J. Simpson case hurt the reputation of policemen.

<u>16</u> (**5.**) The author would like there to be more policemen like Lt. Hosmer.

B. THE RALLYING POWER OF RECORDED MUSIC

(1) Released in 1984, "We Are the World" right away was the fastest-climbing record of the decade. (2) Four million copies were sold within six weeks. (3) Profits from the record, produced by big-name entertainers who volunteered, went to the USA for Africa project. (4) The marketplace success paled, however, next to the social impact. (5) The record's message of the oneness of humankind inspired one of the most massive outpouring of donations in history. (6) Americans pumped $20 million into USA for Africa in the first six weeks the record was out. (7) Within six months, $50 million in medical and financial support was en route to drought-stricken parts of Africa. (8) "We Are the World," a single song, had directly saved lives.

(9) The power of recorded music is not a recent phenomenon. (10) In World War I, "Over There" and other records reflected an enthusiasm for American involvement in the war. (11) Composers who felt strongly about the Vietnam War wrote songs that put their views on **vinyl**.

vinyl plastic used for phonograph records

(12) "The Ballad of the Green Berets" cast American soldiers in a heroic vein, "An Okie from Muskogee" glorified blind patriotism, and there were antiwar songs, dozens of them.

—Vivian, *The Media of Mass Communication*, 4th ed.

_____ **1.** "We Are the World" is the best-selling song of all time.

_____ **2.** "We Are the World" would not have been a popular song if the profits had not gone to a charitable cause.

_5, 6_ **3.** Americans would not have contributed as much to USA for Africa had "We Are the World" not been recorded.

_10_ **4.** "Over There" was a patriotic song supporting U.S. involvement in World War I.

_11, 12_ **5.** During the Vietnam War, there were Americans with strong feelings for the war and Americans with strong feelings against the war.

C. CLONING QUESTIONS MULTIPLY

(1) Would a Michael Jordan clone jump as high as the original? (2) Would a Mother Teresa clone perform the same—or even any—good deeds? (3) As the issue of human cloning settles uneasily into the human consciousness, scientists now have some answers. (4) And just in the nick of time.

(5) Human cloning is **inevitable**, they say, despite grave doubts about the wisdom of such action, despite strong religious and moral restrictions, despite strict bans on government funding. (6) "It's going to happen," said Susan Root, director of human genetics for the National Center for Genome Resources in Santa Fe, New Mexico. (7) "We have to deal with it." (8) Once set in motion, science and technology cannot be stopped, scientists say.

(9) In recent years, sheep, goats, cows and mice have been cloned using cells harvested

inevitable unavoidable

from adult animals. (10) Earlier this month, researchers in South Korea claimed success in cloning a cell taken from a human. (11) Some day soon, someone somewhere will fully clone a human being.

(12) That does not necessarily **herald** a National Basketball Association filled with Michael Jordans, all driving to the basket at the same moment, or a world blessed by multiple Mother Teresas, all feeding hungry multitudes the same meal at the same time. (13) "There are a great number of misperceptions about human cloning and these are the legacies of a long literary and science fiction tradition," said Harold Vanderpool, a **bioethicist** at the Institute for the Medical Humanities at the University of Texas.

—Merzer, "Cloning Questions Multiply," *Miami Herald*

herald signal the coming of
bioethicist someone who studies the ethics of biology and medicine

_3, 5_ **1.** Many Americans oppose the cloning of human beings.

_____ **2.** Susan Root favors the cloning of human beings.

_____ **3.** The South Koreans have cloned sheep, goats, cows, and mice.

_5, 6, 8_ **(4.)** Scientists believe that the cloning of humans cannot be avoided.

_13_ **(5.)** Science fiction has contributed to misunderstandings about cloning.

D. MR. PERFECT

(1) The minister asked for anyone who knew a truly perfect person to stand up. (2) After a long pause a meek-looking fellow in the back stood. (3) "Do you really know a perfect person?" he was asked.

(4) "Yes, Sir, I do," answered the little man.

(5) "Would you please tell the congregation who this rare, perfect person is?" pursued the preacher.

(6) "Yes, Sir, my wife's first husband."

—Bonham, *The Treasury of Clean Jokes*

_3_ **(1.)** The minister is surprised when the man stands up.

_3, 5_ **(2.)** The minister is doubtful that the man really knows a perfect person.

_____ **3.** The man believes that his wife's first husband is perfect.

_____ **4.** The wife believes that her first husband is perfect.

_6_ **(5.)** The man's wife has been comparing him unfavorably with her first husband.

Active Reading Strategy: Inferring the Author's Purpose

The author's purpose is her reason for writing the material. Textbooks, for example, are written to provide information, explain and discuss ideas, and help students improve their skills. Novels may be written to entertain readers with a good story or to convey a message—a theme—or both. Newspaper editorials are written to influence the public's thinking on current issues.

Understanding the author's purpose is essential for effective reading; active readers seek to recognize the author's purpose whenever they are reading.

An author's purpose usually must be inferred. Though textbook writers are likely to explain the purpose and goals of their textbooks, other writers may not come right out and declare their purpose in a direct manner. For example, a writer who is intending to be humorous will probably not start his article by saying, "Get ready to laugh, now, I'm going to say something funny!" Unlike when watching television, where the canned laughter tells the viewer that a program is supposed to be funny, when reading a book or other print material the reader must infer that the writer's purpose is to entertain and amuse. Similarly, a writer whose main purpose is to persuade is not likely to begin her article by stating, "Now I'm going to try to convince you to see things my way!" The reader must infer that the author is intending to influence his thinking and possibly his behavior as well.

Infer the Author's Purpose from the Context and the Content

To infer the author's purpose, active readers make use of all available clues. Start with the material's *context*—where the material is found. When reading in a newspaper, for example, you will infer that front page articles are likely intended to inform (reporting on the news of the day); that articles on the op-ed pages (these are the pages where opinion columns and editorials are located) are intended to persuade; and that the comics are intended to entertain. When reading a textbook, you will normally infer that the author's purpose is to inform, whereas when reading a politician's campaign flyer, you will infer that the author's main purpose is to persuade.

You will also infer the author's purpose from clues within the *content* of the material. Note the subject matter and pay attention to the author's choice of words. Is she discussing a neutral or a controversial subject? Is the writer explaining an idea or promoting a point of view? Is she presenting facts or taking sides in an argument? Is she using neutral language, or emotional language? Is she being serious or is she speaking humorously?

Authors' Three Main Purposes

Though there are many ways to describe an author's purpose, we can divide authors' purposes into three main categories: to inform, to persuade, and to entertain.

To inform. As you have probably inferred, most of the material you will be asked to read for college has been written to inform. Informational material includes material that presents facts, data, and statistics. We will also regard the author's purpose as to inform when she is explaining an idea, a concept, or a theory, or describing someone or something.

Of course, textbooks are not the only source of informational writing. Writing whose main purpose is to inform can also be found in newspapers, magazines, and nonfiction books, and on the Internet.

Let's look at an example of writing whose main purpose is to inform.

The term *index crimes* refers to the eight types of crimes that are reported annually by the Federal Bureau of Investigation (FBI) in its *Uniform Crime Report*. This category of criminal behavior generally consists of those serious offenses that people think of when they express concern about the nation's crime problem. Index crimes include murder, rape, robbery, and assault—all of which are violent crimes committed against people—as well as the property crimes of burglary, theft, motor vehicle theft, and arson.

—Schaeffer, *Sociology*

The previous paragraph is taken from a sociology textbook. The author's primary purpose is to provide the reader with information about index crimes. He tells the reader what an index crime is and lists the crimes that are categorized as index crimes.

To persuade. You will sometimes be asked to read persuasive writing for class, and you will frequently encounter persuasive writing when reading on your own, whether it is in a newspaper, magazine or book, or on the Internet. Persuasive writing is writing intended to influence the reader's thinking and/or behavior. Advertisements are the most obvious example of writing that is intended to influence the reader's behavior. As previously mentioned, newspaper and magazine editorials (opinions written by the editors) and opinion columns are also forms of persuasive writing. Most writing about politics or any controversial subject is likely to be intended to persuade. In short, any writing whose main purpose is to present an author's opinion about something can be considered persuasive writing.

Let's look at an example of a passage whose primary purpose is to persuade.

From where I am sitting today, I am profoundly concerned about our nation's children. Life is far more challenging for children and parents than it was only a generation ago, when I was raising my kids. These days, a host of social forces and trends is putting tremendous pressure on children and their parents: Entertainment media are too often replacing active, child-centered play and social time with peers and family. Constant depictions of violence, aggression, and disrespect toward others are immersing kids in a world where "might makes right." Exposure to frightening news reports that only seem to confirm the violent messages pervading kids' entertainment leave many children fearful and insecure. Aggressive marketing campaigns aimed at kids are pushing a host of products, toys, and values on children, teaching them to value "having" over "being" from an early age. Economic and time pressures on parents are leading them to quick-fix approaches to discipline and to rely on "electronic babysitters" like TVs, Game Boys, and Xboxes. An overemphasis on standardized tests in our schools is robbing children of genuine learning opportunities and resulting in the loss of unstructured play, arts activities, and social time, all of which are essential to their well-being. Childhood as we know it is being stolen from our children, and it is time for us, as concerned parents, grandparents, and citizens, to take it back.

—Carlsson-Paige, *Taking Back Childhood*

The previous paragraph is from a book entitled *Taking Back Childhood.* In the first sentence the author tells us that she is concerned about the welfare of today's children. She lists social forces and trends that she believes are putting pressure on parents and children and promoting unhealthy habits and attitudes. She expresses concern about children's exposure to media and marketing and about schools' overemphasis on standardized testing. She concludes by saying that childhood is being "stolen" from children today and that we—today's adults—must take it back for them. Her main purpose, then, is to persuade the reader that today's children are threatened with a loss of true childhood and that something must be done to restore it.

To entertain. When you read the comics pages of the newspaper or a joke book, you expect to encounter material whose main purpose is to entertain.

Although you may not expect your college reading assignments to be entertaining, you may be pleasantly surprised to find, at times, that you've been assigned to read something that is indeed fun to read and that appears to have been written to entertain the reader. Of course, entertaining writers may also want to make serious points about their subjects. The great Mark Twain, for example, wrote stories and novels that are both highly entertaining and deeply insightful. He is also famous for his witty remarks. Here's a quote from Mark Twain about smoking:

"Giving up smoking is easy . . . I've done it hundreds of times."

Although the statement is intended to be humorous, it also contains a more serious point about the difficulty of stopping smoking and perhaps, more generally, about breaking bad habits.

Let's look at an example of a passage whose primary purpose is to entertain, this one from a modern author.

Everyone thinks they have a really good idea for a restaurant but I've heard some terrible schemes. I even had a few myself.

My first idea was: All You Can Eat for 60 Cents. That didn't work. So I went the other way: All You Can Eat for $1500. That didn't work either. Then I made my fatal mistake: All You Can Eat for Free. Closed after one meal.

My next idea was The Used Footwear Restaurant. Our slogan was, How Would You Like to Enjoy a Nice Hot Meal Eaten Out of Someone Else's Used Footwear? Somehow, it didn't work. Although, after I sold it, it became the very successful fast-food franchise Beef in a Brogan.

Chili Alley was my favorite, and a lot of people got a kick out of it. It was a drive-through chili restaurant. And you didn't even have to slow down. You could drive through at speeds up to 40 miles an hour, and we would shoot the chili at you from a shotgun. Just two dollars. Both barrels, three-fifty. Dry cleaning extra.

—Carlin, *Brain Droppings*

The previous passage is taken from the book *Brain Droppings*, by the comedian George Carlin. We can tell pretty quickly that the author is not being serious or talking about something he really did—in other words, that he is joking around. His main purpose is to amuse and entertain the reader. At the same time, he may be making a point about the multitude of restaurants in today's culture and about the silly schemes people sometimes have for starting a new business.

In sum, most of the material you'll read will have one of the three general purposes we've just reviewed—to inform, to persuade, or to entertain. Keep in mind, however, that authors sometimes write for more than one purpose. For example, a magazine article may be written primarily to inform the reader about a given subject, but may also reflect an author's attitude and opinion about the subject.

Table 9.1 Words That Describe an Author's Tone

When the purpose is to inform	When the purpose is to persuade		When the purpose is to entertain
matter-of-fact (just stating facts)	*Positive*:	*Negative*:	light
objective (not taking sides)	appreciative	accusing	lighthearted
serious	supportive	angry	humorous
straightforward	encouraging	concerned	informal
sincere	enthusiastic	worried	tongue-in-cheek (insincere; not meaning what you say)
earnest	sympathetic	discouraged	flippant (disrespectful; not serious)
formal	affirming	disappointed	
informative	hopeful	harsh	
instructive	optimistic	sarcastic or ironic (mocking or ridiculing)	
	admiring	biting	
		critical	
		harsh	
		pessimistic	

Active Reading Strategy: Inferring the Author's Tone

The author's *tone* is the tone of voice the author would use if he were reading the material aloud—in other words, the tone of voice you imagine as you are reading the material to yourself. The author's tone will be consistent with his purpose. If the author's purpose is to amuse, his tone will be light and humorous. If the author's purpose is to provide information, his tone will probably be serious and objective. The author's tone also reflects his attitude and feeling toward his subject. For example, an author's tone might be described as critical or admiring, pessimistic or optimistic.

There are many words that can be used to describe an author's tone. See Table 9.1 for examples of words that are commonly used to describe tone.

To infer the author's tone, first consider the author's purpose. Purpose and tone go hand in hand. For example, if the author's purpose is to inform, we expect the author to use a neutral tone, such as one of those listed in the first grouping in Table 9.1. Next, pay special attention to the author's choice of words. Is he using words with a negative or positive association? Is he using emotional language? Is the writing formal or informal? Is it personal or impersonal?

Let's consider the tone of the three passages we have used as examples of author's purpose.

The passage about index crimes was written to inform. The author is providing information about index crimes in straightforward, neutral language. We could describe his tone as objective, straightforward, or informative.

The passage about childhood was written to persuade. The author is worried about today's children and critical of cultural forces that are affecting children. Her language is not neutral. She uses emotional words and expressions, such as "robbing children" and "aggressive marketing campaigns." We can describe her tone as concerned, worried, and critical.

The passage about restaurants was written to entertain. The writing is informal, with frequent use of short sentences and incomplete sentences. He writes in first person (using "I"). We can describe his tone as humorous, light, or flippant.

EXERCISE 9.6 PURPOSE AND TONE

Directions: Read each passage and answer the questions that follow it.

A. What would it take to make you really happy? Would you have to be a huge financial success? Have the biggest house in town? Own your own helicopter? That's what advertisers tell us is the key to happiness.

Well, I think they're totally wrong.

Unless you have some innate, personal love of big houses or helicopters, don't let yourself buy into someone else's idea of the good life. If you do, you're in for a big letdown. Because no one but you has any idea what will make you happy.

What you love is as unique to you as your fingerprints. You need to know that because *nothing will make you really happy but doing what you love*. Just look at people who are actually living their dreams. You can see a calm focus in their eyes and patience in their actions. They know they're in the right place, doing the right thing.

—Sher, *Live the Life You Love*

_____c_____ **1.** The author's primary purpose is to:
   a. Inform readers of career opportunities.
   b. Persuade readers to look for new careers.
   c. Encourage readers to consider what will really make them happy.
   d. Criticize advertisers for misleading the public.

_____b_____ **2.** The author's tone is:
   a. Formal and serious.
   b. Personal and encouraging.
   c. Critical.
   d. Excited.

_____b_____ **3.** The main idea of the passage is:
   a. Advertisers cannot be trusted.
   b. Only doing what you love will make you truly happy.
   c. Happiness doesn't come from owning things.
   d. You can tell when someone is living her dream.

_d_   **4.** What is the passage's *primary* logical pattern?
   a. Listing: The passage lists the ways to find satisfying work.
   b. Definition: The author defines happiness.
   c. Compare-contrast: The author contrasts happy people and unhappy people.
   d. Cause-effect: The author explains how doing what you love leads to happiness.

_c_   **5.** The author implies that:
   a. Most people need to earn a lot of money in order to be happy.
   b. Advertisers believe that money is the key to happiness.
   c. Doing what you love is the only way to be truly happy.
   d. We all need pretty much the same things to be happy.

_a_   **6.** Which of the following inferences is *least* supported by the passage?
   a. The author has written advertisements.
   b. The author believes advertisements are misleading.
   c. The author knows people who are living their dreams.
   d. Every person has different needs.

_a_   **7.** *Vocabulary in Context*:
   An *innate* love of something is:
   a. An inner, inborn love.
   b. An unrealistic love; a love that can't be attained.
   c. A feeling you shouldn't have but can't control.

B. The invention of writing is one of the most important landmarks of civilization. It is often said to mark the end of prehistoric times and the beginning of history. This is because writing enabled people to record information accurately, and so helped them to develop a sense of their past.

The first steps toward the development of writing probably took place in Sumer between 4000 BC and 3000 BC. The new cities were rapidly growing and needed a way of keeping records. Pictograms (simple pictures) were used to indicate objects and quantities, such as the amount of grain or cattle owned by a temple. Later the pictures became more stylized and began to look like symbols.

—Chisholm and Millard, *Early Civilization*

_a_   **1.** The authors' primary purpose is to:
   a. Inform the reader of the early history of writing.
   b. Explain why pictograms were used.
   c. Explain why writing developed from picture to symbol.
   d. Present a theory about the origins of written history.

_b_   **2.** The authors' tone is:
   a. Personal and friendly.
   b. Serious and objective.
   c. Informal.
   d. Admiring.

___d___ **3.** The main idea of the passage is:
   a. Writing helped people record the past.
   b. Writing began between 4000 BC and 3000 BC.
   c. Early writing used pictograms.
   d. The invention of writing is one of the most important landmarks of civilization and can be traced back to ancient times.

___a___ **4.** The passage implies that:
   a. Writing enabled people to keep historical records.
   b. Written historical records existed well before 4000 BC.
   c. Written words and letters preceded pictograms and were later replaced by them.
   d. Historians have no idea when writing began.

___d___ **5.** Which of the following inferences is *least* supported by the passage:
   a. Sumer was an important city in ancient times.
   b. The exact date and place of the first use of writing is unknown.
   c. Writing enabled people to become more aware of their history.
   d. The invention of writing led to an increase in warfare.

C. The lottery is now the last hope for all mankind, and the beauty of it is that so many players in this country believe they are born winners.

Joe Jarboe is one of them. He owes me fifty bucks, and he told me just last week, "As soon as I win the lottery I'll pay you back."

"I don't want to wait," I protested.

"It won't be long," he said.

"But Joe, millions of people are playing the lottery. What makes you think you'll win?"

"Because I have hunches that are almost supernatural. Take last month—the winning numbers were eight, seven, three, two, six, one. I played seven, eight, two, zero, three and nine."

"That's nowhere near the winner."

"Right. I learned a lesson. Never play zero on a Friday if it's raining. With just a little more concentration, I figure I'll be staring at a million dollars a year for the rest of my life. Then I'll be happy to pay you back."

"Joe, I think the reason you keep picking wrong numbers is that you're worried about the money you owe me. That's what is driving you crazy."

"You don't understand," he said. "I am determined to have a winning ticket. State lotteries are now the only way the government can provide its citizens with the American dream."

"You're living in a fantasy world," I told him. "Nobody wins the lottery except some porter from the Bronx who says he's not going to quit his job, no matter how much money they give him."

Joe wasn't listening. "I know my turn is coming up. I've been too close for comfort too often. Once I was off by just two numbers. I'm not the only one who thinks the lottery can save him. I have a friend who forgot to pay the IRS last year. He told them they would get their money after the next sweepstakes drawing."

"What did the IRS say?"

"They were happy because they were dealing with a winner. There is a woman who is selling her house in Hoboken, New Jersey, and moving to Princeton because she's sure she's going to split a ten-million-dollar prize with a bus driver in Bayonne."

"But you couldn't do business in this country if everyone said they had to wait for their lottery money to come in."

"Why not? It's the easiest way to have a cash flow. You better watch out, or I may not talk to you when I win the sweepstakes."

"Joe, give me the fifty dollars."

"I don't have fifty dollars."

"Then what do you have?"

"I have a sign."

"What kind of sign?"

"I've had an itch under my left toe for a week. If this isn't a hunch that I am going to be a winner, then I don't know what is. You see, I am not like most people, who have no idea what they're doing. They shouldn't be playing, because for them the lottery is a sucker's game."

—Buchwald, *Lighten Up, George*

_____c_____ **1.** The author's primary purpose is to:
   a. Persuade people not to play the lottery.
   b. Complain about a friend who owes him money.
   c. Amuse the reader with a humorous perspective on people who play the lottery.
   d. Criticize the government for failing to provide economic opportunities for low- and middle-income Americans.

_____d_____ **2.** The author's tone is:
   a. Serious and formal.
   b. Encouraging and admiring.
   c. Harsh and critical.
   d. Light and humorous.

_____c_____ **3.** The main idea of the passage is:
   a. People who buy lottery tickets always expect to win.
   b. You have very little chance of winning the lottery.
   c. Many people have unrealistic hopes about winning the lottery.
   d. The lottery is the last hope for all mankind.

_____d_____ **4.** The passage implies that:
   a. The author's friend will win the lottery sooner or later.
   b. The author's friend will repay him soon.
   c. No one should play the lottery.
   d. People have irrational hopes about winning the lottery.

_____b_____ **5.** Which of the following inferences is *best* supported by the passage:
   a. The author has lost money playing the lottery.
   b. Lottery players should be more realistic about their chances of winning.
   c. The lottery should be abolished.
   d. Lottery players should devise better schemes to improve their changes of winning.

D.

_____ b _____ **1.** The advertisement's primary purpose is to:
  a. Provide the reader with nutritional information.
  b. Persuade the reader to buy Nature Valley energy bars.
  c. Encourage the reader to be more adventurous.
  d. Impress the reader with Dan McKemie's climbing skills.

___c___ **2.** The tone of the advertisement is:
  a. Objective and formal.
  b. Light and humorous.
  c. Appealing and encouraging.
  d. Harsh and critical.

___d___ **3.** The main point the advertisers want to make is:
  a. People who enjoy the outdoors should be well-informed about nutrition.
  b. Always bring some food when you go hiking or climbing.
  c. Nature Valley energy bars are a great bargain.
  d. Nature Valley energy bars are great to have along when you are enjoying an outdoor adventure.

___a___ **4.** The advertisement implies that:
  a. Outdoorsmen prefer Nature Valley over other energy bars.
  b. British Columbia is the best place for outdoor sports.
  c. Dan McKemie is an inexperienced ice climber.
  d. Nature Valley energy bars never freeze.

___b___ **5.** The advertisement leads the reader to infer that:
  a. Nature Valley bars stimulate the flow of adrenaline.
  b. Dan McKemie is the climber in the picture.
  c. The climber in the picture is waiting to be rescued.
  d. Ice climbing is a popular sport in Canada.

EXERCISE 9.7 INFERENCES IN SHORT PASSAGES

Directions: Read each passage and answer the questions that follow it. Base your answers on what is stated and implied in the passage. Use context clues, word structure clues, and the dictionary as well as the vocabulary notes provided to determine the meaning of unfamiliar words.

A. HOW SAFE ARE OVER-THE-COUNTER DRUGS AND DRIVING?

For years, you've read the **dire** statistics on drunk driving; fully half of all fatal collisions or crashes involve alcohol. But with all the publicity that drunk driving justifiably generates, one problem often goes virtually unnoticed—over-the-counter drugs [nonprescription drugs] and driving.

Statistics on the number of crashes or collisions involving over-the-counter drugs are hard to come by. "The law hasn't defined a category for it," says Charles Butler, AAA's

manager of Driver Safety Services. "The information is not part of the standard collision report. These kinds of collisions are frequently attributed to fatigue, inattention, or 'unknown causes.'"

However, experts agree that the effects of medications on driving performance cannot be overlooked. "There are some startling figures," says Dr. Art Kibbe, senior director of pharmacy affairs for the American Pharmaceutical Association. "One in every 10 people admitted to hospitals is admitted because they mismanaged their medications. And one in every four

dire terrible; dreadful

elderly patients is admitted for medication mismanagement. You have to ask yourself, 'How many car wrecks are due to some sort of problems with drugs?' "

Of the more than 1,000 different ingredients in over 300,000 over-the-counter drugs available today, many have the same **debilitating** effect on your alertness, reaction time, and other driving skills that alcohol has. "Some over-

the-counter drugs, like antihistamines with **sedative** qualities, can cause just as much drowsiness as alcohol or illegal drugs and can cause **impairment** to the point where you could easily cause an accident," says Los Angeles pharmacist Rory Richardson.

—Dulles, "How Safe Are Over-the-Counter Drugs and Driving?" *AAA World*

---

debilitating weakening

---

sedative calming; tranquilizing
impairment damage; harm

---

    c   **1.** The author's primary purpose is to:
  a. Persuade the reader not to use over-the-counter drugs.
  b. Analyze the cause of automobile accidents.
  c. Inform the reader of the risks of using over-the-counter drugs while driving.
  d. Compare over-the-counter drugs with alcohol.

    c   **2.** The author's tone is:
  a. Optimistic.
  b. Pessimistic.
  c. Concerned.
  d. Harsh and critical.

    b   **3.** We can infer that the author:
  a. Has probably been arrested for drunk driving.
  b. Believes that the use of over-the-counter drugs sometimes contributes to car accidents.
  c. Has probably had an accident himself while using an over-the-counter drug.
  d. Feels that over-the-counter drugs cause more accidents than alcohol.

    b   **4.** The main idea of the passage is:
  a. Drugs are a more serious problem for drivers than alcohol.
  b. Some over-the-counter drugs can impair a driver's faculties and contribute to auto accidents.
  c. We need more information about over-the-counter drugs and driving.
  d. The use of over-the-counter drugs while driving should be made illegal.

    a   **5.** Which is the *primary* logical pattern used in the passage?
  a. Cause-effect: The passage explains how the use of over-the-counter drugs contributes to auto accidents.

b. Compare-contrast: The passage compares the use of alcohol and drugs.

c. Listing: The passage lists the various over-the-counter drugs that affect a driver's alertness.

d. Chronological order: The passage describes the sequence of events leading to an accident.

6. Read each sentence below. If the statement can be logically inferred from the passage, write Yes on the line before the statement. If the statement is not a logical inference based on the passage, write No.

_____No_____ a. The author feels that drunk driving gets too much publicity.

_____No_____ b. The cause of an automobile collision is always correctly determined.

_____No_____ c. One out of ten automobile collisions is due to mismanaged medication.

_____Yes_____ d. Elderly people make more errors with medication than younger people.

_____Yes_____ e. Like alcohol, antihistamines can affect your alertness and speed of reaction.

B. WINNERS AND LOSERS

Each human being is born as something new, something that never existed before. Each is born with the capacity to win at life. Each person has a unique way of seeing, hearing, touching, tasting, and thinking. Each has his or her own unique potentials—capabilities and limitations. Each can be significant, thinking, aware, and creative being—a productive person, a winner.

The words "winner" and "loser" have many meanings. When we refer to a person as a winner, we do not mean one who makes someone else lose. To us, a winner is one who responds authentically by being **credible**, trustworthy, responsive, and genuine, both as an individual and as a member of a society. A loser is one who fails to respond **authentically**. Martin Buber makes this distinction as he retells the old story of the rabbi who, on his deathbed, is asked if he is ready for the world to come. The rabbi says yes. After all, he will not be asked, "Why were you not Moses?" He will only be asked, "Why were you not yourself?"

Few people are one hundred percent winners or one hundred percent losers. It's a matter of degree. However, once a person is on the road to being a winner, his or her chances are greater for becoming even more so.

—James and Jongeward, *Born to Win*

| **credible** believable; trustworthy | **authentically** honestly; genuinely |

_____d_____ **1.** The authors' primary purpose is to:
a. Entertain the reader with a philosophical story.
b. Persuade the reader to be more honest.
c. Explain why some people are winners and some are losers.
d. Clarify their definitions of winner and loser.

_____a_____ **2.** The authors' tone is:
   a. Optimistic.
   b. Pessimistic.
   c. Sarcastic.
   d. Objective.

_____c_____ **3.** Which of the following would the authors *most* likely consider a winner?
   a. A woman who has just won a tennis tournament
   b. A politician who has just been elected to office
   c. A friend who admits to being upset about another friend's remarks
   d. A student who receives an A on a test

_____a_____ **4.** The main idea of the *first paragraph* is:
   a. Everyone can be a winner.
   b. A winner is someone who is authentic and trustworthy.
   c. Everyone has their own way of seeing things.
   d. We are all different but we're all born with equal abilities.

_____c_____ **5.** Which *two* logical patterns are most important in this passage?
   a. Definition and chronological order
   b. Chronological order and listing
   c. Definition and compare-contrast
   d. Compare-contrast and cause-effect

Explain your answer: _The passage defines winner and loser and contrasts them._
_____

6. Mark each of the following statements Yes or No, according to whether or not the statement may be logically inferred from the passage.

_____No_____ a. A loser is someone who is unable to compete with others.

_____No_____ b. One must be very well educated to be a winner.

_____Yes_____ c. Winners are more honest about their feelings than losers.

_____No_____ d. The story about the dying rabbi makes the point that it is important to imitate those you admire.

_____Yes_____ e. After you have started to act authentically, you probably will continue to do so.

C. CHILDHOOD

As I have discovered by examining my past, I started out as a child. Coincidentally, so did my brother. My mother didn't put all her eggs in one basket, so to speak: she gave me a younger brother named Russell, who taught me what was meant by "survival of the fittest."

I have always felt sorry for only children because they are deprived of the opportunity of being rolled out of bed by a relative. For me, the relative was Russell, with whom I was closer than I ever wanted to be. We slept in one bed in a two-bedroom apartment, where I also got close to music because my marbles kept rolling under the piano.

"Somebody's gonna kill himself on your marbles," my mother would say.

"Only somebody walkin' under the piano," I would reply, trying to show that all my marbles were accounted for.

"Well, don't come runnin' to *me* when your father falls on 'em an' then decides to fall on *you*."

"He falls okay without marbles," I said, thinking of certain Saturday nights.

To be fair to my father, the man spent many years wrestling with a question that no parent has ever been able to answer:

What's wrong with that boy?

For some reason, things that had been endearing when done by Huck Finn lost their charm when done by me. Mark Twain would have appreciated my putting a frog in my father's milk, but my father did not care for a breakfast of **marine** life.

"There's a *frog* in my milk," he noted one morning. "Bill, *you* know how a frog got into my milk?"

"They can really get around," I replied.

"And I wonder how *you'll* be getting around," he said meaningfully.

No matter what threat my father ever made or carried out, I loved him very much, even though he didn't understand me. He did not, for example, understand why one day I painted four butterflies on his boxer shorts. But a child today who decorated Dad's drawers would at once be enrolled in a class in abstract art, and the child's mother would be stopping strangers to say, "My Andrew is an absolute genius at underwear **impressionism**. He just did a jock strap that belongs in **the Louvre!**"

—Cosby, *Childhood*

> **marine** living in water

> **impressionism** a style of painting developed in the nineteenth century
> **the Louvre** a famous Paris museum

---

   a   **1.** The author's primary purpose is to:
   a. Amuse the reader with anecdotes from his childhood.
   b. Let the reader know how difficult it is to have a younger brother.
   c. Explain how children are perceived by adults.
   d. Persuade the reader to become a caring parent.

   c   **2.** The author's tone is:
   a. Serious.
   b. Matter-of-fact.
   c. Humorous.
   d. Sarcastic.

   a   **3.** In the last paragraph, Cosby implies that children today:
   a. Are sometimes regarded by their parents as more talented than they really are.
   b. Are better artists than children of the past.
   c. Are better understood than children of the past.
   d. Do not respect their parents.

   b   **4.** Regarding siblings, the author makes the point that:
   a. Children are better off when they have lots of brothers and sisters.
   b. There are disadvantages to having a brother.
   c. Older siblings have several advantages over younger siblings.
   d. Older siblings like to tease younger siblings.

_____d_____ **5.** In the last paragraph, the author contrasts:

  a. His father's attitude toward him and his mother's attitude toward him.

  b. His brother's artistic talents and his own artistic talents.

  c. The artistic abilities of children today and children in the past.

  d. His father's response to his painting on his underwear and today's parents' response to children drawing on their underwear.

6. Mark each of the following statements Yes or No, according to whether it can be logically inferred from the passage.

_____No_____ a. As a child, Bill Cosby enjoyed playing the piano.

_____Yes_____ b. There are advantages to being an only child.

_____No_____ c. The Cosby family was wealthy.

_____Yes_____ d. Huck Finn liked to play practical jokes.

_____No_____ e. Cosby's father did not know how the frog got into his milk.

EXERCISE 9.8 INFERENCE AND HUMOR

Directions: Read the following passage and answer the accompanying questions.

BEAUTY VS. BEAST

If you're a man, at some point a woman will ask you how she looks. "How do I look?" she'll ask.

You must be careful how you answer this question. The best technique is to form an honest yet sensitive opinion, then collapse with some kind of fatal seizure. Trust me, this is the easiest way out. Because you will never come up with the right answer.

The problem is that women generally do not think of their looks in the same way that men do. Most men form an opinion of how they look in seventh grade, and they stick to it for the rest of their lives. Some men form the opinion that they are irresistible stud muffins, and they do not change this opinion even when their faces sag, their noses bloat to the size of eggplants, and their eyebrows grow together to form what appears to be a giant forehead-dwelling caterpillar.

Most men, I believe, think of themselves as average-looking. Men will think this even if their faces cause heart failure in cattle. Being average does not bother them. This is why men never ask anyone how they look. Their primary form of beauty care is shaving, which is the same form of beauty care that they give to their lawns. If, at the end of his four-minute daily beauty regimen, a man has managed to wipe most of the shaving cream out of his hair and is not bleeding too badly, he feels that he has done all he can, so he stops thinking about his appearance and devotes his mind to more critical issues, such as football.

Women do not look at themselves this way. If I had to express, in three words, what I believe most women think about their appearance, those words would be "not good enough." No matter how attractive a woman may appear to be to others, when she looks at herself in the mirror, she thinks: woof. She thinks that, at any moment, a municipal animal-control officer is going to throw a net over her.

Why do women have such low self-esteem? There are many complex psychological and societal reasons, by which I mean Barbie. Girls grow up playing with a doll proportioned such that, if it were a human, it would be 7 feet tall and weigh 81 pounds, of which 53 pounds would be bosoms. This is a difficult appearance standard to live up to, especially when you contrast it with the standard set for young boys by their dolls . . . excuse me, by their action figures. Most of the action figures that my son played with were hideous-looking. For example, he was very fond of an action figure (part of the He-Man series) called Buzz-Off, who was part human, part flying insect. Buzz-Off was not a looker. But he was extremely self-confident. You could not imagine Buzz-Off saying to the other action figures: "Do you think these wings make my hips look big?"

But women grow up thinking they need to look like Barbie, which for most women is impossible, although there is a multibillion-dollar beauty industry devoted to convincing women that they must try. I once saw an *Oprah* show wherein model Cindy Crawford dispensed makeup tips to the studio audience. Crawford had all these middle-aged women applying beauty products to their faces; she stressed how important it was to apply them in a certain way, using the tips of their fingers. All the women did this, even though it was obvious that, no matter how carefully they applied these products, they would never look remotely like Cindy Crawford.

I'm not saying that men are superior. I'm just saying that you're not going to get a group of middle-aged men to apply cosmetics to themselves under the instruction of Brad Pitt, in hopes of looking more like him. Men would realize that this task was pointless and demeaning. They would find some way to bolster their self-esteem that did not require looking like Brad Pitt. They would say to Pitt: "Oh, *yeah?* Well, what do you know about *lawn care*, pretty boy?"

Of course, many women will argue that the reason why they become obsessed with trying to look like Cindy Crawford is that men, being as shallow as a drop of spit, *want* women to look that way. To which I have two responses: 1. Hey, just because *we're* idiots, that doesn't mean *you* have to be. 2. Men don't even notice 97 percent of the beauty efforts you make, anyway. Take fingernails. I have never once, in more than 40 years of listening to men talk about women, heard a man say, "She has a nice set of fingernails!" Many men would not notice if a woman had upward of four hands.

Anyway, to get back to my original point: If you're a man, and a woman asks you how she looks, you're in big trouble. Obviously, you can't say she looks bad. But you also can't say that she looks great, because she'll think you're lying, because she has spent countless hours, with the help of the multibillion-dollar beauty industry, obsessing about the differences between herself and Cindy Crawford. Also, she suspects that you're not qualified to judge anybody's appearance. This is because you have shaving cream in your hair.

—Barry, "Beauty vs. Beast," *Boston Globe Magazine*

1. What is the author's primary purpose in writing this article?

To amuse the reader with a comparison of how men and women think about their appearance.

2. What is the author's tone?

Light and humorous

3. Which logical pattern is used in the passage? Explain your answer.

Compare-contrast: the author contrasts the ways men and women think about their appearance.

4. According to the author, what do men think about their looks?

Men tend to think they're average-looking.

_____

_____

5. According to the author, what do women think about their looks?

Women think their looks are not good enough.

_____

_____

6. Why are women more critical of their looks than men?

Women have grown up comparing themselves with an unrealistic standard.

_____

_____

7. Is the author more critical of men or women? Explain your answer.

Answers will vary.

_____

_____

8. What can we infer from the passage is the best way for a man to respond when a woman asks him how she looks?

Avoid the question. (sample answer)

_____

_____

SKILLS ONLINE: IDENTIFYING THE AUTHOR'S PURPOSE

 Directions:

1. Choose one of the following topics and find a related Web site or online article whose primary purpose is to inform—to provide information about your chosen topic. Choose a Web site that contains at least one picture or image. Print a page and a picture from the Web site or article. Write "Informative" on that page.

   ■ Food, diet, and nutrition

   ■ Police use of tasers

2. For the same topic, find a related Web site or article whose primary purpose is to persuade. Choose a Web site that contains at least one picture or image. Print a page and a picture from the Web site or article. Write "Persuasive" on that page.

3. Next, explain how you inferred the primary purpose of each Web site. (In other words, what clues within the Web site or article enabled you to determine whether its purpose was to inform or persuade?) You can write your answer on the back of the printed sheet.

4. Finally, write one inference that can be drawn from each of your pictures.

READING 9A

I AM CROW DOG (AMERICAN HISTORY)
by Leonard Crow Dog and Richard Erdoes

Reading 9A is an excerpt from the book *Crow Dog*, which was dictated to Richard Erdoes by Leonard Crow Dog. In telling his story, Crow Dog also tells the story of his people. In the following excerpt, Crow Dog explains some of his beliefs and provides a brief history of his tribe.

Pre-Reading Exercise

Directions: Complete this exercise before reading the passage. Preview the passage and answer the following questions.

1. What is the passage about?
   Crow Dog, a Native American

2. Who is narrating the passage? What can you tell about him from your preview?
   Crow Dog narrates. He is passionate about his people, his culture, and his people's
   history. (sample answer)

3. To which tribe does the narrator belong?
   The Lakotas

4. What have you previously learned about Native Americans?
   Answers will vary.

5. How difficult does the passage seem? Explain.
   Answers will vary.

6. Write three questions whose answers you'd like to find while reading the passage.
   Answers will vary.

Directions: While reading, look for clues to infer author's purpose and tone. Note logical patterns and monitor and clarify your comprehension. Use context, the dictionary, and word structure clues to determine the meanings of unfamiliar words.

Look at things not with the eyes in your face but with the eyes in your heart.

—Leonard Crow Dog

I am Crow Dog. I am the fourth of that 1 name. Crow Dogs have played a big part in the history of our tribe and in the history of all the Indian nations of the Great Plains during the last

two hundred years. We are still making history. I am talking this book because I don't read or write. I never went to school—where they try to make Lakota children into whites, where it takes them eight years to teach you to spell *cat*. Talking and listening, not writing, that's in our tradition. Telling stories sitting around a fire or potbelly stove during the long winter nights, that's our way. I speak English as it forms up in my mind. It's not the kind of English they teach you in school; we don't use five-dollar words. I always think up the story in my mind in my own language. Then I try to put it into English. Our Lakota language is sacred to me. Even now, as I am talking, our language is getting lost among some of us. You can kill a language. The white missionaries and teachers in their schools committed language genocide. We are trying to bring our old language back. Trying to purify it. So now I'm telling my own story in my own way—starting at the beginning.

2   It's a medicine story. White historians say that we came over from Asia, when ice covered the Bering Strait so that one could walk over it. We don't believe this, not only us Lakotas, but nearly all the Native Americans on this turtle continent. If there was any crossing of people on the Arctic ice it was the other way around, from Alaska to Asia. We were always here; we came from this earth. We were put here for a purpose, by Wakan Tanka, the Creator. We were put here in the center of the world, and at the center of these United States. Look at a map. Rosebud, our reservation, is smack in the middle. My story is a spiritual winter count of our people.

We Lakota didn't come from another nation   3 or country. We came from across the Missouri, from three daybreaks and three nights away, from the east. And we Lakota claimed this land; it belongs to us. Before that, so long ago that we can hardly remember it, we came from the land of the Great Lakes. We were then a lake and woodlands people. Then the French gave guns, matchlocks, to the Ojibway. We had only bows and arrows. So we were pushed toward the west. And they had horses and we had not gotten them yet. It was not the Ojibway's fault. It was the white man who started the fighting among the tribes, who pushed Ojibway onto Lakota land, and Crows onto Cheyenne land, Crees on Blackfoot land, always pushing the tribes westward to make room for himself, pushing them with guns and cannons, piling one tribe onto another, stopping only when they reached the western ocean. So for a while, the great prairie became our hunting grounds and we turned into a prairie people, a nation of the Great Plains. We need space to roam, to ride. We are a tipi people. But we are not drifters. We try to stay on our own ground. We are Tunkashila's people. He chose this sacred land for us. Our grandfathers chose it. When the grandfathers had the buffalo and owned this land—the Great Dakota Reservation, as the whites called it in 1868 in the Treaty of Fort Laramie—all our dreams and beliefs and sacred sites were centered here. The wasichu, the white man, always talks about those murderous Sioux, always on the warpath, killing settlers, burning and scalping. But that is not true. We were, and are, a peaceful people. Wolakota means "peace." We even welcomed the wasichu. Only when we saw them building roads through our land, wagon roads at first, and then the railroad, when we watched them building forts, killing off all the game, committing a buffalo genocide, and when we saw them ripping up our Black Hills for gold, our sacred Paha Sapa, the home of the wakinyan, the thunderbirds, only then did we realize that what they wanted was our land. Then we began to fight. For our earth. For our children. That started what the whites call the Great Indian Wars of the West. I call it the Great Indian Holocaust.

4   It began with some of our eastern Dakota cousins, the Sisseton, Santee, Wahpeton, and Yankton. They lived in Minnesota, where they had been put on a reservation. The government, which had taken their land, had promised to feed them. But corrupt white agents stole the food and other supplies. The Dakota were starving to death. The white superintendent told them to eat grass. That started what the whites called the Great Sioux Uprising, the revolt of a desperate, dying people. Out of the prisoners the army took, thirty-eight Dakota warriors were condemned to death and hanged. They sang their death songs. Then the last of our eastern tribes were chased across the Missouri and beyond.

5   It was a killing time. Many hundreds of our people and of the Cheyenne were exterminated, most of them old people, women, and children. They were easy to kill. As one colonel, who was also a clergyman, told his soldiers, "Kill 'em all, big and small, nits make lice."

6   After the Lakota and Cheyenne had wiped out Custer, the soldiers swarmed over our land. So many buffalo were killed that they became almost extinct. They had been our main food. Then we were driven onto the reservations and fenced in.

7   I can trace my ancestry back for nine generations. We Crow Dogs had always had the "earth ear," maka nongeya, having the whole earth for an ear. It means you know what's going to happen before it happens. And you can also listen backward, way back, know the generations gone by. And I have my spirit computer, Inyan Tunka, the ancient rock computer, a finding stone. So I have the rock spirit in me. And I have the wakiksuyapi, a special memory, a hot line to the spirits, the remembrance of long-dead relatives, the understanding of signs. Also I can speak the Lakota language as it was spoken hundreds of years ago. In my dreams I can speak to my ancestors. I carry our history inside me.

—Crow Dog and Erdoes, *Crow Dog*

You, the Reader

Interest Rating. Please rate the interest level of the reading on the following scale (circle one):

5—Very interesting   2—A little boring

4—Fairly interesting   1—Very boring

3—Mildly interesting

Difficulty Rating. Please rate the difficulty level of the reading on the following scale (circle one):

5—Very difficult   2—Fairly easy

4—Fairly difficult   1—Very easy

3—Moderate

Comments: Please explain your ratings and make any other comments you wish about the reading.

Answers will vary.

INFERENCE EXERCISE

Directions: *Three* of the following five statements are logical inferences from the passage. (1) Circle the numbers of the *three* statements that can be logically inferred; and (2) write the number of the paragraph in which you found support for the inference.

_____   **1.** Crow Dog learned to speak English from church missionaries.

___2___   **(2.)** White American historians believe that Native Americans originated in Asia and migrated to North America.

___2___   **(3.)** Rosebud is an Indian reservation in the middle of the United States.

___3___   **(4.)** The Lakota were driven west by the Ojibway Indians, who were better armed.

_____   **5.** In his youth, Crow Dog was a great warrior.

COMPREHENSION QUESTIONS

Directions: For questions 1–5, choose the answer that best completes the statements. For questions 6–10, write your response in the space provided. Base all answers on what you read in the selection. Refer back to the selection as necessary to answer the questions.

___b___   **1.** The authors' primary purpose is to:
   a. Provide a general history of the Native Americans.
   b. Acquaint the reader with some of the history and beliefs of the Lakota.
   c. Argue for the return of native lands to the native peoples.
   d. Convince the reader of the innocence of the Lakota in their wars with the white man.

___a___   **2.** The authors' tone is:
   a. Proud and determined.
   b. Sad and discouraged.
   c. Hopeful.
   d. Impersonal and objective.

___c___   **3.** Regarding language, we can infer that Crow Dog:
   a. Speaks several Indian languages fluently.
   b. Wishes he could read and write.
   c. Is concerned about the disappearance of his native language.
   d. Would prefer to speak English than Lakota.

___c___   **4.** Regarding the origins of his tribe, Crow Dog suggests that:
   a. They migrated from Asia to North America.
   b. They migrated from Canada to the United States.
   c. They came from the Great Lakes region.
   d. They crossed the Bering Strait and then migrated to the Central Plains.

___b___ **5.** Crow Dog states that he possesses *all* of the following *except:*
  a. The "earth ear."
  b. The ability to read minds.
  c. A finding stone or spirit computer.
  d. A special connection to his ancestors.

6. Which logical pattern is primarily used in the passage? Explain your answer.

The passage is mostly chronological, with Crow Dog telling the story of his

tribe.

7. List three Lakota words and their meanings.

Any three: Wakan Tanka—the Creator; wasichu—white man; wolakota—

peace; wakinyan—thunderbirds; maka nongeya—the "earth ear"; Inyan

Tunka—a finding stone; wakiksuyapi—remembrance of deceased relatives.

8. What caused the Great Sioux Uprising, according to Crow Dog?

Corrupt white agents stole the food and supplies that the government

had promised the Dakotas. The Dakotas were starving; the white

superintendent told them to eat grass.

9. What evidence does the passage contain that supports the inference that Crow Dog is a deeply religious man?

Crow Dog regards his native language as sacred. He states that his people

were placed on earth by the Creator for a purpose. He describes his story as a

"spiritual winter count of our people". He considers the land sacred.

He discusses his spirit powers.

10. In your opinion, is Crow Dog justified in blaming the white man for the wars between the whites and the Indians? Explain your answer.

Answers will vary.

VOCABULARY EXERCISES

Pronunciation Guide (see p. 90 for list of phonetic symbols)	
exterminated	(ĕk-stûr'mə-nāt'ĭd)
genocide	(jĕn'ə-sīd')
Holocaust	(hŏl'ə-kôst')
tipi	(tē'pē)

WORDS IN CONTEXT

Directions: Choose the meaning for the boldfaced word that best fits the context.

_____d_____ **1.** The white **missionaries** and teachers in their schools committed language genocide.
   a. Soldiers
   b. Students
   c. Government officials
   d. People sent by a church

_____b_____ **2.** Then the French gave guns, **matchlocks**, to the Ojibway.
   a. Knives
   b. Rifles
   c. Ammunition
   d. Information obtained by spying

_____a_____ **3.** When the grandfathers had the buffalo and owned this land . . . all our dreams and beliefs and sacred **sites** were centered here.
   a. Places
   b. Animals
   c. Travels
   d. Wars

_____c_____ **4.** Out of the prisoners the army took, thirty-eight Dakota warriors were **condemned** to death and hanged.
   a. Put on trial
   b. Pardoned from
   c. Sentenced
   d. Executed

_____c_____ **5.** Many hundreds of our people and of the Cheyenne were **exterminated**.
   a. Saved
   b. Escaped
   c. Killed
   d. Sent away

CONTEXT AND DICTIONARY

Directions: Use context and the dictionary to determine the meaning of the boldfaced word in each sentence. Use word structure clues when applicable.

1. The white missionaries and teachers in their schools committed language **genocide**.

The mass killing of a nation, people, or ethnic group (here a language)

2. We are a **tipi** people.

Cone-shaped tent

3. That started what the whites call the Great Indian Wars of the West. I call it the great Indian **Holocaust.**

A war in which genocide is perpetrated

4. **Corrupt** white agents stole the food and other supplies.

Dishonest; unethical

5. The white **superintendent** told them to eat grass.

Person in charge; commander; chief

6. Kill 'em all, big and small, **nits** make lice.

Young louse

RESPOND TO THE READING

Directions: Write a half-page response to either of the following questions.

1. Discuss your reactions to Crow Dog. Do you admire him? Why or why not?

2. Why did nineteenth-century white Americans treat the Native Americans so badly? Might there have been a more peaceful way to settle the country? What might be done today to improve the quality of life for Native Americans?

WEBQUEST

Directions: Use the Internet to find the answer to the following question. Write your answer on a sheet of paper. Print out the Web page you used for the answer or copy the URL on your sheet.

What important historical event occurred at Wounded Knee, North Dakota?

READING 9B

LISTENING (INTERPERSONAL COMMUNICATION)

by Joseph A. DeVito

Reading 9B is taken from a textbook on interpersonal communication. The passage discusses the importance of listening skills as well as the purposes and benefits of listening. Read the passage to learn about the importance of listening and to find out how good listening skills can help you improve your interpersonal communication and relationship skills.

Pre-Reading Exercise

Directions: Complete this exercise before reading the passage. Preview the passage and answer the following questions.

1. What is the passage about?

   The importance of listening

2. What point about listening does the author make in the introductory paragraph?

   We do a lot of listening; it is an important skill.

3. What information is provided in the bulleted list in paragraph 6?

   The purposes of listening

4. What have you previously read or learned about listening?

   Answers will vary.

5. Are you a good listener? Why or why not?

   Answers will vary.

6. Write three questions about listening or listening skills.

   Answers will vary.

Directions: While reading, look for clues to infer author's purpose and tone. Note logical patterns and monitor and clarify your comprehension. Use context, the dictionary, and word structure clues to determine the meanings of unfamiliar words.

1   Listening is surely one of the most important of all interpersonal communication skills. Just think of your own listening behavior during an average day. You wake up to the alarm radio, put on the television to hear the weather and the news, check your computer and listen to the latest entries on YouTube and the advertising pop-ups, go to school while talking on your cell phone, listen to fellow students and instructors, listen to music or watch television, and listen to family members at dinner. Surely listening occupies a good part of your communication day.

The Importance of Listening: Professional and Relationship Benefits

2   The skills of listening will prove crucial to you in both your professional and relationship lives.

First, in today's workplace, listening is regarded as a crucial skill. For example, one study concluded that in this era of technological transformation, employees' interpersonal skills are especially significant; workers' advancement will depend on their ability to speak and write effectively, to display proper etiquette, and *to listen attentively.* And in a survey of 40 CEOs of Asian and Western multinational companies, respondents cited a lack of listening skills as *the major shortcoming* of top executives.

3   Another important professional benefit of listening is to establish and communicate power. In much the same way that you communicate power with your words or gestures, you also communicate your power through listening.

4   It's also interesting to note that the effective listener is more likely to emerge as a group leader

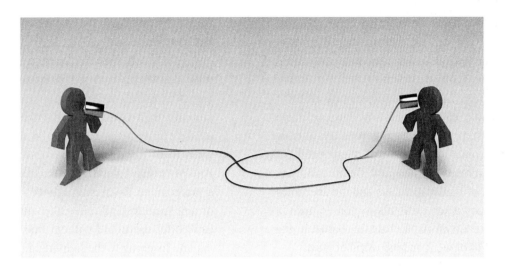

and is often a more effective salesperson, a more attentive and effective healthcare worker, and a more effective manager. Recently medical educators, claiming that doctors are not trained to listen to their patients, have introduced what they call "narrative medicine" to teach doctors not only to listen more effectively but also to recognize how their perceptions of their patients are influenced by their own emotions.

5   And there can be little doubt that listening skills play a crucial role as we develop and maintain a variety of interpersonal relationships. When asked what they want in a partner, women overwhelmingly identify "a partner who listens." And most men would agree that they too want a partner who listens. Among friends, listening skills consistently rank high; in fact, it would be hard to think of a person as a friend if that person was not also a good listener. Children need to learn to listen to their parents and also need their parents to listen to them. And parents need to learn to listen to their children.

6   Another way to appreciate the importance of listening is to consider its purposes and the benefits that accrue for each of these purposes. These purposes, of course, are the same as those of communication generally: to learn, to relate, to influence, to play, and to help.

■ *To learn:* One purpose of listening is to learn, something you do regularly as you listen to lectures in college. You also listen in order to learn about and understand

other people and perhaps to avoid problems and make more reasonable decisions. For example, listening to how your friend dealt with an overly aggressive lover may suggest options to you or to those you know. Listening to your sales staff discuss their difficulties may help you offer more pertinent sales training.

■ *To relate:* One of the communication skills most important to healthy relationships is the ability to listen to friends, romantic partners, family members, colleagues, and just about anyone with whom you come into contact. In fact, women rate listening as one of the most important qualities in a partner. We all use listening to gain social acceptance and popularity and to make people like us. As you know from your own experience, the people you want to talk most with are the people who know how to listen. When you listen attentively and supportively, you communicate a genuine concern for others; it's a way of telling others that you care about them.

■ *To influence:* You also listen to influence other people's attitudes, values, beliefs, opinions, and behaviors. While at first this relationship may seem strange, think about the people who are influential in your life: Very likely these are the people who listen to you, who know you and understand you. You're more likely to follow someone's advice once you feel that you've really been listened to, that your insights and concerns have been heard and understood.

- *To play:* Listening to music or the rustle of leaves often serves a play purpose. Here listening doesn't have to have a profitable outcome; it merely has to be enjoyable for the moment. Listening to the amusing stories of family members and the anecdotes of coworkers will allow you to gain a more comfortable balance between the world of work and the world of play.
- *To help:* Listening to help is something we experience growing up when our parents listen (or, sometimes, don't listen) to our concerns and help us solve our problems. Sometimes just listening—with no advice and no suggestions—proves extremely helpful. Supportive and noninfluential listening helps the other person clarify his or her thoughts and enables them to be seen more objectively. And of course listening is almost always a prerequisite to offering advice or help of any specific kind; after all, you really can't offer useful aid without first knowing and listening to the individual.

—DeVito, *The Interpersonal Communication Book,* 12th ed.

You, the Reader

Interest Rating. Please rate the interest level of the reading on the following scale (circle one):

5—Very interesting	2—A little boring
4—Fairly interesting	1—Very boring
3—Mildly interesting	

Difficulty Rating. Please rate the difficulty level of the reading on the following scale (circle one):

5—Very difficult	2—Fairly easy
4—Fairly difficult	1—Very easy
3—Moderate	

Comments: Please explain your ratings and make any other comments you wish about the reading.

Answers will vary.

INFERENCE EXERCISE

Directions: *Three* of the following five statements are logical inferences from the passage. (1) Circle the numbers of the *three* statements that can be logically inferred; and (2) write the number of the paragraph in which you found support for the inference.

   2, 4   **(1.)** Improving your listening skills is a way to make yourself a more valuable employee.

<u>   6   </u> ②. College students who improve their listening skills are likely to improve their grades.

<u>   </u> **3.** Most top executives achieved their position because they were good listeners.

<u>   </u> **4.** Today's technology makes listening skills less important.

<u>   6   </u> ⑤. Good listening skills contribute to better problem solving.

COMPREHENSION QUESTIONS

Directions: For questions 1–5, choose the answer that best completes the statement. For questions 6–10, write your response in the space provided. Base all answers on what you read in the selection. Refer back to the selection as necessary to answer the questions.

<u>   c   </u> **1.** The author's primary purpose is to:
   a. Amuse the reader with interesting facts about listening.
   b. Provide step-by-step directions for how to become a better listener.
   c. Explain the benefits and importance of listening.
   d. Inform the reader of the risks of poor listening.

<u>   c   </u> **2.** The author's tone is:
   a. Light and cheery.
   b. Harsh and critical.
   c. Informative and sincere.
   d. Worried and concerned.

<u>   d   </u> **3.** The main idea of paragraph 5 is that:
   a. Most women want a partner who listens.
   b. Children learn listening skills from their parents.
   c. Most people don't have good listening skills.
   d. Listening skills are essential to the development and maintenance of interpersonal relationships.

<u>   a   </u> **4.** Regarding romantic relationships, the author states that:
   a. Both men and women want a partner who listens.
   b. Most men do not think listening skills are important in a romantic relationship.
   c. Women are better listeners than men.
   d. Listening skills become less important as a relationship develops.

<u>   d   </u> **5.** Regarding help, the author suggests that all of the following are true *except*:
   a. Parents don't always listen to their children's concerns.
   b. Just listening without giving any advice is sometimes very helpful.
   c. Giving good advice depends on first listening to the individual you are advising.
   d. Children are most helpful to their parents when they listen and do exactly as they are told.

6. What is the primary logical pattern used in the passage? Explain your answer.

Listing: the passage lists the benefits and purposes of listening. [Cause-Effect is also

used in discussing the benefits (effects) of good listening.]

7. What point does the author make about listening and power?

Listening can establish and communicate power.

8. Why are listening skills important to friendships?

Answers will vary.

9. How does listening contribute to learning?

We gain information by listening. We learn about and understand other people by listening.

We can learn from listening to others talk about their experiences. (sample answer)

10. In which careers do you think listening skills are most important? Why?

Answers will vary.

VOCABULARY EXERCISES

Pronunciation Guide (see p. 90 for list of phonetic symbols)	
accrue	(ə-krōō′)
anecdotes	(ăn′ĭk-dōts′)
cited	(sīt′ĭd)
crucial	(krōō′shəl)
etiquette	(ĕt′ĭ-kĭt′)
prerequisite	(prē-rĕk′wĭ-zĭt)

WORDS IN CONTEXT

Directions: Choose the meaning for the boldfaced word that best fits the context.

____b____ **1.** The skills of listening will prove **crucial** to you in both your professional and relationship lives.
   a. Interesting
   b. Of great importance
   c. Difficult
   d. Fortunate

_a_   **2.** And in a survey . . . respondents **cited** a lack of listening skills as the major shortcoming of top executives.
   a. Mentioned
   b. Saw
   c. Predicted
   d. Remembered

_b_   **3.** And in a survey . . . respondents cited a lack of listening skills as the major **shortcoming** of top executives.
   a. Strength; advantage
   b. Weakness
   c. Interest
   d. Goal or target

_d_   **4.** Another way to appreciate the importance of listening is to consider its purposes and the benefits that **accrue** for each of these purposes.
   a. Are learned
   b. Are needed
   c. Cause
   d. Accumulate

_c_   **5.** And of course listening is almost always a **prerequisite** to offering advice or help of any specific kind . . .
   a. Problem
   b. Solution
   c. Requirement
   d. Situation

CONTEXT AND DICTIONARY

Directions: Use context and the dictionary to determine the meaning of the boldfaced word in each sentence. Use word structure clues when applicable.

1. Listening is surely one of the most important of all **interpersonal** communication skills.

Between people; of relationships

2. For example, one study concluded that in this era of technological **transformation** . . .

Change

3. . . . workers' advancement will depend on their ability to speak and write effectively, to display proper **etiquette**, and to listen attentively.

Manners; appropriate ways of behaving

4. Listening to your sales staff discuss their difficulties may help you offer more **pertinent** sales training.

Relevant; to the point; related to the matter at hand

5. Listening to the amusing stories of family members and the **anecdotes** of co-workers will allow you to gain a more comfortable balance between the world of work and the world of play.

Personal stories or accounts

RESPOND TO THE READING

Directions: Write a half-page response to either of the following questions.

1. Evaluate your own listening skills. What are your strengths and weaknesses as a listener? How might your listening skills be improved?

2. Discuss a situation from your own experience in which effective—or ineffective—listening played an important role. Who was involved? What was the situation? How did effective or ineffective listening contribute to what happened?

WEBQUEST

Directions: Use the Internet to find the answer to the following question. Write your answer on a sheet of paper. Print out the Web page you used for the answer, or copy the URL on your sheet.

Find a Web site that provides tips for effective listening. On your paper, write down the five tips that you think are most helpful, and briefly explain why you think they are helpful.

CHAPTER 9 REVIEW

Inference

Inference is the reasoning process by which we interpret and draw conclusions. We sometimes refer to this process as "reading between the lines." Inference is a natural reasoning skill that we use everyday.

Inference is an important part of the reading process. Reliable inferences—inferences that are based on sound reasoning—are essential for good reading comprehension.

Literal vs. Inferential Levels of Comprehension

We can think of reading comprehension as having two levels. At the *literal level* we understand what is actually stated in the material. At the *inferential level* we interpret and draw conclusions from what is stated.

Good inference is always based on sound reasoning. The challenge for active readers is to become more aware of the inferences that they're making and to monitor them so that they become more attuned with the writer's intended meanings.

Inferring Author's Purpose and Tone

The author's purpose is her reason for writing the material. Inferring the author's purpose is essential for effective reading. Using clues from the context and content of the material, active readers seek to recognize author's purpose whenever they are reading. Three common purposes are: *to inform, to persuade,* and *to entertain.*

The author's *tone* is the tone of voice the author would use if he or she were reading the material aloud. The author's tone will be consistent with his purpose. Tone can generally be described as positive, negative, or neutral.

Skills Online: Identifying Author's Purpose

Readings

Reading 9A: I Am Crow Dog (American History)	Reading 9B: Listening (Interpersonal Communication)

CHAPTER TESTS

TEST 9.1 INFERENCE

Directions: The passage below is followed by five statements. *Three* of the five statements are logical inferences. (1) Circle the numbers of the *three* statements that can be logically inferred from the passage; and (2) indicate which sentence or sentences in the passage support the inferences by writing the sentence number(s) on the line before the inference.

(1) "Don't let the bedbugs bite" is an old-fashioned refrain, but it's timely advice. (2) Bedbugs, which had seemingly been controlled in the U.S., are on the rise. (3) In New York City, for instance, the housing preservation department recorded only two bedbug case in 2002; in 2006, nearly 1,200 cases popped up. (4) Elsewhere across the continent, these wingless pests are thriving—hiding in mattress creases and bedroom furniture, then crawling out at night to suck the blood of those who slumber, often leaving itchy skin welts behind. (5) Why the comeback? (6) After World War II, better household hygiene and the liberal use of pesticides helped kill most bedbugs in the United States. (7) By the 1970s, though, many insecticides had been proved hazardous to human health, so they were used less frequently. (8) Bedbugs also got a boost from growing numbers of international travelers, whose luggage carried the tiny stowaways to the U.S. (9) Fortunately, bedbugs aren't know to transmit pathogens. (10) But these parasites can cause bugged-out people to panic. (11) Pesticides work but, if overused, can do more harm than good.

—Mairson, "They're Back," *National Geographic*

<u>2, 3, 6</u> (**1.**) Bedbug cases in the U.S. declined after World War II but have risen recently.

<u>9</u> (**2.**) Bedbugs are unlikely to make you ill.

_____ **3.** Bedbugs are more common in the U.S. than in other countries.

_____ **4.** Resuming the use of hazardous pesticides is the only way to control bedbugs.

<u>4</u> (**5.**) Bedbugs can't fly.

TEST 9.2 PURPOSE AND TONE

Directions: Read the passage and answer the questions that follow it.

Writer Esmeralda Santiago was 13 when her mother decided to move from Puerto Rico to Brooklyn with her eight children.

The move was frightening. New York seemed dark, cold and forbidding compared to the tropical countryside of Santiago's homeland, where, she writes, the air smelled of "peppermint, rosemary, and verbena." She spoke little English and knew nothing of mainland customs.

But Santiago, now 52 and the author of two acclaimed memoirs and other works, believes that the difficult transition between two cultures allowed her to blossom in ways that she might otherwise not have.

It also gave her singular insights into the immigrant experience, particularly that of Latinos, a diverse group projected to account for a quarter of the U.S. population by 2050. Through her writing, Santiago speaks eloquently for the nation's newcomers.

"My writing is about people who are voiceless, who would otherwise not see themselves in the literature of the United States," she says. "I feel very strongly that if you don't exist in the arts of a culture, you're invisible. The arts are what express the soul of who we are and that expresses our humanity."

Her works explain—in vivid detail both painful and funny—that crossing the bridge between two cultures in not an easy journey.

"Yes, it was hard, yes, it was painful, and yes, we suffered," she says of her own journey. "But ultimately, more good came out of it."

—Baker, "Caught Between Cultures," *AARP Bulletin*

___c___ **1.** The author's primary purpose is to:
   a. Provide information about immigration.
   b. Encourage immigration into the United States.
   c. Inform the reader about Esmeralda Santiago, a successful immigrant.
   d. Encourage the reader to read Santiago's memoirs and other writings.

___a___ **2.** The author's tone is:
   a. Sympathetic.
   b. Discouraged.
   c. Critical.
   d. Matter-of-fact.

___d___ **3.** The passage implies that:
   a. Esmeralda was the youngest child in her family.
   b. Esmeralda was the oldest child in her family.
   c. Esmeralda's mother moved her family to New York so her children could get a better education.
   d. Immigrating contributed to Esmeralda's becoming a writer.

___c___ **4.** Which of the following inferences is *best* supported by the passage:
   a. Most of the Latinos in the United States have immigrated from Puerto Rico.
   b. Most immigrants do not appreciate the importance of literature.
   c. The Latino population in the United States is growing rapidly.
   d. Literature about the Latino population in the United States is increasing rapidly.

TEST 9.3 INFERENCE

Directions: Read the following passage and complete the accompanying exercises.

When my grandmother was raising me in Stamps, Arkansas, she had a particular routine when people who were known to be whiners entered her store. Whenever she saw a known complainer coming, she would call me from whatever I was doing and say conspiratorially, "Sister, come inside. Come." Of course I would obey.

My grandmother would ask the customer, "How are you doing today, Brother Thomas?" And the person would reply, "Not so good." There would be a distinct whine in the voice. "Not so good today, Sister Henderson. You see, it's this summer. It's this summer heat. I just hate it. Oh, I hate it so much. It just frazzles me up and frazzles me down. I just hate the heat. It's almost killing me." Then my grandmother would stand stoically, her arms folded, and mumble, "Uh-huh, uh-huh." And she would cut her eyes at me to make certain that I had heard the lamentation.

At another time a whiner would mewl, "I hate plowing. That packed-down dirt ain't got no reasoning, and mules ain't got good sense. . . . Sure ain't. It's killing me. I can't ever seem to get done. My feet and my hands stay sore, and I get dirt in my eyes and up my nose. I just can't stand it." And my grandmother, again stoically with her arms folded, would say, "Uh-huh, uh-huh," and then look at me and nod.

As soon as the complainer was out of the store, my grandmother would call me to stand in front of her. And then she would say the same thing she had said at least a thousand times, it seemed to me. "Sister, did you hear what Brother So-and-So or Sister Much to Do complained about? You heard that?" And I would nod. Mamma would continue, "Sister, there are people who went to sleep all over the world last night, poor and rich and white and black, but they will never wake again. Sister, those who expected to rise did not, their beds became their cooling boards, and their blankets became their winding sheets. And those dead folks would give anything, anything at all for just five minutes of this weather or ten minutes of that plowing that person was grumbling about. So you watch yourself about complaining, Sister. What you're supposed to do when you don't like a thing is change it. If you can't change it, change the way you think about it. Don't complain."

It is said that persons have few teachable moments in their lives. Mamma seemed to have caught me at each one I had between the age of three and thirteen. Whining is not only graceless, but can be dangerous. It can alert a brute that a victim is in the neighborhood.

—Angelou, *Wouldn't Take Nothing for My Journey Now*

___a___   **1.** The author's primary purpose is to:
    a. Share an important lesson she learned from her grandmother.
    b. Ridicule people who complain.
    c. Explain why people like to complain.
    d. Share with the reader an amusing story from her childhood.

___d___   **2.** The author's tone is:
    a. Sympathetic.
    b. Harsh and angry.
    c. Light and humorous.
    d. Earnest and appreciative.

___c___   **3.** We can infer from the passage that:
    a. The author's grandmother had many brothers and sisters.
    b. The author's mother died at a young age.
    c. The author was raised in a rural area.
    d. The author was raised in a large city in Arkansas.

<u> c </u> **4.** Which of the following inferences is *least* supported by the passage?
    a. The author's grandmother rarely complained.
    b. The author's grandmother was an important influence during her childhood.
    c. The author liked working in her grandmother's store.
    d. The author rarely complains.

<u> b </u> **5.** The author's grandmother believed that:
    a. Her granddaughter complained too much.
    b. Life is a gift to be appreciated.
    c. You can always change things rather than complain about them.
    d. Life is to be endured rather than enjoyed.

6. Mark each of the following statements Yes or No, according to whether it can be logically inferred from the passage.
    <u>Yes</u> a. The author sometimes referred to her grandmother as Mamma.
    <u>No</u> b. The author had no other family.
    <u>Yes</u> c. Brother Thomas liked to complain about the heat.
    <u>No</u> d. When you don't like something, the first step to take is to change the way you think about it.
    <u>Yes</u> e. Whining about a problem can lead to further harm.

You, the Reader: Chapter 9 Wrap-up

Directions: Use one or two of the following questions to write a half-page response to Chapter 9.

- What were the most important things you learned from this chapter? How will you use what you have learned from this chapter?
- How have you changed your reading habits in response to this chapter?
- What strategies most help you to make good inferences while reading?
- What parts of the chapter did you find most engaging? What questions do you have about the chapter?

PEARSON
myreadinglab™

For support in meeting this chapter's objectives, go to MyReadingLab and select *Inference*.

Critical Reading

LEARNING OBJECTIVES

In Chapter 10 you will learn to:

- Distinguish factual statements from opinion statements
- Evaluate information sources
- Evaluate authors' arguments

CHAPTER CONTENTS

Pre-Reading Exercise for Chapter 10

Directions: Preview the chapter and answer the following questions.

1. What is the chapter about?

   Critical reading: fact vs. opinion; evaluating information sources; evaluating arguments

2. What is a factual statement?

   A statement that can be determined to be true or false

3. What are some strategies for evaluating an author's argument?

   Consider author's purpose, intended audience, bias, evidence; evaluate author's logic;

   look for emotional appeals and propaganda

4. What have you previously learned about critical reading?

   Answers will vary.

5. How do you determine whether or not to believe something you read?

   Answers will vary.

6. Write two questions about the content of this chapter.

   Answers will vary.

It has been said that we live in the information age, but what exactly does this mean? Well, for one thing, it means that people living today have access to a great deal more information than people of any previous era. A child today who can read and use a computer has access to more information at any given moment than the most advanced scholars of a century ago did in their entire lifetimes!

It also means that people today are required to process more information than people of previous times, on a daily basis. From the time they wake up in the morning until the time they go to bed at night, most Americans are in contact with one information source or another—whether it's television, radio, the Internet, newspapers, magazines, books, or their cell phone—more than half of the time.

All this implies that anyone living today needs to have the ability to evaluate the information that's coming his or her way. Is the information useful? Is it accurate? We also need to be aware of how others are using information to influence our thinking and behavior. The average American is exposed to hundreds or even thousands of advertisements on a daily basis. To evaluate the ideas and information that come our way requires critical thinking.

Critical thinking is the process by which we analyze and evaluate the ideas and information to which we are exposed. (The word *critical* has several meanings. In the term *critical thinking*, *critical* does not mean "finding fault with." It means "exercising skillful and careful judgment.") Critical thinking requires the use of inference, interpretation, and judgment. Clearly, critical thinking is essential to success in virtually any career or field of study in today's world. Many college educators believe that the primary goal of a college education is the development of critical thinking skills.

Critical reading is the process by which we analyze and evaluate the ideas and information we encounter in our reading material. Active readers are critical readers. This means that they evaluate what they read. They question what they read. Is the material credible? Is it useful? Critical readers do not assume that what they read is true just because they read it in a book, magazine, newspaper, or on the Internet.

Critical reading enables you to connect what you read with real life. When you read critically, you think of the author as another human being communicating information or sharing his or her ideas, feelings, and insights with you. You relate the reading material to your own ideas, feelings, and knowledge. You think about the application of the author's material to your own life and experience or to the world around you.

In this chapter, we will explore the complex process of critical reading, building on the skills that you have developed through your work with the previous chapters of the text. Critical reading involves recognition of the author's purpose and assessment of how well the author has achieved his purpose. Critical reading also involves distinguishing between fact and opinion, and assessing how well an author supports her opinion. Active readers assess their own opinions as well, and are willing to modify them after exposure to new information and new ways of thinking about the subject.

Active Reading Strategy: Distinguishing Fact from Opinion

Active readers are careful to distinguish fact from opinion in their reading material. The distinction is important because as critical readers, we respond very differently to the presentation of factual material than we do to expressions of opinion. What then, is the basic difference between fact and opinion?

Facts

What is a fact? The word *fact* is usually used to refer to something that is considered to be real or true. Whether or not a statement is true or accurate, however, is not always easy to assess. For example, we all accept it as fact that the Earth is round. How do we know for sure? In actuality, the Earth is not perfectly round: it is a bit flatter at its poles and bulges a bit around the equator. So, is it a "fact" that the Earth is round?

Facts are not always as clear and simple as we would like them to be.

As critical readers, we recognize that facts are not always easy to determine. Normally, however, we will not need to take the time and trouble to verify an author's facts. When evaluating what we read, we consider a statement to be factual as long as the statement is *capable* of proof or disproof. In other words, *a factual statement is one that can be determined to be correct or incorrect*—either by direct observation, experimentation or referral to other sources of information. We don't have to prove the Earth's roundness ourselves to know that it is possible to determine whether or not the Earth is round.

Examples of factual statements include:

Historical fact	Cortes conquered Mexico.
Scientific fact	The sun is 93 million miles from the Earth.
Statistics	The population of the United States is 310 million.
Description	The house was painted green and yellow with hot pink shutters.
Statements of events	Sarah left for school at 8 o' clock.

Although you may not be sure of the accuracy of any of the previous statements, you can regard them as factual statements because you know that they can be proved or disproved.

Opinions

In contrast, *statements of opinion express an author's particular point of view about his subject, and therefore can never be proved to be correct or incorrect.* Opinion statements express an author's beliefs and ideas and reflect his values and feelings. You can agree or disagree with an opinion statement, but you can never prove it or disprove it. Active readers know that an author's values and opinions may be different from their own and will not automatically discount an author's opinion simply because it is different from theirs.

Examples of opinion statements include:

Personal preference	Vanilla ice cream tastes better than chocolate.
Values statements	Nothing is more important than getting a good education.
Judgments	Michael Jordan is the best basketball player of all time.
"Should" statements	No one should be allowed to own a handgun.
Predictions	Ten years from now almost all jobs will be computer related.
Speculation	With better pitching, the Twins would have finished first last year.
Unproven theory	Our daydreams and night dreams are probably related to each other.

Note that although you may agree or disagree with any of the preceding statements, you cannot verify or disprove them. Also note that wording is sometimes a clue to an opinion statement. Words like "better" and "more important" usually indicate personal judgment or values—in other words, an opinion.

Opinions can't be proved, but some opinions are more justified than others. For example, the opinion that Michael Jordan is the best basketball player of all time is easier to support than the opinion that Michael Jordan would make a great U.S. president. We also give more credence to the opinions of experts. You are more likely to accept the theory that daydreams and night dreams are related when it is proposed by a psychologist who has researched the subject than, let's say, when it has been suggested by a classmate who has never studied psychology. The network weather reporter's opinion that it will rain tomorrow is probably more trustworthy than your English teacher's predictions about the weather (at the same time, your English teacher's opinion on how to improve your writing is probably more trustworthy than the weather reporter's). In any case, active readers are careful to recognize opinion statements as such and respond to them differently from the way they respond to factual statements. They will consider how well the author has supported her opinion and will decide whether or not, based on the strength of the author's argument and their own knowledge and beliefs, they believe the opinion to be justified.

Although not all statements can be neatly categorized as fact or opinion, distinguishing fact from opinion is an important first step toward a critical evaluation of what you read. The next four exercises will provide practice with distinguishing fact from opinion. As you read the statements, remember that it is not your job to determine whether or not the statement is true. Your job is to determine whether the statement is a factual statement (in other words, the statement is capable of proof or disproof) or a statement of opinion (the statement cannot be proved or disproved).

> **Factual statements** are capable of proof or disproof.
> **Opinion statements** cannot be proved or disproved.

EXERCISE 10.1 FACT VS. OPINION

Directions: Mark each statement F (factual statement) or O (opinion statement).

___F___ **1.** The modern public school movement began in the 1830s in Massachusetts.

___O___ **2.** The 1830s was a wonderful time to live.

___O___ **3.** Perhaps the most important function of political polls is to clarify the issues that concern voters.

___F___ **4.** In 1972, two Washington reporters covered the Watergate break-in and linked the crime to the White House.

—Vivian, *The Media of Mass Communication,* 9th ed.

___O___ **5.** Every culture needs its poets.

___O___ **6.** REM was undoubtedly one of the best pop groups of the 1990s.

___F___ **7.** When we communicate nonverbally, we sometimes do so unconsciously.

F **8.** In intimate conversation, North Americans typically stand 1½ to 4 feet apart.

—Henslin, *Essentials of Sociology,* 3rd ed.

F **9.** Erik Erikson was one of the first modern psychologists to propose a life span approach to psychological development.

—Wade and Tavris, *Invitation to Psychology,* 4th ed.

O **10.** The best way to avoid police problems is to hire the right people in the first place.

EXERCISE 10.2 FACT VS. OPINION

Directions: Mark each statement F (factual statement) or O (opinion statement).

O **1.** The U.S. Constitution is the greatest legal document of all times.

F **2.** At age 18, all American citizens are eligible to vote in state and national elections.

F **3.** Nineteenth-century doctors relied on the drugs that were available then—chiefly quinine, opium, and morphine.

O **4.** Nineteenth-century doctors should have had a better understanding of the addictive powers of opium and morphine.

O **5.** Doing what you love to do is the key to happiness in life.

O **6.** Within twenty-five years, the United States will elect its first woman president.

F **7.** Britain, India, and Israel have already elected women to lead their nations.

F **8.** Ozone, the primary component of smog, is a gas formed when nitrogen oxide and hydrocarbons combine in sunlight.

O **9.** The threat to the ozone layer is the single most important environmental issue of our time.

F **10.** The Industrial Revolution began in Great Britain, where in 1765 the steam engine was first used to run machinery.

—Henslin, *Essentials of Sociology,* 3rd ed.

EXERCISE 10.3 FACT AND OPINION IN PARAGRAPHS

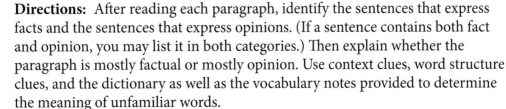

Directions: After reading each paragraph, identify the sentences that express facts and the sentences that express opinions. (If a sentence contains both fact and opinion, you may list it in both categories.) Then explain whether the paragraph is mostly factual or mostly opinion. Use context clues, word structure clues, and the dictionary as well as the vocabulary notes provided to determine the meaning of unfamiliar words.

1. (1) The world will soon start to run out of conventionally produced, cheap oil. (2) If we manage somehow to overcome that shock by shifting the burden to coal and natural gas, the two other primary fossil fuels, life may go on more or less as it has been—until we start to run out of all fossil fuels by the end of this century. (3) And by the time we have burned up all that fuel, we may well have rendered the planet unfit for human life. (4) Even if human life does go on, civilization as we know it will not survive, unless we can find a way to live without fossil fuels.

—Goodstein, *Out of Gas*

Which sentences contain facts? None (there is a buried fact in sentence 2: coal and natural gas are fossil fuels)

Which sentences contain opinions? All

Is the paragraph mostly fact or opinion? Explain your answer.
The paragraph is virtually all opinion. The author is predicting and speculating about running out of oil and other fossil fuels.

2. (1) Although the importance of proteins in the body should not be underestimated, it is carbohydrates that supply us with the energy needed to sustain normal daily activity. (2) Carbohydrates actually can be **metabolized** more quickly and efficiently than proteins can. (3) They are a quick source of energy for the body because they are easily converted to glucose, the fuel for the body's cells. (4) These foods also play an important role in the functioning of internal organs, the nervous system, and the muscles. (5) They are the best fuel for endurance athletics because they provide both an immediate and a time-released energy source since they are digested easily and then consistently metabolized in the bloodstream.

—Donatelle, *Health: The Basics*, 6th ed.

metabolize process; convert

Which sentences contain facts? All

Which sentences contain opinions? 1 and 5

Is the paragraph mostly fact or opinion? Explain your answer.
The paragraph is mostly factual, presenting information about carbohydrates. Some opinion is mixed into the first and last sentence where the author evaluates the relative importance of the nutrients.

3. (1) Few animals, however, have ever been as successful as the lions. (2) The most recent of the *Panthera*, lions evolved on the African savannahs only 700,000 years ago, probably to the **consterna-tion** of our ancestors, and soon thereafter—long before our ancestors thought of doing anything similar—the lions colonized the rest of the planet. (3) Until very recently lions were almost everywhere that glaciers were not. (4) They lived in North and South America, all across Asia and

consternation dismay; bewilderment or shock

down into India; they lived in Europe and on the British Isles; they lived in the Middle East and throughout the continent of Africa, where of course they remain to this day. (5) Australia and the Pacific Islands were about the only places the lions hadn't found.

—Thomas, *The Tribe of Tiger*

Which sentences contain facts? 2–5 _____

Which sentences contain opinions? 1 (and an opinion is inserted into sentence 2:

"probably . . .") _____

Is the paragraph mostly fact or opinion? Explain your answer.

The paragraph is mostly factual, presenting information about lions and their history.

The first sentence expresses an opinion comparing the lions' success with other animals.

4. (1) With dozens of missions now in the works, there has never been a more fascinating time for space exploration. (2) The missions are intended to help us better understand our universe, whether we are investigating life on Mars or searching for solar systems beyond ours. (3) They even seek to **avert** mass destruction on Earth that's due to an asteroid possibly headed our way. (4) Some people find these to be expensive efforts that amount to scarcely anything of **tangible** value. (5) But judging from the missions described here, I contend that, with each one, we'll gain a greater understanding of our world, the worlds unnumbered around us and our relationship to them.

—Tyson, "Where We're Headed," *USA Today Weekend Magazine*

avert prevent; avoid	**tangible** definite; actual; material

Which sentences contain facts? 2, 3, 4 _____

Which sentences contain opinions? 1 and 5 _____

Is the paragraph mostly fact or opinion? Explain your answer.

The paragraph mixes facts and opinions. The author expresses his opinions about the

importance of space exploration. Sentences 2–4 provide "soft" facts in describing the

intention of the space missions and reporting other people's views (which are their opinions).

5. (1) Nothing that we know about the early humans is as awesome as what they painted in the depths of caves. (2) Prehistorians first learned about these paintings in 1875, when an amateur archaeologist was hunting bones and tools in a cave at Altamira near the northern coast of Spain. (3) His little daughter, whom he'd brought along for company, wandered into a nearby chamber. (4) Holding up her candle, she saw paintings on the ceiling of two dozen nearly life-size bison, drawn in yellow, red, brown, and black. (5) The paintings are so masterful that experts quickly—wrongly—called them modern fakes.

—Davis, *The Human Story*

Which sentences contain facts? 2–5 _____

Which sentences contain opinions? 1 _____

Is the paragraph mostly fact or opinion? Explain your answer.

The paragraph starts with an opinion statement, but most of the paragraph is factual,

describing the discovery of cave paintings.

EXERCISE 10.4 FACT AND OPINION IN PARAGRAPHS

Directions: After reading each paragraph, identify the sentences that express facts and the sentences that express opinions. (If a sentence contains both fact and opinion, you may list it in both categories.) Then explain whether the paragraph is mostly factual or mostly opinion. Use context clues, word structure clues, and the dictionary, as well as the vocabulary notes provided, to determine the meaning of unfamiliar words.

1. (1) Families in the United States have changed dramatically over the past fifty years. (2) In the 1950s, the norm was a working father and a mother at home with two or more school-aged children. (3) Today only 68 percent of children who are under eighteen years old live in families with two parents. (4) Seldom does a mother remain at home until her children finish high school. (5) Families today include mothers working while fathers stay at home with the children, single-parent families, families with two working parents, remarried parents, childless marriages, families with adopted children, gay and lesbian parents, extended families, grandparents raising grandchildren, and unmarried couples with children.

—Johnson et al., *Foundations of American Education*, 14th ed.

Which sentences contain facts? 2–5

Which sentences contain opinions? 1 ("dramatically")

Is the paragraph mostly fact or opinion? Explain your answer.

The passage is entirely factual except for the insertion of the word "dramatically" in

sentence 1. The paragraph lists the ways families have changed and the various

compositions of today's families.

2. (1) The challenge in every relationship, every conversation, is to find ways to be as close as you want to be (and no closer) without that closeness becoming **intrusive** or threatening your freedom and your sense that you are in control of your life. (2) In this, relationships between daughters and mothers are like all relationships, only more so. (3) They combine, on one hand, the deepest connection, the most comforting closeness, with, on the other, the most **daunting** struggles for control. (4) Each tends to overestimate the other's power while underestimating her own. (5) And each yearns to be seen and accepted for who she is while seeing the other as who she wants her to be—or as someone falling short of who she should be.

—Tannen, *You're Wearing That?*

intrusive invading one's privacy

daunting challenging

Which sentences contain facts? None

Which sentences contain opinions? all

Is the paragraph mostly fact or opinion? Explain your answer.

The paragraph expresses the author's opinion about relationships and specifically the

mother-daughter relationship.

3. (1) Obviously, if we are spending immense amounts of time and money in successfully teaching children to read but they in turn are choosing *not* to read, we can only conclude that something is wrong. (2) In concentrating exclusively on teaching the child *how* to read, we have forgotten to teach him to *want* to read. (3) There is the key: desire. (4) It is the prime mover, the magic ingredient. (5) There is no success story written today—whether in the arts, business, education, athletics—in which desire does not play the leading role. (6) Somehow we lost sight of the teaching **precept**: What you make a child love and desire is more important than what you make him learn.

—Trelease, *The Read-Aloud Handbook*

precept principle; rule

Which sentences contain facts? None

Which sentences contain opinions? All

Is the paragraph mostly fact or opinion? Explain your answer.

The author expresses his opinion regarding the importance of desire in the process of

learning to read.

4. (1) Personal liberty is perhaps the single most important characteristic of American democracy. (2) The Constitution itself was written to ensure life and liberty. (3) Over the years, however, our concepts of liberty have changed and evolved from freedom *from* to freedom *to*. (4) The Framers intended Americans to be free from governmental **infringements** on freedom of religion and speech, from unreasonable search and seizure, and so on. (5) The addition of the Fourteenth Amendment to the Constitution and its emphasis on equal protection of the laws and subsequent passage of laws guaranteeing civil rights, however, expanded Americans' concept of liberty to include demands for freedom to work or go to school free from discrimination. (6) Debates over how much the government should do to guarantee these rights or liberties illustrate the conflicts that continue to occur in our democratic system.

—O'Connor and Sabato, *American Government: Continuity and Change,* 2006 ed.

infringement violation; trespass

Which sentences contain facts? 4, 5, 6

Which sentences contain opinions? 1, 2, 3

Is the paragraph mostly fact or opinion? Explain your answer.

The paragraph moves from opinion to fact. In discussing changes in our concepts of liberty,

the authors generalize and make interpretations that go beyond the realm of fact (1–3). The

last sentence is a "soft" fact—debates show conflict.

5. (1) The *Iliad* is not only a prime example of early literature but also one of the treasures of human culture. (2) The **epic** poem is traditionally **attributed** to Homer, who may have lived in the ninth century B.C.E. (3) For a long time, classical scholarship tended to believe the poem was composed over several centuries and therefore could not be attributed to one poet. (4) Indeed, when it comes to ancient works, conclusively assigning authorship to a single individual is difficult, but as the traditional joke says, "If it wasn't by Homer, it may have been written by somebody else named Homer." (5) Nothing is definitively known about this poet except that, according to legend, he was blind. (6) More recent scholarship, in any case, suggests the poem is too unified *not* to have been the work of a single genius. (7) Like *Gilgamesh* before it, the numerous versions of the *Iliad* probably circulated for many years until a definitive form of the epic was **compiled** by one individual, perhaps a man named Homer.

—Janaro and Altshuler, *The Art of Being Human,* 8th ed.

epic long narrative
attribute regard as produced by

compile put together

Which sentences contain facts? <u>2, 3, 4, 5, 6</u>

Which sentences contain opinions? <u>1, 4, 7</u>

Is the paragraph mostly fact or opinion? Explain your answer.

<u>The paragraph mixes fact and opinion. Some of the factual statements are "soft" facts—</u>

<u>statements of what someone said or believed (which was their opinion).</u>

Active Reading Strategy: Evaluating Sources of Information

 Critical readers want to know that the information they read is reliable. When reading information, they ask the following questions:

- Is the source normally reliable?
- What is the original source of the information?
- How current (up to date) is the information?
- Can the information be verified in other sources?
- Is the information complete?
- Does the author have any reason to present inaccurate or incomplete information?

However, even critical readers do not usually go to the trouble of verifying an author's facts. You may regard the information you read as reliable if the *source* of the information is reliable. This means that the publisher or publication is trustworthy (for example, a textbook or government Web site). It also means that the author or authors have made a reasonable effort to verify their facts and are presenting the information without bias.

Let's consider the reading materials that commonly serve as sources of information.

Textbooks. When you are reading a textbook, you are likely to treat the information as reliable for a variety of reasons. Authors of textbooks are experts in their fields. Their purpose in writing the text is to convey a breadth of information about their discipline. They are supported by their publisher's staff in making every effort to ensure the accuracy of their information. The information in the text has probably been reviewed by other professors from the same discipline. Let's also note that in most cases the information in a textbook can easily be compared with information in other textbooks on the same subject.

This does not mean, of course, that all of the information in a textbook is completely accurate. With new studies and new information constantly forthcoming, no textbook can be completely up to date.

Trade Books. Trade books are books written for the general public (for example, a biography of a popular historical figure or a book about how to lose weight). They are sold for general readership in bookstores and can be found in public and college libraries. Most nonfiction trade books are reliable sources of information. They are usually carefully reviewed and edited before publication. However, many trade books are written to persuade or influence the reader, and critical readers will be cautious when assessing the author's purpose. If the author has a bias or wants to influence the reader's opinion or behavior, the information in the book may not be entirely reliable.

Newspapers. Newspapers provide current information on a daily or weekly basis. Traditional newspapers are usually reliable sources of information. The primary purpose of any major newspaper is to report the news as accurately as possible. News reporters have been trained to provide accurate information and to do so without bias. Other newspeople will likely be reporting on the same events, which will provide a check on the accuracy of the reported information.

This doesn't mean, however, that 100 percent of the information found in the newspaper is true. Journalists make mistakes—every paper routinely prints corrections for previous errors—and, occasionally, a journalist deliberately publishes false information (these occasions are rare and are discovered sooner or later by other journalists).

Critical readers should also recognize that there are some newspapers whose information cannot be trusted. They are referred to as *tabloids*, and include publications such as the *National Enquirer* and *Star Magazine*. These publications are often sold at supermarket checkout counters, boasting headlines such as "Elvis Alive and Well in Arkansas," or "Woman Marries Shark." Their purpose is not to report the news, but to satisfy readers' appetites for scandal and oddity. They are clearly not reliable sources of information.

Magazines and Journals. News magazines are comparable to newspapers in their reliability, and many other magazines may be reliable sources of information as well. However, some magazines are less concerned with the accuracy of their information than they are with making a sensational appeal to the reader. Professional journals, on the other hand, are highly reliable sources of information. The articles in these journals have been written by experts in their fields and are only accepted for publication after a careful examination by other experts.

The Internet. The Internet provides access to a seemingly infinite amount of information. Some of the information found on the Internet is reliable, and some of it is not. This is because anyone can publish information on the Internet without review or verification. For example, anyone can post information on Wikipedia, the popular online encyclopedia, without the immediate approval or checking of a single other person. Wikipedia relies on its readers to correct errors, which means that when inaccurate information is published on Wikipedia, it will remain there until someone realizes the information is wrong and corrects it.

The critical reader will therefore be especially careful when reading information on the Web. Before accepting information on the Web as reliable, ask yourself the following questions:

- Who created the Web site, and for what purpose?
- What information is provided on the Web site about the author? Is there reason to think that the author is knowledgeable about her subject and unbiased?
- What is the original source of the information?
- When was the Web site created? Is the information up to date?
- Can the information be verified by consulting other reliable sources?

It is also worth noting that your college library probably has a database of reliable online publications which may not be accessible through commonly used search engines like Google. Check with your college librarian to find out how you can access these databases.

EXERCISE 10.5 EVALUATING SOURCES OF INFORMATION

Directions: Write a critical reading question that you might ask (see the questions on p. 480) when reading information from each of the following sources.

1. A Wikipedia article on the origin of the marshmallow

Who contributed the information? Can the information be verified through other

sources? (sample answer)

2. Recommendations for saving files from a computer science textbook published in 1998

Is the information up to date? (sample answer)

3. An article in a tabloid newspaper on a recent sighting of a live dinosaur

Is the source normally reliable? Does the author have a reason to present inaccurate

information? Can the information be verified in other sources? (sample answer)

4. A magazine article on your current U.S. senator written by a member of the opposing party who is planning to run against him in the next election

   Is the information complete? Does the author have reason to present inaccurate

   or incomplete information? (sample answer)

5. Information about auto safety on the Web site of an automobile dealership

   Can the information be verified in other sources? Does the author have a reason to

   present inaccurate or incomplete information? (sample answer)

EXERCISE 10.6 EVALUATING SOURCES OF INFORMATION

Directions: Imagine you were trying to find reliable information on the following five topics. From the choices provided, select the most reliable source of information for each given topic. Then in the space provided, briefly explain your answer.

1. The effectiveness of Vitamin C in preventing colds

   _____ the Web site of a company that sells vitamins and other supplements

   __✔__ a health textbook published in 2009

   _____ an article from a 2005 issue of *Time* magazine

   Explain: The textbook is reasonably current and can normally be considered an

   objective source. (sample answer)

2. The voting record of your current congressman

   _____ the congressman's autobiography

   _____ an article about the congressman in your local newspaper

   __✔__ a government Web site that lists voting records

   Explain: Government records can normally be trusted for accurate information on

   voting records.

3. The amount of sleep required by children between the ages of 5 and 8

   __✔__ a recent research report on children's sleep published in a psychology journal

   _____ a psychology textbook published in 2003

   _____ a Wikipedia article on sleep

   Explain: Journal articles are evaluated before they are accepted for publication.

   A recent one would have more current information than a 2003 textbook. (sample

   answer)

4. The causes of the Vietnam war

_____✔_____ an American history textbook published in 2005

_____ a study of the war written by an American who opposed the war

_____ an interview with a general who served in the war published in 2008 in a popular magazine

Explain: __The war was controversial, and the textbook should be the most objective__

__of these sources. Ideas about the causes of the war haven't changed__

__much since 2005. (sample answer)__

5. The current elephant population in Africa and India (how many elephants there are)

_____✔_____ a 2010 *National Geographic* report on African and Indian elephants

_____ a 2007 biology textbook

_____ an undated Web site of an organization that advocates for animal rights

Explain: __*National Geographic* is an objective source, and the article is recent. The__

__Web site may have more current information but the date is uncertain and its__

__information may not be as reliable. (sample answer)__

Active Reading Strategy: Evaluating Arguments

Critical readers respond to opinion statements much differently from the way they respond to factual statements. Though we generally accept factual statements from reliable sources, critical readers never accept an author's opinion without first examining his argument. Instead, they analyze the argument and evaluate how well the author has supported his opinion.

When you hear the word *argument*, you perhaps think of a disagreement, a verbal dispute. However, the word *argument* also refers to an author's opinion and the reasons or reasoning that support the opinion. When we analyze an argument, in other words, we examine the support that an author provides for his opinion. As we have stated, critical readers do not reject an author's opinion simply because it is different from their own. They analyze the author's evidence and reasoning and evaluate how well the author has argued his position, taking the following considerations into account.

1. *What is the author's purpose?* When reading an argument, we know that the author's general purpose is to persuade. The critical reader also wants to know the author's specific purpose in writing his argument. What exactly is the author trying to persuade his audience to do or to think (buy a product, vote for a candidate, form an opinion about a controversial subject)? As you learned in Chapter 9, authors do not always come right out and state their purpose; we should now add that an author may state a purpose but also have other purposes beyond those stated—a "hidden agenda." Regardless of what the author declares, the active reader will want to make careful inferences about the author's specific purpose when reading opinion and argument.

2. *Who is the intended audience?* Authors often write for a general audience, meaning that they are writing for anyone and everyone who might read their material. However, authors sometimes write for a more limited group of readers. Advertisers, for example, target certain age groups (teenagers, seniors) or a particular gender (men or women). Similarly, writers of argument may also aim their arguments at specific groups of people.

3. *What is the author's bias?* A bias is a slant, leaning, or inclination that an individual has about an issue. We all have biases, though we may not always like to acknowledge them. Biases reflect our feelings and point-of-view about a given topic and can prevent us from being completely impartial when thinking, writing, or discussing the subject. Even authors who are attempting to be impartial may have at least some bias when writing about a controversial topic. For example, most articles you will find on gun control are at least slightly biased toward one side or the other—either in favor of more gun control or in favor of less gun control.

When evaluating an argument, then, it is important to identify the author's bias as well as your own. Sometimes the author's wording provides clues to bias. Words that have positive connotations (associations) indicate a favorable attitude toward the subject, whereas use of words with negative connotations indicates an unfavorable attitude toward the subject. For example, an author who describes gun control laws as *unpatriotic* is using a word with a negative connotation and thus revealing a negative attitude toward these laws.

4. *What evidence does the author provide?* Critical readers will examine the information or evidence an author uses to support his argument. Evidence is factual information that may include personal experience, examples and statistics. Critical readers evaluate whether the author has provided enough evidence to warrant his conclusions. They will ask if the evidence supports the conclusions in a logical manner. They will also ask if there is evidence the author hasn't mentioned that would contradict his conclusions. For example, an author who has lost a family member to gun violence might write an argument in favor of stricter gun control laws. But as tragic as the loss is, the author's personal loss by itself isn't sufficient evidence to conclude that gun control laws should be strengthened.

5. *Is the author's argument logical?* Critical readers carefully examine the author's reasoning. Is his reasoning logical? Do his conclusions logically follow from his evidence? Watch for *fallacies*, or faulty logic, as you read. For example, the statement that "guns don't kill people, people kill people" is an illogical argument against gun control, since no one would argue that guns kill without a human being operating them.

6. *Does the author use emotional appeals or propaganda techniques?* Writers will sometimes try to influence readers through an emotional appeal. They may appeal to the reader's sympathy or try to evoke other positive emotions. On the other hand, they may try to arouse negative emotions such as fear or anger. Although emotions are important, critical readers will recognize emotional appeals as such, and will evaluate the extent to which they contribute to the author's purpose and point. The writer who is sharing the loss of a loved one will certainly enlist the reader's sympathy but must also provide objective evidence to create a compelling argument in favor of stricter gun control laws.

Writers will sometimes also make use of propaganda techniques (see the box on p. 487). Propaganda is the spreading of ideas, information, or rumors to achieve a specific purpose (like selling a product). Propaganda techniques attempt to influence and manipulate the reader in order to serve the author's agenda. They are most effective when they go undetected. Propaganda techniques can be powerful because they can reach subconscious parts of the reader's mind. Name-calling is one example of a propaganda technique. When Republicans called Barack Obama a *socialist* during the last presidential campaign, they were using name-calling, hoping that, because most American voters have a negative connotation for the word *socialist*, they would not vote for Obama. Even though we know rationally that name-calling is not a valid form of argument, we may still be affected by its use.

Propaganda techniques are used frequently in advertising and political campaigns but can also be found in virtually any form of argumentative writing. The critical reader will identify these techniques and beware of their ability to influence his opinion. Propaganda techniques are suspicious forms of argument.

Let's read and analyze an example of argumentative writing. The following passage is from *Points of View*, a Web site that presents arguments on controversial issues.

MARIJUANA SHOULD BE LEGALIZED

Marijuana is a mild intoxicant, not unlike alcohol. Its use is no more dangerous or addictive than drinking beer, wine or liquor. Nonetheless, hundreds of thousands of Americans are arrested each year for possession of marijuana—rather than for its distribution or production—creating a vast population whose only crime was to imbibe a mildly intoxicating substance at their own risk. Further, possession of marijuana should be legalized as a means of combating illegal drug dealers for whom marijuana sales produce a set of prospective customers for more dangerous drugs, such as heroin or methamphetamines.

Consider that wine is served at official functions in the White House. Perhaps, the only debate about this intoxicating substance has been whether French wines or only American varieties should be served. No one doubts that drinking enough wine can lead to intoxication, that some people are prone to alcoholism, and that people who drink too much make dangerous drivers. Still, it is served at functions at 1600 Pennsylvania Avenue.

By keeping marijuana outside the law, the federal government passes up the opportunity to regulate the purity of the substance and to tax it, pushing hundreds of thousands of people into the underworld to obtain their unregulated supplies of a mild intoxicant.

Arguments against legalizing marijuana can usually be applied with equal validity to legal substances such as alcohol and tobacco: alcohol and tobacco can be addictive, can lead to financial or social problems when used in excess, and can lead to serious health problems. Would legalizing marijuana encourage its use by children, as is often alleged, any more than the widespread beer advertisements on television depict drinking alcohol as an integral part of adult life?

—Ford and Walter, "Marijuana Should Be Legalized," *EBSCO Host*

Common Propaganda Techniques

Name-calling.   *Name-calling* is the deliberate use of a negative term or label to create an unfavorable opinion of your opponent(s) and is frequently used in political campaigns. The technique is used to arouse fear of or prejudice against a person or group.
Example: Republicans calling Barack Obama a *socialist*

Bandwagon.   *Bandwagon* is the attempt to convince the audience to follow the crowd—to agree or join in because that's what everyone else is doing or thinking. Bandwagon appeals to the herd instinct and the desire to be on the winning side. Bandwagon also plays on the fear of loneliness—that you will be left out if you don't join in and do what everyone else is doing.
Example: A Burger King advertisement that says, "America loves burgers, and we're America's Burger King."

Assertions.   *Assertions* are emphatically stated opinions that are presented as facts. When an advertisement or politician uses assertion, the listener or reader is asked to accept the assertion without questioning or further explanation or reasoning.
Example: A CVS advertisement that says, "We're the best, we're the best, CVS!"

Glittering Generalities.   *Glittering generalities* are general statements that make use of words with positive connotations to form a general, positive association with the author's ideas or suggestions. They appeal to commonly held values. They are usually too vague to be proved or disproved.
Example: Obama's campaign slogan, "Change we can believe in"

Cardstacking.   Cardstacking is the presentation of only one side of an argument. When cardstacking is used, the author attempts to persuade his audience by presenting the information that is favorable to his argument and omitting any information unfavorable to his argument. Cardstacking can be found in almost any advertisement. Have you ever seen an ad that discusses the weaknesses of its product or the benefits of competing products?
Example: An article about gun control that only includes information to support one side

Testimonial.   A testimonial is the endorsement of a product or candidate by a popular or appealing person. Testimonials are usually done by famous people, but they are sometimes done by ordinary people with whom the audience may identify. Testimonials attempt to influence the audience by association. Advertisers who use testimonials believe that the audience is more likely to purchase a product if it is associated in their minds with someone they admire. Testimonials are, of course, common in advertisements, and are also used with increasing frequency in political campaigns.
Example: Michael Jordan appearing in an advertisement for Hanes underwear

Analysis:

What is the author's purpose?

The author's purpose is to convince the reader that marijuana should be legalized because it is comparable to and no more harmful than alcoholic beverages.

Who is the intended audience?

The passage is written for a general audience. However, it is aimed particularly at readers who are interested in considering both sides of the debate regarding legalization of marijuana (we can infer this because the article appears on a Web site that present both sides of controversial issues).

What is the author's bias?

The author is clearly in favor of legalizing marijuana. He believes that marijuana is comparable to alcoholic beverages and should be treated as they are.

What evidence does the author provide?

The author provides no hard evidence to support his position. He refers to the numbers of people arrested for marijuana possession, but this information does not directly support his argument. He describes some of the problems associated with alcohol use, but this information serves more as part of his logical argument than as direct evidence to support his position.

Is the author's argument logical?

Much of the author's argument is logical. We know that alcohol can be addictive and contributes to dangerous driving. If marijuana is no more addictive and harmful than alcohol, his argument is a logical one. Unfortunately, he fails to demonstrate that marijuana use does not carry greater risks than alcohol use, so the logic of his argument rests simply on his assertion that it is so.

Does the author use emotional appeals or propaganda?

The author's argument rests on his assertion that marijuana is "a mild intoxicant, not unlike alcohol," whose use is no more dangerous than alcohol use. He attempts to elicit sympathy for those arrested for marijuana possession. He asserts that legalizing marijuana would be a way of fighting illegal drug dealers but does not back up this assertion with any evidence.

EXERCISE **10.7** EVALUATING ARGUMENTS

Directions: Critically read each passage and answer the questions that follow. Use context clues, word structure clues, and the dictionary as well as the vocabulary notes provided to determine the meaning of unfamiliar words.

A. DANGEROUS DRIVING: WITH RISKS OBVIOUS, TIME TO GET SERIOUS ABOUT BAN ON CELL PHONES WHILE DRIVING

Few of us want to admit it, but the real solution to the dangers of talking on a cell phone while driving is to ban this multitasking.

Cell phone users have tried to explain how they can do it. They are careful. They use a hands-free device. And so on.

But by now, the danger is well documented.

The National Safety Council now is advocating states completely ban cell phone use while behind the wheel. And in the meantime, the council advises, businesses should ban employees from using their cell phones while driving on company business.

The group's executive director compares it to drunken driving: When talking on a cell phone, drivers are four times more likely to get in a car accident.

This is not a stretch to believe. We see how inattentive and reckless drivers are when they have a cell phone pressed to their ear—or are furiously texting on their phone while negotiating traffic.

And hands-free phone activity is just as risky, contends the safety council.

Nonetheless, it is a hard admission for many drivers, or they wouldn't be doing it. It was easier to admit that we all should be required to wear seat belts—though passing seat belt laws was a long effort.

But putting on a seat belt was a temporary nuisance and just took some getting into the habit. Not allowing ourselves to use the cell phone while behind the wheel seems a far tougher challenge to conquer.

Like seat belts and helmets for motorcyclists, it is the right thing to do. It is even more important than those, in fact, because a reckless driver on a cell phone affects not just himself but endangers other drivers.

Six states now limit cell phone use to hands-free devices while driving. None bans driving and talking altogether.

It is time. Kansas legislators, while they are discussing restrictions to protect teen drivers, should begin a debate about a cell phone ban for all drivers.

We all need protection—from ourselves.

—*The Hutchinson News*

1. What is the author's purpose?

To argue for a ban on cell phones while driving

2. Who is the intended audience?

Kansas citizens and legislators (sample answer)

3. What is the author's bias?

The author favors a complete ban on cell phone use while driving. He feels people

don't want to admit the risk. (sample answer)

4. What evidence does the author provide to support his conclusions?

The author refers to a National Safety Council report advocating the ban. He points

out how inattentive drivers are when using cell phones. He states that drivers are four times more likely to have an accident while talking on a cell phone. He states

that six states have limited cell phone use to hands-free devices. No hard data is

offered. (sample answer)

5. Is the author's argument logical? Why or why not?

Answers will vary. The author compares the cell phone ban with the seat belt law.

6. Does the author use emotional appeals or propaganda techniques? If so, to which emotions does the author appeal? Which propaganda techniques does he use?

The author appeals to fear (pointing out danger) and conscience (admitting to the

truth, "right thing to do," endangering others). "It is the right thing to do" is an assertion.

7. Do you agree with the author that cell phone use while driving should be banned? Why or why not?

Answers will vary.

B. SUPPLEMENTS NEED REGULATION TO KEEP KIDS SAFE FROM STEROIDS

America should get its head out of the sand and face up to the growing use of steroids and questionable dietary supplements by adolescents.

The sports-supplement business, now a $20-billion-a-year industry, continues to grow by leaps and bounds with next to no controls. Teenagers who want to enhance their athletic ability or their body image can buy the latest new muscle-building compounds at their local drugstore or on the Internet, even though neither they nor their parents know much about the active ingredients. These substances—neither food nor drug under the law—carry less **stringent** labeling requirements.

That's just one thing that has to change.

It isn't only the Yankees' Alex Rodriguez or the Dodgers' Manny Ramirez who look for an edge with performance-enhancing drugs. In **credible** studies, 12 percent of boys and 8 percent of girls have reported using steroids or dietary supplements on a weekly basis. The Centers for Disease Control and Prevention has documented that steroid use among high school athletes has more than doubled in the past two decades. And that may not include those who use them **inadvertently** with dietary supplements, some of which now appear to include them.

In this week's issue of *Sports Illustrated,* David Epstein and George Dohrmann report on a study that found 25 percent of the 58 sports supplements tested contained steroids or stimulants that had been banned by the World Anti-Doping Agency. Of particular concern are weight-loss aids and workout boosters.

Don't blame the Food and Drug Administration. Congress passed legislation in 1994 that essentially allows the supplement industry to regulate itself, with predictable results.

stringent strict
credible reliable; believable

inadvertently unintentionally

Supplements don't have to be approved by the FDA. The agency only has the authority to remove them from drugstores if they're proved to be dangerous—but with such loose controls over the ingredients, it's nearly impossible to track which items might be routinely causing harm.

President Barack Obama has talked about the need to revamp the FDA. That should include giving it more authority to regulate the supplement industry. In the meantime, there are three steps Congress should take to have an immediate positive impact. Manufacturers of sports and dietary supplements should be required to:

- List the active ingredients and the country of origin for all of their products. (Many of the ingredients now come from Asia.)

- Report incidents that indicate a problem with a product to the FDA within two weeks.

- Take the advice of the American Medical Association and give risky supplements, especially those targeting young users, the same scrutiny as prescription drugs. Supplements that don't face that scrutiny should be prohibited from sale to minors.

Some supplement providers offer products that are beneficial to consumers. But overall, manufacturers are bombarding Americans of all ages with pitches for dubious products. It's past time for America to muscle up and stop getting pushed around by the supplement industry.

—San Jose Mercury News

1. What is the author's purpose?

To argue for the regulation of the use of supplements, especially those containing

steroids.

2. Who is the intended audience?

The article is intended for a general audience and is especially aimed at parents

and others who are concerned about adolescents. (sample answer)

3. What is the author's bias?

The author is anti-supplement and pro-regulation. (sample answer)

4. What evidence does the author provide to support his conclusions?

He cites studies showing the percentage of boys and girls using supplements. He

cites CDCP documentation of increased steroid use. He cites an SI report finding

banned steroids or stimulants in sports supplements.

5. Is the author's argument logical? Why or why not?

Answers will vary. The author documents the use of steroids and supplements but

presumes that the solution lies in regulation. His recommendations move from

general to specific to general, without much direct support. He lumps all supplements

together.

6. Does the author use emotional appeals or propaganda techniques? If so, to which emotions does the author appeal? Which propaganda techniques does he use?

The author appeals to fear and concern for teenagers using supplements. He

presents the supplement industry as a bully. He starts with an assertion ("America

should get its head out of the sand"). He uses cardstacking—except for one general

sentence, he presents only one side of the issue. (sample answer)

7. Do you agree with the author that supplement use needs to be more strictly regulated? Why or why not?

Answers will vary.

C. SECURING SATISFACTION

Customer satisfaction is a well-established value in most companies, but what about employee satisfaction? One of the best ways for a company to engage its employees, gain their commitment, and improve their job satisfaction is to give them a voice. BBVA, Spain's second-largest bank, accomplishes this by including employees in the performance evaluation process. Not only is one's own self-evaluation considered, but co-workers also answer 35–64 questions about each employee's performance. Infosys Technologies in Bangalore, India, started a Voice of Youth program, which gives top-performing twenty-somethings a seat on its management council. At Ritz-Carlton hotels across the world, after every employee hears a daily "wow story" of someone in the company who went to customer service extremes, managers then open the floor for employees to discuss issues from what cleaner the housekeeping staff prefers to their own stories about guest experiences. By approaching employees as internal customers who deserve the same level of service, these companies are likely to create a level of commitment and devotion in their employees that will keep them—and the customers they serve—satisfied.

—Ebert and Griffin, *Business Essentials,* 7th ed.

Many companies solicit direct feedback from employees through surveys, performance evaluations, or company meetings in which employees have the opportunity to voice their problems and opinions on a regular basis.

1. What is the authors' purpose?

To argue for companies to give their employees a voice—to seek "employee

satisfaction" (sample answer)

2. Who is the intended audience?

Business owners and executives, and business students (sample answer)

3. What is the authors' bias?

The authors are pro-employee. (sample answer)

4. What evidence do the authors provide to support their conclusions?

The authors cite three examples: a bank in Spain (includes employees in the

performance evaluation process); an Indian company (gives seats on its management

council to top-performing twenty-somethings); Ritz-Carlton (employees share stories

and experiences).

5. Is the authors' argument logical? Why or why not?

Answers will vary. The argument is appealing, but the examples don't constitute "proof"

of anything.

6. Do the authors use emotional appeals or propaganda techniques? If so, to which emotions do the authors appeal? Which propaganda techniques do they use?

The authors appeal to sympathy or concern for employees. The second sentence is

an assertion. The use of the examples is a bit of bandwagon and also cardstacking.

7. Should companies be as concerned with employee satisfaction as they are with customer satisfaction? Why or why not?

Answers will vary.

8. Why might businesses not want to give their employees more of a voice?

Answers will vary.

EXERCISE 10.8 EVALUATING BOTH SIDES OF AN ARGUMENT

Directions: In this exercise you will read two opposing views on the question "Should the minimum drinking age be lowered?" Critically read each passage and answer the questions that follow. Use context clues, word structure clues, and the dictionary as well as the vocabulary notes provided to determine the meaning of unfamiliar words.

A. THE MINIMUM DRINKING AGE SHOULD BE LOWERED

Old Enough for War, Old Enough for Alcohol

For better or worse, American society has determined that upon turning 18 teenagers be- come adults. This means they can enlist [in the military], serve, fight and potentially die for their country. And while the "fight for your country" argument is a powerful one, it only begins to capture the essence of adulthood. Most importantly, at age 18 you become legally responsible for your actions. You can buy and smoke cigarettes even though you know that, in time, they will probably give you lung cancer. You may even purchase property, strike binding legal contracts, take out a loan, vote, hold office, serve on a jury, or adopt a child. But strangely at 18, one cannot buy a beer. While that may be an injustice to those choosing to serve their country, the more serious consequence is the postponement of legal **culpability**. In most other countries, the age of **majority** coincides with the legal drinking or purchasing age.

Critics are quick to point out that 18 is not an age of majority, but one step amongst many that together mark the gradual path to adulthood. This argument notes that young adults cannot drink until 21, rent cars until 25, run for the U.S. Senate until they are 30, and run for President until 35. This is, the critics suggest, evidence of a graduated legal adulthood. But this argument falls flat. First, rental car companies are not legally prevented from renting cars to those under 25; this is a decision made by insurance companies. In fact, some rental companies do rent to those under 25, and the associated higher rates compensate for that potential **liability**. Second, age requirements for these high public offices are more appropriately seen as exceptions to full adulthood, rather than **benchmarks** of adulthood. Finally, and most importantly, the Constitution speaks to the legal age of majority only once and that is in the 26th Amendment to the Constitution where, "The right of citizens of the US, who are 18 years of age or older, to vote shall not be denied or abridged . . . on account of age." . . .

—Watkins, *Teens at Risk*

culpability responsibility
majority legal age of adulthood

liability obligation to pay for damages
benchmark standard; reference point

1. What is the author's purpose?

To argue that the drinking age should be lowered to 18

2. Who is the intended audience?

A general audience; all voters; politicians (sample answers)

3. What is the author's bias?

The author favors a lower drinking age (sample answer)

4. What evidence does the author provide to support her conclusions?

She points to military service at 18. She reminds the reader that you can vote, enter

legal contracts, purchase property and buy cigarettes at age 18. She says that

in other countries the drinking age is the same as the age of majority.

She cites the Constitution's reference to voting age.

5. Is the author's argument logical? Why or why not?

Answers will vary. The author effectively lists the many things you can do at age 18.

But do these logically imply that you should also be able to drink at that age? She

also attempts to refute some counterarguments.

6. Does the author use emotional appeals or propaganda techniques? If so, to which emotions does the author appeal? Which propaganda techniques does she use?

The argument that you can die for your country at age 18 carries some emotional

appeal. Her reference to other countries is a bandwagon technique. The first sentence

is an assertion.

7. Before you read the passage, what was your opinion regarding the legal drinking age?

Answers will vary.

B. KEEP THE DRINKING AGE AT 21

A group of 120 college presidents is pushing to lower the drinking age to 18, in an effort to curb binge drinking on campus. They've got an impressive name, the Amethyst Initiative, named after the ancient Greek words that mean "not intoxicated."

These college leaders hope that a lower drinking age will encourage more responsible drinking. They also think it will cut the excessive, **furtive**, forbidden thrill of drinking—"pregaming," in kidspeak—before a frat party or other public appearance. But we think these top academics forgot their Econ 101. Legalizing something generally invites more indulgence, not less.

Yes, binge drinking is widespread, entrenched and **pernicious**. And that is surely frustrating for college officials. But their strategy reeks of surrender.

Kids under age 21 don't drink because it's illegal. And they won't stop drinking if it is legal. Another problem with lowering the drinking age: Surveys—and experience—suggest that making alcohol abundant and available to 18-year-olds also opens the spigot wider for 17- and 16-year-olds and even younger teens.

The current age threshold doesn't stop many underage college students from drinking, but there's evidence that the higher drinking age

has curbed some binge drinking. In 1984, when Congress effectively **mandated** the 21-year-old age limit, 45.4 percent of college students engaged in binge drinking, which is defined as five or more drinks in a row at any point in a two-week period. That's according to Monitoring the Future, which conducts an annual national survey of drug and alcohol use by young people. By 2006, that figure was 40.2 percent. Meanwhile, the percentage of students who reported drinking every day fell by more than a quarter.

Statistics on the effects of the higher drinking age on driving fatalities are even more dramatic. As legal drinking ages have gone up, the number of young people ages 16 to 20 killed in alcohol-related crashes has plummeted by nearly 60 percent—from 5,224 in 1982 to 2,121 in 2006. This even as the number of young people killed in non-alcohol-related crashes has increased by 34 percent.

Some of that drop is **attributed** to other factors, including safer cars and increasing seat belt usage and greater awareness of the perils of drinking and driving. But the trends are known and predictable: When states lowered their drinking ages in the 1970s, alcohol-related crashes involving teens rose. Do the math. Does anyone doubt that putting alcohol in legal reach of

furtive secretive; sneaky
pernicious very harmful

mandate command; require
attribute assign; explain

18-year-olds wouldn't instantly result in more accidents and drunken driving deaths?

The argument most often trotted out to defend this proposal is fairness: If an 18-year-old is old enough to fight in a war, he or she should also enjoy the right to drink. That sounds like a compelling **rationale**. Except it's wrong. Society confers different rights and responsibilities at different ages—in many places, even a 24-year-old can't rent a car, for instance. The right to join the military and fight at 18 doesn't automatically qualify you for every other right and privilege of adulthood, particularly if experience and statistics show that it's a bad idea.

Those college presidents are right to be alarmed about underage drinking on campus. But we'd rather see them pouring their energies into making sure that authorities enforce local laws against serving or selling to minors. And making sure that residence hall advisers are riding herd, not looking the other way. And pioneering new campaigns to convince college kids that they risk their health, and their lives, with heavy drinking.

Lowering the drinking age would transfer responsibility—and in some cases legal liability—from colleges and their presidents to the immature shoulders of 18-year-olds.

That would be **lethal** and unwise.

—*Chicago Tribune*

rationale reason; argument	**lethal** deadly

1. What is the author's purpose?

   To argue that the drinking age should be kept at 21

2. Who is the intended audience?

   General audience and college leaders (sample answer)

3. What is the author's bias?

   The author is against lowering the drinking age and favors stricter enforcement
   of drinking laws.

4. What evidence does the author provide to support his conclusions?

   He refers to surveys that suggest that making alcohol available to 18-year-olds
   encourages younger people to drink; he cites data showing a reduction in binge
   drinking when the age 21 limit was mandated, as well as data on reduced
   driving fatalities at that time.

5. Is the author's argument logical? Why or why not?

   Answers will vary. Some of the author's data seems convincing. However, he
   himself admits that other factors contributed to the reduction in driving fatalities.

6. Does the author use emotional appeals or propaganda techniques? If so, to which emotions does the author appeal? Which propaganda techniques does he use?

   There is a fear factor in the author's argument (see last line) and a bit of chastising

   in his reference to surrender. The question at the end of paragraph 7 has a

   bandwagon element.

7. Compare the two arguments in Passage A and Passage B. Which author best justifies his/her opinion? Explain your answer.

   Answers will vary.

8. Having read and evaluated both sides of the argument, what is your opinion? Should the drinking age be lowered? Explain your answer.

   Answers will vary.

EXERCISE 10.9 CRITICAL READING: ADVERTISEMENT

Directions: Study the following advertisement and answer the questions that follow.

1. What is the purpose of the advertisement?

   To sell Burberry clothing

2. Who is the intended audience?

   adolescents and young adults (sample answer)

3. Does the ad contain any factual information? If so, what is it?

No, other than the company name. (sample answer)

4. To what emotions does the ad appeal? Explain your answer.

The desire to be attractive; the desire to be "cool" and in fashion while maybe a

little offbeat, with a little attitude. (sample answer)

5. What propaganda techniques does the ad use? Explain how the ad uses them.

Bandwagon, testimonial (implied by the picture, with Emma Watson modeling

Burberry fashions)—the ad implies that you will be more attractive, part of the hip

crowd—maybe even a celebrity—if you buy Burberry clothes/outerwear. (sample

answer).

6. In your opinion, is the ad effective? Why or why not?

Answers will vary.

EXERCISE 10.10 CRITICAL READING

Directions: Use the critical reading strategies you have learned in this chapter to read and analyze each passage. Then answers the questions that follow. Use context clues, word structure clues, and the dictionary as well as the vocabulary notes provided to determine the meaning of unfamiliar words.

A. COMMUNITY COLLEGES: CHALLENGES OLD AND NEW

I attended a junior college in Oakland, California. From there, with fresh diploma in hand, I transferred to a senior college—a college in Ft. Wayne, Indiana, that had no freshmen or sophomores.

I didn't realize that my experimental college matched the vision of some of the founders of the community college movement. In the early 1900s, they foresaw a system of local colleges that would be accessible to the average high school graduate—a system so extensive that it would be unnecessary for universities to offer courses at the freshman and sophomore levels.

A group with an equally strong opinion questioned whether preparing high school graduates for entry to four-year colleges and universities should be the goal of junior colleges. They insisted that the purpose of junior colleges should be vocational preparation, to equip people for the job market as electricians and other technicians. In some regions, where the **proponents** of transfer dominated, the admissions requirements for junior colleges were higher than those of Yale. This debate was

| **proponent** supporter; one in favor of |

Community colleges have opened higher education to millions of students who would not otherwise have access to college because of cost or distance.

never won by either side, and you can still hear its echoes today.

The name *junior* college also became a problem. Some felt that the word *junior* made their institution sound as though it weren't quite a real college. A struggle to change the name ensued, and several decades ago *community* college won out.

The name change didn't settle the debate about whether the purpose was preparing students to transfer to universities or training them for jobs, however. Community colleges continue to serve this dual purpose.

Community colleges have become such an essential part of the U.S. educational system that about two of every five of all undergraduates in the United States are enrolled in them. Most

students are *nontraditional* students: Many are age 25 or older, are from the working class, have jobs, and attend college part time.

To help their students transfer to four-year colleges and universities, many community colleges work closely with top-tier public and private universities. Some provide admissions guidance on how to enter **flagship** state schools. Others coordinate courses, making sure that they match the university's title and numbering system, as well as its **rigor** of instruction and grading. More than a third offer honors programs that prepare talented students to transfer with ease into these schools.

The challenges that community colleges face are the usual ones of securing adequate budgets in the face of declining resources, continuing an open-door policy, meeting changing job markets, and maintaining quality instruction. New challenges include meeting the shifting needs of students, such as the growing need to teach students for whom English is a second language and to provide on-campus day care for parents.

—Henslin, *Sociology: A Down-to-Earth Approach,* 9th ed.

flagship	the largest or best in a group or system
rigor	difficulty; strictness of standards

1. Does the passage consist mostly of fact or opinion? Explain your answer.

The passage is primarily factual. It begins with the author's personal experiences

and goes on to provide information about community colleges and what they do.

(sample answer)

2. Is the information in the passage reliable? Why or why not?

Answers will vary. There is very little data in the passage and much of the information

is couched in general terms. Mostly the information is not controversial and the source

seems reliable.

3. What is the author's primary purpose?

To discuss the role and challenges of community colleges (sample answer)

4. Does the author have a bias toward his subject? If so, what is it?

The author is sympathetic to his subject (community colleges) but does not

seem to favor either side in the transfer vs. vocational debate. (sample answer)

5. According to the author, what are the two purposes that community colleges serve?

Preparing students to transfer and training them for a specific career

6. What is the author's opinion of community colleges? How well does he support his opinion?

The author believes that community colleges serve an essential purpose in the

U.S. educational system. (sample answer)

Answers will vary. The author presents a lot of information about what community

colleges do but not much about how successful they are.

7. In your opinion, should the primary goal of community colleges be to prepare students for jobs or prepare them to transfer to four-year schools? Explain your answer.

Answers will vary.

B. PERCEPTIONS AND THE REALITY OF CRIME

We've all heard the statistics. By the time a teenager turns eighteen, he or she has witnessed 40,000 dramatized murders and 200,000 other acts of violence on television and in the movies. So what difference does it make?

Public concern about exposure to violence, even if fictionalized, has resulted in the addition of ratings for movies, video games, and even television shows over the years. But these ratings have not had the desired result, because movies, games, and television programs with violent content often do rather well in attracting their target audience: young people. And the number of these programs has increased in recent years, despite the negative attention.

A federal study documented a number of **unsavory** practices, such as showing previews

| **unsavory** objectionable; morally unfit |

for R-rated films to audiences waiting to see a PG-rated movie. Young shoppers and viewers were easily able to buy M-rated video games, gain entrance into R-rated films, and purchase CDs labeled with parental advisories. Efforts to pressure the entertainment industry to limit their marketing campaigns and placement of ads in magazines and programs aimed at younger audiences have had only modest success.[a]

What is the evidence to show that these practices negatively impact children? **Anecdotal** evidence suggests that some school shootings in recent years and other senseless acts of violence have been committed by young people who were **enthralled** by violent entertainment and who idolized unsavory characters in movies, often obtaining the same weapons their "heroes" used.[b] Scientific studies attempt to measure exposure to violence and its effects on behavior in a more systematic way. In general they have found that exposure to violence has an impact on people, but its extent is not clear or uniform. For example, studies have found that the more television a viewer watches the more likely he or she is to believe that murder rates are higher than they really are; studies have also shown that greater exposure to **depictions** of violence often leads to more aggressive behavior and **desensitization** to violence among young people.[c] It appears that some people are more **susceptible** to media portrayals of violence than are others, and this is likely the result of individual differences, the mix between *actual* violence in the lives of young persons (at home, in school, in the community), and the presence of nonviolent role models in their lives.

Notes

a. Federal Trade Commission, *Marketing Violent Entertainment to Children: A Report to Congress* (Washington, DC: Federal Trade Commission, 2002).

b. Betsey Streisand, "Lawyers, Guns, Money: Hollywood under New Probe May Have a Lot to Hide," *U.S. News & World Report* (June 14, 1999).

c. Donald L. Diefenba and Mark D. West, "Violent Crime and Poisson Regression: A Measure and a Method for Cultivation Analysis," *Journal of Broadcasting & Electronic Media* (summer 2001); American Academy of Pediatrics, "Media Violence," *Pediatrics* (November 2001).

—Albanese, *Criminal Justice*, 4th ed.

---

anecdotal based on individual accounts
enthralled captivated; fascinated

depiction showing
desensitization becoming less sensitive
susceptible easily influenced

---

1. Does the passage consist mostly of fact or opinion? Explain your answer.

The passage is primarily factual. The author begins with statistics about exposure

to TV violence and later refers to studies and anecdotal evidence. (sample answer)

2. Is the information in the passage reliable? Why or why not?

Answers will vary. The author provides the source notes for his references and

they are reliable sources.

3. What is the author's primary purpose?

To explore the relationship between media and violence and present information

from various studies about their relationship (sample answer)

4. Does the author have a bias toward his subject? If so, what is it?

   Answers will vary. The author seems to be seeking an objective voice. He does seem

   skeptical about the value/success of interventions. He is also critical of some movie

   marketing techniques.

5. According to the author, why have efforts to screen young people from media violence been unsuccessful?

   He says that violent movies, games, and TV shows attract young people. Also, the

   rating rules are not well enforced. The entertainment industry has not been

   very cooperative. (sample answer)

6. What evidence does the passage contain that supports the idea that exposure to violence in the media is harmful to children and teenagers?

   Anecdotal evidence connects school shootings with media violence. Scientific

   studies show that exposure to violence has an impact on people. Exposure to

   media violence desensitizes young people to violence. (sample answer).

7. Is the information in the passage sufficient to convince you that more should be done to protect young people from viewing violence in the media? Do you believe that watching media portrayals of violence can affect the viewer's behavior? Why or why not?

   Answers will vary.

SKILLS ONLINE: CRITICAL READING

 Directions:

1. Choose a controversial issue that is of interest to you. You may choose an issue that you have read about in this chapter or any other issue that is currently under public debate. (Suggestion: if you are not sure what issue you'd like to work with, go to *www.ProCon.org* for a list of current issues.)

2. Find one online article that argues for one side of the issue and one online article that argues for the other side of the issue. For each article, answer the following questions:
   a. What is the author's purpose?
   b. Who is the intended audience?
   c. What is the author's bias?
   d. What evidence does the author provide to support his position on the issue?
   e. Is the author's argument logical?
   f. Does the author use emotional appeals or propaganda?

3. Identify which article you think presented a more effective argument and explain why.

4. Based on the work you've done in steps 1 through 3, write a paragraph explaining your current opinion about the issue.

5. Print copies of all the Web pages you used and turn them in along with your answers to the preceding questions.

READING 10A

VIOLENT VIDEO GAMES PUT TEENS AT RISK (SOCIOLOGY)

by Kristin Kalning

Reading 10A is taken from a book entitled *Teens at Risk*. In this article, the author discusses a study in which brain scans were administered to teenagers who had just played video games, comparing those who had played games with violent content with those who had played games without violent content. Read the article to learn about the study and to find out what conclusions the author draws from it.

Pre-Reading Exercise

Directions: Complete this exercise before reading the passage. Preview the passage and answer the following questions.

1. What is the passage about?

   The passage is about the effect of violent video games on teenagers.

2. What do you think will be discussed in the first major section (under the heading "Brains Are Scanned")?

   Brain scan evidence of the effects of violent video games

3. What do you think will be discussed in the second major section (under the heading "Parents Should Be Aware of the Study Results")?

   Concerns parents should/might have regarding the effects of violent video games

4. What information is provided in the boxed figure (labeled "Brain Scan Results")?

   The figure compares the brain scans of adolescents who played violent video games with

   those who played nonviolent video games.

5. What experience do you have with video games? What have you previously read or learned about video games?

   Answers will vary.

6. Write three questions about video games.

   Answers will vary.

   _____

   _____

   Directions: Use the critical reading strategies you have learned in this chapter to read and analyze the passage. Use context, the dictionary, and word structure clues to determine the meanings of unfamiliar words.

Violent Video Games Put Teens at Risk

1   Can video games make kids more violent? A new study employing state-of-the-art brain-scanning technology says that the answer may be yes.

2   Researchers at the Indiana University School of Medicine say that brain scans of kids who played a violent video game showed an increase in emotional arousal—and a corresponding decrease of activity in brain areas involved in self-control, inhibition and attention.

3   Does this mean that your teenager will feel an uncontrollable urge to go on a shooting rampage after playing "Call of Duty"?

Brains Are Scanned

4   Vince Mathews, the principal investigator on the study, hesitates to make that leap. But he says he does think that the study should encourage parents to look more closely at the types of games their kids are playing.

5   "Based on our results, I think parents should be aware of the relationship between violent video-game playing and brain function."

6   Mathews and his colleagues chose two action games to include in their research—one violent the other not.

7   The first game was the high-octane but non-violent racing game "Need for Speed: Underground." The other was the ultra-violent first-person shooter "Medal of Honor: Frontline."

8   The team divided a group of 44 adolescents into two groups, and randomly assigned the kids to play one of the two games. Immediately after the play sessions, the children were given MRIs [magnetic resonance imaging scans] of their brains.

9   The scans showed a negative effect on the brains of the teens who played "Medal of Honor" for 30 minutes. That same effect was not present in the kids who played "Need for Speed."

10   The only difference? Violent content.

11   What's not clear is whether the activity picked up by the MRIs indicates a lingering—or worse, permanent—effect on the kids' brains.

12   And it's also not known what effect longer play times might have. The scope of this study was 30 minutes of play and one brain scan per kid, although further research is in the works.

13   OK. But what about violent TV shows? Or violent films? Has anyone ever done a brain scan of kids that have just watched a violent movie?

14   Someone has. John P. Murray, a psychology professor at Kansas State University, conducted a very similar experiment, employing the same technology used in Mathews' study. His findings are similar.

15   Kids in his study experienced increased emotional arousal when watching short clips from the boxing movie "Rocky IV."

Parents Should Be Aware of the Study Results

16   So, why is everyone picking on video games? Probably because there's a much smaller body of research on video games. They just haven't been around as long as TV and movies, so the potential effects on children are a bigger unknown. That's a scary thing for a parent.

17   Larry Ley, the director and coordinator of research for the Center for Successful Parenting,

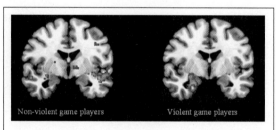

Non-violent game players   Violent game players

In a recent research study, adolescents played two different types of video games for 30 minutes. Teens that played the violent game (right) showed increased activity in the amygdala, which is involved in emotional arousal.

Radiological Society of North America

which funded Mathews' study, says the purpose of the research was to help parents make informed decisions.

18   "There's enough data that clearly indicates that [game violence] is a problem," he says. "And it's not just a problem for kids with behavior disorders."

19   But not everyone is convinced that this latest research adds much to the debate—particularly the game development community. One such naysayer is Doug Lowenstein, president of the Entertainment Software Association [ESA].

20   "We've seen other studies in this field that have made dramatic claims but turn out to be less persuasive when objectively analyzed."

21   The ESA has a whole section of its Web site dedicated to the topic of video game violence, which would suggest that they get asked about it—a lot.

22   And they've got plenty of answers at the ready for the critics who want to lay school shootings or teen aggression at the feet of the game industry. Several studies cited by the ESA point to games' potential benefits for developing decision-making skills or bettering reaction times.

23   Ley, however, argues such studies aren't credible because they were produced by "hired guns" funded by the multi-billion-dollar game industry.

24   "We're not trying to sell [parents] anything," he says. "We don't have a product. The video game industry does."

25   Increasingly parents are more accepting of video game violence, chalking it up to being a part of growing up.

26   "I was dead-set against violent video games," says Kelley Windfield, a Sammamish, Wa.–based mother of two. "But my husband told me I had to start loosening up."

27   Laura Best, a mother of three from Clovis, Calif., says she looks for age-appropriate games for her 14-year-old son, Kyle. And although he doesn't play a lot of games, he does tend to gravitate towards shooters like "Medal of Honor." But she isn't concerned that Kyle will become aggressive as a result.

28   "That's like saying a soccer game or a football game will make a kid more aggressive," she says. "It's about self-control, and you've got to learn it."

29   Ley says he believes further research, for which the Center for Successful Parenting is trying to arrange, will prove a cause-and-effect relationship between game violence and off-screen aggression.

30   But for now, he says, the study released last week [on November 29, 2006] gives his organization the ammunition it needs to prove that parents need to be more aware of how kids are using their free time.

31   "Let's quit using various Xboxes as baby-sitters instead of doing healthful activities," says Ley, citing the growing epidemic of childhood obesity in the United States.

32   And who, really, can argue with that?

—Kalning, "Violent Video Games Put Teens at Risk," *Teens at Risk*

You, the Reader

Interest Rating. Please rate the interest level of the reading on the following scale (circle one):

5—Very interesting   2—A little boring

4—Fairly interesting   1—Very boring

3—Mildly interesting

Difficulty Rating. Please rate the difficulty level of the reading on the following scale (circle one):

5—Very difficult   2—Fairly easy

4—Fairly difficult   1—Very easy

3—Moderate

Comments: Please explain your ratings and make any other comments you wish about the reading.

Answers will vary.

CRITICAL READING EXERCISE

1. What is the author's purpose?

   The author wants to show that violent video games can make kids more aggressive

   and to encourage parents to limit or eliminate their use. (sample answer)

2. Who is the intended audience?

   Parents; anyone concerned about children and teenagers. (sample answer)

3. What is the author's bias?

   The author is against violent video games. (sample answer)

4. What evidence does the author provide to support her point of view?

   The author cites an Indiana University study that found differences in brain scans

   of kids who played violent video games and those playing nonviolent games. She

   also cites a similar study from Kansas State University with violent film watching.

5. Is the author's argument logical? Why or why not?

   Answers will vary. The author is cautious in her interpretation of the study results.

   She does acknowledge counterarguments.

6. Does the author use emotional appeals or propaganda? If so, to which emotions does she appeal? Which propaganda techniques does she use?

The author is appealing to parents' concerns for their children's welfare and safety.

There are no testimonials, but she does quote parents and relies on Larry Ley as an

expert. The question at the end is a kind of assertion. (sample answer)

7. Do you agree with the statement that violent video games put teens at risk? Why or why not?

Answers will vary.

COMPREHENSION QUESTIONS

Directions: For questions 1–5, choose the answer that best completes the statement. For questions 6–10, write your response in the space provided. Base all answers on what you read in the selection. Refer back to the selection as necessary to answer the questions.

___b___ **1.** The study conducted by researchers at the Indiana University School of Medicine determined that:
   a. Video games do not affect the human brain.
   b. The brains of teenagers who played violent video games showed increased emotional arousal and decreased self-control.
   c. The brains of teenagers who played violent video games showed decreased emotional arousal and increased self-control.
   d. The brains of teenagers who played nonviolent video games showed an effect similar to the brains of teenagers who played violent games.

___d___ **2.** The Indiana University study did *not* determine:
   a. The long term effects of playing violent video games.
   b. The effects of longer playing times.
   c. The effects of playing a nonviolent game.
   d. Both a and b.

___b___ **3.** The reader can infer that "Call of Duty" is:
   a. A nonviolent video game.
   b. A violent video game.
   c. A violent movie.
   d. The most popular video game.

_d_

4. We can tell from the information in the "Brain Scan Results" box on p. 504 that:
   a. There are no differences in the brain scans of children who play violent video games and children who play nonviolent video games.
   b. There are no differences in the brain scans of children who play video games and children who don't play video games.
   c. Children who play violent video games show increased arousal in several sections of the brain.
   d. The amygdala is a part of the brain that is associated with emotional arousal.

_d_

5. Larry Ley advises parents to:
   a. Let their children decide for themselves which video games to play.
   b. Only let children play violent games as a reward for good behavior.
   c. Observe their children after they play violent video games to see if they are affected by them.
   d. Encourage their children to choose activities that are healthier than video games.

6. What were the results of John Murray's study of kids who watched violent movies?

The kids experienced increased emotional arousal when watching short clips

from _Rocky IV._

7. According to the studies cited by the ESA, what are some of the benefits of playing video games?

The ESA studies claim that playing games can contribute to better

decision-making skills and improved reaction times.

8. According to Larry Ley, why aren't the ESA's studies showing video games' benefits credible?

He claims they're biased; that they were produced by "hired guns." He says

the video game industry is selling a product and wants to use these studies

to support their aim.

9. What is the attitude toward violent video games of the parents quoted in this article?

One parent was against the games but was convinced by her husband to

accept them. Another parent wasn't concerned about her son playing violent

games; she felt children have to learn self-control for themselves.

10. In your opinion, is the Indiana University research on violent video games reliable? Why or why not?

Answers will vary.

VOCABULARY EXERCISES

Pronunciation Guide (see p. 90 for list of phonetic symbols)

epidemic	(ĕp'ĭ-dĕm'ĭk)
inhibition	(ĭn'hĭ-bĭsh'ən)
naysayer	(nā'sā' ər)
obesity	(ō-bē'sĭ-tē)
rampage	(răm'pāj')

WORDS IN CONTEXT

Directions: Choose the meaning for the boldfaced word that best fits the context.

_a_   **1.** Does this mean that your teenager will feel an uncontrollable urge to go on a shooting **rampage** after playing "Call of Duty"?
 a. Outbreak; spree
 b. Lesson
 c. Control
 d. Game

_c_   **2.** The team divided a group of 44 adolescents into two groups, and **randomly** assigned the kids to play one of the two games.
 a. Carefully
 b. Forcefully
 c. Without plan or design; arbitrarily
 d. Intending to influence the results

_c_   **3.** Several studies **cited** by the ESA point to games' potential benefits for developing decision-making skills or bettering reaction times.
 a. Criticized
 b. Created
 c. Mentioned; referred to
 d. Planned

___b___   **4.** Ley, however, argues such studies aren't **credible** because they were produced by "hired guns" funded by the multi-billion-dollar game industry.
a. Finished
b. Reliable; trustworthy
c. Wrong; inaccurate
d. Likeable; attractive

___d___   **5.** And although he doesn't play a lot of games, he does tend to **gravitate** towards shooters like "Medal of Honor."
a. Avoid or fear
b. Imitate
c. Play
d. Be attracted; move

CONTEXT AND DICTIONARY

Directions: Use context and the dictionary to determine the meaning of the boldfaced word in each sentence. Use word structure clues when applicable.

1. . . . and a corresponding decrease of activity in brain areas involved in self-control, **inhibition** and attention.

Restraint; holding back or holding down (an emotion, desire, etc.)

2. One such **naysayer** is Doug Lowenstein, president of the Entertainment Software Association [ESA].

Someone who says no; one who opposes or denies

3. "We've seen other studies in this field that have made dramatic claims but turn out to be less persuasive when **objectively** analyzed."

Impartially; based on facts rather than personal feelings or preferences

4. "Let's quit using various Xboxes as babysitters instead of doing healthful activities," says Ley, citing the growing **epidemic** of childhood obesity in the United States.

A widespread disease or problem

5. "Let's quit using various Xboxes as babysitters instead of doing healthful activities," says Ley, citing the growing epidemic of childhood **obesity** in the United States.

Extreme fatness

RESPOND TO THE READING

 Directions: Write a half-page response to either of the following questions.

1. Do you believe that playing violent video games or watching violent movies encourages violent behavior? Why or why not?

2. If you were a parent, would you allow your children to play violent video games? Why or why not? What healthier free-time activities might you encourage your children to pursue?

WEBQUEST

 Directions: Use the Internet to find the answer to the following question. Write your answer on a sheet of paper. Print out the Web page you used for the answer or copy the URL on your sheet.

Find one other study that examined the effect of playing violent video games on real-life aggression. What were the results of that study?

READING 10B

GLOBAL WARMING: COMING TO YOUR BACKYARD (ENVRONMENTAL SCIENCE)

by Roger Di Silvestro

You are undoubtedly aware of current concerns about global warming. In this article, taken from a wildlife magazine, the author argues that we will feel the effects of global warming very directly—in our backyards and even at our dinner tables. Read the passage to learn about and to evaluate the author's concerns regarding global warming.

Pre-Reading Exercise

Directions: Complete this exercise before reading the passage. Preview the passage and answer the following questions.

1. What is the passage about?
   Global warming and its effects

2. List two or three concerns about global warming that the author will discuss.
   Answers will vary. Possible answers include disease-carrying insects,

   more pollen, more toxic plants, invasive plants, drier regions, crop problems.

3. Why is increased plant growth a threat for people with allergies?
   Increased plant growth suggests increased pollen production.

4. What have you previously read or learned about global warming?
   Answers will vary.

5. How might global warming affect your life?
Answers will vary.

6. Write three questions about global warming.
Answers will vary.

Directions: Use the critical reading strategies you have learned in this chapter to read and analyze the passage. Use context, the dictionary, and word structure clues to determine the meanings of unfamiliar words.

Global Warming: Coming to Your Backyard

1   If you're accustomed to thinking of global warming as something happening out there—say, in the Arctic or the Antarctic or high in the atmosphere—you may be in for a shock. Recent scientific studies indicate that global warming is likely soon to sneak into your backyard in the guise of burgeoning numbers of disease-carrying insects, escalating amounts of hay-fever-inducing pollen and faster growing and more toxic poison ivy. And it's not just your backyard that will be affected. You're likely to find that your dinner table feels the heat, too.

2   Global warming is caused by a buildup of atmospheric gases increasingly emitted by human activities—mostly the burning of fossil fuels. Most prominent among these gases is carbon dioxide (CO_2), used by plants in photosynthesis, the process by which they turn sunlight into vegetable energy. Given the critical link between plants and CO_2, it makes sense that scientists would study how higher levels of the gas will affect plants. What they are finding is a warning to us all.

Spread of Invasive Plants

3   Consider woody vines, such as Japanese honeysuckle, kudzu, English ivy and other invasive plants that climb backyard fences and trees throughout the nation. In a [2006] study done in North Carolina, Duke University biologists used pipes to

> Increased plant growth suggests increased pollen production, unwelcome news to hay fever victims.

pump carbon dioxide into circular areas of forest, each about 100 feet in diameter. The biologists raised the CO_2 in the air to the level anticipated for our atmosphere by 2050 if CO_2 emissions continue unchanged—about 585 parts per million, "a level never before reached in all of human history," says William Schlesinger, dean of the Nicholas School of the Environment and Earth Sciences at Duke University. Presently, atmospheric CO_2 is at about 372 parts per million, the highest concentration in at least 420,000 years, as indicated by studies of gases trapped in ancient ice.

4   After five years of experimenting, biologists found that one woody vine—poison ivy—under increased CO_2 grew at two and a half times its normal rate. More ominously, the ivy produced a more powerful version of urushiol, the chemical that causes a rash in some 80 percent of people who come in contact with the plant, producing more than 350,000 reported U.S. cases of blistered skin yearly.

5   Increased plant growth suggests increased pollen production, unwelcome news to hay fever victims, because that pollen will lead to an "appreciable increase in hay fever and asthma, which should alarm us all," Schlesinger says. A Harvard study released [in 2006] found that ragweed pollen production increased 55 percent under increased levels of CO_2. Another study, conducted by the University of Oklahoma between 1999 and 2001, found that in tall-grass prairie plots in which temperature was artificially raised, ragweed pollen production grew 84 percent. Considering that a single ragweed plant under current conditions can release up to a billion pollen grains in one season, for a nationwide annual ragweed pollen production of an estimated 100 million tons, these increases are formidable. In the Duke CO_2 studies, Schlesinger says, pines increased pollen production up to three-fold, another escalating threat to hay fever victims.

Increased Insect Populations

6   Global warming researchers have predicted for years that the interior regions of continents will become drier as temperature rises.

Insects, too, are likely to be invigorated by warmer climates. "Long, cold winters have the potential to smack back insect populations," Schlesinger says. The shorter, warmer winters resulting from global warming could lead to more insects, he says, including disease-carrying mosquitoes. A warmer world is also likely to produce more robust tick populations, compounding the threat ticks pose as carriers of Lyme disease.

7   The Union of Concerned Scientists, on its website, reports that insects typical of southern parts of the United States are likely to shift north as climate warms. One insect that already appears to be moving north is the bean leaf beetle, which feeds on soybeans and carries a virus that causes disease in soybeans. Another likely to make the shift is the corn earworm, one of the most destructive crop pests in North America, a threat to a wide variety of crops, from corn to cabbage to eggplants and tomatoes. Presently, it cannot survive most winters north of Kansas and Virginia. It does reach as far north as Canada in summer, but generally too late to cause extensive damage. If warmer winters allow it to live year-round in more northerly areas, it will pose a greater threat to crops. To combat such pests, farmers are likely to use more pesticides, further jeopardizing the health of rivers and streams.

Crop Problems

8   Bruce Hungate, a climate ecologist and professor of biological sciences at Northern Arizona University, notes a more subtle effect of global warming: Studies in Florida show that faster plant growth produces a decline in plant nutritional value. As a result, insects have to eat more plant matter to get the same amount of nutrients. Gardeners thus may find themselves fighting an escalating war against increased numbers of backyard insect pests, each seeking a greater amount of plant food. Crop plants also lose nutrient value as atmospheric CO_2 increases, Hungate says. He points, for example, to a study in Japan which found that the nutritional value of rice declined with more atmospheric CO_2.

9   In addition, the regions in which crops grow may change. In a study published [2006] in the Proceedings of the National Academy of Sciences, scientists predict an 80 percent drop in U.S. production of high-quality wine grapes because of a higher frequency of extremely hot days. "In a nutshell, extreme heat could wipe out many areas of high-quality wine production in the U.S.," Hungate says.

10   Global warming researchers have predicted for years that the interior regions of continents will become drier as temperature rises. This change could make the American Midwest less

suitable for corn and wheat, while Canada may become more productive. "If I were a farmer in Saskatchewan or Manitoba, I'd be thinking this global warming might not be all bad," Schlesinger says. "If I were a farmer in Iowa, I'd be thinking about a change in life."

11   Under the effects of global warming, U.S. corn crop yields could drop by as much as 42 percent, according to figures from the Environmental Protection Agency (EPA). The news isn't all bad: Soybean crops could actually increase by up to 15 percent, depending on the specific effects of global warming on precipitation and other factors. On the other hand, soybeans also could decline by as much as 46 percent, according to EPA warnings.

Such shifts in regions of crop production, 12 with increases in transportation costs, could change the price of foods ranging from breakfast cereals to donuts to bread.

—Di Silvestro, "Global Warming: Coming to Your Backyard,"
National Wildlife

You, the Reader

Interest Rating. Please rate the interest level of the reading on the following scale (circle one):

5—Very interesting   2—A little boring

4—Fairly interesting   1—Very boring

3—Mildly interesting

Difficulty Rating. Please rate the difficulty level of the reading on the following scale (circle one):

5—Very interesting   2—A little boring

4—Fairly interesting   1—Very boring

3—Mildly interesting

Comments: Please explain your ratings and make any other comments you wish about the reading.

Answers will vary.

CRITICAL READING EXERCISE

1. What is the author's purpose?

To make readers aware of some of the potential dangers and negative effects

of global warming

2. Who is the intended audience?

General audience, environmentally conscious people

3. What is the author's bias?

It appears he may be an environmentalist.

4. What evidence does the author provide to support his point of view?

Studies done at Duke University; study published in the Proceedings of the National

Academy of Sciences; studies at Harvard University, University of Oklahoma, and in

Florida

5. Is the author's argument logical? Why or why not?

Yes, he uses scientific studies and articles to back up his opinion. (sample answer)

6. Does the author use emotional appeals or propaganda? If so, to which emotions does he appeal? Which propaganda techniques does he use?

The author uses negative connotations to instill fear in the reader.

He uses cardstacking, presenting only threats, with no solutions or alternatives.

He makes occasional assertions.

7. Do you agree with the author's predictions regarding the effects of global warming? Why or why not?

Answers will vary.

COMPREHENSION QUESTIONS

Directions: For questions 1–5, choose the answer that best completes the statement. For questions 6–10, write your response in the space provided. Base all answers on what you read in the selection. Refer back to the selection as necessary to answer the questions.

b **1.** At the beginning of the passage, the author implies that many people:
   a. Have never heard of global warming.
   b. Think of the effects of global warming as far away from them.
   c. Are more worried about global warming than they should be.
   d. Don't care about global warming because they've heard too much about it.

b **2.** The current concentration of CO_2 in our atmosphere is:
   a. About 585 parts per million.
   b. About 372 parts per million.
   c. About 2050 parts per million.
   d. At its lowest level since scientists began measuring it.

_d_   **3.** University studies have found that:
   a. Ragweed pollen production has been declining.
   b. CO_2 levels do not affect pollen production.
   c. Ragweed plants produce less pollen when the weather is warmer.
   d. Increases in CO_2 levels increase the production of pollen.

_c_   **4.** Which of the following is *not* true about the effect of global warming upon insects?
   a. Insect populations will increase with warmer weather.
   b. Insects found typically in the south will shift north as climate warms.
   c. Mosquito and tick populations will decrease in North America.
   d. Insects will pose a greater threat to crops as the weather gets warmer.

_a_   **5.** Why are scientists concerned about drier climates in the interior regions of continents?
   a. Some farming regions may become less productive.
   b. Insect populations increase in drier climates.
   c. Allergy problems increase in drier climates.
   d. Farming will become impossible in the American Midwest.

6. What causes global warming?

Buildup of atmospheric gases emitted by human activities

7. According to the author, how will global warming affect your dinner table?

Climate shifts in regions of crop production could increase food prices. The

nutrient value of some foods may decline. Foods may contain more pesticides.

8. What were the findings of Duke University researchers regarding the effects of increased CO_2 on poison ivy?

Poison ivy grew at two and a half times its normal rate, and it produced a

more powerful version of urushiol.

9. Name two insects that the author identifies as threats to farm crops and list the crops that these insects can harm.

Bean leaf beetle—soybeans; corn earworm—wide variety of crops,

including corn, cabbage, eggplants, and tomatoes

10. Which of the effects of global warming described in the passage do you find most alarming? Why?

Answers will vary.

VOCABULARY EXERCISES

Pronunciation Guide (see p. 90 for list of phonetic symbols)

burgeoning	(bûr' jən-ĭng)
ecologist	(ĭ-kŏl'ə-jĭst)
formidable	(fôr'mə-də-bəl)
guise	(gīz)
jeopardizing	(jĕp'ər-dīz-ĭng)
ominously	(ŏm' ə-nəs-lē)
subtle	(sŭ'təl)

WORDS IN CONTEXT

Directions: Choose the meaning for the boldfaced word that best fits the context.

__b__ 1. . . . global warming is likely soon to sneak into your backyard in the guise of **burgeoning** numbers of disease carrying-insects . . .
   a. Small
   b. Increasing
   c. Decreasing
   d. Unusual

__a__ 2. . . . faster growing and more **toxic** poison ivy.
   a. Harmful; poisonous
   b. Faster growing
   c. Hard to notice
   d. Uncommon

__d__ 3. Consider woody vines, such as Japanese honeysuckle, kudzu, English ivy and other **invasive** plants that climb backyard fences and trees throughout the nation.
   a. Growing along the ground; low
   b. Poisonous
   c. Useful
   d. Invading; intruding into new areas

__b__ 4. Insects, too, are likely to be **invigorated** by warmer climates.
   a. Made warmer
   b. Energized
   c. Weakened
   d. Destroyed; eliminated

__c__ 5. . . . farmers are likely to use more pesticides, further **jeopardizing** the health of rivers and streams.
   a. Investigating
   b. Caring for; maintaining
   c. Endangering
   d. Improving

CONTEXT AND DICTIONARY

Directions: Use context and the dictionary to determine the meaning of the boldfaced word in each sentence. Use word structure clues when applicable.

1. ... global warming is likely soon to sneak into your backyard in the **guise** of burgeoning numbers of disease-carrying insects ...

   Appearance; form

2. ... **escalating** amounts of hay-fever-inducing pollen ...

   Increasing

3. ... escalating amounts of hay-fever-**inducing** pollen ...

   Causing; encouraging

4. Most **prominent** among these gases is carbon dioxide (CO_2), used by plants in photosynthesis, the process by which they turn sunlight into vegetable energy.

   Well known, outstanding

5. Most prominent among these gases is carbon dioxide (CO_2), used by plants in **photosynthesis**, the process by which they turn sunlight into vegetable energy.

   The process by which plants turn sunlight into vegetable energy

6. More **ominously**, the ivy produced a more powerful version of urushiol, the chemical that causes a rash in some 80 percent of people who come in contact with the plant ...

   Threateningly; menacingly

7. Considering that a single ragweed plant ... can release up to a billion pollen grains in one season ... these increases are **formidable**.

   Of discouraging size; intimidating

8. A warmer world is also likely to produce more **robust** tick populations ...

   Strong and healthy; hardy, vigorous

9. Bruce Hungate, a climate **ecologist** and professor of biological sciences at Northern Arizona University, notes a more subtle effect of global warming ...

   Environmental biologist who studies interactions between organisms and their

   environment

10. Bruce Hungate, a climate ecologist and professor of biological sciences at Northern Arizona University, notes a more **subtle** effect of global warming ...

    Not obvious; not easy to notice

RESPOND TO THE READING

Directions: Write a half-page response to either of the following questions.

1. Discuss the ways that global warming might affect you, your community, and your state over the next ten to twenty years.

2. Do you believe that global warming is as serious a threat as the author suggests? Why or why not? What can be done to deal with the problems associated with global warming?

WEBQUEST

Directions: Use the Internet to find the answer to the following question. Write your answer on a sheet of paper. Print out the Web page(s) you used for the answer or copy the URL(s) on your sheet.

What evidence do scientists have that global warming is indeed occurring?

CHAPTER 10 REVIEW

Active readers are critical readers. *Critical reading* is the process by which we analyze and evaluate the ideas and information we encounter in our reading material.

Fact vs. Opinion

Distinguishing factual statements from opinion statements is an important part of critical reading. A *factual statement* is a statement that can be determined to be true or false. An *opinion statement* reflects an individual point of view that can never be proved or disproved.

Evaluating Sources of Information

Critical readers evaluate the source of the information they are reading. A reliable source is one that is unbiased and has made a reasonable effort to verify its information.

Evaluating Arguments

Critical readers are careful to analyze and evaluate the arguments, or opinions, that they read, asking the following questions: *What is the author's purpose? Who is the intended audience? What is the author's bias? What is the author's evidence? Is the argument logical? Does the author use emotional appeals and propaganda techniques?*

Skills Online: Critical Reading

Readings

Reading 10A: Violent Video Games Puts Teens at Risk (Sociology)

Reading 10B: Global Warming: Coming to Your Backyard (Environmental Science)

CHAPTER TESTS

TEST 10.1. FACT VS. OPINION

Directions: Mark each statement F (factual statement) or O (opinion statement).

O **1.** Individuals should have a wide range of work experiences in order to make a decision about a career.

O **2.** Podcasts will become increasingly popular over the next five years.

F **3.** Calvin Coolidge was the first president to appear on radio on a regular basis.

O **4.** Perhaps the most important point to recognize about e-mail in the workplace is that the nature of business e-mail is dramatically different from that of personal e-mail.

F **5.** Neurons do not directly touch each other, end to end.

F **6.** Police salaries vary by jurisdiction and are related to the size of the police department and the cost of living in different parts of the country.

—Albanese, *Criminal Justice,* 3rd ed.

F **7.** In 2007 a contaminated ingredient imported from China began killing pets in the United States.

—Vivian, *The Media of Mass Communication,* 9th ed.

O **8.** All high school graduates should attend at least two years of college.

O **9.** Dogs make better pets than cats.

F **10.** Throughout history, a number of things—gold or silver coins, paper money, cattle, and even beads, stones, and red parrot feathers—have served as money.

—Gregory, *Essentials of Economics,* 4th ed.

TEST 10.2. FACT AND OPINION IN PARAGRAPHS

Directions: After reading each paragraph, identify the sentences that express facts and the sentences that express opinions. (If a sentence contains both fact and opinion, you may list it in both categories.) Then explain whether the paragraph is mostly factual or mostly opinion.

1. (1) Marc Draisen has seen the future for suburban communities, and for many, he said, it is troubling. (2) They will grapple with serious water shortages. (3) They will battle worsening traffic. (4) And they will lose acres upon acres of fields and farmland.

—Lazar and Carroll, "Warnings of a Crowded Future," *The Boston Globe*

Which sentences contain facts? _____None_____

Which sentences contain opinions? _____All_____

Is the paragraph mostly fact or opinion? Explain your answer.

The paragraph is all opinion: speculation about the future of suburban communities.

---

2. (1) Where rainfall is very sparse, desert forms. (2) The driest biome on Earth, most deserts receive well under 25 cm (9.8 in.) of precipitation per year, much of it during isolated storms months or years apart. (3) Some deserts, like Africa's Sahara and Namib deserts, are mostly bare sand dunes; others, like the Sonoran Desert of Arizona and northwest Mexico, receive more rain and are more heavily vegetated. (4) Because deserts have low humidity and relatively little vegetation to insulate them from temperature extremes, sunlight readily heats them in the daytime, but daytime heat is quickly lost at night. (5) As a result, temperatures vary widely from day to night and across seasons of the year.

—Withgott and Brennan, *Essential Environment: The Science Behind the Stories*, 2nd ed.

Which sentences contain facts? _____All_____

Which sentences contain opinions? _____None_____

Is the paragraph mostly fact or opinion? Explain your answer.

The passage is entirely factual. It provides information about deserts.

---

3. (1) One specific similarity between work and school is that the same misconceived question is regularly posed in both places. (2) Douglas McGregor reminded us that "How do you motivate people?" is not what managers should be asking. (3) Nor should educators: children do not need to be motivated. (4) From the beginning they are hungry to make sense of their world. (5) Given an environment in which they don't feel controlled and in which they are encouraged to think about what they are doing (rather than how well they are doing it), students of any age will generally exhibit an abundance of motivation and a healthy appetite for challenge.

—Kohn, *Punished by Rewards*

Which sentences contain facts? _____2, 4_____

Which sentences contain opinions? _____All_____

Is the paragraph mostly fact or opinion? Explain your answer.

The passage is primarily opinion, with some facts mixed in. The author presents his view about how children's education should be approached. The only facts are that Douglas McGregor made a statement (which expresses his opinion) and the generalization in sentence 4 that children want to understand the world.

TEST 10.3. EVALUATING ARGUMENTS

Directions: Critically read the following passage and answer the questions that follow.

SHOULD ALL STUDENTS BE BILINGUAL? YES!

Yes, all students should be bilingual. Unfortunately, in the United States very few students become truly proficient in a foreign language. That is one reason for the shortage of foreign language and bilingual teachers.

Before the world wars, many immigrants in the United States used their native languages daily while they learned English. But the world wars and isolationist policies created a climate in which it was unpopular to speak anything but English. In some cities, fines were imposed on anyone caught speaking a foreign language in public business.

Many descendants of immigrants never learned their parents' or grandparents' native languages—in my case, Polish and German—because of these attitudes. My grandparents and parents, pressured by society, did not understand the importance of passing on their languages to me.

Learning a foreign language involves more than learning how to read, write, and speak. More important, it teaches students about a culture. Lack of understanding of cultural differences causes intolerance and war.

The people of the United States and the world need to be, not just tolerant, but accepting of other cultures. We need to embrace and celebrate our many cultures. Studying a foreign language and becoming bilingual opens one's mind to new thinking and creates new opportunities to communicate with other people.

Language can be the key to a lasting peace between enemies. Learning another language is the best way to make friends.

Students in many other countries learn at least one foreign language in their public schools. In the United States, few schools even offer a foreign language in elementary school.

As global businesses and trade expand, the need to know a second language is growing tremendously. Many businesses in other countries want to do business with us. Their salespeople speak English and know our customs. We need people who know other languages and cultures so that our exports will increase and our economy will become stronger.

Learning another language may also spill over into other areas. Research shows that bilingualism leads to cognitive advantages that may raise scores on some intelligence tests.

Studies also show a correlation between knowing two languages and linguistic abilities that may facilitate early reading acquisition. That, in turn, could boost academic achievement.

—Johnson et al., *Foundations of American Education*, 14th ed.

1. What is the authors' purpose?

To argue that American students should be bilingual

2. Who is the intended audience?

General audience; educators; policy-makers

3. What is the authors' bias?

The authors favor Americans knowing more than one language.

4. What evidence do the authors provide to support their conclusions?

Students in many other countries learn at least one foreign language; global

business is increasing; research shows cognitive advantages to being bilingual.

Studies show correlation between bilingualism and linguistic abilities that may

facilitate early reading acquisition.

5. Is the authors' argument logical? Why or why not?

Answers will vary. The various pieces of the authors' argument seem to make

sense, but it's not clear that they add up to their conclusion.

6. Do the authors use emotional appeals or propaganda techniques? If so, to which emotions do the authors appeal? Which propaganda techniques do they use?

Assertions are used throughout passage; also, the authors use cardstacking,

presenting only one side of the argument. References to what other countries are

doing is a type of bandwagon technique.

7. Do you agree with the authors that all students should be bilingual? Why or why not?

Answers will vary.

TEST 10.3. CRITICAL READING

Directions: Use the critical reading strategies you have learned in this chapter to read and analyze the following passage. Then answers the questions that follow.

Does Laughter Enhance Health?

Remember the last time you laughed so hard that you cried? Remember how relaxed you felt afterward? Scientists are just beginning to understand the role of humor in our lives and health. For example, laughter has been shown to have the following effects.

- Stressed-out people with a strong sense of humor become less depressed and anxious than those whose sense of humor is less well developed.

- Students who use humor as a coping mechanism report that it predisposes them to a positive mood.

- In a study of depressed and suicidal senior citizens the patients who recovered were the ones who demonstrated a sense of humor.

- Telling a joke, particularly one that involves a shared experience, increases our sense of belonging and social cohesion.

Laughter helps us in many ways. People like to be around others who are fun-loving and laugh easily. Learning to laugh puts more joy into everyday experiences and increases the likelihood that fun-loving people will keep company with us.

Psychologist Barbara Fredrickson argues that positive emotions such as joy, interest, and contentment serve valuable life functions. Joy is associated with playfulness and creativity. Interest encourages us to explore our world, which enhances knowledge and cognitive ability. Contentment allows us to savor and integrate experiences, an important step in achieving mindfulness and insight. By building our physical, social, and mental resources, these positive feelings empower us to cope effectively with life's challenges. While the actual emotions may be transient, their effects can be permanent and provide lifelong enrichment.

Laughter also seems to have positive physiological effects. A number of researchers, such as Lee Berk, M.D., and Stanley Tan, M.D., have noted that laughter sharpens our immune sys-

tems by activating T-cells and natural killer cells and increasing production of immunity-boosting interferon. It also reduces levels of the stress hormone cortisol.

In one experiment, Fredrickson monitored the cardiovascular responses of human subjects who suffered fear and anxiety induced by an unsettling film clip. Some of them then viewed a humorous film clip, while others did not. Those who watched the humorous film returned more quickly to their baseline cardiovascular state, which indicates that laughter may counteract some of the physical effects of negative emotions.

—Donatelle, *Health: The Basics*, 6th ed.

1. Does the passage consist mostly of fact or opinion? Explain your answer.

The passage is a mix of fact and opinion, with fact dominating. Most of the passage is repeating information from studies. Some of the passage reflects the author's opinion and another psychologist's opinion regarding the benefits of laughter. (sample answer)

2. Is the information in the passage reliable? Why or why not?

Answers will vary. The source is reliable and her sources are, but there's not a lot of hard data.

3. What is the author's primary purpose?

The author wants to show that laughter is good for your health. (sample answer)

4. Does the author have a bias toward her subject? If so, what is it?

The author favors laughing. (sample answer)

5. According to the author, how does laughter contribute to good health?

Laughter reduces stress, enhances mood, and strengthens social connections. Laughter sharpens our immune system by activating T-cells and natural killer cells and by increasing production of interferon. It reduces cortisol, a stress hormone. (sample answer)

6. Does the author present sufficient evidence to support the conclusion that laughter enhances health? Why or why not?

Answers will vary. The only direct evidence linking laughter to health is in the last two paragraphs. The information in the first few paragraphs is substantial but general and focused more on feelings than on physical health.

7. Do you believe that laughter contributes to good health? Why or why not?

Answers will vary.

_____

_____

You, the Reader: Chapter 10 Wrap-up

Directions: Use one or two of the following questions to write a half-page response to Chapter 10.

- What were the most important things you learned from this chapter? How will you use what you have learned from this chapter?

- How have you changed your reading habits in response to this chapter?

- Which strategies or habits best help you to read critically? Explain your answer.

- What parts of the chapter did you find most engaging? What questions do you have about the chapter?

PEARSON
myreadinglab

For support in meeting this chapter's objectives, go to MyReadingLab and select *Critical Thinking*.

definitely worth the effort. He was born in Merigold, Mississippi, the child of migrant workers who followed the crops through America's heartland. By the age of five, he was picking cotton, asparagus, and beets alongside his family. Living in noisy labor camps, dusty tents, and once even under a tree, was the norm. "I just accepted it," says Nane. What else could he do? He'd never known anything different.

5   The day his grandfather died, a life that was simply hard turned bad. The patriarch, Don Pancho, returned home from a long day of chopping beets with a short-handled hoe. Soon after, he collapsed. Twelve-year-old Nane held his seventy-two-year-old grandfather in his arms, begging him not to die, but it was too late.

6   After Don Pancho's death, Nane's family fell apart. His father began to drink, and jobs became more scarce. Nane felt his father's pain as he bowed his head before the bosses and searched for work. He wanted nothing more than to escape, but there was nowhere to go. He decided if he couldn't run from his pain, he'd numb it. At twelve years of age, he started sniffing glue. By thirteen he'd smoked his first joint. When he was seventeen he tried LSD. He returned from Vietnam a heroin addict.

7   During a short jail sentence for drug use, he took a hard look at himself. He knew if he didn't change his path, he'd wind up like the gangsters and drug dealers around him: in prison for a very long time, or dead.

8   When he got out of jail, Nane used the GI Bill to attend Fresno City College and transfer to the University of California, Santa Cruz. As he studied, he gained perspective on his life. He understood that the same despair that had nearly destroyed him was running rampant in the barrios. Without help, and with few choices, many young boys were destined to repeat the mistakes he had lived, and kill each other or self-destruct.

9   Nane chose to help. He went out into the streets and started talking to kids. It was that simple. He hung out with them, counseled them, and talked to them about better ways of living, alternatives to prison or death. To reach the kids better, he decided to walk his talk: he conquered his own drug addictions.

10   But the way out of addiction and despair was "one step forward and two steps back." One day Nane reached the low point in his life. He had lost twelve relatives and friends in twelve years, including his two brothers; his childhood hero, Uncle Pancho; and his grandmother. Finally, all he could feel was the pain. "I didn't know how to let go of the tragedies in my life," he said. Desperate to escape, Nane overdosed and was near death.

11   As he was rushed to the hospital's emergency room, Nane had a vision in which he could actually see his brother Leo at the end of a tunnel of flashing light. "Go back, go back," Leo said. "It's not your time." Then he saw his other brother, Tavo, who said the same thing.

12   "When I finally woke up, I realized the Creator had given me the opportunity to see my brothers and to know they were okay," Nane remembers. "After that I could let go of the pain."

13   The next day he went to the cemetery and prayed quietly with his brothers. "I realized that I needed to deal with my own life—to move forward," he said. From then on, Nane found strength from being spiritually connected through

traditional Native American ceremonies. He sought guidance from tribal elders, and also spoke more with people of different faiths. "I began to focus on my own mission in life," Nane says, "to better our communities and to stop the violence among our young people."

14 Nane founded Barrios Unidos working from the trunk of his car. The group was to provide new role models for the youth of America. It was 1977, and he was twenty-seven years old. While his wife sold tacos to make ends meet, he and his small band of volunteers pursued their dream: providing youth with a world free of violence, drugs, and alcohol abuse. They went to schools, walked the barrios, and worked late into the night. After a while, Barrios Unidos moved into a small office, then used grant money to buy a computer so they could write applications for other grants. Soon their message spread, as did their impact.

15 Today, Barrios Unidos has a room full of computers and a staff of twenty-six people in several chapters across the country. They offer extensive programs and free food and counseling to those in need. Three summer Kids' Klub programs reach out to the youngest residents of the barrios. To foster an entrepreneurial spirit, Barrios Unidos started a silk-screening business run by teens. The proceeds of the business help fund their initiatives.

16 One of their most exciting projects is the Cesar Chavez School for Social Change in Santa Cruz, near where Cesar organized in the fields of Pajaro Valley. Here, future community leaders are raised in the tradition of Cesar Chavez, Martin Luther King, and Mahatma Gandhi. Nineteen-year-old Miriam Garcia is grateful to Nane and others at Barrios Unidos for making it possible for her to attend the school. "I look forward to becoming a creator of positive change in my community," she says.

17 Of course there is still much to do. Some days, Barrios Unidos may seem to be losing the battle. Youth crime in our country is projected to more than double over the next decade, fueled in large part by gang activity. The FBI reports nearly 1.5 million young people are now involved in gangs. For Nane, and Barrios Unidos, that means more lives to turn around, more young people who need more choices for the future. Nane finds hope in young people like Alejandro Vilchez, who is a young father and a warrior for peace. "My father taught me to be a man," says Alejandro. "Nane taught me to be a warrior for change."

18 At fifty-one, Nane is still the guiding spirit of his organization. He works in the office, travels across the country giving speeches and raising funds, and meets with children of the barrios. And he always takes time to pray, honoring the Creator.

19 In the kitchen of his modest home, Nane snuggles his ten-year-old grandson close and talks of his hopes for peace. "Not for me," he says, "maybe not for my children. But if we all keep working toward it, maybe for my grandson's children."

—Townsend, "Viva! Barrios Unidos,"
from *Stone Soup for the World*

You, the Reader

Interest Rating: Please rate the interest level of the reading on the following scale (circle one):

5—Very interesting 2—A little boring

4—Fairly interesting 1—Very boring

3—Mildly interesting

Difficulty Rating: Please rate the difficulty level of the reading on the following scale (circle one):

5—Very difficult 2—Fairly easy

4—Fairly difficult 1—Very easy

3—Moderate

Comments: Please explain your ratings and make any other comments you wish about the reading.

Answers will vary.

COMPREHENSION QUESTIONS

Directions: For questions 1–5, choose the answer that best completes the statement. For questions 6–10, write your response in the space provided. Base all answers on what you read in the selection. Refer back to the selection as necessary to answer the questions.

a **1.** Nane began Barrios Unidos in:
   a. Santa Cruz.   c. Fresno.
   b. Mississippi.   d. San Mateo.

b **2.** We can infer from the passage that Nane's grandfather:
   a. Was well educated.   c. Was an alcoholic.
   b. Worked as a migrant farmer. d. Died from a stroke.

d **3.** Nane's attitude toward the future can best be described as:
   a. Pessimistic.   c. Uncertain.
   b. Unrealistic.   d. Cautiously optimistic.

a **4.** The primary purposes of Barrios Unidos are to:
   a. Provide role models and constructive activities for barrio youths.
   b. Help alcoholics and drug addicts overcome their addictions.
   c. Teach religious and spiritual values.
   d. Raise funds and raise public awareness regarding the problems caused by poverty in America.

c **5.** What of the following was not mentioned in the passage as a reason why Nane started Barrios Unidos?
   a. His spiritual beliefs.
   b. His experiences as a drug addict.
   c. His experiences as an alcoholic.
   d. His vision in the emergency room.

6. What is a barrio?

A Hispanic neighborhood or community

7. Why does the author feel that Nane is an appropriate name for Daniel Alejandrez?

Nane means "walks in peace"; he fights violence and promotes peace through his work.

8. Why did Nane become a drug addict?

After his grandfather died, his family fell apart. He turned to drugs to cope with his pain.

9. What are some of the problems that make it difficult for organizations like Barrios Unidos to accomplish their goals?

   They work in poor, drug-ridden communities. Many of the teens there are addicts,

   criminals, or gang members. Their resources are inadequate. (sample answer)

10. In your opinion, can organizations like Barrios Unidos succeed in helping troubled youth? Why or why not?

    Answers will vary.

VOCABULARY EXERCISES

Pronunciation Guide (see p. 90 for list of phonetic symbols)

entrepreneurial	(ŏn'trə-prə-nûr'ē-əl)
initiatives	(ĭ-nĭsh'ə-tĭvz)
patriarch	(pā'trē-ärk')

WORDS IN CONTEXT

Directions: Choose the meaning for the boldfaced word that best fits the context.

__c__ 1. He was born in Merigold, Mississippi, the child of **migrant** workers who followed the crops through America's heartland.
   a. Factory   c. Moving from place to place
   b. Skilled   d. Unemployed

__b__ 2. He understood that the same **despair** that had nearly destroyed him was running rampant in the barrios.
   a. Excitement   c. Violence
   b. Hopelessness   d. Career

__d__ 3. To foster an **entrepreneurial** spirit, Barrios Unidos started a silk-screening business run by teens.
   a. Educational   c. Curious
   b. Normal   d. Business; profit-seeking

__d__ 4. The **proceeds** of the business help fund their initiatives.
   a. Officers   c. Activities
   b. Organization   d. Earnings

__a__ 5. Youth crime in our country is **projected** to more than double over the next decade, fueled in large part by gang activity.
   a. Predicted, expected   c. Caused
   b. Built up to   d. Featured, transformed

CONTEXT AND DICTIONARY

Directions: Use context and the dictionary to determine the meaning of the boldfaced word in each sentence. Use word structure clues when applicable.

1. The **patriarch**, Don Pancho, returned home from a long day of chopping beets with a short-handled hoe.

    Male head of family

2. As he studied, he gained **perspective** on his life.

    Broader viewpoint; better understanding

3. He understood that the same despair that had nearly destroyed him was running **rampant** in the barrios.

    Widespread

4. He sought guidance from tribal **elders**, and also spoke more with people of different faiths.

    Seniors; older people

5. They offer **extensive** programs and free food and counseling to those in need.

    Large; comprehensive; wide in scope

6. The proceeds of the business help fund their **initiatives**.

    New enterprises

RESPOND TO THE READING

Directions: Write a half-page response to either of the following questions.

1. What causes young Americans to experiment with addictive drugs? How can the problem of drug abuse be remedied?

2. Write about an important experience or event that significantly changed your life. Tell what happened and explain how your life changed as a result of this experience or event.

WEBQUEST

Directions: Use the Internet to find the answers to the following questions. Write your answers on a sheet of paper. Print out the Web page(s) you used for the answers or copy the URL(s) on your sheet.

Who are the Crips? Where are they located? When did they originate?

READING 12

WHO ARE THE POLICE? (CRIMINAL JUSTICE)
by Jay Albanese

Reading 12 is taken from a criminal justice textbook. Read the selection to find out who is doing police work today, and to discover what the characteristics of good police work are.

Pre-Reading Exercise

Directions: Complete this exercise before reading the passage. Preview the passage and answer the following questions.

1. What is the passage about?

   Police officers: who they are and what makes good police work

2. How has the make-up of our police departments been changing?

   More women and minorities are being hired.

3. List two of the characteristics of good police work.

   Any two: attentiveness, reliability, responsiveness, competence, manners, fairness

4. What have you previously learned about police work?

   Answers will vary.

5. What questions do you have about police work?

   Answers will vary.

6. Does the passage seem interesting? Why or why not?

   Answers will vary.

1   People in law enforcement in the United States are a diverse group totaling more than 1 million sworn officers and civilians. In 1987 the Bureau of Justice Statistics began the Law Enforcement Management and Administrative Statistics (LEMAS) program, which is a nationwide survey of state and local police agencies employing one hundred or more officers that is conducted every three years. According to the most recent survey, local police departments employed an average of 16 officers per 10,000 city residents, but varied from 8 to more than 78 officers per 10,000 residents. This shows that the relative size of police departments varies considerably.

Females in Police Work

2   In addition, a growing proportion of these officers are women. Until recent decades, women and those of certain heights, weights, and backgrounds were excluded from police work. The 1972 amendments to Title VII of the Civil Rights Act of 1964 made its provisions applicable to *both* public (e.g., police) and private sector employers. The act prohibits discrimination on the basis of gender, and it also mandates that gender must be shown to be a "bona fide occupational qualification" if women are not hired or promoted on the same basis as men. Therefore, an employer must prove that there is a significant difference in the performance of men versus women if they are not to be hired or assigned in the same manner.

3   Although the idea of women in police work is more than a century old, it has only been during the last forty years that women have been hired and assigned in the same manner as men. The guidelines of the Equal Employment Opportunity Commission (EEOC) also have helped to eliminate discrimination on the basis of gender. Under these guidelines both public and private employers "must demonstrate that any requirement for employment or promotion is specifically related to some objective measure of job performance." Although there has been criticism of the EEOC for a sluggish enforcement record, the guidelines have helped to eliminate arbitrary police qualifications such as minimum height requirements, unless they can be shown to affect job performance.

Minorities in Police Work

4   The result of these trends is that police officers are increasingly diverse. Female officers now make up 11 percent of all local police, African Americans nearly 12 percent, and Hispanic Americans more than 9 percent of the total. These figures vary by size of police agency. For example, the percentage of female officers ranged from 4 percent in places with fewer than 2,500 to 16.5 percent in jurisdictions of 500,000 or more. The total of 51,000 female police officers nationwide represents an increase of 9 percent since 2000. Police recruits are increasingly college graduates, and many have had internship experiences within police agencies. In addition, many larger police departments now recruit prospective officers from outside their own jurisdiction, in an attempt to obtain better-qualified recruits and have their department more closely reflect the makeup of their community.

5   A detailed job analysis of the tasks performed by New York City police officers, for example, identified forty-two distinct tasks that police officers carry out. As a result, all police exams, interviews, and other testing must be based on these performance criteria. This requirement ensures that the officers chosen will conform to the qualifications for the job, rather than to stereotypes not based in fact. Nevertheless, job expectations change. The growth of community policing, for example, requires police to work with the noncriminal public more than ever before and makes crime prevention as important a goal as the apprehension of law violators. Police researcher Stephen Mastrofski has identified six characteristics that summarize current expectations of "good service" from police officers:

Characteristics of Good Police Work

- Attentiveness—vigilance and accessibility to the public and to their concerns.

- Reliability—predictable and error-free police service when called upon.
- Responsiveness—"client-centered" service that always provides a good faith effort by police.
- Competence—use of police legal authority and discretion in acceptable ways.
- Manners—interaction with the public in a respectful way.
- Fairness—enforcement of the law and treatment of suspects in an even-handed manner.

These six characteristics reflect the belief   6
that police work requires much more than the application of the law in the community. The quality of police service is increasingly scrutinized, because the manner in which police tasks are carried out is considered as important as the tasks themselves. This situation has placed increased emphasis on the way in which police officers are selected and trained.

—Albanese, *Criminal Justice*, 4th ed.

You, the Reader

Interest Rating: Please rate the interest level of the reading on the following scale (circle one):

5—Very interesting	2—A little boring
4—Fairly interesting	1—Very boring
3—Mildly interesting	

Difficulty Rating: Please rate the difficulty level of the reading on the following scale (circle one):

5—Very difficult	2—Fairly easy
4—Fairly difficult	1—Very easy
3—Moderate	

Comments: Please explain your ratings and make any other comments you wish about the reading.

Answers will vary.

COMPREHENSION QUESTIONS

Directions: For questions 1–5, choose the answer that best completes the statement. For questions 6–10, write your response in the space provided. Base all answers on what you read in the selection. Refer back to the selection as necessary to answer the questions.

___d___ **1.** The most recent LEMAS survey discovered that:
  a. Police departments in small towns have a higher relative size.
  b. Police departments in small towns have a lower relative size.
  c. No police department has more than 78 officers.
  d. The size of police departments varies significantly.

___a___ **2.** The Civil Rights Act of 1964 requires employers to:
  a. Prove gender performance differences if hiring a man over a woman.
  b. Hire an equal number of men and women.

c. Hire a certain percentage of women each year.

d. Increase their number of female employees on an annual basis.

_c_ **3.** The author states that the EEOC guidelines:

a. Have had little effect on police hirings.

b. Have been strictly enforced to ensure equal treatment for men and women.

c. Have helped to remove unfair job qualifications.

d. Have been criticized for eliminating important job qualifications.

_a_ **4.** We can conclude from the information in the passage that:

a. Most police officers today are white and male.

b. Hispanic American police officers outnumber African American police officers.

c. There are twice as many women in the police today than there were ten years ago.

d. More women officers are hired by small towns than by large cities.

_b_ **5.** Community policing emphasizes:

a. Strict and consistent law enforcement.

b. Crime prevention.

c. Frequent arrests.

d. Control of juvenile offenders.

6. What is LEMAS?

The Law Enforcement Management and Administrative Statistics program is a nation-

wide survey of police agencies with a minimum size of 100 officers. It is conducted

every three years.

7. What do the EEOC guidelines require of employers?

EEOC requires employers to prove that their job qualifications are related to some

objectively measurable aspect of job performance.

8. How are police recruits today different from police recruits of the past?

They are more diverse. More are college graduates. Many have done internships in

police agencies. Many are recruited from outside the department's jurisdiction.

9. How have job expectations for police officers changed in recent years?

Police are expected to work with the public more and focus on crime prevention.

Today's officers are expected to be attentive, reliable, responsive, competent, fair,

and respectful.

10. In your opinion, what are the characteristics of a good police officer?

Answers will vary.

VOCABULARY EXERCISES

Pronunciation Guide (see p. 90 for list of phonetic symbols)

arbitrary	(är′bĭ-trĕr′ē)
bona fide	(bō′nə fīd′)
criteria	(krī-tîr′ē-ə)
stereotypes	(stĕr′ē-ə-tīps′)

WORDS IN CONTEXT

Directions: Choose the meaning for the boldfaced word that best fits the context.

___d___ **1.** The act . . . **mandates** that gender must be shown to be a "bona fide occupational qualification" if women are not hired or promoted on the same basis as men.
   a. Prevents.   c. Sets a time for
   b. Makes a difference between   d. Requires; orders

___a___ **2.** The act . . . mandates that gender must be shown to be a "**bona fide** occupational qualification" if women are not hired or promoted on the same basis as men.
   a. Real, genuine   c. Normal; typical
   b. Not important   d. Unfair

___c___ **3.** . . . many larger police departments now recruit **prospective** officers from outside their own jurisdiction . . .
   a. Local   c. Future; potential
   b. Senior   d. Unskilled

___a___ **4.** As a result, all police exams, interviews, and other testing must be based on these performance **criteria**.
   a. Standards   c. Of the future
   b. History   d. Investigations

___b___ **5.** . . . and makes crime prevention as important a goal as the **apprehension** of law violators.
   a. Understanding   c. Study
   b. Arrest   d. Destruction

CONTEXT AND DICTIONARY

Directions: Use context and the dictionary to determine the meaning of the boldfaced word in each sentence. Use word structure clues when applicable.

1. Although there has been criticism of the EEOC for a **sluggish** enforcement record . . .

   Slow; not energetic

2. . . . the guidelines have helped to eliminate **arbitrary** police qualifications such as minimum height requirements, unless they can be shown to affect job performance.

Having no reasonable basis

3. . . . the officers chosen will conform to the qualifications for the job, rather than to **stereotypes** not based in fact.

Fixed ideas of a group that do not allow for individual variations

4. Attentiveness—**vigilance** and accessibility to the public and to their concerns.

Watchfulness, alertness

5. Attentiveness—vigilance and **accessibility** to the public and to their concerns.

Availability; approachability

6. Competence—use of police legal authority and **discretion** in acceptable ways.

Judgment; discrimination

7. The quality of police service is increasingly **scrutinized**, because the manner in which police tasks are carried out is considered as important as the tasks themselves.

Carefully watched

RESPOND TO THE READING

Directions: Write a half-page response to either of the following questions.

1. Would you make a good police officer? Why or why not?

2. How can today's police departments better serve their communities?

WEBQUEST

Directions: Use the Internet to find the answer to the following question. Write your answer on a sheet of paper. Print out the Web page you used for the answer or copy the URLs on your sheet.

What education and training are required to become a police officer in your state?

READING 13

TELEVISION IN TRANSITION (COMMUNICATION/MEDIA)

by John Vivian

Reading 13 is an excerpt from the textbook *The Media of Mass Communication*. Mass media are the forms of communication, such as television, radio, and the Internet, which reach very large audiences. The word *media* is the plural form of the word *medium*—which means "a method of communication." In this passage, the author discusses television's relationship with other media, past and present, and speculates about the future of television as well. He also discusses television's importance and its influences on today's culture. Read the passage to learn about the author's ideas regarding television's ongoing role in our lives.

Pre-Reading Exercise

Directions: Complete this exercise before reading the passage. Preview the passage and answer the following questions.

1. What is the passage about?

   Television: its cultural role and its current issues

2. What questions does the author raise about the future of television?

   Can the TV industry reinvent itself?

   Can it get on top of the new technology?

   Will television be subsumed or replaced by new competition?

3. Write a goal question for the second heading of the passage, "Cultural Role of Television." What do you expect to learn from this section?

   What is the cultural role of television?

4. Does the author believe that television is about to disappear? How can you tell?

   He does not believe it will disappear soon. He says, in paragraph 8, that no one is predicting

   its imminent disappearance.

5. What have you previously read or learned about television?

   Answers will vary.

6. How much television do you watch? Which kinds of programs do you enjoy?

   Answers will vary.

1 Once, television was so influential that its cultural influence was described as "a molder of the soul's geography." The question now is whether television as a medium can retain its social role amid a changing technological environment.

Television Industry in Crisis

2 Television transformed the mass media. In the 1950s, television, the new kid on the block, forced its media elders, notably movies, radio and magazines, to reinvent themselves or perish. Year by year television entrenched itself in the latter 20th century, first as a hot new medium, then as the dominant medium. Now the industries that developed around television technology are themselves in crisis. They have been overtaken by innovations in delivering video through other channels. Can the television industry reinvent itself? Can the industry get on top of the new technology? Or will television as an industry find itself subsumed, perhaps even replaced, by new competition? High drama is being played out even as you read this chapter.

Cultural Role of Television

3 Despite questions about how the U.S. television industry will adapt to an era of iPods, blogs and online gaming, the medium itself is hardly on its deathbed. Almost every U.S. household has at least one television set. On average, television is playing about seven hours a day in those households. Many people, sometimes millions, still shape their leisure time around when CBS runs *CSI*. Somewhere around 134 million people assemble ritual-like for the Super Bowl.

4 As a medium, television can create cultural icons, as Budweiser has demonstrated time and again. A generation remembers the Bud frog, then "Whazzup?" became an icon greeting. Even though many advertisers are shifting their spending to alternative media, Procter & Gamble spends $1.7 billion touting its wares on television, General Motors $1.3 billion.

5 For important messages to U.S. citizens, President Bush, even though visibly uncomfortable with television, has no more effective pulpit. It is rare for a candidate for public office not to use television to solicit support. For information, millions of people look to network news—and also Jon Stewart, Oprah Winfrey, David Letterman and Conan O'Brien.

6 Fictional television characters can capture the imagination of the public. Perry Mason did wonders for the reputation of the legal profession in the 1960s. Then Mary Tyler Moore's role as a television news producer showed that women could succeed in a male-dominated business. Roles played by Alan Alda were the counter-macho model for the bright, gentle man of the 1970s. The sassy belligerence of Bart Simpson still makes parents shudder.

Enduring Television Effects

7 Although television can be effective in creating short-term impressions, there also are long-term effects. Social critic Michael Novak, commenting on television at its heyday, called television "a molder of the soul's geography." Said Novak: "It builds up incrementally a psychic structure of expectations. It does so in much the same way that school lessons slowly, over the years, tutor the unformed mind and teach it how to think." Media scholar George Comstock made the point this way: "Television has become an unavoidable and unremitting factor in shaping what we are and what we will become."

8 Whether the influence ascribed to television by Novak and Comstock will survive the fast-changing media landscape of the 21st century remains to be seen. Nobody, however, is predicting the imminent disappearance of television. The question is whether the television industry will lose its legacy as a mass medium to technological innovations from new media of mass communication.

—Vivian, *The Media of Mass Communication*, 9th ed.

You, the Reader

Interest Rating: Please rate the interest level of the reading on the following scale (circle one):

5—Very interesting   2—A little boring

4—Fairly interesting   1—Very boring

3—Mildly interesting

Difficulty Rating: Please rate the difficulty level of the reading on the following scale (circle one):

5—Very difficult   2—Fairly easy

4—Fairly difficult   1—Very easy

3—Moderate

Comments: Please explain your ratings and make any other comments you wish about the reading.

Answers will vary.

_____

COMPREHENSION QUESTIONS

Directions: For questions 1–5, choose the answer that best completes the statement. For questions 6–10, write your response in the space provided. Base all answers on what you read in the selection. Refer back to the selection as necessary to answer the questions.

_____d_____ **1.** According to the passage, fictional TV characters:
  a. Have only a temporary effect on viewers.
  b. Have little impact on adult viewers.
  c. Are useful in advertisements.
  d. Capture the public imagination and influence our social images.

_____c_____ **2.** How has television impacted older media (movies, radio, magazines)?
  a. Television has had no effect on them.
  b. Television has contributed to their growth and success.
  c. Television forced them to change in order to survive.
  d. Television has affected movies but has had no real effect on radio or other media.

_____b_____ **3.** The main idea of paragraph 7 is that:
  a. Television is effective in making short term impressions.
  b. Television has long-term effects on our minds and outlooks.
  c. Scholars believe that television is a dangerous medium.
  d. We learn more from television than we do from school.

_____b_____ **4.** The passage suggests that:
  a. The impact of TV is less important for politicians today than it was ten years ago.
  b. Politicians use TV to influence public opinion.

        c. TV has little impact on public opinion on serious issues.
        d. TV's impact is always short term.

___a___ **5.** Regarding the future of television, the reader may conclude that:
        a. Television will be affected by changes in technology and new media.
        b. Television will continue to grow in popularity for many years.
        c. Changes in technology and media will have no effect on television.
        d. Television sets will soon start to disappear from American households.

6. According to the author, why is today's television industry in crisis?

The technological environment is changing. Video can now be delivered through

other media.

7. What evidence of television's ongoing popularity does the passage contain?

Almost every U.S. household has at least one TV set. On average, television is

playing seven hours daily in those homes. Many people plan around the *CSI*

schedule. About 134 million watch the Super Bowl.

8. In paragraph 4, the author refers to the Bud frog in order to make what point about television?

Television can create cultural icons.

9. Which media were television's chief competitors in the past? Which are television's chief competitors today?

In the past: movies, radio, and magazines

Today: iPods, blogs, and online gaming; the Internet

10. In your opinion, how important an influence does television have on society? Explain your answer.

Answers will vary.

VOCABULARY EXERCISES

Pronunciation Guide (see p. 90 for list of phonetic symbols)
        belligerence   (bə-lĭj'ər-əns)
        incrementally   (ĭn'krə-mĕnt' ə-lē)
        innovations   (ĭn'ə-vā'shənz)

WORDS IN CONTEXT

Directions: Choose the meaning for the boldfaced word that best fits the context.

___b___ **1.** In the 1950s, television . . . forced its media elders, notably movies, radio and magazines, to reinvent themselves or **perish**.
  a. Move   c. Join
  b. Die   d. Discover

___c___ **2.** . . . first as a hot new medium, then as the **dominant** medium.
  a. New   c. Powerful; influential
  b. Enduring forever   d. Cold

___b___ **3.** Now the industries that developed around television technology are themselves in **crisis**.
  a. A stage of rapid growth   c. No longer existing
  b. A difficult, unstable situation d. Completion

___c___ **4.** They have been overtaken by **innovations** in delivering video through other channels.
  a. High costs   c. Changes; new methods
  b. Competition   d. Mistakes

___d___ **5.** It is rare for a candidate for public office not to use television to **solicit** support.
  a. Pay for   c. Research; analyze
  b. Represent   d. Seek; ask for

CONTEXT AND DICTIONARY

Directions: Use context and the dictionary to determine the meaning of the boldfaced word in each sentence. Use word structure clues when applicable.

1. Year by year television **entrenched** itself in the latter 20th century . . .
Securely established

2. Or will television as an industry find itself **subsumed**, perhaps even replaced, by new competition?
Taken over; included within a larger group

3. As a medium, television can create cultural **icons**, as Budweiser has demonstrated time and again.
Images; representations; symbols

4. The sassy **belligerence** of Bart Simpson still makes parents shudder.
Aggressiveness; quarrelsomeness; wanting to fight attitude

5. It builds up **incrementally** a psychic structure of expectations.
In small increases; bit by bit

6. Whether the influence **ascribed** to television by Novak and Comstock will survive the fast-changing media landscape . . .
Attributed; credited

7. Nobody, however, is predicting the **imminent** disappearance of television.

About to happen; likely to happen soon

RESPOND TO THE READING

Directions: Write a half-page response to either of the following questions.

1. What would your life be like if there were no television? If you never watched television, what might you do with that time?

2. Discuss the future of television. Do you think that the use of new technologies, like iPods, cell phones, blogs, and video games, will replace television watching?

WEBQUEST

Directions: Use the Internet to find the answers to the following questions. Write your answers on a sheet of paper. Print out the Web page(s) you used for the answers or copy the URL(s) on your sheet.

How many television sets does the average American family own?

Which age group watches the most television?

READING 14

MINDS OF THEIR OWN: ANIMALS ARE SMARTER THAN YOU THINK (NATURE)

by Virginia Morell

Reading 14 is taken from a *National Geographic* feature article on animal intelligence. In this excerpt, the author describes her visit with Irene Pepperberg, a highly regarded researcher, and Alex, a parrot with whom Pepperberg worked for thirty years. Read the article to learn about Alex's abilities and what they tell us about animal minds.

Pre-Reading Exercise

Directions: Complete this exercise before reading the passage. Preview the passage and answer the following questions.

1. What is the passage about?

   Irene Pepperberg's research with Alex the parrot

2. Who is Alex? What will you learn about him from reading the passage?

   Alex is an African gray parrot who Pepperberg was teaching language.

3. When did Pepperberg begin her research with Alex?

   1977

4. What other animals are mentioned in the passage?

   Chimpanzees, dogs, dolphins, sheep, scrub jays, archerfish, bonobos, gorillas

5. What have you previously read or learned about animal intelligence?
   Answers will vary.

6. Does the passage seem interesting? Why or why not?
   Answers will vary.

1   In 1977 Irene Pepperberg, a recent graduate of Harvard University, did something very bold. At a time when animals still were considered automatons, she set out to find what was on another creature's mind by talking to it. She brought a one-year-old African gray parrot she named Alex into her lab to teach him to reproduce the sounds of the English language. "I thought if he learned to communicate, I could ask him questions about how he sees the world."

2   When Pepperberg began her dialogue with Alex, who died last September at the age of 31, many scientists believed animals were incapable of any thought. They were simply machines, robots programmed to react to stimuli but lacking the ability to think or feel. Any pet owner would disagree. We see the love in our dogs' eyes and know that, of course, Spot has thoughts and emotions. But such claims remain highly controversial. Gut instinct is not science, and it is all too easy to project human thoughts and feelings onto another creature. How, then, does a scientist prove that an animal is capable of thinking—that it is able to acquire information about the world and act on it?

3   "That's why I started my studies with Alex," Pepperberg said. They were seated—she at her desk, he on top of his cage—in her lab, a windowless room about the size of a boxcar, at Brandeis University. Newspapers lined the floor; baskets of bright toys were stacked on the shelves. They were clearly a team—and because of their work, the notion that animals can think is no longer so fanciful.

4   Certain skills are considered key signs of higher mental abilities: good memory, a grasp of grammar and symbols, self-awareness, understanding others' motives, imitating others, and being creative. Bit by bit, in ingenious experiments, researchers have documented these talents in other species, gradually chipping away at what we thought made human beings distinctive while offering a glimpse of where our own abilities came from. Scrub jays know that other jays are thieves and that stashed food can spoil; sheep can recognize faces; chimpanzees use a variety of

tools to probe termite mounds and even use weapons to hunt small mammals; dolphins can imitate human postures; the archerfish, which stuns insects with a sudden blast of water, can learn how to aim its squirt simply by watching an experienced fish perform the task. And Alex the parrot turned out to be a surprisingly good talker.

5   Thirty years after the Alex studies began, Pepperberg and a changing collection of assistants were still giving him English lessons. The humans, along with two younger parrots, also served as Alex's flock, providing the social input all parrots crave. Like any flock, this one—as small as it was—had its share of drama. Alex dominated his fellow parrots, acted huffy at times around Pepperberg, tolerated the other female humans, and fell to pieces over a male assistant who dropped by for a visit. ("If you were a man," Pepperberg said, after noting Alex's aloofness toward me, "he'd be on your shoulder in a second, barfing cashews in your ear.")

6   Pepperberg bought Alex in a Chicago pet store. She let the store's assistant pick him out because she didn't want other scientists saying later that she'd deliberately chosen an especially smart bird for her work. Given that Alex's brain was the size of a shelled walnut, most researchers thought Pepperberg's interspecies communication study would be futile.

7   "Some people actually called me crazy for trying this," she said. "Scientists thought that chimpanzees were better subjects, although, of course, chimps can't speak."

8   Chimpanzees, bonobos, and gorillas have been taught to use sign language and symbols to communicate with us, often with impressive results. The bonobo Kanzi, for instance, carries his symbol-communication board with him so he can "talk" to his human researchers, and he has invented combinations of symbols to express his thoughts. Nevertheless, this is not the same thing as having an animal look up at you, open his mouth, and speak.

9   Pepperberg walked to the back of the room, where Alex sat on top of his cage preening his pearl gray feathers. He stopped at her approach and opened his beak.

10   "Want grape," Alex said.

11   "He hasn't had his breakfast yet," Pepperberg explained, "so he's a little put out."

12   Alex returned to preening, while an assistant prepared a bowl of grapes, green beans, apple and banana slices, and corn on the cob.

13   Under Pepperberg's patient tutelage, Alex learned how to use his vocal tract to imitate almost one hundred English words, including the sounds for all of these foods, although he calls an apple a "ban-erry."

14   "Apples taste a little bit like bananas to him, and they look a little bit like cherries, so Alex made up that word for them," Pepperberg said.

15   Alex could count to six and was learning the sounds for seven and eight.

16   "I'm sure he already knows both numbers," Pepperberg said. "He'll probably be able to count to ten, but he's still learning to say the words. It takes far more time to teach him certain sounds than I ever imagined."

17   After breakfast, Alex preened again, keeping an eye on the flock. Every so often, he leaned forward and opened his beak: "Ssse . . . won."

18   "That's good, Alex," Pepperberg said. "Seven. The number is seven."

19   "Ssse . . . won! Se . . . won!"

20   "He's practicing," she explained. "That's how he learns. He's thinking about how to say that word, how to use his vocal tract to make the correct sound."

21   It sounded a bit mad, the idea of a bird having lessons to practice, and willingly doing it. But after listening to and watching Alex, it was difficult to argue with Pepperberg's explanation for his behaviors. She wasn't handing him treats for the repetitious work or rapping him on the claws to make him say the sounds.

22   "He has to hear the words over and over before he can correctly imitate them," Pepperberg said, after pronouncing "seven" for Alex a good dozen times in a row. "I'm not trying to see if Alex can learn a human language," she added. "That's never been the point. My plan always was to use his imitative skills to get a better understanding of avian cognition."

23   In other words, because Alex was able to produce a close approximation of the sounds of

some English words, Pepperberg could ask him questions about a bird's basic understanding of the world. She couldn't ask him what he was thinking about, but she could ask him about his knowledge of numbers, shapes, and colors. To demonstrate, Pepperberg carried Alex on her arm to a tall wooden perch in the middle of the room. She then retrieved a green key and a small green cup from a basket on a shelf. She held up the two items to Alex's eye.

24   "What's same?" she asked.

25   Without hesitation, Alex's beak opened: "Co-lor."

26   "What's different?" Pepperberg asked.

27   "Shape," Alex said. His voice had the digitized sound of a cartoon character. Since parrots lack lips (another reason it was difficult for Alex to pronounce some sounds, such as *ba*), the words seemed to come from the air around him, as if a ventriloquist were speaking. But the words—and what can only be called the thoughts—were entirely his.

28   For the next 20 minutes, Alex ran through his tests, distinguishing colors, shapes, sizes, and materials (wool versus wood versus metal). He did some simple arithmetic, such as counting the yellow toy blocks among a pile of mixed hues.

29   And, then, as if to offer final proof of the mind inside his bird's brain, Alex spoke up. "Talk clearly!" he commanded, when one of the younger birds Pepperberg was also teaching mispronounced the word green. "Talk clearly!"

30   "Don't be a smart aleck," Pepperberg said, shaking her head at him. "He knows all this, and he gets bored, so he interrupts the others, or he gives the wrong answer just to be obstinate. At this stage, he's like a teenage son; he's moody, and I'm never sure what he'll do."

31   "Wanna go tree," Alex said in a tiny voice.

32   Alex had lived his entire life in captivity, but he knew that beyond the lab's door, there was a hallway and a tall window framing a leafy elm tree. He liked to see the tree, so Pepperberg put her hand out for him to climb aboard. She walked him down the hall into the tree's green light.

33   "Good boy! Good birdie," Alex said, bobbing on her hand.

34   "Yes, you're a good boy. You're a good birdie." And she kissed his feathered head.

35   He was a good birdie until the end, and Pepperberg was happy to report that when he died he had finally mastered "seven."

—Morell, "Minds of Their Own: Animals Are Smarter Than You Think," *National Geographic*

You, the Reader

Interest Rating. Please rate the interest level of the reading on the following scale (circle one):

5—Very interesting   2—A little boring

4—Fairly interesting   1—Very boring

3—Mildly interesting

Difficulty Rating. Please rate the difficulty level of the reading on the following scale (circle one):

5—Very difficult   2—Fairly easy

4—Fairly difficult   1—Very easy

3—Moderate

Comments. Please explain your ratings and make any other comments you wish about the reading .

Answers will vary.

COMPREHENSION QUESTIONS

Directions: For questions 1–5, choose the answer that best completes the statement. For questions 6–10, write your response in the space provided. Base all answers on what you read in the selection. Refer back to the selection as necessary to answer the questions.

<u>b</u>   **1.** In the 1970s, scientists believed that animals:
    a. Could learn language and reason out problems if properly trained.
    b. Were not capable of thought.
    c. Had feelings similar to human feelings but were unable to express them.
    d. Were capable of thinking but unable to learn language.

<u>c</u>   **2.** Pepperberg's main goal was to:
    a. Develop a close relationship with Alex to show that he had human feelings.
    b. Teach Alex to talk.
    c. Learn about animal thinking.
    d. Prove that animals can learn language.

<u>c</u>   **3.** Alex demonstrated the ability to do all of the following except:
    a. Imitate almost one hundred words.
    b. Practice pronunciation of new words.
    c. Count to twelve.
    d. Distinguish colors and shapes.

<u>a</u>   **4.** We can tell from the passage that parrots:
    a. Are social animals.
    b. Prefer to be by themselves than with other parrots.
    c. Are the smartest of all birds.
    d. Can use sign language and symbols to communicate with humans.

<u>a</u>   **5.** It appears that Alex:
    a. Learned by practicing and was willing to practice in order to learn.
    b. Only practiced when he was rewarded with food.
    c. Only practiced when he was rewarded with praise and attention.
    d. Imitated the sounds of words but didn't know what any of them meant.

6. Give two examples of animal behavior that reflect higher mental abilities.

Any two: good memory; a grasp of grammar and symbols; self-awareness;

understanding others' motives; imitating others; being creative

7. Why does Alex call an apple a "ban-erry?"

Apples taste like bananas to him and look like cherries.

8. Why did Pepperberg let the store assistant pick out the parrot she would use in her experiments?

She didn't want to be accused of choosing an especially smart bird.

9. Why did Pepperberg choose to work with a parrot instead of a chimp, gorilla, or bonobo?

<u>Parrots can talk.</u>

10. Which of Alex's abilities do you find most interesting and impressive? Why?

<u>Answers will vary.</u>

VOCABULARY EXERCISES

Pronunciation Guide (see p. 90 for list of phonetic symbols)

automatons	(ô-tŏm'ə-tənz)
avian	(ā'vē-ən)
futile	(fyo͞ot'l)
ingenious	(ĭn-jēn'yəs)
tutelage	(to͞ot'l-ĭj)

WORDS IN CONTEXT

Directions: Choose the meaning for the boldfaced word that best fits the context.

b   **1.** At a time when animals still were considered **automatons**, she set out to find what was on another creature's mind by talking to it.
   a. Creatures that can only live in the wilderness
   b. Beings that act automatically without thinking
   c. Very intelligent creatures
   d. Cruel and dangerous beings

a   **2.** . . . gradually chipping away at what we thought made human beings **distinctive** while offering a glimpse of where our own abilities came from.
   a. Different   c. Famous; well-known
   b. Smart   d. Powerful; controlling

b   **3.** . . . most researchers thought Pepperberg's interspecies communication study would be **futile**.
   a. Successful; highly productive   c. Very important
   b. Useless; unsuccessful   d. Poorly planned

d   **4.** Under Pepperberg's patient **tutelage**, Alex learned how to use his vocal tract to imitate almost one hundred English words . . .
   a. Medical care   c. Laboratory
   b. Criticism   d. Teaching

b   **5.** "My plan always was to use his imitative skills to get a better understanding of avian **cognition**."
   a. Feeling   c. Conflict
   b. Thinking   d. Health

CONTEXT AND DICTIONARY

Directions: Use context and the dictionary to determine the meaning of the boldfaced word in each sentence. Use word structure clues when applicable.

1. They were simply machines, robots programmed to react to **stimuli** but lacking the ability to think or feel.

   Things that elicit responses, that cause reactions

2. Bit by bit, in **ingenious** experiments, researchers have documented these talents in other species . . .

   Clever; inventive

3. . . . where Alex sat on top of his cage **preening** his pearl gray feathers.

   Cleaning and trimming; grooming

4. "My plan always was to use his imitative skills to get a better understanding of **avian** cognition."

   Bird

5. "He knows all this, and he gets bored, so he interrupts the others, or he gives the wrong answer just to be **obstinate**."

   Stubborn

RESPOND TO THE READING

Directions: Write a half-page response to either of the following questions.

1. Discuss your experiences with one of your pets or your observations of other animal behavior. What have you observed that might be evidence of animal thinking or intelligence?

2. In your opinion, which animal or animals are the most intelligent? Explain why you think so.

WEBQUEST

Directions: Use the Internet to find the answer to the following question. Write your answer on a sheet of paper. Print out the Web page you used for the answer or copy the URL on your sheet.

Which animals do scientists believe are the most intelligent?

READING 15

THE MARSHMALLOW TEST (PSYCHOLOGY)

by Carey Goldberg

Reading 15 is adapted from a recent newspaper report on "the marshmallow test," an important psychological experiment first carried out in the 1960s by Walter Mischel. The article reports on current attempts to use brain scans to build on the findings from the original experiment. Read the article to learn about the marshmallow test and what it tells us about success and the human mind.

Pre-Reading Exercise

Directions: Complete this exercise before reading the passage. Preview the passage and answer the following questions.

1. What is the passage about?

   The marshmallow test, a psychological experiment about delayed gratification

2. What challenge is given to a 4-year-old child in the marshmallow test?

   The child can eat the marshmallow right away or wait and get two.

3. What area in the brain is associated with delaying gratification and keeping track of goals?

   The anterior prefrontal cortex

4. What have you previously read or learned about self-control or delayed gratification?

   Answers will vary.

5. Write three questions about the marshmallow test or delayed gratification.

   Answers will vary.

6. Does the passage seem easy to understand, or difficult? Explain your answer.

   Answers will vary.

1   It is a simple test, but has surprising power to predict a child's future. A 4-year-old is left sitting at a table with a marshmallow or other treat on it and given a challenge: Wait to eat it until a grown-up comes back into the room, and you'll get two. If you can't wait that long, you'll get just one.

2   Some children can wait less than a minute, others last the full 20 minutes. The longer the child can hold back, the better the outlook in later life for everything from SAT scores to social skills to academic achievement, according to classic work by Columbia University psychologist Walter Mischel, who has followed his test subjects from preschool in the late 1960s into their 40s now.

3   From church sermons to parenting manuals, "the marshmallow test" has entered popular culture as a potent lesson on the rewards of self-control. It has also raised deep psychological research questions: What is involved in delaying gratification? Why does it correlate with success in life? Why do people fail at it?

4   Now neuroscientists, using high-tech brain scans, are seeking to answer these questions by examining what goes on in the brain when a person aces or flunks marshmallow-type tasks. They aim to use their findings to figure out how to train people to control themselves better, whether that means focusing on the potential pitfalls of a mortgage broker's pitch or concentrating on the calorie count of a brownie.

5   "Brain imaging provides a very exciting and important new tool," Mischel said. What matters, he said, is not which areas of the brain light up on scans, but the clues that brain activity may provide to the psychological mechanisms involved: Is the problem in how you perceive a temptation, for example, or in an underlying inability to stop yourself?

6   Most recently, Yale University researchers found that delaying gratification involves an area of the brain, the anterior prefrontal cortex, that is known to be involved in abstract problem-solving and keeping track of goals. For example: You want to drive across town, so you find your keys, start your car, and navigate the route, all while

that critical brain region keeps the overarching trip goal in your mind.

7   The brain scan findings from 103 subjects suggest that delaying gratification involves the ability to imagine a future event clearly, said Jeremy Gray, a Yale psychology professor and coauthor of the study in the September edition of the journal *Psychological Science*. You need "a sort of 'far-sightedness,' to put it in a single word," he said.

8   In the coming months, researchers plan to perform brain scans on 40 of the original subjects of Mischel's marshmallow test, said John Jonides, a psychology professor and brain imager at the University of Michigan who is working with Mischel on the project.

9   If brain differences are found between good and poor delayers, he said, they could suggest effective avenues for training. For example, if brain regions involved in attention make a difference, poor delayers could be trained to focus their attention more effectively and fight distractions.

10   "Or, if we find that the problem seems to be associated with regions involved in ridding your short-term memory of unwanted information (i.e., getting the marshmallow out of mind so that you can wait for two of them), then perhaps training to improve control over short-term memory might be something to try," Jonides said in an e-mail.

11   Mischel, among others, believes that the key to delaying gratification may lie in the ability to "cool the hot stimulus," he said in a telephone interview. He and colleagues are exploring the possibility of teaching children that skill in schools.

12   Over and over, research is showing that the trick is to shift activity from "hot," more primitive areas deep in the brain to "cool," more rational areas mainly in the higher centers of the brain, he said.

13   There are many ways to cool a hot stimulus, said Mischel, who is president of the Association for Psychological Science. Say you are determined to resist the chocolate cake at a restaurant. You must distract yourself from the waiter's dessert tray. You can also focus on long-term consequences and make them "hot"—by vividly

imagining your future tummy and hip bulges—or think of the cake in the cooler abstract, as a thing that will make you fat and clog your arteries.

14 In the marshmallow test, he said, "the same child who can't wait a minute if they're thinking about how yummy and chewy the marshmallow is can wait for 20 minutes if they're thinking of the marshmallow as being puffy like a cotton ball or like a cloud floating in the sky."

15 Neuro-economists, who use brain scans to shed light on economic decision-making, are also exploring the "cool brain hot brain" theory, said Daniel Benjamin, an assistant professor of economics at Cornell University.

16 If that model is borne out, he said, it could hold important implications for economics. Economists traditionally think that people's preferences naturally reflect their best interests. But if their impulsive brain leads them to make poor choices, "then there's a whole realm of situations where some kind of intervention, whether by government or by employers, might be appropriate," he said.

17 Already, he said, such thinking is leading to experiments like the website stickk.com, which tries to help people use their "cool" brain to overcome impulses by letting them stake money on goals they aim to achieve. If a user wants to lose 20 pounds, for example, he might choose to put $200 down and receive $10 back each week he loses 1 pound.

18 Such experiments are exciting, Benjamin said, because they avoid paternalistic government intervention. Instead, "They allow individuals themselves, during cool periods, to regulate the way they will behave during hot periods."

19 Research has found that the ability to delay gratification is linked not just to cool headedness and farsightedness, but to intelligence as well. The relationship appears complex, however; intelligence is hard to define, and when a child is both smart and good at delaying, it is hard to distinguish cause from effect.

20 Four-year-olds who ace the marshmallow test may then translate their self-control into academic effort that makes them score higher on intelligence tests; or, it could be that being smart helped them figure out how to distract themselves from the marshmallow.

21 Mischel emphasized that though intelligence is related to doing well on marshmallow tests, it is by no means the whole answer.

22 As many people know, "It's quite possible to be very smart and not able to inhibit your impulses," he said.

—Goldberg, "The Marshmallow Test," *Boston Globe*

You, the Reader

Interest Rating: Please rate the interest level of the reading on the following scale (circle one):

5—Very interesting   2—A little boring

4—Fairly interesting   1—Very boring

3—Mildly interesting

Difficulty Rating: Please rate the difficulty level of the reading on the following scale (circle one):

5—Very difficult   2—Fairly easy

4—Fairly difficult   1—Very easy

3—Moderate

Comments: Please explain your ratings and make any other comments you wish about the reading.

Answers will vary.

COMPREHENSION QUESTIONS

Directions: For questions 1–5, choose the answer that best completes the statement. For questions 6–10, write your response in the space provided. Base all answers on what you read in the selection. Refer back to the selection as necessary to answer the questions.

<u> c </u>   **1.** The marshmallow test is a predictor of an individual's ability to:
a. Form meaningful long-term relationships.
b. Solve mathematical problems.
c. Delay gratification.
d. Distinguish right from wrong.

<u> c </u>   **2.** Neuroscientists are currently trying to:
a. Get people to eat fewer marshmallows.
b. Teach children to do better on the marshmallow test.
c. Help people improve their self-control.
d. Help people improve long-term memory.

<u> a </u>   **3.** Brain scan findings indicate that:
a. The ability to delay gratification is associated with the ability to imagine future events.
b. Self-control cannot be learned.
c. People who succeed in delaying gratification have larger brains than people who are unable to delay gratification.
d. Short-term memory is associated only with the anterior prefrontal cortex.

<u> d </u>   **4.** The ability to delay gratification is linked with all of the following *except*:
a. Intelligence
b. Far-sightedness
c. Cool headedness
d. Athletic ability

<u> b </u>   **5.** The reader may conclude that:
a. The marshmallow test has been given to children all over the world.
b. There is more to learn about the differences between good and poor delayers.
c. There were forty children in Mischel's original experiment.
d. Poor delayers have poor short-term memories.

6. What are the most important findings of the marshmallow test experiments?

Delayed gratification—self-control—is correlated with success in life. (sample answer)

7. What are some questions about delayed gratification that researchers are hoping to answer?

What is involved in delaying gratification? Why does its correlate with success in life?

Why do people fail at it?

8. What is a "hot stimulus"? Give an example.

A hot stimulus evokes a response in a primitive part of the brain—an impulsive,

emotional, nonrational response, a sensory desire. Examples will vary (chocolate

cake is mentioned in the passage).

9. According to Mischel, how can you cool a hot stimulus?

Distract yourself; focus on long-term negative consequences; think of the stimulus

in the cooler abstract.

10. If you had been given the marshmallow test as a child, would you have passed?
Explain.

Answers will vary.

VOCABULARY EXERCISES

Pronunciation Guide (see p. 90 for list of phonetic symbols)

gratification	(grăt'ə-fĭ-kā'shən)
neuroscientists	(nŏŏr'ō-sī'ən-tĭsts)
paternalistic	(pə-tûr'nə-lĭs' tĭk)

WORDS IN CONTEXT

Directions: Choose the meaning for the boldfaced word that best fits the context.

_a_   **1.** Why does it **correlate** with success in life?
   a. Correspond; have a direct relationship
   b. Interfere; block
   c. Cause good luck
   d. Result from; come from

_a_   **2.** . . . all while that critical brain region keeps the **overarching** trip goal in
   your mind.
   a. Main; big   c. Typical
   b. Impossible   d. Hard to see or imagine

_c_   **3.** . . . the key to delaying gratification may lie in the ability to "cool the hot
   stimulus," . . .
   a. Marshmallow   c. Something that excites
   b. Disease   d. Control

_c_   **4.** . . . the trick is to shift activity . . . to "cool," more **rational** areas mainly
   in the higher centers of the brain . . .
   a. Excitable   c. Logical; using reason
   b. Emotional   d. Familiar

_d_   **5.** As many people know, "It's quite possible to be very smart and not able
   to **inhibit** your impulses," he said.
   a. Like or love   c. Desire
   b. Express   d. Restrain; control

CONTEXT AND DICTIONARY

Directions: Use context and the dictionary to determine the meaning of the boldfaced word in each sentence. Use word structure clues when applicable.

1. . . . "the marshmallow test" has entered popular culture as a **potent** lesson on the rewards of self-control.

Powerful; convincing

2. What is involved in delaying **gratification**?

Satisfaction; pleasure

3. Now **neuroscientists**, using high-tech brain scans, are seeking to answer these questions . . .

Scientists who study the nervous system

4. . . . all while that **critical** brain region keeps the overarching trip goal in your mind.

Important; essential

5. . . . or think of the cake in the cooler **abstract**, as a thing that will make you fat and clog your arteries.

Idea separated from the material object; concept or conception

6. . . . they avoid **paternalistic** government intervention.

Acting like a father; controlling; taking authority or responsibility for others

7. . . . they avoid paternalistic government **intervention**.

Interference; coming between to influence

RESPOND TO THE READING

Directions: Write a half-page response to either of the following questions.

1. Discuss a situation in which you used self-control or delayed gratification in order to achieve a long-term goal. What temptation did you resist? How did you resist it? What long-term goal were you working toward?

2. In your opinion, what are the most effective ways to develop self-control and the ability to delay gratification?

WEBQUEST

Directions: Use the Internet to find the answer to the following question. Write your answer on a sheet of paper. Print out the Web page you used for the answer or copy the URL on your sheet.

List five strategies for developing self-discipline.

Understanding Word Structure: Common Roots

Roots are the central parts of words. The roots of many English words derive from Latin and Greek. Recognizing the root in a word gives you a valuable clue to its meaning. For example, if you know that the root *somn* means "sleep," you will have no trouble learning and remembering that insomnia means "inability to sleep." Thus, a knowledge of common roots is a helpful aid to vocabulary growth.

Studying roots is similar to studying prefixes, but there are a few noteworthy differences:

- It is sometimes harder to identify the root of a word because the root may appear anywhere in the word—the beginning, middle, or end.
- Some roots have several spellings.
- Most roots cannot be looked up in the dictionary as easily as prefixes can.

In this Appendix, we will review twenty common word roots. (See Table AP.2 on pp. 565–566 for an expanded list of roots.) Study the meaning of the root in each of the following boxes and note the accompanying example words. After studying each box, list two other words containing that root. Review exercises are provided after every five roots.

See Instructor's Manual

1. aud, audit   hear   audible, auditorium
Audible means "capable of being *heard*."
An *auditorium* is a place where people *hear* someone speak, sing, and so on.

_____   _____

2. bio   life   biology, antibiotic
Biology is the science of *living* things and *life* processes.
An *antibiotic* kills *live* bacteria that cause illness.

_____   _____

3. cess, cede   go   proceed, procession
To *proceed* is to *go* forward.
A *procession* is a group of people *going* forward.

_____   _____

4. chron   time   synchronize, chronology

To *synchronize* is to set at the same *time*.
A *chronology* is a record of events in *time* order.

_____   _____

5. cred   belief   credible, discredit

Credible means "*believ*able."
To *discredit* means "to negate *belief* in someone or something."

_____   _____

APPENDIX EXERCISE 1 PRACTICE WITH ROOTS

Directions: For sentences 1–5, use the meaning of the root in the word in italics to complete the sentences. For sentences 6–10, fill in the missing root.

1. A *credulous* person will __believe__ anything you tell him.

2. When a doctor tests your *audition*, he is testing your __hearing__ .

3. The *biosphere* is that part of our planet where __life__ is found.

4. When flood waters *recede*, they __go__ back.

5. A *chronic* illness is one that lasts a long __time__ .

6. Dogs can hear sounds that are in __aud__ *ible* to humans.

7. A new __bio__ *graphy* of Elvis Presley will be published next year.

8. A __chrono__ *meter* is an instrument that measures time.

9. In the astrological cycle, the sign Aries *pre* __cedes__ the sign Taurus.

10. The attorney challenged the witness's __cred__ *ibility*.

6. dict   speak, say   predict, dictaphone

To *predict* is to *say* that an event will occur.
A *dictaphone* is a machine you *speak* into.

_____   _____

7. duct, duce   lead, carry   conductor, introduce

The *conductor leads* the orchestra.
To *introduce* is to *lead* to, or *lead* into.

_____   _____

8. fac(t), fic(t)   do, make   factory, fiction

A *factory* is a place where goods are *made*.
Fiction is literature *made* up by the author.

_____   _____

| 9. graph | write, draw | biography, graphics |

A *biography* is a *written* account of someone's life.
Computer *graphics* involves *drawing* on the computer.

_____   _____

| 10. miss, mit | send | mission, transmit |

A *mission* is something one is *sent* on to accomplish.
To *transmit* a message is to *send* it.

_____   _____

APPENDIX EXERCISE 2 PRACTICE WITH ROOTS

Directions: For sentences 1–5, use the meaning of the root in the word in italics to complete the sentence. For sentences 6–10, fill in the missing root.

1. The root *manu* means "hand." The word *manufacture* originally meant ____make____ by hand.

2. To *remit* payment on a bill is to ____send____ the payment in.

3. The root *ver* means "truth." We hope that when a jury delivers its *verdict*, it will ____speak____ the truth.

4. To *seduce* is to ____lead____ someone on sexually.

5. A *graphologist* analyzes your hand ____writing____.

6. Nothing could *in* ____duce____ Mike to go to the party.

7. Many parents do not like to be *contra* ____dict____ *ed* by their children.

8. Have you ever considered writing your *autobio* ____graph____ *y*?

9. The rocket ship was *e* ____mit____ *ting* strange signals.

10. Many foods today use *arti* ____fic____ *ial* sweeteners.

APPENDIX EXERCISE 3 MATCHING

Directions: Using the roots as clues, match the words on the left with their meanings on the right. Do not consult a dictionary.

_c_ 1. auditory   a. carry off, kidnap

_f_ 2. symbiosis   b. historical record

_d_ 3. intercede   c. having to do with hearing

_j_ 4. credence   d. go between

_b_ 5. chronicle   e. creating a mental picture

_i_ 6. diction   f. interdependent living

_a_ 7. abduct   g. one who does good

_g_ 8. benefactor   h. one sent as an ambassador

_e_ 9. graphic   i. speech

_h_ 10. emissary   j. belief

11. mor(t)   die, death   immortal, mortician
Immortal means "never *dying*."
A *mortician* is someone who prepares *dead* bodies for their funerals.

12. path   1. feeling   1. sympathy
                    2. disease   2. pathology
To have *sympathy* is to have *feelings* for someone.
Pathology is the study of *disease* and its causes.

13. phon(o), phone   sound   phonics, symphony
Phonics is the study of the *sounds* used in a language.
In a *symphony*, the *sounds* of many instruments are heard.

14. port   carry   transport, portable
To *transport* goods is to *carry* them from one place to another.
A *portable* object is one that can be *carried*.

15. scrib(e), script   write   inscription, scribble
An *inscription* is something *written*.
Scribble is careless *writing*.

APPENDIX EXERCISE ▮4▮ PRACTICE WITH ROOTS

Directions: For sentences 1–5, use the meaning of the root in the word in italics to complete the sentence. For sentences 6–10, fill in the missing root.

1. A *psychopath* is someone with a ____diseased____ mind.

2. On a canoe trip, the distance you must ____carry____ your canoe is called your *portage*.

3. *Mortality* rates are ____death____ rates.

4. The *scriptures* are holy ____writings____ .

5. A *dictaphone* records the ____sound____ of your voice.

6. Another word for the military draft is *con* ____script____ *ion* (in the past, the names of the young men to be drafted were written down).

7. A *post*____mort____ *em* examination was needed to determine the exact cause of death.

8. When we got off our plane, we were unable to find a ____port____ *er* to help us with our luggage.

9. As a former alcoholic, John felt a great deal of *em*____path____ *y* for others still struggling with their drinking.

10. Before CDs and cassette tapes, people listened to music on ____phono____ *graphs*.

---

16. spect, spic   look, see   spectacle, conspicuous

A *spectacle* is an event worth *seeing*.
To be *conspicuous* is to be easily *seen* or obvious.

_____   _____

---

17. tract   pull, draw   tractor, retract

A *tractor pulls*.
To *retract* is to *draw* back.

_____   _____

---

18. ven(t), vene   come   convene, invent

When people *convene*, they *come* together or meet.
When something is *invented*, it *comes* into being.

_____   _____

---

19. viv, vit   live, life   survive, vital

To *survive* means "to continue to *live*."
Vital means "necessary for *life*."

_____   _____

| **20.** voc, voke | call, voice | vocal, revoke |

Vocal means "using the *voice.*"
To *revoke* means "to *call* back."

APPENDIX EXERCISE 5 PRACTICE WITH ROOTS

Directions: For sentences 1–5, use the meaning of the root in the word in italics to complete the sentence. For sentences 6–10, fill in the missing root.

1. A *convivial* person is someone who is ____live____ ly.

2. When you are *attracted* to someone you are ____drawn____ toward them.

3. To *evoke* a memory is to ____call____ it forth.

4. *Introspection* is ____looking____ within yourself.

5. People ____come____ together for a *convention.*

6. Someone who watches events is a ____spect____ ator.

7. A bad tooth may need to be *ex* ____tract____ ed.

8. Who *pro* ____voke____ d the argument?

9. When his best hitter started to argue with the umpire, the manager *inter* ____vene____ d.

10. It is important to eat foods rich in essential ____vita____ mins.

APPENDIX EXERCISE 6 MATCHING

Directions: Using the roots as clues, match the words on the left with their meanings on the right. Do not consult a dictionary.

__d__ 1. vitality		a. expel, carry away
__f__ 2. spectrum		b. tighten, pull together
__b__ 3. contract		c. strong dislike
__e__ 4. vociferous		d. health
__g__ 5. advent		e. noisy
__i__ 6. morgue		f. range of visible light
__c__ 7. antipathy		g. beginning, coming into being
__j__ 8. phonology		h. note at end of a letter
__a__ 9. deport		i. place where bodies are kept
__h__ 10. postscript		j. study of sounds of a language

Use Table AP.1 as a review of common roots.

Table AP.1 Common Roots

Root	Meaning	Example
1. aud, audit	hear	audible
2. bio	life	biology
3. cess, cede	go	proceed
4. chron	time	synchronize
5. cred	belief	credible
6. dict	speak, say	predict
7. duct, duce	lead, carry	conductor
8. fac(t), fic(t)	do, make	factory
9. graph	write, draw	biography
10. miss, mit	send	mission
11. mor(t)	die, death	immortal
12. path	feeling, disease	sympathy, pathology
13. phon	sound	phonics
14. port	carry	transport
15. scrib, script	write	inscription
16. spect, spic	look, see	spectacle
17. tract	draw, pull	tractor
18. ven(t), vene	come	convene
19. viv, vit	life	survive
20. voc, voke	call, voice	vocal

Table AP.2 Expanded List of Roots

Roots in boldface type have been reviewed in this Appendix.

Root	Meaning	Example
ann, enn	year	anniversary, perennial
arch	rule	monarchy
aqua	water	aquarium
astro, aster	star	astronaut, asteroid
aud, audit	hear	audible, auditorium
bio	life	biology
cap, cept	take, have	capture, reception
cess, cede	go	process, recede
chron	time	synchronize
cred	belief	credible
cur	run	current

(*continued*)

Table AP.2   (continued)

Root	Meaning	Example Word
dict	speak, say	predict
duct, duce	lead, carry	conductor, induce
fac(t), fic(t)	make, do	factory, fiction
fer	bear	transfer
geo	earth	geography
graph	write, draw	biography
gress, grad	step	progress, gradual
iatr(o)	medicine	pediatrician
ject	throw	eject
loc	place	location
loq	talk	eloquent
mater	mother	maternal
meter	measure	odometer
miss, mit	send	mission, transmit
mor(t)	die, death	immortal
mot, mob	move	motion, mobile
pater	father	paternal
path	feeling, disease	sympathy, pathology
ped	children	pediatrician
ped, pod	foot	pedal, tripod
pel, puls	push	propel, propulsion
phon	sound	phonics
port	carry	transport
rupt	break	disrupt
scop(e)	look	telescope
scribe, script	write	inscribe, inscription
sect	cut	dissect
spect, spic	look	spectator
ten, tain	hold	retention, retain
terr	earth	territory
the(o)	god, religion	monotheism
tract	draw, pull	tractor
ven(t), vene	come	convene
ver	truth	verdict
vert, verse	turn	invert, reverse
vis, vid	see	vision, video
viv, vit	life	survive, vital
voc, voke	call, voice	vocal, provoke
vor	eat	carnivorous

Credits

TEXT CREDITS

CHAPTER 1

Page 35: Excerpt from "Milk." *The World Book Encyclopedia* © 1993 World Book, Inc. http://www.worldbookonline.com. By permission of the publisher. All rights reserved. **Page 36:** Excerpt from "Money." *The World Book Encyclopedia* © 1993 World Book, Inc. http://www.worldbookonline.com. By permission of the publisher. All rights reserved.

CHAPTER 2

Page 61: From Webster's New World College Dictionary, 4th Edition. Reproduced with permission of John Wiley & Sons, Inc. **Page 77:** Copyright © 2010 by Houghton Mifflin Harcourt Publishing Company. Reproduced by permission from *The American Heritage College Dictionary*, Fourth Edition. **Page 81:** Copyright © 2010 by Houghton Mifflin Harcourt Publishing Company. Reproduced by permission from *The American Heritage College Dictionary*, Fourth Edition. **Page 85:** Copyright © 2010 by Houghton Mifflin Harcourt Publishing Company. Reproduced by permission from *The American Heritage College Dictionary*, Fourth Edition. **Page 85:** Copyright © 2010 by Houghton Mifflin Harcourt Publishing Company. Reproduced by permission from *The American Heritage College Dictionary*, Fourth Edition. **Page 90:** Copyright © 2010 by Houghton Mifflin Harcourt Publishing Company. Adapted and reproduced by permission from *The American Heritage Dictionary of the English Language*, Fourth Edition. **Page 85:** Copyright © 2010 by Houghton Mifflin Harcourt Publishing Company. From *The American Heritage College Dictionary*, Fourth Edition.

CHAPTER 3

Page 125: Copyright © 2010 by Houghton Mifflin Harcourt Publishing Company. Reproduced by permission from *The American Heritage College Dictionary*, Fourth Edition. **Page 126:** Copyright © 2010 by Houghton Mifflin Harcourt Publishing Company. From *The American Heritage College Dictionary*, Fourth Edition.

CHAPTER 4

Page 164: Excerpt from "The Indispensable Man" reprinted from *Commentary*, December 1997, by permission; copyright © 1997 by Commentary, Inc. **Page 163:** From "What's Up with Boys?" by Georgia Orcutt from *Boston Parents' Paper*, a publication of Dominion Enterprises, Inc., February 2009, p. 14. Copyright © 2009. Used by permission.

CHAPTER 5

Page 221: From "Why Lincoln Matters" by Michael Beschloss. Used by permission of the author. **Page 246:** "New Ways to Stop Crime" © 2009 David Baldacci. Initially published in *Parade Magazine*, August 2, 2009. All rights reserved. Used by permission of *Parade* and The Aaron Priest Literary Agency. **Page 257:** From "Get a Better Mood Fast" by Michael O'Shea in *Parade*, August 23, 2009. Copyright © 2009 Parade Publications. All rights reserved. Used by permission.

CHAPTER 6

Page 267: From "Sun Alert!" in ChemMatters, April 1998, 16(2): 4–6. Reprinted with permission from ChemMatters magazine at www.acs.org/chemmatters, American Chemical Society. **Page 276:** From "How Invisibility Cloaks Work" on www.howstuffworks.com. Reprinted courtesy of HowStuffWorks.com. **Page 264:** From "The Game that Ruth Built" by Peter Keating from *The Boston Globe*, May 7, 2006. Used by permission of the author. **Page 264:** From "HealthStyle Cheat Sheet" by Emily Listfield in *Parade*, January 7, 2009. Copyright © 2009 Parade Publications. All rights reserved. Used by permission. **Page 269:** From "Teenagers Need Help to Form Better Sleep Habits" by Dr. Darshak Sanghavi. Originally appeared in *The Boston Globe*, June 21, 2005. Used by permission of the author. **Page 287:** "Waking Up to Our Dreams" from *Parade*, October 28, 2007. © 2007 Robert Moss.

Initially published in *Parade Magazine*. All rights reserved. Used by permission of *Parade* and the author.

CHAPTER 7

Page 328: From "Without a Map" by Naila Moreira from *The Boston Globe*, October 9, 2006. Used by permission of the author. **Page 356:** From "Viva! Barrios Unidos" by Peggy R. Townsend from *Stone Soup for the World*, edited by Marianne Larned, published by Three Rivers Press. Copyright © 2002 by Marianne Larned. Used by permission. www.soup4world.com.

CHAPTER 8

Page 357: From "Working in the Schools" by Jonathan Alter from *Stone Soup for the World*, edited by Marianne Larned, published by Three Rivers Press. Copyright © 2002 by Marianne Larned. Used by permission. www .soup4world.com. **Page 379:** From "Born to Be Wild" in *The Nevada Daily Mail*, August 23, 1998. Used by permission. **Page 380:** Excerpt from "Wright Brothers." *The World Book Encyclopedia* © 1993 World Book, Inc. http://www.worldbookonline.com. By permission of the publisher. All rights reserved.

CHAPTER 9

Page 428: From "Fossil Discovery Fills a Piece of Evolutionary Puzzle" by Gareth Cook in *The Boston Globe*, April 6, 2006, © 2006 The Boston Globe. All rights reserved. Used by permission and protected by the Copyright Laws of the United States. The printing, copying, redistribution, or retransmission of the Content without express written permission is prohibited. **Page 443:** "How Safe Are Over-the-Counter Drugs and Driving?" by Wink Dulles. Used by permission of the Wink Dulles estate. **Page 448:** "Beauty vs. Beast" by Dave Barry from *The Miami Herald*, February 1, 1998. Used by permission of Dave Barry. **Page 451:** *From Crow Dog: Four Generations of Sioux Medicine Men* by Leonard Crow Dog and Richard Erdoes. Copyright © 1995 by Leonard Crow Dog and Richard Erdoes. Reprinted by permission of HarperCollins Publishers. **Page 466:** From "They're Back" in *National Geographic*, May 2007, Vol. 211, Issue 5. Reprinted by permission of National Geographic Society. **Page 431:** From "Do the Right Thing" by Tom McNichol in the San Jose Mercury News. Used by permission of the author. **Page 432:** From "Cloning Questions Multiply" from *Miami Herald*, December 26, 1998. Copyright © The Miami Herald, 1998. Used by permission. **Page 467:** From "Caught Between Cultures" by Beth Baker from *AARP Bulletin*, July/August 2000. Used by permission of the author.

CHAPTER 10

Page 477: From "Where We're Headed" by Neil deGrasse Tyson in *USA Weekend*, July 6–8, 2007. Used

by permission of the author. **Page 493:** "The Minimum Drinking Age Should Be Lowered" (Old Enough for War, Old Enough for Alcohol) from *Teens at Risk*, 2006, Greenhaven Press. Used by permission of Choose Responsibility, www.chooseresponsibility. org. **Page 490:** "Supplements Need Regulation to Keep Kids Safe from Steroids" from *San Jose Mercury News*, May 20, 2009. Copyright © 2009 by the *San Jose Mercury News*. Reproduced with permission of *San Jose Mercury News* in the format Textbook via Copyright Clearance Center. **Page 495:** "Keep the Drinking Age at 21" from *The Chicago Tribune*, September 15, 2008. Copyright © 2008 Chicago Tribune. All rights reserved. Used by permission and protected by the Copyright Laws of the United States. The printing, copying, redistribution, or retransmission of the Material without express written permission is prohibited. **Page 486:** From Points of View: Legalization of Marijuana from http://web.ebscohost. com/pov/delivery?hid=104&sid=de84a511-5b23, courtesy of EBSCO Publishing, Inc. **Page 489:** "Dangerous Driving: With risks obvious, time to get serious about ban on cell phones while driving" from *The Hutchinson News*, January 15, 2009. Reprinted by permission of TMS Reprints. **Page 512:** "Global Warming: Coming to Your Backyard" by Roger Di Silvestro from National Wildlife, Vol. 45, February-March 2007. Used by permission of the National Wildlife Federation. **Page 523:** From "Should All Students Be Bilingual?" by Douglas Ward from NEA Today, May 2002. Used by permission of the author and the National Education Association.

ADDITIONAL READINGS

Page 529: "Viva! Barrios Unidos" by Peggy R. Townsend from *Stone Soup for the World*, edited by Marianne Larned, published by Three Rivers Press. Copyright © 2002 by Marianne Larned. Used by permission. www.soup4world.com. **Page 546:** "Minds of Their Own: Animals Are Smarter Than You Think" from *National Geographic*, March 2008. Reprinted by permission of National Geographic Society. **Page 552:** "The Marshmallow Test: Brain Scans Could Yield Vital Lessons in Self-Control" by Carey Goldberg from *The Boston Globe*, October 22, 2008. Used by permission.

PHOTO CREDITS

Page 2: Cartoon copyrighted by Mark Parisi, printed with permission, www.offthemark.com. **Page 17:** Kiselev Andrey Valerevich/Shutterstock. **Page 18:** Ivy Close Images/Alamy. **Pages 25:** Yuri Arcurs/ Shutterstock. **Page 55:** Courtesy of Apnex Medical. **Page 60:** Cartoon copyrighted by Mark Parisi, printed with permission, www.offthemark.com. **Page 94:** Hulton Archive/Getty Images. **Page 99:** Tom Mc Nemar/Shutterstock. **Page 136:** OJO Images Ltd/ Alamy. **Page 181:** With permission of Dr. Elizabeth Loftus. **Page 188:** ph: Mark Fellman/TM & Copyright © 20th Century Fox. All rights reserved/Courtesy Everett Collection. **Page 234:** Annabella Bluesky/ Photo Researchers. **Page 239:** Mark Lennihan/AP Images. **Page 247:** © Katherine Lambert. **Page 276:** Tachi Laboratory, Keio University and The University of Tokyo. **Page 295:** Michael Newman/PhotoEdit. **Page 329:** Foto Factory/Shutterstock. **Page 330:** Flip Schulke/Black Star/Newscom. **Page 336:** Topham/ The Image Works. **Page 342 (left):** North Wind Picture Archives/Alamy. **Page 342 (right):** akg-images/Newscom. **Page 394:** Handout/MCT/Newscom. **Page 401 (top):** Robnroll/Shutterstock. **Page 401 (bottom):** www.CartoonStock.com. **Page 416 (top left):** Gorich/Shutterstock. **Page 416 (top right):** luxorphoto/Shutterstock. **Page 416 (middle left):** Luis Santos/Shutterstock. **Page 416 (middle right):** 101imges/Shutterstock. **Page 416 (bottom both):** Kalim/Shutterstock. **Page 417:** Keith Birmingham/ ZUMA Press/Newscom. **Page 418:** PEANUTS © 1992 Peanuts Worldwide LLC. Dist. By UNIVERSAL UCLICK. Reprinted with permission. All rights reserved. **Page 442:** NATURE VALLEY® is a registered trademark of General Mills and is used with permission. Photography: Hermann Erver/Look/Getty Images and Chris Sheehan. **Page 452:** National Anthropological Archives, Smithsonian Institution Museum [GN 03218b]. **Page 459:** Ben Greer/ Istockphoto. **Page 492:** Chad McDermott/ Shutterstock. **Page 497:** Courtesy of Advertising Archives. **Page 499:** Jack Hollingsworth/Thinkstock. **Page 504 (top):** s70/ZUMA Press/Newscom. **Page 504 (bottom):** Courtesy of RSNA and Dr. Vincent P. Mathews. **Page 512:** Robert Clare/Alamy. **Page 513:** Matthew Veldhuis/Shutterstock. **Page 529:** Condor 36/Shutterstock. **Page 534:** Darrin Klimek/ Thinkstock. **Page 546:** Rick Friedman/Corbis. **Page 552:** Elena Elisseeva/Shutterstock.

Index

Additional Readings

READING 11

VIVA! BARRIOS UNIDOS (HUMAN INTEREST)

by Peggy R. Townsend

Reading 11 is taken from the book *Stone Soup for the World*. In this excerpt, the author recounts the experiences that led a man named Daniel Alejandrez to create Barrios Unidos, a nonprofit organization dedicated to the prevention of inner-city gang violence. Read the excerpt to learn about the obstacles Alejandrez had to overcome in his own life in order to help others.

Pre-Reading Exercise

Directions: Complete this exercise before reading the passage. Preview the passage and answer the following questions.

1. What is the passage about?

   A man called Nane and the organization he founded—Barrios Unidos

2. What can we tell about Nane from the first paragraph?

   He's an unusual man. He is fighting the problems that plague inner-city youth.

3. What are some things we can tell from previewing the passage about Nane's life?

   He had a difficult life. His family fell apart after his grandfather died. He was in jail for drug use.

   He had a vision while in a hospital.

4. What have you previously read or learned about the problems facing young people growing up in poor neighborhoods?

   Answers will vary.

5. Do you know anyone who has overcome an addiction problem? What helped them to do it?

   Answers will vary.

6. In your opinion, what motivates people to help others?

   Answers will vary.

1   His grandmother called him Nane, meaning "Walks in Peace." It's an unusual name for one who spends his days in the toughest neighborhoods of the country. Then again, Nane is a rather unusual man. His real name is Daniel Alejandrez. In barrios throughout the nation, he fights the violence and addictions that are killing America's youth.

2   The barrio where he started his work lies in the shadow of the Giant Dipper rollercoaster in Santa Cruz, California. It's a tiny neighborhood filled with rundown homes and broken dreams. Drug dealers stand on every corner, gang graffiti litters the walls, and most of the tourists who pass by on their way to the nearby amusement park don't even notice it exists.

3   It is here that Nane began Barrios Unidos. He combines messages of hope and understanding with practical programs like job training and computer courses, as well as art classes. "Kids aren't born gang members or racists," he says. "They become that way." But Nane can tell you from personal experience that they don't have to.

4   His voice is so soft that a listener has to lean in very close to hear the story of his life, but it is